Gone Beyond

The Tsadra Foundation Series
published by Snow Lion Publications

Tsadra Foundation is a U.S.-based nonprofit organization that was founded in 2000 in order to support the activities of advanced Western students of Tibetan Buddhism, specifically those with significant contemplative experience. Taking its inspiration from the nineteenth-century nonsectarian Tibetan scholar and meditation master Jamgön Kongtrül Lodrö Tayé, Tsadra Foundation is named after his hermitage in eastern Tibet, Tsadra Rinchen Drak. The Foundation's various program areas reflect his values of excellence in both scholarship and contemplative practice, and the recognition of their mutual complementarity.

This publication is part of Tsadra Foundation's Translation Program, which aims to make authentic and authoritative texts from the Tibetan traditions available in English. The Foundation is honored to present the work of its fellows and grantees, individuals of confirmed contemplative and intellectual integrity; however, their views do not necessarily reflect those of the Foundation.

Tsadra Foundation is delighted to ally with Snow Lion Publications in making these important texts available in the English language.

GONE BEYOND

The Prajñāpāramitā Sūtras,

The Ornament of Clear Realization,

and Its Commentaries in the Tibetan Kagyü Tradition

VOLUME TWO

Translated and introduced by

Karl Brunnhölzl

SNOW LION PUBLICATIONS
ITHACA, NEW YORK

Snow Lion Publications
P. O. Box 6483
Ithaca, NY 14851 USA
(607) 273-8519
www.snowlionpub.com

Printed in USA on acid-free recycled paper.

Typeset by Stephanie Johnston based on a design by Gopa & Ted2, Inc.

ISBN-10: 1-55939-357-2
ISBN-13: 978-1-55939-357-7

Library of Congress Cataloging-in-Publication Data

Dkon-mchog-yan-lag, Źwa-dmar V, 1525-1583.
[Mṅon par rtogs pa'i rgyan gyi 'grel pa. English]
Gone beyond : the Prajñāpāramitā sūtras, the Ornament of clear realization, and its commentaries in the Tibetan Kagyü tradition / translated and introduced by Karl Brunnhölzl.
p. cm. -- (The Tsadra foundation series)
Includes index.
ISBN-13: 978-1-55939-356-0 (v. 1 : alk. paper)
ISBN-10: 1-55939-356-4 (v. 1 : alk. paper)
ISBN-13: 978-1-55939-357-7 (v. 2 : alk. paper)
ISBN-10: 1-55939-357-2 (v. 2 : alk. paper)
1. Abhisamayālaṅkāra--Commentaries--Early works to 1800. 2. Tripiṭaka. Sūtrapiṭaka. Prajñāpāramitā. Pañcāviṃśatisāhasrikā--Commentaries--Early works to 1800. 3. Bka'-rgyud-pa (Sect)--Doctrines--Early works to 1800. I. Brunnhölzl, Karl. II. Title.
BQ1955.D5613 2010
294.3'85--dc22

2010029531

Contents

Abbreviations:

AA *Abhisamayālaṃkāra*

ACIP Asian Classics Input Project (www.acip.org)

Ālokā Haribhadra's *Abhisamayālaṃkārālokā*

AS *Asiatische Studien*

BT Karma Trinlépa's commentary on the AA (Ka rma phrin las pa phyogs las rnam rgyal 2006a)

CE The Fifth Shamarpa's commentary on the AA (Dkon mchog yan lag 2006)

CZ Conze's translation of *The Large Sūtra on Perfect Wisdom*

D Derge Tibetan Tripiṭaka

J Johnston's Sanskrit edition of the *Ratnagotravibhāgavyākhyā*

JAOS *Journal of the American Oriental Society*

JG The Seventh Karmapa's commentary on the AA (Chos grags rgya mtsho n.d.)

JIABS *Journal of the International Association for Buddhist Studies*

JIBS *Journal of Indian and Buddhist Studies* (Indogaku Bukkyōgakku Kenkyū)

JIP *Journal of Indian Philosophy*

JNS The Eighth Karmapa's commentary on the AA (Mi bskyod rdo rje 2003)

LN Butön's commentary on the AA (Bu ston 2001)

LSSP Tsongkhapa's commentary on the AA (Tsong kha pa 1985)

LTWA Library of Tibetan Works and Archives

MCG Mipham Rinpoche's commentary on the AA ('Ju mi pham rgya mtsho 1984)

MPZL Dongag Tenpa'i Nyima's commentary on the AA (Mdo sngags bstan pa'i nyi ma 1986)

NSML Ngawang Kunga Wangchug's commentary on the AA (Ngag dbang kun dga' dbang phyug 1987)

P Peking Tibetan Tripiṭaka (Tokyo-Kyoto: Suzuki Research Foundation, 1956)

PBG Patrul Rinpoche's word commentary on the AA (Dpal sprul 'jigs med chos kyi dbang po 1997)

PEW *Philosophy East and West*

PK Padma Karpo's commentary on the AA (Padma dkar po 1991)

PSD Patrul Rinpoche's general topics of the AA (Dpal sprul 'jigs med chos kyi dbang po 1997)

RT Rongtön's commentary on the AA (Rong ston shes bya kun rig 1988)

SC The Third Karmapa's *Table of Contents of the Abhisamayālaṃkāra* (Rang byung rdo rje 2004a)

SLG Padma Karpo's *Gate for Entering the Prajñāpāramitā Scriptures* (Padma dkar po 1974)

STT The Third Karmapa's *Synopsis of the Eight Chapters of Prajñāpāramitā* (Rang byung rdo rje 2004b)

Taishō Taishō Shinshū Daizōkyō (The Chinese Buddhist Canon), ed. J. Takakusu and K.Watanabe. Tokyo: Taishō Shinshū Daizōkyō Kanko kai, 1970

TBRC Tibetan Buddhist Resource Center (www.tbrc.org)

TJ *Tibet Journal*

TOK Jamgön Kongtrul Lodrö Tayé's *Treasury of Knowledge* (Kong sprul blo gros mtha' yas 1982)

Vivṛti Haribhadra's *Abhisamayālaṃkāravivṛti*

Vṛtti Āryavimuktisena's *Abhisamayālaṃkāravṛtti*

WZKS *Wiener Zeitschrift für die Kunde Südasiens*

YT Yagtön's commentary on the AA (G.yag ston sangs rgyas dpal 1994)

An Aspiration
by H.H. the Seventeenth Karmapa, Ogyen Trinley Dorje

You realize that whatever appears dawns within the play of the mind
And that mind itself is the dharmakāya free of clinging.
Through the power of that, you, the supreme siddhas, master apparent existence.
Precious ones of the Kagyü lineage, please bestow excellent virtue.

Through the heart of a perfect buddha awakening in you,
You possess the blossoming glorious qualities of supreme insight.
You genuine holder of the teachings by the name Dzogchen Ponlop,
Through your merit, the activity of virtue,

You publish the hundreds of flawless dharma paintings
That come from the protectors of beings, the Takpo Kagyü,
As a display of books that always appears
As a feast for the eye of intelligence of those without bias.

While the stream of the Narmadā[1] river of virtue
Washes away the stains of the mind,
With the waves of the virtues of the two accumulations rolling high,
May it merge with the ocean of the qualities of the victorious ones.

This was composed by Karmapa Ogyen Trinley Dorje as an auspicious aspiration for the publication of the precious teachings called The Eight Great Texts of Sūtra and Tantra *by the supreme Dzogchen Ponlop Karma Sungrap Ngedön Tenpe Gyaltsen on April 18, 2004 (Buddhist Era 2548). May it be auspicious.*

Foreword
by H.H. the Seventeenth Karmapa, Ogyen Trinley Dorje

In Tibet, all the ravishing and beautiful features of a self-arisen realm—being encircled by ranges of snow mountains adorned by superb white snowflakes and being filled with Sal trees, abundant herbs, and cool clear rivers—are wonderfully assembled in a single place. These wonders make our land endowed with the dharma the sole pure realm of human beings in this world. In it, all aspects of the teachings of the mighty sage, the greatly compassionate teacher skilled in means, are perfectly complete—the greater and lesser yānas as well as the mantrayāna. They are as pure and unblemished as the most refined pure gold; they accord with reasoning through the power of things; they dispel the darkness of the minds of all beings; and they are a great treasury bestowing all benefit and happiness one could wish for, just as desired. Not having vanished, these teachings still exist as the great treasure of the *Kangyur*, the *Tengyur*, and the sciences, as well as the excellent teachings of the Tibetan scholars and siddhas who have appeared over time. Their sum equals the size of the mighty king of mountains, and their words and meanings are like a sip of the nectar of immortality. Headed by Dzogchen Ponlop Rinpoche with his utterly virtuous and pure intention to solely cherish the welfare of the teachings and beings, many dedicated workers of Nitartha *international*, striving with devotion, diligence, and prajñā, undertook hardships and made efforts over many years to preserve these teachings and further their transmission, and restore them. In particular, they worked toward the special purpose of propagating the excellent stream of teachings and practices of the unequaled Marpa Kagyü lineage, the great family of siddhas, in all directions and times, like the flow of a river in summertime. Through these efforts, the *Eight Great Texts of Sūtra and Tantra* publication series, inclusive of all the essential meanings of the perfectly complete teachings of the victor, is magically manifesting as a great harvest for the teachings and beings. Bearing this in mind, I rejoice in this activity from the bottom of my heart and toss flowers of praise into the sky. Through this excellent activity may the intentions of our noble forefathers be fulfilled in the expanse of peace.

Karmapa Ogyen Trinley Dorje
Gyütö Ramoche Temple
July 19, 2002 (Buddhist Era 2547)

INTRODUCTION

This second volume on the Kagyü commentaries on the *Abhisamayālaṃkāra* contains a translation of Chapters Four to Eight of the AA with the corresponding sections of the commentary *A Concise Explanation of the* Abhisamayālaṃkāra by the Fifth Shamarpa, Göncho Yenla[2] (1525–1583). As in the first volume, these are supplemented by three layers of additional explanations found in the Eighth Karmapa's commentary JNS. The Karmapa's corresponding (1) direct comments on the last five chapters of the AA and (2) his subcommentary on Haribhadra's *Vivṛti* (if different from and/or more extensive than CE) are included in the endnotes to the respective sections of CE. (3) Appendix I contains JNS's extensive general discussions of the major subjects in Chapters Four to Eight as well as many supplementary topics, such as the classifications of afflictive and cognitive obscurations and the manner of relinquishing them, ultimate reality and buddhahood representing permanent entities that perform functions, the five great Madhyamaka reasonings, dependent origination, the four stages of yoga, the discussion about whether there are three or four kāyas, and enlightened activity. In addition, the endnotes include selected relevant passages from other commentaries (BT, PK, SC, LN, YT, RT, LSSP, PSD, PBG, and NSML). Appendix II includes the charts that are relevant to the last five chapters of the AA as well as an overview of its eight topics and seventy points. The remaining appendices provide translations of the Third Karmapa's STT and *Stanzas That Express Realization* (summarizing the path of prajñāpāramitā based on the thirty-seven dharmas concordant with enlightenment), the definitions of the eight topics and seventy points of the AA according to JG, JNS, CE, STT, SLG, and LSSP/PSD, Jamgön Kongtrul Lodrö Tayé's (1813–1899) presentation of paths and bhūmis in his TOK, brief biographies of the Third, Seventh, and Eighth Karmapas as well as the Fifth Shamarpa, and the text of the AA proper.[3]

In brief, this volume contains a four-tier structure of commentaries on the AA—(1) CE on its own, CE's endnotes with (2) JNS on the AA as well as (3) JNS on the *Vivṛti*, and (4) JNS's general topics in Appendix I. In addition, there are the excerpts from the other commentaries mentioned above.

Overview of Chapters Four to Eight

The complete training in all aspects

The complete training in, or full realization of, all aspects refers to actually engaging in the practice of all the points in the three knowledges. It is the combined familiarization with all entities, all paths, and all aspects, including their respective knowledges, as being without nature in order to realize the three knowledges. The AA discusses the 173 aspects of all three knowledges in terms of practicing, realizing, and mastering them in their entirety.

The eleven points of the complete training in all aspects

(1) "All aspects" refers to that with which bodhisattvas must familiarize themselves—the 173 aspects of all three above knowledges (AA IV.1–5). Here, "aspects" refers to the particular instances of cognition or wisdom that focus on particular focal objects, which in this case means all the facets of the four realities of noble ones from the perspective of the mahāyāna, the various stages of the bodhisattva path, and the qualities of the final fruition. In particular, the focusing on the four realities differs from the manner of doing so in the other yānas because it eliminates all extremes and reference points with regard to these four realities as entertained by non-Buddhists as well as by śrāvakas and pratyekabuddhas. Thus, all these "aspects" are not aspects in terms of seeming reality (such as outer objects or impermanence), but represent aspects in terms of ultimate reality—they are nothing but the distinctive forms in which the mind that familiarizes with and realizes emptiness, the two kinds of identitylessness, the lack of arising of the three knowledges, and so on appears. In more detail, among these 173 aspects, the twenty-seven aspects in terms of the knowledge of entities and the thirty-six aspects in terms of the knowledge of the path represent the specific ways in which bodhisattvas focus on the four realities as the path. Among the 110 aspects of the knowledge of all aspects, the first set of thirty-seven consists of the dharmas concordant with enlightenment. The second set of thirty-four consists of various sets of samādhis (the three doors to liberation, the eight liberations, the nine meditative absorptions of progressive abiding, the four readinesses of the path of seeing) and the ten pāramitās. The final set of thirty-nine describes the nature and the qualities of buddhahood, such as the ten powers and the four fearlessnesses. The description of all these aspects is followed by two verses about the general characteristics of the persons who are suitable recipients for the teachings on prajñāpāramitā (IV.6–7).

(2) The nature of this training or the manner in which bodhisattvas familiarize with these aspects consists of the five natural and the fifteen situational

trainings (IV.8–11). The former are practiced on an ongoing basis from the path of accumulation up through the end of the tenth bhūmi, while the latter are only engaged in during certain phases of the path.

The next four points refer to the preliminary factors of the actual trainings. (3) First, there are the fourteen distinct qualities (IV.12ab) that result from cultivating the above twenty trainings. These include vanquishing the power of māras, never being born in the unpleasant realms, firm bodhicitta, the ability to establish many beings in perfect enlightenment, and the promotion of their vast welfare.

(4) On the other hand, while being engaged in said trainings, bodhisattvas need to know and eliminate forty-six flaws (IV.12cd). These obstacles to properly familiarizing with and realizing prajñāpāramitā consist of three main groups—twenty flaws that depend on oneself (such as being distracted in various ways, misconceptions about prajñāpāramitā, and causes for abandoning the mahāyāna), twenty-three flaws in terms of various ways in which teacher and student can be incompatible, and three flaws that depend on others (various activities of māras).

(5) The defining characteristics of the mahāyāna training in all aspects (IV.13–31) consist of (a) the characteristic of supreme knowledge in terms of each one of the three knowledges of bodhisattvas, which demonstrates the capacity of the mahāyāna training to produce the final realization of buddhahood. (b) The characteristic of supreme activity indicates the capacity of this training to accomplish the vast welfare of others. (c) The characteristic of distinctiveness shows that śrāvakas and pratyekabuddhas do not possess such consummate capacities. (d) The characteristic of the nature of the training that possesses these distinctive features (a)–(c) is instantiated by sixteen aspects in terms of the three knowledges.

(6) The first temporary result of such training is the mahāyāna path of accumulation, which is called "the factors conducive to liberation" (IV.32–34). In general, it consists of gathering the accumulations and, in particular, of five faculties—the skill in the means to abide in signlessness through eliminating signs and characteristics by way of confidence in the three jewels; vigor with regard to the pāramitās; mindfulness of bodhicitta; nonconceptual samādhi; and the prajñā of knowing all aspects of phenomena. Classified in another way, the lesser, medium, and great levels of the path of accumulation are the four foundations of mindfulnesss, the four correct efforts, and the four limbs of miraculous powers.

(7) The next path is the path of preparation, which represents the factors conducive to penetration (IV.35–37). In this chapter, its four levels of heat up through the supreme dharma are taught from the perspective of the activities of bodhisattvas during subsequent attainment (in the chapter of the

knowledge of all aspects, they were taught from the perspective of their realizations in meditative equipoise). Throughout these levels, the focal objects are all sentient beings, on whom one focuses through seeing oneself and all others as equal, refraining from evil, abiding in the pāramitās, maturing sentient beings, and so on. One also establishes others in such activities and rejoices in their doing so.

(8) The persons who cultivate the complete training in all aspects are the irreversible learning bodhisattvas (IV.38–59). Bodhisattvas of sharp faculties achieve twenty signs of being irreversible from eventually attaining buddhahood already on the path of preparation. Those of medium faculties attain sixteen signs of such irreversibility on the path of seeing, which consist of special expressions of physical and verbal conduct as the natural outflow of the realizations during the sixteen moments of this path. Those of duller faculties show eight signs of said irreversibility on the path of familiarization, which are this path's profundity in terms of arising, ceasing, suchness, and so on.

(9) The training in realizing saṃsāra and nirvāṇa as equality (IV.60) consists of not conceptualizing these two in any way because all phenomena are equally empty and dreamlike. This training is the cause of the dharmakāya.

(10) The training in pure realms means to manifest one's own pure buddha realm, which consists of pure beings and a pure environment with unsurpassable qualities (IV.61). This training is the cause of the sambhogakāya.

(11) The tenfold training in skill in means (IV.62–63) matures others and is the cause of one's enlightened activity in this pure realm.

The culminating training

The culminating training, or culminating clear realization, represents the highest forms of familiarization with all entities, all paths, and all aspects as being without nature, which take place on the paths of preparation, seeing, and familiarization, respectively. In other words, it consists of the various levels of "breakthrough experiences" and their signs that manifest on the progressive paths of bodhisattvas as the results of their cultivating the complete training in all aspects.

The eight points of the culminating training

(1) The culminating training of the level of heat of the path of preparation (V.1) arises from the cause of having cultivated the complete training in all aspects on the path of accumulation. It is taught through the twelve signs during both the waking state and in dreams that signal its attainment.

(2) The culminating training of the level of peak (V.2) is taught by way of sixteen examples that demonstrate the increase in merit on this level in comparison with the level of heat. These examples show that bodhisattvas on the

level of peak, through not being separated from the mental engagement of all phenomena as being dreamlike, engage in prajñāpāramitā and teach it to others, which is far more meritorious than the merits in any of said examples.

(3) The culminating training of poised readiness (V.3) is taught by way of the stability of not regressing into the paths of śrāvakas or pratyekabuddhas through never abandoning the three knowledges (by virtue of dedicating them to buddhahoood) or the welfare of sentient beings.

(4) The culminating training of the supreme dharma (V.4) is taught by way of the immeasurable extent of the two accumulations of merit and wisdom that characterize the samādhi of continuously settling on the threefold lack of nature of the three knowledges.

(5) The culminating training of the path of seeing is discussed by starting with the four sets of the nine imputational conceptions about apprehender and apprehended that are the factors to be relinquished through seeing (V.5–16). The two sets of conceptions about the apprehended are in terms of the objects that bodhisattvas regard as something to be engaged in (the paths and fruitions of the mahāyāna) versus the objects from which they need to withdraw (the paths and fruitions of the hīnayāna). The two sets of the conceptions about the apprehender are, respectively, in terms of ordinary beings taking persons to be substantially existent and noble beings taking them to be imputedly existent. This is followed by discussions of the causes of enlightenment (enlightenment being understood as the actual nature of the culminating training of the path of seeing), its nature, and the manner of familiarizing with it (V.17–21). Unlike the explicit explanations in the sūtras on the individual remedies for the implied four sets of conceptions, the AA explicitly discusses the latter, while their remedies are implied. Thus, the AA gives no details of the remedies, but only summarily refers to the uninterrupted path and the special path (called "the lion's sport") of the path of seeing (V.22–23).

(6) The culminating training of the path of familiarization is explained by starting with its special way of training in samādhi through alternating and skipping various meditative states, called "crossing in one leap" (V.24–25). Among the four sets of the nine innate conceptions about the apprehender and the apprehended to be relinquished through familiarization4 (V.26–34), the two sets of the conceptions about the apprehended are about what is to be engaged by bodhisattvas (the prajñāpāramitā teachings, their qualities, and the paths related to them) and what is to be rejected by them (not mentally engaging in and familiarizing with prajñāpāramitā or doing so in wrong ways). The two sets of the conceptions about the apprehender refer to imputations (mere persons) and the mere causes for such imputations (mere appearances). This section concludes with the limitless qualities that arise from the culminating training of the path of familiarization (V.35–36) and support the bodhisattvas on this level, enabling them to swiftly become buddhas.

(7) The culminating training of the final uninterrupted path of the path of familiarization (V.37–38) is the "vajralike samādhi" during the very last moment of the tenth bhūmi, which overcomes the most subtle obscurations (the last remainder of the ālaya-consciousness). Here, this training is equated with the knowledge of all aspects (which manifests immediately after it) and is described through its abundance of merit.

(8) Finally, this chapter speaks about sixteen mistaken notions in terms of the two realities seeming to be contradictory (V.39–42). These subtle qualms represent the specific factors to be relinquished during the vajralike samādhi and pertain to its focal object (the lack of entities), its dominant factor (the prajñā of mindfulness), and its aspect (all reference points and characteristics being at peace).

The serial training

As for the serial training in a general sense, it is a brief overview of the sequential nature of the entire path, emphasizing the progressive stabilization of momentary and culminating insights in terms of all the different aspects of the three knowledges. More specifically, it refers to being able to train in all these aspects together in a very swift sequential manner due to one's great familiarity with them.

The thirteen points of the serial training

This training is taught through (1)–(6) practicing the six pāramitās (VI.1a) in the manner of not observing the three spheres. This represents conduct (or the consummate training), in which merit is primary.

The six recollections (VI.1b) represent the path of the union of view and conduct (or the consummate way of thinking) and consist of recollecting the three jewels—(7) the Buddha (the aspects of the knowledge of all aspects), (8) virtuous, nonvirtuous, and neutral dharmas, and (9) the saṃgha of irreversible bodhisattvas; (10) ethics and (11) giving as the bases of the six pāramitās; and (12) taking the noble ones who appear as deities as one's witnesses on the path. The specific manner of familiarizing with all these recollections is to lack recollection and mental engagement.

(13) The training in realizing the nature of the lack of entity (VI.1c) represents the training in equality and the general view for all thirteen aspects of the serial training, which means to primarily familiarize with nonconceptual wisdom.

The instantaneous training

The instantaneous training, or the clear realization in a single instant, refers to a bodhisattva's simultaneous realization of all aspects of the three knowledges in the vajralike samādhi during the last moment of the tenth bhūmi, which is immediately followed by the attainment of buddhahood. This training is the natural culminating outflow of the serial training, in particular due to having cultivated all the pāramitās in a sequential manner. In terms of its nature, the instantaneous training cannot be divided, but by way of its general characteristics, isolates, or distinct capacities, it is fourfold.

The four points of the instantaneous training

(1) The instantaneous training in terms of nonmaturation (VII.1–2) refers to being in the process of becoming free from the most subtle stains that are the impregnations of negative tendencies. This means that each uncontaminated phenomenon includes all other infinite uncontaminated phenomena. Therefore, if a single one of them becomes free from these subtle stains, all uncontaminated phenomena will be free from them.

(2) The instantaneous training in terms of maturation (VII.3) refers to this very training being about to become buddha wisdom after being freed from said impregnations. This means that, in a single instant, personally experienced wisdom dawns as the matured true nature of prajñāpāramitā, which overcomes even the most subtle stains. The inseparability of subject and object at this point represents the knowledge of all aspects.

(3) The instantaneous training in terms of the lack of characteristics (VII.4) means that, through dwelling in the insight that all phenomena arise in a dreamlike fashion, the knowledge of all aspects is manifested in one single instant of discovering the lack of characteristics of these dependently originating phenomena.

(4) The instantaneous training in terms of nonduality (VII.5) means that, upon awakening from sleeplike ignorance, phenomena are no longer seen as the duality of apprehender and apprehended. Thus, the true reality of the purity of nondual mind is seen in one single instant.

The dharmakāya

The last topic discusses the final fruition of the four trainings—buddhahood—as the three (or four) kāyas and their enlightened activity. The primary buddhakāya is the dharmakāya. In terms of its nature and purity, it is referred to as the svābhāvikakāya; in terms of its enjoyment of the dharma of the mahāyāna, as the sāmbhogikakāya; and in terms of its manifesting in all kinds of pure and impure forms in various realms, as the nairmāṇikakāya.

The four points of the dharmakāya

(1) The svābhāvikakāya (VIII.1–11) refers to twofold purity—the dharmadhātu being primordially pure and also having become free from all adventitious stains. This includes the attainment of the twenty-one sets of uncontaminated qualities, which account for a buddha's all-pervading and permanent activity for the vast and inexhaustible welfare of all sentient beings.

(2) The sāmbhogikakāya (VIII.12–32) is always endowed with the five certainties in terms of body, realm, retinue, teaching the mahāyāna, and time. In the AA, it is described through the thirty-two major and the eighty minor marks, including their causes on the path.

(3) The nairmāṇikakāya (VIII.33) is of three types—(a) artistic nairmāṇikakāyas (great artists, scientists, healers, and so on); (b) incarnate nairmāṇikakāyas (any animate or inanimate manifestations by buddhas for the welfare of beings); and (c) supreme nairmāṇikakāyas who display the twelve deeds of a buddha (such as Buddha Śākyamuni). Though all these manifestations of the nairmānikakāya arise and cease in great variety, the continuum of their common activity represents an uninterrupted stream for as long as saṃsāra lasts.

(4) The effortless and nonconceptual enlightened activity of buddhahood (VIII.34–40) depends on the dominant condition of the wisdom dharmakāya. In brief, it consists of the twenty-seven aspects of establishing beings in the support of the path, the path itself, and the fruition of this path.[5]

The last two verses of the AA respectively summarize the eight topics into six (taking the three knowledges as one point) and three (taking the three knowledges and the four trainings as one point, respectively).

Translation:

A CONCISE ELUCIDATION OF THE *ABHISAMAYĀLAṂKĀRA*

(Topics Four to Eight)

The Fourth Chapter, on the Complete Training in All Aspects

2.3.1.2.2. The four trainings (the means)

This has four parts:

1) The complete training in all aspects (familiarizing with the aspects of the three knowledges in a combined manner)[6]
2) The culminating training (the consummation of that)
3) The serial training (familiarizing with these [aspects] in a sequential manner)
4) The instantaneous training (familiarizing with these [aspects] in a simultaneous manner)

2.3.1.2.2.1. The complete training in all aspects (familiarizing with the aspects of the three knowledges in a combined manner)

This has two parts:

1) Presenting the connection
2) Detailed explanation of the clear realizations

2.3.1.2.2.1.1. Presenting the connection

Following the instructions on the nine dharmas that define the knowledge of entities, the four trainings are explained. In the first three chapters, in order to understand the three knowledges by way of their defining characteristics, they were primarily taught by defining them in terms of their causes, objects, natures, factors to be relinquished, being remedies, and so on. However, though there are some statements about the aspects of the paths of seeing, familiarization, and so on [in these chapters], they are only partial. Therefore, {79a} in order to overcome the antagonistic factor [of the three knowledges]—clinging to characteristics—and to realize their threefold lack of arising, these chapters [on the four trainings] teach the familiarization with all aspects of the three knowledges without exception in the manner of them being remedies. If the term "complete training in all aspects" is used in a wider sense, it applies to all four trainings because they are alike in terms of familiarizing with the 173 aspects [of all three knowledges].[7] With respect to a single given factor to be relinquished, the first three trainings arise in an alternating way. [In order to gain mastery over the remedies, beginning with] the path of accumulation, one cultivates [the complete training in] all aspects [as the beginning of] the invalidating remedy of the factors to be relinquished through seeing. The culminating training [takes place in the manner of having gained mastery over the remedy. Its beginning] on the path of preparation represents the portion that is the relinquishing remedy [of the factors to be relinquished through seeing]. The serial training [is undertaken in order to gain stability in the mastery over the remedy. It begins] during the subsequent attainment [of the meditative equipoise of the level of heat of the path of preparation], which preceded this [culminating training, and] represents the distancing remedy. [The same alternating way applies for the paths of seeing and familiarization] The sustaining remedy—the path of liberation—is not taught here.[8] From among these [three trainings], the one that is taught first is the complete training in all aspects—familiarizing [with these aspects] in order to gain [experiential] mastery over [one's preceding] realization of the three knowledges through studying and reflecting. This is the meaning of Subhūti teaching, "This mother is the pāramitā of what is not . . ."[9]

2.3.1.2.2.1.2. Detailed explanation of the clear realizations

This has two parts:

1) The general presentation of the training
2) Instruction on the complete training in all aspects proper

2.3.1.2.2.1.2.1. The general presentation of the training

This has four parts:

1) The aspects to familiarize with
2) The persons who familiarize
3) The nature of the training
4) The preliminary factors of the training

2.3.1.2.2.1.2.1.1. The aspects to familiarize with

This has two parts:

1) Brief introduction
2) Detailed explanation

2.3.1.2.2.1.2.1.1.1. Brief introduction

This has two parts:

1) General [topic]
2) [Meaning of] the text

2.3.1.2.2.1.2.1.1.1.1. General topic

The "aspects" in this context refers to the aspects in the twofold division of focal objects and aspects. Though prajñāpāramitā is free from arising, abiding, and ceasing, in terms of the manners of familiarizing with this, the focal objects are what are expressed as "the three [kinds of] nonarising" [of the three knowledges]. As for the aspects, {79b} there are two [kinds]—the aspects of the seeming (such as consciousness appearing as the aspects that [look like] outer objects) and the aspects of the ultimate. [The latter] do not appear as the aspects of the arising, ceasing, and so on of mistaken outer objects, but their own nature is self-awareness and they appear in the manner of luminosity. From among these, here, the latter [are explained]. Though focal objects and aspects are of the same nature ultimately, they are explained as aspects from the point of view of becoming increasingly more luminous through the progression of becoming free from adventitious stains. Therefore, the aspects of the three knowledges that are the objects of familiarization on [the level of] engagement through aspiration and the aspects of the knowledge of all aspects that are the objects of familiarization on the paths of training are not actual aspects, but merely similar in type. Still, the training in familiarizing with them is the one that fulfills this definition in all respects. One may think here that there is the possibility of a mahāyāna path of familiarization on which one familiarizes with personal identitylessness[10] through familiarizing with the aspects of the knowledge of entities. [However,] the [latter] has the characteristics of regarding [the four realities] as [their sixteen aspects,] such as impermanence. Therefore, bodhisattvas do not deliberately familiarize with these, but, through their familiarizing with the nonarising of entities, [they realize personal identitylessness in the manner of] the lower [realizations] being incorporated in the higher, just as the realization of personal identitylessness is implicitly clearly present if phenomenal identitylessness is realized.[11]

2.3.1.2.2.1.2.1.1.1.2. Meaning of the text

> **The specific instances of cognizing entities**
> **Represent the defining characteristic of "aspects."**
> **By virtue of the three kinds of omniscience,**
> **They are asserted as three kinds.** [IV.1]

The individually arising **specific instances** of the insights **of cognizing** the **entities** to be known (the three kinds of nonarising) in a direct or approximately concordant manner **represent the defining characteristic of "aspects."**

If divided in general, it is said, "**By virtue of the three kinds of omniscience, they are asserted as three kinds** [with regard to the three knowledges]."[12]

2.3.1.2.2.1.2.1.1.2. Detailed explanation

This has three parts:

1) The twenty-seven aspects of the knowledge of entities
2) The thirty-six aspects of the knowledge of the path
3) The 110 aspects of the knowledge of all aspects

2.3.1.2.2.1.2.1.1.2.1. The twenty-seven aspects of the knowledge of entities

> **Beginning with the aspect of nonexistence**
> **Up through the aspect of immovability,**
> **Four for each one of the realities**
> **And fifteen of them for the path are taught.** [IV.2]

If each of these [three sets of aspects of the three knowledges] are subdivided, [the twenty-seven aspects of the knowledge of entities], **beginning with the aspect of nonexistence up through the aspect of immovability**, {80a} **are taught** as **four** aspects of focusing on **each one of the** first three **realities**, respectively, **and** [the remaining] **fifteen of these** aspects focus on the reality of **the path**. The sūtras say:

> Subhūti, the mother is the pāramitā of what is not existent because space is not existent.[13]

From among these, the four aspects of focusing on the reality of suffering are (1) *not existing* as a permanent entity [like space]; (2) phenomena *not arising*; (3) *being free* from a self; and (4) *not being crushed* due to being unobservable. The four [aspects] of the reality of the origin [of suffering] are (5) *being without abiding* because of not being a produced basis; (6) *[being like] space* because of the afflictions lacking arising and ceasing; (7) *being inexpressible* through words because of being free from examination and analysis; (8) *being without* the four *name* skandhas. The four [aspects] of the reality of cessation are (9) *not going* anywhere and not being something to be attained by having gone [anywhere]; (10) *nothing being removed* newly since [the afflictions] are primordial peace; (11) *being inexhaustible* by virtue of being the nature of phenomena; and (12) *being without arising* by virtue of not being established primordially. [In due order,] these [twelve correspond to] the characteristics, such as impermanence, that are stated in the abhidharma.

From among the fifteen aspects of the reality of the path, the following four are the aspects of focusing on the uncontaminated path as the remedy for the afflictions—(13) *there being no agent* who attains the fruition; (14) *there being no cognizer* since there is no self; (15) *there being no transition* in terms of adopting and rejecting; and (16) *there being no subduing* of factors to be relinquished that are naturally empty. These [correspond to] the four characteristics (such as path) [of the reality of the path in the abhidharma]. The [above aspects] teach that [bodhisattvas] focus on the four realities in accordance with the path of the disciples, [that is, the śrāvakas,] and that [the fomer's] mental aspects are superior to those [of the latter].

Following that, in accordance with the pratyekabuddhas, {80b} [bodhisattvas] focus on the path that is the remedy for the conceptions about the apprehended, which is twofold. (a) The five aspects of focusing [on the path] during [contaminated] subsequent attainment are the aspects of (17) the apprehended being without nature, *like a dream*; (18) its not arising from a real cause, *like* a reverberation or *an echo*; (19) its mere aspect being unceasing, *like an optical illusion* or a shadow; (20) its being primordial peace, *like a mirage*; (21) its being naturally pure, *like an illusion*. (b) The six aspects of focusing [on the path] during uncontaminated meditative equipoise are the aspects of (22) *there being no afflicted phenomena* to be rejected; (23) *there being no purified* entities to be adopted; (24) luminosity—being *without* any basis for *being tainted* by the latent tendencies of these [afflictions]; (25) *there being no reference points* of any divisions, such as form; (26) consequently, *there being no conceit* about [one's own] realization;[14] (27) *being immovable* since there is absolutely no deterioration through apprehending anything as nonempty.[15]

Also these mental aspects of bodhisattvas are superior to [those of] the pratyekabuddhas. As for conceptions, there are the two portions—(1) imputational and (2) innate ones.[16] The first are twofold—(1a) the conceptions that apprehend [by conflating] terms and their referents and cling to the duality of apprehender and apprehended and (1b) the false imagination of dualistic appearances. In due order, these obscure the two purities and represent factors to be relinquished through seeing and familiarization, respectively, in the mahāyāna. (2) The latter [conceptions] consist of (2a) the actual [innate ones] and (2b) their latent tendencies, which bear the name "impregnations of negative tendencies." By dividing (2) in terms of being those that obscure the seeing of [the wisdoms of] suchness and variety, respectively, they represent [the obscurations of] attachment [during meditative equipoise] and obstruction [during subsequent attainment].[17] In due order, these are relinquished through the two wisdoms of the meditative equipoise and the subsequent attainment of the end of the continuum. Pratyekabuddhas are not able to relinquish the [innate conceptions], but relinquish merely the clinging to the imputed apprehended in terms of apprehender and apprehended being different in substance. {81a} For they relinquish the clinging to what appear as referents as being actual outer referents during the subsequent attainment of the path of familiarization and [relinquish] the clinging to these appearances as being of the nature of consciousness during the meditative equipoise [of this path].[18]

2.3.1.2.2.1.2.1.1.2.2. The thirty-six aspects of the knowledge of the path

> **In terms of the cause, the path, suffering,**
> **And cessation, in due order,**
> **They are said to be eight, seven,**
> **Five, and sixteen.** [IV.3]

By virtue of focusing **in terms of** the realities of the origin of suffering (**the cause), the path, suffering, and cessation, in due order**, the aspects of realizing **them are said to be eight, seven, five, and sixteen.** The sūtras say:

> . . . because desire is unobservable . . .[19]

Among these, the eight aspects of focusing on the reality of the origin are as follows. The remedies for its threefold aspect "cause"[20] (which consists of striving for objects, clinging desire, and liking to be reborn) are the three aspects of (1) *being free from desire*, (2) *not abiding* by virtue of no striving, and (3) *peace* of characteristics. The remedies for the three poisons as the threefold [aspect] "origin" are (4)–(6) the three [kinds of] lack of the three poisons [*lack of greed, hatred, and dullness*]. The remedy for the origin of dualistic appearances (the single [aspect] "arising") is (7) the single [aspect of the] *subsiding* of the cause *of the afflictions*—clinging to duality. The remedy for clinging to sentient beings—the views about a real personality (the single [aspect] "condition")—is (8) the single [aspect of realizing] the *lack of sentient beings*.

[Among] the seven [aspects] of the path, (9) *being immeasurable* and (10) *being disconnected from the two extremes* represent the "path" that opens up the opportunity for all sentient beings progressing to enlightenment because of disconnecting them from the two extremes [of saṃsāra and one-sided nirvāṇa] through prajñā and compassion. (11) *Not being different* and (12) *no clinging to superiority* refer to the "appropriateness" of realizing that all phenomena are not different because there is no clinging to the paths of śrāvakas and pratyekabuddhas being superior. (13) *Nonconceptuality* and (14) *being unassessable* refer to the "accomplishment" of not conceptualizing the two [kinds of] identity because the nature of phenomena is unassessable through mind. {81b} (15) *Lacking attachment* means to realize the phenomena under "appropriateness" as being spacelike. For this, no justification is set forth.

The five [aspects] of suffering are its four specific characteristics (16) "*impermanence*," (17) "*suffering*," (18) "*being empty*," and (19) "*identity-less*" as well as (20) its one general characteristic of *not* viewing these as any [*characteristics*].

[Among] the sixteen [aspects] of cessation, the three realizations of (21) *the internal* [sense faculties], (22) *the external* [objects], and (23) *both* as *being emptiness* refer to [the aspect] "cessation." The eight realizations of (24) *emptiness*, (25) *the great*, (26) *the ultimate*, (27) *conditioned phenomena*, (28) *unconditioned phenomena*, (29) *what is beyond extremes*, (30) *what is without beginning and end*, [and (31) *what is not rejected*] as *being emptiness* refer to [the aspect] "peace." The one realization of (32) *the primordial nature* as *being emptiness* refers to [the aspect] "excellence." The three realizations of (33) *all phenomena*, (34) *specifically characterized phenomena*, and (35) *the unobservable* as *being emptiness* refer to the manner of "final deliverance." The one realization of (36) *the nature of nonentities* as *being emptiness* refers to "final deliverance." For, by virtue of these [sixteen] aspects of wisdom being free from clinging to their corresponding [sixteen objects], they realize them as being emptiness. These [aspects] are the remedies for the conceptions about the apprehender.[21]

2.3.1.2.2.1.2.1.1.2.3. The 110 aspects of the knowledge of all aspects

> **Starting with the foundations of mindfulness**
> **And ending with the aspects of buddhahood,**
> **In approximate concordance with the reality of the path,** [IV.4ac]

The aspects of realizing the actuality of **the realities** in the mind streams **of** [the three kinds of] noble persons on **the path** teach the actual aspects of the knowledge of entities and the knowledge of the path and the **approximately concordant** aspects of the knowledge of all aspects. Within the scope of the knowledge that all aspects are without arising, the knowledges that entities and the path are without arising are included too. It is in terms of this [that the next lines say:]

> **And distinguished through the threefold omniscience** [IV.4d]

> **Of disciples, bodhisattvas,** {82a}
> **And buddhas, in due order,**
> **They are asserted as thirty-seven,**
> **Thirty-four, and thirty-nine.** [IV.5]

The sūtras say:

> . . . because body, feelings, mind, and phenomena are unobservable . . .[22]

You may wonder, "But isn't this a repetition of the above explanations on the aspects of [the knowledges of] entities and the path?" There is no flaw since the above [explanations were given] in terms of [the limited scope of these aspects in] the bodhisattvas' own mind streams, whereas here [these aspects] are presented by way of a buddha's mind possessing them, [with their nature being all-encompassing]. Or, above, they were [explained] by way of their characteristics, matching them with the basic nature of the four realities, while here they are presented by way of practicing the path.[23]

This has three parts:

1) [Explaining] the thirty-seven aspects that are in common with the knowledge of entities
2) [Explaining] the thirty-four aspects that are in common with the knowledge of the path
3) Explaining the uncommon thirty-nine aspects of the knowledge of all aspects[24]

1) Explaining the thirty-seven aspects that are in common with the knowledge of entities

This has seven parts:

a) The path of examining entities
b) The path that arises from effort
c) The path of training in samādhi[25]
d) The path of preparing for clear realization
e) The path of connecting with clear realization
f) The path of clearly realizing the realities
g) The path that is conducive to pure final deliverance

1a) [The path of examining entities] consists of the [four] foundations of mindfulness of (1) the body (the support for the clinging to a self); (2) feelings (the support for the clinging to the enjoyments of this self); (3) mind (the support for apprehending the things of this self) and mental factors (the supports for apprehending the self as afflicted and purified); and (4) [virtuous and nonvirtuous] phenomena, such as confidence and attachment. Through prajñā [one is mindful of them] as being, in due order, impure, suffering, impermanent, and identityless. In terms of the body, one familiarizes with the inner one (the five sense faculties), the outer one (their objects), and the one that is both (the sense organs) as being impure, just as a body in a charnel ground (its specific characteristic), {82b} and being without nature (its general characteristic). The feelings, minds, and phenomena that focus on and arise based on these three [aspects of the] body are also threefold each by virtue of this bodily division. The manner of familiarizing [with them in terms of their general and specific characteristics] corresponds to the above one.

1b) By virtue of having become familiar with this, [there follows the path that arises from effort]. One produces vigor in order to (5) relinquish any nonvirtues that have [already] arisen; (6) not give rise to any that have not yet arisen; (7) increase the virtues that have arisen; and (8) give rise to those that have not yet arisen. With regard to each one, first, through the striving of wishing to perform them, one makes efforts in calm abiding and superior insight. How is vigor produced as the remedy for faintheartedness and agitation? One cultivates it by way of collecting the mind through prajñā and settling the mind within that through calm abiding. As for "virtue" and "nonvirtue" here, the mother [sūtras] say that they refer to mental nonengagement and engagement, respectively.

1c) By virtue of having become familiar with this, a one-pointed mind arises, which consists of (9) the samādhi based on the striving of devoted application; (10) the samādhi based on the vigor of constant application; (11) the samādhi based on the mind having attained samādhi before; and (12) the samādhi based on the analysis of phenomena through prajñā. Once this [one-pointed mind] has arisen, one also attains miraculous powers. [There are] five flaws in this [training in samādhi]—laziness; forgetting the instructions; dullness and agitation; not applying the mind due to these [—dullness and agitation—] having subsided; applying the mind in the form of being discursive due to these [two] not having subsided.[26] The remedies for laziness consist of cultivating the four samādhis of striving, vigor, confidence, and suppleness. The four remedies for the remaining four [flaws] are recollection, alertness, application, and the equanimity of naturally settling the mind. Thus, one cultivates the eight applications that relinquish [the five flaws]. These three {83a} [paths (1a–1c)] are primarily cultivated starting from the lesser, middling, and greater paths of accumulation, respectively.

1d) By virtue of having become familiar with this, [on the path of preparing for clear realization one develops] (13) the confidence of having trust in enlightenment; (14) the vigor of applying oneself to the conduct of bodhisattvas; (15) the mindfulness of not forgetting one's focal objects; (16) the samādhi of mind not being discursive; and (17) the prajñā of discriminating phenomena. Progressively, one gains power over them through the respectively preceding ones. This means that one, [in due order,] familiarizes with the [four] realities in the manner of having trust in them; thus being enthusiastic about realizing them; not forgetting them after having realized them; dwelling one-pointedly in what is not forgotten; and being certain about their meaning.

1e) By virtue of having become familiar with this, [on the path of connecting with clear realization] the five antagonistic factors lack of confidence, laziness, forgetfulness, distraction, and dullness are overcome, and (18)–(22) the five faculties become very powerful. The manner of familiarizing is as before. These two [sets of faculties and powers] are cultivated starting on [the levels of] heat and peak and on [the levels of] readiness and supreme dharma [of the path of preparation, respectively].[27]

1f) By virtue of having become familiar with this, [on the path of clearly realizing the four realities one practices the seven branches of enlightenment]—(23) the correct mindfulness of not forgetting the basic nature; (24) the prajñā that thoroughly discriminates phenomena and overcomes conceptions; (25) the vigor that swiftly accomplishes the supernatural knowledges; (26) the joy that satisfies body and mind through the increase in the illumination of the dharma; (27) the suppleness of attaining the bliss of a workable body and mind; (28) the one-pointed samādhi in which the abundance of wisdom arises; and (29) the equanimity that is nonconceptual wisdom. These represent the [five] branches such as the matrix of enlightenment. [The branch of] the matrix of enlightenment is mindfulness; [the branch of enlightenment's] nature is the thorough analysis of phenomena; [the branch of] final deliverance is vigor; [the branch of its] benefit is joy; and the branch of the lack of affliction consists of the remaining [three]. In each one of them one focuses on the four realities and then familiarizes with these [realities] as what is to be understood, {83b} to be relinquished, to be manifested, and to be relied on in one's mindstream, respectively.

1g) By virtue of having become familiar with this, [the path that is conducive to pure final deliverance—the eightfold path of the noble ones—arises.[28] It consists of] (30) the correct view of realizing the basic nature, just as it is; (31) through the power of that, the [correct] thoughts of understanding the meanings of the sūtra collections and so on; (32) the [correct] speech of pure verbal actions; (33) the [correct] aims of action—pure physical actions; (34) the [correct] livelihood that is pure of verbal flattery, physical pretense, and so on; (35) the [correct] effort of not being weary of relinquishing the cognitive obscurations for a long time; (36) [correct] mindfulness as the remedy for dullness and agitation; and (37) [correct] samādhi as the remedy for the obscurations of meditative absorption that obscure the supernatural knowledges and so on. These represent the branches of the path of the noble ones, such as delimitation. This means that [correct] view delimits the realization[29] of the path of seeing. [Correct] thought and speech make others understand.

The triad of [correct] speech, aims of action, and livelihood instills trust in the view, ethics, and the reduction of necessities, respectively. The remaining three make up the branch of remedy. The manner of familiarizing with these is as with the branches of enlightenment and this familiarization [takes place] from the second bhūmi onward.

2) Explaining the thirty-four aspects that are in common with the knowledge of the path

This has six parts:

a) The path of the remedies
b) The path of manifesting[30]
c) The path of blissfully abiding amidst visible phenomena
d) The supramundane path
e) The path of relinquishment
f) The path of buddhahood

2a) [The path of the remedies] consists of the three samādhis of (1) emptiness, (2) wishlessness, and (3) signlessness that focus on the three objects that represent the two kinds of identity, the five skandhas as the basis of these two identities, and the subsiding of this basis, respectively. The cause of wishlessness is to familiarize with everything conditioned being impermanent and all conceptions being suffering; {84a} the cause of emptiness is to familiarize with identitylessness; and the cause of signlessnes is to familiarize with nirvāṇa as [all] conceptions being utterly at peace. These [three doors] also include [all sixteen] aspects of the four realities—the first door [includes the aspects of] being empty and identityless; the second door, impermanence, suffering, and [all aspects] of the origin of suffering; and the third door, the eight [aspects] of cessation and the path.[31]

2b) [The path of manifesting consists of the first three of the eight liberations.] (4) Looking at form through what possesses form means to manifest all kinds of [outer] forms of the container and its contents, be they big, small, beautiful, or ugly, and so on, without being free from attachment to one's own form, or, even if one is free from it, without the notion of form being eliminated. (5) Looking at form through what is formless means to manifest outer forms as before through being free from attachment to one's own form, or, even if one is not free from it, with the notion [of form] being eliminated (these two are the doors that liberate from the obscurations of manifesting). (6) [The liberation of notions of] specific beauty means that, from among three [things], such as a copper, a silver, and a golden vase, (a) one focuses on the silver vase and regards it as being both beautiful and ugly in dependence on [each one of] the other two; (b) one looks at it as being connected with the other two; and (c) likewise looks at [the notion of] being ugly being related to [the notion of] being beautiful.[32] This is applied in the same way to all phenomena and represents the liberation from the obscurations of desiring to manifest only beautiful [forms and disliking to manifest ugly ones].

2c) [The path of blissfully abiding amidst visible phenomena consists of the remaining five liberations, which are] (7)–(10) the four formless [absorptions] and (11) the meditative absorption of the cessation of [primary] minds and mental factors. [The former four represent the liberations from] the cravings for relishing these respective levels [of meditative absorption] and [the latter one is] the liberation from feelings and discrimination.[33] Adding the three above [liberations] to these, {84b} they make up the eight liberations. In the system of the mahāyāna, the physical support for attaining them for the first time is a human one, while sustaining an already arisen one [among these liberations] is also possible in supports within the form realm. The mental support is the same [in both cases]—relying on the highest form of the fourth dhyāna.

2d) [The supramundane path] consists of the nine meditative absorptions of progressive abiding—(12)–(15) the four dhyānas; (16)–(19) the four formless [absorptions]; and (20) the meditative absorption of cessation. The first eight are the supports of the supramundane path. The latter one [is presented as] the supramundane path by virtue of being its subsequent attainment, or in terms of being its nature. The difference between the meditative absorptions [(16)–(20)] and [these same absorptions in the context of the eight] liberations lies in their being the uninterrupted paths and the paths of liberation, respectively.

2e) [The path of relinquishment] consists of (21)–(24) the four readinesses of the path of seeing.[34]

2f) [The path of buddhahood] consists of (25)–(34) the ten pāramitās.

The [particular] explanation of the meditative absorption of cessation in this context has two parts:

a) The system of the hīnayāna
b) The system of the mahāyāna

2fa) The system of the hīnayāna has two parts:

1) Supports
2) Nature

2fa1) The physical supports are as above.[35] As for the mental supports, the support for entering [this meditative absorption] is the Peak of Existence because [its very subtle] flux of minds and mental factors is easy to stop. When one rises [from the meditative absorption of cessation, this rising] is based on [a mental support that is] either the pure [form of the] Peak of Existence or the [uncontaminated] Nothing Whatsoever.

2fa2) Since feelings and discriminations are coarse, through eliminating them minds and mental factors within the body are stopped. This is asserted as being virtuous and a nonassociated formation. One engages in it for as long as one is propelled [into it] through the motivational forces of either the [non-returners] who witness with the body or the arhats who are liberated by virtue of the aspects of both [prajñā and samādhi].

2fb) The system of the mahāyāna has two parts:
1) Common
2) Uncommon

2fb1) The common [meditative absorption of cessation] is the mere cessation of feelings and discrimination—it accords with the one of the śrāvakas, and bodhisattvas do not dwell in it for more than seven days.[36] {85a}

2fb2) The uncommon [system] has two parts:
a) The Madhyamaka [system]
b) The [Mere] Mentalist system

2fb2a) In the first one, it is taught that [the meditative absorption of cessation] is attained from the sixth bhūmi onward. On the seventh bhūmi, [bodhisattvas] are able to enter it and rise [from it in a single moment] all by themselves. On the eighth bhūmi since there is no clinging to characteristics even during subsequent attainment, when they rise [from it], they must be raised by the buddhas. [This meditative absorption of cessation] consists of characteristics and reference points having been put to an end within suchness through prajñāpāramitā.

2fb2b) In the system of the Mere Mentalists, in terms of those learners who have not previously gone through inferior paths, [the meditative absorption of cessation] exists from the subsequent attainment of the path of seeing onward and consists of the seven collections [of consciousness] having been put to an end within the ālaya-consciousness through wisdom. Though wisdom is not this [absorption's] own nature, wisdom exists [in it] in an uninterrupted manner. In terms of nonlearners, it consists of the buddha wisdom of all adventitious stains having ceased within ālaya-wisdom, and there is no rising from that. In the *[Abhisamay]ālaṃkāra* here, [the meditative absorption of cessation] should be asserted in accordance with both these systems of Madhyamaka and Mere Mentalism.[37]

3) Explaining the uncommon thirty-nine aspects of the knowledge of all aspects
This has seven parts, which are the aspects of
a) The ten powers
b) The four fearlessnesses

c) The four discriminating awarenesses
d) The eighteen unique qualities
e) Suchness
f) Self-arising
g) Buddhahood

3a) [The ten powers] consist of knowing (1) what is the case (such as possessions arising from generosity) and what is not the case (their arising from avarice); (2) all processes without exception of maturational results [arising from] contaminated actions; (3) the various distinct inclinations of sentient beings; (4) [all] the many [ways in which] worldly realms[38] come into existence and perish, as well as their respective superiority and inferiority; {85b} (5) the faculties [of beings] (such as confidence) as being superior (sharp) or nonsuperior (dull and medium); (6) the paths on which to proceed to all three kinds of enlightenment; (7) afflicted phenomena (such as relishing the obscurations of meditative absorption) and purified phenomena (the lack of characteristics connected to these [meditative absorptions] and rising [from them] in a timely fashion); (8) the recollection of the past states of innumerable lifetimes of oneself and others [and thus guiding them on the various yānas]; (9) the manner of the deaths, transitions, and rebirths of all sentient beings; and (10) the termination of the contaminations of the two obscurations. Among these, the first one possesses the power to overcome the māras who deceive one about the means of [attaining] the higher realms; the second one, those who deceive one about what is not a refuge being a refuge; the seventh one, those who deceive one about uncontaminated pure [samādhis]; and the remaining, those who deceive one about the final deliverance of the mahāyāna.

3b [The four fearlessnesses] consist of (11)–(12) the two statements of realization and relinquishment (one's own welfare), proclaiming in the middle of those who surround one, "I am a buddha" and "I have terminated all contaminations," and (13)–(14) the two statements about the factors to be relinquished and the path (the welfare of others), proclaiming, "The two obscurations obstruct liberation and omniscience" and "Through the all-knowledge and the knowledge of the path, resepectively, the path is the final deliverance in the form of śrāvaka and pratyekabuddha [arhats] and perfect enlightenment." These are "fearlessnesses" because [they are proclaimed as fearlessly as a lion roars in the midst of other animals and] there is not even a little bit of dispute in accordance with the dharma about them.

3c) The discriminating awarenesses of (15) phenomena (knowing all synonyms of causal phenomena—the supports) and (16) meanings (knowing what is to be expressed or the resultant phenomena that are supported [by the former]) are the two knowledges of what is to be explained. {86a} The discriminating awarenesses of (17) semantics (through expressing a given [term] it will be understood in the languages of the respective country) and (18) self-confidence (knowing the divisions of phenomena, such as whether they exist substantially or imputedly) are the two knowledges of the means of explanation.

3d) [The eighteen unique qualities] consist of (a) the six [aspects of] the unique conduct of [a buddha] never being involved in any (19) mistakenness in terms of the body (such as jumping around together with a mad elephant); (20) useless chatter (such as laughter or lamentation); (21) deterioration of mindfulness (such as not doing what is to be done or being too late); (22) mind that is not settled in meditative equipoise, no matter whether resting in or rising from samādhi; (23) discriminations in terms of saṃsāra and nirvāṇa being different; and (24) indifference of forsaking those to be guided through lacking examination [as to whether the time to guide them is right or not]; (b) the six [aspects of] unique realization of there never being any deterioration of (25) the striving to teach the dharma; (26) the vigor to accomplish what is to be done for those to be guided; (27) the mindfulness of teaching the dharma without having to think; (28) the samādhi of the nature of phenomena; (29) the prajñā of immeasurable wisdom; and (30) being liberated from all factors to be relinquished; (c) the three [aspects of] unique enlightened activity—wisdom preceding and following the enlightened activities of [a buddha's] (31) body (guiding sentient beings through one's physical attire, conduct, and so on); (32) speech (teaching the dharma that is fruitful); and (33) mind (wisdom following all sentient beings); and (d) the three [aspects of] unique wisdom—(34)–(36) the vision of wisdom operating with regard to all phenomena in the three times without attachment (by virtue of knowing their suchness) and without obstruction (by virtue of knowing their variety).

3e) (37) Suchness is the very nature of the nirvāṇa explained by all buddhas. {86b}

3f) (38) What is self-arising is the wisdom of knowing the entire variety of phenomena by virtue of the dependent origination that consists of the manifestation[39] of suchness.

3g) (39) [In buddhahood] there is no appearance of anything other than solely the nature of the fully perfect realization of all aspects of these phenomena.[40]

2.3.1.2.2.1.2.1.2. The persons who familiarize

> **Those who lived up to their duties toward the buddhas,**
> **Planted roots of virtue in relation to them,**
> **And are protected by spiritual friends**
> **Are the vessels for listening to her.** [IV.6]

> **Since they attended to the buddhas, asked them,**
> **And engaged in generosity, ethics, and so on,**
> **These genuine beings are held to be the vessels**
> **For taking her up, retaining her, and so on.** [IV.7]

You may wonder, "Who are the persons to familiarize with prajñāpāramitā?" **Those who lived up to their duties toward the** previous **buddhas** by paying service to and honoring them; **planted roots of virtue in relation to these** buddhas [through making offerings and so on]; and, [through having purified and trained their mind streams,] **are protected** through [always] being taken care of **by** [these buddhas as their] **spiritual friends are the vessels for listening to her**—profound prajñāpāramitā. **Since they attended to the buddhas** as spiritual friends; **asked them** about the meaning of prajñāpāramitā; **and engaged in** the [ten] pāramitās of **generosity, ethics, and so on** [for many eons], **these genuine beings are held** [by the buddhas] **to** [now] **be the vessels for** not only listening [to prajñāpāramitā], but also not being afraid upon hearing her, **taking her up** readily, **retaining her** words and meanings, **and so on** (that is, practicing and realizing her).[41] The sūtras say:

> Those sons and daughters of good family who come to hear this mother rendered service to and honored the past victors, planted roots of virtue in relation to these tathāgatas, and were taken care of by spiritual friends. . . .[42]

2.3.1.2.2.1.2.1.3. The nature of the training[43]

This has two parts:

1) The five natural trainings
2) The fifteen situational trainings

2.3.1.2.2.1.2.1.3.1. The five natural trainings

> **Because of not abiding in form and so on,**
> **Because of having stopped involvement in them,**
> **Because of their suchness being profound,**
> **Because of their being difficult to fathom,** [IV.8]

> **Because of their being immeasurable,** [IV.9a]

(1) **Because of not abiding in form and so on** ([everything] up through the knowledge of all aspects) through clinging; (2) **because of having stopped involvement in them**; (3) **because of their suchness being profound**; (4)

because of their suchnesses **being difficult to fathom**; and (5) **because of their** suchness {87a} **being immeasurable**, in due order, [these indicate] the five samādhis of putting an end to the clinging to the apprehended; putting an end to the clinging to the apprehender; and realizing that [the knowledges of] entities, the path, [and all] aspects are without arising. [These samādhis] are referred to as the trainings that bear their names in accordance with what is respectively practiced [in them]. They exist from the path of accumulation up through the end of the continuum.

2.3.1.2.2.1.2.1.3.2. The fifteen situational trainings

> **Because of realization being slow and full of hardships,**
> **Because of the prophecy, irreversibility,**
> **Final deliverance, no obstructions,** [IV.9bd]
>
> **Being close to enlightenment, swift,**
> **The welfare of others, without increase and decrease,**
> **Not seeing dharmas or nondharmas and so on,**
> **Not seeing the inconceivability of form and so on,** [IV.10]
>
> **Because of not conceiving the characteristics**
> **Or the being of form and such,**
> **Bestowing precious fruitions,**
> **Purity, and a set period of time.** [IV.11]

(6) **Because of** the **realization** of the mother **being slow and full of hardships** due to the possibility of fear of the mother arising; (7) **because of** obtaining **the prophecy** about perfect enlightenment due to not being afraid of the mother; (8) because of **irreversibility** due to swiftly retaining the mother upon hearing her; (9) because of **final deliverance** from the opposites of the mother, such as the two levels [of śrāvakas and pratyekabuddhas]; (10) because of **no obstructions** to enlightenment—the coarse conceptions that are the factors to be relinquished through seeing; (11) because of **being close to enlightenment** by virtue of having newly attained uncontaminated phenomena; and (12) because of becoming **swiftly** enlightened, in due order, [these respectively indicate] the seven samādhis of bodhisattvas who dwell on the path of accumulation and are of dull faculties; on [the levels of] heat; peak; poised readiness; and the supreme [dharma of the path of preparation]; on the path of seeing; and on the second through the seventh bhūmis. They are referred to as the practices of these respective [aspects].

(13) Because of accomplishing **the welfare of others** (turning the wheel of dharma and encouraging them [to practice]); (14) because of seeing that

the nature of phenomena is **without increase and decrease**; (15) because of **not seeing dharmas** (white actions) **or nondharmas** (black actions) **and so on**; (16) because of not being conceited by virtue of **not** [even] **seeing the inconceivability of form and so on**; and (17) **because of not conceiving the characteristics or the being of form and such**, these are the five distinctive features of bodhisattvas who dwell on the eighth bhūmi, {87b} which are [again] referred to as the practices of these respective [aspects].

(18) Because of **bestowing** the six **precious fruitions** (from stream-enterer up through perfect buddhahood)[44] to others; (19) because of **purifying** the subtle stains of the impregnations of negative tendencies; **and** (20) because of not reducing **a set period of time** in terms of months or years for which one has vowed to write down the mother and so forth, [in due order, these indicate] the samādhis of the ninth and the tenth bhūmis and the activities of bodhisattvas from the path of accumulation up through the seventh bhumi, which are [again] referred to as the practices of these respective [aspects].[45] The sūtras say:

> When bodhisattvas do not abide in form and so on, they practice yoga with regard to form . . .[46]

2.3.1.2.2.1.2.1.4. The preliminary factors of the training

This has four parts:

1) [Knowing] the qualities
2) [Knowing] the flaws
3) [Knowing] the defining characteristics
4) Knowing the factors conducive to liberation

2.3.1.2.2.1.2.1.4.1. Knowing the qualities

> **The qualities are fourteenfold,**
> **Such as vanquishing the power of māras.** [IV.12ab]

[The fourteen qualities that result from the twenty trainings] are discussed in order to give rise to enthusiasm for familiarizing with the mother.[47] Though they are attained starting with the path of accumulation, in their proper form they [only exist] from the path of preparation onward.[48] The sūtras say:

> Bhagavan, through whose power are evil māras unable to create obstacles for bodhisattvas . . .?[49]

The fourteen [qualities] **are** (1) **vanquishing the power of māras** through the blessings of the Buddha; (2) being considered by the minds of the buddhas; (3) being seen by the eyes of the buddhas; (4) being close to enlightenment; (5) never being born in the unpleasant realms until reaching [the level of] irreversibility; (6) not being separated from the buddhas; (7) not being separated from uncontaminated phenomena, such as the six pāramitās; {88a} (8) becoming a buddha in the southern or northern countries and being praised by all buddhas for engaging in this way; (9) fully completing uncontaminated phenomena; (10) not rejecting the mother and great joy and bliss arising upon hearing about her; (11) one's vow [of bodhicitta] being firm and thus unalterable by māras; (12) being able to establish many beings in perfect enlightenment; (13) seizing consummate maturation; (14) being able [to promote] the vast welfare of sentient beings.[50]

As an elaboration on the phrase "during the last five hundred [years]" in the corresponding sūtra passages,[51] the duration during which the teachings remain is explained. According to what the *Bhadrakalpikā[sūtra]* says, the teachings remain for five thousand years after the teacher's passing away. [Within] this [timespan, the first] three times five hundred [years] represent the time of realization, during which [the followers of these teachings] attain mainly [the fruitions of] arhats, nonreturners, and stream-enterers, respectively. [The next] three times five hundred [years] represent the time of practice—[practicing] mainly [the trainings of] prajñā, samādhi, and ethics, respectively. [The following] three times five hundred years are the time of the scriptures, during which mainly abhidharma, sūtra, and vinaya, respectively, are taught. [Finally, there is] one [last period of] five hundred [years] during which [monastics just] bear the mere [outer] signs of being ordained, while lacking the genuine view and conduct. At the present time of the mighty victor [Mikyö Dorje] being forty-one years old [1547 CE], according to the Kālacakra system 2,425 [years] have passed since the teacher has passed away. Therefore, among the five hundred [years] of [mainly practicing] samādhi, 425 have passed and seventy-five are left.[52]

2.3.1.2.2.1.2.1.4.2. Knowing the flaws

These forty-six flaws are stated because they are the obstacles to familiarizing with the mother that must be [known and] eliminated.

> **The flaws** {88b} **are to be known**
> **As four sets of ten plus six.** [IV.12cd]

These exist from the path of accumulation up through the seventh bhūmi, but mainly on [the paths of] accumulation and preparation. The *[Prajñāpāramitā]-saṃcayagāthā* says:

> Not promoting the welfare of beings, they will deteriorate
> As swift as lightning—this is the work of māra.[53]

The forty-six [flaws] are (1) overly belated self-confidence; (2) overly quick [self-confidence]; (3) [while writing down the mother,] yawning, being agitated, and kicking each other;[54] (4) a distracted mind; (5) being attached to other letters; (6) rising from one's seat and leaving without having gotten a taste of the mother; (7) giving explanations on a text while yawning; (8) intending to cast away the rootlike mother and train in the branchlike sūtra collections of śrāvakas and pratyekabuddhas; (9) for the sake of gain and honor, casting away the mother and then training in the inferior sūtra collections; (10) casting away the mother and then searching for the knowledge of all aspects in these inferior sūtra collections; (11) just as vassal kings vying with a cakravartin, considering the sūtra collections of śrāvakas and pratyekabuddhas as equal to the mother and then training in the sūtra collections of śrāvakas and pratyekabuddhas; (12) just as considering a precious gem and a trinket as equal, casting away the mother that one has found and intending to search for the knowledge of all aspects in the sūtra collections of śrāvakas and pratyekabuddhas; (13) when engaging in the mother, inflational conceptual self-confidence about phenomena from form up through the knowledge of all aspects; (14) clinging to nonentities as being the mother; (15) clinging to letters as being the mother; (16) clinging to what is without letters as being the mother; (17) when engaging in the dharma, giving rise to many object-related activities; (18) mentally engaging in village men and women and their various actions; {89a} (19) savoring gain and honor; (20) casting away the mother and then searching for skill in means in sūtras of śrāvakas and pratyekabuddhas procured by māra; (21) in the context of engaging the dharma of the mother, the one who explains being vigorous and the listener being without vigor; (22) the one who explains desiring gain and honor and the listener not desiring so; (23) the one who explains possessing the twelve qualities of abstinence and the listener not possessing them; (24) the one who explains giving away material things, making efforts in virtue, and being of sharp faculties, and the listener being miserly, lazy, and of dull faculties; (25) the one who explains knowing the twelve branches of a buddha's speech and the listener not knowing them; (26)–(30) these [last] five [situations] being reversed; (31) either master or disciple possessing skill in means and the other one not possessing it; (32) likewise, [either one] having attained dhāraṇī or not; (33) striving or not striving to engage in the dharma of the mother; (34) being free or not being free from the five obscurations; (35) being afraid of saṃsāra and thus desiring nirvāṇa right now or not desiring so; (36) making efforts alone without a companion or not making efforts [in this manner]; (37) the one who explains not liking to be followed and the listener [liking to] follow; (38) making or not making efforts in engaging in the dharma for the sake of the slightest material goods; (39) going or not going to places that can be life-threatening; (40) going or not going to places where one is deprived of livelihood; (41) the one who explains going to places where there is plenty of livelihood and the listener refusing to follow; (42) the one who explains attempting to go to frightening places and the listener refusing to follow; (43) the one who explains looking full of attachment at villages where there is plenty of alms and the listener refusing to follow; {89b} (44) doubt about the mother arising and abandoning her when māras, in order to turn one away from the mother, cause a schism, saying, "My conduct corresponds to this mother, but yours does not"; (45) training in [some kind of] mother that is fabricated through the power of these [māras]; and (46) one's mind being altered by evil māras in the disguise of śrāmaṇas, who thus make one have confidence in them.[55]

2.3.1.2.2.1.2.1.4.3. The defining characteristics to be known

This has two parts:

1) General [topic]
2) [Meaning of] the text

2.3.1.2.2.1.2.1.4.3.1. General topic

This has two parts:

1) General presentation of defining characteristics
2) Explanation of the topic at hand

2.3.1.2.2.1.2.1.4.3.1.1. General presentation of defining characteristics

As for defining characteristics, something like "the heat of fire" is a specific characteristic. Something like "being impermanent" is a general characteristic. What entails many isolates in dependence on singling out [certain aspects of] a single entity is a defining characteristic in terms of a division. To exclude underinclusion, overinclusion, and so on is a defining characteristic in terms of eliminating discordant types. What does not exist ultimately, but is put forth in order to eliminate doubts from the perspective of [certain] mental states, is a defining characteristic in terms of eliminating wrong ideas. Among these, the one explained here is the first one.

2.3.1.2.2.1.2.1.4.3.1.2. Explanation of the topic at hand

This passage [of the AA about the defining characteristics of the training] does not identify [defining characteristics, definienda, and their instances] that actually fulfill the definition of portraying something to be portrayed. You may wonder, "So what is identified [here]?" Since the instances and the definiendum [in this case] are the same in terms of both the meaning and the equivalent terms, in actual fact they are indeed not different. Nevertheless, for example, the single term "to boil" is suitable to be used in both [phrases that refer to] the object and the agent—"that which boils [something]" and "that which is boiled." Likewise, the single term "defining characteristic" is stated with the intention of its being connected to both the agent and the object—"that which defines" and "that which is defined." Therefore, the three [defining characteristics of] knowledge, distinctiveness, and activity are what define [the training] (being used as the agents [that define]), while the characteristic of the nature [of the training] is what is defined (being used as the object [that is defined]). These two [ways of using the term "defining characteristics"] represent what makes one understand and what is to be understood, just as a reason and its probandum. {90a} You may wonder, "How do they define [the training]?" The characteristic of knowledge and the characteristic of activity respectively define it in the sense of the two capacities of giving rise to realization (one's own welfare) and enlightened activity (the welfare of others) existing within the training in the three knowledges. Thus, they represent exclusions of nonpossession. The characteristic of activity eliminates the [qualm of] wondering, "Do these two capacities also exist in the trainings of śrāvakas and pratyekabuddhas?" Thus, it defines that [these two capacities] exist only in this [training of bodhisattvas], which is an exclusion of possession by others.[56] Both the training and the capacities that are based on it are identified as the instance that is defined.[57]

2.3.1.2.2.1.2.1.4.3.2. Meaning of the text

This has two parts:

1) Brief introduction
2) Detailed explanation

2.3.1.2.2.1.2.1.4.3.2.1. Brief introduction

> **What defines should be known**
> **As the defining characteristic, which is threefold**
> **(Knowledge, distinctiveness, and activity),**
> **And what is defined is the nature.** [IV.13]

In order to cultivate this [mahāyāna] training [by way of adopting the above qualities and rejecting the flaws], its defining characteristics must be known. Therefore, they are stated [here as follows]. **What defines** it **should be known as the defining characteristic** of the training. This defining characteristic that defines it **is threefold**—it consists of the defining characteristics of **knowledge, distinctiveness, and activity. What is defined** through the sixteen [aspects of] **the nature** of the training that has these three [characteristics] **is** to give rise to the three knowledges. As for "**and**" [in IV.13d], it is said [to indicate] that not only the above [three characteristics] but also this one [—the nature—] is a defining characteristic.[58] The boundary lines of these defining characteristics range from the path of accumulation up through the end of the continuum.

2.3.1.2.2.1.2.1.4.3.2.2. Detailed explanation

This has four parts:

1) [The defining characteristic of] knowledge, which demonstrates the capacity to produce the final realization
2) [The defining characteristic of] distinctiveness, which demonstrates that śrāvakas and pratyekabuddhas do not possess this consummate capacity
3) [The defining characteristic of] activity, which demonstrates the capacity to accomplish the vast welfare of others
4) The defining characteristic of the nature—the training that possesses these distinctive features

2.3.1.2.2.1.2.1.4.3.2.2.1. The defining characteristic of knowledge, which demonstrates the capacity to produce the final realization

This has three parts:

1) The defining characteristic of knowledge in terms of the knowledge of entities
2) The defining characteristic of knowledge in terms of the knowledge of the path
3) The defining characteristic of knowledge in terms of the knowledge of all aspects

2.3.1.2.2.1.2.1.4.3.2.2.1.1. The defining characteristic of knowledge in terms of the knowledge of entities

> **The Tathāgata appearing,**
> **The world having the character of not being perishable,**
> **The conduct of the minds of sentient beings,**
> **Their being concentrated and moving outside,** [IV.14]

The aspect of inexhaustibility,
Being endowed with attachment and so on, vast,
Great, immeasurable,
Consciousness being indemonstrable, [IV.15]

Mind being invisible,
Consciousnesses being discerned as coming forth and so on,
Knowing these as aspects
Of suchness, and furthermore [IV.16]

The sage realizing suchness
And communicating it to others—
These make up the defining characteristic of knowledge
In the context of the all-knowledge. [IV.17]

[The sixteen aspects of the defining characteristic of knowledge in terms of the knowledge of entities] are (1) **the Tathāgata appearing** from the mother; (2) {90b} in true reality, **the world** of the five skandhas **having the character of not being perishable** either momentarily or by way of a continuum [coming to its end]; (3) **the conduct of the minds of sentient beings** being immeasurable; (4) **these** minds **being concentrated** inside; (5) these minds **moving outside** and thus being distracted; (6) their having become the unconditionedness of the freedom [from obscurations]—**the aspect of inexhaustibility** of these minds; (7) the mind **being endowed with** afflictions (**attachment** and so on); (8) **and so on** referring to being free from attachment and so on; (9) mind being **vast** by virtue of being the essence of the nature of phenomena; (10) mind being **great** by virtue of pervading everything; (11) mind being **immeasurable** by virtue of lacking any foundation; (12) **consciousness being indemonstrable** as "This is it" by virtue of lacking any specific characteristics; (13) **mind being invisible** even to the eyes of the tathāgatas; and (14) **consciousnesses being discerned as coming forth** (engaging in objects by way of affirmation) **and so on**, that is, being withdrawn (engaging by way of negation).

Here, the assertions that the self and the world are permanent, impermanent, both, or neither depend on a starting point. The assertions that the self and the world have an end, do not have [an end], both, or neither depend on an end point. The assertions that buddhas [still] manifest after having passed away, do not manifest, both, or neither depend on nirvāṇa. The assertions that body and life-force are one or different depend on body and life-force. Among these, [the self and the world] being permanent and not having an end as well as [buddhas still] manifesting after having passed away refer to "coming forth" (views about permanence). {91a} Their opposites refer to "being withdrawn" (views about extinction). [The above instances of] both [of these possibilities] refer to "being scattered"—the view of the Nirgranthas (affirmation). [The above instances of] neither [of these possibilities] refer to "being closed"—the view of the Vātsīputrīyas (negation). The Vaiśeṣikas view body and life-force as one, and the Sāṃkhyas view them as different, with the former representing an affirmation and the latter being a negation. These represent the meanings of the sixty-two views of non-Buddhists[59] at the time when [the Buddha] turned the wheel of dharma in Jambudvīpa, which were put forward [to him] by dividing them into these fourteen extremes. Since all of them start with [the assumption of] a self, in the absence of [a self as] the basis of [the above] distinctive features, such features are not justified. However, with [the Buddha] having in mind that it would be pointless [in the given situations] if he refuted [the self as] the basis of such features, his answers [to the questions addressed to him in the form of the above fourteen extremes] were undecided. Therefore, to relate them [here] to distinct persons [or schools] is only [done] in order to elucidate [certain] aspects. However, [in general,] all of them represent non-Buddhist views, which are without object and illusionlike.[60]

Furthermore, [the last two aspects are] (15) **knowing these** five skandhas **as aspects of suchness and** (16) **the sage realizing** the **suchness** of phenomena **and communicating it to others. These make up the defining characteristic of knowledge in the context of** the training in **the all-knowledge** [with its nature of] being devoid [of the afflictions] and so on.[61] [This means that] this training has the capacity to know these [above sixteen] objects.[62] The sūtras say:

> This profound mother gives rise to the tathāgatas . . .[63]

2.3.1.2.2.1.2.1.4.3.2.2.1.2. The defining characteristic of knowledge in terms of the knowledge of the path

> **Emptiness, signlessness,**
> **Relinquishment of desires,**
> **No arising, no ceasing, and so on,**
> **The nature of phenomena being unperturbed,** [IV.18]
>
> **Nonformation, nonconceptualization,**
> **Distinction, and nonexistence of defining characteristics—**
> **These are asserted as the defining characteristic of knowledge**
> **In the context of the knowledge of the path.** [IV.19]

[The sixteen aspects of the defining characteristic of knowledge of the knowledge of the path are] (1) the mother's **emptiness** of reference points; (2) the **signlessness** of causes; (3) the **relinquishment of desires** for results; {91b} (4) **no** new **arising**; (5) **no ceasing** of something that existed before; **and so on**—the six [features of] there being (6) no afflicted phenomena; (7) no purified phenomena (such as confidence); (8) no entities to be relinquished; (9) no nature of nirvāṇa; (10) no foundation that is the dharmadhātu; and (11) no existence [of the latter] as a changeable phenomenon; (12) **the nature of phenomena being unperturbed** by the superimpositions and denials of humans and gods; (13) **not** being **formed** through causes; (14) therefore, **not conceptualizing** anything whatsoever; (15) the **distinction** of defining characteristics (such as emptiness); **and** (16) **defining characteristics not existing** ultimately. The attainments of the clear illumination of **these** [sixteen] **are asserted as the defining characteristic of knowledge in the context of** the training in **the knowledge of the path** [with its nature of] being hard to be done and so on.[64] The sūtras say:

> This profound mother has the defining characteristic of emptiness . . .[65]

2.3.1.2.2.1.2.1.4.3.2.2.1.3. The defining characteristic of knowledge in terms of the knowledge of all aspects

> **Abiding through relying**
> **On one's own dharma, to be honored,**
> **To be respected, to be pleased,**
> **To be worshipped, lacking an agent,** [IV.20]
>
> **Being the knowledge that engages everywhere,**
> **Showing what is invisible,**
> **The world's aspect of emptiness,**
> **The one who indicates, makes known, makes visible,** [IV.21]
>
> **And shows inconceivability and peace,**
> **As well as the cessation of the world and discriminations—**
> **These are said to be the defining characteristic of knowledge**
> **In terms of the principle of the knowledge of all aspects.** [IV.22]

[The sixteen aspects of the defining characteristic of knowledge of the knowledge of all aspects are] (1) the buddhas of the three times **abiding through relying on** the mother—the **dharma** that is realized on **one's own**; that, [when] they teach [this dharma of the mother], she is (2) **to be honored,** (3) **to be respected,** and (4) **to be pleased;** (5) that the mother66 is **to be worshipped;** (6) these [factors] **lacking an agent** ultimately; (7) **being the knowledge** of wisdom **engaging** in knowable objects **everywhere;** (8) **showing** that **what is invisible** as anything whatsoever by way of characteristics is true reality; (9) the **aspect of emptiness of the world** of the seeming; (10) [the buddhas] being **the ones who** first **indicate** this as emptiness from the perspective of studying; (11) {92a} [next,] **make** it **known** from the perspective of reflection; (12) **make** it directly **visible** from the perspective of meditation; (13) **show** it to be not just nonexistence [but] **inconceivable; and** (14) show it to be the **peace** of reference points, **as well as** (15) **the cessation of** the apprehended—**the world** of the seeming, **and** (16) the cessation of the apprehender—the **discriminations** of the seeming. The attainments of the clear illumination of **these** [sixteen] **are said to be the defining characteristic of knowledge** that exists **in terms of the principle of** the training in **the knowledge of all aspects** with its nature of focal object and so on.[67] The sūtras say:

> The tathāgatas abide through relying on this dharma that is the mother.[68]

2.3.1.2.2.1.2.1.4.3.2.2.2. The defining characteristic of distinctiveness, which demonstrates that śrāvakas and pratyekabuddhas do not possess this consummate capacity

This has two parts:

1) Brief introduction
2) Detailed explanation

2.3.1.2.2.1.2.1.4.3.2.2.2.1. Brief introduction

> **The defining characteristic of distinctiveness**
> **Is explained by way of the sixteen moments**
> **That have the realities as their sphere and are distinguished**
> **Through the distinctive features of inconceivability and so on.**
> [IV.23]

[This verse] explicitly teaches that the [sixteen moments of the mahāyāna] path of seeing are more distinguished [than the ones of śrāvakas and pratyekabuddhas]. By virtue of this, one is able to understand that also the [mahāyāna] paths of familiarization and nonlearning are more eminent.

2.3.1.2.2.1.2.1.4.3.2.2.2.2. Detailed explanation

> **Being inconceivable, being incomparable,**
> **Transcending all measure and calculation,**
> **Incorporating all noble ones, being what the wise know,**
> **The knowledge not in common,** [IV.24]
>
> **Swift knowledge, lacking decline and increase,**
> **Engaging, being completely accomplished,**
> **Focusing, foundation,**
> **Completeness, being held,** [IV.25]
>
> **And lacking any relishing are to be known**
> **As the sixteen distinctive features**
> **Through which this special path**
> **Is distinguished from other paths.** [IV.26]

These sixteen distinctive features [of the mahāyāna path of seeing] consist of four kinds of focusing on each one of the four realities. First, through the power of boundless prajñā, one realizes that [this prajñā] (1) **is inconceivable,** (2) **incomparable,** (3) **transcends all** mental **measuring and** (4) is beyond all **calculations** with numbers. Secondly, it (5) **incorporates** the qualities of **all noble ones**; (6) **is what those** who are **wise** about the actualities of suchness and variety {92b} **know**; (7) is **the** supreme **knowledge** (prajñā) **not in common** with śrāvakas and pratyekabuddhas; and (8) attains supernatural **knowledge swift**er than śrāvakas and pratyekabuddhas. Thirdly, it (9) **lacks decline** (denial) **and increase** (superimpositions); (10) **engages** in the mother through being pure of the three spheres; (11) **completely accomplishes** the two accumulations [of merit and wisdom]; and (12) **focuses** on all phenomena in a nonconceptual way. Fourthly, it means (13) being endowed with the **foundation** of the path—the supreme disposition; (14) being the **completeness** of all the branches of the path; (15) **being held**, that is, embraced, by skillful means; **and** (16) **lacking any relishing** of relinquishment and realization. Therefore, these **are to be known as the sixteen distinctive features through which this special path is distinguished from other paths** because it realizes phenomenal identitylessness without exception.[69] The sūtras say:

> Form is inconceivable . . .[70]

2.3.1.2.2.1.2.1.4.3.2.2.3. The defining characteristic of activity, which demonstrates the capacity to accomplish the vast welfare of others

> **Representing benefit, happiness, protection,**
> **The refuge and place of rest for humans,**
> **An aid and an island,**
> **Acting as the leader,** [IV.27]
>
> **Being spontaneously present, having the character of not manifesting**
> **The fruition through the three yānas,**
> **And, lastly, the activity of being a resource**[71]**—**
> **These represent the defining characteristic of activity.** [IV.28]

[The eleven defining characteristics of activity] are (a) the three [activities] of training in the all-knowledge—(1) **representing** the **benefit** of all beings in their next lives as well as (2)–(3) their **happiness** and constant **protection** from suffering in this life; (b) the [seven] activities of training in the know-ledge of the path—(4) being **the refuge for** beings (such as **humans**) through establishing them in [the nirvāṇa] without remainder; (5) being their **place of rest** in putting an end to their clinging to real existence [as the cause of suffering]; (6) being the **aid** [lit. "friend in battle"] that makes them realize existence and peace as equality [in that they are empty]; **and** (7) the **island** of continuous welfare—accomplishing the welfare of oneself and others; (8) **acting as the leader** for beings because of being free from craving for one's own welfare; (9) the two welfares **being spontaneously present** without effort; and (10) {93a} **having the character of not manifesting the fruition** (the true end)[72] despite final deliverance being attained **through** the paths of **the three yānas; and, lastly,** (11) [the activity] of training in the knowledge of all aspects—**the activity of being a resource** for beings (such as turning the wheel of dharma). **These** eleven **represent the defining characteristic of activity.**[73] The sūtras say:

> You should know that bodhisattva mahāsattvas are the benefit of the world . . .[74]

2.3.1.2.2.1.2.1.4.3.2.2.4. The defining characteristic of the nature—the training that possesses these distinctive features

This has three parts:

1) The four trainings in the all-knowledge
2) The five [trainings] in the knowledge of the path
3) The seven [trainings] in the knowledge of all aspects

2.3.1.2.2.1.2.1.4.3.2.2.4.1. The four trainings in the all-knowledge

> **Being devoid of afflictions, signs, characteristics,**
> **And antagonistic factors and remedies,** [IV.29ab]

[The four defining characteristics of the nature of training in the all-knowledge] are **being devoid of** (1) **afflictions** (such as attachment); (2) their **signs** (improper physical and verbal [behavior]); (3) their **characteristics** (improper mental engagements); **and** (4) **antagonistic factors and remedies** (the cognitive obscurations of conceptions about existence and peace, respectively).

2.3.1.2.2.1.2.1.4.3.2.2.4.2. The five trainings in the knowledge of the path

> **Hard to be done, devoted in an exclusive manner,**
> **Aim, nonobservation,** [IV.29cd]

> **Refraining from clinging,** [IV.30a]

[The five defining characteristics of the nature of training in the knowledge of the path] are (5) conduct being devoid[75] of being **hard to be done** since it liberates sentient beings who are primordially nonexistent; (6) the view that is **devoted in an exclusive manner,**[76] since everything is realized to be of one taste with the dharmadhātu; (7) the **aim** of the three greatnesses;[77] (8) **nonobservation** of the three spheres; and (9) **refraining from clinging** even to the mother.

2.3.1.2.2.1.2.1.4.3.2.2.4.3. The seven trainings in the knowledge of all aspects

> **What is discerned as the focal object,**
> **Being antagonistic, unobstructed,**
> **Without ground, without going and arising,** [IV.30bd]

> **And not observing suchness—**
> **This sixteenfold nature**
> **Is defined as something like a definiendum,**
> **And thus is held to be the fourth defining characteristic.** [IV.31]

[The five defining characteristics of the nature of training in the knowledge of all aspects] are (10) all aspects being **what is discerned as the focal object**; (11) this—the ultimate—**being antagonistic** to mistaken appearances; (12) engaging in all knowable objects in an **unobstructed** manner; (13) suchness being **without** any **ground** or place for mistakenness; (14) being **without** coming and **going**; (15) being without **arising** and ceasing; **and** {93b} (16) **not observing**

suchness as anything other than itself. **This nature** of the training—the **sixteen** facets of the subject that is the wisdom devoid of reference points—**is defined** through the previous three [defining characteristics] **as something like** the basis that is **a definiendum, and thus is held to be the fourth defining characteristic.** "Something like" means that ["definiendum" here] is merely a conventional term.[78] The sūtras say:

> Bodhisattva mahāsattvas will be of the nature of being free from [the need to] eliminate desire, hatred, and ignorance . . .[79]

2.3.1.2.2.1.2.1.4.4. Knowing the factors conducive to liberation

This has two parts:

1) Nature
2) Divisions

2.3.1.2.2.1.2.1.4.4.1. Nature

> **Being skilled in the full accomplishment**
> **Of signlessness, generosity, and so on,**
> **Within this complete realization of all aspects,**
> **Are asserted as the factors conducive to liberation.** [IV.32]

In general, among the factors conducive to merit and the factors conducive to liberation, the former refer to the virtues of those who have not entered the path, while the latter [are the virtues that] liberate from suffering. They are "partial" since one merges with a part of such [liberation], and they are "concordant" since they are unchanging [in this regard].[80] They mainly arise from studying and reflecting, but there are also [some] that arise from meditation. Their physical supports are humans on the three continents (except for hermaphrodites, neuters, and those with the actions of immediate consequence) and desire gods. As for their mental supports, they can arise in any one of the dhyānas.[81]

Here, in particular, making efforts and **being skilled in the full accomplishment of** the aspect of means (being **generous** with all material goods **and so on** [up through generating the knowledge of all aspects] through aspiring that all phenomena are **signless) are asserted as the factors conducive to liberation**, which are the preliminaries to **this** training in familiarizing with **all aspects** in a combined manner in order to **realize** them [all to be nonarising].[82] The sūtras say:

> Bodhisattva mahāsattvas, starting with their first generation of bodhicitta, never lack the mind of the knowledge of all aspects and, in this way, practice generosity, but do not turn this into signs . . .[83]

2.3.1.2.2.1.2.1.4.4.2. Divisions

This has two parts:

1) Division in terms of objects {94a}
2) Division in terms of faculties

2.3.1.2.2.1.2.1.4.4.2.1. Division in terms of objects

> **They are fivefold—the confidence of focusing on the Buddha and so on,**
> **The vigor whose sphere consists of generosity and so on,**
> **The mindfulness of the consummate intention,**
> **Nonconceptual samādhi,** [IV.33]
>
> **And the prajñā of knowing**
> **Phenomena in all aspects.** [IV.34ab]

[The factors conducive to liberation] **are fivefold** [in terms of focusing on five] objects—(1) **the confidence of focusing on** the three jewels of **the Buddha** and so on; (2) **the vigor whose sphere consists of** the pāramitās (**generosity and so on**); (3) **the mindfulness of** focusing on **the consummate intention** (such as the generation of bodhicitta); (4) the **samādhi** of being **nonconceptual** with regard to distractions; **and** (5) **the prajñā of** being able to **know all aspects** of **phenomena.** [Unlike on the path of preparation, here these five] are not [yet considered as the five] faculties since it is not definite that they arose from meditation.

2.3.1.2.2.1.2.1.4.4.2.2. Division in terms of faculties

> **It is held that perfect enlightenment is easy to realize**
> **By those who are sharp, and hard to realize by the dull.** [IV.34cd]

It is held that perfect enlightenment is easy to realize by those who are of **sharp** faculties ([those who realize it] through mahāyāna confidence so on). However, perfect enlightenment is **hard to realize by those** of **dull** faculties ([those with] the confidence of śrāvakas and pratyekabuddhas).[84] The sūtras say:

> Bodhisattva mahāsattvas, not lacking in the mother and skill in means, bring to mind the buddhas of the three times . . . but do not turn these into signs . . . [85]

2.3.1.2.2.1.2.2. Instruction on the complete training in all aspects proper

This has three parts:

1) The levels of its arising
2) The supports that are the irreversible persons
3) The nature of the training to be cultivated

2.3.1.2.2.1.2.2.1. The levels of its arising

This has two parts:

1) The actual [topic]
2) The ancillary topic

2.3.1.2.2.1.2.2.1.1. The actual topic

> **The focal object of heat here**
> **Is praised as being all sentient beings.**
> **This is described as ten aspects,**
> **Such as an equal mind towards them.** [IV.35]
>
> **Through oneself turning away from evil**
> **And abiding in generosity and so on,**
> **One establishes others in these two,**
> **Praises them, and makes them conform,** [IV.36]
>
> **Which represent reaching the peak. Likewise, poised readiness**
> **Is the knowledge of the realities within oneself and others.**
> **The supreme dharma is likewise to be understood**
> **Through maturing sentient beings and so on.** [IV.37]

After having comprehended the three knowledges through studying and reflecting, when one familiarizes with the aspects that are approximately concordant with these [knowledges] in a combined manner, the path of preparation arises. What is taught [here] is the part that is the subsequent attainment [of this path]. Generally speaking, **the focal object of heat here is praised as being all sentient beings.** [In detail,] **this is described as** the **ten aspects** of heat, **such as** (1) focusing **on these** sentient beings as being the **equality** of oneself and others [without some being close and others distant], which is the **mind** of bodhicitta; focusing on them through (2) love and compassion; (3) a mind [that seeks their] benefit without pride and deceit; (4) [a mind] without anger; (5) a mind without harmful intentions; {94b} and [focusing on them] as being (6) one's father and mother, (7) brothers and sisters, (8) [sons and daughters], (9) friends, and (10) relatives and same kin.

Through oneself turning away from evil and abiding in the pāramitās **(generosity and so on), one** also **establishes other** sentient beings **in these two** [activities], **praises** practicing in **this** way, **and** mentally **conforms** with those who practice **them** [through rejoicing], **which represent** [the aspects] of **having reached the peak.**

Just **like** making efforts in the two [kinds of] welfare on [the level of] peak, [the aspects] at the time of **poised readiness** have the nature of focusing on one's own four **realities,** likewise establishing others too in **the knowledge of these** [realities], and thus [cultivating them] **within** both **oneself and others;** [giving rise to] the four fruitions [of stream-enterers and so on]; and giving rise to the flawless consciousness of the mahāyāna.

Just **like** the ones before, also **the supreme dharma is to be understood through** oneself **maturing sentient beings.** The words "**and so on**" [include] giving rise to pure buddha realms; supernatural knowledges; the wisdom of the knowledge of all aspects; consummate lifetime; upholding the genuine dharma so that it remains; connecting others too with this, commending them for abiding in it, and so on.[86] The sūtras say:

> Bodhisattvas should rest in a mind of equality toward sentient beings . . .[87]

2.3.1.2.2.1.2.2.1.2. The ancillary topic

Here [it should be mentioned that] the respective descriptions of the paths of preparation, seeing, and familiarization in the first six chapters are not repetitive. In the first three [chapters, they are presented] from the perspective of the view of entities, the path, and [all] aspects being without arising. In the latter three [chapters], they are presented from the perspectives of [both] the familiarization with [these paths] (in order to attain mastery [over the remedies]; [manifest] this attainment; and gain stability [in this attainment], once it has been attained,[88] respectively) and their conduct (the six pāramitās). {95a} Or, among the four [kinds of] repetition (repetition of words, repetition of meanings, flawed, and flawless), these [repetitions] here are flawless because they are taught in dependence on other beings to be guided [being present at a given time]. As Dignāga says [in his *Prajñāpāramitārthasaṃgraha*]:

> This very same point is repeated
> Again, based on other points.[89]

2.3.1.2.2.1.2.2.2. Explaining the supports that are the irreversible persons

This has two parts:

1) Brief introduction
2) Detailed explanation

2.3.1.2.2.1.2.2.2.1. Brief introduction

Right **from** attaining the path of preparation of **bodhisattvas**, they will be **irreversible** from [eventually] attaining perfect enlightenment.[90] Therefore, it is said:

> **Starting from the branches of penetration**
> **Up through the paths of seeing and repeated exercise,**
> **The bodhisattvas who dwell on these**
> **Are the irreversible assembly here.** [IV.38]

One cannot give a presentation of these [signs] by way of the reasons[91] of dialecticians, such as being certain about the three modes through valid cognition.[92] They are also not presented merely by virtue of the collection of the causes for finally becoming a buddha being present either. Therefore, from seeing the signs that are taught **here** during the subsequent attainment [of bodhisattvas], one infers that the causes for perfect enlightenment are present in the mind streams of these persons in an uninterrupted way. In other words, one gives rise to certainty based on scriptures.

2.3.1.2.2.1.2.2.2.2. Detailed explanation

This has three parts:

1) [The signs of irreversibility of those on the path of] preparation
2) [The signs of irreversibility of those on the path of] seeing
3) The signs of irreversibility of [those on the path of] familiarization

2.3.1.2.2.1.2.2.2.2.1. The signs of irreversibility of those on the path of preparation

This has two parts:

1) Brief introduction
2) Detailed explanation

2.3.1.2.2.1.2.2.2.2.1.1. Brief introduction

> **By virtue of speaking of twenty kinds of signs,**
> **Such as turning away from form and so on,**
> **[There are] the characteristics of irreversibility**
> **Of** {95b} **those who dwell on the branches of penetration.** [IV.39]

2.3.1.2.2.1.2.2.2.2.1.2. Detailed explanation

> **Turning away from form and so on,**
> **Termination of doubt and unfavorable states,**
> **Oneself abiding in virtue**
> **And establishing others in it,** [IV.40]
>
> **Generosity and so on that are based on others,**
> **No indecisiveness even about profound actuality,**
> **The body being loving and so on,**
> **Not being associated with fivefold obscuration,** [IV.41]
>
> **Overcoming all latencies,**
> **Mindfulness and alertness,**
> **Clean robes and so on,**
> **The body not being infested with parasites,** [IV.42]
>
> **Mind being without crookedness, assuming**
> **Abstinence, lacking greed and so on,**
> **Proceeding by being endowed with the nature of phenomena,**
> **Searching for the hells for the welfare of the world,**[93] [IV.43]
>
> **Others being unable to lead one astray,**
> **Realizing, "This is māra,"**
> **When māra teaches another path,**
> **And the conduct that pleases the buddhas—** [IV.44]

[Among the twenty signs of irreversibility of bodhisattvas on the path of preparation, the first eleven are the signs] of those who dwell on [the level of] heat—(1) **turning away from** clinging to **form and so on** as entities; (2) **termination of doubt** (that is, wondering about bad views whether they are good); (3) termination of being born in the eight **unfavorable states** (the three unpleasant realms, barbarians, long-living gods without discrimination among the gods of Great Fruition,[94] people with wrong views who scorn cause and result, [places] empty of the Buddha's words and the four kinds of retinue, and being [mentally or physically] handicapped so as to not understand the meaning [of the dharma]); (4) **oneself abiding in** the ten virtues **and establishing others in them**; (5) engaging in **generosity and so on that are based on** the welfare of **others**; (6) **no indecisiveness even about profound actuality**—the fundamental nature; (7) **the** triad of **body**, speech, and mind **being** endowed with **love** ("**and so on**" refers to the actions that arise through this); (8) **not being associated with fivefold obscuration** (striving for sense pleasures; malice; drowsiness and torpor; agitation and regret; doubt); (9) **overcoming all latencies** of views; (10) being endowed with **mindfulness and alertness** in all one's conduct; and (11) being **clean** since one's **robes** are without lice eggs **and so on**, that is, one has few diseases and no bad odor.

[The next six are the signs of those who dwell] on [the level of] peak—(12) **the body not being infested with** the eighty thousand kinds of **parasites**; (13) **mind being without** the **crookedness** of inferior mindsets; (14) **assuming** the twelve qualities of **abstinence** (the three in terms of food: alms, a single seat, and not taking [food] later; {96a} the three in terms of robes: [wearing the dress of] a dung sweeper, [only] wool, and [only] three robes; the four in terms of abode: living as a hermit, without roof, under trees, and in charnel grounds; and the two in terms of conduct: [sleeping in] a sitting position, and [leaving] the ground as it is);[95] (15) **lacking greed and so on**, that is, being free from the antagonistic factors of the six pāramitās; (16) **proceeding by being endowed with** the mother—**the nature of phenomena**; and (17) **searching for the hells for the welfare of the world** and being fearless even when born there.

[The next two are the signs of those who dwell] on [the level of] poised readiness—(18) **others** than one's spiritual friends, such as māra's magical creations, **being unable to lead one astray** into wrong ways; and (19) **realizing, "This is māra," when māra teaches** inferior paths **other** than the bodhisattva **path**.

[The last one is the sign of those who dwell on the level of the supreme dharma]—(20) **the conduct that pleases the buddhas** (engaging in the six pāramitās by way of not observing the three spheres).[96]

> **By virtue of these twenty signs,**
> **Those who dwell on heat, peak,**
> **Poised readiness, and the supreme dharma**
> **Do not turn away from perfect enlightenment.** [IV.45]

The sūtras say:

> Those bodhisattvas who have turned away from form . . . should be known as irreversible . . .[97]

2.3.1.2.2.1.2.2.2.2.2. The signs of irreversibility of those on the path of seeing

This has two parts:

1) Brief introduction
2) Detailed explanation

2.3.1.2.2.1.2.2.2.2.2.1. Brief introduction

> **The sixteen moments of readiness**
> **And cognition on the path of seeing**
> **Should be known as the characteristics**
> **Of irreversible bodhisattvas.**[98] [IV.46] {96b}

2.3.1.2.2.1.2.2.2.2.2.2. Detailed explanation

This has four parts in terms of focusing on the four realities:

1) [The signs of focusing on the reality of suffering]

> **Turning away from discriminating notions of form and so on,**
> **Firmness of mind, turning away**
> **From both the inferior yānas,**
> **Dissolution of the branches of the dhyānas and so on,** [IV.47]

These four are (1) **turning away from discriminating notions** about the characteristics **of form and so on**; (2) **firmness of** the **mind** of bodhicitta; (3) **turning away from** the mental engagements of **both the inferior yānas**; and (4) attaining the meditative absorptions (**the dhyānas and so on**), but having **dissolved the branches of** being reborn without control in the [corresponding god realms].[99]

2) [The signs of focusing on the reality of the origin of suffering]

> **Lightness of body and mind,**
> **Skill in means in using what is desirable,**
> **Constantly pure conduct,**
> **Purity of livelihood,** [IV.48]

These are (5) **lightness of body and mind** rising [and operating] by virtue of being free from afflicted phenomena; (6) being embraced by **skill in means** (such as generosity) even **in** situations when **using desirable** sense pleasures; (7) **constantly pure conduct**[100] in terms of oneself not relishing sense pleasures; and (8) sustaining oneself through **purity of livelihood** by virtue of not engaging in the five [kinds of] wrong livelihood, bringing [others] under one's power, giving predictions, and so on. As the *Ratnāvalī* says:

> Corrupt ethics is to control the senses
> For the sake of honor and gain.
> Flattery is to speak pleasant words
> For the sake of honor and gain.

Indirect appeal is to praise
The things of others in order to obtain them.
Being devious is to put down
Others for the sake of one's gain.

Desiring gain through gain
Is to praise what one obtained earlier.[101]

3) [The signs of focusing on the reality of cessation]

With regard to the skandhas and so on, obstacles,
The accumulations, the battle
Of the faculties and so on, . . . [IV.49ac]

These are the four of stopping connecting and so on with any (9) talk about **the skandhas and so on** (dhātus and āyatanas) as well as **obstacles** (such as kings and robbers); (10) talk about village **crowds;**[102] (11) talk about **the** afflicted **faculties and so on** (their consciousnesses and objects); {97a} and (12) talk about **the battles of** war.[103]

4) [The signs of focusing on the reality of the path]

. . . and greed and so on,
Stopping to dwell on [IV.49cd]

Connecting and being occupied with them,
Observing not the least phenomenon,
Certainty about one's own bhūmi
And dwelling on the triple bhūmi, [IV.50]

As well as renouncing one's life for the sake of the dharma—
These sixteen moments
Are the signs of irreversibility
Of the intelligent who dwell on the path of seeing. [IV.51]

These are the four of (13) **stopping to dwell on** first **connecting and** then continuously **being occupied with** talk about **greed and so on** (the antagonistic factors of generosity and so on), that is, not to speak [about them]; (14) **observing not** even **the least** seeming **phenomenon** as being established ultimately; (15) **certainty about one's own** abiding on the first **bhūmi and dwelling on the triple** path of one's own **bhūmi** (the uninterrupted path, the path of liberation, and the special path); and (16) daring to even **renounce**

one's own **life for the sake of the** genuine **dharma** remaining and so on. The characteristics of abiding in **these sixteen moments are the signs of irreversibility of the intelligent who dwell on the path of seeing.**[104] The sūtras say:

> Bodhisattvas turn away from discriminating notions of form . . .[105]

Here, as an elaboration on "the faculties and so on" [in line IV.49c], the explanation of the [twenty-two] faculties has four parts:

1) Division
2) On which levels they exist
3) Manner of relinquishment
4) Objects

1) The division is twofold:

a) Purified [faculties]
b) Afflicted faculties

1a) [The purified faculties] are eight—(1)–(5) those that wield power over mundane purity (the five such as confidence) and (6)–(8) the [three] that wield power over uncontaminated purity (the faculty that makes everything unknown known—the five such as confidence at the time of the path of preparation; the faculty of knowing everything—the same five of noble learners; and the faculty of being endowed with knowing everything—the same five of nonlearners).

1b) [The afflicted faculties] are fourteen—(9)–(13) those that wield power over experiencing results (the five faculties that are feelings—[physical] pleasure and suffering, mental pleasure and displeasure, and equanimity); {97b} (14)–(19) the six faculties that wield power over objects (the five sense [faculties] and the mental faculty); (20) the life faculty, which wields power over the body remaining; and (21)–(22) the two that wield power over birth (the male and female [sexual] faculties).

2) In the desire realm, all afflicted faculties exist. In the form realm, among these, the male and female ones, [physical] suffering, and mental displeasure do not exist. In the formless realm, [only] the three of life, mind, and equanimity exist. As for the [physical] supports of these faculties, in the desire realm, all eight atomic substances are present; in the form realm, [all] except smell and taste; and in the formless realm, [the others] rely on the life [faculty].

3) [In terms of their] contaminated parts, each one among the following four—the mental faculty, mind pleasure, mental pleasure, and equanimity—contains factors to be relinquished through seeing, factors to be relinquished through familiarization, and factors not to be relinquished.[106] In mental displeasure, there are both factors to be relinquished through seeing and factors

to be relinquished through familiarization. The five sense faculties, the male and female ones, and the ones of life and [physical] suffering are factors to be relinquished through familiarization alone. The contaminated [five faculties] such as confidence and, according to the mahāyāna, also the contaminated faculty that makes everything unknown known are factors to be relinquished through familiarization. As for the [physical] supports of the faculties, all eight [atomic substances] are factors to be relinquished through familiarization.

4) In the desire realm, there are six objects; in the form realm, [all] except smell and taste; and in the formless realm, only phenomena.[107]

2.3.1.2.2.1.2.2.2.2.3. The signs of irreversibility of those on the path of familiarization

This has five parts:

1) The nature of this path in general
2) The manner of familiarizing with it
3) The particular division of the path of familiarization
4) Rebuttal of objections to further increase
5) Rebuttal of objections to cause and result

2.3.1.2.2.1.2.2.2.2.3.1. The nature of this path in general

> **The path of familiarization is profound**
> **And such profundity is in terms of emptiness and so on.**
> **This profundity is the state of being liberated**
> **From the extremes of superimposition and denial.** [IV.52]

The path of familiarization of noble bodhisattvas **is profound** because the sūtras say: {98a}

> This matrix that perfects all buddha qualities, once bodhisattvas abide in it . . . is profound—it is a synonym for emptiness, signlessness, wishlessness, nonformation, nonarising, freedom from desire, cessation, nirvāṇa . . . and all dharmas.[108]

Thus, its **profundity** of lacking any basis for adventitious stains **is in terms of emptiness and so on.** This is also the ground, the fruition, and the yāna. As for **this profundity**, the meaning of the sūtra passage "[Bodhisattvas] both turn away from form and demonstrate nirvāṇa"[109] is as follows. The profound dharmadhātu **is the state of being liberated from the extremes of superimposition** (its being an entity) **and denial** (its not being nirvāṇa) because it is beyond any objects of mind and consciousness.[110]

2.3.1.2.2.1.2.2.2.2.3.2. The manner of familiarizing with it

> **The path of familiarization consists of the repeated**
> **Reflections, verifications, and absorptions**
> **During the branches of penetration,**
> **The path of seeing, and the path of familiarization itself.** [IV.53]

The manner in which bodhisattvas familiarize with such profundity consists of **the paths of familiarization**. By virtue of progressively dwelling in **the branches of penetration, the path of seeing, and the path of familiarization itself**, [these levels of the path of familiarization] **consist of** familiarization by way of **repeated reflections** on this profundity during the first period; directly **verifying** it through self-aware prajñā during the second period; **and** being **absorbed** in it during the third period. The [corresponding] sūtra [passage] is provided below.[111]

2.3.1.2.2.1.2.2.2.2.3.3. The particular division of the path of familiarization

> **Because it is an uninterrupted continuum,** [IV.54a]

If the direct realization of the naturally pure dharmadhātu is subsequently divided because self-aware wisdom **is** permanent in that **it** exists as **an uninterrupted continuum** right from the start, {98b} it is divided from the perspective of wisdom becoming manifest in an increasingly lucid manner by virtue of its, respectively, becoming free a little bit, becoming more free, and becoming greatly free from the stains that obscure it.

> **It is treated as ninefold**
> **Through its lesser, medium, and great degrees**
> **Being further divided into lesser and so on.** [IV.54bd]

The sūtras say:

> If bodhisattva mahāsattvas repeatedly reflect on, verify, and are absorbed in these profundities . . . countless, immeasurable, and infinite roots of virtue will grow.[112]

Elaborating on this, in the sūtras, [Subhūti] asks, "What is the difference between countless, immeasurable, and infinite?"[113] The meaning of the answer to this is that

> **The descriptions as countless and so on** [IV.55a]

are mere names, which

> **Do not hold out in terms of the ultimate.** [IV.55b]

The sūtras say:

> In these dharmas, any difference to be made through meaning or letters is unobservable.[114]

In terms of the seeming, the sage asserted

> **Them to be the true[115] natural outflows of compassion.** [IV.55cd]

However, **in terms of the seeming, the sage asserted** that these descriptions were given with the intention of **the** [various kinds of] inexpressible merit arising from the dependent origination that is **the natural outflow of** the great **compassion** of the buddhas.[116] [The sūtras say]:

> This inexpressibility is a teaching that is the natural outflow of the great compassion of the Tathāgata.[117]

2.3.1.2.2.1.2.2.2.2.3.4. Rebuttal of objections to further increase

This has two parts:

1) The qualm
2) The answer

2.3.1.2.2.1.2.2.2.2.3.4.1. The qualm

> **In the inexpressible entity**
> **Decrease and increase are not tenable.**
> **Through the progression[118] called "familiarization,"**
> **What could decrease and what could be obtained?** [IV.56]

"**In** the actual way of being of **entities—the inexpressible** and unconditioned dharmadhātu—**decrease and increase are not tenable.** Therefore, [since] they have the nature of the [dharmadhātu], **what** factors to be relinquished in **the progression called "familiarization" could decrease and what** remedies **could be obtained?** It follows that they are not obtained."[119] The sūtras say:

> If there is no increase or decrease in the inexpressible actuality, {99a} there will be no increase or decrease of the pāramitās, such as generosity, either.[120]

2.3.1.2.2.1.2.2.2.2.3.4.2. The answer

> **In the same way as enlightenment**
> **This [path] accomplishes the desired goal.**
> **Enlightenment has the defining characteristic of suchness,**
> **Which is also asserted as the defining characteristic of this.** [IV.57]

There is no such flaw. **In the same way as** the fruition—perfect **enlightenment**—accomplishes the welfare of those to be guided, also **this** dharmadhātu **accomplishes the desired goal** of the clear realizations of those to be guided increasing and their factors to be relinquished becoming terminated. The reason for this being **asserted** in such a way is that the fruition—**enlightenment—has the defining characteristic of suchness** and that suchness **also** has **the defining characteristic of this** enlightenment because these two are the same.[121] The sūtras say:

> Just like the suchness of all phenomena, thus is unsurpassable perfect enlightenment.[122]

2.3.1.2.2.1.2.2.2.2.3.5. Rebuttal of objections to cause and result
This has two parts:
1) The dispute
2) The answer

2.3.1.2.2.1.2.2.2.2.3.5.1. The dispute

> **Enlightenment through an earlier mind**
> **Is not reasonable, nor is it through a later one.** [IV.58ab]

"Ultimately, the dharmadhātu and **enlightenment** are indeed one, but we see that [the path of familiarization] **is not reasonable** even with regard to being the cause of buddhahood on the level of the seeming. For **through earlier** moments of generating the **mind** [of bodhicitta]—the cause of buddhahood—**not** being in touch with **later ones** and vice versa, the accumulation of virtue does not take place, and without that, the fruition does not arise."[123] The meaning of this refers to [the following passage from] the sūtras:

> The first generating of bodhicitta is not in touch with a later generating of bodhicitta . . .[124]

2.3.1.2.2.1.2.2.2.2.3.5.2. The answer

This has two parts:

1) Answering through an example
2) Explaining the signs of those on the path of familiarization that arise from this [path]

2.3.1.2.2.1.2.2.2.2.3.5.2.1. Answering through an example

> **In accordance with the example of an oil lamp,** [IV.58c]

Though enlightenment is not generated through each individual moment of mind, by virtue of their depending on each other there is mere dependently originating arising on the level of the seeming. {99b} Though the wick **of an oil lamp** is not burned through each individual one of the earlier or later moments [of its flame], it is directly perceived that the wick is burned in dependence on both [these moments. Thus, the arising of enlightenment through the path of familiarization] is to be understood **in accordance with this example.** The sūtra passage is obvious in [the above line of] the text.[125]

2.3.1.2.2.1.2.2.2.2.3.5.2.2. Explaining the signs of those on the path of familiarization that arise from this path

> **The eightfold nature of phenomena is profound.** [IV.58d]

> **Its profundity lies in arising, ceasing,**
> **Suchness, what is to be cognized,**
> **Cognition, engagement, nonduality,**
> **And skill in means.** [IV.59]

Immediately after having realized the generation of ultimate bodhicitta [on the path of seeing], the path of familiarization—the realization of **the eightfold profound nature of phenomena**—arises. After having presented this [profundity in general], in particular there are eight [aspects to it] that are realized. **Its profundity lies in** (1) dependently originating **arising**; (2) **ceasing** because of the seeming not being established ultimately; (3) very subtle **suchness**; (4) **what is to be cognized**—the actual way of being of the two realities; (5) the primordial **cognition** of realizing this actual way of being; (6) the **engagement** of not engaging in anything; (7) what is to be realized and what realizes it **not** being different or **dual** ultimately; **and** (8) the **skill in means** of being a buddha primordially and yet demonstrating becoming a buddha again.[126] The sūtras say:

The profound dependent origination of bodhisattva mahāsattvas awakening into unsurpassable enlightenment is amazing.[127]

2.3.1.2.2.1.2.2.3. The nature of the training to be cultivated

This has three parts:

1) The cause of the dharmakāya—[the training in] the equality of existence and peace
2) The cause of the sambhogakāya—[the training in] pure realms
3) The cause of enlightened activity—the training in skill in means

2.3.1.2.2.1.2.2.3.1. The cause of the dharmakāya—the training in the equality of existence and peace

This has two parts:

1) General [topic]
2) [Meaning of] the text

2.3.1.2.2.1.2.2.3.1.1. General topic

The saṃsāra in this [line IV.60b] consists of all kinds of mistaken appearances, and nirvāṇa is their nature—emptiness. As for the manner of [their] equality if a mistaken subject focuses on the single object that is suchness, [saṃsāric] existence [seems to take place]. If an unmistaken subject focuses on it, peace is happening. However, ultimately since the nature of this object is neither of these two, [the training here] is to not conceptualize it as either of them. {100a} The training in familiarizing with this exists from the path of accumulation onward since what is taught here is the training in completely realizing all aspects and not the other [three trainings]. The direct appearance [of this particular training] in the mind stream [occurs] from the eighth bhūmi onward.[128]

2.3.1.2.2.1.2.2.3.1.2. Meaning of the text

This has two parts:

1) The actual [training]
2) Removing qualms

2.3.1.2.2.1.2.2.3.1.2.1. The actual training

> **Since phenomena are dreamlike,**
> **[Saṃsāric] existence and peace are not conceptualized.** [IV.60ab]

Since imaginary **phenomena are dreamlike,** [bodhisattvas] **are** familiarizing [with equality] through **not conceptualizing** [saṃsāric] **existence and peace**

as any kind of existing entity or nonimplicative negation, respectively.[129] The sūtras say:

> If prajñāpāramitā increases through familiarizing with it during daytime, it also increases through familiarizing with it during dreams. Why? Because they cannot be conceptualized as dreams and daytime.[130]

2.3.1.2.2.1.2.2.3.1.2.2. Removing qualms

> **The refutations[131] of the qualms about karma**
> **Not existing and so on are just as explained.** [IV.60cd]

One may think, "Just as no results arise from actions in a dream, no results arise from conceptual virtues [in the waking state] either because these two are alike [in that all phenomena are dreamlike and lack a nature of their own]." There is no flaw here in terms of **the qualms about** the accumulation of **karma** and its results **not existing and so on** because **the refutations of** [these qualms] **are just as explained** and contained in the sūtras. They say that, without conceptualization, there is no foundation for karma and thus no result, but if one conceptualizes upon awakening, results arise even from actions in a dream. The sūtras [start with Śāriputra] asking, "If [all phenomena] are said to be dreamlike, there is no accumulation or decrease of karma." The answer is, "Without a focal object, karma does not arise . . ." and "However, if one thinks about it upon awakening, there will be accumulation or decrease of it."[132]

2.3.1.2.2.1.2.2.3.2. The cause of the sambhogakāya—the training in pure realms

> **The world of sentient beings is impure,**
> **And so is the world that is the environment.**
> **By virtue of accomplishing the purity of those,**
> **The purity of a buddha realm [appears].** [IV.61]

For example since **the world of sentient beings** (the adventitious stains) **is** not mixed with suchness, {100b} once this is realized, these stains vanish like a rainbow, **and so is the impure world** (such as the unpleasant realms) **that is the environment** and appears from the perspective of mistakenness. **By virtue of** having eliminated mistakenness through the dependent origination of compassion for **those** [beings] and thus **accomplishing**, and familiarizing with,

the pure container, which already existed before, through making it clearly manifest, **a buddha realm** that actually fulfills this function appears in **the pure** mind.[133] This is primarily taken to be a sambhogakāya realm, [but] in the sūtras, it is described through examples from the perspective of mistakenness:

> This great earth will be made of blue beryl . . .[134]

2.3.1.2.2.1.2.2.3.3. The cause of enlightened activity—the training in skill in means

This has two parts:

1) Prajñā as the root
2) The manner in which it becomes skill in means through being embraced by compassion

2.3.1.2.2.1.2.2.3.3.1. Prajñā as the root

> **As for the object and this training,** [IV.62a]

[This training] is identified as **this** realization of existence and peace as equality that entails the full joining[135] of two [factors]—**the object** (prajñāpāramitā—suchness without arising and ceasing) **and** the subject (self-aware wisdom).[136] The sūtras say:

> How should bodhisattva mahāsattvas . . . familiarize with the buddhadharmas . . . ?

The answer to this is:

> They should familiarize with all phenomena, such as form, being empty . . .[137]

The manner of familiarizing with this is as [stated in *Bodhicaryāvatāra*]:

> Through familiarity with the latent tendencies of emptiness,
> The latent tendencies of entities will be relinquished.
> Through familiarity with "utter nonexistence,"
> These too will be relinquished later on.[138]

2.3.1.2.2.1.2.2.3.3.2. The manner in which it becomes skill in means through being embraced by compassion

> **Overcoming the hordes[139] of enemies,**
> **Not abiding, hitting just as [intended],**
> **Uncommon characteristic,** [IV.62bd]
>
> **Not becoming attached, not observing,**
> **Having terminated characteristics and aspiration prayers,**
> **The sign of this, and being unlimited**
> **Represent the tenfold skill in means.** [IV.63]

[The ten ways of training in skill in means] **are** (1) through this [prajñā] being embraced by compassion, **overcoming the enemies**—the four māras (the māra of the five skandhas, the māra of the afflictions that fetter in saṃsāra, the māra who is the lord of death, and the devaputra māra—the ruler of [the gods] who have power over others' emanations);[140] {101a} (2) **not abiding** in the emptiness of peace; (3) dedicated virtues **hitting** perfect enlightenment, like skilled archers shooting **just as** they please;[141] (4) the [bodhisattva's] **characteristic** of not forsaking sentient beings, which is **uncommon** in comparison with śrāvakas and pratyekabuddhas; (5) the stains of sentient beings **not becoming attached** [to the bodhisattvas], though [the latter] mix in with [the former]; (6) teaching by way of **not observing** any phenomena; (7) **having terminated** views about **characteristics**; (8) having terminated the path[142] of looking at the fruition in a way of having **aspirations** for it; (9) not entertaining characteristics about the prophecy by the victors, which is **the sign of this** being endowed with skill in means; **and** (10) knowing **unlimited** enumerations of knowable objects. Through adding "**skill in means**" at the end of each one of these, [this training] is **tenfold.**[143] The sūtras say:

> And, having overcome the four māras and the two levels . . .[144]

> **This is the fourth chapter, on the complete realization of all aspects, in *The Treatise on the Pith Instructions on Prajñāpāramitā, Called* The Ornament of Clear Realization.**

This is the commentary on **the fourth chapter in the** versified ***Treatise on the Pith Instructions on Prajñāpāramitā, Called* The Ornament of Clear Realization.**

The Fifth Chapter, on the Culminating Training

2.3.1.2.2.2. The culminating training (the consummation of the [complete training in all aspects])

This has two parts:

1) Presenting the connection
2) Detailed explanation of the clear realizations

2.3.1.2.2.2.1. Presenting the connection

[The culminating training] is the consummation of the complete training in all aspects through [the latter] serving as the remedy for the factors to be relinquished. [The culminating training] refers to familiarizing [with the complete training in all aspects] in the manner of gaining mastery [over it], which is the meaning of [the passage] in the sūtras [that starts with] the discussion of the signs of irreversibility [in dreams and so on]. [The various levels of] the culminating training do not need to be preceded by the entire [training in] all aspects {101b} because they are presented from the perspective of what constitutes and does not constitute the factors to be relinquished and their remedies, respectively, on the [distinct] levels of the respective paths.[145]

2.3.1.2.2.2.2. Detailed explanation of the clear realizations

This has four parts:

1) [The culminating training of the path of] preparation
2) [The culminating training of the path of] seeing
3) [The culminating training of the path of] familiarization
4) The culminating training of the uninterrupted path

2.3.1.2.2.2.2.1. The culminating training of the path of preparation

This has four parts:

1) Heat
2) Peak
3) Poised readiness
4) The supreme dharma

2.3.1.2.2.2.2.1.1. Heat

> **Even in dreams, all phenomena**
> **Are regarded as dreamlike and so on—**
> **The signs of the training of having reached culmination**
> **Are asserted as twelvefold.** [V.1]

[The culminating training of heat] is taught by way of its signs. The six signs in dreams are that, (1) through the power of aspiring during daytime that all phenomena are appearing yet empty, **even in dreams, all phenomena are regarded as dreamlike and so on**; (2) any liking for the inferior mindsets [of śrāvakas and pratyekabuddhas] does not arise; (3) the tathāgatas teach the dharma [among limitless retinues of monastics, gods, nāgas, and so on]; (4) their magical creations, [such as radiating light,] proliferate; (5) oneself teaches the dharma to sentient beings, who are tormented by suffering; and (6) upon seeing the unpleasant realms, one gives rise to the intention, "I will purify my own buddha realm so that these [unpleasant realms] do not exist in it." The six signs during the waking state are (7) being able to pacify harm by fire and so on through words of truth, saying, "May this be pacified if I am irreversible"; (8) being able to dispel harm by nonhuman beings in the same manner; (9) attending to a spiritual friend without being overwhelmed by any inner or outer [obstructing] conditions; (10) always training in the mother; (11) not clinging to any phenomena at all; and (12) being close to buddha enlightenment. Thus, **the signs of the training of having reached** the **culmination** of the meditative equipoise of heat **are asserted as twelvefold.**[146] The sūtras say:

> Even in dreams, bodhisattva mahāsattvas . . . regard all phenomena as dreamlike.[147]

2.3.1.2.2.2.2.1.2. Peak

> **By comparing it in many ways,**
> **Such as the virtue of worshipping as many buddhas**
> **As there are beings in Jambudvīpa,**
> **Increase is sixteenfold.** [V.2]

[The culminating training of peak is taught] by way of the increase of merit, **such as** (1) **the virtue of** someone **worshipping**, for as long as they live, **as many beings as there are in Jambudvīpa** who all have become **buddhas.** {102a} ["Such as" includes] (2) worshipping as many beings as there are in a trichiliocosm who all have become buddhas; the seven virtues of having established as many sentient beings as there are in Jambudvīpa in (3) mundane excellencies (such as [the ten virtues,] the dhyānas, and the formless [absorptions]) and [the fruitions of] (4) stream-enterer, (5) once-returner, (6) nonreturner, (7) arhat, (8) pratyekabuddha, and (9) unsurpassable enlightenment; and (10)–(16) the seven virtues of having established as many beings as there are in a trichiliocosm in these respective [fruitions]. **By comparing it in** these **many ways** with the sixteen virtues as taught [here], the meditative equipoise of peak is the **sixteenfold increase** in merit [that is even greater] than [the merits in] these respective examples. This is obvious from the [corresponding] passages in the sūtras.[148]

2.3.1.2.2.2.2.1.3. Poised readiness

> **The unsurpassable perfection**
> **Of the dharmas of the three omnisciences**
> **And the nonabandonment of the welfare of sentient beings**
> **Are described as "stability."** [V.3]

[The culminating training of poised readiness is taught] by way of the stability of not regressing from the mother. Due to **the unsurpassable** virtue of **perfecting** all the aspects **of the dharmas of** natural buddhahood without exception through **the three omnisciences and the nonabandonment of the welfare of** other **sentient beings**, the meditative equipoise of poised readiness does not involve any regressing into [the paths of] śrāvakas or pratyekabuddhas. Therefore, it **is described as "stability."**[149] The sūtras say:

> May those persons who belong to the bodhisattvayāna . . . perfect the buddhadharmas.[150]

2.3.1.2.2.2.2.1.4. The supreme dharma

> **By using the examples of a four-continent world,**
> **A chiliocosm, a dichiliocosm, and a trichiliocosm,**
> **This samādhi is expressed**
> **Through the abundance of merit.** [V.4]

[The culminating training of the supreme dharma] has the nature of settling in the threefold lack of nature. [The sūtras] say that one may be able to gauge **a four-continent world, a chiliocosm** (one thousand such [worlds]), **a dichiliocosm** (one thousand such [chiliocosms]), **and a trichiliocosm** (one thousand such [dichiliocosms]) through just a single tip of hair. But the merit of the generation of bodhicitta that is endowed with rejoicing is immeasurable. {102b} **By using these examples, the samādhi** of the supreme dharma **is expressed through the abundance of** [its] **merit.**[151] The sūtras say:

> Their merit of generating bodhicitta that is endowed with rejoicing is immeasurable.[152]

2.3.1.2.2.2.2.2. The culminating training of the path of seeing

This has two parts:

1) The factors to be relinquished
2) The remedies

2.3.1.2.2.2.2.2.1. The factors to be relinquished

This has two parts:

1) Brief introduction
2) Detailed explanation

2.3.1.2.2.2.2.2.1.1. Brief introduction

This has two parts:

1) [The conceptions about] the apprehended
2) [The conceptions about] the apprehender

2.3.1.2.2.2.2.2.1.1.1. The conceptions about the apprehended

> **One should know that the two**[153] **conceptions about the apprehended—**
> **In terms of engagement and withdrawal—**
> **Are ninefold each and that their character**
> **Is [to apprehend] objects not as they are.** [V.5]

The two [sets of] **conceptions about the apprehended** are those that apprehend the objects **of engagement** (the path and fruition of the mahāyāna) **and** the objects of **withdrawal** (the paths and fruitions of the hīnayāna) as what are to be adopted and to be rejected, respectively. **One should know that,** through the classifications of these objects, **each** of these two [sets of conceptions] has as a **ninefold** [subdivision] **and that** the reason for their being mistaken lies in all of them **not** focusing on the **object** that is the basic nature, just **as it is**. Therefore, **the character** of these [apprehending] subjects is to be equally mistaken states of mind.[154] The sūtras say:

Having rejoiced . . . one should dedicate this in such a way that one has neither any notion of duality nor any notion of nonduality . . . Not only the mother is nonconceptual, but form too . . .[155]

2.3.1.2.2.2.2.2.1.1.2. The conceptions about the apprehender

The two conceptions about substantially and imputedly existent sentient beings
Are asserted as the ones about the apprehender.
Divided by ordinary beings and noble ones,
Each one of them is ninefold. [V.6]

If apprehended referents do not exist like that,
Can these two be asserted as the apprehenders of anything?
Thus, their characteristic is the emptiness
Of a nature of an apprehender. [V.7]

Divided by what exists in the mind streams of **ordinary beings and noble ones, sentient beings** are the bases of imputing phenomenal identity, that is, the minds that entail dualistic appearances. The former's **conceptions** apprehend [sentient beings] as **substantially** [existent] **and** the latter's [conceptions] apprehend them as merely **imputedly existent**. [Respectively, these] **are asserted as the two** conceptions **about the apprehender. Each one of them is ninefold** in terms of their objects. The meaning of mistakenness is as follows. **If apprehended referents** (objects) **do not exist** either substantially or imputedly, **like**wise, to **assert** that **these two** conceptions **apprehend** such objects through **anything** is not suitable. For if apprehended objects {103a} do not exist ultimately, what apprehends them in this way is not beyond mistakenness [either].[156] Therefore, **their characteristic is the emptiness of an apprehender's** own **nature.**[157] The sūtras say:

Since space is void, sentient beings should be seen as void.[158]

2.3.1.2.2.2.2.2.1.2. Detailed explanation

This has two parts:

1) [The conceptions about] the apprehended
2) [The conceptions about] the apprehender

2.3.1.2.2.2.2.2.1.2.1. The conceptions about the apprehended

This has two parts:

1) The objects of engagement
2) The objects of withdrawal

2.3.1.2.2.2.2.2.1.2.1.1. The objects of engagement

Nature, disposition,
Perfect accomplishment of the path,
Unmistakenness about the focal object of consciousness,
Antagonistic factors and remedies, [V.8]

One's own realization, agent,
Its activity, and the result of activity—
Being based on the factors of engaging in these,
Conceptions are asserted as ninefold. [V.9]

[The nine objects of engagement of bodhisattvas are] (1) the **nature** of the object—enlightenment; (2) uncontaminated wisdom—the mahāyāna **disposition** of focusing on this [enlightenment]; (3) **perfect accomplishment of the path** through that; (4) **unmistakenness** by virtue **of consciousness** in meditative equipoise lacking any **focal object** [that represents] the seeming; (5) rejecting and adopting **antagonistic factors and remedies**, respectively; (6) the bodhisattvas' **own realizations**; (7) [their being] the **agent** of relinquishing their own welfare; (8) **its activity**—accomplishing the welfare of others; and (9) **the result of** [this] **activity**—the two accumulations. Since there are **the** nine **factors of engaging in these**, the **conceptions based on** them **are asserted as ninefold.**[159] The sūtras teach the remedy by way of nonconceptuality:

> The mother is utterly void.[160]

2.3.1.2.2.2.2.2.1.2.1.2. The objects of withdrawal

Realizations being deficient
Due to falling into existence or peace,
Lacking being mentored,
The aspects of the path being incomplete, [V.10]

Progressing by virtue of another condition,
Turning away from the aim,
Being limited, variety,
Being ignorant about abiding and engaging, [V.11]

And subsequent pursuing—
The conceptions about these are ninefold,
Being based on the factors of withdrawal
As they arise in the minds of śrāvakas and so on. [V.12]

[The nine objects of bodhisattvas to withdraw from are] (1) the **realizations** of śrāvakas and pratyekabuddhas **being deficient due to falling into** the objects that are **existence or peace**; (2) **lacking being mentored** through skill in means; (3) most of **the aspects of the path** to accomplish buddhahood **being incomplete**; (4) having to **progress** again in the mahāyāna **by virtue of another condition** and not through one's own power; (5) **turning away from the aim** to be strived for—the fruition that is the knowledge of all aspects; (6) relinquishment **being limited**; (7) realization {103b} entailing a **variety** of clinging to characteristics; (8) **being ignorant about abiding** in the knowledge of all aspects **and**, through that, about **engaging** in the welfare of others; and (9) the five [pāramitās], such as generosity, **following after**[161] prajñāpāramitā. **The conceptions about these are ninefold, being based on the factors of withdrawal as they arise in the minds of śrāvakas and so on.**[162] The sūtra [passage starts] with the example of the sun and the moon performing their functions for the four continents and following [these continents], [with prajñāpāramitā doing the same for the other five pāramitās].[163]

2.3.1.2.2.2.2.2.1.2.2. The conceptions about the apprehender

This has two parts

1) Apprehending substantial existence
2) Apprehending imputed existence

2.3.1.2.2.2.2.2.1.2.2.1. Apprehending substantial existence

> **The first about the apprehender should be known**
> **In terms of seizing and discarding,**
> **Mental engagement,**
> **Adhering to the three realms,** [V.13]
>
> **Abiding, clinging,**
> **Imputing phenomenal entities,**
> **Attachment, remedy,**
> **And impairment of proceeding as one wishes.** [V.14]

The first [set of conceptions] **about the apprehender** [as a substantially existent person] **should be known in terms of** the conceptions that focus on the following nine [mental states] as being substantially existent—(1) **seizing and discarding** objects (such as form), respectively; (2) **mental engagement** in these [objects]; (3) through that, **adhering to the three realms** (minds and mental factors); (4) **abiding**—apprehending form and so on as being really existent; (5) **clinging** to them; (6) **imputing** nonexistent **phenomenal entities** as being substantially existent; (7) **attachment**—clinging to the three spheres; (8) apprehending even the **remedies** for that as substantially existent; **and** (9) **impairment of proceeding** to the buddhabhūmi **as one wishes.**[164] The sūtras say:

> The mother does not seize or discard any phenomena whatsoever.[165]

2.3.1.2.2.2.2.2.1.2.2.2. Apprehending imputed existence

> **No final deliverance according to the aim,**
> **Identifying the path as not being the path,**
> **Ceasing and arising,**
> **Being conjoined and not being conjoined with entities,** [V.15]
>
> **Abiding, destroying the disposition,**
> **The absence of striving and the cause,**
> **And observing opposing forces**
> **Are the other conceptions about the apprehender.** [V.16]

[The second set of conceptions about the apprehender as an imputed individual refers to] (1) **no final deliverance** into the knowledge of all aspects **according to the** subject focusing on its own **aim**; (2) **identifying** inferior **paths as not being** one's own **path**; (3) results **arising and** their causes **ceasing**; (4) **being conjoined** with imputed entities **and not being conjoined with** substantial **entities**; (5) destroying the **abiding** in form and so on through that; {104a} (6) [naturally] **destroying the dispositions** of śrāvakas and pratyekabuddhas; (7) **the absence of striving** for the six pāramitās; (8) ultimately, [the absence] of the path—**the cause**; **and** (9) [the absence of] **observing** māras—the **opposing forces** to engaging in the mother—as mere imputations. These nine **are the other conceptions about the apprehender.**[166] The sūtras say:

> The mother proceeds on the even path to where the knowledge of all aspects is.[167]

2.3.1.2.2.2.2.2.2. The remedies

This has two parts:

1) [Explaining] the result of freedom—enlightenment
2) Explaining the means for freedom—the path of seeing itself

2.3.1.2.2.2.2.2.2.1. Explaining the result of freedom—enlightenment

This has two parts:

1) The causes for attainment
2) Identifying enlightenment

2.3.1.2.2.2.2.2.2.1.1. The causes for attainment

> **Pointing out the enlightenment of others,**
> **Entrusting the cause for this,**
> **And the cause for its uninterrupted attainment**
> **With its characteristic of an abundance of merit.** [V.17]

The three causes for the direct realization of natural purity that represent the means for being free from the stains of clinging to duality are (1) **pointing out** through a prophecy that **others** will attain **enlightenment**; (2) **entrusting the cause for this**—prajñāpāramitā—to others; **and** (3) **the cause** or path **for its uninterrupted attainment**—the self-aware nonconceptual wisdom that is endowed with nonreferential compassion and thus has the **characteristic of an abundance of merit.**[168] The sūtras say:

> Bodhisattvas undergo hardships . . .[169]

2.3.1.2.2.2.2.2.2.1.2. Identifying enlightenment

This has three parts:

1) The actual topic
2) Removing qualms
3) The manner of familiarizing with it

2.3.1.2.2.2.2.2.2.1.2.1. The actual topic

> **The wisdom of the termination and the nonarising**
> **Of the stains is called "enlightenment,"**
> **But these two should be understood, in due order,**
> **By virtue of the lack of termination and the lack of arising.** [V.18]

Termination refers to the realization of it being certain that there are no **stains and nonarising** refers to the realization that wisdom is free from arising, abiding, and ceasing—**the wisdom of** these two becoming manifest **is called "enlightenment."** This is the mere attainment of the dharmakāya. However, on the path of familiarization, through dualistic appearances ceasing in a progressive manner, the dharmakāya is completed progressively. {104b} This applies to the basic nature as follows. [For example,] a subject that is mistaken through the disease [of jaundice] may see the object, a conch shell, as yellow, and, if that disease is removed, see it as white. However, within that object, a conch shell, there is no termination of yellow and no new arising of white. Likewise, **these two** meanings [of termination and nonarising] **should**

be understood, in due order, according to this example, **by virtue of the lack of termination** of stains **and the lack of arising** of wisdom.[170] The sūtras say:

> The mother was not terminated, is not terminated, and will not be terminated.[171]

2.3.1.2.2.2.2.2.2.1.2.2. Removing qualms

This has two parts:

1) Objection
2) Answer

2.3.1.2.2.2.2.2.2.1.2.2.1. Objection

[The objection here] appears in the minds of realists, who think, "A stain that is a real entity is overcome through a newly arisen remedy. Otherwise, the conventional expression 'attaining enlightenment' is not suitable."[172]

2.3.1.2.2.2.2.2.2.1.2.2.2. Answer

> **In the nature without cessation,**
> **Through the path called "seeing,"**
> **What could be terminated that is born by conception**
> **And what nonarising could be attained?**[173] [V.19]
>
> **That phenomena exist and, at the same time,**
> **The cognitive obscurations of the teacher**
> **Are terminated—this claim by others**
> **I consider as amazing.** [V.20]

The basic nature does not accord [with what realists think]. **In** this **nature** of the ālaya-wisdom that is **without** any efforts toward the **cessation** of stains, **through the path called "seeing** its own nature," **what** factors to be relinquished **could be terminated that are born by conception and what nonarising could be attained** newly? Neither is the case because[174] this is similar to a dream not happening once one wakes up. Thus, the *[Tathāgata]-mahākaruṇānirdeśasūtra* says:

> Termination is not a termination through remedies—
> By virtue of having been terminated before, they are terminated later.

The *Uttaratantra* states:

Its true nature of being changeless
Is the same before as after.[175]

Other than this principle, [some people] assert that obscuring **phenomena** really **exist and** accept [these phenomena] in their own system as **cognitive** objects. **At the same time,** {105a} [they claim that] **the obscurations of the teacher**—the Buddha—with regard to [these objects] **are terminated.** About such a philosophical system that makes [internally] contradictory **claims,** [Maitreya] expresses his concern, saying, "**I consider this as amazing.**" As for the reason for this [concern] if [the stains] were really established, one would not be able to relinquish them. As the *Mūlamadhyamakakārikā* explains:

A nature that changes into anything else
Is never justified.[176]

2.3.1.2.2.2.2.2.2.1.2.3. The manner of familiarizing with it

There is nothing to be removed in this
And not the slightest to be added.
Actual reality is to be seen as it really is—
Whoever sees actual reality is liberated. [V.21]

In terms of progressively engaging in the [three kinds of] enlightenment of the three yānas, the view of the śrāvakas, the view of the pratyekabuddhas, and the Madhyamaka view [about what enlightenment is] are as follows. The first one refers to the liberation from afflictive obscurations by virtue of being free from clinging to a self in relation to the skandhas. The second one is the freedom from the coarse [duality of] apprehender and apprehended by virtue of realizing that apprehender and apprehended are not other in substance. The third one is the realization of phenomenal identitylessness by virtue of a bodhisattva's entire clinging to duality having been put to an end, and, through having familiarized [with phenomenal identitylessness], any consciousnesses with dualistic appearances having disappeared too. This is stated [in the scriptures] as follows:

Neither existent, nor nonexistent, [nor] neither existent nor nonexistent,
Nor having the character of both—
Being liberated from the four extremes
Is what is realized by Mādhyamikas.[177]

To explain the meaning of this [verse], among the following two systems, those who propound *Rangtong* Madhyamaka (*Svātantrikas and *Prāsaṅgikas) say, "It is explained by way of any clinging to suchness being unsuitable because no matter what one clings to, it does not go beyond the clinging to duality." The main point in venerable [Maitreya's], Asaṅga's, and his brother's own system is that, {105b} since suchness never becomes a dualistically appearing object, there is no concern that any clinging to real existence with regard to it could arise. Rather, the meaning of this verse here is to point out the very nonexistence of all seeming phenomena as anything whatsoever, such as being existent, nonexistent, both, or neither. The *Uttaratantra* says:

> Because they see that, due to mind's natural luminosity, the afflictions lack a nature . . .[178]

Therefore since there are no stains **in this** [buddha] heart—the pure other-dependent, the ālaya-wisdom—**there is nothing to be removed and** since it is of beginningless time, **not the slightest** wisdom **to be added** newly. "But how does one familiarize with it then?" One familiarizes in the manner of **actual reality**—one's own mind as such—seeing itself **as it really is.** At that point, with all dualistic clinging having vanished if **actual reality** without the duality of what is looked at and what looks at it is **seen**, the path of seeing is attained and one **is liberated.** The *[Prajñāpāramitā]saṃcayagāthā* says:

> The bodhisattva who realizes dependent origination
> Through this prajñā as being without arising and without extinction,
> Just as the rays of the sun free from clouds dispel darkness,
> Will overcome the density of ignorance and attain the self-arisen.[179]

This accords with what the *Laṅkāvatārasūtra* states:

> By relying on mere mind,
> One does not imagine outer objects.
> By resting in the focal object of suchness,
> One should go beyond mere mind too.
>
> Having gone beyond mere mind,
> One must even go beyond nonappearance.
> The yogin who rests in nonappearance
> Sees the mahāyāna.[180]

2.3.1.2.2.2.2.2.2.2. Explaining the means for freedom—the path of seeing itself

This has three parts:

1) The actual relinquishing remedy—the uninterrupted path
2) The sustaining remedy—the path of liberation
3) The distancing remedy—the special path {106a}

2.3.1.2.2.2.2.2.2.2.1. The actual relinquishing remedy—the uninterrupted path

> **That in which generosity and so on**
> **Are mutually combined with each other**
> **And which consists of poised readiness**
> **In one single moment is the path of seeing here.** [V.22]

After the [manifest] factors to be relinquished through seeing have been invalidated during the phase of [the supreme dharma of] the path of preparation, [there follows] the means to relinquish their seeds.[181] It is **that** wisdom **in which** the pāramitās (**generosity and so on**) **are mutually combined with each other** (all five pāramitās except for the one [with which they are combined], respectively)[182] **and which consists of** the four [instances of] **poised readiness in one single moment** on the path of seeing. This **is the path of seeing here.**[183] The sūtras say:

> Bodhisattvas dwell in each one of the pāramitās, such as generosity, and the others become completely perfect.[184]

2.3.1.2.2.2.2.2.2.2.2. The sustaining remedy—the path of liberation

The realization of the sixteenth [moment] is the actual [sustaining remedy], while the other [fifteen moments of] cognition are approximately concordant [with it].

2.3.1.2.2.2.2.2.2.2.3. The distancing remedy—the special path

> **Then, after having been absorbed**
> **In the samādhi of the lion's sport,**
> **Dependent origination is examined**
> **In its progressive and reverse orders.** [V.23]

Through having attained the path of seeing, one trains in **the samādhi of the lion's sport**—[the nine meditative absorptions of progressive abiding] from the first dhyāna up through [the meditative absorption of] cessation and from [the meditative absorption of] cessation down to the first dhyāna. **After having been absorbed in** this, during its subsequent attainment **dependent origination is examined in its progressive** [saṃsāric] **and reverse** [nirvāṇic] **orders.** The sūtras say:

> Bodhisattva mahāsattvas . . . are absorbed in the samādhi of the lion's sport . . . discriminate "formations due to the condition of ignorance," . . .[185]

There follows a critical analysis of dependent origination, which has three parts:
1) The basis of division
2) Explanation of the term
3) Divisions

1) The basis of division [is expressed in the *Mahāyānasūtrālaṃkāra*]:

> Therefore, what is this particular kind of darkness
> Of not seeing what exists and seeing what does not exist?[186]

[These lines address] dualistic appearance—nonafflicted ignorance. This refers to saṃsāra, which is primordially nonexistent. Therefore, ultimately, it has neither beginning nor end. Conventionally, it is as follows:

> Though beginningless, it entails an end.[187] {106b}

2) The explanation of the term [dependent origination] refers to the dependence on conditions and the infallible origination of causes and results.

3) Divisions
This has two parts:
a) The individual divisions
b) Teaching their presentation

3a) From the perspective of mistakenness, causes and results circle in an inexhaustible manner. [The twelve links of dependent origination are] (1) afflicted ignorance, which is twofold in being a factor to be relinquished through seeing and a factor to be relinquished through familiarization. The first one refers to the ignorance about the [four] realities that occurs as the accompanying factor of the mental sixth [consciousness] alone. The second one occurs as both the accompanying factor of the afflicted mind and the accompanying factor of the mental sixth [consciousness]. The latter one is again twofold—ignorance about reality and ignorance about objects. Among these, the one taught in the context of dependent origination here is the first one188 because it functions as the motivational force that propels one into another existence. (2) [Karmic] formations are the actions of body, speech, and mind that are motivated by this [ignorance]. (3) Consciousness refers to the phase of the seeds of these actions dwelling within the ālaya-consciousness and the result of this—[the ālaya-consciousness] connecting with a womb. (4) Name and form mean that the other four skandhas are accomplished after that [connection]. (5) The six āyatanas refer to the development of each one of the [six sense faculties]. (6) Contact means that the triad of object, sense faculty, and consciousness comes together, so that change with regard to the object is eliminated. Thus, there are six [kinds of] contact [by virtue of] the eye up through the mind coming together [with their respective objects]. (7) Feelings are the agreeable, painful, and neutral experiences due to contact. These are twofold—physical sensations and mental feelings. (8) Craving means being attached to pleasant and unpleasant feelings as something to be adopted and rejected, respectively. In terms of the three realms, craving is threefold. (9) Grasping refers to the striving to search for these [feelings as what are to be adopted and rejected, respectively]. The four [kinds of] appropriating grasping here are attachment to what is desirable; the sixty-two wrong views; being conceited about ethics and spiritual disciplines; and attachment to a self. {107a} (10) Becoming[189] means that, through the karmic seeds of the [latter] two within the ālaya[-consciousness] being awakened, their potency has become powerful. This is fourfold—the becoming of the past; the becoming of birth; the becoming of dying; and the becoming of the intermediate state. (11) Birth refers to [the process] from entering the location into which one is reborn up though feeling it [fully]. Birth is fourfold—[through] eggs, wombs, warmth and moisture, and in a miraculous way. (12) Aging and death refer to the changes in lifespan, faculties, form, strength, memory, prajñā, and well-being, as well as to timely and untimely deaths.

3b) The dependent origination of purified phenomena consists of the cessation of ignorance up through the cessation of aging and death. The twelve links [as presented above] are given in terms of womb birth—the first two among them represent one's previous lifetime; the last two, one's next lifetime; and the remaining ones, the present state. In brief, it is as [Nāgārjuna's *Pratītyasamutpādahṛdaya*] says:

> The first, the eighth, and the ninth are afflictive;
> The second and the tenth are karmic;
> And the remaining seven are suffering.[190]

2.3.1.2.2.2.2.3. The culminating training of the path of familiarization

This has three parts:

1) The path of familiarization that is the remedy
2) The conceptions that are the factors to be relinquished
3) The qualities that are based [on this path]

2.3.1.2.2.2.2.3.1. The path of familiarization that is the remedy

This has two parts:

1) General [topic]
2) [Meaning of] the text

2.3.1.2.2.2.2.3.1.1. General topic

This has two parts:

1) The meditative absorption of crossing in one leap that is the remedy
2) The manner in which it relinquishes the factors to be relinquished

2.3.1.2.2.2.2.3.1.1.1. The meditative absorption of crossing in one leap that is the remedy

Being preceded by the preparatory [samādhi of the] lion's sport, which suppresses the seeds of the factors to be relinquished through familiarization, the uninterrupted path that fully eradicates them is the actual crossing in one leap. (a) As for the lesser [crossing in one leap], its manner of meditating accords with the lion's sport. (b) [During] the medium [crossing in one leap], having risen from the first dhyāna, one enters cessation, and from there, the second [dhyāna]. In this manner, one alternates the other eight [meditative absorptions of] progressive abiding with cessation.{107b} One rises from the [last] cessation [in this sequence] through [assuming the state of] mind of the Peak of Existence, and, after having risen [in this way], will come out of being in meditative equipoise altogether. With the latter two states of mind being taken as one, [medium crossing in one leap contains] seventeen states [of meditative absorption]. (c) [During] the great [crossing in one leap], one reenters cessation and then rises from it into subsequent attainment, next [enters] the Peak of Existence and rises again [into subsequent attainment]. Thus, [great crossing in one leap contains] eighteen [meditative states]—nine meditative absorptions alternated with illusionlike subsequent attainments. When [additionally] divided by the upward progression [in the same manner, there are] thirty-six. Lesser, medium, and great crossing in one leap are each further divided into lesser, medium, and great [levels, with these nine levels matching] a bhūmi each. The preparatory stages of these [levels] (the lion's sport) are also equal in number and are merely based on said meditative absorptions. Their nature is the path of familiarization as accomplishment as taught [in verse 25] in the second chapter.

2.3.1.2.2.2.2.3.1.1.2. The manner in which it relinquishes the factors to be relinquished

The factors that are relinquished here are the ones that obscure the purity from adventitious [stains, which consist of] what entails dualistic appearance as well as the clinging to apprehender and apprehended as being mere imputations, which is produced by the [former. These factors] are divided into four sets of nine through their respective objects. Each one of these [nine] is divided into greater, medium, and lesser, which are each further divided into greater, medium, and lesser.

2.3.1.2.2.2.2.3.1.2. Meaning of the text

> **After the twofold progressing and returning through**
> **The nine absorptions, including cessation,**
> **The intermittent consciousness belonging to the desire [realm],**
> **Which is not in meditative equipoise, is assumed.** [V.24]
>
> **Through crossing over one, two,**
> **Three, four, five, six, seven, and eight,**
> **The meditative absorption of crossing in one leap consists of**
> **Proceeding up through cessation in disparate ways.** [V.25]

After the twofold progressing upward **and returning** back down **through the nine absorptions, including cessation**, during the lesser crossing in one leap, the great crossing in one leap entails **assuming the intermittent consciousness belonging to the desire** [realm], **which is not in meditative equipoise** but in subsequent attainment. **Through crossing over one, two, three, four, five, six, seven, and eight** of the [first] eight meditative absorptions of progressive abiding by alternating them with [said mind of] subsequent attainment, the manner of **the meditative absorption of crossing in one leap consists of proceeding up through** entering **cessation** {108a} by alternating meditative equipoises and subsequent attainments **in disparate ways**. The medium [crossing in one leap] is not taught in the text.[191] The sūtras say:

> . . . they enter into the samādhi of crossing in one leap.[192]

2.3.1.2.2.2.2.3.2. The conceptions that are the factors to be relinquished

This has two parts:

1) [Conceptions about] the apprehended
2) [Conceptions about] the apprehender

2.3.1.2.2.2.2.3.2.1. The conceptions about the apprehended

This has two parts:

1) [The objects of] engagement
2) [The objects of] withdrawal

2.3.1.2.2.2.2.3.2.1.1. The objects of engagement

> **With regard to being concise, detailed, not mentored**
> **Through not being protected**[193] **by the buddhas,**
> **Lacking the qualities of the three times,**
> **And the threefold excellent path—** [V.26]
>
> **These first conceptions about the apprehended**
> **Have the aspects of the training as their sphere.** [V.27ab]

[The first set of] nine [among the innate] conceptions [about the apprehended], which cling to the following objects as something to engage in, are **with regard to** (1) nondual wisdom **being concise;** (2) the general [and specific] characteristics of the bearers of the nature of phenomena being **detailed;** (3) those who do not train in the mother **not** being **mentored through not being protected by the buddhas,** but those who train being mentored through being protected; (4)–(6) the opposite of apprehending the mother as **lacking the qualities** of the buddhas **in the three times** being born [from her]—the three conceptions about the buddhas of the three times being born [from her]; **and** (7)–(9) **the threefold excellent path**—engagement through aspiration, the impure [bhūmis], and the pure [bhūmis]. Among the twofold **conceptions about the apprehended, these** are the **first.** Since they represent **the** cognitive aspects and **their** objective **spheres**[194] at the time **of the training** in the mother, they are objects and subjects that are mere imputations.[195] The sūtras say:

> What is the suchness of form? . . . It refers to all phenomena in brief and in detail.[196]

2.3.1.2.2.2.2.3.2.1.1. The objects of withdrawal

> **It is asserted that the second ones have the engagements**
> **Of minds and mental factors as their objects.** [V.27cd]
>
> **These conceptions about the nonarising of the mind,**
> **Not mentally engaging in the heart of enlightenment,**
> **Mentally engaging in the hīnayāna,**
> **Not mentally engaging in perfect enlightenment,** [V.28]

Familiarizing, not familiarizing,
The opposites of these,
And not being in accord with true reality
Should be known as those on the path of familiarization. [V.29]

[As for the second set of nine among the innate conceptions about the apprehender, which cling to their objects as something to be rejected,] **minds and mental factors** that entail dualistic appearances are the subjective conceptions that **engage** their objects.[197] Therefore, **it is asserted** by the Bhagavān **that they** are the primary factors to be relinquished. Their objects are (1) **the nonarising of the mind** of bodhicitta; (2) **not mentally engaging in the heart of enlightenment**[198]—the mother; (3) **mentally engaging in the hīnayāna**; (4) **not mentally engaging in perfect enlightenment** (that which bears the nature [of this mother]; (5) pondering, "Is the knowledge of all aspects attained through intensely **familiarizing** [with this mother]; {108b} (6) pondering, "Is it attained through **not familiarizing** [with her]?"; (7)–(8) **the opposites of these**—pondering, "Is it attained no matter whether one has familiarized or has not familiarized [with this mother]?" and pondering, "Is it attained through something that is neither familiarization nor nonfamiliarization [with this mother]?"; **and** (9) wondering about suchness, the ālaya-wisdom, "Is it **not** the **true reality** of **being in accord with** the basic nature?" These nine **conceptions** of regarding the proliferating conceptions that are the [above nine] mental factors as flaws **should be known as the** factors to be relinquished that exist **on the path of familiarization.**[199] [The sūtras] say:

> By all means, bodhisattvas should familiarize with engaging in prajñāpāramitā so that the phenomena of minds and mental factors do not stir.[200]

2.3.1.2.2.2.2.3.2.1. The conceptions about the apprehender

This has two parts:
1) The imputations
2) The causes of imputation

2.3.1.2.2.2.2.3.2.1.1. The imputations

The first ones about the apprehender are to be known
In terms of having imputed sentient beings as their sphere,
Imputed phenomena, not being empty,
Attachment, and the character of discrimination. [V.30]

They are further proclaimed with regard to
The formation of entities, the three yānas,
The impurity of offerings,
And disordered conduct. [V.31]

The first [nine innate] conceptions about the apprehender **are proclaimed to be known** as **the apprehending** of and clinging to mere imputations **in terms of** the following objects—(1) **having as their sphere** the apprehension of **sentient beings** (the bases of imputing phenomenal identities) as merely **imputed** consciousnesses; (2) the **imputed phenomena** that appear to those [consciousnesses]; (3) clinging to mere seeming appearances as being existent, that is, **not being emptiness**; (4) **attachment** to focal objects; (5) phenomena having **the character of** being **discriminated** by prajñā; (6) clinging to **the formation of entities**; (7) clinging to **the three yānas** as being distinct; (8) those who are not merged with the mother being **impure** objects for **offerings**; **and** (9) **disordered conduct** (such as generosity) by virtue of conceiving of the three spheres.[201] [The sūtras] say:

> If a self, sentient being, soul, or person is not observed, how can they be imputed as the dhātu of a self, the dhātu of a sentient being, the dhātu of a soul, or the dhātu of a person? Thus, through not imputing any phenomena, the knowledge of all aspects will be attained.[202]

2.3.1.2.2.2.2.3.2.1.2. The causes of imputation {109a}

Having imputed sentient beings and the cause of these
As their objects, the other nine kinds [of conceptions]
That are associated with the path of familiarization
Are its antagonistic factors by virtue of being overcome through
it. [V.32]

In terms of ignorance about the three obscurations
Of the three omnisciences, respectively,
The path of peace, being conjoined with
Or disjoined from suchness and so on, [V.33]

Being unequal, suffering and so on,
The nature of the afflictions,
And nonduality, these conceptions
Are asserted as the last ones. [V.34]

[Verse V.32] represents the introductory passage. The **imputations** of **sentient beings** as phenomenal identities **and** the subject—dualistically appearing consciousness—that is **the** basis or **cause of** imputing **these** [beings], **by virtue of being overcome through this** path of familiarization **are the antagonistic factors that are associated with the** remedial **path of familiarization** as its factors to be relinquished. They are explained as **the nine kinds** of [innate] conceptions about the apprehender that are **other** than the preceding ones. **These** nine **conceptions** [operate] **in terms of ignorance about** the following objects—(1)–(3) **the three obscurations of** the pure nature of **the three omnisciences** [knowing] the essential character, just as it is,[203] of the relinquishment [that is accomplished] through the three knowledges; (4) **the path of peace** of the three yānas; (5) [having doubts as to] the mother **being conjoined with or disjoined from** the nature of phenomena (**suchness and so on**); (6) **unequaled** relinquishment and realization; (7) the four realities of **suffering and so on**; (8) **the nature of the afflictions** (being terminated and nonarising); **and** (9) the actuality of the **nonduality** of apprehender and apprehended. These conceptions about the apprehender **are asserted as the last ones.**[204] [The sūtras] say:

> The knowledge of all aspects is the one of the tathāgatas.[205]

2.3.1.2.2.2.2.3.3. The qualities that are based on this path

> **When these pestilences have become extinguished,**
> **It is like breathing freely again after a long time.**
> **All the consummate qualities that accomplish**
> **The happiness of beings in all aspects,** [V.35]
>
> **Just like rivers [feeding] into the great ocean,**
> **Sustain these mahāsattvas,**
> **Who are embellished with the desired fruition,**[206]
> **From all sides.** [V.36]

When these cognitive obscurations, which are like **pestilences, have become extinguished** through the medicinelike wisdom that is free from reference points, this [state of] relinquishment **is like breathing freely** and having gained one's well-being **again** through being relieved from the hardships of a disease **after a long time**. Therefore, **all the consummate** inexhaustible **qualities** of such bodhisattvas **that accomplish** the temporary and ultimate **happiness of beings in all aspects, just as rivers** feeding **into the great ocean,** arise uninterruptedly and moreover {109b} **sustain these mahā**bodhi**sattvas,**

who are beautified and courageous through the attainment of **the fruition** of being the supreme among bipeds, **from all sides.** This means that these bodhisattvas will swiftly become buddhas. The sūtras say:

> Just like leaves, flowers, and fruits, bodhisattvas will nourish all sentient beings.[207]

2.3.1.2.2.2.2.4. The culminating training of the uninterrupted path

This has two parts:

1) The actual culminating training of the uninterrupted path
2) Removing qualms about the focal objects and aspects of this path

2.3.1.2.2.2.2.4.1. The actual culminating training of the uninterrupted path

> **It is compared to the virtues of having established**
> **The people in a trichiliocosm**
> **In the consummate realizations of disciples**[208] **and rhinos**
> **And on the flawless [bhūmi] of bodhisattvas.** [V.37]
>
> **Through such an abundance of merit**
> **This uninterrupted samādhi**
> **Immediately before attaining buddhahood**[209]
> **Is the knowledge of all aspects.** [V.38]

The vajralike samādhi is what overcomes the stains of the impregnations of negative tendencies, that is, the seeds of false imagination which are the obscurations of attachment and obstruction. It is the wisdom at the end of the continuum [of bodhisattvas on the tenth bhūmi] and is taught here through examples [that refer to this] samādhi of the uninterrupted path. **It is compared to the virtues of having established** all **the people in a trichiliocosm in the consummate realizations of** śrāvaka **and rhino**like pratyekabuddha [arhathood] **and on the flawless** bhūmi **of bodhisattvas** (the first bhūmi), all of which do not even come close to a hundredth of [the merit of] this samādhi. Between the vajralike samādhi that is accomplished **through such an abundance of merit** and **buddhahood** there is no interruption through obscurations. Therefore, **this uninterrupted samādhi is** the wisdom that is **the knowledge of all aspects.**[210] The sūtras say:

> Even if all sentient beings in a trichiliocosm were to dwell on the levels of śrāvakas . . . their merits would not even come close to a hundredth of the merit of a bodhisattva who has engaged in enlightenment.[211]

2.3.1.2.2.2.2.4.2. Removing qualms about the focal objects and aspects of this path

This has two parts:

1) Explaining the focal objects and aspects
2) Eliminating wrong ideas about them

2.3.1.2.2.2.2.4.2.1. Explaining the focal objects and aspects

This has two parts:

1) The presentation of causes and conditions in general
2) Explaining the meaning of the text

2.3.1.2.2.2.2.4.2.1.1. The presentation of causes and conditions in general

A cause is that which appropriates a result and produces the nature of a result. [Causes] are divided into six. An enabling cause produces the nature of a result that is other than itself. {110a} Simultaneous causes are mutual causes and results, such as the four elements in a single collection. A cause of similar outcome produces a factor to be relinquished that resembles it in terms of type and concordance with its own level. Congruent causes are primary minds and their accompanying mental factors, which aid each other. An omnipresent cause is a preceding omnipresent factor of a given level that produces a subsequent afflicted phenomenon [of this level]. Maturing causes consist of nonvirtues and contaminated virtues.

A condition is that which produces the distinctive features of a result. [Conditions] are divided into four. The last five causes are causal conditions. A former moment of mind is the immediate condition of the following one. Objects such as forms are the object conditions of consciousness. Enabling causes are [equivalent to] dominant conditions. Therefore, causes and conditions can also [be said to] be equivalent, such as when a vase is produced from clay.[212]

2.3.1.2.2.2.2.4.2.1.2. Explaining the meaning of the text

> **The lack of entity is asserted as the focal object of this,**
> **Mindfulness as its dominant factor,**
> **And peacefulness as its aspect.** [V.39ac]

The focal object of this wisdom of the meditative equipoise of mahāyāna noble ones **is asserted as the lack of entity** of the seeming, such as arising and ceasing; **mindfulness** or the prajñā of meditation, **as its dominant factor**; **and peacefulness** in terms of reference points and characteristics (that is, self-aware wisdom), **as its aspect**. These are presented as mere conventionalities because, ultimately, no causes, conditions, and so on can be presented with regard to suchness.[213] The sūtras say:

> The focal object of the knowledge of all aspects is the lack of entity . . .[214]

2.3.1.2.2.2.2.4.2.2. Eliminating wrong ideas about them

This has two parts:

1) The manner in which wrong ideas arise
2) The manner in which they are eliminated

2.3.1.2.2.2.2.4.2.2.1. The manner in which wrong ideas arise

> **. . . In this regard,**
> **Those who talk a lot dispute** [V.39cd]

In this regard of the Bhagavān's teachings on the path, **those** dialecticians whose minds cannot cope with the inconceivable manner of the variety of the dependent origination of the seeming appearing from the nature of ultimate true reality {110b} in an inexhaustible way **talk a lot** and **dispute**, saying, "If the entities of the seeming do not exist, [everything] from the focal objects of the path up through the familarization with the mother is not tenable." In the sūtras, these qualms are raised through Subhūti's questions and then answered by the teacher, [the Buddha]. Though there is no actual dispute in this situation, it resembles bringing up certain doubts.[215]

2.3.1.2.2.2.2.4.2.2.2. The manner in which they are eliminated

> **About the justification of the focal object,**
> **The identification of the nature of this,**
> **The wisdom of the knowledge of all aspects,**
> **The ultimate and the seeming,** [V.40]
>
> **The training, the three jewels,**
> **The means, the realization of the sage,**
> **Mistakenness, the path,**
> **Remedies and antagonistic factors,** [V.41]
>
> **Defining characteristic, and familiarization.**
> **Those people's utterances about these sixteen**
> **Are asserted as the wrong ideas**
> **About the knowledge of all aspects.** [V.42]

[The sixteen qualms here are eliminated as follows.] (1) Since conditioned phenomena are mistaken appearances, it is **justified** that **the focal object** of the meditative equipoise of the great noble ones is the lack of entity. (2) Since there is no phenomenon other than the dharmadhātu, it is justified that **the nature of this** wisdom is **identified** as the lack of entity. (3) Since the nature of phenomena engages in the basic nature of all phenomena, it is justified as **the wisdom of the knowledge of all aspects.** (4) Since they serve as prajñā and means, respectively, for each other, **the ultimate** reality **and the seeming** reality are justified. As the *Mūlamadhyamakakārikā* says:

> Without relying on the conventional,
> The ultimate cannot be taught.[216]

(5) **The training** in the six pāramitās is justified because it is performed for the sake of enlightenment. (6)–(8) **The three jewels** are justified—the jewel of the Buddha because of realizing true reality; the jewel of the dharma because of suchness being enlightenment; and [the jewel of] the saṃgha because of training in enlightenment in a nonreferential manner. (9) Skill in **means** is justified because of engaging without observing the three spheres. (10) **The realization of the sage** is justified because of seeing with certainty that there are no reference points. {111a} (11) **Mistakenness** is justified because, no matter whether form and so on are apprehended as permanent or impermanent, this represents clinging. (12) **The path** that makes one attain the knowledge of all aspects is justified because it trains in all paths. (13)–(14) **Remedies** are justified **and antagonistic factors** are justified because, in terms of the seeming, what is to be adopted and what is to be rejected arise. (15) Since all phenomena are of one taste as the dharmadhātu, it is justified as **the defining characteristic.** (16) To familiarize with the mother is justified because **familiarization** means not mentally engaging in anything whatsoever. These **are asserted as** the eliminations of **the sixteen wrong ideas** that represent **those people's utterances** who are mistaken **about** these [points], that is, their wrong views that arise **about the knowledge of all aspects.**[217]

> **This is the fifth chapter, on the culminating training,** ***in The Treatise on the Pith Instructions on Prajñāpāramitā, Called*** **The Ornament of Clear Realization.**

This is the commentary on **the fifth chapter in the** versified ***Treatise on the Pith Instructions on Prajñāpāramitā, Called*** **The Ornament of Clear Realization.**

The Sixth Chapter, on the Serial Training

2.3.1.2.2.3. The serial training (familiarizing with the [aspects of the three knowledges] in a sequential manner)

This has two parts:

1) Presenting the connection
2) Explaining the clear realization

2.3.1.2.2.3.1. Presenting the connection

After the antagonistic factors of the culminating training have been relinquished, the path of liberation increases progressively. As the *Dharmadhātustava* says:

> Just as when the waxing moon
> Is seen more in every moment,
> Those who've entered on the bhūmis,
> See its increase step-by-step.[218]

[This chapter] is an elaboration on the sūtra [passage] on the elimination of the sixteen wrong ideas, in which [the Tathāgata] says that he became a buddha after having realized all phenomena as having the nature of the lack of entity.[219]

2.3.1.2.2.3.2. Explaining the clear realization

This has three parts: {111b}

1) The six pāramitās (the conduct, in which merit is primary)
2) The six recollections (the path of the union [of view and conduct])
3) The training in equality (the view—primarily familiarizing with wisdom)

2.3.1.2.2.3.2.1. The six pāramitās (the conduct, in which merit is primary)

> **By way of generosity up through prajñā,** [VI.1a]

(1)–(6) [Among the thirteen elements of the serial training, the first six] refer to engaging in [the six pāramitās] from **generosity up through prajñā** in the manner of not observing the three spheres. As for prajñā, in its essence, it indeed represents the view. However since any meditation and conduct must be embraced by it, it is included in any of them.

2.3.1.2.2.3.2.2. The six recollections (the path of the union of view and conduct)

> **The recollections of the Buddha and so forth,** [VI.1b]

[The six recollections] are **the recollections of** (7) **the Buddha** (the aspects of the knowledge of all aspects) **and so forth**—(8) virtuous, nonvirtuous, and neutral dharmas; (9) the saṃgha of irreversible bodhisattvas; (10) ethics; (11) giving; and (12) the noble ones who are born as deities.[220] One recollects these and familiarizes with them by way of the lack of recollection and nothing to mentally engage in. One familiarizes with this yoga through relying on the three jewels; taking generosity and ethics as the basis of the six pāramitās; and taking deities as one's witnesses.

2.3.1.2.2.3.2.3. The training in equality (the view—primarily familiarizing with wisdom)

> **And the nature of the lack of entity,**
> **The serial activity is asserted.** [VI.1cd]

(13) The nature of familiarizing with the aspects [of the three knowledges in a] combined [manner] is the yoga of equality, which has **the nature of lacking** being tainted by any **entity** in terms of clinging to characteristics. **The serial activity** or training **is asserted by way of** these [thirteen].[221] The sūtras say:

> Bodhisattvas exert themselves in the serial activity, the serial training, and the serial practice.[222]

> **This is the sixth chapter, on the serial training, in *The Treatise on the Pith Instructions on Prajñāpāramitā, Called* The Ornament of Clear Realization.**

This is the commentary on **the sixth chapter in the** versified ***Treatise on the Pith Instructions on Prajñāpāramitā, Called* The Ornament of Clear Realization.**

The Seventh Chapter, on the Instantaneous Training

2.3.1.2.2.4. The instantaneous training (familiarizing with the [aspects of the three knowledges] in a simultaneous manner)

This has two parts:

1) Presenting the connection
2) Explaining the clear realization

2.3.1.2.2.4.1. Presenting the connection

{112a} Through all reference points of the yogas of combined familiarization [—the three preceding trainings—] having been eliminated without exception, this is the training of being made a buddha in an instant. It is an elaboration on [the passage in the sūtras that] discusses the manner of cultivating the six pāramitās through not observing them.[223]

2.3.1.2.2.4.2. Explaining the clear realization

This has four parts:

1) [The instantaneous training in terms of] nonmaturation (being in the process of becoming free from the stains of the impregnations of negative tendencies)
2) [The instantaneous training in terms of] maturation (being about to become buddha wisdom after being free from these [stains])
3) [The instantaneous training in terms of] the lack of characteristics
4) The instantaneous [training] in terms of nonduality

2.3.1.2.2.4.2.1. The instantaneous training in terms of nonmaturation (being in the process of becoming free from the stains of the impregnations of negative tendencies)

> **By virtue of each one, such as generosity,**
> **Including all that is uncontaminated,**
> **The sage's realization in a single instant**
> **Is to be understood.** [VII.1]

Each uncontaminated phenomenon (**such as generosity** and ethics) **includes all uncontaminated** phenomena that fill space. Therefore, if a single one [of them] becomes free from the most subtle stains, all will be free from these [stains]. **By virtue of** and in accordance with this, suchness is realized without remainder through the **realization** of **the sage's** wisdom **in a single instant.** This **is to be understood** as the vajralike wisdom. The sūtras say:

> How do bodhisattvas . . . complete the six pāramitās through generating a single mind?[224]

Realizing everything through realizing one is taught through the following example:

> **Just as a waterwheel driven by a person**
> **Through just a single spot to step on**
> **Turns simultaneously in its entirety,**
> **So does wisdom in a single instant.**[225] [VII.2]

2.3.1.2.2.4.2.2. The instantaneous training in terms of maturation (being about to become buddha wisdom after being free from these stains

> **When abiding in the state of the true nature**
> **Of all matured spotless phenomena,**
> **At that point prajñāpāramitā is born—**
> **The wisdom in one single instant.**[226] [VII.3]

The nature **of all spotless** purified **phenomena** is the ālaya-wisdom—**prajñāpāramitā**. Though it is indeed the case that it is primordially untainted by any stains, through self-aware wisdom being affected by ignorance suchness is not seen in a fully complete manner. However, {112b} personally experienced wisdom **is born** as **the state of the true nature** (prajñāpāramitā) in the **matured** manner of the wisdom at the end of the continuum overcoming even the most subtle stains. By virtue of not going beyond that very [state] and being its nature, subject and object having become inseparable represents the very knowledge of all aspects. **At that point**, the **one single instant** that precedes this [knowledge of all aspects] is **the wisdom** at the end of the continuum. Thus, Nāgārjuna's [*Dharmadhātustava*] states:

> On the fifteenth day of waxing,
> Eventually the moon is full.
> Just so, when the bhūmis' end is reached,
> The dharmakāya's full and clear.[227]

The sūtras say:

> After bodhisattvas have engaged in the knowledge of the path and attained all dharmas in a fully complete manner, they attain the knowledge of all aspects.[228]

2.3.1.2.2.4.2.3. The instantaneous training in terms of the lack of characteristics

> **Through abiding in phenomena being dreamlike**
> **By way of having engaged in generosity and such,**
> **The lack of characteristics of phenomena**
> **Is discovered in one single instant.** [VII.4]

The dependent origination of the correct seeming flows forth from the mother in a naturally spontaneous manner. Consequently, at the time of this meditative equipoise, **through abiding in** [the fact of] all[229] **phenomena** of vast **engagement (such as generosity)** arising in a **dreamlike** fashion, the knowledge of all aspects is manifested **in one single instant** of **discovering the lack of characteristics of** these **phenomena.**[230] The sūtras say:

> Bodhisattvas abide in the five appropriating skandhas as being like a dream . . . or a magical creation, and thus engage in the six pāramitās.[231]

2.3.1.2.2.4.2.4. The instantaneous training in terms of nonduality

> **With not even a dream and the seeing of it**
> **Being perceived in a dualistic fashion,**
> **The true reality that is the nonduality of phenomena**
> **Is seen in one single instant.** [VII.5]

For example since **a dream** (the object) is consciousness **and the seeing of it** (the subject) is also consciousness, they do not exist as two different [phenomena], but still occur as two—subject and object. Likewise, within the [ordinary waking] state that is [actually] the sleep of ignorance, apprehender and apprehended appear as two different [phenomena]. Upon awakening since any dream or any seeing of such a [dream] does not occur, there is **no perceiving** of apprehender and apprehended **in a dualistic fashion.** Likewise,[232] upon awakening from ignorance, including its latent tendencies, without seeing **phenomena** as the duality of existence and nonexistence, {113a} this is the training that makes one **see the true reality that is the** purity of **nondual** mind **in one single instant.**[233] The sūtras say:

> When engaging in the mother, bodhisattvas do not see a dream, nor do they see the seer of a dream.[234]

These [four] divisions [of the instantaneous training] are made in terms of the single vajralike samādhi—the wisdom at the end of the continuum—possessing [four] aspects of distinct capacities.

> **This is the seventh chapter, on the instantaneous training, in *The Treatise on the Pith Instructions on Prajñāpāramitā, Called* The Ornament of Clear Realization.**

This is the commentary on **the seventh chapter in the** versified ***Treatise on the Pith Instructions on Prajñāpāramitā, Called* The Ornament of Clear Realization.**

The Eighth Chapter, on the Dharmakāya

2.3.1.2.3. Explaining the dharmakāya (the fruition)

This has two parts:

1) Presenting the connection
2) Detailed explanation of the divisions

2.3.1.2.3.1. Presenting the connection

Through having made the path—the yogas of the four trainings—a living experience, the aspects [of the three knowledges and the four trainings] have become more and more lucid. In this way, just as one's own darkness is dispelled through one's own light, the dharmakāya, which is the direct realization of all three nonarisings [of the three knowledges], will be attained. This is the meaning that is taught by elaborating on the sūtra passages on the fourfold instantaneous training.[235]

2.3.1.2.3.2. Detailed explanation of the divisions

This has two parts:

1) General [topic]
2) [Meaning of] the text

2.3.1.2.3.2.1. General topic

This has two parts:

1) Presenting the enlightened mind [that represents the dharma]kāya
2) The manner in which it knows what is to be known

2.3.1.2.3.2.1.1. Presenting the enlightened mind that represents the dharmakāya

The ālaya-wisdom (the great mother or the sugata heart) is also called "dharmadhātu wisdom." Since various wisdoms of perfect dependent origination appear, in the mantra[yāna], it is also taught as "the wisdom kāya that is endowed with the supreme of all aspects." This is the dharmakāya or the svābhāvikakāya, which represents the basis for [further] divisions.[236] Within this [fundamental kāya], the aspect of luminosity that was never tainted by any stains primordially is mirrorlike wisdom—the sāmbhogikakāya. {113b} The aspect of its nonreferential great love pervading all sentient beings equally is the wisdom of equality. In terms of the aspect of various dependent originations appearing to it, it is discriminating wisdom. In terms of the aspect of the enlightened activity through which it accomplishes the welfare of all sentient beings, it is all-accomplishing wisdom—the nairmāṇikakāya.[237] Therefore, it is by virtue of being free from stains (such as the ālaya-consciousness) that these respective wisdoms appear, but it is not the case that those [stains] transform into these [wisdoms]. For example, this is just as sunlight comes forth by virtue of clouds being dispelled, but it is not that the clouds have transformed into sunlight.[238] These [wisdoms] are divided in terms of buddhahood's own basic nature. However, as for the rūpakāyas, their melodious speech, and their activities (all of which appear to the beings to be guided), the aspect of the enlightened activity that exists for [these beings as] the objects that are its recipients consists of [certain] aspects of the dualistic appearances in the very mind streams of those to be guided.

2.3.1.2.3.2.1.2. The manner in which it knows what is to be known

Ultimately, one cannot give any presentation of meditative equipoise and subsequent attainment with regard to the wisdom of buddhas. However, from a conventional perspective, they [always] dwell in meditative equipoise alone. At the point [of buddhahood] since dualistic appearances including their seeds do not exist [anymore], the seeming does not appear for this wisdom, just as falling strands of hair do not appear if one is free from blurred vision. You may think, "But then [buddha wisdom] would not be omniscience." There is no flaw because [this wisdom] knows the actual way of being of phenomena—the entirety of what is certain to exist—which is just like knowing the fundamental nature of the four realities. Thus, Nāgārjuna says:

> Likewise, seeming consciousnesses,
> Once one's eyes of insight are opened
> And one has parted from the sleep of ignorance,
> Are not seen at the time of being awake.[239]

As for knowing [phenomena's] way of appearing, this way of appearing consists of [certain aspects in] the mind streams of those to be guided appearing as rūpakāyas, appearing as teaching the dharma, and so on.[240] {114a}

2.3.1.2.3.2.2. Meaning of the text

This has four parts:

1) [Explaining] the svābhāvikakāya
2) [Explaining] the sāmbhogikakāya
3) [Explaining] the nairmāṇikakāya
4) Explaining enlightened activity

2.3.1.2.3.2.2.1. Explaining the svābhāvikakāya

This has two parts:

1) Brief introduction
2) Detailed explanation

2.3.1.2.3.2.2.1.1. Brief introduction

> **Those who have attained purity in every respect**
> **And the uncontaminated dharmas,**
> **Theirs is the svābhāvikakāya of the sage,**
> **Which bears the characteristic of the nature of these.** [VIII.1]

The dharma-**svābhāvikakāya of the sage**[241] refers to **the** aspect of **having** naturally **attained** all **the uncontaminated dharmas** there are **and** [the aspect of] being **pure** of stains from the start **in every respect** being blended into a single inseparable **nature**. It is this actuality **which bears the characteristic of the** lack of characteristics.[242] The sūtras say:

> . . . the lack of characteristics should be understood as the Tathāgata . . .[243]

2.3.1.2.3.2.2.1.2. Detailed explanation

This has three parts:

1) Explaining each one of the 140 uncontaminated dharmas[244]
2) Distinguishing dispassion and the knowledge through aspiration in terms of their focal objects
3) Instruction on the meanings of [all-]pervading and permanent

2.3.1.2.3.2.2.1.2.1. Explaining each one of the 140 uncontaminated dharmas

> **The factors concordant with enlightenment, the immeasurables,**
> **The liberations, the ninefold**
> **Progressive meditative absorptions,**
> **The ten totalities,** [VIII.2]

The āyatanas of overpowering,
Divided into eight kinds,
Dispassion,[245] **knowledge through aspiration,**
The supernatural knowledges, the discriminating awarenesses,
[VIII.3]

The four purities in all respects,
The ten masteries, the ten powers,
The four fearlessnesses,
The three ways of nothing to hide,[246] [VIII.4]

The threefold foundation of mindfulness,
The true nature of being without forgetfulness,
The latent tendencies being overcome,
Great compassion for beings, [VIII.5]

The eighteen qualities that are said
To be unique to a sage,
And the knowledge of all aspects—
The dharmakāya is described as these. [VIII.6]

You may wonder, "What are the uncontaminated dharmas?" They are [the twenty-one sets of qualities that are] taught as the [dharmas] concordant with enlightenment up through the dharmakāya. For all paths are attained through progressively becoming free from the stains [that cover] the subject of [the wisdom that cultivates] these [paths] and are thus divided by being a little bit free [from such stains] up through being free from all of them.[247]

[Among these qualities,] (1) **the factors concordant with enlightenment**, (2) **the** [four] **immeasurables**, (3) **the** [eight] **liberations**, (4) and **the ninefold progressive meditative absorptions** were already taught [above].

(5) **The ten totalities** are the samādhis of the four elements, the four [primary] colors, and [the two formless meditative absorptions of infinite] space and consciousness, [which are discussed in three parts]:

a) Support
b) Manner of meditation
c) Meaning of the term

a) [Their support] is the actual fourth dhyāna.

b) As for the manner of meditation, for the first [totality of] earth, a focal support is not mentioned. During the others, one respectively focuses on [the remaining three elements; the four colors; space; and consciousness as instantiated by] a vessel filled with water, a blazing fire, and wind touching one's body; some blue, yellow, red, and white discs; a cavity the size of a cubit or four fingerwidths; {114b} and the light of a lamp shining on the surface of a wall. Then, one brings to mind the respective names and so on of these [ten] and meditates that they, respectively, pervade all phenomena. [In due order,] the signs of stability in these [meditations] include such things as a fan of precious gems or a red woolen cloth[248] abiding in the sky; being immovable in one's posture; the colors that are one's focal support soaring up into the sky and then appearing there like fans of precious gems; a cavity that one has produced expanding as if being [all of] space; and intense lucidity illuminating all directions—these are the signs of accomplishment. The signs of nonaccomplishment include [appearances] such as water with bubbles; fire with smoke; wind with vapor; with regard to the four [colors] (such as blue), flowers without anthers and stalks; and not being able to produce cavities and [things] appearing as obstructive. Later, once one is familiar [with these], immediately upon seeing the respective focal object, the [corresponding] samādhis will be very clear. [Further fruitions include being able to] multiply one's single [form] and so on, walk on water and in space, sink into the earth, blaze with fire, move swiftly like the wind, transform the ground into [being made of precious substances] (such as beryl), walk through walls unimpededly, and greatly distancing oneself from sleep and dullness.

c) [Totality means] to expand infinitely and without interruption.[249]

(6) As for **the** [eight] **āyatanas of overpowering**, the first two [kinds of] overpowering mean that one, through considering oneself as [possessing] form, looks at (a) small (sentient beings as the contents) and (b) large outer forms (the world as the container), [each one in their] good (divine) and bad (human) [varieties], respectively. By overpowering these forms, one knows them through calm abiding and sees them through superior insight. The next two [kinds of] overpowering refer to (c)–(d) looking [at said small and large outer forms, respectively,] in the same manner through considering oneself to be formless. [Thus, the first two and the second two among] these four are derivatives of the first two [among the eight] liberations, respectively. {115a} [During the last] four kinds of overpowering, through solely considering oneself to be formless, one looks at the outer forms that display as colors, such as (e) both natural blue and manufactured blue, and does so in a way of blue light streaming forth from them, thus knowing and seeing them through overpowering them. The same goes for looking at (f) yellow, (g) white, and (h) red. Thus, they are **divided into eight kinds**—four in terms of shape and four in terms of color. The sūtras also give two examples for each of these colors in terms of their being natural and manufactured, respectively. The meaning of the term is to overpower focal objects because of gaining mastery over them.[250]

Next, [there follow] (7)–(10) **dispassion, knowledge through aspiration,**[251] **the** [six] **supernatural knowledges**, and **the** [four] **discriminating awarenesses.**

(11) **The four purities in all respects** are (a) complete purity in terms of the body by virtue of having gained mastery over adopting [physical forms as one pleases], dwelling [in them as long as one pleases], and abandoning [them in a timely fashion]; (b) complete purity in terms of focal objects by virtue of having gained mastery over magically creating and transforming them; (c) complete purity of the mind by virtue of having gained mastery over samādhi; and (d) complete purity of knowledge by virtue of having gained mastery over wisdom.[252]

(12) **The ten masteries** are (a) being able to live for eons by virtue of having blessed one's *lifespan*; (b) *mind* being able to engage in samādhi as one pleases; (c) being able to shower down rains of *necessities* and possessions; (d) something like causing the *karma* to be experienced in the [two] higher realms being experienced in the desire [realm]; (e) being able to take *birth* [as one pleases], such as [being born] in the desire [realm] without regressing from the dhyānas; (f) being able to transform earth into water, water into earth, and so forth through sheer *creative willpower*; (g) one's *aspiration prayers* for the inexhaustible welfare of others being accomplished; (h) displaying infinite *miraculous powers* for the sake of guiding those to be guided; (i) the *wisdom* of the [four] discriminating awarenesses; and (k) teaching the *dharma* in accordance with the thinking [of those to be guided].[253]

(13)–(14) **The ten powers** and **the four fearlessnesses** [have been taught above]. {115b}

(15) **The three ways of nothing to hide** refer to there never being any need to conceal anything from others because the conduct of the three doors [of the body, speech, and mind of buddhas] is utterly pure. Thus, amidst their retinues, they speak straight from the heart.

(16) **The threefold foundation of mindfulness** refers to equanimity in terms of not having the three [kinds of] distraction (attachment, aversion, or both, respectively) toward those who listen to the dharma with respect, without respect, or both [(sometimes with and sometimes without respect)].

(17) **The true nature of** the deeds of **being without forgetfulness** [in the sense of] never missing the [right] time for [accomplishing] the welfare of sentient beings is that [these deeds] bear fruits [accordingly].

(18) By virtue of **the latent tendencies** of the two obscurations **being overcome**, throughout [all periods of] movement or stillness body and speech are changeless in never [exhibiting any] conduct that is not [in accordance with] omniscience.

(19) **Great compassion** beholds all **beings** six times during day and night, [thinking,] "Who flourishes and who is in decline?"

(20) **The eighteen qualities that are said to be unique to a sage** [have also been taught above].

(21) After the enlightenment of the three kāyas has been found, **the knowledge of all aspects** cuts through the doubts of all sentient beings.

The dharmakāya is described through all of **these** [qualities] being perfectly complete.[254] The sūtras say:

> Subhūti asked, "What are these uncontaminated dharmas?" The Buddha said, "They are the thirty-seven dharmas concordant with enlightenment . . ."[255]

2.3.1.2.3.2.2.1.2.2. Distinguishing dispassion and the knowledge through aspiration in terms of their focal objects

> **The dispassion of śrāvakas means avoiding**
> **The afflictions of people upon being seen [by them].**[256]
> **The dispassion of the victor refers to extinguishing**
> **The stream of their afflictions in villages and so on.** [VIII.7]
>
> **The Buddha's knowledge through aspiration**
> **Is held to be effortless, free from attachment,**
> **Unobstructed, remaining forever,**
> **And solving all questions.** [VIII.8]

The view of **the dispassion of śrāvakas** and pratyekabuddhas **means** merely **avoiding the** conditions for the arising of **afflictions** in others and their own mind streams merely being without [afflictions]. **The dispassion of the victor** (the Buddha) **refers to** the samādhi that has the power of completely relinquishing[257] **the afflictions** in the mind streams **of** the many [beings] to be guided (such as [human] **people**) and **extinguishing the stream of the afflictions** of **the** persons who live **in villages and so on** through merely entering these [places]. {116a}

As for the knowledge through aspiration of śrāvakas and pratyekabuddhas, it refers to [their having made] aspiration prayers due to aspiring to know certain knowable objects. By virtue of being preceded by [such aspiration prayers], they [eventually come to] know the matters they aspired for. **The Buddha's knowledge through aspiration is held to** operate in a manner that is primordially **effortless, free from attachment, and unobstructed**; to **remain** in meditative equipoise **forever; and**—from within that state—to be capable of **solving all questions** of those who have doubts.[258]

2.3.1.2.3.2.2.1.2.3. Instruction on the meanings of all-pervading and permanent

> **Once the cause has come to maturity,**
> **For whomever and whenever,**
> **It will unfold[259] as beneficial**
> **Activity to them.** [VIII.9]
>
> **Though the god of rain[260] may send rainfalls,**
> **An unsuitable seed will not grow.**
> **Likewise, though buddhas come forth,**
> **The unsuitable will not come to enjoy any good.** [VIII.10]
>
> **By virtue of the vastness of activity like that,**
> **Buddhahood is described as "all-pervading."** [VIII.11ab]

You may wonder, "If the dharmakāya is present in an effortless manner primordially, why does it not appear to all sentient beings? Isn't it that there are buddhas without the welfare of others happening?" **Once the cause**—having cultivated the yoga of equality through realizing the stains to be adventitious—**has come to maturity**, being fostered through the conditions of the confidence and so on of those to be guided, **for whomever** among them **and whenever** they are guided, when enlightened **activity benefits** them through eliminating their stains and increasing their realizations, **it** [—the dharmakāya—] **will unfold to those** to be guided in accordance with their pure appearances. [To give] an example for the manner in which not all sentient beings see it in this way, **though** the king **of the gods may send rainfalls** without any bias and fruits are produced from fertile seeds through that, no fruit **will grow** from **an unsuitable seed** (such as a rotten one). **Likewise, though buddhas come forth** throughout the three times in an incessant manner, **the unsuitable** who are obscured by ignorance **will not come to enjoy** and attain **any good** fruitions. Therefore, just because the dharmakāya does not appear to the consciousnesses [of certain beings], it is not the case that it is not all-pervading and permanent. It is **by virtue of the vastness of** its **activity** being **like the** divine rainfalls that **buddhahood is described as "all-pervading."** {116b} The *Uttaratantra* says:

> Unconditioned and effortless . . .[261]

Accordingly, [the next two lines state]:

> **By virtue of being inexhaustible,**
> **It is also declared to be "permanent."**[262] [VIII.11cd]

2.3.1.2.3.2.2.2. Explaining the sāmbhogikakāya

This has two parts:

1) Brief introduction
2) Detailed explanation

2.3.1.2.3.2.2.2.1. Brief introduction

> **Since this [kāya] of the sage, whose character lies in**
> **The thirty-two major marks and the eighty minor marks,**
> **Enjoys the mahāyāna,**
> **It is held to be the sāmbhogikakāya.** [VIII.12]

In a buddha's own actual way of being, the major and minor marks of wisdom blaze. In mahāyāna noble ones, major and minor marks inferior to these appear, while in śrāvakas and so on, even coarser ones than the [latter appear]. Therefore, in terms of the sāmbhogikakāya that is an appearance for others since **this** [kāya] **of the sage, whose character lies in the thirty-two major marks and the eighty minor marks, enjoys** solely **the** dharma of the **mahāyāna, it is held to be the sāmbhogikakāya.**[263] The sūtras say:

> The kāyas of the buddha bhagavāns are adorned with the thirty-two marks of a great being . . .[264]

2.3.1.2.3.2.2.2.2. Detailed explanation

This has two parts:

1) [Explaining] the major marks
2) Explaining the minor marks

2.3.1.2.3.2.2.2.2.1. Explaining the major marks

> **It is marked with wheels on hands and feet, and has tortoiselike feet.**
> **Fingers and toes are joined by webs,**
> **Hands and feet are soft and supple,**
> **The body has seven convex surfaces,** [VIII.13]

Long fingers, broad heels, and is tall and straight.
It has nonprotruding ankles, body hairs that point upward,
Antelopelike calves, long and beautiful arms,
And is the supreme of those whose sexual organ is covered by a sheath. [VIII.14]

The skin has a golden hue and is delicate.
It has well-grown body hairs, each one single by itself and curling to the right,
The face is adorned with the ūrṇā hair, and the upper body is lionlike.
It has evenly rounded shoulders, with compact flesh in between, [VIII.15]

And even unpleasant tastes appear as the most delicious tastes for it.
Its figure has symmetrical proportions like a nyagrodha [**tree**]**,**
It has an uṣṇīṣa on the head, a large and beautiful tongue,
A melodious voice like Brahmā, jaws like a lion, [VIII.16]

Very white teeth of equal size, well arranged,
And in a complete set of forty,
Dark-blue eyes, and eyelashes like those of a magnificent heifer.
These are the thirty-two marks. [VIII.17]

[The thirty-two major marks] are each taught [here] by way of three [points]—the former actions that are their causes,[265] the natures of these marks, and the fruitions for which they are portents.

(1) Through the causes that consist of previously having escorted the gurus, praised listening to the dharma, and paid respect to stūpas, **hands and feet are marked with** thousand-spoked **wheels**, which look like being carved in ivory and are the portents of having a large retinue.

Likewise, (2) through [the buddhas] having been firm in their vows, the soles of their **feet** are even **like** the belly of a **tortoise**, [which is the portent] of being immovable.

(3) Through having become familiar with the four means of attracting [those to be guided], **fingers and toes are joined by webs** between them, which do not prevent wearing finger rings (just as in geese). [These are the portents] of the retinue swiftly gathering.

(4)–(5) Through having provided delicious and abundant food and drinks for others, **hands and feet are soft and supple** and {117a} **the body has seven**

convex surfaces due to the two soles of the feet, the two palms of the hands, the two shoulders, and the nape of the neck showing no concavities, but being level with the other [neighboring areas of the body].[266] These two are the portents of obtaining delicious solid food and drinks.

(6)–(8) Through having liberated those who were bound, the **fingers** are **long**, that is, of the same size as the length of the soles. Through having protected life, the **heels** are **broad**, that is, protruding to [the extent of] a quarter [of the length] of the foot. Through having abandoned killing, the height of the body is **tall** (ten and a half cubits [as measured] in ordinary humans and thus seven cubits more)[267] **and straight**, that is, not being bent over or crooked. These three [are the portents] of having a long life.

(9)–(10) Through having undertaken virtuous dharmas, the kneecaps and **ankles** are **not protruding**. Through having increased the undertaking of virtue, the tips of the **body hairs point upward**. These two [are the portents] of being endowed with unequaled dharmas.

(11) Through having taken up the activities of the sciences, arts, and crafts and having passed them on to others, the **calves** are proportioned and rounded **like** the calves of a wild deer, that is, an **antelope**. [This is the portent] of swiftly seizing [the unequaled dharmas].

(12) Through not having been miserly, the **arms** are **beautiful and** so **long** that the palms reach the kneecaps when standing upright, [which is the portent] of necessities being plenty and kept under control.

(13) Through not having separated dear ones, having encouraged others [to adopt] pure [sexual] conduct, and having guarded secret words, just like the all-knowing steed, [the buddhas] **are the supreme of those whose sexual organ is covered by a sheath**, [which is the portent] of having many sons.[268]

(14)–(15) Through having supplied clothes and seats for others, **the skin** is shining with **a goldlike hue, and**, through having provided houses and estates, **is delicately** grown and soft. These two [are the portents] of obtaining clothes, seats, mansions, and stately estates.

(16)–(17) Through having relinquished hustle and bustle, the **body hairs** are **well grown, each one single by itself** (with no two in a single pore), **and** {117b} **curling to the right**. Through having paid proper services to preceptors, masters, parents, and so on, at the place between the eyebrows, **the face is adorned with the ūrṇā hair**—thirty-two white, soft, and very fine hairs that radiate light [more intense than that of the sun and the moon].[269] These two [are the portents] of being unequaled.

(18)–(19) Through having spoken nice words in answer to being put down, **the upper body is lionlike** in being expanded greatly. Through having adopted excellent explanations accordingly, its **shoulders** are broad and **evenly rounded**. These two [are the portents] of being unassailable.

(20)–(21) Through having provided medical treatment and services, the **flesh in between** [the shoulders] **is compact**, the throat is round, and the chest [is compact].[270] Through having provided elixirs and beneficial foods, **even tastes** that are **unpleasant** for ordinary people **appear as the most delicious tastes for this** [body]. These two [are the portents] of having few diseases.

(22)–(23) Through having provided pleasure groves for others, **its figure has symmetrical proportions like a nyagrodha** tree,[271] since its height and arm span are equal in size. Through having provided temples, **it has a** round **uṣṇīṣa on the head**, which curls to the right and protrudes four finderwidths. These two [are the portents] of having great might and power.

(24)–(25) Through having spoken only nice words and in a gentle manner, the **tongue** is **large and beautiful**—[when extended, it] covers [the entire face up to] the hairline and the ears. Through having made everybody understand the genuine dharma, just **like** the melodious **voice** of **Brahmā,**[272] the speech is heard far away outside in just the way [it is heard] inside. These two [are the portents] of having the speech that is endowed with the five branches. These five branches are (a) knowing and understandable; (b) delightful to listen to; (c) profound and melodiously pitched; (d) captivating; (e) coherent and clear.

(26) Through having relinquished meaningless words, the **jaws** are round and broad **like** those of **a lion**, {118a} [which is the portent] of everybody listening to one's words.

(27)–(28) Through having paid respect to all beings, the **teeth** are **very white**. Through pure livelihood, the teeth are **of equal size**, without [some] being long and [others] short. These two [are the portents] of a retinue from before and so on.

(29)–(30) Through having spoken nothing but true words, the teeth are **well arranged** [that is, even and without gaps]. Through having relinquished slandering, the teeth are **in a complete set of forty**. These two [are the portents] of the retinue being indivisible.

(31)–(32) Through having looked [upon all beings] with loving eyes, the white and dark [parts] of the **eyes** are not mixed, with the dark area being somewhat **dark-blue**. Through having looked [upon all beings] without desire, anger, or ignorance, the **eyelashes** are not tangled, **like those of a magnificent** lead bull. These two are the portents of being handsome in every respect. Thus, **these are the thirty-two marks.**[273]

[The next verses] instruct on their causes:

As for the causes that accomplish
These respective marks,
Through completing them
These marks will be possessed in full. [VIII.18]

What are these [causes]?

> **Escorting the gurus and so on,**
> **Firmness with regard to vows,**
> **Relying on the means of attraction,**
> **Providing magnificent things,** [VIII.19]
>
> **Liberating those to be killed,**
> **Undertaking and increasing virtue,**
> **And so on—these are the causes that accomplish**
> **These marks according to the sūtras.** [VIII.20]

These were already commented on [above].

2.3.1.2.3.2.2.2.2.2. Explaining the minor marks

> **The sage's nails are copper-colored,**
> **Glossy, and prominent. His fingers and toes are**
> **Rounded, compact, and tapering.**
> **His veins do not protrude and are free from knots.** [VIII.21]
>
> **His ankles do not protrude and his feet are equal [in size].**
> **He walks with the stride of a lion, an elephant,**
> **A goose, and a lordly bull, and walks by keeping to the right [side],**
> **Elegantly, and upright. The limbs of his body are well rounded,** [VIII.22]
>
> **Smooth, slender,**
> **Clean, soft, and pure.**
> **His genitals are fully developed**
> **And his figure is beautiful and stately.** [VIII.23]
>
> **His steps are even and his eyes**
> **Are pure. His body is beautifully youthful,**
> **Not sunken, with full [flesh],**
> **And very firm.** [VIII.24]
>
> **His limbs are well proportioned**
> **And his vision is unobscured and pure.**[274]
> **His belly is round, smooth, unmarred,**
> **And slender.**[275] **His navel is deep** [VIII.25]

And winds to the right.
He is beautiful to behold from all sides,
His conduct is clean,
And his body is free from black moles. [VIII.26]

His hands are as soft as cotton wool
And the lines on his palms are glossy, deep, and extensive.
His face is not too long
And his lips are red like a bimba berry. [VIII.27]

His tongue is supple, slender,
And red. His voice is like thunder,
Sweet, and gentle. His eyeteeth are round,
Sharp, white, equal [in size], [VIII.28]

And tapering. His nose is prominent
And supremely pure.
His eyes are wide, with well-developed eyelashes,
And like the petals of a lotus. [VIII.29]

His eyebrows are elongated, smooth,
And shiny, and their hairs are of equal length.
His arms are long and muscular, and his ears
Are equal and completely unimpaired. [VIII.30]

His forehead is well shaped
And broad, and his head is large.
His hair is as black as a black bee,
Thick, smooth, not shaggy, [VIII.31]

Not unruly, and has a fragrant smell
That captivates the minds of people.
[His hands and feet show] endless knots and swastikas.
These are held to be the minor marks of a buddha.[276] [VIII.32]

[Among the eighty minor marks,] the first set of ten is as follows. (1) Through being free from formations, **the sage's nails are copper-colored.** (2) Through being endowed with a mind [that seeks] the benefit and happiness [of sentient beings], his nails are **glossy.** (3) Through being of high caste, his nails are **prominent.** (4) Through being without evil deeds, **his fingers and toes are rounded.** (5) Through having accumulated virtue, his fingers and toes are

compact. (6) Through having accomplished virtue, the tips of his fingers and toes are **tapering**. (7) Through having well guarded his livelihood, {118b} **his veins do not protrude** above the skin. (8) Through being without [the knots of] the afflictions, his veins **are free from knots**. (9) Through being endowed with the dharma of voidness, **his** inner **ankles do not protrude**. (10) Through being without rivals, **his feet are equal**, without any difference in length or width.

The second set of ten: (11) Through being the lion among humans, **he walks with the** majestic **stride of a lion**. (12) Through being the elephant among humans, [he walks with the] straight [stride of] **an elephant**. (13) Through moving in space, [he walks with the stride] of **a goose** bird. (14) Through being the leader of humans, [he walks with the stride] of **a lordly bull** who guides his retinue. (15) Through being endowed with the proper approach [of circumambulating], he arrives from **the right** side and returns from the right. (16) His stride is **elegant** to watch. (17) Through his mind being without deceit, he walks with his body **upright**. (18) Through showing pure qualities, **his body is** majestic and **well rounded**. (19) Through being without wrongdoing, his body is **smooth** without any stains. (20) Through teaching the dharma in accordance with those to be guided, his body is slim and has a **slender** waist.

The third set of ten: (21) Through his conduct being pure, his body is **clean**. (22) Through his mind being gentle, his body is **soft**, that is, pleasant to touch. (23) Through his mind being pure, his body is **pure**. (24) Through having perfected the dharma of the vinaya, **his** thirty-two marks[277] **are fully developed**. (25) Through his qualities being beautiful and stately, **his figure is** large, that is, **beautiful and stately**. (26) Through his mind being even with respect to everything, **his steps are even** in length. (27) **His eyes are** of **pure** sight. (28) Through teaching the gentle dharma, **his body is beautifully youthful**. (29) Through his mind being dauntless, his body is **not sunken**. (30) Through having purified all nonvirtue, his flesh is lush, that is, **full**.

The fourth set of ten: (31) Since he has overcome rebirth, his body is not slack, but **very firm**. (32) Through teaching dependent origination [in a finely distinguishing manner], **his limbs** {119a} **are well proportioned**, that is, their respective length is just appropriate. (33) **His vision is pure** since it is **unobscured** in that his eyes [are not affected by] blurred vision, any occurrence of eye discharge, and so on. (34) Through being surrounded by disciples with ethics, **his belly is round**. (35) Through being without the flaws of saṃsāra, his waist is **slender**. (36) Through being without pride, his belly is **unmarred**, that is, his intestines are without indentations. (37) Through his teaching the dharma being inexhaustible, his belly is without any elevations, that is, **smooth**. (38) Through his realization of the profound dharma, the bottom of the cavity of **his navel is deep**. (39) Through disciples who adopt his instructions [accordingly] having gathered, the lines in his navel **wind to the right**.

(40) Through a saṃgha with beautiful conduct having gathered, his physical conduct **is beautiful to behold from all sides.**

The fifth set of ten: (41) The **conduct** of **his** three gates **is clean.** (42) Through being free from black dharmas, **his body is free from moles** and **black** marks on his flesh. (43) Through teaching dharmas that are convenient to practice, **his hands are as soft as cotton wool.** (44) Through having found the great [radiant] training in virtue, **the lines on his palms are glossy** and shining. (45) Through abiding firmly [in the profound dharma], the lines of his palms are **deep.** (46) Through teaching the dharma of patience, the lines of his palms are **extensive.** (47) Through sustaining the trainings in their most subtle form, the shape of **his face is not too long.** (48) Through sending out his reflections into the world, **his lips are red like a bimba** flower and have the appearance of a reflection.[278] (49) Through guiding with gentle words, **his tongue is** pliant and **supple.** (50) Through being endowed with a host of subtle qualities, his tongue is **slender.**

The sixth set of ten: (51) Through the dharma of the vinaya that is difficult to fathom, his tongue is **red.** (52) Through not having any fear, he is endowed with the magnificence of a **voice like thunder.** {119b} (53) Through having disciples who speak gently, **his voice is sweet and gentle.** (54) Through being beyond any bondage to [saṃsāric] existence, **his eyeteeth are round.** (55) Through guiding those who are difficult to guide, his eyeteeth are **sharp.** (56) Through the white dharma of the vinaya, his eyeteeth are **white.** (57) Through dwelling in equality, his eyeteeth are **equal** in length and so on. (58) Through teaching clear realization in a progressive manner, the tips of his eyeteeth are **tapering.** (59) Through dwelling on the mountain of prajñā, **his nose is prominent.** (60) Through being associated with disciplined clean persons [around him], his nose is without stains and thus **supremely pure.**

The seventh set of ten: (61) Through being endowed with the vast buddhadharmas, **his eyes are** long and **wide.** (62) Through leading the assemblies of sentient beings, **his eyelashes are well developed.** (63) Through delighting the women among gods, asuras, and so on, the black and white [parts] of his eyes are [properly] set apart, **like the petals of a lotus.** (64) Through beholding [the conditions of beings] throughout the future, **his eyebrows are elongated** due to being connected left and right. (65) Through guiding [beings] in a smooth way, his eyebrows are **smooth.** (66) Through being endowed with the shine of virtue, his eyebrows are **shiny.** (67) Through knowing all flaws, **the hairs** of his eyebrows **are of equal length** and so on. (68) Through warding off harm, **his arms are long and muscular.** (69) Through being victorious over the afflictions, **his ears are equal** in size and [at the same] level. (70) Through guiding [beings] with an [ever] unimpaired motivation,[279] his ears are **completely unimpaired** by deafness and so on.

The eighth set of ten: (71) Through having purified all views, his hairline is prominent, that is, **his forehead is well shaped.** (72) Through taming opponents [in debate], his forehead is **broad.** (73) Through having completed genuine aspiration prayers, **his head is large,** like an umbrella. {120a} (74) Through having put an end to pleasures related to objects [of attachment], there are no white **hairs** on his head and their color **is as black as a black bee.** (75) Through the latencies to be relinquished [through the paths of seeing and familiarization] having been terminated, his hair is **thick.** (76) Through having internalized the essence of the teachings with a gentle mind, his hair is **smooth.** (77) Through his mind being undisturbed [by afflictions], his hair is **not shaggy.** (78) Through lacking abusive speech, his hair does not stand on end, that is, it is **not unruly.** (79) Through having accomplished the fragrance of the branches of enlightenment, **his hair has a fragrant smell** and thus **captivates the minds of people.** (80) On his hands and feet there are **endless knots,** [swastikas], the eight auspicious substances,[280] rectangular patterns,[281] and so on. **These are held to be the minor marks of a buddha.**[282]

2.3.1.2.3.2.2.3. Explaining the nairmāṇikakāya

> **The perpetual nairmāṇikakāya of the sage**
> **Is the one through which various benefits**
> **For the world are performed equally**
> **Until the end of existence.** [VIII.33]

[Nairmāṇikakāyas are of three kinds—] (1) artistic nairmāṇikakāyas, such as the emanation of a masterful vīnā player in order to guide Pramudita, the king of the gandharvas; (2) incarnate nairmāṇikakāyas that appear as any manifestations as one pleases, such as ships, bridges, medicines, fruits, waterfalls, [or various animals]; (3) [supreme] nairmāṇikakāyas of great enlightenment who display the twelve deeds and so on, [such as Buddha Śākyamuni]. Thus, **the nairmāṇikakāya of the sage is the one through which various benefits for the world are performed equally** (simultaneously) through various guiding physical forms for certain [beings] to be guided **until the end of existence.** Therefore, it arises **perpetually.**[283] The sūtras say:

> Through the enlightened activities of various manifestations of the Buddha . . . the welfare of sentient beings is promoted.[284]

2.3.1.2.3.2.2.4. Explaining enlightened activity

This has two parts:

1) Brief introduction to enlightened activity in terms of its actual way of being
2) Detailed explanation of its way of appearing

2.3.1.2.3.2.2.4.1. Brief introduction to enlightened activity in terms of its actual way of being

> **Likewise, it is held that its activity**
> **Is perpetual until the end of saṃsāra.** [VIII.34ab]

Just **like** the nairmāṇikakāya is perpetual, **it is held that** the **activity** of dharmadhātu wisdom—natural luminosity—{120b} **is perpetual until the end of saṃsāra** because it is permanent.[285]

2.3.1.2.3.2.2.4.2. Detailed explanation of its way of appearing

> **The activity of pacifying beings,**
> **Establishing them in the fourfold means of attraction,**
> [VIII.34cd]
>
> **Realizing afflicted phenomena**
> **And purified phenomena,**
> **The true nature of the welfare of sentient beings,**
> **The six pāramitās,** [VIII.35]
>
> **The buddha path, emptiness**
> **Of a nature, the termination of duality,**
> **Symbols, nonobservation,**
> **Maturing living beings,** [VIII.36]
>
> **The bodhisattva path,**
> **Putting an end to clinging,**
> **Attaining enlightenment, pure**
> **Buddha realms, definitiveness,** [VIII.37]
>
> **The immeasurable welfare of sentient beings,**
> **The qualities of attending to buddhas and so on,**
> **The branches of enlightenment, actions**
> **Being never lost, seeing reality,** [VIII.38]

Relinquishing mistakenness,
The manner of its nonsubstantiality,
Purification, the accumulations,
Conditioned and unconditioned phenomena [VIII.39]

Being understood as nondifferent,
And establishing in nirvāṇa—
The enlightened activity of the dharmakāya
Is held to be twenty-sevenfold. [VIII.40]

The **twenty-seven** actions [of the dharmakāya] that occur effortlessly are as follows.

(1) The one [activity] of establishing [those to be guided] in the support of the path consists of **pacifying** the sufferings of the **beings** in the unpleasant realms, the desire realm gods' clinging to desirous objects, and the views about the Brahmā [realm]s.

The two [activities of] establishing human beings on the path of accumulation consist of (2) **establishing them in the fourfold means of attraction** and (3) [making them] **realize afflicted phenomena and purified phenomena**, which are to be rejected and adopted, respectively, through studying and reflecting.

The four [activities of] establishing them on the path of preparation consist of [establishing them in] (4) the four immeasurables as **the true nature of** the path to **the welfare of sentient beings**; (5) **the six pāramitās**; (6) **the buddha path** (the ten virtues); and (7) knowing all phenomena to be the **emptiness of a nature**.

The one [activity of] establishing them on the path of seeing is [to establish them in] (8) **the** primordial **termination of** all **dualistic** phenomena.

The eighteen [activities of] establishing them on the path of familiarization consist of [establishing them in] (9) conventional phenomena being mere imputed **symbols**; (10) **nonobservation** of the three spheres; (11) being able to **mature** other **living beings**; (12) **the bodhisattva path** that is not in common with śrāvakas and pratyekabuddhas; (13) **putting an end to** the fixation of **clinging**; (14) being able to display the [first] ten [among the twelve] deeds [of a buddha], such as **attaining enlightenment**; (15) being able to purify **pure buddha realms** (container and contents); (16) the **definitiveness** of becoming a certain buddha in a certain [buddha] realm in one's next life; (17) being able to accomplish **the immeasurable welfare of sentient beings**; (18) being able to **attend to** the **buddhas** of the ten directions **and so on** (paying honors and service to them) and knowing **the qualities** [of doing so]; (19) completing **the branches of** being able to attain great **enlightenment** in this lifetime; (20) virtuous **actions being never lost** by virtue of the attainment of buddhahood being definite; (21) being able to **see** true **reality** {121a} in an instant; (22) **relinquishing** fourfold **mistakenness**, such as clinging to permanence; (23) **the manner of** bringing about **its nonsubstantiality**—[annihilating] the seeds of false imagination; (24) completing the uncontaminated dharmas of **purification**; (25) completing **the** two **accumulations**; (26) equality by virtue of **conditioned** (saṃsāra) **and unconditioned phenomena** (nirvāṇa) **being understood as nondifferent.**

The one [activity of] establishing them in the fruition consists of (27) **establishing** them **in** the nonabiding **nirvāṇa.**[286] The sūtras say:

> After bodhisattvas have appeased the sufferings of hell beings . . .[287]

> **This is the eighth chapter, on the dharmakāya, in *The Treatise on the Pith Instructions on Prajñāpāramitā, Called* The Ornament of Clear Realization.**

This is the commentary on **the eighth chapter in the** versified ***Treatise on the Pith Instructions on Prajñāpāramitā, Called* The Ornament of Clear Realization.**

2.3.2. Teaching the [eight topics] as six for persons interested in the intermediate version

> **The characteristic, the training in it,**
> **Its highest degrees, its progression,**
> **Its final conclusion, and its maturation—**
> **This is another summary in six points.** [IX.1]

This summary is another one **in six points**, with the three knowledges being taken as one [point]—**the characteristic** of prajñāpāramitā being that ground, path, and fruition are inseparable. The four trainings are **the training** that makes one realize **this** [characteristic], **its highest degrees, its progression, and its final conclusion.** The **maturation** of these trainings refers to the one [point of the] fruition—the dharmakāya—[which means] seeing the dharmakāya's own face.[288]

2.3.3. Teaching them as three for persons interested in the brief version

> **The threefold object (the cause),**
> **The fourfold training,**
> **And the fruition (the dharmakāya and enlightened activity)—**
> **This is another summary in three points.** [IX.2]

This summary is another one **in three points**, with **the object** (ālaya-wisdom or mother prajñāpāramitā), from which the adventitious stains (which are like blurred vision) are eliminated and which is divided into the **three** knowledges in terms of isolates, being taken as one [point]. **The cause**[289] for realizing the seeming stains (which obscure this [object] {121b} and are like the horns of a rabbit) for what they are is the yoga of familiarizing with nonarising. Divided by way of its progressive development, it consists of **the fourfold training**, which is [also] taken as one [point]. Through this, after mistaken appearing and its objects have become pure, **the fruition (the dharmakāya and enlightened activity)** means that [prajñāpāramitā] has become aware of its own nature by itself, [which is likewise taken as] one [point].[290]

3. Conclusion

> **This completes** ***The Treatise on the Pith Instructions on Prajñāpāramitā, Called*** **The Ornament of Clear Realization, composed by Lord Maitreyanātha.**

This completes the versified ***Treatise on the Pith Instructions on Prajñāpāramitā, Called*** **The Ornament of Clear Realization, composed by Lord Maitreyanātha.** It was [first] translated [into Tibetan] and edited by the Indian paṇḍita Vidyākaraprabhā[291] and the great editor-translator Bandé [Gawa] Baldseg. [The final Tibetan edition] was excellently prepared by Indian junior paṇḍitas, such as glorious Amaragomī, and the fully ordained monk and translator [Ngog] Loden Shérab.

When the ocean suddenly overflows in front of fragile sentient
beings in danger of [dying from] thirst,
The flurry of their anguish and [urge to] drink will be at peace, but
how [could this happen] otherwise?
Likewise since some beings of inferior insight who wish to easily
realize the meaning of the mother
Fail to understand the guru's vast and profound excellent
explanations, I composed this droplike [commentary].[292]

When explaining the hidden meaning of clear realization,
Scholars who fall into the explicit meaning of emptiness
Are finished off—so come here
And look at this treatise!

Therefore, [all] the actions of having composed this [commentary]
and others rejoicing in it,
Reading it, studying it, reflecting on it, and making it a living
experience, {122a}
In order to dry out the ocean of the suffering and the stains of
mistakenness of infinite sentient beings,
Should be dedicated to the mind's nature of luminosity in a way
that is pure of the three spheres.

Having been urged by his mind thinking about benefiting himself and all others, the Fifth Shamarpa finished this [commentary] at the age of twenty-three (during the eighth month of the Lightning[293] Sheep Year [1547]). Through the virtue of this, may the intentions of the unequaled guru be fulfilled and the teachings of exegesis and practice thus remain for a long time.

May the glory of auspiciousness blaze and be the ornament of the world!

Appendix I: Selected General Topics from JNS

4) The training in the complete realization of all aspects

A) The focal objects and aspects of this training[294]

The bases or focal objects of the training in all aspects are the four realities.[295] According to the large, medium, and brief prajñāpāramitā sūtras, their respective instances are described as follows. The reality of suffering consists of the resultant factors that consist of the five contaminated skandhas. The reality of the origin of suffering consists of the factors that consist of the causes of these contaminated skandhas. Though cessation refers to the true nature of the mind that operates by being primordially endowed with twofold purity, in accordance with common consensus it is presented as this very nature of the mind as it becomes pure of the respective parts of the adventitious stains. There are two ways in which it becomes pure of these stains—the mundane reality of cessation (the weakening of the seeds of the afflictions through mundane paths) and the supramundane reality of cessation (the actual relinquishment of the seeds to be relinquished through the paths of the noble ones). The reality of the path consists of the five paths of ordinary beings and noble ones.

The aspects in question here are the aspects in the pair of "focal objects" and "aspects," which must be explained as distinctive features of cognition (the perceiving subject). This corresponds to Dharmakīrti's detailed explanation of establishing the two ways in which mind appears (apprehender and apprehended) as nothing but different aspects of cognition, and thus establishing even outwardly-oriented kinds of cognition as self-awareness.[296] Thus, though there are no independently established "aspects" other than consciousness if these aspects are classified in terms of what they depend on, they are twofold—aspects of the seeming (such as aspects of outer objects) and aspects of the ultimate (such as the aspects of the threefold lack of arising with regard to the three knowledges). Here, "aspects" are explained in terms of the latter because this is the context of explaining that the aspects with which to familiarize consist of the very mind that cognizes said threefold lack of arising through studying and reflecting. As for the three kinds of cognitive aspects of the three knowledges, those that actually fulfill this definition exist in the mind streams of the noble ones of the mahāyāna (the subjects that directly perceive them), while the aspects that are approximately concordant with these exist even in the mind streams of bodhisattvas on the level of engagement through aspiration (the subjects that study and reflect). Nevertheless, even those approximately concordant aspects are objects of familiarization that fulfill this definition because it is explained that the mahāyāna training that fulfills this definition exists on the paths of accumulation and preparation. The aspects of training that fulfill this definition must be divided into either being or not being actual objects of familiarization because the cognitive aspects that realize said threefold lack of arising on the buddhabhūmi are the aspects of the three knowledges that fulfill this definition, but are not actual objects of familiarization during the mahāyāna training (since the buddhabhūmi is the fruition of this training). However, this does not mean that the division into the 173 aspects of the three knowledges with which to familiarize (as explained in the fourth chapter of the AA) is untenable because they refer to familiarizing with the continua of the aspects that are similar in kind to said respective aspects on the buddhabhūmi. The familiarization with these continua of aspects is referred to by the conventional phrase "familiarizing through aspects in terms of aspiration."

You may wonder, "If bodhisattvas familiarize with the aspects of the knowledge of entities, does one not have to accept a mahāyāna path of familiarization on which one familiarizes with personal identitylessness?" When noble bodhisattvas familiarize with the nonarising of entities, the realization of personal identitylessness is included in this familiarization in the manner of the lower realizations being incorporated in the higher. But they do not deliberately familiarize with personal identitylessness as having the aspect of personal identitylessness because what has this aspect of personal identitylessness is explained as one of the aspects that represent reference points, while bodhisattvas do not mentally engage in any characteristics that represent reference points whatsoever. For example, when the aspects of the knowledge of entities of bodhisattvas are explained, it is not the sixteen aspects (such as impermanence) as stated in the abhidharma that are explained, but what are explained as the objects of familiarization are the aspects of phenomenal identitylessness as stated in the prajñāpāramitā sūtras. "But aren't these two sets of aspects explained to be equivalent?" Once the aspects of phenomenal identitylessness appear, the realization of personal identitylessness is included in these in the manner of the lower being incorporated in the higher because the aspects of phenomenal identitylessness eliminate the opposites of personal identitylessness too. It is with this in mind that the aspects as stated in the abhidharma and the prajñāpāramitā sūtras, respectively, are matched according to their orders. However, it is not the case that the aspects of the freedom from reference points are explained as what have the sixteen aspects of impermanence and so on because the aspects of the freedom from reference points as stated in the prajñāpāramitā sūtras are realizations that make one go beyond said sixteen aspects of the abhidharma. Others say, "But then this is not a familiarization with the threefold lack of arising through training in the three knowledges because it is solely cognitive aspects that are asserted as the objects of familiarization." There is no flaw—by way of familiarizing with cognitive aspects, one is perfectly able to present this as the familiarization with the threefold lack of arising because the realization of the aspect of the nature of phenomena is presented as the realization of the nature of phenomena, just as the appearing of the aspect of blue is presented as the cognition of blue.

In brief, the focal objects here are the three kinds of nonarising (with regard to the three knowledges), while the aspects consist of the mental states that, through their respective modes of apprehending said focal objects, take them as their apprehended objects. Understood in this way, earlier Tibetans applied the conventional term "referent" to the bases and focal objects with regard to which superimpositions are cut through, while they used the conventional term "cognitive aspects" for the aspects that cut through these superimpositions. Therefore, both the objects of familiarization of the training and what is to be experienced by personally experienced wisdom are solely cognitive aspects. Thus, the aspects that actually fulfill this definition are necessarily cognitions. Dölpopa Sherab Gyaltsen says:

> The explanation of earlier Tibetans that the dharmadhātu is the aspect of a referent is not the system of the mahāyāna because the dharmadhātu is the wisdom that is free from any reference points of referents and cognitions whatsoever. But if you label the revealing of the dharmadhātu through wisdom as an aspect that is a referent, I will not dispute about [mere] words.

In brief since there is not the slightest nature of a focal object that is other than its aspect, this very aspect is inseparable from cognition's own nature. However, the aspects in the threefold division of "aspects, signs, and characteristics" in the context of the signs of irreversibility[297] are not the aspects in the twofold division of focal objects and aspects that is discussed here. Therefore, the former are not suitable as the aspects that are taught here, while the latter are not suitable as the aspects in said threefold division.

B) Afflictive obscurations, cognitive obscurations, and obscurations of meditative absorption[298]

The definition of an obscuration in general is that which obscures perfect wisdom. Though the term "obscuration" may apply to both that which is obscured and that which obscures, the obscurations that are taught here are in terms of that which obscures. The two divisions of what is neutral—obscuring and unobscuring[299]—are not equivalent with the two obscurations here because they are not explained in terms of that which obscures.

Obscurations can be divided into those that obscure calm abiding and those that obscure superior insight (which will be explained below under the obscurations of meditative absorption), or into those that obscure qualities and those that obscure wisdom. Since the obscurations that obscure superior insight and those that obscure wisdom come down to the same essential point, they consist of the obscurations that obscure the wisdom of realizing personal identitylessness and the wisdom of realizing phenomenal identityless. The first of these are the afflictive obscurations and the second represent the cognitive obscurations.

1) Explaining the afflictive obscurations has three parts:

a) Definition
b) Division
c) The boundary lines of relinquishing the afflictive obscurations

1a) The definition of the afflictive obscurations is "the kind of obscurations that obscure the attainment of either of the two nirvāṇas of śrāvakas and pratyekabuddhas."

1b) They are divided into
a) those that obscure the attainment of the nirvāṇa with remainder
b) those that obscure the attainment of the nirvāṇa without remainder

1ba) The first consist of the afflictive obscurations that agitate the mind stream and those that are latencies.

1bb) The latter are the karmic and the maturational afflictive obscurations. The afflictive obscurations as explained here are definite in number because they relate to the definite number of the two kinds of nirvāṇa of śrāvakas and pratyekabuddhas. The nirvāṇa of śrāvakas and pratyekabuddhas that fulfills this function is the nirvāṇa without remainder, while the nirvāṇa with remainder is not presented as the one that actually fulfills this function because it is not liberation from saṃsāra yet.

As for the afflictive obscurations that obscure these inferior nirvāṇas, those that agitate the mind stream are any among the triad of karmas, afflictions, and maturations that bind in saṃsāra, including their seeds. Among these three, the afflictions plus their seeds that serve as the motivations for the karmas which propel one into saṃsāra are explained as being mainly the obscurations of attaining just the nirvāṇa with remainder. The karmas that are motivated by these afflictions and the skandhas of suffering that are the maturations of these karmas obscure the attainment of the nirvāṇa without remainder. As for the afflictive obscurations that are latencies, they are the latencies that are planted by the afflictions and serve as the causes for assuming birth in saṃsāra. Instances of these latencies are the ones in the mind streams of noble bodhisattvas that lack the capacity to agitate their mind streams and yet have the capacity to function as the causes for completing their being born in saṃsāra. This division in terms of afflictions that agitate the mind stream and the latencies that are planted by these afflictions represents the twofold division of the afflictive obscurations that is made in terms of the factors to be relinquished on the path of bodhisattvas. However, in terms of the factors to be relinquished on the inferior paths, there is no such twofold division of the afflictions into the afflictive obscurations that agitate the mind stream and those that are the capacity to take birth, but they are taken as one set and relinquished together in combination. Bodhisattvas distinguish between the two and deliberately relinquish those that agitate the mind stream, while not deliberately relinquishing the causes for taking birth.

Others may wonder, "Isn't it that the afflictive obscurations that are the causes for taking birth are relinquished as a matter of course, once the capacity to agitate the mind stream has been relinquished?" If one familiarizes with personal identitylessness as the remedy for those afflictive obscurations that agitate the mind stream, the capacity of the causes for taking birth is relinquished as a matter of course. However, bodhisattvas relinquish the capacity that agitates the mind stream, but do not relinquish the capacity of the causes for taking birth in saṃsāra. For through the force of familiarizing with phenomenal identitylessness as the remedy for the cognitive obscurations, the afflictive obscurations (plus their seeds) that agitate the mind stream cease on their own, but the causes for taking birth do not cease on their own. "But then it follows that bodhisattvas generally do not relinquish the latencies of the afflictive obscurations." This is not the case—in terms of relinquishment in general, they relinquish them as a matter of course while relinquishing the cognitive obscurations. As for temporarily not relinquishing said afflictive obscurations in a deliberate manner, this means that the causes for taking birth do not function as manifest obstructions to realizing phenomenal identitylessness. As for bodhisattvas not striving to deliberately relinquish these causes for taking birth, the path to realizing personal identitylessness (which deliberately relinquishes the afflictions that are the capacity to take birth in saṃsāra) does not serve as a remedy for the cognitive obscurations—it is the path that serves as the remedy for the afflictive obscurations alone, which is not the path that bodhisattvas primarily strive for. These causes for taking birth represent fully qualified afflictive obscurations because they are factors that obstruct the attainment of the inferior nirvāṇas, and because the uninterrupted path of directly realizing personal identitylessness is the type of remedy that eradicates the seeds of these afflictive obscurations that are latencies. However, though they are fully qualified afflictive obscurations, they are not fully qualified afflictions because they exist in the mind streams of noble bodhisattvas and lack the capacity to agitate the mind stream.

1c) The boundary lines of relinquishing the afflictive obscurations

In terms of the inferior yānas, once the nirvāṇa with remainder is manifested, both the afflictive obscurations that agitate the mind stream and those that are latencies have been relinquished without exception because their remedy (the vajralike samādhi) has fully rendered them into something that has the property of not arising anymore. Though the maturational obscurations have been relinquished at that point too, one is not free from them because one is not free from the skandhas of suffering that were propelled through previous karma and afflictions. In other words, though no new contaminated karma is accumulated, the results of old contaminated karmas have not yet been rendered into something that has the property of not arising anymore. *Bodhicaryāvatāra* IX.45cd says:

> However, one sees the efficacy of actions
> Even in those who lack afflictions.

The nirvāṇa that consists of the time of being without the remainder of the skandhas, which is free from the entire triad of karma, afflictions, and maturations, is presented as the nirvāṇa that actually fulfills this function.

In terms of the mahāyāna, the portion of the capacity of the afflictions that binds in saṃsāra is relinquished on the first bhūmi since mastery over eradicating the seeds of this capacity is gained during the dharma readiness of suffering of the mahāyāna path of seeing of those bodhisattvas who have previously not gone through inferior paths. The capacity of the afflictions that are latencies has two portions—factors to be relinquished through seeing and factors to be relinquished through familiarization in the mahāyāna. The first portion is relinquished simultaneously with the relinquishment of the 108 cognitive obscurations that are to be relinquished through seeing. The second portion (the latencies of the afflictions that are factors to be relinquished through familiarization) are relinquished simultaneously with the relinquishment of the 108 cognitive obscurations that are factors to be relinquished through familiarization.

Here, the following difficult point is to be understood. It may be said, "It is said here that (one portion of) the latencies of the afflictions is relinquished on the first bhūmi. But isn't it that the existence of the afflicted mind on the impure bhūmis of those who have previously not gone through inferior paths must be accepted?" Its existence is accepted because the afflicted mind and the latencies of the afflictions are not the same. In the case of the primary affliction of the views about a self, according to the mahāyāna it is for the reason of the afflicted mind existing that the views about the skandhas as a personal self, which are present within innate mental states, arise through the mental consciousness. They are relinquished through the path of seeing and represent afflictive obscurations. However, the ālaya being viewed as an identity by the afflicted mind is presented as referring to a phenomenal identity and as being a cognitive obscuration. Since this latter viewing occurs in assocation with the portion of the sixth consciousness that is planted by the afflictions that bind in saṃsāra, the sheer latencies of this afflicted viewing are relinquished together with the 108 conceptions that are the cognitive obscurations to be relinquished through seeing, with the same applying to their relinquishment through the path of familiarization. However, through relinquishing said viewing of the ālaya as an identity, the latencies existing within the ālaya are not necessarily relinquished. For this reason, "the afflicted mind not having changed state" is presented as the impure bhūmis. "But then these latencies of viewing the ālaya as a phenomenal identity are not the fully qualified afflicted mind because they are not conceptions that cling to a personal self. For the afflicted mind must necessarily be what discriminates the ālaya as a self. As the *Triṃśikākārikā* says:

> What operates based on the [ālaya-consciousness]
> Is the consciousness called "mentation,"
> Which has it as its focal object, its nature being self-centeredness.
> It is always associated with the four afflictions,
> And is obscuring yet neutral.[300]

"Since it says here, 'It is always associated with the four afflictions,' these must be presented as the latencies of the afflictions." This is not the case because the latencies of the afflictive obscurations function as the motivating forces of the karmas for taking birth, whereas the latencies of viewing the ālaya are the ones that are solely internally oriented toward the ālaya.[301]

2) Explaining the cognitive obscurations has three parts:

a) Definition
b) Division
c) The boundary lines of relinquishing the cognitive obscurations

2a) The definition of the cognitive obscurations is "the kind of obscurations that obscure the attainment of omniscience."[302]

2b) They are divided into
- a) the cognitive obscurations that are factors to be relinquished on the pratyekabuddha path
- b) the cognitive obscurations that are factors to be relinquished solely on the mahāyāna path

2ba) The first are the cognitive obscurations that bear the name "conceptions about the apprehended" and are taught in AA II.29c ("Afflictive, cognitive, and [the obscurations] of the three paths") and AA II.8a ("Through the conceptions about apprehended referents being relinquished"). With regard to this, Asaṅga and Vasubandhu on the one hand and Āryavimuktisena and Haribhadra on the other differ in their ways of identification. According to the former, pratyekabuddhas possess the remedies for the conceptions about the apprehended among the four conceptions about the apprehender and the apprehended that are explained in the AA, whereas the remedies for the conceptions about the apprehender exist only in the noble ones of the mahāyāna. The mental states that cling to the imputed apprehended as being real are the conceptions about the apprehended and the mental states that cling to the imputed apprehender as being real are the conceptions about the apprehender. However, the remedy that relinquishes the conceptions about the apprehender is nondual wisdom alone. Therefore, pratyekabuddhas only have the wisdom of realizing that there is nothing apprehended, but since they lack the wisdom of realizing nonduality, they lack the stage of yoga of realizing that there is no apprehender.[303]

Āryavimuktisena and Haribhadra hold the following. Pratyekabuddhas do not possess the remedies that relinquish the conceptions about the apprehender and the apprehended that are explained in the AA as the factors to be relinquished through seeing and familiarization in the mahāyāna. The conceptions about the apprehender and the apprehended that are explained as the factors to be relinquished on the mahāyāna path must be relinquished through the wisdom of directly realizing that both apprehender and apprehended are empty of a nature of their own. For pratyekabuddhas, it is not like this—they lack the wisdom of realizing that both apprehender and apprehended are empty of a nature of their own, but rely on the mere wisdom of realizing that they are empty of being other. Therefore, the conceptions about the apprehended that are the cognitive obscurations to be relinquished on the path of the pratyekabuddhas consist of the clinging to the very conceptions that cling to the duality of apprehender and apprehended. Here, the conceptions that cling to the apprehended consist of clinging to what appear as referents as being actual outer referents. The conceptions that cling to the apprehender consist of clinging to these appearances as being of the nature of consciousness. The conceptions about the apprehended are relinquished through the wisdom of the subsequent attainment of the path of familiarization of pratyekabuddhas, while the conceptions about the apprehender are relinquished through the wisdom of the meditative equipoise of this path. However, these two conceptions about the apprehender and the apprehended are not included in the conceptions that are taught in AA I.25cd ("Based on being associated with the four conceptions in due order") because these four are explained to be the factors to be relinquished through the paths of seeing and familiarization in terms of the culminating training of bodhisattvas alone.

As for the manner in which pratyekabuddhas relinquish said two conceptions about the apprehender and the apprehended, the clinging to appearances as being outer referents, which is present in innate conceptions, is represented by the philosophical system of the Vaibhāṣikas. The clinging to appearances as being mind is found in the philosophical systems of the Real Aspectarians and the Sautrāntikas, and also the manner in which the Sāṃkhyas assert appearances to be of the nature of mind accords with that. The Sautrāntikas and the Sāṃkhyas hold that appearances are internal, but that there are causes on the outside that project them into the mind. The reasoning that refutes the assertions that there are apprehended referents on the outside is an argument of the nonobservation of something that is suitable to appear,[304] which is the Mere Mentalists' reasoning of refuting outer referents. Based on this reasoning, the pratyekabuddhas negate that apprehender and apprehended are different in substance. Through this, they arrive at the realization of the lack of something apprehended, which enables them to relinquish the above-mentioned triad of karmic, afflictive, and maturational obscurations that obstruct the liberation of pratyekabuddhas. When the Real Aspectarians' and Sautrāntikas' clinging to appearances as being mind is refuted by the False Aspectarians, they refute the apprehender through the reason that there is nothing apprehended. The pratyekabuddhas also refute the apprehender based on this reasoning and their purpose in doing so is as follows. Though the conceptions about the apprehender do not represent obstructions to attaining the liberation of pratyekabuddhas, they are obstructions to thoroughly analyzing what is to be known by pratyekabuddhas. Therefore, they are refuted and relinquished. "So do pratyekabuddhas then realize nondual wisdom?" The position of Asaṅga and Vasubandhu that pratyekabuddhas do not realize this wisdom was taught above. However, Āryavimuktisena and Haribhadra assert that pratyekabuddhas do realize this wisdom because they explain this well by way of the passages of "being untainted, no reference points, and no conceit about realization."[305] Here, the intention behind saying that pratyekabuddhas realize nondual wisdom is that they do so because apprehender and apprehended in terms of outer referents are phenomena that depend on each other (that is, without referents, there is no apprehender of such referents either). However, such is not said in terms of pratyekabuddhas relinquishing the phenomenal identity that consists of the internally oriented apprehender which arises as having the nature of apprehending self-aware experience as objects. Therefore, if the respective wisdoms of pratyekabuddhas and bodhisattvas are not distinguished in terms of their levels of the nonduality of apprehender and apprehended being coarse and subtle, respectively, all systems become mixed up.

2bb) The cognitive obscurations that are solely relinquished on the path of the mahāyāna are twofold:

1) the conceptions, plus their seeds, that cling to characteristics and obstruct the thorough analysis of what is to be known
2) the impregnations of the negative tendencies of the entirety of the two obscurations

2bb1) The first are twofold:

a) those that are the factors to be relinquished through the mahāyāna path of seeing[306]
b) those that are the factors to be relinquished through the final culminating training

2bb1a) The first consist of (a) the conceptions that are the cognitive obscurations to be relinquished on the mahāyāna path of seeing and (b) the appearances by virtue of clinging to the duality of apprehender and apprehended.

2bb1b) The second are the factors to be relinquished through the uninterrupted culminating training alone. The instances of these consist of the "ground of the latent tendencies of ignorance" that is explained as the cause for śrāvaka arhats, pratyekabuddha arhats, and bodhisattvas who have attained mastery taking rebirth in saṃsāra. The ignorance of this ground consists of the latent tendencies of both afflicted and nonafflicted ignorance. These latent tendencies are divided into two—those that obscure attaining the wisdom of knowing suchness in meditative equipoise and those that obscure attaining the wisdom that knows variety in subsequent attainment. Their remedies are the prajñā of seeing suchness and the prajñā of seeing variety, respectively. The first one of these relinquishes the obscurations of attachment during meditative equipoise and the second one relinquishes the obscurations of obstruction during subsequent attainment.

2bb2) The impregnation of the negative tendencies of the entirety of the two obscurations is the ālaya—it consists of the impregnations of the negative tendencies that function as the foundations of any given obscurations after these obscurations themselves have been relinquished in a progressive manner. At the end of the process of these impregnations too having become exhausted progressively, bodhisattvas finally relinquish the ālaya-consciousness in the vajralike samādhi (being divided into preparation and main part) through the uninterrupted culminating training. At this point, it is asserted that the impregnations of negative tendencies are completely relinquished. Here, though the impregnations of the negative tendencies of the afflictions are latent tendencies of the afflictions, they are not suitable as any one of the two kinds of afflictive obscurations (those that agitate the mind stream and their latencies that cause rebirth) because the defining characteristics of these two are not complete in them. The impregnations of the negative tendencies of the obscurations of meditative absorption are presented as obscurations of meditative absorption because they are obscurations that obstruct the calm abiding of the buddhabhūmi.[307]

2c) The boundary lines of relinquishing the cognitive obscurations has two parts:

a) the boundary lines of relinquishing the first type of cognitive obscurations (2bb1)

b) the boundary lines of relinquishing the second type of cognitive obscurations (2bb2)

2ca) The conceptions about characteristics that obstruct the thorough analysis of what is to be known are not relinquished by the śrāvakas because the scriptural collections of the śrāvakas do not explain a path to relinquish them. Also, when the presentation of the path of the śrāvakas is explained in the mahāyāna scriptural collection, there are no explanations of any scriptural passages or reasonings that refute apprehender and apprehended being different in substance. Thus, the śrāvakas lack the realization that there is nothing apprehended.

As for the pratyekabuddhas, there is no separate scriptural collection on the manner in which they progress on the path—their manner of progressing on the path needs to be found in the scriptural collections of śrāvakas and bodhisattvas. Though the śrāvaka scriptures lack any scriptural passages or reasonings that refute apprehender and apprehended being different in substance, in the mahāyāna scriptural collection that is not shared with the śrāvakas one finds such scriptural passages and reasonings that refute apprehender and apprehended being different in substance with regard to the manner in which pratyekabuddhas progress on the path. Therefore, it is explained that, upon the attainment of pratyekabuddha arhathood, the conceptions about the apprehended that cling to characteristics are relinquished and that these conceptions about the apprehended must be relinquished from the pratyekabuddha path of familiarization onward. Thus, it is asserted that a portion of the first type of cognitive obscurations is also relinquished by pratyekabuddha arhats.

In terms of the mahāyāna, the conceptions about apprehender and apprehended[308] are twofold—(1) the conceptions that apprehend by conflating terms and their referents and cling to the duality of apprehender and apprehended and (2) the false imagination of dualistic appearances. Since the capacity to eradicate the seeds of (1) exists from the dharma readiness of suffering on the path of seeing onward, they have been relinquished from the dharma cognition of suffering onward. As for (2), the latent tendencies that produce conceptions of dualistic appearances and represent factors to be relinquished through seeing are relinquished simultaneously with the relinquishment of the factors to be relinquished through seeing. Those of them that represent factors to be relinquished through familiarization are relinquished simultaneously with the relinquishment of the factors to be relinquished through familiarization.

As for the impregnations of the negative tendencies of these latent tendencies, they are relinquished through the vajralike samādhi because the eradication of the latent tendencies of dualistic appearances is only certain for a perfect buddha.

2cb) The boundary lines of relinquishing the second type of cognitive obscurations (2bb2—the impregnations of negative tendencies) were stated implicitly just above.

Through summarizing the above-mentioned first basic twofold division into the obscurations of calm abiding and the obscurations of superior insight into a single point, they are taught to be the obscurations of meditative absorption.

This has three parts:

1) Definition
2) Division of their instances
3) The boundary lines of relinquishment

1) The definition of the obscurations of meditative absorption is "the kind of obscurations that obstruct the manifesting of the calm abiding and the qualities of the buddhabhūmi."

2) They are divided into two
a) the obscurations that obstruct mundane calm abiding
b) the obscurations that obstruct supramundane calm abiding

2a) By virtue of the division into the eight mundane meditative absorptions (four each in the form and formless realms), these obscurations are eightfold.

Or, by virtue of the division into the five supernatural knowledges, they are fivefold.

2b) By virtue of the divisions of the eight liberations, the ten totalities, the eight kinds of overpowering, and so on, which bodhisattvas have in common with śrāvakas and pratyekabuddhas, the obscurations that obstruct these are of an equal number. The obscurations that obstruct the ultimate pāramitā of dhyāna, which is not in common with śrāvakas and pratyekabuddhas, are explained to be overcome through the power of knowing all the distinctions of meditative absorption and so on.

In brief, however slow that may be, bodhisattvas relinquish the afflictive obscurations simultaneously with the 108 conceptions that are factors to be relinquished through familiarization, whereas the (remaining) obscurations of meditative absorption and cognitive obscurations are relinquished through the vajralike samādhi alone.[309]

The following must be understood here. Other people may wonder, "Then the relinquishments of śrāvakas and pratyekabuddhas would not be complete in bodhisattvas from the first bhūmi onward because śrāvakas and pratyekabuddhas have relinquished the afflictive obscurations that are latencies, whereas bodhisattvas from the first bhūmi onward have not relinquished them." The answer to this is twofold—analogous applicability of the reason and the actual answer. First, the same flaw would apply to the position of these people too who do assert that śrāvakas and pratyekabuddhas have relinquished the māra of the skandhas and the afflicted mind, whereas these two have not been relinquished on the first bhūmi and above. Therefore, for their position, it also follows that the relinquishments of śrāvakas and pratyekabuddhas are not complete in bodhisattvas from the first bhūmi onward.

Second, the actual answer is as follows. The obscurations to be relinquished on the path of bodhisattvas are twofold—afflictive and cognitive obscurations. The first are necessarily only those afflictive obscurations that bind in saṃsāra because the afflictive obscurations that are latencies are not asserted to be factors to be relinquished by bodhisattvas. For these latencies are definitely needed as aids for the path of bodhisattvas and thus have the nature of not being relinquished. The cognitive obscurations to be relinquished by bodhisattvas are twofold—the conceptions of clinging to apprehender and apprehended being different in substance and the latent tendencies of mere dualistic appearances. The latter are not deliberately relinquished through the path of bodhisattvas because they do not deliberately familiarize with the phenomenal identitylessness of the apprehended as their remedy and because they do not eradicate the latent tendencies of the dualistic appearances of apprehender and apprehended for as long as the accumulation of merit is not completed. Therefore, to the very extent that the distinctive features of the afflictive and cognitive obscurations to be relinquished on the path of bodhisattvas are relinquished by śrāvaka and pratyekabuddha arhats, the relinquishment of these obscurations is complete starting with the first bhūmi of those bodhisattvas who have not previously gone through inferior paths. This much is sufficient for being able to present the scope of the relinquishment and realization of śrāvakas and pratyekabuddhas being complete in these bodhisattvas. However, it is not that bodhisattvas must have relinquished everything that those arhats have relinquished in order to present the relinquishment of arhats as being complete in said bodhisattvas. For it is not asserted that the factors to be relinquished by bodhisattvas consist of all the factors to be relinquished on the paths of śrāvakas and pratyekabuddhas. This is just as it is not asserted that, in terms of the scope of realization, bodhisattvas realize everything that śrāvakas and pratyekabuddhas realize.

In terms of the definite number of obscurations, they are well known as threefold—afflictive obscurations, cognitive obscurations, and obscurations of meditative absorption. As for the latter obscurations, they indeed[310] contain the portions of both the predominantly afflictive obscurations that consist of the afflictions of the desire realm and the two higher realms which obscure mundane and supramundane dhyānas and the cognitive obscurations that consist of the obscurations of the powers of the three kinds of noble ones (such as the obscurations that prevent bodhisattvas from entering the king of samādhis). However, those that mainly obscure dhyānas and samādhis are therefore included in the category of the afflictive obscurations. Those that mostly obscure the qualities of freedom[311] and maturation of a buddha are therefore included in the category of the cognitive obscurations. To explain the obscurations of meditative absorption as a separate third category of obscurations is in order to understand the diverse specifics of the obscurations. In the mantrayāna and elsewhere, other identifications of the obscurations of meditative absorption appear as well.[312]

C) The 110 aspects of the knowledge of all aspects[313]

1) The thirty-seven aspects of the knowledge of entities (the dharmas concordant with enlightenment)

1a) The four foundations of mindfulness

This has two parts:

a) Their nature

b) Practicing them

1aa) Their nature has three parts:

1) Essence
2) Cause
3) Result

1aa1) The essence of these foundations is the mindfulness that is associated with the prajñā of thoroughly discriminating phenomena. When divided, there are four foundations of mindfulness because there are four focal objects—body, feelings, mind, and phenomena. The purpose of the foundations of mindfulness that are taught here is to counteract clinging to the body as being pure, feelings as being happiness, mind as being permanent, and phenomena as having any identity. In brief, they refer to the special prajñā of discriminating whether one's actions are or are not linked with mindfulness. Therefore, they are foundations since they are not just some mere recollections of simply something that comes to mind[314] without being in meditative equipoise. Their boundary lines range from the lesser path of accumulation up through the buddhabhūmi.

1aa2) The causes for the arising of the foundations of mindfulness are two—the meditation on the repulsiveness of the body as the remedy for desire and the familiarization with the movement of exhalation and inhalation as the remedy for thoughts. If desire is predominant, one meditates on the former, and if thoughts are, one uses the latter (such as counting one's exhalations and inhalations). The details of these meditations are clarified in the *Abhidharmakośa* and so on.

1aa3) The result lies in there being the purpose of engaging in the four realities. According to *Madhyāntavibhāga* IV.1, through the foundation of the mindfulness of the body, one understands that the impregnations of the negative tendencies of the body are the all-pervasive suffering and therefore engages in understanding suffering. Through the mindfulness of feelings, one familiarizes with the fact that all feelings (the causes of craving) are suffering. Based on that, one engages in relinquishing craving (their result) and thus engages in relinquishing the origin of suffering. Through the mindfulness of mind, one familiarizes with the fact that mind (the basis for clinging to an identity) is impermanent and therefore engages in manifesting the cessation in which the clinging to mind as a permanent identity has ceased. Through the mindfulness of phenomena, one is not ignorant about the actuality of all phenomena being identityless and therefore engages in cultivating the path of realizing that all phenomena are identityless.

1ab) Practicing these mindfulnesses has two parts:

1) Meditating in the common manner
2) Meditating in the uncommon manner

1ab1) The first is twofold—meditating through examining the specific characteristics and the general characteristics, respectively. The first is explained as familiarizing with the body being impure, feelings being suffering, mind being impermanent, and phenomena being identityless. The second refers to familiarizing with the first three of the four seals of dharma (everything conditioned is impermanent; everything contaminated is suffering; and all phenomena are empty and identityless).

1ab2) Among the four foundations of mindfulness, the first one can be cultivated in two ways—mentally engaging in aspirational imagination and true reality, respectively. The first one is done by cultivating the notion of repulsiveness and the second one consists of familiarizing with the fact that one's own body is full of the thirty-six impure substances (*Ratnāvalī* II.66). The second foundation is to familiarize with all feelings being suffering, just like an illusion. The third one is to familiarize with mind being impermanent, just like a water bubble. The fourth one is twofold—meditating in an exclusive manner and in combination. First, through focusing on the phenomena other than the body, feelings, and mind, one familiarizes with their being impermanent, suffering, empty, and identityless. The second manner means to meditate like that by focusing on all the three (body, feelings, and mind) together. This manner of meditating is the one during subsequent attainment. If one meditates on body, feelings, mind, and phenomena during meditative equipoise, one does so in the manner of familiarizing with their lack of nature.[315]

1b) The four correct efforts
This has two parts:
 a) Their nature
 b) Practicing them

1ba) Their nature has three parts:
 1) Essence
 2) Cause
 3) Result

1ba1) Their essence is the enthusiasm to rid oneself of the factors to be relinquished that have already arisen and to adopt the remedies for that, all of which is based on having adopted the four foundations of mindfulness. "Correct" has the meaning of "unmistaken." "Relinquishment"[316] refers to relinquishing nonvirtue. Though there are two kinds of relinquishing and two kinds of accomplishing here, all four are labeled from just the one point of view of "relinquishment," just as one says, "a castle has collapsed" even if just one side of it has collapsed. The boundary lines range from the middling path of accumulation up through buddhahood.

1ba2) The causes for these four efforts are the foundations of mindfulness. As *Madhyāntavibhāga* IV.2 says:

> Once antagonistic factors and remedies
> Have been understood in all aspects,
> The vigor in order to relinquish them
> Arises in four kinds.

1ba3) The result consists of the relinquishment of the remaining factors that are to be relinquished through the foundations of mindfulness (as stated in *Mahāyānasūtrālaṃkāra* XVIII.46).

1bb) The practice of these four is indicated in the sūtras:

> Bodhisattvas give rise to striving. They make efforts. They produce vigor. They seize their minds. They correctly settle them.

The first two refer to the armorlike vigor and the one of application. The third one means vigor with body and mind. The fourth one refers to superior insight. The fifth one means calm abiding. Correct effort in each one of these five is cultivated in order to relinquish nonvirtue and adopt virtue. As for the meanings of "virtue" and "nonvirtue," the mother sūtras say that, temporarily, these refer to the actions that are motivated by the three times and the actions that are free from these three. Ultimately, nonvirtue is mental engagement and virtue is mental nonengagement. There is no need to be worried that this is not correct because it is not in accord with the abhidharma. The presentation of virtue and nonvirtue in the abhidharma is the system of the sūtras of expedient meaning, while their presentation in the mother sūtras is the definitive meaning that is to be taken literally. For mental engagement and nonengagement are taught to be "nonvirtue" and "virtue," respectively, with the intention that suchness is not clearly perceived as long as there is mental engagement. According to Chinese masters and others, by implication of this statement of mental nonengagement being virtue, to stop all mental engagement (no matter whether it is good or bad) is the genuine means to attain liberation.

1c) The four limbs of miraculous powers
This has two parts:
  a) Their nature
  b) Practicing them

1ca) Their nature has three parts:

1) Essence
2) Cause
3) Result

1ca1) The essence or definition of the limbs of miraculous powers is the mind dwelling one-pointedly on a focal object, which arises based on having adopted the four correct efforts (as stated in *Mahāyānasūtrālaṃkāra* XIV.11). The four limbs are the samādhis of striving, vigor, mind, and analysis. In due order, these refer to the mind dwelling one-pointedly on a focal object through relying on the dominant conditions of striving, vigor, the previous mind of samādhi, and analyzing prajñā. Thus, such dwelling in samādhi is fourfold because there are four different dominant conditions. Therefore, the result of a one-pointed mind that arises based on these four conditions is the ability to miraculously manifest all kinds of bodies. It is in this sense that one speaks of "miraculous powers." By virtue of being the causes for these miraculous powers, striving and so on are called "limbs" (lit. "feet"). They exist from the great path of accumulation up through buddhahood.

1ca2) The cause for their arising is to familiarize with applying the eight remedies that relinquish the five flaws (as stated in *Madhyāntavibhāga* IV.3–6ab). The first flaw—laziness about training in samādhi—is relinquished through the first four remedies in the following way. Based on confidence in the benefits of samādhi, striving arises; this gives rise to vigor, which eventually results in the complete suppleness of a workable body and mind. As for the remaining four flaws, the remedy for forgetting the instructions is mindfulness because it makes one not forget the conceptions in terms of focal objects and aspects. The remedy for dullness and agitation is the alertness of recognizing when they arise. The remedy for not applying the remedies for dullness and agitation is the intention that makes one think of the remedies. As the remedies for dullness, one needs to cultivate superior insight and its causes, and, as the remedies for agitation, calm abiding and its causes. For the *Ālokā* says that mentally engaging in things that make one joyous (the qualities of buddhahood and so on) relinquishes dullness, while mentally engaging in things that make one weary (such as impermanence) relinquishes agitation. As the remedy for overapplying these remedies and thus being distracted, one familiarizes with the equanimity of naturally resting within the union of calm abiding and superior insight.

1ca3) The results of these four limbs are listed in *Mahāyānasūtrālaṃkāra* XVIII.55. One attains the five visions and the six supernatural knowledges (the latter being the causes for teaching the instructions). Through the mind dwelling one-pointedly on its focal object, one is able to display all kinds of magical powers. All aims of one's aspiration prayers become fulfilled, and one attains the ten masteries.[317] In addition, the *Śrīmālādevīsūtra* says that one sees all the tathāgatas who dwell in the ten directions.

1cb) The practice of these four is to focus on all phenomena and familiarize with the aspect that they are without nature. The *Ratnakūṭa* says:

> The samādhis of bodhisattvas are remedies because they relinquish all connections with latent tendencies. The samādhis of bodhisattvas are the prajñā that transcends the entire world.

There are also other sources, such as *Abhidharmakośa* VI.49, which say that one focuses on respectively higher versus lower mundane levels of samādhi and familiarizes with them as being respectively more peaceful, excellent, and liberating versus being coarse, bad, and like a thick wall preventing liberation.

1d) The five faculties
This has two parts:
  a) Their nature
  b) Practicing them

1da) Their nature has three parts:
  1) Essence
  2) Cause
  3) Result

1da1) The faculties that are taught here refer to the power of giving rise to purified phenomena, which is based on having adopted the factors conducive to liberation. When divided, there are five such faculties (confidence, vigor, mindfulness, samādhi, and prajñā) because their five focal objects are unsurpassable enlightenment; the six pāramitās as the conduct for attaining it; studying; calm abiding; and superior insight, respectively (as stated in *Mahāyānasūtrālaṃkāra* XVIII.56). They are also said to be faculties because one gains power over striving through confidence, and power over the vigor of application through striving (as *Madhyāntavibhāga* IV.6cd says). Said five faculties exist from the level of heat of the path of preparation up through buddhahood.

1da2) Their cause is the path of accumulation (as *Madhyāntavibhāga* IV.6cd says).

1da3) Their result is to give rise to the five powers (as per *Madhyāntavibhāga* IV.7cd).

1db) Practicing them has two parts:
  1) Meditating in the common manner
  2) Meditating in the uncommon manner

1db1) Through confidence, one familiarizes with the sixteen aspects of the four realities in the manner of trusting them. Through vigor, one familiarizes with them by being enthusiastic. Through mindfulness, one familiarizes with them by not forgetting the conceptions in terms of focal objects and aspects. Through samādhi, one familiarizes with them by mind being one-pointed with regard to its focal object. Through prajñā, one familiarizes with them in the manner of discriminating focal objects and aspects.

1db2) Through confidence, one familiarizes with the two sets of the sixteen focal objects and aspects of the four realities on the two levels in the manner of trusting them while not observing them.[318]

1e) The five powers

Their nature consists of the five faculties having come to possess the power to overcome their antagonistic factors, which is based on having adopted said five faculties. This is the reason why they are called "powers" (as stated in *Mahāyānasūtrālaṃkāra* XVIII.57cd). Their causes are the five faculties. Their result is giving rise to the first bhūmi and beyond (*Mahāyānasūtrālaṃkāra* XVIII.57a). To practice them is the same as for the five faculties.

1f) The seven branches of enlightenment
This has three parts:
  a) Essence
  b) Cause
  c) Result

1fa) Essence has five parts:
  1) Definition
  2) Division
  3) Meaning of the term
  4) Example
  5) Boundary lines

1fa1) Their definition is "that which arises based on having adopted the supreme dharma and serves as aids for enlightenment."

1fa2) As *Madhyāntavibhāga* IV.8cd–9 says, there are seven branches of enlightenment, which are included in five—the branches of (1) matrix, (2) nature, (3) final deliverance, (3) benefit, and (5) lack of affliction. (1) The branch of the matrix is mindfulness because it functions as the cause of enlightenment. (2) The branch of nature is to thoroughly discriminate phenomena because this is the nature of great enlightenment. (3) The branch of final deliverance is vigor because it finally delivers from the state of saṃsāra to the state of nirvāṇa. (4) The branch of benefit is joy because (according to the Sautrāntikas) joy benefits the mind and bliss benefits the body, and (according to the Vaibhāṣikas) both benefit the mind. (5) The branch of the lack of affliction is threefold—the branches of its (a) foundation, (b) matrix, and (c) nature. (a) Suppleness is the branch that is the foundation of the lack of affliction because it relinquishes the causes for the afflictions—the impregnations of negative tendencies. (b) Samādhi is the branch that is the matrix of the lack of affliction because it is the attainment of the change of state that consists of the lack of afflictions. (c) Equanimity is the branch that is the nature of the lack of affliction because it is the lack of any afflictions whatsoever. When counted as the seven branches of the path to enlightenment, the above branches (5a)–(5c) become branches (5)–(7).

1fa3) As for the meaning of the term "branches of enlightenment" (Tib. byang chub yan lag), it refers to "being purified" (*byang*) in the sense of antagonistic factors being purified. It refers to "being realized" (*chub*) because suchness is internalized. It says "branches" because they represent parts of enlightenment, just like the limbs of the body.

1fa4) Bodhisattvas on the path of seeing are like cakravartins and the seven branches of enlightenment resemble the seven insignia of his kingdom (as stated in *Mahāyānasūtrālaṃkāra* XVIII.59–63). Mindfulness conquers as yet unconquered knowable objects, just as his precious wheel conquers as yet unconquered lands. Prajñā simultaneously overcomes all characteristics of conceptions, just as the precious elephant overcomes all enemies. Vigor swiftly progresses toward enlightenment, just as the precious horse travels across the earth that is surrounded by oceans. Joy about the increase in the illumination of the dharma satisfies, just as the precious jewel delights through its special radiance. Since suppleness means being liberated from all obscurations, bliss is attained, just as a cakravartin experiences bliss with the precious queen. Samādhi fulfills the intended aims of bodhisattvas, just as the wealth of a cakravartin comes from the precious minister. Through eliminating antagonistic factors through equanimity, bodhisattvas dwell in every situation as they please, always being at their best by virtue of dwelling in nonconceptual wisdom during meditative equipoise and in its subsequent attainment, just as the precious general delights a cakravartin by way of warding off the armies of opponents.

1fa5) The boundary lines of these seven branches are that they exist from the first bhūmi up through buddhahood.

1fb–c) Their causes and results have already been explained in the earlier and later sections on the path of seeing. The manner of practicing them is not taught here—since the wisdom of the first bhūmi is of the nature of being self-arisen, it cannot be made a living experience through mundane studying, reflecting, or meditating.

1g) The eightfold path of the noble ones
This has three parts:
a) Essence
b) Cause
c) Result

1ga) Essence has four parts:
1) Definition
2) Division
3) Meaning of the term
4) Boundary lines

1ga1) The definition of the eightfold path of the noble ones is "that which arises from having adopted the seven branches of enlightenment and serves as aids for the path of the noble ones."

1ga2) It is presented as eightfold because it has eight different natures. The common yāna's system of presenting them is explained in the relevant texts (the *Vivṛti* just lists the eight) and the system of the mahāyāna is as follows. According to the *Bodhipakṣanirdeśasūtra*, correct view means to see all phenomena as equal, nondual, and indivisible. Correct thought is to see all phenomena as always nonexistent, inconceivable, and unexaminable. Correct speech is to see all phenomena as inexpressible. Correct aims of action refer to seeing that all phenomena are without actor and object of action. Correct livelihood is to not write down the names and so on of all phenomena. Correct effort means to accomplish all phenomena in the manner of being without effort and accomplishment. Correct mindfulness is to see the lack of mindfulness and mental engagement with regard to all phenomena. Correct samādhi means to naturally rest in meditative equipoise and to be free from agitation because all phenomena are unobservable, thus seeing them in a nonobserving manner.

According to *Madhyāntavibhāga* IV.10–11, these eight are summarized into the four branches of (1) delimitation, (2) making others understand, (3) instilling trust in others, and (4) remedy. (1) Correct view is the branch of delimitation because it delimits the actuality that has already been seen on the path of seeing. (2) Both correct thought and speech are the branch of making others understand because the speech that arises from correct thought demonstrates the actuality that one has realized to others. (3) The branch of instilling trust in others is threefold. Through correct speech, trust in the pure view is instilled. Through correct aims of actions, trust in pure ethics is instilled because one knows how not to engage in any improper actions of body, speech, and mind. Through correct livelihood, trust in reducing necessities is instilled because one knows how to relinquish wrong ways of livelihood. Wrong livelihood is fivefold—corrupt conceited ethics; flattery; snatching the possessions of other people after they gave them up or are disowned through one's own influence; indirectly appealing to receive the possessions of others through praising these possessions; and trying to receive large gifts in reward through first giving a little bit oneself. Furthermore, the *Saṃvaraviṃśakavṛtti*[319] (on line 11d) explains that keeping impure things, pounding sesame seeds, pressing mustard seeds, farm work, and so on are also wrong ways of livelihood for monastics. (4) The branch of the remedy is also threefold. Correct effort functions as the remedy for the afflictions that are factors to be relinquished through familiarization. According to Vasubandhu's *Madhyāntavibhāgabhāṣya*,[320] correct mindfulness serves as the remedy for the secondary afflictions of dullness and agitation. Correct samādhi serves as the remedy for the antagonistic factors of attaining mastery over special qualities (such as the five visions and the six supernatural knowledges) because it functions as the remedy for the obscurations of meditative absorption. The *Saṃvaraviṃśakavṛtti* (on line 15a) explains the obscurations of meditative absorption to be fivefold.[321]

1ga3) The meaning of the term "eightfold (or the eight branches of the) path of the noble ones" is as follows. The persons on it are "noble ones" because they have gone far beyond those who have not attained the path of seeing. It is a "path" because it makes one progress to the city of nirvāṇa. It is referred to as being "eightfold" or having "eight branches" because these are the parts of the path of the noble ones, just like the limbs of the body.

1ga4) Some say that the eightfold path of the noble ones exists from the second bhūmi onward. In this case, it follows that this path does not exist on the path of seeing because it only exists from the second bhūmi onward. However, this is rejected by *Mahāyānasūtrālaṃkāra* XIV.36:

> It is held that the children of the victors,
> Simultaneously with the path of seeing,
> Always attain all the various kinds
> Of the factors concordant with enlightenment.

Therefore, the eight branches of the path of the noble ones exist from the second moment of the first bhūmi up through buddhahood.

1gb) The cause from which these eight branches arise consists of the seven branches of enlightenment—they represent the arising of the path of familiarizing with fully knowing the reality that is seen on the path of seeing.

1gc) The results of the eightfold path of the noble ones are the results of the two paths of seeing and familiarization.[322]

2) The thirty-four aspects of the knowledge of the path

This has six parts:
a) The path of the remedies
b) The path of manifesting
c) The path of blissfully abiding amidst visible phenomena
d) The supramundane path
e) The path of relinquishment
f) The path of buddhahood[323]

2a) The path of the remedies
This has two parts:
a) The doors to liberation that are to be known
b) The doors to liberation that are the path

As for these doors existing in these two ways, *Mahāyānasūtrālaṃkāra* XVIII.78ab says:

> Samādhi should be understood as threefold—
> In terms of apprehended, apprehender, and nature.[324]

2aa) As for the doors to liberation that are to be known, *Mahāyānasūtrālaṃkāra* XVIII.80bd says:

> As the causes for samādhi,
> The four epitomes of the dharma
> Were taught to bodhisattvas.[325]

The four epitomes of the dharma are stated in *Mahāyānasūtrālaṃkāra* XVIII.81:

> For the intelligent ones, these four
> Have the meaning of nonexistence, the meaning of conception,
> The meaning of imagination,
> And the meaning of conceptions being at peace.

Accordingly, (1) all conditioned phenomena mean that there is nothing that exists permanently. (2) The three realms are contaminated, everything contaminated is conception, and all conception means suffering. (3) All phenomena are just imagined as identities through conception, but the meaning of identity equals the meaning of the lack of specific characteristics. (4) Nirvāṇa means conceptions being at peace. Master Dignāga's *Praise to Mañjuśrī*[326] says:

> Not realizing conceptions—
> This so-called "saṃsāra"—is nothing whatsoever.
> Since you are free from conceptions,
> You are always nirvāṇa.

The first two epitomes represent the door to liberation that is wishlessness; the third one, the door of emptiness; and the fourth one, the door of signlessness. Or, (according to the *Vṛtti* and *Ālokā*) the sixteen aspects of the four realities (such as impermanence) correspond to the three doors of liberation that are to be known as follows. The aspects "empty and "identityless" of the reality of suffering represent the door of emptiness; the eight aspects of the realities of cessation and the path represent the door of signlessness; and the aspects "impermanent" and "suffering" of the reality of suffering as well as the four aspects of the reality of its origin represent the door of wishlessness.[327]

2ab) The doors to liberation that are the path are taught in the *Vivṛti* follows. The remedy for the five wrong views (such as the views about a real personality) is the door of emptiness—the nature of the aspects "empty" and "identityless." The remedy for the conceptions that are affected by these views as their causes is the door of signlessness—the nature of the aspects of the realities of cessation (the nature of signlessness) and the path (that which eliminates conceptions about signs). The remedy for wishing for the three realms is the door of wishlessness—the nature of the aspects "impermanent" and "suffering" and of those of the origin of suffering.

2b–c) The path of manifesting and the path of blissfully abiding amidst visible phenomena

Higher abhidharma

The eight liberations (three as the path of manifesting and five as the path of blissfully abiding) that arise in the mind streams of bodhisattvas are explained in two points:

a) The support of a person's mind stream in which they arise
b) Determining the eight liberations that arise in such a mind stream

2ba) The physical support for the first arising of the eight liberations is a human one, and the physical support for sustaining them once they have arisen can also be one in the form realm because they have the same physical supports as the meditative absorption of cessation. As for the mental support, the liberations arise in the meditative absorption that is the highest form of the fourth dhyāna because without this meditative absorption, one is not even able to manifest the first one among the eight liberations. You may wonder what the difference between the fourth dhyāna and its highest form is. In order to speak of the highest form of said dhyāna, it needs to be preceded by the attainment of all nine meditative absorptions of progressive abiding without regressing from them. For the highest form of the fourth dhyāna must possess the capacity to enter the actual four formless absorptions without relying on their four preparatory stages and the capacity to definitely enter the meditative absorption of cessation without relying on the Peak of Existence. Otherwise, it would be contradictory for the eight liberations to rely on the highest form of the fourth dhyāna.

2bb) Determining the eight liberations that arise in such a mind stream

This has three parts:

1) Definition
2) Division of each of their instances
3) The manner of practicing them

2bb1) The eight liberations are the meditative absorptions that are accomplished through the highest form of the fourth dhyāna and make one turn one's back on saṃsāra.

2bb2) The definition of (1) the liberation of looking at form through what possesses form is a meditative absorption that is accomplished through the fourth dhyāna as its specific mental support and specifically consists of the samādhi that is congruently associated with prajñā and immersed in looking at outer forms in their variety without having eliminated the notion of form with regard to oneself. The definition of (2) the liberation of looking at form through what is formless is the same except for replacing the last phrase by "looking at outer forms by way of having eliminated any notion of form with regard to oneself." The definition of (3) the liberation of notions of specific beauty is the same except for replacing the last phrase with "one-pointedly looking at outer forms by way of being endowed with the three notions of preparation and actual stage."[328] The definitions of (4)–(7) the liberations of the four formless absorptions are the same except for replacing the last phrase with "being liberated from the obscurations of craving for the taste of the formlessness of their respective levels." The definition of (8) the liberation of the meditative absorption of cessation is the same except for replacing the last phrase with "being liberated from the obscurations of meditative absorption that obstruct the cessation of discrimination and feelings."

2bb3) The manner of practicing them

First, by relying on the highest form of the fourth dhyāna, one relinquishes the obscurations of meditative absorption that obstruct looking at outer forms in their variety without having eliminated the notion of form with regard to oneself. Once these obscurations have been relinquished, one speaks of "having attained the first liberation." Likewise, by relying on this highest form of the fourth dhyāna, one relinquishes the obscurations of meditative absorption that obstruct looking at various forms by way of having eliminated any notion of form with regard to oneself. Then, again relying on said dhyāna, as the remedy for the obscurations of meditative absorption that appear as the aspects of liking to manifest beautiful forms and disliking to manifest ugly ones, one familiarizes with the two notions pertinent to the time of preparation. After said obscurations have been relinquished through these two notions, once the one-pointed notion of beauty has been attained during the actual stage of this meditative absorption, this is called "having manifested the third liberation." Then, again relying on said dhyāna, one turns one's back on the craving for the respective levels of the four formless absorptions. Once that is accomplished, one speaks of "having manifested the liberations of the four formless absorptions." Finally, again relying on the highest form of the fourth dhyāna, one relinquishes the obscurations of meditative absorption that obstruct the meditative absorption of cessation's being based on this fourth dhyāna. Once said obscurations have been relinquished, this is called "having manifested the liberation of cessation." In brief, in terms of their self-isolates, the eight liberations are not presented as the supramundane path, but they must definitely be practiced through relying on the supramundane path. For otherwise, it is hard to explain a reason for why non-Buddhists do not possess them. Also, as long as the supramundane path has not been attained, the formless absorptions and the meditative absorption of cessation are unable to rely on the actual fourth dhyāna. For the scriptural proofs of this, see the *Śrāvakabhūmi* and the *Bahubhūmivastu*.[329]

Lower abhidharma

As presented in *Abhidharmakośa* VIII.32ab, the nature of the first two liberations is repulsiveness and they are based on the mental supports of either of the first two actual dhyānas (here the remedy for the attachment to the colors and so on of the desire realm is to meditate by relying on the first dhyāna, and the remedy for the attachment to the colors and so on of the first dhyāna is to meditate by relying on the second one). As for their objects, the first three liberations focus on the forms of the desire realm (*Abhidharmakośa* VIII.34a).

As per *Abhidharmakośa* VIII.37cd, the four liberations of the formless absorptions can arise in persons within all three realms, but the other four arise only in the men and women on the three continents (i.e., except Uttarakuru).

(1) In the first liberation, the manner of familiarizing with its aspect is to give rise to the notion of one's own body being a skeleton, and, through that, familiarize with all outer sentient beings and nonsentient forms as being skeletons. This is taught in the *Sūryagarbhasūtra*.

(2) In the second liberation, the manner of familiarizing with its aspect is twofold—(a) the manner of eliminating the notion of form and (b) the manner of establishing the notion of formlessness (as mentioned in the commentary on the *Abhidharmasamuccaya* and explained in the *Sūryagarbhasūtra*). (a) Through relying on an actual formless absorption, one does not give rise to any notion of form with regard to one's own body. By way of that, one then looks at outer sentient beings and nonsentient forms as appearing as the aspect of repulsiveness. However, when looking at outer forms, one must rise from one's formless absorption because one is not able to look at outer forms while resting in such an absorption. (b) One meditates that a strong wind emits from one's mouth and nose, which reduces one's body—visualized as a skeleton—to dust and scatters it. Through familiarizing oneself with this for a long time, there will be no appearance of form with regard to one's own body. Then, one looks at outer sentient beings and nonsentient forms as appearing as the aspect of repulsiveness.

(3) According to *Abhidharmakośa* VIII.32c, the nature of the third liberation is the virtuous mental factor of detachment and it must arise based on the mental support of the actual fourth dhyāna. As for the manner of familiarizing with its aspect, by way of having cultivated the notion of there being no forms, one familiarizes with the notions of forms being mutually dependent, mutually connected, and mutually of one taste. In order to cultivate this third liberation, the attainment of the second one is necessary as a branch of it. For by virtue of the notion of there being no inner form, it is not different in substance from the four kinds of overpowering in terms of blue and so on. The manners of familiarization of the first three liberations are presented here according to the commentary on the *Abhidharmasamuccaya*. According to the *Sūtra of the Omnipresent Noble Dharmas*,[330] all eight liberations are explained as the wisdoms of resting in meditative equipoise with regard to all phenomena.

(4)–(7) The respective actual and preparatory stages of the four formless absorptions represent both the natures and the mental supports of the fourth through the seventh liberations, respectively. As for their focal objects, according to *Abhidharmakośa* VIII.21ab and VIII.34bd, the uncontaminated actual formless absorptions that serve as these liberations are unable to focus on the first three and a half of the four realities of any levels that are respectively lower than them. They focus on the four realities of their own respective levels, the four realities of higher levels, and the respective subsequent readiness and subsequent cognition of the reality of the path on the respective lower levels. As for the manner of familiarizing with their aspects, one familiarizes with them by thinking, "Space is infinite" and so on.

(8) As for the meditative absorption of cessation, in terms of the śrāvakas, according to *Abhidharmakośa* VI.43cd and VI.64a, the ones who enter this absorption are the nonreturners who witness with the body and the arhats who are liberated by virtue of both aspects (prajñā and samādhi). Ordinary beings, stream-enterers, once-returners, and the arhats who are liberated through prajñā alone do not enter it for the following reasons. Ordinary beings have not attained the path of the noble ones; stream-enterers, once-returners, and said arhats have not attained the state of mind of the Peak of Existence; and these four have not relinquished all obscurations of meditative absorption. The *Viniścayasaṃgrahaṇī* explains that both learner and nonlearner pratyekabuddhas who have relinquished the obscurations of meditative absorption enter the meditative absorption of cessation. Rhinolike pratyekabuddhas do not enter the meditative absorption of cessation on their path of learning because they must progress in a single session from heat up through the knowledge of termination and nonarising. According to *Abhidharmakośa* II.44ab, buddhas also enter the meditative absorption of cessation, while bodhisattvas cannot enter the meditative absorption of cessation because they must become buddhas through giving rise to the following thirty-four moments in an uninterrupted manner—the sixteen readinesses and cognitions of the path of seeing; the nine uninterrupted paths of the path of familiarization; and the nine paths of liberation of the path of familiarization.

As for the physical supports of the persons who enter this meditative absorption, its first arising can only happen in humans in the desire realm. Once it has arisen, it can be sustained in the physical supports within both the desire and the form realms because it can be accomplished in a support within the desire realm and then manifested in a support within the form realm (*Abhidharmakośa* II.44cd). The meditative absorption of cessation cannot be manifested in a support within the formless realm. For there are no bodies in this realm and, according to the *Abhidharmasamuccaya*,[331] no efforts to enter this absorption. Its mental supports are twofold—those for entering it and those for rising from it. According to *Abhidharmakośa* II.43b and VIII.33bd, the first one is the state of mind of the Peak of Existence because it is very subtle and thus its flux of minds and mental factors is easy to stop. One can rise from this meditative absorption by either relying on a pure state of mind of the Peak of Existence or the uncontaminated formless absorption of Nothing Whatsoever.

As for the actual meditative absorption of cessation, it is presented in five parts. (a) The basis within which cessation takes place is the body. For the hīnayāna system does not assert the ālaya or suchness as the basis for such a cessation and it holds that the meditative absorption of cessation is witnessed with the body. (b) According to *Abhidharmakośa* II.41bd and VIII.43a, the factors to be ceased are all minds and mental factors. (c) As for the manner of ceasing, one sees that feelings and discrimination are distractions since they are coarse. Thus, one first prepares through the mind resting in the subsiding of feelings and discriminations and then enters the meditative absorption of cessation in the manner of stopping the minds and mental factors of the Peak of Existence (*Abhidharmakośa* II.43b). (d) According to *Abhidharmakośa* II.43c, the nature of this meditative absorption is virtuous and its karmic maturation can be experienced in the next lifetime, in any lifetime after that, or its experience can be uncertain (that is, when the practitioner attains nirvāṇa in the present lifetime). Among the triad of matter, mind, and nonassociated formations, it is asserted to be a nonassociated formation. This is said to be the case in terms of the state of the body (which is primordially without awareness) during this cessation because all minds and mental factors have ceased. You may wonder if this is not contradictory to this cessation being explained as a meditative absorption. It is not contradictory because it is explained as a meditative absorption or equipoise by virtue of the elements of the body being put into equipoise when one is absorbed in it and because it is a case of the name of the cause being given to the result. (e) As for the time, one is able to rest in this meditative absorption for as long as one propels one's mind in this way. Vasubandhu explains that the reason for it being labeled as one of the "liberations" is that one turns one's back on all formations.

2d) The supramundane path

The general topic of the dhyānas and formless absorptions was explained above.[332] As for the explanation of the meditative absorption of cessation in the mahāyāna, it has two parts:

a) The Yogācāra system
b) The Madhyamaka system

2da) The Yogācāra system has two parts:

1) The persons who enter it in which realms
2) Identifying the nature of this meditative absorption

2da1) Unlike in the above explanation in terms of inferior persons, the ones who enter this meditative absorption are not identified here as the nonreturners who witness with the body and the arhats who are liberated by virtue of the aspects of both prajñā and samādhi. In the mahāyāna, the persons who enter it are twofold—learners and nonlearners.

As for the learners, those who have not previously gone through inferior paths must necessarily enter it only from the subsequent attainment[333] of the path of seeing onward because they are not able to enter it without having attained this path. Therefore, in terms of this meditative absorption of cessation that is asserted by the Yogācāras and exists already below the sixth bhūmi,[334] one must give a presentation of the meditative absorption at the time of entering the nine meditative absorptions of progressive abiding, such as "crossing in one leap" and "the lion's sport," up through the fifth bhūmi. This is the true intention of the AA and its commentaries. However, if one had to explain the meditative absorption of cessation as it is found in the AA and its commentaries in accordance with Madhyamaka alone, there is the following flaw. The meditative absorption of cessation of the Madhyamaka system cannot be manifested as long as the sixth bhūmi has not been manifested. However, in that case, it follows that there are no meditative absorptions of "crossing in one leap" and "the lion's sport" of the second and the following bhūmis. In terms of the self-isolate of this meditative absorption, it is not explained as wisdom, but it is not the case that one is not able to relinquish the seeds of the obscurations through engaging in the meditative absorption of cessation because there is the uninterrupted arising of nonconceptual wisdom for as long as one engages in this meditative absorption.

In terms of the nonlearners in the mahāyāna, buddhas enter the meditative absorption of cessation for the following reasons. It is impossible for them to rise from the meditative absorption in which the seven kinds of consciousnesses plus their associated mental factors (the factors to be ceased) have ceased within mirrorlike wisdom (the basis of cessation). The texts of Maitreya and Asaṅga clearly state that buddhas have this kind of meditative absorption of cessation, and also the *Vṛtti* explains it accordingly.

As for the realms in which this meditative absorption is entered, this happens only in the desire and form realms, but not in the formless realm because there is no need for it there. In terms of the hīnayāna, there is the difficult point of the first arising of this meditative absorption being accomplished in a human support and then manifested later in the form realm, but in terms of noble bodhisattvas, there is no such difficult point. Without such bodhisattvas having freed themselves from the attachment to the portion of the afflictions that serves as the cause for their taking rebirths on lower levels, they are able to manifest the minds of the actual meditative states of higher and higher levels of existence. Therefore, for them, it is not contradictory to take rebirth on some lower levels while not regressing from the actual meditative states of higher levels.

2da2) The nature of this meditative absorption

It is the nonassociated formation that is a label for the state in which the seven kinds of consciousnesses plus their associated mental factors (the factors to be ceased) have ceased within the ālaya (the basis of cessation) through the supramundane path (the means of cessation). With regard to this state, some assert that supramundane wisdom is interrupted, but this is greatly mistaken. If the wisdom of the supramundane path is asserted as what is to be ceased within this state of the meditative absorption of cessation, what could be more unreasonable than that? They may say, "If one asserts that supramundane wisdom is not actually ceased, but is interrupted through its own force, this contradicts the fact that the supramundane path ceases what is to be ceased in the state of having entered the meditative absorption of cessation. For if the supramundane path (the means of cessation) is interrupted, the meditative absorption of cessation is not able to cease what is to be ceased. Thus, it is by having in mind that nonconceptual wisdom is necessarily the mental consciousness that we assert supramundane wisdom being ceased here." However, in this case, nonconceptual wisdom would be a consciousness that is based on the dominant condition of the mental sense faculty. If this is accepted, it would either be based on any one of the first six consciousnesses having ceased immediately before its own arising or it would be based on the afflicted mind. For it is not explained that anything except for these seven can function as the mental sense faculty that is the dominant condition of the mental consciousness.[335] In brief, nonconceptual wisdom is not necessarily the mental consciousness, just like the wisdoms of the meditative equipoises of those who dwell on the bhūmis.

2db) The Madhyamaka system

What is called "meditative absorption of cessation" in the Madhyamaka system and is explained in the *Daśabhūmikasūtra* and the *Madhyamakāvatāra* does not exist in śrāvakas and pratyekabuddhas because the meditative absorption that is explained in the Madhyamaka system must be attained through the power of prajñāpāramitā. Nevertheless, one is not able to present this meditative absorption merely by virtue of being the nonconceptual wisdom of the assembly of reference points (the factors to be ceased) having ceased within suchness (the basis of cessation) because then it would follow that also the mahāyāna paths of seeing and familiarization that are based on the preparatory stages of the dhyānas are this meditative absorption of cessation. Therefore, its definition is the nonconceptual wisdom that is specified through being preceded by its specific cause (the bhūmi that mainly consists of the pāramitā of dhyāna) and in which all characteristics of reference points (the factors to be ceased) have ceased without exception within suchness (the basis of cessation) through the power of prajñāpāramitā.

As for its boundary lines, it is attained from the sixth bhūmi onward. On the seventh bhūmi, bodhisattvas are able to enter it and also rise from it through their own power in a single instant, just as they please. On the eighth bhūmi, they are able to enter it in this way, but they are not able to rise from it through their own power because they need to be raised from it by the buddhas. Also, the inability of bodhisattvas on the eighth bhūmi to rise from the meditative absorption through their own power lies in their being able to blend meditative equipoise and subsequent attainment in an inseparable way by virtue of all conceptions that cling to characteristics having utterly subsided even during subsequent attainment. Furthermore, though they, on the eighth bhūmi, have attained the ability to be absorbed in the nature of phenomena all the time if they were to relinquish the cognitive obscurations without fully completing the accumulation of merit, they would not be able to eventually promote the welfare of sentient beings through the two rūpakāyas. Therefore, they need to be raised from this meditative absorption by the buddhas.[336]

D) The signs of irreversibility[337]

The sūtras say:

> Bodhisattvas who are endowed with these aspects, signs, and characteristics should be known to be irreversible from perfect enlightenment . . .[338]

In this passage, "aspects" refer to nature reasons; "signs," to result reasons;[339] and "characteristics," to reasons in terms of the collection of causes being complete in number. This is explained in two parts:

1) Formulating the basic reason
2) The manner in which this serves as a reason

1) Formulating the basic reason has three parts:

1a) The meaning of the subject in question

In general, it is from the mahāyāna path of preparation onward that one speaks of irreversibility. According to Āryavimuktisena and Haribhadra, those who are of sharpest faculties and endowed with the respective distinctive signs are irreversible from the path of preparation onward; those who are of medium faculties and endowed with the respective signs, from the paths of seeing and familiarization onward; and those who are of dull faculties and endowed with the respective signs, from the eighth bhūmi onward. However, the great scholar Kamalaśīla says that being of dull faculties is impossible after having attained the bhūmis.

So who is taken as the subject in question in the above-mentioned reasonings? It is not the bodhisattvas who dwell on the paths of preparation, seeing, and familiarization as just explained who are presented as such subjects. For, from the perspective of the disputants in this context, the disposition of said bodhisattvas is already identified as the mahāyāna disposition and thus needs not to be established through reasons. Therefore, it is explained that it is the bodhisattvas with uncertain dispositions who are presented as the subjects here—if these bodhisattvas are endowed with the respective signs, they are explained to be irreversible, and if they are not so endowed, they can revert from their states. You may object, "But that means that those with uncertain dispositions who are on the mahāyāna paths of seeing and familiarization would also revert if they are not endowed with such signs." There is no flaw because, once the mahāyāna paths of seeing and familiarization are attained, it is impossible for the respective signs of irreversibility to not arise at their respective times. However it is taught that, though bodhisattvas whose disposition is certain as the mahāyāna disposition have no doubts about their irreversibility from the path of preparation onward, bodhisattvas with uncertain dispositions do have doubts about their irreversibility even up to attaining the eighth bhūmi.

1b) The probandum

This can refer to proving a convention or proving a fact. The first one means to prove that someone is irreversible from perfect enlightenment by virtue of the power of their motivation and the training motivated by it. The second means proving that, in the person who is the subject in question, the attainment of nirvāṇa is suitable to not be interrupted by any other yānas and that the wisdom of great nirvāṇa is suitable to arise.

1c) Identifying the reason

In terms of meditative equipoise, the reason serves as a reason from one's own perspective, while during subsequent attainment it serves as a reason from the perspective of others—perceiving the qualities of irreversibility is put forward as the reason for someone being a person who is endowed with these qualities. The approach of the *Vivṛti* is to divide the twenty signs of irreversibility on the path of preparation by way of the four levels of this path. On this, some say that it contradicts the sūtras to divide these twenty signs up, whereas others say that the intention of the sūtras lies in even any single one among these signs being able to prove that someone is an irreversible person on the path of preparation. However, these statements are to be examined by the learned.

In terms of the signs of irreversibility serving as reasons during subsequent attainment, in order to prove a convention the relevant scriptural passage itself is given as a reason, and in order to prove a fact the meaning of this passage is given as a reason. Thus, the first kind of argument is phrased as, "Bodhisattvas with uncertain dispositions on the path of preparation who are endowed with the aspects, signs, and characteristics that are taught in the passage starting with 'Bodhisattvas have turned away from discriminating notions of form and so on . . .'[340] (the subject in question) are temporarily irreversible from perfect enlightenment because the sūtras say that they are irreversible." The second argument is phrased as, "For the same bodhisattvas (the subject), it is suitable for perfect enlightenment to arise without being interrupted by other yānas because the collection of the causes for this enlightenment is complete in number."

2) The manner in which this serves as a reason has three parts:

a) The manner in which it serves as a reason for certain persons
b) The manner of recollecting the three modes
c) Identifying the probative argument

2a) First, it is necessary that, based on an actual example, both disputants have already established the connection between the signs of being irreversible from perfect enlightenment and those who possess these signs. Otherwise, as stated in *Pramāṇavārttika* III.475ab, there would be an infinite regress in terms of such examples. In particular, the defender must have certainty about such distinctive signs meaning irreversibility from perfect enlightenment. Otherwise, there would be the flaw that is stated in *Pramāṇavārttika* III.476d–477ab:

> Through perceiving speech and movements,
> The minds of others would not be inferred,
> Because there is no connection to oneself.

Therefore, to serve as a reason from one's own perspective is called "an argument in the context of one's own welfare," which here means to infer from the signs in one's meditative equipoise that one's own realization is irreversible. To serve as a reason from the perspective of others refers to inferring from the signs during the subsequent attainments of other persons (which are approximately concordant with the realizations in the meditative equipoises of these others) that their realizations are irreversible.

2b) The manner of recollecting the three modes
The subject property is established through perceptual valid cognition. The entailment can only hold up for the challenger through being based on a concordant example by way of the trusted scriptural passages in AA IV.39–45. For said irreversibility is a very hidden object and therefore cannot be established through the perception of anybody else but those who abide on the special

path in question and buddhas. Therefore, though great bodhisattvas on the ten bhūmis teach all kinds of genuine dharmas, they do not prophesy others being irreversible in terms of enlightenment because this is beyond their sphere. You may think, "If the connection in terms of the entailment relies only on scripture, this contradicts the above explanation that this connection must already be established in one's mind stream." This is not contradictory because it is not contradictory that the connection in terms of the entailment is established in one's mind stream by way of trusted scripture serving as the reason. In brief, whoever is endowed with the signs of irreversibility is necessarily irreversible from enlightenment because one trusts the words of the Tathāgata (scriptures that are pure through the threefold analysis) which say that someone is irreversible if they are endowed with these signs.

2c) Identifying the probative argument

Pramāṇavārttika I.7a says:

> Results arise from the collection of [their] causes.

To apply this reasoning here, the probative argument is formulated as follows: "As for bodhisattvas with uncertain dispositions on the path of preparation (the subject), their conduct is preceded by the seeming kinds of bodhicitta, great loving-kindness, compassion, and the prajñā of realizing emptiness because they are endowed with special ways of conduct during subsequent attainment (such as even searching out the hells for the welfare of others and being unaffected by the activities of māras)." In this reasoning, the subject property is established through the reason of directly seeing the results of irreversibility. Or "For said bodhisattvas (the subject), it is suitable for the wisdom of the knowledge of all aspects to arise in their mind streams without being interrupted by other yānas because the collection of the causes for the knowledge of all aspects is complete in number." Here, the subject property is established through a nature reason. In this way, in terms of the wording, what is formulated here is the reason of the wisdom of the knowledge of all aspects being suitable to arise, but in terms of the meaning, this comes down to a sign or reason of irreversibility. You may wonder, "But the texts on reasoning explain that to establish the definite arising of something through it being suitable to arise as being a mistaken entailment. Therefore, one is not able to prove the definite arising of irreversibility through its being suitable to arise." In general, it is true that one is not able to prove the definite arising of something through its being suitable to arise, which is in terms of there still being (potential) obstructions to its being suitable to arise. However, in the case of irreversibility here, this approach comes down to proving the definite arising of irreversibility, which is in terms of there being no obstructions to its being suitable to arise. Therefore, Atiśa's *Prajñāpāramitāpiṇḍārthapradīpa* says:

> If one infers about oneself, this is only an argument
> Of nature in terms of the collection of the causes.
> If others infer, they do so through both
> Nature and result reasons.
>
> The purpose of such inferences
> Is to stop being fainthearted
> About oneself and to stop
> The arising of contempt for others.[341]

Thus, this is a good explanation.

E) The twenty-two faculties[342]

This has three parts:

1) Identifying the faculties
2) The manner in which these faculties exist on certain levels
3) The manner in which these faculties cease on certain paths

1) Identifying the faculties has two parts:

a) Division of the faculties
b) The manner in which certain persons possess them.

1a) There are twenty-two faculties, but they are included in two:

a) The purified faculties
b) The afflicted faculties.

1aa) The purified faculties are eight in number—(1)–(5) the five of confidence, vigor, mindfulness, samādhi, and prajñā; (6) the faculty that makes everything unknown known; (7) the faculty of knowing everything; and (8) the faculty of being endowed with knowing everything. As for the meaning of the latter three, according to the śrāvaka system (6) the faculty that makes one know everything unknown is presented as the set of nine faculties of those on the path of seeing (the five faculties such as confidence; the mental faculty; the faculty of pleasant physical sensations; the faculty of pleasant mental feelings; and the faculty of equanimity). (7) The faculty of knowing everything consists of the same set of nine on the path of familiarization, and (8) the faculty of being endowed with knowing everything consists of the same set on the path of nonlearning (see *Abhidharmakośa* II.9ab). According to the mahāyāna, as per the revised edition of the *Prajñāpāramitāsūtra in Twenty-five Thousand Lines*, (6) the faculty that makes everything unknown known consists of the five faculties (such as confidence) that exist on the path of preparation; (7) the faculty of knowing everything consists of these same five faculties as they exist in noble learners; and (8) the faculty of being endowed with knowing everything (or that guards knowing everything) consists of these five as they exist in the four kinds of nonlearners (śrāvaka and pratyekabuddha arhats, bodhisattvas, and buddhas).

1ab) The afflicted faculties are fourteen—(9)–(13) the five faculties of feelings (the faculties of pleasure, suffering,[343] mental pleasure, mental displeasure, and equanimity); (14)–(18) the five sense faculties; (19) the life faculty; (20) the mental faculty; and (21)–(22) the male and female sexual faculties. As for pleasure (9), it exists in the desire realm and the first dhyāna, but not in the second dhyāna (as explained below). As an exceptional case, the mental feeling of pleasure in the third dhyāna is presented as (9) the faculty of pleasure and not as (11) the faculty of mental pleasure, which only exists in the desire realm and the first two dhyānas. (13) The faculty of equanimity is presented as a single type of feeling that is not differentiated in terms of body and mind because it does not arise through examining an object, but in both cases occurs merely through the supports that are its specific objects (body or mind) being complete. The *Śrāvakabhūmi*[344] explains that the difference between physical sensations and mental feelings is that the former are congruently associated with any of the five sense consciousness, while the latter are so associated with the mental consciousness. (14)–(18) The five sense faculties consist of internal translucent minute particles and have the power of giving rise to the consciousnesses that are able to apprehend forms, sounds, smells, tastes, and tangible objects. (19) The life faculty is what provides the lifespans of beings in the three realms. (20) The mental faculty consists of self-awareness and has the power of giving rise to the consciousness that is able to apprehend phenomena. (21)–(22) The male and female faculties are the sexual parts of the body sense faculty.

The *Viniścayasaṃgrahaṇī*[345] explains that sixteen of these twenty-two faculties are substantially existent, while six are imputedly existent. As for the latter, the three supramundane faculties (6)–(8) are imputed onto the above respective sets of nine faculties (such as confidence); the life faculty is imputed onto the factor that is a certain continuum of time; and the male and female faculties are imputed onto the body sense faculty (some also say that these two are substantially existent and represent particular instances of the body sense faculty in general).

1b) The manner in which certain persons possess them

According to *Abhidharmakośa* II.21ac, ordinary beings in the desire realm can have a maximum of nineteen faculties (all except the three supramundane faculties), that is, with all their physical and mental faculties being complete, possessing both the male and female sexual faculties (that is, being a hermaphrodite), and being without deterioration of their roots of virtue. Through this, one implicitly understands how many faculties the various beings on the nine levels of saṃsāra may possess. According to *Abhidharmakośa* II.21cd, the śrāvakas who are on the paths of seeing or familiarization each have nineteen faculties—the former lack the last two supramundane faculties; the latter lack the first and the last one of the supramundane faculties; and both lack either one of the two sexual faculties. Bodhisattvas on the path of seeing can have nineteen faculties, that is they lack either one of the two sexual faculties as well as the first and the last one of the supramundane faculties according to the mahāyāna. In general, it is possible for a mere person on the path of seeing to have all twenty-two faculties because śrāvaka arhats who have entered the mahāyāna path of seeing have the faculty of being endowed with knowing everything. In this way, the respective manner in which persons on the other paths possess certain faculties is understood implicitly.

2) The manner in which these faculties exist on certain levels

In the desire realm, all fourteen afflicted faculties exist. On the first dhyāna level, the faculty of mental displeasure does not exist because this dhyāna is what delivers one from it. Also, the male and female faculties do not exist on this level because one is free from desire for desirable objects. According to the Vaibhāṣikas (*Abhidharmakośa* II.12bc), the faculty of suffering does not exist on this level either. However, according to the system of the *Viniścayasaṃgrahaṇī*, there are eleven faculties on the first dhyāna level because it says:

> Why is the faculty of suffering not relinquished in the first dhyāna? Because it is not free from the impregnations of negative tendencies that accord with this factor.[346]

Furthermore, *Abhidharmakośa* I.30bd explains that, in the form realm, the nose and tongue sense faculties exist despite there being no objects for them and thus no corresponding consciousnesses. Therefore, according to the śrāvaka system, on the first dhyāna level there are eleven faculties through subtracting mental displeasure and the two sexual faculties.

On the second dhyāna level, the faculty of suffering does not exist either because one has become free from physical suffering. Nor does the faculty of pleasure exist because pleasures of body and mind are both nonexistent.

There is no mental ease on this level because there is only what is called "joy." As for the difference between the faculty of mental pleasure[347] (which exists here) and joy, mental pleasure is superior, whereas mere joy is not mental pleasure because joy is explained as the striving for the experience of pleasant feelings even if pleasant feelings are not experienced. Furthermore, on this second dhyāna level, there is no faculty of physical pleasure because there are no sense consciousnesses. For their congruently associated mental factors examination and analysis[348] related to this level do not exist (*Abhidharmakośa* II.31bd), which necessarily means the lack of the corresponding consciousnesses since these are always associated with such examination and analysis (*Abhidharmakośa* I.32ab). Therefore, without such consciousnesses, there is necessarily no physical pleasure. You may wonder, "But then it follows that, from the second dhyāna onward, there is no perception of forms, sounds, or tangible objects by visual, auditory, or body consciousnesses." Though these three consciousnesses do not exist from the second dhyāna level onward, according to *Abhidharmakośa* VIII.13ac, when beings on this level look at perceptible form and so on, these objects are appropriated through these beings' activating the visual consciousness and so on of the first dhyāna level. Therefore, on the second dhyāna level, there are nine faculties (that is, subtracting pleasure and suffering, mental displeasure, and the two sexual faculties).

On the third dhyāna level, the faculty of mental pleasure does not exist because there is no joy. This is necessarily the case because the mental factor of examination with regard to joy is mental pleasure (*Abhidharmakośa* VIII.29d). Therefore, though the faculty of mental pleasure that exists on the second dhyāna level is not present on the third one, there are nine faculties because it is explained that the faculty of pleasure exists on this level.

On the fourth dhyāna level, in addition to the faculties that do not exist up through the third dhyāna, the faculty of pleasure does not exist either because one has been delivered from it. Thus, there are eight faculties on the fourth dhyāna level. As *Abhidharmakośa* II.15ac says:

> In the formless [realm], dying means
> That the [faculties of] life, mind, and equanimity
> Come to an end; in the form [realm], eight do so.[349]

In this context, there are many ways of critical analysis in terms of whether the faculties of physical and mental pleasure exist or do not exist on the second and third dhyāna levels as well as in terms of distinguishing two types of joy (being or not being one in nature with the faculty of mental pleasure), but I will not elaborate on these for fear of being too verbose.

3) The manner in which these faculties cease on certain paths

When the path of seeing has arisen, the five faculties that are factors to be relinquished through seeing cease. According to *Abhidharmakośa* II.13, each one among the mental faculty and the three feelings—the faculty of pleasure (mental ease), mental pleasure, and equanimity—has three parts, consisting of those that are factors to be relinquished through seeing, those that are factors to be relinquished through familiarization, and those that are not factors to be relinquished. As for mental displeasure, it has two parts—those that are factors to be relinquished through seeing and those that are factors to be relinquished through familiarization. Therefore, the factors to be relinquished through seeing are five. The nine factors to be relinquished through familiarization alone are the seven that possess form (the five sense faculties and the two sexual faculties), the life faculty, and the faculty of suffering. As for the five faculties such as confidence, they are not factors to be relinquished through seeing. In their contaminated forms, they are factors to be relinquished through familiarization, and in their uncontaminated forms, they are not factors to be relinquished at all. As for the three supramundane faculties, they are never relinquished. In this way, the factors to be relinquished through familiarization are explained to be nineteen. According to the mahāyāna, there are twenty faculties that are factors to be relinquished through familiarization because the contaminated seeds that are a portion of the faculty that makes everything unknown known and exist in the mind streams of noble ones are factors to be relinquished through familiarization.

As for the ancillary question of the cessation of the faculties that are contained in certain levels, in the desire realm there are four—the mental faculty and the three faculties of pleasure, mental pleasure, and equanimity. On the first and second dhyāna levels, the mental faculty and the two faculties of mental pleasure and equanimity cease. On the third dhyāna level, the mental faculty and the two faculties of pleasure and equanimity cease. On the fourth dhyāna level, the mental faculty and the faculty of equanimity cease. In the formless realm, the same two faculties cease.

As for the sense organs as the physical supports of the sense faculties, they are composed of material particles that consist of all eight or fewer among the eight atomic substances (the four elements, color, smell, taste, and being a tangible object).[350] In the desire realm, all eight of these are present; in the form realm, only six (except smell and taste because there is no desire for food); and in the formless realm, obviously none. These eight atomic substances do not cease through the power of the arising of the path of seeing, but are solely factors to be relinquished through familiarization (*Abhidharmakośā* I.40ab). As for the objects of the six sense faculties (the five sense objects and phenomena), in the desire realm, all six exist; in the form realm, only four (except smell and taste); and in the formless realm, only phenomena. As for the five sense faculties, they do not cease through the power of the arising of the path of seeing either because they are solely factors to be relinquished through familiarization.

F) Ultimate reality and buddhahood as permanent entities that perform functions

1) Emptiness, the nature of phenomena, and the sugata heart as existing functional entities[351]

To teach the "nonbeing" or "the lack of nature" of entities (such as form) from the perspective of people who entertain reference points is done for a purpose. To teach "the lack of nature" as "the nature" is not a presentation as the nature of something in the sense that it is the very nature of the lack of nature itself. Rather, it means that the lack of nature is not something other than the nature of the lack of nature, which is nothing other than the meaning of "the emptiness of emptiness." This meaning represents the final system of those who assert that everything is empty of a nature of its own. However, some *Shentongpas* who do not know how to speak properly of *Shentong* claim it to be "the entity of the nonexistence of entities" and assert that the lack of nature is established as the nature of the lack of nature, thus being an existent. Those people do not speak in accordance with Maitreya. That the phenomena of seeming reality are empty of a nature of themselves is exclusively explained by him as their not abiding as any nature of their own, while the nature of the lack of nature never turns into anything else than a nonimplicative negation. Therefore, to proclaim an implicative negation in terms of the nature of the lack of nature being a remainder is not the system of the *Shentongpas*.

What the supreme proponents of *Shentong* say is that the ultimate perfect nature, which *has* a nature, is the nature that actually fulfills this function. But when such is said, this nature is not nonempty either and the existence of this nature is not something that consists of or is included in reference points and characteristics. Therefore, it does not fall in any extremes of reference points. Since said existence abides ultimately, it is free from all extremes of permanence and extinction. However, to teach said nature as the nature of the nonexistence of seeming entities and to teach it as the nature that is the existence of the ultimate entity must be understood as being what entails an intention and this intention, respectively. To teach said nature as the nature of the nonexistence of entities is done from the perspective of people who entertain reference points and out of the concern that these people may become afraid of emptiness. From the perspective of the noble ones without reference points, the very same nature is explained as the nature that is the existence of an entity. Therefore, the explanation of the ultimate perfect nature as the nature of the nonexistence of entities is the expedient meaning and its explanation as the nature that is the existence of an entity is the definitive meaning.

As for "the existence of an entity" in this context, some say indeed, "If the emptiness that is ultimate reality and actually fulfills that function is explained as an entity, why should that be any different from those who propound (really existing) entities?" However, the entity in this context is an "existent entity" among the triad of "nonexistent entity," "bad entity," and "existent entity" that is differentiated in all three mother sūtras.[352] The fact that this is an entity is clearly evident in all of the Sugata's sūtras and tantras of definitive meaning because they explain that this kind of emptiness that is the buddha heart performs the functions that are represented by the distinctive qualities of this very buddha heart. Thus, the nature of phenomena as described in this way is definitely an entity. It is said nowadays that one does not belong to the Mādhyamikas if one accepts suchness as an entity. However, in that case, it would be reasonable that venerable Maitreya and master Asaṅga do not belong to the ranks of the Mādhyamikas either. For the former and master Asaṅga explain in the *Uttaratantra* root text and its commentary that the vajra of suchness is an entity and furthermore explain this entity to be pure, permanent, and blissful. If this referred to the nonexistence of any entity (or a nonentity), how could it be suitable as being pure, permanent, and blissful?

Some people with wrong ideas say, "The purity, permanence, and bliss that consist of the pāramitās of purity, permanence, and bliss are by no means purity, permanence, and bliss." However, these people just try to come up with some faulty objections to dispute the perfect Buddha (Maitreya) and his disciples. To deal with the pāramitās of purity, permanence, and bliss by omitting the word "supreme"[353] from them is a mistaken understanding. Let's take "supreme permanence" as an example of the unmistaken meaning to be understood through these pāramitās. What is taken as the basis here is everything that is both permanent and supreme (or highest). From among these phenomena, what is explained as the pāramitā of permanence is to be endowed with the attainment of the nature of the state of there being nothing to which one could possibly progress higher or which could become more eminent than that.

Some people may ask, "If, according to you, the distinctive feature of said state is attained through the phenomenon that is taken to be the basis of this feature, what would be the reason for asserting the attainer of this state as not being such an attainer, or not existing, earlier?" To these people one cannot teach any answer other than the words that they proclaim themselves and in which their minds are thoroughly trained—they say:

> Just as, for example, the pāramitā of the supreme self is not a self, the permanence of the pāramitā of supreme permanence is not permanence . . .

This just represents a lengthy discussion through talking in a flawed way. As for the self that is the pāramitā of the supreme self, though it is neither a personal self nor a phenomenal identity, it is not unsuitable to accept it as the ultimate self because it is what the Buddha (Maitreya) and his disciples accept as the supreme self. Likewise, though it is true that the permanence of the pāramitā of supreme permanence is not the permanence that represents a knowable phenomenon, the permanence of what is not a knowable object and is the nature of phenomena is explained by the Buddha (Maitreya) and his disciples exclusively as permanent, but not as impermanent. Therefore, one should not raise lengthy discussions through talking in a flawed way.

2) Buddhahood and enlightened activity[354]

The beings to be guided focus on the dominant condition of primordially established buddhahood, which has the nature of the dharmakāya (and the other two kāyas) being of the essential character of the nonreferential wisdom of enlightenment since it abides as changeless suchness. It is merely through such focusing that these beings' desired goal or function is accomplished by way of generating the mind of bodhicitta through the triad of completion, maturation, and purification, which is eventually suitable to appear as the special actualities of the rūpakāyas and the dharmakāya in accordance with these beings having gathered the accumulations of merit and wisdom, respectively. To elaborate on the meaning of this, the *Uttaratantra* says:

> Liberation has the characteristic of being inseparable
> From all the aspects of innumerable,
> Inconceivable, and stainless qualities.
> This liberation is the Tathāgata.
>
> Suppose there were some painters,
> [Each] an expert in a different [body part],
> So that whatever part is known by one of them
> Would not be understood by any other one.
>
> Then a mighty king would hand
> Them a canvas and order,
> "All of you, on this [canvas]
> Paint my portrait!"

Upon having heard [this order] from him,
They would start their painting work,
[But] then one among these dedicated workers
Would leave for another country.

With him having gone to another country,
Due to his absence, the painting
Would not be completed in all its parts—
Such is the example that is given.

The painters that appear in such a way
Are said to be generosity, ethics, patience, and so on,
While the emptiness endowed with
The supreme of all aspects is the painting.[355]

The meaning of this is as follows. "All aspects" of the knowledge of all aspects do not exist as conventional numbers. Or they are "innumerable" because the aspects of the ultimate knowledge of all aspects are limitless. Since the knowledge of all aspects does not concord in type with the nature of consciousness, it is "inconceivable." It is "stainless" because the inseparable aspects or nature of this knowledge of all aspects represent supreme purity. It is "inseparable from" all consummate "qualities." "Liberation" is what possesses these "defining characteristics." "That which is liberation is the Tathāgata" because the single nature that is labeled with various names from the perspective of isolates (such as "tathāgata," "enlightenment endowed with these four qualities," and "the seven vajra points, such as the basic element") is unconditioned and permanent.[356] This nature of phenomena is not something unconditioned and permanent in the sense of merely negating its being conditioned and impermanent, though it is distinguished through negating these two. It is unconditioned in the sense of not being conditioned through specifically characterized conditional formations, and it is permanent in the sense of not being something like an impermanent phenomenon that represents an entity which appears for (ordinary) mental states. "But then it follows that this permanent and unconditioned enlightenment and tathāgata entail the triad of agent, object, and action because it is explained here that it is endowed with the activities of promoting the vast welfare of oneself and others, such as said qualities and enlightened activities. You accept the reason, the entailment is established through valid cognition, and if you say, 'I accept,' this is invalidated through Dharmakīrti's reasoning in *Pramāṇavārttika* II.23cd:

Because there is no reversal in what is permanent,
It is hard to realize any capacity [of it]."

The answer to this is that it is true in terms of the instance-isolates of what is permanent and unconditioned. However, in terms of their meaning-isolates, if what is permanent and unconditioned comes together with the other-dependent that is dependent origination, for the reason of the nature of phenomena being profound, it can also become a foundation for the triad of agent, object, and action.[357] Moreover, Dharmakīrti's statement that the triad of agent, object, and action is not feasible for what is permanent and unconditioned was made in terms of what is permanent and unconditioned and is a nonentity, but not in terms of what is permanent and unconditioned and is an entity. "But isn't any common locus for 'entity' and 'what is permanent' excellently negated by Dharmakīrti?" Of course he refuted this thoroughly, but the permanent and unconditioned entity in his refutations and the permanent and unconditioned entity that is asserted here are not alike. As for how they are not alike, from the perspective of the consciousnesses and their objects that are impaired by ignorance (the seeming) there are all these factors that appear for non-Buddhist and Buddhist proponents of entities as if they actually appeared, are mistaken by them as if they actually existed, and are superimposed by them as if they were real. However, in these factors, there is nothing real, undeceiving, valid, or permanent, but they are definitely nothing but unreal, deceiving, nonvalid, and impermanent. Whatever is impermanent keeps changing and perishes at its very own point in time. Thus, in actual fact, it is unreal and therefore deceiving. It is not valid since the eyes that see the nature of phenomena realize its being without validity. It is by way of entailing said change that it appears as if performing a function, which is why it is called an "entity." Such an entity refers to what appears in the innate mental states of worldly beings and dialecticians as what is able to perform a function. It is in terms of this kind of entity that a common locus of "entity" and "what is permanent" is negated.

As for this kind of permanent entity, there are the two situations of Mādhyamikas determining the self-empty bearers of the nature of phenomena and determining the other-empty nature of phenomena. In the first situation since what performs a function by way of being impermanent and changing is not something that is genuinely able to perform a function, entities that simply appear as if they perform a function are not genuine entities in this sense of truly performing a function. In fact, there is nothing whatsoever that serves as such an entity, as is illustrated by *Pramāṇavārttika* III.360:

> Once entities are analyzed through this,
> In true reality their nature does not exist
> Because they do not have a nature
> Of unity or multiplicity.

Thus, Dharmakīrti negates all that appears as an entity, but he does not affirm the lack of entity. For, in true actuality, something being the lack of entity or the existence of the lack of entity is impossible. Since there is no need to affirm the lack of entity and, if it were affirmed, one would not go beyond characteristics and reference points, to do so is flawed. Nevertheless, as for the manner in which the nature of phenomena and the Tathāgata are permanent entities, ultimately, as the object of self-aware wisdom, liberation—the Tathāgata endowed with the four qualities—abides as an entity that is able to perform functions. It is permanent because a situation of it becoming interrupted is impossible, that is, liberation and the Tathāgata can never be reversed and change into something else. Also, the intention of glorious Dignāga and Dharmakīrti is nothing but this—the opening lines of the *Pramāṇasamuccaya* say:

> To the one who embodies valid cognition and wishes to benefit beings,
> The teacher, the Sugata and protector, I pay homage.

Thus, the fruition that arises from the cooperative cause which consists of the consummate motivation and application of this motivation—the teacher who has the character of being the Sugata in terms of his own welfare and performing the activity of protection in terms of the welfare of others—is clearly described as an entity.[358] In accordance with this, the opening verse of the *Pramāṇavārttika* says:

> To the embodiment of profundity and vastness
> In which the web of conceptions is eliminated,
> The ever-excellent one, whose light
> Radiates everywhere, I pay homage.

Thus, it teaches on the entity that performs the function of the light rays of the profound and vast kāyas radiating, and the phrase "radiates everywhere" indicates that this radiating is not something intermittent, but is displayed permanently.[359]

Here, some people may think, "Expressions such as 'the ultimate, peaceful, and supramundane permanent entity' are just deceptive words, but such deceptive words exist in the scriptures of the followers of Śiva[360] too." Of course these words appear there, but what is spoken about here is not at all similar to the deceptive words through which these texts teach because "ultimate," "peaceful," and "supramundane" are not identified in the same way. For the "ultimate" of the followers of Śiva refers to the self that is considered through a fivefold view;[361] their "peace (Śiva)" refers to the state of Īśvara[362] and the like; and their "supramundane" refers only to not tasting the suffering and happiness of the desire realm. Thus, even in terms of the seeming, these kinds of "ultimate" and so on represent the false seeming and just refer to those who are even less at peace than those who are not at peace. On the other hand, the "ultimate" in this system here refers to the entity of identitylessness from the perspective of the genuine great noble ones who are more eminent than Śiva, with no entities or nonentities whatsoever being observed before their minds. "Peace" means the stream of mind and mental factors being at peace, and "supramundane" refers to all factors of formations having been relinquished.

In brief, the permanent entity that is explained in the texts of the followers of Śiva and so on is the superimposition of a permanent entity onto certain aspects of the apprehensional modes of the two obscurations that obstruct liberation. But here we deal with the permanence of primordial liberation and the entity that is the remedy which purifies the two obscurations. For the mother sūtras say that this entity, which is the knowledge of all aspects, purifies the obscurations in the mind streams of the three kinds of beings to be guided and then brings forth its own children—the four kinds of noble ones. Thus, one should not deny it by saying, "There is no such permanent entity." Consequently, simply using the same word "permanent entity" does not make the meaning the same.

Again, some people may think, "In general, it is not justified for the permanent entity that represents the supreme actuality to be named in accordance with how it abides ultimately." This is the worst kind of thinking because they think that one one has to say the opposite of what is the case through the power of entities. For this reason, one needs to understand the permanent entity that is negated by Dignāga and Dharmakīrti and the permanent entity that is asserted by them without mixing them. Thus, it is clear in all great sūtras, tantras, and treatises that tathāgata, enlightenment, and Mahāmudrā are permanent entities. Since these are very hidden objects, the above people are not able to gain certainty in their minds if they do not put their trust into such scriptural reasons. Therefore, they should rely on these reasons.

"But how does permanent liberation—the dharmadhātu, emptiness—produce the entity that performs the function of promoting the welfare of others?" In the above example in the *Uttaratantra*, when the one painter who is the expert in painting heads is missing among the painters who are each skilled in painting a particular body part, the painted form of the king will not be complete in that it lacks the head. Likewise, on the path of learning, the stains that obscure permanent liberation are removed and liberation is excellently accomplished through the means (such as the ten pāramitās) that produce the appearance of the two genuine kāyas. Therefore, the genuine permanent emptiness that has been accomplished through its being endowed with all aspects of the means is described as the entity that is able to perform functions and serves as the kāya or the form of the nature of phenomena. For, without each and every aspect of said means being complete, the two kāyas of perfect buddhahood will not clearly manifest.

Thus, with the pure mirrors of the mind streams of the beings to be guided serving as the remedial factors and through the power of the dependent origination within the facet of their minds that is the lucid and aware cognition which is close to the nature of genuine liberation and accords in its realization with the nature of phenomena, the obscurations of sentient beings are relinquished in dependence on the aspects of the rūpakāyas appearing in said facet of their minds by virtue of permanent liberation—the Tathāgata—functioning as the dominant condition for such appearance. Since the functions such as generating the remedies arise or are accomplished naturally, despite the Tathāgata's being permanent, by way of profound dependent origination, the triad of agent, object, and action is justified. The example to illuminate that this is justified is as follows. Though all seeming and ultimate phenomena are permanent emptiness, it is seen that, through the principle of dependent origination, the triad of agent, object, and action operates in a conventional manner on the level of the seeming. This is the way in which the Yogācāra masters present this justification and its example to the Niḥsvabhāvavādins.[363]

Some people will say here, "It is not justified that the *Svātantrika and *Prāsaṅgika masters refer to emptiness as 'permanent.'" But then, it would be likewise unjustified for the mother sūtras to exclusively speak of emptiness as being unconditioned because emptiness is not permanent. The reason is accepted, the entailment is established through valid cognition, and if these people say, "We accept," they are in direct contradiction to the sūtras. Therefore, in accordance with the intention of the victor Maitreya, even a bodhisattva of the Madhyamaka model texts—master Śāntideva—says in *Bodhicaryāvatāra* IX.35–37:

> Just as a wish-fulfilling jewel and a wish-fulfilling tree
> Fully satisfy [all] desires,
> Likewise, appearances of the victors are seen
> Because of their aspiration prayers and those to be guided.
>
> For example, when a worshipper of Garuḍa
> Has built a pillar and passed away,
> It still neutralizes poisons and such
> Even when he has long been dead.
>
> Likewise, through following enlightening conduct,
> The pillar of the victor is built too.

It continues to promote all welfare
Even after the bodhisattva has passed beyond.

The meaning of this is that there is no actual activity that a wish-fulfilling jewel or a wish-fulfilling tree performs—it is not that they in fact practice generosity by magically creating all that is needed and desired according to whatever wishes someone may have. Nevertheless, the hopes of persons who intensely focus on such a wish-fulfilling jewel or a wish-fulfilling tree are fulfilled accordingly. In such a case, it is by virtue of the interaction of a wish-fulfilling jewel and a person focusing on it meeting that the performance of activity—the arising of all that is desired—appears. Likewise, it is through the power of (a) the pure mind streams of those to be guided, (b) the attainment of the permanent genuine entity of the Tathāgata, and (c) the full completion of the aspiration prayers of this Tathāgata (which entail the function of promoting the welfare of sentient beings) that it is not contradictory for the Tathāgata to be a permament entity and yet, from the perspective of those to be guided, to appear as the kāyas of the victor that arrive and leave, come and go, and so on. "But then it follows that it is not this permanent entity that performs the triad of agent, object, and action because what function as the support for the triad of agent, object, and action are the mere appearing aspects of what appears as said kāyas in the pure mind streams of those to be guided." This reason just perfectly proves our point here because the aspects of the kāyas of the victor are excellently cast by virtue of the dominant condition that is the profound natural outflow of the dharmadhātu which exists as the permanent entity of the Tathāgata.

Some people may continue, "But when something permanent casts an aspect, if it does so with activity, that contradicts its being permanent, and if it does so without activity, how could it cast an aspect?" The answer to this has two parts—the equal applicability of the reason to opposite cases and the actual answer. First, by the same token, it follows that a specifically characterized object does not cast an aspect toward consciousness either because, in its own timespan, a single and momentary specifically characterized object does not perform any activity in terms of an agent and what is acted upon. The entailment is accepted and the subject property is established through valid cognition. If these people say, "I accept," the following applies. When said momentary specifically characterized object casts an aspect, if it does so with activity, the position that the own timespan of this specifically characterized object is a partless moment is ruined because it possesses an activity that entails parts. That is, if this object casts its aspect with activity, for the very reason of this activity entailing parts it then follows that there are two moments in this object's own timespan of a single moment—its own time and the moment in which it casts its aspect. If that is accepted, the position of a specifically characterized phenomenon whose own timespan is momentary is ruined, so how would it cast an aspect? Also, if a specifically characterized object were to cast its aspect without any formational activity within its own timespan, the above objection by these people—that it is contradictory for something permanent to perform activity in terms of an agent and what is acted upon—applies to them as well.

The actual answer is as follows. An aspect is cast by the power of the existence of a cause that casts this aspect. However, as for a cause that casts an aspect, it can exist either permanently or impermanently. The first case is the ultimate existence that actually fulfills the function of existence, while the second one is just ostensible seeming existence. One may use reasonings such as "Something permanent does not cast an aspect—if it possesses activity, this contradicts being permanent," or "If something impermanent casts an aspect, how could it do so since it is something that has already ceased once it has arisen?" This means that, ultimately, the notion of an aspect being cast by anything—be it permanent or impermanent—cannot withstand analysis through reasoning. Nevertheless, the manner in which the permanent nature of phenomena casts aspects and the manner in which the impermanent bearers of this nature cast aspects should be understood through the principle of illusionlike profound dependent origination. This is how this should be understood according to what is said in the Madhyamaka system.

Furthermore, there is no need to panic about the statement, "It is contradictory for something permanent to perform activity." Though it is well known in dialectics that it is contradictory for activity to exist without an agent, this is not contradictory if analyzed through reasoning. As in the above example in the *Bodhicaryāvatāra*, someone may think, "I must pacify diseases such as leprosy through building a garuḍa pillar." By virtue of this thought, the thinker builds this pillar, and then the builder passes away. But even after a long time has elapsed, this pillar still performs the function of pacifying poison and so on. Likewise, through the profound view and conduct of learner bodhisattvas on the ten bhūmis, they accomplish the pillar that eventually becomes clearly perceptible as the victor's permanent genuine kāya free from obscurations. It is the rūpakāyas of the victor, which approximately concord with this pillar, that promote the welfare of sentient beings in terms of the triad of agent, object, and action, whereas the continua of the bodhisattvas who are the accomplishers of these kāyas of the victor have come to an end by their passing into complete nirvāṇa at the end of the continuum of the ten bhūmis. Nevertheless, by virtue of the pillar that has been accomplished by them remaining permanently, the promotion of the welfare of sentient beings is performed permanently too. Therefore, it is established that being permanent and activity are not contradictory.[364] Again, others may say, "This quote from the *Bodhicaryāvatāra* represents an explanation about acitivity being permanent, but its meaning is not that something permanent performs activity." However, then it just follows that permanent activity (the subject) does not perform activity because it is permanent. The reason is accepted, and the option of saying, "I accept" is excluded through the above claim.[365]

G) Training in the equality of saṃsāra and nirvāṇa[366]

This has four parts:

1) The nature of saṃsāra and nirvāṇa
2) The manner in which they are equal
3) The boundary lines of when this training is generated
4) Removing objections

1) The sūtras say:

> If prajñāpāramitā increases through familiarizing with it during daytime, it also increases through familiarizing with it during dreams. Why? Because these cannot be conceptualized as dreams and daytime.[367]

Here, the word "dream" refers to saṃsāra and "having awakened" or "daytime" means nirvāṇa. Just as the states of dream and being awake are distinguished through sleep, the difference between saṃsāra and nirvāṇa lies in being affected or not affected by ignorance. As for the saṃsāra and nirvāṇa taught here, the two Vimuktisenas, Ratnākaraśānti, and others hold them to be the antagonistic factors (conceptions) and remedial nonconceptual wisdom, respectively. The sūtras assert that saṃsāra consists of all kinds of mistaken appearances, while nirvāṇa is their nature—emptiness:

> This is mistaken appearance,
> Just as experiencing a dream.
>
> If you awake from the sleep of ignorant mistakenness,
> Saṃsāra is unobservable.
> Therefore, buddhahood means
> To not give rise to any mind about anything.

Or, in this context, Ratnakīrti identifies saṃsāra as the appearances that bear the aspects of the three realms and nirvāṇa, as perfect buddhahood.[368]

Saṃsāra appears as if one comes into this existence in any one among the three realms from one's last life under the sway of karma and then goes on from this life into some other existence within these realms. Nirvāṇa means the unconditioned state of being free from any aspects of the three realms—saṃsāric existence being at peace. In terms of the definitive meaning, saṃsāra is not established. It is not something permanent because that would be without the functions of saṃsāra. Nor is it something impermanent because what is momentarily impermanent is not something that can circle as saṃsāra—it is without coming and going. You may say, "There is no saṃsāra in any individual momentary impermanent phenomenon, but there is the saṃsāra that is an impermanent continuum." However since there is no continuum other than the individual moments, there is no saṃsāra that is an impermanent continuum either.

2) As for the manner in which saṃsāra and nirvāṇa are equal, Dölpopa Sherab Gyaltsen explains:

> The equality of existence and peace of abiding in the actuality of the nature of phenomena is stated in the *Mūlamadhyamakakārikā*:
>
> > Whatever is the limit of nirvāṇa,
> > That is the limit of saṃsāra.
> > There is not the slightest difference
> > Between these two, not even a subtle one.[369]
>
> The limit that is nirvāṇa and the true limit of saṃsāra are both of one taste as the nature of phenomena, great natural emptiness, and the perfect [nature]. Therefore, they are equality. In accordance with this, the Bhagavān said in the mantrayāna in the *Two Part [Hevajratantra]*:
>
> > This is the abode of buddhas,
> > Bodhisattvas, and vajra holders.
> >
> > This is what is called "saṃsāra"
> > And nothing but this is nirvāṇa.
> > Nirvāṇa will not be realized as something else
> > By relinquishing saṃsāra.[370]
>
> The abode in which all buddhas dwell is the dharmadhātu, which is called "ultimate existence and saṃsāra" because it is the prajñā of all aspects—the great being empty. Its nature is great nirvāṇa, but

> there is no nirvāṇa that is the relinquishment of what appears as the aspects that consist of the three existences. Such existence and peace are of one taste and therefore equality. Also, [the statements] in the mother [sūtras] such as "Forms are pure and thus results are pure" represent the same essential point as when it is said that everything is of the same single taste. Other explanations [about the equality of saṃsāra and nirvāṇa]—the seeming being equal to the ultimate, or saṃsāra and nirvāṇa being equal in that they are empty in the sense of extinction—are a far cry from the intention of the victor.

In my opinion, just like realizing that all phenomena are not established as entities (similar to dream appearances), saṃsāra is not established as the entity of saṃsāra and therefore not conceptualized as saṃsāra. Nor is nirvāṇa conceptualized as nirvāṇa since it is not established as a seeming entity. Saṃsāra and nirvāṇa are equal by virtue of being alike or equal in terms of nonconceptuality's own nature. The ending "-ity" in "equality" is added to indicate their nature when speaking of these aspects (what appear as saṃsāra and nirvāṇa). Or, from another point of view, from the perspective of an unmistaken subject, the object that is emptiness—peace in every respect—appears. From the perspective of a mistaken subject, the object that is saṃsāra—mistaken appearances—appears. Both of these objects are equal in that they appear by virtue of different subjects (as saṃsāra and nirvāṇa, respectively), but it is not that there are two different objects. Therefore, it is certain that this is the meaning of equality.

3) As for the boundary lines of when this training is generated: One cultivates the sheer training in the equality of saṃsāra and nirvāṇa from the level of heat of the path of preparation onward because one attained poised readiness for the dharma of nonarising. The actual training in equality appears in a mind stream on the eighth bhūmi. According to the *Vṛtti*, its fully complete form exists solely at the end of the continuum of the ten bhūmis.

4) Removing objections has four parts:

a) The sūtra passage about the consequence of there being no accumulation of karma

Śāriputra's question, "If all phenomena are said to be dreamlike, there is no accumulation or decrease of karma" is answered by saying, "If one thinks about it upon awakening, there will be accumulation or decrease of it."[371] This refers to the following qualm: "It follows that there is no accumulating of virtuous or nonvirtuous karmas because all phenomena are nothing but dreamlike." This is countered by the reply of the entailment being uncertain: "It is not the case that results are not experienced if actions are accumulated in dreams because it is explained that results arise if these actions are revived in one's mind after the dream."

b) The sūtra passage about the consequence that the Tathāgata needs to accumulate karma
The question, "Does then even the Tathāgata accumulate karma through producing thoughts at the time of awakening?" is answered by saying, "The Tathāgata is free from thoughts and conceptions." This refers to the following qualm: "It follows that even tathāgatas can accumulate karma because they mentally revive actions later." This is countered by saying that the subject property does not apply: "On the buddhabhūmi there is no cognition that revives actions. For meditative equipoise and subsequent attainment are not separate at this point and these very actions do not exist. The second reason applies because actions do not arise without focal objects. The reason applies because the mother sūtras teach that buddhas do not have any focal objects."

c) The sūtra passage about the consequence of contradicting the scriptures
The question, "If the Bhagavān says that all focal objects are empty, why would actions arise with a focal object?" is answered by saying, "One needs to focus on the very lack of focal objects . . ." This refers to the following qualm: "It follows that it is not tenable for karma to be accumulated even in a mind stream with focal objects because the Bhagavān said that all karmas and sentient beings are empty." If this statement is examined, the answer is to accept it. But according to common worldly consensus, the entailment is uncertain: "This statement by the Bhagavān was made in terms of those who are free from focal objects, but not in terms of those who entertain focal objects."

d) The sūtra passage about the consequence of accumulating karma in dreams
The question, "If, in a dream, bodhisattva mahāsattvas were to practice generosity . . . would this result in great enlightenment?" is answered by saying, "Śāriputra, as the mahāsattva Maitreya, who has experienced this face to face . . . is present, ask him." This refers to the following qualm: "It follows that actions are accumulated even in dreams because there are focal objects in dreams. The Bhagavān accepts the entailment, the subject property is established through direct perception, and if it is said, 'I accept,' this is eliminated through valid cognition." Ultimately, this is accepted. But in terms of the seeming, there is no entailment because the accumulation of actions in dreams exists. This is what Āryavimuktisena and Haribhadra assert,[372] but Dölpopa argues as follows:

> Here this answer of there being no entailment in terms of the seeming ("The accumulation of actions in dreams exists") is not pure. Noble Mañjuśrī says:

> Merit [comes] from benefiting sentient beings,
> And evil from harming sentient beings.
> For those without benefiting or harming,
> There are no actions and no results.

This explains that actions without any benefit or harm for others do not yield results, which means that there are no actions in dreams because there are no entities. As for [a dream action] yielding a result, if it is conceptualized after one has woken up, this refers to the mind of the waking time being the one that accumulates the action. Implicitly, this means that one is not able to accumulate actions in dreams because one is under the sway of sleep. As it is said:

> The dreaming mind is impaired by sleep.
> Therefore, the result is dissimilar.

This explains that there is a difference between actions during the waking state and actions in dreams in that they yield or do not yield results, respectively. Since [Haribhadra] explains the opposite of this here, he is wrong.

H) The meaning of "vanquishing māras"[373]

This has three parts:

1) The nature of the four māras
2) Their definite number
3) The boundary lines of vanquishing them

1) In general, the mere term "māra" refers to the obstacles for attaining the permanent state of enlightenment. (a) The māra of the skandhas refers to the five appropriating skandhas. (b) The māra of the afflictions consists of the afflictions that fetter in saṃsāra and the karmic actions motivated by them. Here, one needs to understand that the latencies of the afflictions in the mind streams of noble bodhisattvas are not presented as the māra of the afflictions because these are neither suitable as the motivational forces of the karmas that propel one into saṃsāric existence nor as what revives the karmas motivated by them. (c) The māra of death means to die under the sway of the karmas and afflictions that fetter in saṃsāra. (d) The devaputramāra is that which creates the obstacles for bringing together the roots of virtue in order to go beyond the other three māras just explained. The *Saddharmasmṛtyupasthānakārikā* says that the ruler of the gods who have power over others' emanations and his wife shoot five kinds of flower arrows at the beings of the desire realm, through which their minds become joined with the five kinds of sense pleasures. As

for what is metaphorically described here as having form, in terms of the definitive meaning what is symbolized by said flowers refers to certain factors that dwell in these beings' respective own mind streams—the three factors that make one faint, dull, and strive for desirable objects, as well as envy and miserliness. Malice and desirous attachment are symbolized by the evil māra and his wife, respectively, just as the māra who is the lord of death is symbolized by his messengers (for example, in *Bodhicaryāvatāra* II.42ab). To explain these afflictions that are symbolized by the five arrows and so on from the perspective of their self-isolates, they are not different from the māra of the afflictions, but it is the functions of these particular afflictions that are named "devaputramāra." The purpose of giving them this name lies in indicating that they only exist on the levels of the desire realm, but not in the two higher realms. In general, the reasons for labeling something with the name "māra" are that it creates obstacles or hindrances, blocks something, terminates certain causes, or makes one die. If one wishes for a detailed explanation of the term, one needs to do so by following the meaning of the Sanskrit.[374]

2) As for the definite number of four māras, that which dies refers to the five appropriating skandhas—the māra of the skandhas. That through which these die is the power of karma and afflictions—the māra of the afflictions. The nature of dying is that one's life-force comes to an end in an uncontrollable manner—the māra of death. That which creates obstacles to transcending death is to entertain desire for what is desirable—the devaputramāra. The *Vastusaṃgrahaṇī* explains that the māra of the lord of death, the devaputramāra, the māra of the afflictions, and the māra of the skandhas are presented in terms of creating hindrances to, by virtue of living for a long time, accomplishing many temporary special features and thus attaining the final fruitions of the nirvāṇas with and without remainder.[375]

3) According to the śrāvakas, the boundary lines of vanquishing these māras are as follows. When the inferior fruition of arhathood with remainder is manifested, three māras are vanquished. For the afflictions and their seeds have been relinquished and the devaputramāra is vanquished too because arhathood is preceded by the fruition of a nonreturner and thus is necessarily rendered free from attachment to the desire realm. As for the devaputramāra that consists of the manifest attachment for what is desirable, it can also be relinquished through mundane paths, but the relinquishment of the devaputramāra by way of rendering it into something that does not arise again only happens at the time of attaining the fruition of a nonreturner. Or those approaching nonreturners who have previously become free from attachment also have vanquished the devaputramāra. Some say, "The devaputramāra is vanquished from the śrāvaka path of seeing onward because the confidence

of trust in the three jewels is attained." The gist of the explanation that the clear realization of the three jewels arises is that it was given with the intention that one's realization on the path of seeing is indivisible through māra activity (such as making one faint). However, merely through this, one is not able to relinquish the devaputramāra because it does not make one free from desire for what is desirable. Some others assert, "When the highest level of the fourth samādhi is attained, one goes beyond the māra of death because one is able to bless the formations of one's lifespan." This appears to be a point to be examined. Once the nirvāṇa without remainder is attained, one goes beyond the manifest māra of the skandhas because the skandhas that are the karmic maturations propelled by karma and afflictions have come to an end. Though this is the case, the māra of the skandhas is already vanquished from the time of attaining the nirvāṇa with remainder onward. For, at that time, through the power of the remedies, the appropriating skandhas have been rendered into something that does not arise again in later lifetimes.

According to the mahāyāna, even if one has not gone through any of the inferior paths previously, all four māras are vanquished from the first bhūmi onward because the relinquishment of śrāvaka arhats is complete. At that point, as long as the skandhas that were propelled by one's previous karma and afflictions are not left behind, though they have been rendered into something through which subsequent sufferings of aging, sickness, and dying do not arise, it is not taught that one is free from the two māras of the skandhas and death that were propelled by one's previous karma and afflictions. Also, the devaputramāra is vanquished on the mahāyāna path of preparation because the clear realization of the three jewels is attained, and because it is possible for the uninterrupted path that relinquishes this māra to arise in such a mind stream. It is also taught, "The māra of the skandhas is vanquished starting from the eighth bhūmi of those who have not gone through any of the inferior paths previously because the ability to manifest the vimuktikāya is attained." However, this appears to be difficult. As for the "vimuktikāya," in the buddhakāya there are the two aspects of having relinquished the obscurations and of having completed the qualities. The *Uttaratantra* explains that, in terms of the first one, the buddhakāya is the vimuktikāya. As for the indicator of the ability to manifest this kāya from the eighth bhūmi onward, bodhisattvas are able to rest in meditative equipoise in the nature of phenomena at all times from this bhūmi onward. For this reason, it must be explained that there is the ability to manifest said kāya before the triad of completion, maturation, and purification has been completed. However, if one presents the māra of the skandhas as being relinquished merely through being able to manifest the vimuktikāya, then this ability to manifest the vimuktikāya would equally be able to relinquish the cognitive obscurations. Also, if the māra of the skandhas is not relinquished as long as the ability to manifest the vimuktikāya is not attained, it would follow that the skandha māra is not relinquished merely through attaining the śrāvaka nirvāṇa without remainder because the ability to manifest the vimuktikāya is not attained through that. Furthermore, according to the above position, one would have to assert the "māra of the skandhas" as the māra that obstructs the manifesting of the vimuktikāya. But in this case, it would follow that the vimuktikāya is manifested at the time of the inferior nirvāṇa without remainder because the māra of the skandhas has been vanquished.

Some other people say, "The vanquishing of all four māras without exception happens simultaneously with buddhahood." If this is said by having the impregnations of the negative tendencies of all four māras in mind, the boundary line for their relinquishment would be like that. However, it amounts to a very absurd flaw if these māras are identified as their respective impregnations of negative tendencies. Yet others say, "The afflictive obscurations that are latencies represent the māra of the afflictions, and the skandhas as the results that concord with the causes that are these latencies represent the māra of the skandhas." In terms of the inferior paths, this is not contradictory, but in terms of noble bodhisattvas, these two are not suitable as māras. A bodhisattva's afflictive obscurations that are latencies are not presented as a māra—they do not obstruct perfect enlightenment because they are its cause in that they are of the nature of the knowledge of the path. It may be that the boundary line of the relinquishment of the māra of the skandhas is identified in the above way by having in mind the inconceivable death and transition, when a body is assumed under the influence of the latent tendencies of ignorance. The *Uttaratantra* indeed teaches on this by using the term "māra of death," but this is not the actual māra of death because it is not the death as classified within the four māras. If it were the actual māra of death, then it would follow that both uncontaminated karma and the latent tendencies of ignorance are the māra of the afflictions and that the skandhas of a mental nature, which arise from these two, are also a māra. So what are they then? The buddhakāya is explained as permanent, stable, peaceful, and changeless. From among the reverse aspects of these four, the reverse aspect of changelessness is presented as "the māra of death," while the changeless kāya itself is presented as "the state of deathlessness." As *Uttaratantra* II.66cd says:

> For, in the attainment of deathless peace,
> The māra of death does not stir.

There is yet another assertion, saying, "Under the bodhi tree, the Bhagavān vanquished the devaputramāra at dusk. At dawn, through the vajralike samādhi, he vanquished the māra of the afflictions without exception. In Vaiśālī, he vanquished the māra of death because he blessed the formations of his lifespan for three months. In Kuśinagara, he vanquished the māra of the skandhas because he manifested the nirvāṇa without remainder." In this case, obviously, the devaputramāra and the māra of the afflictions were vanquished through the path of learning, while the māras of the skandhas and death were relinquished after having become a buddha.

In general, the manner of relinquishing the four māras and the identification of their natures is as described. However, in the *Vivṛti* here ("Through having gone beyond any phenomena that are obstacles . . ."),[376] this is presented in terms of relinquishing the impregnations of negative tendencies. For this is the context of explaining the manner in which the māras are vanquished on the buddhabhūmi.

5) The culminating training

A) The four conceptions to be relinquished on the path of seeing and their remedies[377]

1) General explanation

The conceptions about the apprehended that are factors to be relinquished through seeing by bodhisattvas are discussed in terms of (1) their objects; (2) their nature; (3) being taught as antagonistic factors of the path of seeing of bodhisattvas; (4) their division; and (5) the reason for presenting them as (mistaken) conceptions. (1) The objects of these conceptions are buddhahood and the hīnayāna nirvāṇa being taken as what are to be adopted and rejected, respectively. The manner of engagement for the sake of great enlightenment and the manner of withdrawal from the extreme of mere individual peace have the nature of nonreferentiality and referentiality, respectively. (2) The nature of these conceptions about the apprehended is thus to operate by way of adopting the dharmas of bodhisattvas (AA V.8–9) and rejecting those of śrāvakas and pratyekabuddhas (AA V.10–12). (3) One may think, "The mental states that focus on said dharmas and thus adopt or reject them, respectively, are not tenable as factors to be relinquished by bodhisattvas. For they engage in their objects in the correct way (adopting the dharmas of the mahāyāna and rejecting those of the hīnayāna)." However, these two kinds of conceptions about the apprehended are factors to be relinquished through seeing because they are imputational conceptions that engage in the basic nature, which is the only true object, in mistaken ways. In this way, these conceptions are just like afflictions. (4) By way of their objects, the conceptions about the apprehended in terms of engagement and withdrawal are divided into nine each. (5) The reason for presenting them as mistaken conceptions is that there are no real entities that serve as the natures of what appear as referents. Therefore, by virtue of these conceptions being completely unrelated to any such entities, but operating through sheer mistakenness, they appear in ways that deviate from true reality. Thus, both these conceptions of engagement and withdrawal should be understood as having the nature of focusing on what is not the ultimate object as it actually is.

The conceptions about the apprehender are treated under the same five points. (1) They have two distinct kinds of objects since they are based on the minds of ordinary beings apprehending persons as substantially existent, while the minds of noble ones apprehend persons as imputedly existent. (2) The nature of such mental states is to be conceptions of clinging to the apprehender since they cling to their objects as being substantially and imputedly existent, respectively. (3) They are antagonistic factors of the path of seeing because they obstruct the arising of the culminating training of the path of seeing. (4) Also, these conceptions are divided into nine each by way of their objects. (5) When analyzed by reasoning, the apprehended referents—the entities that serve as the objects—of these conceptions about the apprehender do not exist as having any nature in accordance with the ways in which they are apprehended by these conceptions. Thus, they are not actually apprehended by any such conceptions at all. For this reason, these conceptions about the apprehender lack the nature of apprehenders and therefore the basic nature appears to them in ways that are mistaken. Consequently, it should be understood that their nature is not to realize the ultimate object as it is—they are delusive.

In the AA, lines V.6ac teach which persons possess which type of these two conceptions about the apprehender, and the objects that they conceive in these ways are indicated as "sentient beings." What is explicitly taught here is that sentient beings are the objects of conceptions about substantial existence with regard to persons. What is implicitly taught is that sentient beings are the objects of conceptions about substantial existence with regard to phenomena—the bases that are imputed as persons. Furthermore, the two conceptions about the apprehender in this context definitely apply to ordinary beings and noble ones, respectively. On the meaning of this, earlier Tibetans say, "There are the two possibilities of conceptions in terms of the twofold apprehending of the substantial and imputed existence of objects or in terms of the twofold apprehending of the substantial and imputed existence of the subject (the conceptions). From among these, the two conceptions about the apprehender that are taught here are in terms of objects because this is the context of explaining the conceptions that are the factors to be relinquished through seeing. Otherwise, if said conceptions were explained in terms of the subject, there would be the flaw of the consequence that the conceptions of apprehending the subject as substantially existent, which exist in noble ones and are factors to be relinquished through familiarization, must be relinquished here on the path of seeing. Also since apprehending the subject (conceptions) as imputedly existent exists in ordinary beings too, it would follow that this must be relinquished here as well." These two consequences are simply unrelated to the matter at hand and are even refuted as the theses of opponents in Āryavimuktisena's *Vṛtti* and Haribhadra's *Ālokā*,[378] which quotes the respective passages from the *Vṛtti*. In brief, from a merely general perspective, they explain that ordinary beings' conceptions of apprehending imputed existence, such as thinking, "All phenomena are identityless," are mental engagements in terms of aspiration. But here, the question of having or lacking conceptions of apprehending imputed existence refers to ordinary beings lacking those conceptions of apprehending imputed existence that are mental enagements in terms of true reality. Therefore, only noble ones have the conceptions of apprehending imputed existence that are taught here. As for the conceptions of apprehending substantial existence, when noble ones make certain statements that may suggest that they too have such conceptions, they only make such statements in terms of sheer worldly conventions, but not by virtue of actually having such conceptions.

Some people may think, "Therefore, this statement by Āryavimuktisena and Haribhadra that ordinary beings lack conceptions of apprehending imputed existence and that noble ones lack conceptions of apprehending substantial existence is made in terms of conceptions about objects. But it is not a teaching on the conceptions about substantial and imputed existence in terms of conceptions about the subject definitely applying to ordinary beings and noble ones, respectively." This is not the case. For, in general, the presentation of conceptions about the apprehended (the object) is explained within the context of these conceptions about the apprehended themselves and not as the above people assert. Here, however, we deal with the explanation of the conceptions about the apprehender (the subject). Therefore, in this context, Āryavimuktisena and Haribhadra did not cast away the topic at hand, which consists of the conceptions about the apprehender (the subject). Furthermore, the issue of whether authoritative persons, in this context, have or have not given presentations of a division into the four conceptions about the apprehender by way of distinguishing between object and subject is difficult to analyze. Also, even if such presentations were given, from a mere general point of view one is able to present the following. From the perspective of both subject and object, both ordinary beings and noble ones definitely possess the two conceptions about substantial and imputed existence in their respective ways.

In this context here, to apprehend substantial existence refers to the conceptions that focus on the primary minds and mental factors of a person and cling to them as being substantially existent. As for the conceptions of apprehending imputed existence, though said minds and mental factors are not taken to exist as coarse substances, a person is imputed onto these sheer aspects of minds and mental factors and is conceived as existing to merely that extent. Among these latter conceptions, there are two types—the conceptions about the apprehender that apprehend, in an imputational manner, the bases for imputing a person as being phenomena and the conceptions about the apprehender that apprehend, in an imputational manner, what is imputed as being a person.

The outcome of this explanation is that the statement of the two conceptions about the apprehender here definitely applying to ordinary beings and noble ones, respectively, is only made in terms of the factors to be relinquished through seeing because this statement is made in terms of the context of explaining these very factors. It is made for the sake of realizing personal identitylessness because it is made primarily in terms of only the relinquishment of the conceptions of apprehending a person as substantially or imputedly existent. The noble ones do not have any conceptions of apprehending a person as substantially existent because they directly realize the lack of any substantial identity of a person. One may think, "But then the apprehending of substantial existence taught here would not be a cognitive obscuration that is a factor to be relinquished through the mahāyāna path of seeing alone. For śrāvaka noble ones have relinquished it too since they realize personal identitylessness." The śrāvaka noble ones' mere relinquishment of the conceptions of apprehending a person as substantially existent refers to their not apprehending the person that is the mere collection of the five skandhas as being substantially existent. Therefore, it is not from this perspective that said conceptions here are presented as being cognitive obscurations that are factors to be relinquished through the mahāyāna path of seeing alone. Rather, the difference is that it is the conceptions of apprehending each one of the five skandhas as substantially existent that are relinquished here in this context of the factors to be relinquished through seeing. Therefore, this is the reason for presenting the apprehensions of persons as substantially existent as being cognitive obscurations that are factors to be relinquished through seeing here. For example, through explicitly explaining that something like apprehending a person as independent and single and so on represents an apprehension of substantial existence and an afflictive obscuration, implicitly the apprehension of substantial existence that is a cognitive obscuration is taught. You may wonder what the purpose of such a teaching is. It is given because both the personal identity of apprehending the five skandhas as "me" and the imputed phenomenal identity of apprehending the skandhas as being really existent are relinquished simultaneously in this context of the mahāyāna here.

As for the conceptions of apprehending imputed existence that are discussed in this context, they do not exist in ordinary beings because they have not realized personal identitylessness. These conceptions do not exist in mahāyāna noble ones either. For they do not have any conceptions of apprehending real existence that would allow for imputing a person onto the skandhas since they attained the mahāyāna path of seeing. Therefore, the conceptions of apprehending imputed existence exist only in śrāvaka and pratyekabuddha noble ones because they realized personal identitylessness, but did not relinquish the apprehension of real existence that allows for imputing a person onto the skandhas. Furthermore, the conceptions of apprehending imputed existence that are mental engagements in true reality with regard to phenomena do not exist in a manifest form in either ordinary beings or noble ones. That they do not exist in ordinary beings is easy to understand. That they do not exist in śrāvaka and pratyekabuddha noble ones either is because they have not directly realized phenomenal identitylessness. In addition, the conceptions of apprehending imputed existence that are mental engagements in true reality with regard to persons also do not exist in these noble ones. Likewise, in mahāyāna noble ones, the manifest conceptions of apprehending imputed existence that are mental engagements in true reality with regard to phenomena do not exist either because they attained the mahāyāna path of seeing. Furthermore, the conceptions of apprehending phenomena as substantially or really existent that are factors to be relinquished through the mahāyāna path of seeing also exist in śrāvaka and pratyekabuddha noble ones because they still possess the apprehension that the bases of imputing a person—the skandhas—are really existent. "But didn't the paṇḍitas of old explain that śrāvaka and pratyekabuddha noble ones have relinquished the apprehension of persons as real substances? With this explanation, would they then not have relinquished the apprehension of a real existence of phenomena that allows for imputing a person onto the skandhas?" This is not the case. For though they have put an end to apprehending persons as substantially real, they did not put an end to apprehending as substantially real the phenomena that are the bases of imputing persons. This is just as in the case of the Vaibhāṣikas realizing that a coarse phenomenon (such as a vase) is not substantially existent, but not realizing that the individual particles of this vase are also not substantially existent. To give a further example, Āryadeva explains that pratyekabuddhas realize forms and sounds to not be really existent, but they do not realize forms and sounds to be identityless. Also, all the teachings that mahāyāna noble ones do not have any manifest apprehending of real existence and substantial existence are given with the intention of these noble ones having attained the path of seeing on which phenomenal identitylessness is seen directly.

In brief, the conceptions that are taught here—those of apprehending sentient beings as substantially existent and those of apprehending persons as imputedly existent refer to personal identities and phenomenal identities, respectively. Thus, some say, "It is obvious that it does not apply in this context to present all conceptions that are taught here as being cognitive obscurations. Atiśa's *Prajñāpāramitāpiṇḍārthapradīpa* says:

> Afflictive obscurations and cognitive obscurations,
> And some assert them as both.[379]

Thus, he says that the conceptions of apprehending substantial existence are presented as afflictive obscurations and the conceptions of apprehending imputed existence as cognitive obscurations. Or each one of them contains both portions of obscurations. The vajra of reasoning, Chaba Chökyi Sengé, accepts the conceptions of apprehending imputed existence as factors to be relinquished through seeing and then asserts that they exist in noble ones. This is the same as saying, 'My mother is a barren woman.'" The above is indeed said in terms of the factors to be relinquished through the mahāyāna path of seeing, but there is no contradiction here. The excellent explanations of Dagdéwa Sengé Gyaltsen[380] say that this is noncontradictory because the conceptions of apprehending imputed existence that exist in śrāvaka noble ones are explained as factors to be relinquished through the mahāyāna path of seeing.

2) Analysis of some difficult points

In general, all presentations of conceptions that are explained in the AA and its commentaries are divisions in terms of the conceptions that apprehend by conflating terms and their referents and the conceptions in this context here also refer to this type. These conceptions are not identified from the perspective of their afflictive elements, but primarily identified from the perspective of their nonafflictive elements. They are classified as twofold—conceptions about the apprehender and conceptions about the apprehended. For the objects of all conceptions are definite as these two—apprehender and apprehended—and thus conceptions conceive of these two. The conceptions whose objects are the apprehended are explained from the perspective of the conceptions that apprehend what is apprehended as phenomena and the conceptions whose objects are the apprehenders are explained from the perspective of the conceptions that apprehend these apprehenders as persons. Among the first, phenomena as the apprehended objects are not identified from the perspective of the class of afflicted phenomena, but from the perspective of the class of purified phenomena, which are twofold—those of the mahāyāna and those of the hīnayāna. It is from these two objective supports that the two conceptions about the apprehended in terms of engagement and withdrawal, respectively, derive. As for the conceptions whose objects are the apprehenders, they can be divided into two in terms of afflicted and purified phenomena, and there are conceptions that apprehend in this way. Here, however, they are not divided in this way, but the conceptions about the apprehender are classified as two by way of dividing them in terms of persons and the phenomena that are the bases of imputing persons.

Thus, the presentation of the conventional terms of the four conceptions—the two conceptions about the apprehended in terms of engagement and withdrawal and the two conceptions about the apprehender in terms of apprehending persons and individuals as substantially and imputedly existent, respectively—is made in terms of the factors to be relinquished through seeing. However, these conventional terms are not used for the conceptions that are the factors to be relinquished through familiarization. For, in the latter context, engagement and withdrawal as in the context of the path of seeing through dividing the objects of the conceptions about the apprehended into those of the mahāyāna and those of the hīnayāna do not clearly appear in the sūtras. Also, the difference between the conventional terms of the two kinds of conceptions about the apprehender in the context of the path of familiarization is explained as being based on the noble ones imputing persons and the causes for such imputations, respectively, but not through the conventional term "substantial existence." It is also not suitable to explain them in such a way. For if the first kind of the conceptions about the apprehender that are factors to be relinquished through familiarization were to be explained as an apprehension of substantial existence, it would be an apprehension of real existence. However, if it is explained like that, it would follow that there is no first kind of the conceptions about the apprehender that are factors to be relinquished through familiarization because the conceptions that apprehend persons as substantially existent have already been rendered into something that does not arise again from the mahāyāna path of seeing onward, just as the conceptions of apprehending any personal identity. You may wonder, "So which are the conventional terms that are applied to the four conceptions that are factors to be relinquished through familiarization?" Āryavimuktisena and Haribhadra apply the conventional terms of the two conceptions about the apprehended that are based on (a) mere entities and (b) purified phenomena, respectively, and the two conceptions about the apprehender that cling to (a) persons as being mere imputations and to (b) the causes for imputing such persons as likewise being mere imputations. The differences in terms of the boundaries for applying these conventional terms is implied in this.

Furthermore, in general, all the many conceptions that there are can be divided into two—states of mind of clinging to real existence and states of mind of clinging to the lack of real existence. The conceptions of clinging to real existence are again twofold—imputational and innate. The first are exclusively factors to be relinquished through seeing and the latter are exclusively factors to be relinquished through familiarization. In the conceptions of clinging to the lack of real existence, there is no imputational element because such does not exist without being imputed through philosophical systems. However, absolute insistence that, for this reason, the conceptions that are factors to be relinquished through familiarization are necessarily innate is not warranted either, as is illustrated by the imputational state of mind of clinging to characteristics with regard to emptiness, which exists in the mind streams of bodhisattvas on the path of familiarization. You may wonder, "So is it definite that the instances of the innate clinging to real existence are exclusively factors to be relinquished through familiarization? And if that is definite, do they occur in the mind streams of mahāyāna noble ones?" The instances of the innate clinging to real existence are exclusively factors to be relinquished through familiarization and they do not occur in the mind streams of mahāyāna noble ones because these have directly realized that all phenomena lack real existence. "But then it follows that the innate clinging to real existence represents a factor to be relinquished through seeing." This does not follow because to render the innate clinging to real existence into something that does not arise anymore depends exclusively on the path of familiarization. Therefore, though said clinging has not been relinquished on the path of seeing, it does not become manifest on the path of familiarization. This is just as in the case of the conceptions of apprehending imputed existence that are mental engagements in true reality with regard to phenomena—they have not been rendered into something that does not arise anymore on the path of seeing, but do not become manifest on the path of familiarization.[381]

Also, this explanation that conceptions about substantial existence exist in ordinary beings and that conceptions about imputed existence exist in noble ones is an explanation that these must exist in the mind stream of a single psychophysical support in a progressive manner in terms of this support representing a mahāyāna ordinary being or noble one, respectively. It may be said, "But isn't it explained that the conceptions of apprehending imputed existence that are taught here exist in the mind streams of śrāvaka noble ones? For Ratnākaraśānti's *Śuddhamatī* explains:

> The second conception about the apprehender, which is based on sentient beings existing in an imputational manner, is the one of the noble ones because śrāvakas and pratyekabuddhas have not relinquished it."[382]

He indeed explains it in this way, but to do so refers to the conceptions of apprehending imputed existence that exist in the mind streams of śrāvaka and pratyekabuddha noble ones being close to arising in the mind streams of mahāyāna noble ones. Therefore, it is in order to render these conceptions into something that does not arise anymore that he explains the presentation of the factors to be relinquished and their remedies in terms of the conceptions of apprehending imputed existence here. Thus, the mind streams of śrāvaka arhats are endowed with apprehending phenomena as substantially real and with the conceptions of apprehending imputed existence that are mental engagements in true reality with regard to persons. When they enter the mahāyāna path of seeing, they must relinquish said conceptions about substantial and imputed existence (which are factors to be relinquished) through the remedies that are taught in this section here. For these conceptions must be relinquished and the AA and its commentaries do not teach any remedies other than these here that would serve to relinquish said conceptions.

The outcome of this explanation is that conceptions about substantial existence are presented as being present only in the psychophysical supports of mahāyāna ordinary beings because they are not supported by the mind streams of mahāyāna noble ones. For mahāyāna noble ones have directly realized the lack of real existence and therefore an occasion of some manifest apprehension of real existence occuring in them is absolutely impossible. As for conceptions of apprehending imputed existence, they are presented as being supported by the mind streams of mahāyāna noble ones alone because these conceptions are entertained in terms of the mental engagements in true reality. Consequently, it is contradictory for them to be supported by the mind streams of mahāyāna ordinary beings. You may think, "It is not reasonable for the conceptions of apprehending imputed existence that are mental engagements in true reality and represent factors to be relinquished through seeing to exist in mahāyāna noble ones because they have already been relinquished from the attainment of the mahāyāna path of seeing onward." There is no flaw. In the mind streams of mahāyāna noble ones, the conceptions of apprehending imputed existence have been rendered into something that does not arise anymore and therefore it is impossible for them to arise in the mind streams of these noble ones. However, under the hypothetical assumption of such an arising being possible at all, it is necessarily an arising in the mind streams of noble persons alone because such a conception of apprehending imputed existence must be a conception that is induced by the prajñā of directly realizing the lack of real existence. Thus, it is definite that, when conceptions of apprehending imputed existence arise, they arise in the psychophysical supports of noble ones, but not in the supports of ordinary beings.

3) The remedies of the four conceptions

The remedies that eliminate these conceptions are only taught implicitly in the AA. According to AA I.14d ("four kinds of remedy") as well as the *Ālokā* and the *Vivṛti* on V.7–16, these four sets of nine conceptions correspond to four sets of nine remedies. With the path of seeing being divided into the preparation and the actual part, the preparatory stage does not explicitly appear in the AA. However, both Abhayākaragupta's *Marmakaumudī* and the author of the *Abhidharmakośaṭīkā*[383] refer to the wisdom of the great degree of the supreme mundane dharma as the preparatory stage in this context. You may think, "Then it follows that the preparatory stage of the path of seeing is not a remedy for the factors to be relinquished through seeing because it is the remedy for the factors to be relinquished through the supreme dharma of the path of preparation." There is no such flaw—to be the remedy for the factors to be relinquished through seeing is presented as such from the perspective of being the remedy for the seeds that are to be relinquished through seeing, while the preparation is presented in terms of merely relinquishing the manifest forms of the factors to be relinquished through seeing. The remedy for the factors to be relinquished through seeing that has the nature of such a preparation appears at the time of the supreme dharma of the path of preparation. Since it eliminates the manifest factors that obstruct the direct arising of the wisdom of the path of seeing, this excludes said preparatory stage of the path of seeing not being included in the path of seeing.

The explanation of the four conceptions being gradually relinquished through the four levels of the path of preparation is referred to by the conventional terminology of their "being relinquished in the manner of suppressing the four manifest forms of these conceptions." In particular, when the lesser degree of the supreme dharma has arisen, the four conceptions in their manifest form are subdued, which means that they are rendered into a form that still retains a certain potency. At the time of the arising of the medium supreme dharma, the first two conceptions that retain a certain potency are in the process of being canceled out by being relinquished gradually. When the great degree of the supreme dharma arises, the first two conceptions that retain a certain potency have ceased, while the latter two conceptions that retain a certain potency are in the process of being canceled out by being relinquished gradually. Once the wisdom of the actual path of seeing—the uninterrupted path—arises, the latter two conceptions that retain a certain potency cease, which happens simultaneously with the actual relinquishment of the seeds of all four conceptions. This is a good explanation that has not appeared clearly ever before.

B) Enlightenment[384]

In general, the mahāyāna and hīnayāna agree in asserting that the nature of enlightenment is the wisdom of knowing that the stains to be relinquished are terminated and do not arise again (the reality of cessation). However, the part about which they disagree is as follows. The śrāvakas explain that "great enlightenment" refers to the prajñā that realizes the lack of a personal self having terminated the stains of ignorance—which are the opposite of this prajñā, the subject of this self, not empty of a nature of their own, and previously existent—and rendered them into something that does not arise anymore later. The followers of the mahāyāna say that, through the power of having familiarized with the prajñā of realizing that the stains are empty of a nature of their own, these stains are rendered into something that does not arise anymore even on the level of the seeming, which is called, "realizing them to be without arising." For this reason, the realization that these very stains are without termination is called "great enlightenment." The manner of establishing this great enlightenment through scriptures and reasoning is taught below.

As for the meaning of there being no phenomena except for the dharmadhātu (as it is presented in the scriptures),[385] the False Aspectarians who propound other-emptiness explain that the dharmadhātu must necessarily exist as not being empty of its own nature. For it is ultimate reality, and the reference points of apprehender and apprehended, by virtue of being mistakenness, are empty of a nature of their own and thus do not exist. Due to this explanation, what exists is nondual wisdom alone because it is explained to never abide in any way that is opposite to its own basic true nature. The Niḥsvabhāvavādins who propound self-emptiness say that any phenomena that are mere appearances must be dependently originating. Whatever is dependently originating must not be established by a nature of its own, and whatever is not established by a nature of its own is necessarily free from the extremes of reference points. This freedom from reference points is the dharmatādhātu of the noble ones. It should be understood that there are no phenomena (such as adventitious stains) in any respect that are other than the dhātu which consists of being liberated from any clinging to extremes (such as the Yogācāras saying that this dhātu must exist and so on). If this is understood, it means that, precisely because the obscuring stains do not exist, these stains are suitable to be relinquished. But if the obscuring stains actually existed, they would not be suitable to be relinquished. Thus, it is established that the existence of stains and their relinquishment are contradictory.

Explained in this way, enlightenment in terms of the object is natural purity and enlightenment in terms of the subject is the wisdom of being pure of what is adventitious. As for the first one among these two since all phenomena (such as stains) are naturally pure, the termination of stains, their not arising again, and so on are mere names—they are equivalent to the natural nirvāṇa because they never existed in the first place. The second one refers to the nature of realization on the conventional level—wisdom having eliminated the adventitious stains through directly realizing enlightenment, with its own nature being nothing other than the nonabiding nirvāṇa. As *Mahāyānasūtrālaṃkāra* XXI.58ab says, this enlightenment can be divided into the three kāyas:

> Through the three kāyas you attained
> Great enlightenment in every respect.

Here, there is no disagreement that the svābhāvikakāya is great enlightenment. As for the sāmbhogikakāya and the nairmāṇikakāya, in terms of their actual way of being, there is no dispute as to whether they represent or do not represent enlightenment since the defining characteristics of enlightenment are complete in them. However, in terms of the way in which these two kāyas appear, they are not suitable as actual enlightenment since their way of appearing is something that is contained in the mind streams of sentient beings. Nevertheless, despite this being the case, within their own scope of presumption, those to be guided presume that these two kāyas in their manner of appearing are great enlightenment, just as they presume that a reflection of Indra is the actual Indra.

As for the two inferior kinds of enlightenment of śrāvakas and pratyekabuddhas, the enlightenment of the first ones in terms of the object is as follows. By virtue of the self, which is imputed through the conceptions of clinging to the person as being a self, not existing by nature, the dhātu of consciousness is naturally pure of a personal self. Enlightenment in terms of the subject is the wisdom of being liberated from adventitious afflictions and directly realizing that the dhātu of consciousness is pure of said personal self. As for the enlightenment of pratyekabuddhas, in terms of the object, it is the mere dhātu of cognizance empty of apprehender and apprehended being different. In terms of the subject, it is the wisdom that, through having directly realized this dhātu of cognizance, is liberated from the cognitive obscurations that are the conceptions about the apprehended.

C) The five great reasonings[386]

1) The reasoning of the freedom from unity and multiplicity

a) Formulating the reason

You may wonder how it is realized that the adventitious stains, which consist of apprehender and apprehended, lack real existence. *Pramāṇavārttika* III.360 says:

> Once the entities [of apprehender and apprehended] are analyzed
> by this,
> In true reality, their nature does not exist,
> Because they do not have a nature
> Of unity or multiplicity.

Accordingly, if the adventitious stains are analyzed, they do not exist as real entities because they are free from being a real unity and multiplicity.

b) Proving the subject property

As for the first part of the reason (there being no real unity), some say that phenomena exist as unities by adducing reasons in terms of either coarse phenomena, continua, or minute particles and moments. For example, non-Buddhists say that coarse phenomena are real as partless unities. But they are not real in this way because coarse phenomena have many parts, such as moving versus unmoving, covered versus uncovered, and changing color versus not changing color. *Pramāṇavārttika* I.84–86a says:

> If a hand and so on moves, then the entire [body]
> Would move; because of this and because
> Contradictory actions are unsuitable in what is single,
> It is established otherwise—that [the body has] different [parts].
>
> If one [part] is covered, then all
> Would be covered, or if it is uncovered,
> [All] would be seen. If one [part] is colored,[387]
> [All] would be colored, or it would be cognized as uncolored.
>
> Therefore, a collection does not exist as a unity.

The śrāvakas, such as the Vaibhāṣikas, say, "Since phenomena in the three times are substantially established, they are real as partless single continua." They are not because for eons, years, months, days, moments, and so on, it is necessarily the case that the respective former ones are established through many of the respective latter ones having accumulated. But in themselves, continua and such are nothing but designational imputations, as Śāntideva's *Bodhicaryāvatāra* VIII.101ab says:

> What are called "continuum" and "collection"
> Are delusive, just as a rosary, an army, and so on.

The Sautrāntikas say, "Minute particles are real as partless single unities." They are not—when larger objects are formed by such particles, other particles must join a middle particle either by way of its having six sides (front, back, left, right, top, and bottom) or by way of its only having a single side. In the first case, the thesis of this particle being partless is ruined since it has six parts. In the second case, it would be impossible for larger objects to be formed because nothing other than and beyond the space that a single such particle occupies can be formed. As the second omniscient one, Vasubandhu, says in verse 12 of his *Viṃśatikākārikā*:

> By virtue of six joined together,
> The minute particle would have six parts.
> If the six occupied a single location,
> Their conglomeration would only be a [single] particle.

The Vijñaptivādins say, "Consciousness is real as momentary single unities." It is not because it has many fractions in terms of time. The question here is whether such a momentary entity's meeting the previous moment when it arises, its own abiding, and its meeting the following moment when it ceases are one or different. In the first case, these three do not exist as what produce and what are produced (cause and result) because they are the same in time. In the second case, the thesis of consciousness being real as a single unity is ruined. *Ratnāvalī* I.69 says:

> Just as [examining] whether a moment has an end,
> Examine its beginning and middle.
> Since it has the nature of three moments,
> The world does not abide for a moment.

Furthermore, all entities (such as adventitious stains) have the properties of being conditioned and deceiving, and what is deceiving is necessarily delusive. *Mūlamadhyamakakārikā* XXV.5 and XIII.1cd say:

If nirvāṇa were an entity,
Nirvāṇa would be conditioned.
No unconditioned entity
Whatsoever exists anywhere.
. . .
All formations are deceiving phenomena—
Therefore, they are delusive.

As for the second part of the reason in the reasoning of the freedom from unity and multiplicity if there is no real unity, there is no multiplicity either because multiplicity depends on the accumulation of unities.

c) Proving the entailment
If adventitious stains do not exist as either a unity or a multiplicity, these stains necessarily do not exist as real entities because unity and multiplicity are mutually exclusive and there is no third alternative. Verses 61–62 of mahāpaṇḍita Śāntarakṣita's *Madhyamakālaṃkāra* say:

Any entities that are analyzed
Are without any unity.
Whatever is without unity
Also lacks multiplicity.

Entities with any aspects other
Than just unity and multiplicity
Are not feasible because these two
Exist in a mutually exclusive way.

2) The reasoning that negates arising from the four extremes[388]

a) Formulating the reason
Ultimately since all phenomena are without arising, how could the stains be real? *Mūlamadhyamakakārikā* I.1 says:

Not from themselves, not from something other,
Not from both, and not without a cause—
At any place and any time,
All entities lack arising.

b) Proving the subject property
If the stains were arising, one would have to adduce any of the reasons of them either arising from themselves, from something other, from both, or

without a cause. However, they do not arise from themselves—if something is already established, it need not be produced again, and if it is not established, it cannot produce itself. *Mūlamadhyamakakārikā* VII.13 says:

> Since what arises is unarisen,
> How could it give rise to itself?
> But if it is produced through having arisen,
> With it having arisen, what is there to produce?

Phenomena do not arise from something other either. For if they were to arise from something else that has ceased, it would follow that they are without cause, but if they arise from something that has not ceased yet, cause and result would be simultaneous. *Mūlamadhyamakakārikā* XX.10 says:

> How could what has ceased and vanished
> Give rise to an arisen result?
> How could it be produced through a cause
> That abides joined with its result?

Phenomena also do not arise from something that is in the process of ceasing. If such is claimed from the perspective of the cause being partially ceased and partially unceased, such assumed production through ceased and unceased portions entails the above two flaws, respectively. There is no third alternative either—Āryadeva's *Catuḥśataka* XV.15ab says:

> Since what is in the process of arising is [only] half-arisen,
> What is in the process of arising is not arising.

Mūlamadhyamakakārikā II.1cd says:

> Apart from having moved and not having moved,
> Moving is not perceived.

Phenomena do not arise from both themselves and something other either—if there is no arising from either of these possibilities, how could there be any arising from both? This would be like being multicolored without blue and all the other colors.

Nor do phenomena arise without a cause—they would not be intermittent since they were as *Pramāṇavārttika* I.35ab says:

> Since what is without cause depends on nothing else,
> It would always either exist or not exist.

c) Proving the entailment

Therefore since all phenomena are without arising, how could the stains abide or cease? If there is no abiding and ceasing, there are no entities and conditioned phenomena. If these do not exist, nonentities, unconditioned phenomena, and so on, being mutually dependent just like parents and children, are also just nominal conventional terms. Therefore, how could the stains be real? *Mūlamadhyamakakārikā* VII.22d, 26d, and 33 say:

> What nonarisen could abide?
> . . .
> What nonarisen could cease?
> . . .
> Since arising, abiding, and ceasing
> Are not established, there are no conditioned phenomena.
> Since conditioned phenomena are not established,
> How could unconditioned phenomena be established?

Consequently, in the fundamental nature of the seeming, there is not even an atom of real entities and all phenomena are nothing but not being established as anything whatsoever.

3) The reasoning that negates an arising of existents and nonexistents

The stains are not really arisen because they are free from any arising of existents and nonexistents. *Mūlamadhyamakakārikā* I.6 says:

> For either existent or nonexistent referents
> Conditions are not suitable—
> If something does not exist, of what would they be conditions?
> If something exists [already], what are conditions good for?

4) The reasoning that negates arising from the four possibilities

The stains are without real arising because they do not arise by virtue of refuting the four possibilities, such as many causes producing a single result. Verse 14 of the *Satyadvayavibhāga* says:

> Many do not produce a single entity,
> Many do not produce many,
> A single one does not produce many entities,
> And a single one does not produce a single one either.

Therefore, the cognitions and their objects whose nature it is to be adventitious stains and so on do not even exist as some mere seeming reality. *Madhyamakāvatāra* VI.36cd says:

> Any arising from itself and something other is not reasonable—
> Through this reasoning, [arising] is not even reasonable
> conventionally.[389]

5) The reasoning of dependent origination

The stains are empty of being real entities because they are mere dependent origination. *Mūlamadhyamakakārikā* XXIV.19 says:

> There is no phenomenon
> That is not dependent origination.
> Therefore, there is no phenomenon
> That is not empty.[390]

D) The four stages of yoga[391]

This has three parts:

1) The purpose of presenting the four stages of yoga here
2) Explaining the meanings of each one of these stages of yoga
3) JNS's comments on the *Vivṛti* on the four stages of yoga

1) The purpose of presenting the four stages of yoga here

You may wonder, "How is the teaching on the four stages of yoga related to this context of AA V.20 demonstrating that the position of Buddhist realists is internally contradictory?" The four stages of yoga are presented here by Haribhadra in order to teach the following. If enlightenment is untenable for the faction of Buddhist tīrthikas who assert merely the afflictive obscurations as being really established, it is then equally untenable for all factions up through the Mere Mentalists because they assert knowable objects as being really established. The teaching on the four stages of yoga is an instruction on the manner in which the beings to be guided gradually engage in the mahāyāna path. In the beginning, in order to turn these beings away from non-Buddhist views and make them suitable vessels for teaching phenomenal identitylessness, the first stage of familiarizing with there being no self in the person is in common with the śrāvakas. Then, as for familiarizing with phenomenal identitylessness, there is a progression in terms of increasing subtlety. First, to familiarize with the lack of real existence of outer referents is in common with the pratyekabuddhas and the Real Aspectarian Mere Mentalists. Second, to familiarize with the lack of real existence of the cognitive aspects that are the apprehenders of such (nonexistent) referents is in common with the False Aspectarian Mere Mentalists. Finally, to familiarize with the lack of real existence of an ultimately existent consciousness that is empty of the duality of apprehender and apprehended is the unique position of the Yogācāra-Mādhyamikas.

You may wonder how this progression arises in the mind stream. On the mahāyāna path of accumulation, one uses the reason of the skandhas entailing arising and ceasing, saying, "The appropriating skandhas are not permanent, single, and independent,[392] because they arise and cease." Through the reasoning that arises from the reflection which is induced by that reason, one familiarizes with the appropriating skandhas lacking a self and, based on that, relinquishes the clinging to a personal self. On either one of the levels of heat or peak on the mahāyāna path of preparation, one uses the reason of invariable co-observation, saying, "What appears as blue and the cognition for which blue appears are not different in substance, despite their appearing that way, because they are invariably observed together." Through the reasoning that arises from the reflection which is induced by that reason, one familiarizes with the apprehended being nothing apart from said two aspects (what appears as blue and the cognition for which blue appears) and, based on that, relinquishes the cognitive obscurations that are the conceptions about the apprehended. On either one of the levels of poised readiness or supreme dharma on the mahāyāna path of preparation, one uses the reason of outer referents not really existing, saying, "The aspects that appear as outer referents are not real as the substance of cognition because they do not exist as they appear in all their various forms." Through the reasoning that arises from the reflection which is induced by that reason, one familiarizes with the aspects that appear in said manner as not being real as mind and, based on that, relinquishes the clinging to the apprehended aspects, which appear as if outside, being real as the substance of consciousness.[393] On the mahāyāna path of seeing, one uses the reason of dependent origination, saying, "Self-aware self-luminous consciousness without the duality of apprehender and apprehended does not really exist because it is dependent origination." Through the reasoning that arises from the reflection which is induced by that reason, one familiarizes with this kind of consciousness not really existing either and, based on that, relinquishes the seeds of the cognitive obscurations.[394]

2) Explaining the meanings of each one of these stages of yoga

This has four parts:

a) Explaining the yoga of realizing the nonexistence of a self (the stage of the śrāvakas)
b) Explaining the yoga of realizing the nonexistence of the apprehended (the stage of the pratyekabuddhas)
c) Explaining the yoga of realizing the nonexistence of the apprehender (the stage of the view asserted by the Mere Mentalists)
d) Explaining the yoga of realizing the freedom from reference points (the stage of the view asserted by the Mādhyamikas)

2a) Explaining the yoga of realizing the nonexistence of a self (the stage of the śrāvakas)
This has two parts:

a) Identifying that onto which the self is superimposed
b) Proving that the self does not exist

2aa) Identifying that onto which the self is superimposed
This has two parts:

1) The manner of superimposing
2) The basis of imputation

2aa1) The manner of superimposing a personal self is twofold—the permanent, single, and independent one that is superimposed by the tīrthikas and the inexpressible one that is superimposed by the faction of the Vātsīputrīyas.[395] Candrakīrti's *Madhyamakāvatāra* VI.121 and VI.146 say:

> The tīrthikas impute a self that has an eternal nature, is not an agent,
> Is the experiencer, without qualities, and inactive.
> The differentiations in the systems of the tīrthikas
> Occurred based on minor divisions [of this self].
> . . .
> Some assert a substantially existent person that is inexpressible
> As either the same as or different [from the skandhas], permanent or impermanent, and so on.
> They hold it to be an object known by the sixth consciousness
> And assert that it is the basis of the clinging to an "I."

2aa2) This self is imputed onto the skandhas. *Mahāyānasūtrālaṃkāra* XVIII.92ab says:

> The person is to be described
> As imputedly existent, but not as substantially.

2ab) The probative argument that proves the nonexistence of such a self is the one stated above ("The appropriating skandhas are not permanent, single, and independent because they arise and cease").

2b) Explaining the yoga of realizing the nonexistence of the apprehended (the stage of the pratyekabuddhas)

This consists of the detailed explanation of the reasoning of invariable co-observation, which has two parts:

a) Formulating the reason
b) Identifying the subject, the predicate, and the reason

2ba) Formulating the reason
This has two parts:

1) Refuting what others say
2) Presenting the meaning of our own assertion

2ba1) Some present this reasoning as follows: "Blue and the apprehender of blue do not really exist as different substances because they are invariably observed together." However, these two are different in substance because they are cause and result (what produces and what is produced by it). If it is said that the reason does not apply to the subject, the result of valid cognition as per the Sautrāntikas appears in *Pramāṇavārttika* III.352bd:

> The cause for consciousness appearing in this way
> Is the referent—therefore,
> The referent is asserted to be what is assessed.

Therefore, phenomena that exist as what produces and what is produced by it are necessarily causes and results, respectively, just as fire and smoke. If that is accepted, it follows that apprehender and apprehended are not invariably observed together because they are different in nature. The reason entails the predicate because the *Pramāṇaviniścaya* says:

> This is untenable for what is different in nature . . .[396]

Here, "this" refers to invariable co-observation. If this is accepted, the thesis that blue and the apprehender of blue are invariably observed together is ruined.

2ba2) The correct formulation of this reasoning is as follows: "The aspect of blue and the mind that apprehends it are not real as different substances because, from the perspective of the single substance of mind, apprehender and apprehended are invariably observed together as inseparable, just like the aspect of falling hairs and the cognition of someone with blurred vision that apprehends such an aspect." This reasoning represents the system of those who propound mind as entailing aspects, which explains that there is no outer referent of blue at the time of such a perception, but that the causes of casting the aspect of blue consist of latent tendencies.

2bb) Identifying the subject, the predicate, and the reason
This has three parts:
1) The meaning of the subject
2) The meaning of the predicate
3) The meaning of the reason

2bb1) The subject consists of the aspect of blue and the mind that apprehends it. The *Pramāṇaviniścaya* says:

> What are invariably [co-observed] are the two that consist of the aspect of blue and awareness.[397]

Or it is also suitable to present the aspect of blue alone as the subject because this is in the context of refuting that this aspect of blue is something other than the cognition that apprehends blue.

2bb2) The predicate is the mere refutation of these two (the aspect and the mind that apprehends it) being real as different substances.

2bb3) The meaning of the reason has two parts:
a) The actual meaning
b) Removing objections

2bb3a) The actual meaning has three parts:
a) Identifying the nature of the reason (the instance of the reason at hand)
b) Proving the subject property and the entailment (the definition of the reason)
c) Identifying the type of reason (the definiendum of the reason)

2bb3aa) In the term "invariable co-observation," "co-" means at the same time; "observation" refers to clearly cognizing; and "invariable" means by necessity. Thus, the instance of the reason at hand refers to it being necessarily the case that apprehender and apprehended are invariably cognized or experienced by a single mental substance at the same time. The *Pramāṇaviniścaya* says:

> If one aspect among these two is not observed, there is no observation of the other.[398]

This means refuting a situation such as observing the aspect that represents the apprehended and yet not observing the apprehender.

2bb3ab) As for proving the subject property, by virtue of self-aware perception directly observing the cognition that apprehends an aspect of blue, this aspect of blue is necessarily observed as a matter of course. Also, by virtue of observing the aspect of blue as a matter of course, the cognition that apprehends this aspect of blue is necessarily observed directly. By way of establishing this, the reason applies to the subject.

As for proving the entailment, if apprehender and apprehended (the subject) are different in substance, they cannot be observed together in an invariable manner because there is no connection between apprehender and apprehended, just as in the case of blue and yellow. The *Pramāṇaviniścaya* says:

> This is untenable for what is different in nature because there is no reason for being connected.[399]

Thus, based on the *Pramāṇaviniścaya*'s example of the aspect of two moons appearing for someone with blurred vision, the invariable co-observation of certain aspects and the cognitions that apprehend them is established through valid cognition.[400] Here, it is certain that being and not being real as different substances are directly contradictory. Thus, through refuting with the reason at hand (2bb3aa) that apprehender and apprehended are real as different substances, the entailment of their not being real as different substances is established.

2bb3ac) The type of this reason is a reason of nonobservation, in which an instance that is contradictory in nature is observed.[401]

2bb3b) Removing objections has three parts in terms of the reason
a) not applying to the subject
b) being uncertain
c) being contradictory.

2bb3ba) Some people may say, "It follows that blue and the apprehender of blue are not simultaneous because they are cause and result. If that is accepted, it follows that they are not invariably observed together." Here, the question is whether these people bring up this consequence in terms of a philosophical system that accepts the existence of outer referents. Within the context of such a philosophical system I can only accept their consequence as true. However since I am someone who says that outer referents do not exist, I answer that a blue that is an outer referent does not qualify as the one part of the twofold subject in question here. Also, in the above consequence by these people, the reason does not apply to the subject because the aspect of blue and the cognition that apprehends blue are of the same nature, which is stated in the *Pramāṇaviniścaya*:

> An appearance of blue and so on and the awareness of that are established as not being different.[402]

2bb3bb) Removing objections in terms of the reason being uncertain has three parts:

1) Relinquishing uncertainty in terms of the mind streams of those to be guided and buddha wisdom
2) Relinquishing uncertainty in terms of primary minds and mental factors
3) Relinquishing uncertainty in terms of forms and light

2bb3bb1) Some people may say, "The reason of invariable co-observation is uncertain as to proving that two phenomena are not different substances because the mind streams of those to be guided and the wisdom of a buddha are different in substance, while the reason of invariable co-observation applies to them as well." It is not established that this reason applies to them. If it did apply, it would follow that the self-awareness of experiencing the mind stream of a being to be guided observes the wisdom of a buddha because it observes this being's own mind stream. The reason is established through valid cognition, and if it is said that there is no entailment, the above position that these two are invariably observed together is ruined.

2bb3bb2) Others may say, "The reason of invariable co-observation is uncertain in said respect because primary minds and mental factors are different in substance, while this reason applies to them as well." Minds and mental factors are not different in substance because they are of the same nature in terms of their general type. It may be said that the reason here does not apply to the subject, but *Mahāyānasūtrālaṃkāra* XI.34 states:

> Mind is what appears as twofold:
> It appears as desire and such, and likewise,
> It appears as confidence and so on.
> There is no other phenomenon that is affliction and virtue.

The *Viniścayasaṃgrahaṇī* lists the objections to mind and mental factors being one in substance:

> Because five are not justified,
> Because their states are mistaken,
> Because there are no distinct enabling causes,
> And because it would be contradictory to scripture.[403]

I comment here on the meaning of these quotes in the manner of eliminating some qualms that may be raised against mind and mental factors not being different in substance. These qualms say, "If minds and mental factors are not distinct substances, it follows that the division of the five skandhas is not justified because the skandha of mental factors is not established as different from the skandha of consciousness. If you say that there is no flaw because it is specific temporary states of the mind that are presented as the skandha of mental factors, the question is whether mind and mental factors have different defining characteristics and functions or not. If they have, it follows that they are different in nature, and if they have not, it follows that they are not temporary states and what possesses these states, respectively. In fact, it follows that these two are not tenable as temporary states and what possesses these states.For, according to you, these two are of the same substance and thus do not exist as different functioning causes." Though mind and mental factors are a single substantial continuum, their defining characteristics and functions are different. Therefore, the reason that they do not exist as functioning causes that function as different phenomena—temporary states and what possesses these states, respectively—does not apply. For temporary states and what possesses these states (specific enabling causes such as the mental factors of desire and confidence that observe objects and so on occurring within a single substantial continuum of mind) are established through valid cognition in one's very own mind stream. By virtue of having different defining characteristics and functions, they need not be different in substance, just as the defining characteristics of a wish-fulfilling jewel (being precious and rare) are different and its functions (pacifying poisons and multiplying grains) are different, while the jewel's substance does not need to be different. Also, some may say, "The passage in the sūtras, 'Mind as such is a mental factor' is not reasonable—it contradicts the scriptural passages that explain mind and mental factors as being different in nature." The latter passages are refutations of mind and mental factors being one in nature in each and every specific aspect, but they do not contain any refutation of them being of the same nature in terms of their general type.[404]

2bb3bb3) Some may say, "The reason of invariable co-observation is uncertain as to proving that two phenomena are not different substances because it also applies to forms and light, which are different in substance." The explanations on this reason applying to forms and light are not to be taken literally. If they were to be taken literally, it would follow that light (what illuminates) and form (what is illuminated) are not cause and result because they are simultaneous. If this is accepted, the *Pramāṇaviniścaya* answers:

> Without light, forms would not be observed because there is no mistakenness of the result [arising] from the cause.[405]

2bb3bc) Removing objections in terms of the reason being contradictory

Some may say, "It follows that this reason of invariable co-observation is contradictory because antagonistic factors are necessarily different." If they mean to say that this follows because antagonistic factors are necessarily really existent as different, the reason does not apply. If they mean to say that this follows because they appear as different, there is no entailment.

2c) Explaining the yoga of realizing the nonexistence of the apprehender (the stage of the view asserted by the Mere Mentalists)

This has two parts:

a) Identifying phenomenal identity
b) Establishing its nonexistence

2ca) According to the common yāna, phenomenal identity refers to the pair of apprehender and apprehended. According to the śrāvakas, both coarse apprehended phenomena and the continuum of the apprehender are seeming entities, while both the apprehended phenomena that are minute particles and the moments of the apprehender are ultimate entities. According to the Mere Mentalists, all of these are nothing but seeming entities. Or phenomenal identitylessness refers to all phenomena that bear their own specific characteristics. As it is said:

> The continuum is called "person"
> And what bears characteristics is expressed as "phenomenon."[406]

2cb) All phenomena (the objects) are imputed by false imagination, but not established as having any natures of their own. As for the imagining or apprehending cognition (the subject) itself, it is also established to be nonexistent, which is implied by the nonexistence of the phenomena that are apprehended (the objects).

2d) Explaining the yoga of realizing the freedom from reference points (the stage of the view asserted by the Mādhyamikas)

You may wonder, "What is the gist of Madhyamaka—this philosophical system that is unsurpassed by any others?" As it is said:

> Neither existent, nor nonexistent, [nor] neither existent nor
> nonexistent,
> Nor having the character of both—
> Being liberated from the four extremes
> Is the true reality of learned Mādhyamikas.[407]

Thus, it is the prajñā free from all four extremes of reference points that is explained as the Madhyamaka view. There are two ways of commenting on the meaning of this view:

a) The way of commenting on the intention of Great Madhyamaka that delights the victors and their children

b) The way of commenting on the intention of Madhyamaka that delights the people during the last five hundred years of the Buddhist teachings

2da) As for the first two extremes (being existent and being nonexistent), the first way of commenting says that all imaginary and other-dependent phenomena are not existent because they are nothing but appearances that are delusive in all respects, while actually not existing. However, they are not nonexistent either. For if they never existed right from the start, any being nonexistent in dependence on that is impossible. Also, their being nonexistent refers to the opposite of their being existent, but their very being existent is not established. Therefore, its opposite—their being nonexistent—is not established either. Nor do these imaginary and other-dependent phenomena have the nature of being both existent and nonexistent (the third extreme)—being existent and being nonexistent cannot both apply to a single basis of reference. Since it has been determined already (as just explained) that imaginary and other-dependent bases of reference are neither existent nor nonexistent, a phenomenon that has the nature of being both existent and nonexistent is like the child of a barren woman because entities in which contrary elements are of a single nature are impossible.

Nowadays, some Mere Mentalists who propound *Shentong* and claim this to be Madhyamaka explain "not having the nature of being both existent and nonexistent" to mean that the imaginary does not have the nature of existence, while the other-dependent does not have the nature of nonexistence. This is not a good reasoning—through distinguishing between the aspects of what is correct and false, respectively, merely within the seeming reality of childish beings (such as, "Not being existent from the perspective of being mistaken as a snake, while not being nonexistent from the perspective of appearing as a rope"), "not having the nature of being both existent and nonexistent" is explained by having different instances for each one of the two possibilities of being existent and nonexistent in mind. However, in the context of Great Madhyamaka as taught here if one does not individually distinguish the respective aspects of appearance and imputation of all beings who are affected by ignorance (from those who have not entered the path up through those who have reached the end of the continuum) and yet applies said kind of reasoning at the time of proving that all seeming phenomena which obscure the nature of phenomena do not have the nature of being both existent and nonexistent, one does not go beyond the extreme of being both existent and nonexistent. That is, the imaginary is said to not have the nature of being existent and therefore does not go beyond the extreme of being nonexistent, while the other-dependent is said to not have the nature of being nonexistent and thus does not go beyond the extreme of being existent. In this way, *not having* the nature of being both existent and nonexistent is not established because it follows that, based on each one of these two instances (imaginary and other-dependent), what is established is *having* the nature of being both existent and nonexistent.

In our opinion, all seeming phenomena do not exist as having the nature of being existent, nonexistent, or the combination of both. For if they existed in any of these ways, they needed to exist as being established through a nature of their own. However, apart from not existing in this way (being established through any nature of their own), while merely appearing as being existent, nonexistent, and so on through being imputed by mistaken consciousnesses, there is nothing to be found that is real as some single self-sufficient phenomenon, be it existent or nonexistent. Just to observe the mere imputed aspects of existence, nonexistence, and the combination of both that are imputed by mistaken consciousnesses and to observe the mere appearing aspects of existence, nonexistence, and the combination of both that appear for the innate mistakenness which derives from being habituated to these mistaken consciousnesses does not mean that said aspects necessarily are and exist as they are imputed and appear. For there is not the slightest difference between these aspects and what appears for an insane person, what is observed by impaired sense faculties, objects in a dream, and so on. In brief, all aspects that are imputed and appear by virtue of mistaken consciousnesses are not established as being these respective aspects or existing as them. For they are cognitive aspects that appear for mistaken consciousnesses and are not other than the nature of these mistaken consciousnesses. These consciousnesses are mistaken since such consciousnesses do in fact not exist, which is precisely because they are fictitious or mistaken consciousnesses. Therefore, if such fictitious, delusive, or mistaken consciousnesses are not real as being anything or as existing as anything, it is certain that their objects are not established as being anything or as existing as anything either.

Also, some who boast to be great claim, "In the context of not having the nature of being both existent and nonexistent, the meaning of not being both is that the appearing aspect of these seeming appearances is not nonexistent, while their empty aspect is not existent. For the mantrayāna says:

> Just as the nature is primordially unborn,
> Neither delusive nor real, everything is held

> To be like [a reflection of] the moon in water.
> Therefore, yoginī, understand this!"[408]

To identify existence and nonexistence by claiming the aspect of appearing and the aspect of being empty to be distinct and different contradicts the Madhyamaka boundary lines for presenting the two realities. In any system, if the aspect of appearing and the aspect of being empty are claimed to be either one or different, such claims represent just extremes of reference points. Since there is no aspect of being empty that is other than the aspect of the appearing of the seeming and no aspect of appearing that is other than the aspect of being empty, what is accepted in Madhyamaka is solely the emptiness free from reference points that consists of negating the characteristics of these two aspects being existent by any nature of their own without establishing their nonexistence. However, according to the above claim, through seizing the extreme of existence (appearances not being nonexistent) and the extreme of nonexistence (emptiness not being existent), one refutes a specific feature of the one through the other and vice versa. Thus, the pretense of asserting *not being* both existent and nonexistent by way of this approach in effect results in the claim of *being* both existent and nonexistent. For it is by virtue of the existence and nonexistence, respectively, that are based on each one of two distinct elements (appearance and emptiness) that a different kind of *being* both existent and nonexistent is accepted. Moreover, the meaning of the above quote from the mantrayāna is explained wrongly. What it means is that, just as the reflection of the moon in water does not exist as the moon, seeming phenomena are not established as being or existing in the way they appear. But this passage is not about one part of seeming phenomena being existent, while another part is nonexistent. Therefore, the above interpretation is nothing but flawed.

As for the meaning of the fourth extreme ("not not having the nature of being both"), it refers to not not being both existent and nonexistent either because the nature of not being either existent or nonexistent is impossible. For, as was explained, being both existent and nonexistent is impossible and, consequently, any not being either existent or nonexistent—which is dependent on the former—is impossible too. This means that to present these two options is done by way of their being mutually dependent, so if *being* such a dependent phenomenon (being both existent and nonexistent) is impossible, *not being* said dependent phenomenon is impossible too.[409]

Through being explained in this way, all seeming cognitions and their objects are magical creations by nothing but the states of mind that cling to characteristics. Since these states of mind obstruct the arising of the wisdom without characteristics, in all respects they are factors to be relinquished. Though these states of mind are relinquished, it is solely in the nondual wisdom that is the nature of ultimate reality that there is no clinging to extremes. For it is this very wisdom that completely eradicates said extremes, but this wisdom has the nature of it being impossible for it to entertain any views about extremes about itself, such as its being existent or nonexistent. On the other hand, it is equally impossible for any cognitions of those who possess a mind stream of clinging to extremes to cling to any extremes (such as existence and nonexistence) with regard to this wisdom. For if this wisdom is not even suitable to appear in the form of a mere object generality as an object of any cognitions that cling to extremes, it is certainly impossible for any cognitions of those who possess a mind stream of clinging to extremes to take this wisdom as their basis of analysis and then cling to it as existent, nonexistent, or anything else. For this reason, the reasoning of this really established nondual wisdom lacking or being empty of a nature is not something that can be conceived.

Thus, this is the manner in which both true reality and what appears as if being false reality are free from extremes. If one rests in meditative equipoise in accordance with this manner being just as it is, the seeds of all obscurations are eradicated. By virtue of having realized said manner, just as it is, during such meditative equipoise, its subsequent attainment increases the roots of virtue that make the two kāyas manifest.[410]

2db) As for the way of commenting on the intention of Madhyamaka that delights the people during the last five hundred years of the Buddhist teachings, the great elder Buddhapālita and others explain the following. The reasoning just explained—all seeming phenomena being free of extremes (such as existence and nonexistence)—is used as a preliminary. However, without reflecting on the reasonings that determine nondual wisdom as lacking real existence through refuting all reference points about it (such as its existing, not existing, and so on), merely through forcefully putting an end to the conceptions that cling to extremes in terms of the seeming, one is not able to relinquish the seeds of all conceptions that cling to extremes. However, due to certain purposes, these masters either do not explain the above principle of Great Madhyamaka well or they do not understand its element that consists of the manner through which this principle is as it is. But apart from that, the flaw stated by them does not apply for the following reasons. Nondual wisdom cannot be determined as lacking real existence through any reasonings in the mind streams of those who just see this life and consequently there is no need to determine nondual wisdom in this manner. Therefore, though nondual wisdom is not determined as lacking real existence, once nondual wisdom dawns as unobscured natural luminosity, through becoming familiar with it while resting in it in equipoise for a long time, one is able to eradicate all seeds of conceptions. The *Uttaratantra* says:

> Because they see that, due to mind's natural luminosity, the afflictions lack a nature . . .[411]

When explaining the meaning of this, the *Uttaratantra* continues:

> The [wisdom of] suchness by virtue of
> The realization of the world's true nature of peace
> Is due to the natural complete purity [of the mind]
> And due to the primordial termination of the afflictions.[412]

This explains that, through becoming familiar with the actuality of really established nondual wisdom in the meditative equipoise of resting in it, all obscurations can be relinquished right from the start. Therefore, the *Mahāyānottaratantra* explains that the nondual wisdom which bears the name "uncontaminated dhātu" (the buddha heart) exists solely as the reality that is permanent, stable, and changeless. Since any situation of it being affected by impairments (such as being real or unreal) is impossible, the *Uttaratantra* does not teach any extra remedies for clinging to it as being really existent or clinging to it as lacking real existence.

Therefore, the third stage of yoga consists of the False Aspectarian Mere Mentalists going beyond mere mind, which consists of apprehender and apprehended, and then resting in nondual consciousness, which is nonreferential, lacks appearance, and exists ultimately. In the context of explaining the fourth stage of yoga, it is negated that this nondual consciousness exists ultimately, but it is not affirmed that nondual wisdom lacks real existence. The *Laṅkāvatārasūtra* says:

> Having gone beyond mere mind,
> One must even go beyond nonappearance.
> The yogin who rests in nonappearance
> Sees the mahāyāna.[413]

This verse also teaches the third stage of yoga, with the line "sees the mahāyāna" indicating that the view of the False Aspectarian Mere Mentalists too is a mahāyāna view. Likewise, the third stage of yoga is also taught by the following verse:

> The consciousness that is liberated
> From apprehender and apprehended exists ultimately.
> This is what is proclaimed in the texts of the Yogācāras
> Who have gone to the other shore of mind's ocean.[414]

Differing from the above, according to the Mādhyamikas who guide the beings during the last five hundred years of the Buddhist teachings, one familiarizes one's mind stream with emptiness through the conceptuality that consists of the cognitions in the mind streams of those who just see this life, having analyzed true ultimate reality—"the great being empty," which is genuinely permanent—and found it to be nonexistent. However, these Mādhyamikas say that, having done so, it would represent a form of clinging to extremes if one were to subsequently familiarize with the existence of naturally luminous nondual wisdom, which is obtained through the nature of phenomena and found in the scriptural tradition of the Great Madhyamaka that teaches the definitive meaning of the sūtras and tantras taught by the supreme victor. Therefore, these Mādhyamikas say that resting in meditative equipoise within nondual natural luminosity is a great mistake. But I do not regard this as the supreme system.

Still, saying, "This is the system of the Niḥsvabhāvavādins, such as master Rendawa Shönnu Lodrö,"[415] certain people assert that nothing but sheer emptiness (which is not suitable as anything such as the existence or nonexistence of consciousness free from apprehender and apprehended) is the ultimate basic nature, but that there is no wisdom which is other than nondual consciousness. In our opinion, this assertion evidently does not go beyond Mere Mentalism. The False Aspectarian Mere Mentalists and those who make said assertion accord in that there is no extra nondual wisdom that is other than consciousness. From just that perspective, there is no difference between these people and the False Aspectarian Mere Mentalists—the difference obviously lies in the former asserting that consciousness is empty and devoid of a nature of its own, while the latter do not assert such. Therefore, the Madhyamaka view of these people is that "consciousness empty of apprehender and apprehended does not exist as a nature of its own." On the other hand, they say, "The view of the False Aspectarians is merely that the aspects of appearances are not real as mind." However, these people being so concerned about having to claim this is due to their being afraid of the Madhyamaka view consisting of nondual wisdom. To assert the Madhyamaka view in such a way that the boundary lines of its own system do not surpass the False Aspectarians results in their implicitly being forced to say that what is actually the view of the Real Aspectarians represents the view of the False Aspectarians. In fact, the view of the False Aspectarians is explained in terms of being empty of any apprehender that apprehends the aspect of what appears to it, whereas it is a fraud to present Real and False Aspectarians in terms of the difference of whether the aspect of what appears is real as mind or delusive.[416]

So when the view of the False Aspectarians is explained, it is taught that there is no need for explicitly familiarizing with the fact that the aspects that appear as outer referents despite there being no such referents are not real as mind. Rather, by virtue of having relinquished what apprehends such aspects, it is implicitly established that the latter are naturally relinquished too. If it were otherwise, consider that also the Real Aspectarian Mere Mentalists meditate by thinking, "As for the aspects of seemingly outer referents appearing to cognition despite there being no such referents, they are neither this very cognition appearing out there as the aspects of appearances nor actual outer referents being established in here as the cognitive aspects that appear in the form of such referents. However, these aspects of apprehended objects, which appear under the sway of mistakenness, are nothing but the aspects of nonexistents appearing." If the Real Aspectarians did not meditate in this way, they would not realize that apprehended objects are not established, and if they did not realize this, their meditation would not be suitable to be presented as the stage of the yoga of realizing the nonexistence of the apprehended. During that stage, through thinking, "The aspects of outer referents are aspects of nonexistents appearing," the realization of the aspects of the apprehended not being real as mind exists even in the Real Aspectarians. In brief, according to the above people, the difference between Real Aspectarian and False Aspectarian Mere Mentalists refers to whether the aspect of the apprehended is said to be real or delusive. In my opinion, the difference refers to whether the aspect of the apprehender is said to be real or delusive.[417]

Here I say:

Consciousness being empty of apprehended and apprehender,
    progressively,
Represents the assertions of Real Aspectarians and False
    Aspectarians.
That wisdom is as empty as consciousness
And that wisdom itself is not empty of wisdom's own nature—
These assertions, respectively, represent the difference
Between those who propound Madhyamaka and Great
    Madhyamaka.
In brief, the assertions of nondual consciousness
And nondual wisdom being really established, respectively,
Appear as "Mere Mentalism" and "Madhyamaka"[418]—
The two systems as prophesied by the victor.

3) JNS's comments on the *Vivṛti* on the four stages of yoga[419]

3a) The stage of yoga of realizing the nonexistence of a self
This has three parts:

a) The reasoning that arises from reflection
b) The yoga that arises from meditation
c) The fruition of meditation

3aa) In the appropriating skandhas, there is no self that is established as a nature of its own. For if a self existed, it had to remain without arising and ceasing, but since the basis of imputing a self that is asserted by non-Buddhists and the Vātsīputrīyas is empty by way of arising and ceasing, it is established that the skandhas are without a self.

3ab) Induced by this reasoning, one meditates by thinking, "There is no self," which puts an end to the clinging to a self.

3ac) Having given up this self, these entities of aging and dying, such as the appropriating skandhas devoid of such a self, are phenomena that bear the features of arising and ceasing in terms of dependent origination under the influence of the twelve links. Through focusing on such phenomena, the stage of the yoga of realizing the nonexistence of a self is manifested.

3b) The yoga of realizing the nonexistence of the apprehended

This has the same three parts:

3ba) The reasoning that arises from reflection is that the appearance of blue and the mental state that apprehends this blue do not exist as different substances because these two are invariably observed together by a single mental state.

3bb) The yoga that arises from meditation is to familiarize with, and mentally engage in, that these appearances of referents are nothing but aspects of mere mind, whereas outer material referents do not exist.

3bc) The fruition of meditation is that there is no clinging to the very aspect that is the apprehended because this aspect is not an actual something to be apprehended. Without giving up the clinging to the mind that has the aspect of being the apprehender of said apprehended aspect, the clinging to outer referents is relinquished, which manifests the stage of the yoga of realizing the nonexistence of the apprehended.

3c) The stage of yoga of realizing the nonexistence of the apprehender
This has the same three parts:

3ca) The aspect of the apprehender does not exist because if there is nothing apprehended, there is no apprehender of it either. Through this reasoning that arises from reflection, superimpositions are cut through.

3cb) The yoga that arises from meditation is to mentally engage through having gained certainty in this, thinking, "The aspect of the apprehender does not exist."

3cc) The fruition of meditation is to manifest the stage of the yoga of realizing the nonexistence of the apprehender by virtue of eliminating also the apprehender—the mere cognizance whose nature it is to have the characteristic of being the aspect of the apprehender.

3d) The stage of yoga of realizing the freedom from reference points
This has two parts:
a) Removing slight qualms in this context
b) Explaining the meaning of the words of the *Vivṛti*

3da) In the context of the fourth stage of yoga, though the elimination of the thesis that nondual consciousness empty of apprehender and apprehended exists does not clearly appear in Haribhadra's *Vivṛti*, he speaks of nondual wisdom being twofold—the nominal nondual wisdom whose nature is dependent origination and the nonnominal nondual wisdom whose nature is not dependent origination. In the system of the Niḥsvabhāvavādins, it is nothing but the first one that is presumed to be the ultimate reality that actually fulfills this function. In order to eliminate reference points about this wisdom in terms of thinking that it truly exists, through the reasoning of its being dependently originating they reject that it is a permanent existent. This is expressed in the *Vivṛti* through the passage starting with "Having gained certainty in the sense of thinking that this sheer nondual wisdom . . ."[420] The latter wisdom is a permanent existent and beyond dependent phenomena since reference points and characteristics such as existent and nonexistent are not supported by it. Thus, without adducing any reasonings that eliminate reference points, the *Vivṛti* explains that cognitive obscurations are relinquished through resting in the meditative equipoise of this nondual wisdom having arisen. This is expressed in the passage ". . . is to be experienced personally . . ."[421]

I think that this manner in which Haribhadra comments here appears to represent the unsurpassable system of Yogācāra-Madhyamaka. The Seventh Karmapa[422] comments that the *Vivṛti*, through saying in the context of explaining the third stage of yoga that "also mere cognizance is eliminated,"[423] teaches that the notion of a truly existing nondual consciousness must be eliminated implicitly. In the context of explaining the fourth stage of yoga, by virtue of taking this need to eliminate the notion of a truly existing nondual consciousness as the basis of the explanation, this notion is not mentioned explicitly anymore. Though truly existing nondual wisdom being the actual outcome is taken as the basis here, this nondual wisdom is twofold—from the perspective of others it appears as aspects of dependent origination, and from its own perspective it exists as its self-arisen nature. From among these two, the first one is what eliminates the mistakenness that what appear as the aspects of dependent origination truly are or exist as these aspects.

3db) Explaining the meaning of the words of the *Vivṛti*
This has the same three parts as under (3a)–(3c) above:

3db1) The reasoning that arises from reflection is as follows. Those with a childish mind among the Mādhyamikas gain certainty in the sense of thinking that this reality of a nonimplicative negation—the sheer wisdom in which there is no duality in terms of reference points and characteristics other than this wisdom and there thus not being any second entity—has the nature of existing truly. In order to put an end to such a view, one further analyzes through reasoning, thinking that this reality of nondual wisdom as a nonimplicative negation does not exist because it is dependently originating. Like an illusion, the nondual wisdom that is nominal reality is nothing but without nature. For there is no graver mistakenness than clinging to this wisdom as existent since it means to cling to a nonexistent as being existent.

3db2) As for the yoga that arises from meditation, if analyzed truly, nondual wisdom is free from any conceptualized nature, such as definitely being established as a seeming entity, being a nonentity, being both, or being neither. Through meditating by thinking like that, finally, also the very consciousness that meditates in this way simply ceases on its own, while the permanent existent that is nonnominal nondual wisdom dawns.

3db3) As for the fruition of meditation, you may wonder, "How can it be that, through the power of truly and unmistakenly familiarizing with actual reality, activities are accomplished?" Just as the knowledge in some persons that the appearances that show in the clear and shiny surfaces of gems, silver, and so on are just reflections, what represents the mere appearance by virtue of having relinquished all characteristics of mistakenness is this mental state that appears with an illusionlike character (being a clearly appearing nonexistent)—the nonimplicative negation that is the nominal nondual wisdom. Through having eliminated all reference points with regard to it (such as its existing or not existing), one rests in meditative equipoise in nonconceptuality. At that point, the power of the two accumulations has become special and, through the power of the nature of phenomena, wisdom exists permanently as nonnominal nondual wisdom. Through this, once what is to be experienced personally has arisen truly in accordance with the progressive relinquishments of the obscurations on the respective lower stages of yoga, the yogin perfectly relinquishes the cognitive obscurations, thus manifesting the stage of the yoga of realizing the freedom from reference points.[424]

E) Dependent origination[425]

This has six parts:

1) The nature of dependent origination
2) Divisions
3) Meaning of the term
4) How many lifetimes it takes for one cycle of the causal and resultant links of dependent origination to be completed
5) The distinction in terms of the twelve links being substantially existent or imputedly existent
6) The distinction in terms of the twelve links corresponding or not corresponding to a given level of saṃsāric existence

1) The nature of dependent origination

Since they do not exist by any nature of their own, all phenomena appear in dependence on causes and conditions. All these phenomena are neither created by Īśvara or any other creating agents, nor do they arise from non-concordant causes and conditions, nor from permanent causes. Though these mere appearances do not exist as being established by virtue of dependent connections, they are entities that appear to childish beings as if they were existent. As *Yuktiṣaṣṭikā* 44ab says:

> Those who assert that dependent entities
> Are established in true reality . . .

From the perspective of unmistakenness, the mere phenomena that appear in this way are emptiness, but from the perspective of mistakenness, they are present as appearing to be established in dependence. By virtue of them being present in this way, if one understands the actual nature of being established in dependence, the emptiness in which the two extremes are relinquished is clarified as well. The concluding verse of the *Vigrahavyāvartaṇī* says:

> I pay homage to the incomparable Buddha,
> Who supremely teaches emptiness,
> Dependent origination, and the middle path
> To be of the same meaning.

2) Divisions

This has two parts:
a) The dependent origination of afflicted phenomena
b) The dependent origination of purified phenomena

2a) The dependent origination of afflicted phenomena has two parts:
a) The common division
b) The nature of each part of the division

2aa) The common division has five parts:

2aa1) The basis of the division is the dependent origination whose nature consists of the causes and conditions for circling in saṃsāra.

2aa2) The nature of the division is what appears as the twelve links (such as ignorance).

2aa3) The reason for the division is that the distinct features of what produces and what is produced in terms of the power of causes and results exist as the aspects that are said twelve links. How do these exist? The Vaibhāṣikas assert them to consist of five causes and seven results, while the Mere Mentalists hold them to consist of six causes and six results.

2aa4) The meaning of the division is that, though these links have different natures in terms of substance, their substantial continuum is not different. Therefore, they are of the same general type.

2aa5) The number of the twelve links being definite means that the Bhagavān ascertained them as that many. Some realists say, "So does ignorance have or not have a cause? If it has a cause, it follows that there are thirteen links, and if it has no cause, it follows that saṃsāra has a beginning" and "If aging and death have a result, it follows that there are thirteen links, and if they have no result, it follows that saṃsāra becomes discontinued after one single cycle of the causes and results in the twelve links." This is true for such realists, but said flaws do not apply to me. Ignorance means not seeing. That which is not seen is the actual nature of objects, just as it is because one is ignorant about the actual nature, just as it is, of each one of the four realities or the three characteristics (the imaginary, the other-dependent, and the perfect nature). As *Mahāyānasūtrālaṃkāra* VI.4cd says:

> Therefore, what is this particular kind of darkness
> Of not seeing what exists and seeing what does not exist?

To be ignorant is solely due to not knowing. However, as for the adventitious stains that have many names (such as "formational dhātus," "inconceivable sentient beings," "inconceivable karmas," "infinite and inexhaustible realms of sentient beings," and "stable mistaken appearances"), if analyzed, they are without any beginning and end, without causes and conditions, and so on because they are not established by any nature of their own and yet appear in an adventitious and seeming manner. Whatever is adventitious and seeming and yet appears as if it were a dependent phenomenon is necessarily without causes and conditions and so forth. For such a delusive appearance that looks as if it were an existent phenomenon, though it it is without any nature of its own, is produced by delusive causes and conditions. If it is said that the reason does not apply to the subject, it follows that said appearances are produced because it is certain that results are different from causes (no matter whether these causes and results are real or delusive). If said appearances are produced by delusive causes and conditions, they are necessarily not produced by causes and conditions. For delusive causes and conditions are not actual causes and conditions in the first place, just as delusive causes and conditions for transforming ordinary metal into gold are not the causes and conditions for such a transformation. Therefore, if these adventitious stains themselves (which appear as if produced by causes and conditions and entail the twelve links) never existed in the first place, any analyzing as to whether the link of ignorance among these stains or the link of aging and death have or lack a beginning and an end subsides on its own.

Some may object, "In that case, it follows that ignorance is without a cause, and if it has no cause, the same follows for the remaining links." The consequence of ignorance having no cause does not invalidate what is said here. For if ignorance existed, it would depend on causes and conditions, but it is not claimed here that ignorance exists if analyzed. "In that case, it follows that ignorance does exist because dependent origination exists." When thoroughly scrutinized through reasoning, the reason does not apply to the subject. As for dependent origination, it follows that whatever arises in dependence and is established in dependence[426] is necessarily not existent. For if it existed, it must exist by a nature of its own, but since such a nature does not exist, it just arises as being established in dependence from the perspective of mistakenness, while not existing actually. The reason is established through valid cognition and the entailment is established as follows. Whatever exists from the perspective of mistaken appearances is necessarily nonexistent because it is deceiving in terms of the actual nature of objects, just like the appearance of two moons for people with cataracts. "But then, with the twelve links of dependent origination not existing, it is not justified to give a presentation of them." Though dependent origination does not exist, there is a purpose for the Bhagavān having given such a presentation. Through teaching mistaken and suffering childish beings how the manner of their being mistaken in the form of the twelve links arises from the basis of mistakenness, this mistakenness is put to an end.

Some may wonder, "It may well be like that from the perspective of being without mistakenness, but from the perspective of mistakenness, what are the causes and conditions of ignorance?" They are the preceding continua of the twelve links that are similar in type. "And what are the causes and conditions of these preceding continua of the twelve links?" They are likewise their respectively preceding continua of the twelve links. Some people may object, "But in that case, it follows that there is an infinite regress of the starting point of saṃsāra, which leads to the consequence that the beginning or first point in time of saṃsāra cannot be pinpointed. From that it follows that saṃsāra is not temporary or adventitious because—with the beginning time of saṃsāra being unidentifiable—it exists permanently in a primordial way." This is true for such people who cling to the way things appear, but said flaw does not apply to me. Through the power of mistakenness, it appears that there is an infinite regress of the starting point of saṃsāra. Therefore, the thought, "Saṃsāra exists primordially since it is not temporary" appears for the innate mode of apprehension of the minds of all childish beings. However, if one trains in the texts of Great Madhyamaka, it is not necessarily the case that saṃsāra is something primordially permanent just because it has no identifiable beginning by virtue of it wrongly appearing for one's mistakenness that there is an infinite regress of saṃsāra's starting point. For all conceptions of mistaken appearances are deceiving, just as it may appear for a consciousness that is affected by an illusion or sleep as if many eons occur in between two consecutive moments. Furthermore, though aging and death do not actually have any results, no matter whether the cycle of the twelve links of dependent origination is completed in two or three lifetimes, being propelled into and completing one's next existence function according to such cycles. Therefore, there is no flaw of saṃsāra becoming discontinued at the end of one single such cycle.

In general, these twelve links circle in mutual dependence, just as the parts of a chariot roll. Therefore, through the force of that, saṃsāric existence appears from causes and conditions in the manner of these causes and conditions circling and being in motion. *Ratnāvalī* I.36cd says:

> This maṇḍala of saṃsāra,
> Just as a circling firebrand,
> Circles by entailing mutual causes.

Many Tibetans think that saṃsāra is permanent because there is no ending point of the entire number of sentient beings becoming exhausted. They also think that since there is no starting point of saṃsāra, at the time of its beginning the substantial continuum of saṃsāra represents being permanent in terms of a continuum. However, at the time of saṃsāra's end, through said substantial continuum having been canceled out, its permanent continuum is ceased. However, such thoughts just exhibit the flaws of not having trained in the scriptural tradition of Great Madhyamaka. Thus, under slight analysis through reasoning, sentient beings are not substantially established because it is nothing but the adventitious stains that are labeled as sentient beings. Since there is no substance of sentient beings, there is no substantial continuum of them either. However, under thorough analysis, sentient beings are not even established as mere imputations. For the very basis for such imputations does not exist in the first place and sentient beings are not established in the ways they are imputed. Thus, if they are not even established as imputedly existent, how could they be established as substantially existent? Also, if the substantial continuum of beginningless saṃsāra were permanent at first, it would be impossible for it to revert from being such a permanent entity at any later point (as asserted above). For it is impossible for the natures of being permanent and impermanent to change into the respective other one, just as the sambhogakāya that is permanent in terms of a continuum does not revert from being permanent at any later point.

According to my own understanding, the meaning of saṃsāra being without beginning and end is as follows. It was already explained more than once that its beginning or end does not exist because this very saṃsāra itself is not established. But the position of others—its being without beginning and end meaning that saṃsāra (or the realms of sentient beings) exists from the very beginning and also exists in the end as being interminable—is wrong. In brief, this stance that saṃsāra is infinite, because a time of saṃsāra becoming empty is impossible by virtue of the number of sentient beings not becoming exhausted, is very despicable. It is only for those who are engaged in mistakenness that it appears as if the number of sentient beings does not become exhausted, but if no sentient being whatsoever is seen, an endless inexhaustibility of sentient beings is not observable. As for the manner in which the mere appearance of inexhaustible sentient beings for those who are engaged in mistakenness is not established as these sentient beings actually existing in an inexhaustible manner, it was already explained above. As for whether there is or is not a time when saṃsāra becomes empty if it is explained that saṃsāra does not exist in that it does not abide for even a single moment, there is no need to analyze whether there is or is not a time when it becomes empty. It may be objected, "But in that case, it is absolutely uncertain whether saṃsāra will also occur in the future." I can only accept this because the fact of saṃsāra being established as being "contained" in the first place, since it does absolutely not happen, is expressed by the Bhagavān in the mantrayāna as "Glorious Cakrasaṃvara."[427] Nevertheless, as for saṃsāra temporarily appearing as not becoming empty and so on, by virtue of being habituated to the dependent origination of afflicted phenomena, the inconceivable realms of sentient beings represent the very nature of dependent origination. This nature of dependent origination is a subtle point since the cognitions in the mind streams of those who just see this life cannot conceive it. As it is said:

> Though beginningless, it entails an end.[428]

Thus since saṃsāra has no point of beginning, but an end, it is taught as if it had a closure. However, this is said with a certain intention, which is established through the following as it is found in the scriptural tradition of Great Madhyamaka. A closure of saṃsāra is described there with the intention of it appearing in the end as if the adventitious stains naturally vanish because they are delusive. This statement about the existence of a final closure, while there is no beginning, is the way it actually is because, ultimately, it is impossible for any sentient being to not become a buddha. Many difficult points in the dharma terminology of the definitive meaning will become clear if one properly understands the meaning of this point of whether saṃsāra has or lacks a beginning and an end.

2ab) The nature of each part of the division of the dependent origination of afflicted phenomena has two parts in terms of:

1) the three karmas (virtuous, nonvirtuous, and unmoving) in common and
2) the karmas that will be experienced after having been reborn.

2ab1) From among the twelve links of dependent origination, (1) the definition of ignorance is to be confused. Though there are many ways to divide it, in general, if ignorance is classified, it is of two kinds—afflicted ignorance and nonafflicted ignorance. The ignorance that is presented here as the first among the twelve links of dependent origination is of the first kind because this is the context of explaining the origin of suffering that consists of the afflictions (the other origin being karma). Also, in particular, this ignorance serves as a cause for the karmas that propel one into one's next existence, that is, as a motivational or triggering force at the time of engaging in such karmas. Though ignorance qualifies as being such a motivational force, it is not only the motivational force at the time of engaging in said propelling karmas that is identified as the first link. For the ignorance that is taught here is indeed a propelling factor, but for virtuous karmas, an afflicted motivational force at the time of engaging in them is impossible. As for the ignorance that occurs simultaneously with the latent tendencies that are input by formational karmas, it is not identified as being the first link either because the ignorance that is presented as this link is only the one that propels the skandhas of suffering of the next lifetime, but not the ignorance that is a mere producing factor. In brief, the ignorance that is presented here as the link which propels consists of the ignorance within the group of the six primary afflictions. On the other hand, nonafflicted ignorance is the ignorance about knowable objects that exists in the mind streams of śrāvaka and pratyekabuddha arhats and noble bodhisattvas.

This ignorance that is presented as the first link of dependent origination contains the two portions of what is a factor to be relinquished through seeing and what is a factor to be relinquished through familiarization. For both its portion that consists of what is a factor to be relinquished through seeing and the ignorance that is an accompanying factor of the afflicted mind are able to function as causes for the karmas that propel one into one's next existence, that is, as motivational forces at the time of engaging in these karmas. In particular, with regard to the karmas that propel the skandhas of pleasant realms, there is no such kind of ignorance that is congruently associated with the afflictions and serves as a motivational force at the time of engaging in such karmas because said karmas arise by being congruently associated with the virtuous root that is the lack of ignorance. With regard to the karmas that propel one into unpleasant realms, there exists the motivational force at the time of engaging in these karmas that is the afflicted ignorance which represents a factor to be relinquished through seeing because such karmas are nothing but nonvirtuous, so that this ignorance arises by being congruently associated with either desire or hatred. The meaning of the skandhas, the dhātus, and so on of the unpleasant realms being explained as factors to be relinquished through seeing is also reflected in this point. Therefore, the intention of all this is that, depending on the difference of whether the motivational force at the time of engagement in karma is or is not the ignorance that is congruently associated with afflictions, the first link of dependent origination in terms of the ignorance of proceeding toward unpleasant realms is nonvirtuous, while the one of proceeding toward pleasant realms is neutral.

In brief, the portion of afflicted ignorance that represents a factor to be relinquished through seeing is the ignorance that occurs only as the accompanying factor of the sixth consciousness. For it is the ignorance that is included within the six primary afflictions and is the ignorance of being ignorant about the aspects of the four realities. The portion of afflicted ignorance that represents a factor to be relinquished through familiarization is the ignorance that occurs as the accompanying factor of the afflicted mind because it produces affliction through looking inward and taking the ālaya-consciousness as the object of self-centeredness. This portion of afflicted ignorance does not function as a motivational force for the karmas that complete a rebirth. Within the portion of afflicted ignorance that represents a factor to be relinquished through familiarization there is also a part that is congruently associated with the sixth consciousness. This kind of ignorance is again twofold, consisting of the portion of being ignorant about the four realities and the portion of being ignorant about objects. The first one functions as the motivational force for the karmas that propel the next rebirth, while the latter one does so for the links that complete this rebirth because the first one propels the latent tendencies of the karmas that propel said rebirth, while the latter one is what awakens these propelled latent tendencies. The first one is the ignorance that is the first link of dependent origination, while the latter one is identified as consisting of both craving and grasping.

Some may object, "But if there is an afflicted ignorance that represents a factor to be relinquished through familiarization, it follows that it exists in the mind streams of noble ones. In that case, it follows that they accumulate karmas which propel them into further births, but that is invalidated by the following passage:

> In those who see reality, there is no propelling.
> In those who are free from craving, there is no rebirth."

This does not invalidate what is said here. The statement "In those who see reality, there is no propelling" is made with the intention that the afflicted ignorance that represents a factor to be relinquished through familiarization (the causal first link of dependent origination that serves as the causal motivational force for the karmas that propel one into existence) is overcome at said point of seeing reality and therefore not manifest. Or, though a certain afflicted ignorance that represents a factor to be relinquished through familiarization and may function as the motivational force for propelling and completing karmas exists in the mind streams of noble ones at said point, it does not actually motivate or trigger any propelling or completing karmas. For the unimpededly existing power of being able to propel and complete karmas consists of the afflicted ignorance that represents a factor to be relinquished through seeing, but this ignorance has already been relinquished through the clear realization of personal identitylessness. On the other hand, the afflicted ignorance that represents a factor to be relinquished through familiarization is not able to motivate or trigger any propelling and completing karmas because its power is weak. This is just as in the following example: in an ordinary person with a psychophysical support within the desire realm who does not regress from an actual dhyāna there is the afflicted mind of the desire realm, but this afflicted mind does not motivate or trigger any karmas for being reborn in the desire realm.

Some may object, "But then it would be impossible for noble ones to take birth in saṃsāra because the motivational force for propelling and completing karmas is not possible in their mind streams." There is no flaw here in terms of both hīnayāna and mahāyāna noble ones. As for the first, to illustrate this through śrāvaka noble ones being born on the level of the first dhyāna, though they have no propelling factor that consists of some new afflicted ignorance, their existence on the level of the first dhyāna is completed by way of their connecting with the karmas that complete the countless instances of the afflicted ignorance which propels one into a birth on the level of the first dhyāna and already existed before they saw reality (on the path of seeing). This connecting takes place in such a manner that the links of craving and grasping for a rebirth on the level of the first dhyāna are replaced through the uncontaminated preparatory stage of this dhyāna. As for the mahāyāna noble ones, they do not rely on the link of dependent origination that consists of the afflicted ignorance which binds in saṃsāra, but they deliberately do not relinquish the afflicted ignorance that represents a factor to be relinquished through familiarization and causes them to be reborn in saṃsāra. This is what functions as their causes and conditions of propelling and completing rebirths, through which they take births in saṃsāra as they please.

That this ignorance which is the first one within the twelve links consists of the two portions of what is to be relinquished through seeing and familiarization, respectively, is also established through scripture because the *Yogācārabhūmi* says:

> "How many links do stream-enterers relinquish?" [They relinquish] a portion of all of them, but none of them in their entirety.[429]

As for the manner in which this ignorance functions as the motivational force for formations (the second link), ignorance means to be confused about the self. From this, attachment to this self arises, which in turn leads to the wish for this self to be happy. This wish is twofold—wishing for happiness in this life and later lives, respectively. Through wishing for happiness in this life, one commits nonvirtuous actions, such as killing. Wishing for happiness in later lives is twofold—wishing for pleasant existences within the desire realm and the two higher realms, respectively. Through wishing for happiness in later lives in the desire realm, one accumulates meritorious actions that are included within the levels of the desire realm, such as practicing generosity and keeping ethical discipline. Through wishing for happiness in later lives in the two higher realms, one accumulates unmoving actions, such as the pure dhyānas and formless absorptions. In this way, one is reborn in the respective ones among the three realms.

(2) The link of (karmic) formations consists of the karma that is motivated or triggered by the ignorance just explained and propels one into another existence. It is divided into two—volitional karma and volitioned karma. Here, the Vaibhāṣikas assert the former to be mental karma and the latter to be physical and verbal karmas. All other schools from the Sautrāntikas upward hold both types to be the mental factor intention (or impulse).[430] In this case, volitional karma refers to the intention that serves as the causal motivation, while volitioned karma is the intention that serves as the motivation at the time of actually engaging in an action. The karmic formations that represent the second one among the twelve links definitely refer solely to any of the volitional karmas that accompany the actions of body, speech, and the mental consciousness, whereas the latent tendencies within the ālaya-consciousness are not taken to be the karmas that represent this second link. For the link of karmic formations is presented as the link that propels one into a rebirth (for the reason that it is what inputs said latent tendencies), whereas the latent tendencies that are propelled by this link of karmic formations are presented as the link of how one is propelled into this rebirth (for the reason that they are the causal conditions for suffering).

The karmic formations in question here are threefold—meritorious karma, nonmeritorious karma, and immovable karma. Through these karmas one is propelled into the pleasant existences of the desire realm, unpleasant existences, and the two higher realms, respectively. You may wonder, "What is the meaning of the first two types of karma being movable and the latter being immovable?" The first type does not mean that one moves to another realm by virtue of the power of the maturation of the first two types of karma because it is definite that the maturational results of meritorious karmic formations occur solely within the psychophysical supports of the pleasant existences of the desire realm, while the maturational results of nonmeritorious karmic formations occur only within the psychophysical supports of the unpleasant existences. However, what is seen to move to other levels are the results that concord with said causes (meritorious and nonmeritorious formations, respectively) because the results that concord with merits as their causes (such as riches) are also seen to occur in certain psychophysical supports of the unpleasant existences, while the results that concord with nonmerits as their causes (such as being destitute) are seen to occur in certain psychophysical supports of the pleasant existences too. "Immovable karma" is called that way because it is definite that not only the maturational results of the karmas that propel one into a particular level of the higher realms, but also the results that concord with these causes occur solely within this particular level of these realms, whereas it is impossible for them to move to any other realms.[431] In this context of the twelve links, "formation" is meant to designate the factor of the agent within the coming together of the three elements of agent, object, and action.

(3) The link of consciousness consists of the ālaya-consciousness that serves as the basis into which the latent tendencies of the link of formations are input. This ālaya-consciousness has the two aspects of cause and result. The first one is its seminal aspect—through the power of the latent tendencies of the karmic formations being input into the ālaya-consciousness, the ālaya-consciousness renders the suffering of one's next rebirth into something that is suitable to arise. The second one is its maturational aspect—the skandha of the ālaya-consciousness that, through the potency of these seeds, arises as the beginning of the skandhas of suffering in one's mother's womb.

(4) The link of name and form refers to the four skandhas other than consciousness that progressively develop from the time of consciousness having connected with a womb onward. In the desire and form realms, both name and form exist, but in the formless realm, though the link of name and form exists in a general way, the specific link of form does not. Thus, this link is taught as "name and form" by combining these two into one.

(5) The link of the āyatanas consists of the link of the six inner āyatanas being complete by virtue of name and form having fully developed. Here, some people may say, "It is not tenable to separate the link of name and form from the link of the six āyatanas because they are completed simultaneously in miraculous birth." There is no flaw because the twelve links are presented in terms of womb birth. The reason for this is that the progressive arising of the twelve links exists solely in the process of being born from a womb.

(6) The link of contact is the mental factor of the triad of object, sense faculty, and consciousness meeting and thus delimiting objects. Here, the six objects, six sense faculties, and six consciousnesses are easy to understand. The manner in which these three elements meet and thus delimit objects is by way of momentary consciousness cognizing momentarily changing objects. Contact can be classified as threefold (contact leading to experiences of pleasure, displeasure, or indifference). Or it can be classified as sixfold (contact by virtue of the eye sense faculty up through the mind sense faculty coming together with their respective objects) as well as the two types of contact that occur as the accompanying factors of the afflicted mind and the ālaya-consciousness, respectively.

(7) The link of feelings consists of the agreeable, painful, and neutral experiences in accordance with the objects delimited by contact. When classified, feelings are either fivefold (pleasant and unpleasant physical sensations, pleasant and unpleasant mental feelings, and neutral feelings) or twofold—physical sensations and mental feelings. The former are the sensations that occur as the

accompanying factors of the sense consciousnesses, while the latter are the feelings that occur as the accompanying factors of the mental consciousness. Or one speaks of the feelings based on renunciation (uncontaminated feelings) and the feelings based on clinging (contaminated feelings).

(8) The link of craving refers to being attached to pleasant and unpleasant feelings as something to be adopted and rejected, respectively. This can be classified as threefold—craving for the attainment of pleasure, craving for the relinquishment of suffering, and craving for equanimity as being neither, or craving for what is desirable, craving for existence, and craving for extinction.

(9) The link of grasping means grasping by striving to search for the causes of happiness and suffering. In general, both craving and grasping represent afflictions that function as motivational forces for the karmas that complete the skandhas of suffering. As for the difference between craving and grasping, some say that the *Madhyamakāvatārabhāṣya* explains it as the difference between craving and the latter increase of this craving, but this explanation was given with the intention of the continuum of the consciousness that craves becoming the consciousness that grasps. However, if grasping is explained as the specific feature of the increase of craving not in the sense just described, the difference between the two lies in craving being the striving to attain something, while grasping consists of the attainment of that something. Some also say that craving is desire in the sense of being attached to the nature of feelings, while grasping is desire in the sense of being attached to and striving for searching for the causes of these feelings. Grasping is classified as fourfold—the grasping of being attached to what is desirable (clinging to the five sense pleasures); the grasping onto the sixty-two wrong views; the grasping in terms of being conceited about ethics and spiritual disciplines; and the grasping of those who propound a self (being attached to the notions of a self or a sentient being).

(10) The link of becoming is as follows. After both craving and grasping have revived the latent tendencies of the propelling karmas whose specific result is to be propelled into one's next rebirth and which have been input into the ālaya-consciousness, the potency of these tendencies has become powerful. This means that they now represent what is called "becoming"—being about to be born in the specific realm and level that constitute one's next rebirth. Among the seven types of becoming (hell beings, hungry ghosts, animals, humans, gods, the intermediate state, and the becoming of karma), it is the last one that is presented as the link of becoming here. Becoming can also be classified as fourfold—the becoming of the past; the becoming of dying; the becoming of birth; and the becoming of the intermediate state. The first one refers to one's existence from being born up through the time right before the moment of dying. The second one is the moment of the

mind of dying. The third one refers to the first moment of consciousness in the mother's womb. The fourth one is the state from having died up through being conceived again.[432] As for the timespan of the latter, there appear to be two opinions, with some saying that it lasts for seven days, while others say that it is uncertain.[433] In any case, *Abhidharmakośa* III.13–14 and its *Bhāṣya* say about the features of beings in the intermediate state that their physical appearances resemble those of their next lifetime; they can be seen by others in the intermediate state and through the divine eye; they possess miraculous powers (such as moving through space); all their sense faculties are complete; they can penetrate anything, with nothing offering them any resistance; they cannot be prevented from heading toward their karmically destined next rebirth; and those of the desire realm feed on smells. Furthermore, becoming may be classified as threefold by way of the three realms, and as ninefold in terms of the way of being born—from the desire realm into the desire realm, form realm, and formless realm, respectively, with the same applying to the two higher realms. In detail, through the division of the nine levels of saṃsāra, becoming can be further classified into eighty-one in terms of the nine kinds of birth from each one of these levels into the desire realm up through the nine births from each one of these levels onto the Peak of Existence.

(11) The link of birth refers to the karmically matured skandhas being newly established through connecting with one's specific place of birth. Its classification is taught in *Abhidharmakośa* III.9—humans and animals can be born in all four ways; hell beings, gods, and beings in the intermediate state are only born miraculously; and hungry ghosts are usually born the same way, but can also be born from a womb.[434]

(12) The link of aging and death means that one's age changes and that one's life-force ceases, respectively. You may wonder, "Though there is death in the higher realms, isn't it that they lack aging?" Though they lack the aging of the faculties deteriorating, there is the aging of the substantial continuum of form dwindling through time. As for aging and death being presented together as a single link, this is both in terms of it being possible to die without having aged and to die by it being preceded by aging.

In brief, birth, aging, and death constitute the phase of the results of karmic maturation being manifest. Among these, aging and death represent specific features of this maturation, but not the actual maturation, because they are the results that concord with the causes which are the actual propelling factors. Therefore, these two results are presented from the perspective of the present because they are presented as completed results, just like today's harvest. The four links from name and form up through feelings are presented from the perspective of the future because they are presented as propelled results, just like next year's harvest.

2ab2) As for the presentation of the twelve links in terms of the karmas that will be experienced after having been reborn, the Vaibhāṣika system as described in *Abhidharmakośa* III.20cd–25ab says the following about the twelve links being completed over three lifetimes. All five skandhas at the time of engaging in the afflictions in the last life consist of ignorance. Since ignorance is their chief factor, or because they are included in it, all five skandhas are designated through it. The same needs to be understood for the other links too—all five skandhas at the time of accumulating karma in the last life represent the link of formations. Then, in this life, all five skandhas during the phase of first entering the mother's womb constitute the link of consciousness. Next, all five skandhas during the phase in the womb when the sense gates have not yet developed represent name and form. The five skandhas from the point of the sense faculties having developed up through not being able to delimit objects make up the six āyatanas. The five skandhas from the point of being able to delimit objects up through not knowing the specifics of the causes of happiness and suffering constitute contact. The five skandhas from the point of knowing the specifics of the causes of happiness and suffering up through not being able to engage in intercourse represent feelings. The five skandhas from the point of being able to engage in intercourse up through not taking on the objects of one's desire constitute craving. The five skandhas during the phase of taking on the objects of one's desire represent grasping. The five skandhas during the phase of accumulating the karma that completes the next rebirth are the link of becoming. Then, the five skandhas during the phase of entering the womb of one's mother in the next life constitute birth. Finally, the four links of name and form, the six āyatanas, contact, and feelings of one's next life are included in the link of aging and death. As the *Śālistambasūtra* says:

> That which is the arising of name and form is the arising of aging and death, and it is the same up through feelings.

Abhidharmakośa III.25cd describes the purpose of teaching the completion of the twelve links over three lifetimes in the above way as eliminating the ignorance about one's past, future, and present existences.

2b) The dependent origination of purified phenomena is that which is included in either of the realities of the path and cessation because these are characterized by being what purifies and the state of being purified, respectively. Thus, the cessation in the sense of all twelve links of dependent origination having stopped is the reality of cessation, but it is not that this cessation is independent of causes and conditions because it a result of freedom. You may wonder, "How is this designated as the dependent origination of purified phenomena?" It is designated in this way with the intention of all links from ignorance up through aging and death coming to an end. As *Mūlamadhyamakāvatāra* XXVI.11 explains:

> If ignorance ceases,
> Formations will not arise.
> The cessation of ignorance is by virtue of
> Knowledge having familiarized with true reality.

3) Meaning of the term "dependent origination"

In terms of the definitive meaning, it is what appears based on the mere dependence of what is posited and what posits it. For the detailed explanation of this term, see Candrakīrti's clear presentation in his *Prasannapadā*.[435]

4) How many lifetimes it takes for one cycle of the causal and resultant links of dependent origination to be completed

This completion can happen (a) instanteously or (b) over a longer period of time.

4a) It is possible for all twelve links to be complete in a single moment. According to my guru Karma Trinlépa's excellent explanation on this being explained in the *Abhidharmakośabhāṣya*,[436] it was said with the intention that, based on a karma such as killing under the influence of attachment, all twelve links will be fully complete in the future.

4b) Completion of the twelve links over a longer period of time can be experienced
(a) in one's next rebirth or (b) after any other number of rebirths.

Some say, "In terms of what is experienced in this lifetime, one cycle of the twelve links of dependent origination is completed in a single lifetime." This needs to be examined.[437]

4ba) As for the twelve links being completed in one's next rebirth, there are:
1) the Vaibhāṣika system and
2) the system of the Mere Mentalists

4ba1) As for the the first one, earlier Tibetan masters explain an initial cycle of the twelve links in dependence on one's last life and another cycle in dependence on one's next life (all links thus being completed over three lifetimes). The first one means that, in dependence on the ignorance and the karmic formations of one's last life functioning as the causes, their results are the five links from consciousness up through feelings in this life. The second one means that, in dependence on this life's three links of craving, grasping, and becoming functioning as the causes, their results arise as the two links of birth and aging and death in the next life. In terms of the twelve links thus being completed over three lifetimes, ignorance and formations are presented as the propelling factors; the five links from consciousness up through feelings are the propelled results; the three links of craving, grasping, and becoming are the completing factors; and birth as well as aging and death are the completed results.[438]

Evidently, this is to be analyzed as follows. Some people say, "This cycle of causes and results being completed over three lifetimes is explicitly clear in the sūtras and the above explanation by Tibetan masters is the intention of the *Abhidharmakośabhāṣya*. Thus, the sequence of causes and results is completed two times during three lifetimes." But then, in the above completion over three lifetimes, this life's birth, aging, and death are not propelled results because they are not explained as such results. They are not completed results either because there is the flaw of the causes that complete them (craving, grasping, and becoming) not having preceded them. Thus, there appears to be the flaw of one cycle of causes and results that depends on one's last life and this life being incomplete. Likewise, when it is explained that this life's craving, grasping, and becoming connect one with one's next birth and the aging and death therein, the question is whether, in this latter cycle of the twelve links, there is or is not the ignorance that represents a propelling factor. If it does not exist in this latter cycle, there is the flaw of the twelve links being incomplete in it. But if this ignorance exists in it, the question is whether it is the ignorance of the cycle that depends on one's last life or the ignorance that is an accompanying factor of the craving and grasping that serve to complete one's next life. The first case is untenable since it entails the following flaw. If the ignorance of the first one of the two cycles that are taken to be completed over three lifetimes were suitable as the ignorance in the second cycle, then this ignorance of the first cycle alone would be sufficient as all instances of propelling ignorance as long as one cycles in saṃsāra. The second case is not tenable either because then it would follow that the very causes that complete are causes that propel. Furthermore, some people, for the reason of not accepting the ālaya-consciousness, present the link of consciousness (which is no doubt a cause that propels) as a propelled result and say that next life's name and form, āyatanas, and so on are included in the links of birth, aging, and death. But all such crooked explanations of the meaning of the scriptures represent just the meanings of bad philosophical systems.

In this context, with others not understanding how the twelve links' full cycle of causes and results is completed once over three lifetimes, the oral explanation of the mighty victor, Chötra Gyatso, on this is roughly presented as follows. Last life's links of ignorance, formations, and consciousness have been propelled through last life's three links of craving, grasping, and becoming toward this life's six links of name and form, āyatanas, contact, feelings, birth, and aging and death. Likewise, this life's ignorance, formations, and consciousness are propelled through this life's three links of craving, grasping, and becoming toward next life's six links of name and form, āyatanas, contact, feelings, birth, and aging and death. You may wonder now, "So what is the flawless explanation of the twelve links being completed once over three lifetimes in the Vaibhāṣikas' own system?" It says that, during one lifetime, driven by the motivational force of ignorance, through formations, the potencies of karmas are input into consciousness. During the next lifetime, through being revived by craving and grasping, the potencies of these karmas—becoming—is rendered powerful. During the third lifetime, the remaining six resultant links are completed.

4ba2) According to the system of the Mere Mentalists, the causes and results of one full cycle of the twelve links are completed over two lifetimes. Last life's two links of ignorance and formations propel the four links from name and form up through feelings through implanting them into the ālaya-consciousness as seeds that are suitable to arise later. The latent tendencies of these four propelled links are then, through the two links of craving and grasping, rendered into the link of becoming. "To be rendered into the link of becoming" means that said latent tendencies are revived through craving and grasping. "Revived" means that craving and grasping render into these tendencies factors that are certain to yield maturations in the second moment, just as a seed that has fallen somewhere on the earth is certain to sprout in the second moment by virtue of the conditions of moisture, warmth, and fertilizer. In this way, the specific features that are the flaws resulting from said four propelled results are presented as the completed results—the two links of birth and aging and death. In brief, through the completion of six causes in one's last life, six results in this life are completed.

Furthermore, the following difficult point in this context is to be analyzed. The self-isolate of becoming is not presented as having the nature of propelling karma because this self-isolate is presented as the latent tendencies that are input through the propelling karmas. Without analysis, this becoming is identified as completing karma, but under analysis, it is not so identified because becoming is presented as the phase of the potencies of the completing karmas having entered the latent tendencies of the propelling karmas. Therefore, the link of formations is only that which propels the nature of what is matured, but not that which produces it, whereas becoming is that which produces the nature of what is matured. Explained in this way, at the time of maturation a long time has elapsed after the actual propelling factors have ceased, whereas becoming exists during the entire time from its having rendered the latent tendencies of the propelling karmas into the factors that are certain to yield maturation up through their uninterrupted state of having matured. Thus, becoming's own nature is neutral, but the nature of the propelling factors is either only virtuous or nonvirtuous. Among the factors that revive virtuous and nonvirtuous latent tendencies, all three types of karma (virtuous, nonvirtuous, and neutral) are possible. Explained in this way, both the actual propelling factors and their latent tendencies are presented as maturing causes. The actual maturations (name and form up through feelings), the actual completing factors, and their latent tendencies are causes of similar outcome. Their products (birth, aging, and death) are results that concord with their causes. Under analysis, the actual maturations (such as form) can also be presented as results that concord with their causes in that they depend on their own preceding completing factors.

Some may think here, "According to this explanation of the Mere Mentalists, in which the twelve links are completed once over two lifetimes, the order of these links is not as presented by the Buddha since the three links of craving, grasping, and becoming follow immediately after the link of consciousness." There is no flaw because this enumeration of the order of the twelve links given by the Buddha here represents the manner in which he adapted the hīnayāna scriptures (which explain the twelve links to be completed once over three lifetimes) to the mahāyāna scriptures. Furthermore, one may think, "The Mere Mentalist system here is not in accord with the explanation in the sūtras that craving arises through the condition of feelings because it says that craving and grasping are the factors that produce what is matured, such as feelings." There is no such flaw either because of the following. The intention behind what is said here is that, though there are no three links of craving, grasping, and becoming that constitute the actual completing factors of the four already manifest matured links (such as name and form), during the own time of the continuum of these matured links' own nature and their specific features there arise the three links of craving, grasping, and becoming that represent the factors which produce the subsequent ones of these matured links. Moreover, through explaining that the twelve links are completed once over two lifetimes, it is de facto taught that craving arises from feeling, which is by virtue of having in mind that (in the same way as one's last life and this life are related) the propelling and completing factors for the respective links in one's next life must be acculumated in this life. There is also an example for this being justified. In the psychophysical support of a Brahmakāyika god there arises the craving of relishing the flavor of the feeling within the actual first dhyāna. This craving increases the potencies of the corresponding latent tendencies within the ālaya-consciousness of that god. Through doing so, in this Brahmakāyika god later instances similar in type to the nature of what has matured (this god's name and form) and its particular features (aging and death) that concord with their causes are produced. Therefore, until the potencies of said latent tendencies are exhausted, the maturations produced by them will arise or those that have arisen already are not discontinued.

4bb) In terms of karma being experienced after any other number of rebirths, the sūtras explain that it is possible for the twelve links to be incomplete even up to hundreds of millions of eons.

5) The distinction in terms of the twelve links being substantially or imputedly existent

Earlier Tibetan masters claim, "In terms of two cycles of the twelve links being completed over three lifetimes as per the Vaibhāṣikas, in the first cycle seven links are substantially existent and five are imputedly existent. As for the manner of imputation, craving and grasping are imputed onto elements of ignorance; becoming, onto elements of formations; birth, onto elements of consciousness; and aging and death, onto elements of the four links from name and form up through feelings. In terms of the second cycle, five links are substantially existent and seven are imputedly existent. Here, ignorance is imputed onto elements of craving and grasping; formations, onto elements of becoming; consciousness, onto elements of birth; and the four links from name and form up through feelings, onto elements of aging and death. This distinction into substantial and imputed existence is the Vaibhāṣika system's rationale for two cycles of the twelve links being completed over three lifetimes." On this, Avalokiteśvara Dharmakīrtisamudraśrībhadra[439] says, "This assertion by earlier Tibetans is foolish chatter. No matter whether the links of dependent origination are presented in one or two cycles, they must be presented on the basis of entities, whereas a presentation of these links based on nonentities is not feasible because, in terms of seeming reality, the latter are not able to perform any function. Therefore, in terms of the twelve links being complete once over three lifetimes, the teaching on certain links being of substantial and imputed existence, respectively, is given for small-minded people who think, 'Since the third lifetime's seven links such as ignorance are not explicitly mentioned, it follows that they are left out' and 'Since the middling lifetime's five links such as craving and grasping are not explicitly mentioned, it follows that they are left out.' However, said teaching is of expedient meaning. Therefore, it is only in this sense that the explanation of certain links being of substantial and imputed existence, respectively, is a correct proof for the twelve links being completed once over three lifetimes." It is clear that this single completion over three lifetimes is the *Abhidharmakośa*'s own system since it is stated in lines III.20cd and their *Bhāṣya* that the first two links pertain to one's last life; the next eight, to the present life; and the last two, to the next life.

If this is explained according to the common yāna, one may wonder about the reason for calling this "the dependent origination of afflicted phenomena." The twelve links are designated in this way because they are all included in the three kinds of afflictions in terms of what is afflictive, karmically active, and serves as the basis of afflictions. Ignorance, craving, and grasping are "afflictive afflictions"; formations and becoming are "karmic afflictions"; and the remaining seven links are "afflictions in terms of being bases." The reasons for these, in due order, are that ignorance, craving, and grasping are not only afflictions by nature, but also further searching for and grasping at afflictions; formations and becoming are the karmic activities that are produced by the first three afflictions; and the remaining seven links (such as consciousness) are the bases upon which afflictions or suffering are experienced. This is also expressed in Nāgārjuna's *Pratītyasamutpādahṛdaya* (verse 3):

> From the three, the two arise;
> From these two, the seven arise; and from these seven,
> The three arise—this wheel of existence
> Turns again and again.

6) The distinction in terms of the twelve links corresponding or not corresponding to a given level of saṃsāric existence

This is explained briefly and roughly according to Nāyakaḥ Svayavajra's treatise called *Differentiating Dependent Origination*.[440] The link of ignorance that occurs as an accompanying factor of the afflicted mind is included in the very class of sentient beings in which certain karmas are accumulated because this ignorance is the causal motivational force of the karmas that propel maturation. Also, the link of consciousness is included in the very beings who accumulate certain karmas because the afflicted mind and the ālaya-consciousness are included within the physical supports of the beings who accumulate certain karmas. The link of ignorance that is an accompanying factor of the mental consciousness is mainly taken as belonging to the future level on which one will be reborn—the six propelled and completed results are necessarily included in solely the level on which one will be reborn. The two links of formations and becoming are exclusively included in the level on which one will be reborn. For it is contradictory for the factors that propel the maturations of another level to be the factors that propel the maturations of the present level at hand and it is also contradictory for the factors that produce the maturations of this level to be the factors that produce the maturations of another level. Grasping also corresponds to the level on which one will be reborn because it is definitely nothing but that which revives the maturations of the level on which one will be reborn. Unlike with grasping, there is no certainty for craving that it corresponds to the level on which one will be reborn. For example, when one is born on the first dhyāna level from the desire realm, though the craving in this case is a craving that is based on the feelings of the desire realm, the grasping in this case is the appropriating factor that represents the cause of the feelings of the first dhyāna level. In terms of cultivating causal meditative absorptions, some also assert that, in a psychophysical support of the desire realm, there occurs the craving that craves for the feelings of the dhyānas.

F) The nature of the path of familiarization (lion's sport and crossing in one leap)[441]

This has seven parts:

1) Eliminating the qualms of Tibetan masters in the context of Āryavimuktisena's and Haribhadra's explanation of the samādhi of the lion's sport as the special path of the path of seeing
2) Determining the objects of the meditative absorptions of the preparatory lion's sport and the actual crossing in one leap
3) Reflecting on the manner of entering into meditative absorption through these two samādhis
4) Explaining the manner in which the factors to be relinquished are relinquished through these meditative absorptions that serve as their remedies
5) Removing contradictions to other scriptures
6) JNS's specific comments on the *Vivṛti* on AA IV.24–25
7) The manner in which the conceptions that are factors to be relinquished through familiarization are relinquished

1) Eliminating the qualms of Tibetan masters in the context of Āryavimuktisena's and Haribhadra's explanation of the samādhi of the lion's sport as the special path of the path of seeing

Some Tibetan masters say, "Having in mind that those on the path of seeing are not able to enter the meditative absorption of cessation, the *Vṛtti* says:

> The path of familiarization consists of the nine meditative absorptions of progressive abiding. These consist of the meditative absorptions of crossing in one leap . . .[442]

This and the explanation that the lion's sport belongs to the path of seeing while the crossing in one leap is the path of familiarization contradict the sūtras because the sūtras say that these two samādhis represent the pāramitā of dhyāna among the other five pāramitās that are included in prajñāpāramitā.

Not only are the above explanations in contradiction with the sūtras, they also contradict the claims of the people who give such explanations. For these two samādhis represent the pāramitā of dhyāna, whereas said people explain the dhyāna on the path of seeing as the six sets of six pāramitās. Though they think that one does not enter the meditative absorption of cessation on the path of seeing, they explain the samādhi of the lion's sport as belonging to the path of seeing. In fact, this samādhi is distinguished by engaging in the nine meditative absorptions of progressive abiding in both their progressive and reverse orders. In addition, the sūtra passage on the dissolution of the branches of dhyāna of irreversible bodhisattvas on the path of seeing (AA IV.47d) says that such bodhisattvas engage in the eight liberations and the nine meditative absorptions.[443] If that is accepted, everybody from stream-enterers up through pratyekabuddhas is able to attain this." "Furthermore, it is explained that if śrāvakas and pratyekabuddhas too enter the meditative absorption of cessation, all the qualities of relinquishment and realization of śrāvakas and pratyekabuddhas are included in the mahāyāna path of seeing. In addition, it very absurdly follows that the path of familiarization consists of the nine meditative absorptions, and it is equally absurd to think that the nine meditative absorptions consist of the path of familiarization. Therefore, 'crossing in one leap' is the detailed explanation of the lion's sport, but this samādhi itself is included in the path of familiarization[444] alone."

Such statements are not justified. The misinterpretation of these people that Āryavimuktisena's and Haribhadra's position entails thinking that bodhisattvas with the clear realization of the path of seeing are not able to enter the meditative absorption of cessation is an obvious case of said people themselves not having arrived at clear realization because the texts of Āryavimuktisena and Haribhadra are very clear about bodhisattvas being able to enter the meditative absorption of cessation after having attained the mahāyāna path of seeing. The above-mentioned flaw of it following that the path of familiarization consists of the nine meditative absorptions does not apply either. For it is the meaning of the mother sūtras that the 108 conceptions that are the cognitive obscurations of the path of familiarization are relinquished through the eighty-nine meditative absorptions of progressive abiding on the second up through the tenth bhūmis.[445] In unison, powerful paṇḍitas such as Āryavimuktisena, Haribhadra, Ratnākaraśānti, and Abhayākaragupta commented in accordance with the explanation in the sūtras that the samādhi of the lion's sport that constitutes the special path of the path of seeing and the lion's sport that is the preparation for the actual meditative equipoises of the path of familiarization are different. These are the masters whom we follow here, but not some impudent and defiant Tibetans who cannot bear being accused of denigrating Āryavimuktisena through their above criticism and thus feel pressed to claim that the Āryavimuktisena who was the disciple of Vasubandhu, the second omniscient one, was not the Āryavimuktisena who composed the *Vṛtti*.[446]

2) Determining the objects of the meditative absorptions of the preparatory lion's sport and the actual crossing in one leap

In terms of the path of familiarization, the objects of the lion's sport (the preparation) and the crossing in one leap (the actual samādhi) are the nine meditative absorptions of progressive abiding. Among these, the four dhyānas and four formless absorptions have already been explained above.[447] As for ascertaining the meaning of the meditative absorption of cessation, this has six parts:

a) The persons who enter it
b) The realms in which it is entered
c) The levels that are its mental supports
d) The factors to be ceased that it makes cease
e) Its own nature
f) The timespan for which it is entered

2a) In terms of the śrāvakas, according to *Abhidharmakośa* VI.43cd and 64a, those who enter this meditative absorption are only those nonreturners who are bodily witnesses and the arhats who are liberated through both prajñā and samādhi.[448] The *Viniścayasaṃgrahaṇī* explains that pratyekabuddhas also enter the meditative absorption of cessation.[449] In terms of the mahāyāna, the *Viniścayasaṃgrahaṇī*[450] says that irreversible bodhisattvas and buddhas enter this meditative absorption. It is well known from Bhāvaviveka's *Madhyamakaratnapradīpa*[451] that bodhisattvas of sharp faculties attain buddhahood in three incalculable eons, while those with medium and dull faculties do so in seven and thirty-three such eons, respectively. In terms of those of dull faculties, the paths of accumulation and preparation together last for three incalculable eons, and each one of the ten bhūmis lasts for three such eons. According to *Mahāyānasūtrālaṃkāra* XIV.29cd and 44ab, for those of sharp faculties, the three periods of engagement through aspiration (the paths of accumulation and preparation), the seven impure bhūmis, and the three pure bhūmis, respectively, each last for one incalculable eon. The same is said in the *Bodhisattvabhūmi*,[452] which adds that "incalculable eon" refers to being beyond sixty great eons. According to the *Ālokā*, during the first incalculable eon, everything from the level of accumulation up through the first bhūmi is completed; the second eon lasts from the second to the seventh bhumis; and the third one, from the eighth bhūmi up through buddhahood. About the sixth and seventh bhūmis, *Madhyamakāvatāra* VI.1cd and VII.1b says:

> The [bodhisattva] who sees the true reality of dependent origination
> Dwells in prajñā and thus attains cessation.
>
> [The bodhisattva] enters cessation in a single instant.

In agreement with this, the *Daśabhūmikasūtra* says:

> From the sixth bodhisattvabhūmi onward, they enter the meditative absorption of cessation of bodhisattvas. Bodhisattvas who dwell on the seventh bodhisattvabhūmi enter the meditative absorption of cessation in each mental instant, but this is not called "having manifested cessation."[453]

These statements are made with the intention of whether said bodhisattvas are able or not to enter this meditative absorption in the manner of being without any characteristics. However, in general, bodhisattvas are able to enter the meditative absorption of cessation from the path of seeing onward—the prajñāpāramitā sūtras say that irreversible bodhisattvas enter the meditative absorption of the first dhyāna up through the meditative absorption of cessation.[454]

2b) As for the realms in which the meditative absorption of cessation is entered, in terms of the śrāvakas, one first enters it in the desire realm and then enters it in the form realm later. The *Abhidharmasamuccaya* says:

> The meditative absorption of cessation is supramundane—it is produced among humans. After it has been produced among humans, it is manifested either among humans or in the form realm. In the formless realm it cannot be manifested.[455]

Abhidharmakośa VI.44cd agrees on this. Such a presentation is in terms of the śrāvakas, who do not accept the ālaya-consciousness. According to the Mere Mentalists, one first enters the meditative absorption of cessation in the desire realm and then enters it in all three realms later. The *Viniścayasaṃgrahaṇī* says:

> If the ālaya-consciousness is presented, the manifestation [of this meditative absorption] should be regarded as happening in all [three realms].[456]

2c) The levels that are its mental supports
This has two parts:
a) The supports for entering it
b) The supports for rising from it

2ca) The *Abhidharmakośabhāṣya* on II.43b[457] says that the support for entering the meditative absorption of cessation is solely the level of Neither Discrimination Nor Nondiscrimination. Thus, after having attained the mental state of the Peak of Existence, through mentally engaging in the nature of phenomena the meditative absorption of cessation arises once the subtle mental elements of the Peak of Existence have ceased (due to the latter's great subtlety, its flux of primary minds and mental factors is easy to stop). The *Koṣṭilaparipṛcchāsūtra* says:

> How many causes and how many conditions are there for resting in meditative equipoise in the expanse of signlessness? There are two—not mentally engaging in any signs and mentally engaging in the expanse of signlessness.

The *Śrāvakabhūmi* explains that the meditative absorption of cessation arises from mentally engaging in feelings and discriminations as being coarse and in freedom from these as being peaceful.

2cb) As *Abhidharmakośa* VIII.33cd says, the supports for rising from the meditative absorption of cessation are either the pure state of mind of the Peak of Existence or the uncontaminated level of Nothing Whatsoever.

2d) The factors to be ceased that it makes cease
The meditative absorption of cessation ceases the seven collections of consciousness plus their accompanying mental factors as appropriate. The *Abhidharmasamuccaya* says:

> What is the cessation of discriminations and feelings? It is the cessation of those phenomena that are the unstable minds and mental factors as well as some of the stable ones, [which occurs] through the mental engagement of the preceding discrimination of abiding in peace of someone who is free from the desire of the āyatana of Nothing Whatsoever and moves above the Peak of Existence.[458]

The *Sūtrasamuccaya* by the arhat Dharmatrāta says:

> "Moving above" is the manifestation of no arising and no ceasing.

In the above quote, "peace" refers to all three lower noble ones of the śrāvakayāna (stream-enterers, once-returners, and nonreturners).

Or the factors to be ceased refer to all reference points being ceased. As the *Madhyamakāvatārabhāṣya* on VII.1 says:

> Since the meditative absorption of cessation is the meditative absorption in the true end, suchness is called "cessation" because all reference points cease in it.[459]

2e) Its own nature

The Mere Mentalists assert it to to be the cessation of the factors to be ceased (the seven collections of consciousness plus their accompanying mental factors) within the ālaya-consciousness. However, this is not tenable—since there is no ālaya-consciousness on the buddhabhūmi, there would be no meditative absorption of cessation on this level. Therefore, the nature of this meditative absorption is the cessation of the entirety of reference points within nondual wisdom or profound emptiness (the basis of cessation).

The śrāvakas assert the nature of this meditative absorption as consciousness having been made to cease within the body. The *Dharmadattāparipṛcchāsūtra* says:

> The consciousness of this [meditative absorption] is not separated from the body.

2f) The timespan for which it is entered

As for śrāvakas and pratyekabuddhas, *Laṅkāvatārasūtra* II.209cd says:

> Once they have attained the body of samādhi,
> They do not awake for eons.

As for bodhisattvas, the *Sūryagarbhasūtra* says:

> Bodhisattvas rest in meditative absorption between one and seven days. If they were to rest longer in meditative absorption, their bodhisattva conduct would deteriorate.[460]

The *Mahākaruṇāpuṇḍarīkasūtra* states:

> Bodhisattvas who are obstructed [from buddhahood] by a single birth spend ten intermediate eons by resting in the meditative absorption of cessation.

3) Reflecting on the manner of entering into meditative absorption through the two samādhis of lion's sport and crossing in one leap

a) As for the lion's sport (the preparation), the sūtras say:

> Subhūti, what is the samādhi of the lion's roar of bodhisattva mahāsattvas? Subhūti, bodhisattvas free from desire, free from evil and nonvirtuous dharmas, abide by practicing the first dhyāna, which entails examination and analysis, arises from detachment, and is endowed with joy and bliss . . . Having risen from the meditative absorption of the āyatana of Neither Discrimination Nor Nondiscrimination, they enter the meditative absorption of cessation. Having risen from the meditative absorption of cessation, they enter the meditative absorption of the āyatana of Neither Discrimination Nor Nondiscrimination . . . Having risen from the second dhyāna, they enter the first dhyāna.[461]

b) As for the lesser crossing in one leap,[462] the sūtras say:

> What is the samādhi of crossing in one leap of bodhisattva mahāsattvas? Subhūti, bodhisattvas free from desire, free from evil and nonvirtuous dharmas, abide by practicing the first dhyāna, which entails examination and analysis, arises from detachment, and is endowed with joy and bliss . . . Having risen from the meditative absorption of the āyatana of Neither Discrimination Nor Nondiscrimination, they abide by practicing the cessation of discriminations and feelings. Having risen from the meditative absorption of cessation, they enter the first dhyāna.

c) As for the medium crossing in one leap, the sūtras say:

> Having risen from the first dhyāna, they enter the meditative absorption of cessation. Having risen from the meditative absorption of cessation, they enter the second dhyāna . . . Having risen from the meditative absorption of the āyatana of Neither Discrimination Nor Nondiscrimination, they enter the meditative absorption of cessation.

d) As for the great crossing in one leap, the sūtras say:

> Having risen from the meditative absorption of cessation, they adopt a state of mind of not being in meditative equipoise. From that state of mind of not being in meditative equipoise, they enter

> the meditative absorption of cessation. Having risen from the meditative absorption of cessation, they adopt a state of mind of not being in meditative equipoise. From that state of mind of not being in meditative equipoise, they enter the meditative absorption of Neither Discrimination Nor Nondiscrimination . . . From that state of mind of not being in meditative equipoise, they enter into the meditative absorption of the first dhyāna. Having risen from the first dhyāna, they adopt a state of mind of not being in meditative equipoise.

a) As for the first one (the preparatory lion's sport) among these four phases, it is the meditative absorption in which one travels through the nine meditative absorptions of progressive abiding in their given progressive (upward) and reverse (downward) orders, without skipping any of them or alternating them with any other mental states. When divided, in terms of the division into eighty-one actual samādhis of crossing in one leap from the second up through the tenth bhūmis, there are accordingly eighty-one preparatory samādhis of the lion's sport (as preparations for each one of those samādhis of crossing in one leap). When divided in terms of the number of distinct meditative states within said sequence of the lion's sport, there are eighteen. Some also speak of seventeen meditative states by counting the two meditative absorptions of cessation during the upward and downward progressions, respectively, as one.

b) The lesser crossing in one leap is the meditative absorption in which one travels through the nine meditative absorptions of progressive abiding in their progressive (upward) order, without skipping any of them or alternating them with any other mental states. As for their division, they are asserted to be definitely only nine in number. Some say, "Preceded by the preparatory lion's sport, in order to attain the medium crossing in one leap one enters the nine meditative absorptions of progressive abiding in both their given progressive (upward) and reverse (downward) orders." In this context, some assert that there are eighteen meditative states, which is answered by others saying, "There are not eighteen meditative states because there is no meditative absorption of cessation of progressing downwards. For having risen from the meditative absorption of cessation of progressing upward, one enters the meditative absorption of Neither Discrimination Nor Nondiscrimination." Some say, "This does not invalidate the existence of eighteen meditative states because these two meditative absorptions of cessation are separated through a state of mind of the desire the realm." Yet others say, "Something like the samādhi of the lion's sport that bears the name of lesser crossing in one leap, is not interspersed with any eliminating of phenomena of concordant or discordant classes, and does not drop certain phenomena is not the actual crossing in one leap because it does not match the explanation of the term 'crossing in one leap' in any way." Though there is no lineaege of explaining the term "crossing in one leap" for said samādhi, it is tenable to explain it as "crossing in one leap" because the Bhagavān used this conventional term for it in the prajñāpāramitā sūtras. Here, some also say, "The lesser crossing in one leap is not the actual crossing in one leap. Rather, just as one points out a racing course for horses, it demonstrates the arena for crossing in one leap."

c) Medium crossing in one leap initially consists of sixteen meditative states through cultivating the first eight meditative absorptions of progressive abiding by alternating each one of them with the meditative absorption of cessation. Finally, by virtue of a state of mind of the Peak of Existence, one rises from the last cessation in this sequence. After having risen from the Peak of Existence, one manifests a state of mind of not being in meditative equipoise. Here, said rising from the meditative absorption of cessation into the state of mind of the Peak of Existence is adduced as the seventeenth meditative state in terms of it being a "slight exiting" from the former, while they are one in substance. Different from that, the subsequent state of mind of the desire realm of not being in meditative equipoise is just the ancillary state that marks the boundary line between the medium and the great crossing in one leap (and thus not counted as a separate meditative state). The reverse order of these meditative states begins as follows. From said state of mind of the desire realm, one assumes a state of mind of the Peak of Existence, which then comes to rest in the meditative absorption of Neither Discrimination Nor Nondiscrimination. After that, starting to progress downward, again, from the meditative absorption of Neither Discrimination Nor Nondiscrimination, one enters the meditative absorption of cessation. In this manner, alternating each one of the four formless absorptions and the four dhyānas with the meditative absorption of cessation continues all the way down through the first dhyāna, which results in thirty-four meditative states altogether. Finally, there is a state of mind of the desire realm, making thirty-five.[463] Some say, "The medium crossing in one leap is eighteenfold. Apart from the first sixteen as described above, the seventeenth is the slight exiting from the meditative absorption of cessation into the Peak of Existence, while the eighteenth is the state of mind of the desire realm after having been in the Peak of Existence." Others say, "Medium crossing in one leap has twenty meditative states—in addition to the first sixteen above, there are the slight exiting at the end of cessation, the manifesting of a state of mind of the desire realm, cessation, and again a state of mind of the desire realm." These statements must be examined by matching them with the sūtras.

Here, some Tibetans say, "The explanation in the mother sūtras that the rising from cessation relies on the state of mind of the Peak of Existence (see

2cb above) appears also in the system of characteristics. As *Abhidharmakośa* VIII.33cd says, it is stated in this way in terms of manifesting a state of mind of rising from meditative absorption, whereas the term 'slight exiting' is not found in the terminology of the land of the noble ones."[464] In answer to this, when others search for what the purpose for a "slight exiting" might be, some say, "It is for the sake of manifesting a state of mind of the desire realm. For right after having alternated the two final very peaceful states of the Peak of Existence and the following meditative absorption of cessation, one is not able to manifest a state of mind of the desire realm, whereas one is able to do so through slightly exiting from said states. Also since the mental consciousness has ceased in the meditative absorption of cessation, when one rises from this cessation one must rise through the state of mind at the end of the Peak of Existence." Others claim, "The purpose of manifesting a state of mind of the desire realm in the phase of medium crossing in one leap is to alternate cessation with cessation. As for the purpose of alternating cessation and cessation since there is no slight exiting on the sixth bhūmi and below, from a momentary cessation one is not able to reenter cessation in an instant. However, through the power of slight exiting, one is able to enter from one momentary cessation into another one. Therefore, the boundary line between such former and later cessations must be marked by a state of mind of the desire realm." Yet others say, "The reason for manifesting a state of mind of the desire realm right after the slight exiting is that it is done for the sake of examining whether one is able to alternate cessation and a state of mind of the desire realm."

These statements are to be analyzed a bit. In general, it is the system of the hīnayāna that one must rely on the states of mind of either the Peak of Existence or the level of Nothing Whatsoever when one rises from the meditative absorption of cessation. According to the mahāyāna, no matter whether one enters or rises from the meditative absorption of cessation, any entering and rising through having gained mastery over nonconceptual wisdom is explained as the aspect of having gained self-control. Furthermore, in this context of the medium crossing in one leap, to alternate cessation with cessation is not the intention of the sūtras, the AA, and its commentaries because something like that does not clearly appear in the sūtras. Some say, "According to the presentation of twenty meditative states, it is evidently clear that cessation and cessation are taken as alternating phenomena." However, without the sūtras dividing cessation in terms of a basis of alternation and the phenomenon that alternates with it, it is a mistake to make a presentation of two cessations as alternating phenomena. Some may think, "In the AA, the medium crossing in one leap does not clearly appear except for just one indirect phrase (line V.25d), but the *Vivṛti* brings it out well by saying, 'After having manifested such a consciousness of not being in meditative equipoise, one enters cessation.'"[465] However, this is the *Vivṛti's* commentary on the great crossing in one leap. Also, there is no need for a state of mind of the desire realm to mark the boundary between a former and a later cessation as held in the above position. Since that boundary is already marked by the slight exiting into the Peak of Existence, there is no need for it to be marked again by a state of mind of the desire realm.

In brief, this statement of "entering the meditative absorption of cessation from cessation" is made in terms of progressing upward and downward through the eighteen meditative states on the basis of alternating all of them with cessation. To take the medium crossing in one leap as eighteen meditative states accords with the sūtra in one hundred thousand lines, but in terms of the seventeen meditative states according to the sūtras in twenty-five thousand and eight thousand lines, one does not enter the meditative absorption of cessation from cessation. Rather, the great translator Ngog has coined the conventional term "slight exiting" for the following. When one, coming from the Peak of Existence of the upward progression, goes back into entering the Peak of Existence of the downward progression, one rises again by virtue of a state of mind of the Peak of Existence.[466] According to my leader, Karmake Kīrti Abdhi,[467] this point is clearly explained in the sūtra in eighteen thousand lines.

Also, the above statement that, "without said slight exiting, through the peaceful states of mind of cessation and the Peak of Existence one is not able to manifest a state of mind of the desire realm" is not tenable. For both the sūtras and the commentaries explain that one is able to manifest a state of mind of the desire realm after cessation, saying, "One enters cessation and then a state of mind of not being in meditative equipoise." Furthermore, it may be said, "Said cessation is a cessation that is produced by the Peak of Existence and thus is the final state of peacefulness. For this reason, by virtue of this cessation, one is not able to enter a state of mind of the desire realm." This is not the case either—a meditative absorption of cessation that is not produced by the Peak of Existence is not possible anyway. Therefore, according to the just-mentioned position, there accrues the flaw of it following that one, without slightly exiting from the meditative absorption of cessation that one has entered from the Peak of Existence, is not able to rise into the phase of subsequent attainment. Also, it is not tenable to say, "This slight exiting is the training in the dexterity of samādhi to enter cessation in one instant." For even without said slight exiting, there are no other obstacles for bodhisattvas making all characteristics cease within the state of wisdom free from reference points. Therefore, the excellent explanation of Karmaka Tathāgata[468] on the purpose of slightly exiting into the Peak of Existence is that this is for the sake of engaging in the very peaceful samādhi of the medium crossing in one leap.

d) Great crossing in one leap is presented as the eighteen meditative states of alternating each one of the nine meditative absorptions of progressive abiding with the state of mind of the desire realm, which is done in both upward and downward progression, thus making thirty-six. Śrī Karmakaḥ says that the state of mind of the desire realm here is identified as the pure subsequent attainment of bodhisattvas, but that this is meant in terms of each moment.[469]

4) Explaining the manner in which the factors to be relinquished are relinquished through these meditative absorptions that serve as their remedies

As for the clear realization subsequent to the invalidation of the seeds of the conceptions that are to be relinquished through familiarization, the preparatory path of the lion's sport first suppresses these seeds, while the actual crossing in one leap (the uninterrupted path) eradicates them fully later. According to AA IV.54bd, by virtue of the division of their factors to be relinquished, said preparatory and uninterrupted paths of the path of familiarization also must each be divided into nine:

> It is treated as ninefold
> Through its lesser, medium, and great degrees
> Being further divided into lesser and so on.

During the preparatory stage, in terms of the ninefold division of each one of the first two conceptions about apprehender and apprehended, these two sets of nine are gradually relinquished through two sets of nine preparations. Some may object, "But then the nine conceptions that are factors to be relinquished through seeing must equally be relinquished gradually through the progression of the four paths." This is not the case because it appears in the AA that the factors to be relinquished through seeing are not relinquished through nine lesser, medium, and great[470] remedies, while the factors to be relinquished through familiarization are gradually relinquished through nine lesser, medium, and great remedies. This kind of preparatory lion's sport is the pāramitā of dhyāna that is a subdivision of the six pāramitās with which prajñāpāramitā is endowed. This pāramitā of dhyāna consists of the nine meditative absorptions of progressive abiding that are congruently associated with the prajñā of directly realizing emptiness. By virtue of its having the nature of engaging in these meditative absorptions in their progressive and reverse orders, it directly invalidates the seeds of the conceptions that are the factors to be relinquished through familiarization. Therefore, it is called "the lion's sport." Consequently, there are as many instances of the preparatory lion's sport as there are uninterrupted paths of the actual crossing in one leap from the second up through the tenth bhūmis.

The actual crossing in one leap is explained as lesser, medium, and great. As its specific factors to be relinquished, the lesser crossing in one leap eradicates the seeds of any of the three great degrees of the conceptions that are factors to be relinquished through familiarization. Accordingly, this lesser crossing in one leap is presented as threefold[471] by virtue of its having lesser, medium, and great degrees. As its specific factors to be relinquished, the medium crossing in one leap eradicates the seeds of any of the three medium degrees of the conceptions that are factors to be relinquished through familiarization (as before, this medium crossing in one leap is also threefold). As its specific factors to be relinquished, the great crossing in one leap eradicates the seeds of any of the three lesser degrees of the conceptions that are factors to be relinquished through familiarization (this greater crossing is threefold too). You may wonder, "How does one match the thirty-six conceptions about the apprehender and apprehended (which are listed in the sūtras and the AA and have the nature of being factors to be relinquished through familiarization) with these lesser, medium, and great crossings in one leap, each of which is again explained to be threefold?" Dharmasvāmin Śrī Karmakaḥ says that each one of the four conceptions is divided into nine by way of its objects. Being further divided by way of the three realms, this makes 108. These are then divided by the nine levels (or bhūmis) of the path of familiarization. Through likewise dividing the 108 remedies for said conceptions through the nine levels of crossing in one leap, these two sets are matched as factors to be relinquished and their remedies, respectively.

Some great ones think, "This manner of matching factors to be relinquished and remedies is not justified. For on each one of the nine bhūmis of the path of familiarization, one would then relinquish nine sets of 108 factors to be relinquished by focusing on the three realms, together 972. Also, with the 108 remedies that relinquish the 108 conceptions on each bhūmi being divided into nine levels of crossing in one leap, there would equally be 972 remedies. Thus, adding the factors to be relinquished and their remedies in this context, there would be 1,944, which means being endless." Then, they put forth their own system: "The 108 conceptions are summarized into nine through their division in terms of greater, medium, and lesser degrees. Thus, they are relinquished in the manner of the nine levels of the actual crossing in one leap being their respective nine remedies."

Others say, "The ninefold divisions of the factors to be relinquished through seeing would then also be divided into lesser, medium, and great, which means that their remedies must equally be divided into nine in terms of lesser, medium, and great." This is not the same case because one is able to relinquish the 108 conceptions to be relinquished through seeing merely through directly seeing the nature of phenomena. But on the path of familiarization, the corresponding conceptions to be relinquished must be relinquished through the power of familiarizing with what has already been seen directly. "But then the path of seeing's later instances of poised readiness (after the dharma readiness with regard to suffering) would be meaningless." They are not—though the 108 factors to be relinquished through seeing with regard to suffering are simultaneously relinquished through the dharma readiness of suffering, it is established that the 108 factors to be relinquished through seeing with regard to the origin of suffering must be relinquished through the dharma readiness of the origin of suffering and so on.

Some say, "In general, when the meditative absorptions of crossing in one leap are explained as the culminating training of the path of familiarization, the state of mind of the desire realm, the Peak of Existence, and the meditative absorption of cessation are not suitable as crossing in one leap. For in the dharma of characteristics, it is explained to be impossible for the mind of the desire realm and the Peak of Existence to be uncontaminated states and the meditative absorption of cessation is explained to be a nonassociated formation." This flaw does not apply because "the consciousness that is included in the desire realm" is explained here as a state of mind of not being in meditative equipoise, which is further explained to be the wisdom of subsequent attainment, but does not refer to a state of mind that is congruently associated with the afflictions of the desire realm. Also, Haribhadra explains that the state of mind of the Peak of Existence is presented as uncontaminated in terms of bodhisattvas who are skilled in means. Furthermore, the prajñāpāramitā sūtras state that the meditative absorption of cessation that is taught here is nothing but nondual wisdom.

In brief, as for the meaning of bodhisattvas who are skilled in means, the Yogācāras say, "Since the uncontaminated nondual wisdom of bodhisattvas is nothing but the wisdom that is free from reference points, it does not apprehend any reference points or characteristics. As for the element of lucid aware experience, which is the nature of said states of mind of the desire realm and the Peak of Existence, in terms of mere dependent origination it is not contradictory for it to arise as the nature of wisdom free from reference points." The meaning of the śrāvakas not being skilled in means is that their uncontaminated wisdom arises as entailing the sixteen aspects of impermanence and so on, which are taken as the apprehended objects by way of the mode of apprehension of this wisdom. However, their mental consciousnesses of the desire realm and the Peak of Existence are not able to take said aspects as their objects in this way.

The outcome of this explanation here is that the purpose of lesser, medium, and great crossing in one leap lies in their being the factors that eradicate the great, medium, and lesser seeds, respectively, of the conceptions to be relinquished through familiarization. Once the bhūmis are attained, the meditative absorption of cessation of the mahāyāna (the prajñā of realizing emptiness) exists in an uninterrupted continuous manner. Also, except for said mind of the desire realm, from the perspective of this prajñā of directly realizing nonduality all the meditative absorptions in this crossing in one leap (which serve as the bases of alternating and the phenomena with which they are alternated) are of one taste. You may wonder, "So what are the features that divide the different meditative absorptions of progressive abiding, such as the first dhyāna?" They are divided by virtue of certain distinct features such as the remedial branches of examination and analysis that put an end to the reference points of clinging to characteristics during the preparatory stage and the branches of benefit (such as mental joy, physical bliss, and mental joy without physical bliss). Examples of this include the distinct features of uncontaminated wisdom as based on the first and second dhyānas, respectively.

5) Removing contradictions to other scriptures

Abhidharmakośa VIII.18c–19ab explains:

> Traveling back and forth through the eight levels in two
> manners,[472]
> In succession, through leaping over one [level],
> And by way of proceeding to a third one of different type
> Is the meditative absorption of crossing in one leap.

The meaning of this has four parts:

a) Distant preparation
b) Proximate preparation
c) Actual crossing in one leap
d) Physical support

5a) The distant preparation consists of sequentially entering the eight meditative absorptions (the four dhyānas and the four formless absorptions) in their contaminated form in their progressive order and the same eight in their uncontaminated form in the reverse order. Thus, the manner of entering the eight meditative absorptions is divided into two here—contaminated and uncontaminated.

5b) The principle during the proximate preparation is to leap from one meditative absorption to the next but one, skipping the respective one in between.

Thus, first one enters the actual contaminated first dhyāna. Then, by skipping the second dhyāna, one enters the actual contaminated third dhyāna. Next, by skipping the fourth dhyāna, one enters the contaminated formless absorption of Infinite Space. Finally, by skipping Infinite Consciousness, one enters the contaminated absorption of Nothing Whatsoever, and then reverses the entire process in the same manner. Secondly, one likewise sequentially enters the uncontaminated first dhyāna, skips the second one, enters the uncontaminated third one, skips the fourth one, enters uncontaminated Infinite Space, skips Infinite Consciousness, enters uncontaminated Nothing Whatsoever, and reverses that process too.[473]

5c) During the actual crossing in one leap, one first enters the actual contaminated first dhyāna. Then, by skipping the second dhyāna, one enters the actual uncontaminated third dhyāna. Next, by skipping the fourth dhyāna, one enters contaminated Infinite Space. Finally, by skipping Infinite Consciousness, one enters uncontaminated Nothing Whatsoever. In such a manner of progressing, one alternates between the distinct types of contaminated versus uncontaminated meditative absorptions and, on each step, progresses to the respective third meditative absorption in such a sequence, but never proceeds to the respective fourth one. The *Abhidharmakośabhāṣya* on this says:

> It is impossible to skip two meditative absorptions and enter the fourth one [in sequence] because it is too distant.[474]

Finally, this entire process is reversed in the same manner.

5d) As for the physical support, this meditative absorption of crossing in one leap is only entered by those humans of sharp faculties who are liberated through both prajñā and samādhi, but not by anybody else.

Thus, it is only in terms of the mere name "crossing in one leap" that the presentation of crossing in one leap and its preparation as explained in the texts of the hīnayāna and the presentation of crossing in one leap as explained in the prajñāpāramitā sūtras (consisting of the preparatory lion's sport and the actual crossing in one leap) concord. However, the meaning of this name differs in said two presentations in that each has its own distinct defining characteristics.[475]

6) JNS's specific comments on the *Vivṛti* on AA IV.24–25[476]

This has three parts:

a) Detailed explanation
b) Summary of the meaning of crossing in one leap
c) The nature of the culminating training of the path of familiarization

6a) Detailed explanation

This has two parts:

a) Explanation of the preparatory samādhi of the lion's sport
b) Explanation of the actual samādhi of crossing in one leap

6aa) Explanation of the preparatory samādhi of the lion's sport

Bodhisattvas on the path of familiarization progress from the first dhyāna up through cessation in the progressive order and then return from cessation down to the first dhyāna in the reverse order. Thus, through said two progresssive and reverse orders of ascending and descending as just explained, they enter meditative absorption by progressing and returning through the nine meditative absorptions—the four dhyānas, the four formless absorptions, and the one that has the characteristic of cessation. There is a commentarial system that relates this entire passage to the lion's sport. In another Tibetan system, only the phrase "Bodhisattvas . . . return from cessation down to the first dhyāna" is related to the preparatory lion's sport, while the passage "Thus, through said two . . . has the characteristic of cessation" is said to teach the lesser crossing in one leap. Under examination, the former accords with the facts.

6ab) Explanation of the actual samādhi of crossing in one leap

As for the lesser crossing in one leap since it accords with the ascending and descending of the lion's sport, it is easy to understand and thus is not explained in the *Vivṛti*.[477]

As for the medium crossing in one leap, bodhisattvas again enter the meditative absorption of the first dhyāna and, after having risen from it, they enter cessation. Likewise, by alternating each of the eight meditative absorptions up through Neither Discrimination Nor Nondiscrimination with cessation, they finally enter the meditative absorption of cessation. Having risen from that cessation, they rest in meditative equipoise by focusing on the adjacent meditative absorption of the Peak of Existence, which represents the cessation of the previous one. Thus, in this medium crossing in one leap, there are eight steps in terms of the four dhyānas being alternated with four cessations; eight steps in terms of the four formless absorptions being alternated with four cessations (together sixteen); and the seventeenth step of the slight exiting into the Peak of Existence. Only that many steps are in order here, whereas the assertion by those who are not familiar with the *Vivṛti* that cessation too alternates with cessation is wrong.[478]

As for the great crossing in one leap, preceded by the medium crossing in one leap, great bodhisattvas rest in a consciousness that engages in the desire realm, which has the nature of being a boundary line between the sessions of the nine meditative absorptions of progressive abiding. Through the power of their skill in means, there is a manner of these bodhisattvas entering meditative absorption again—after first having manifested such a consciousness of the desire realm that is not in meditative equipoise, they enter cessation. From this cessation, they again enter the state of not being in meditative equipoise. After this state of mind of the desire realm, they skip only cessation and enter the āyatana of Neither Discrimination Nor Nondiscrimination. From this Peak of Existence, they enter the state of not being in meditative equipoise. From there, they skip two meditative absorptions (cessation and the Peak of Existence) and enter the āyatana of Nothing Whatsoever. Then, they enter the state of not being in meditative equipoise. Likewise, by gradually skipping up to eight meditative absorptions, they finally enter the first dhyāna as the ninth step. From that, they enter the state of not being in meditative equipoise. Thus, it is very clear in the *Vivṛti* that there are two times nine steps plus a single final state of mind of the desire realm, making nineteen altogether.

6b) Summary of the meaning of crossing in one leap
According to this explanation, starting with cessation, bodhisattvas descend by progressively skipping one and so forth from among the formless absorptions and dhyānas and then produce a session of a state of mind of the desire realm. Again, from that state, they progressively reenter the dhyānas and formless absorptions by alternating each one with said state of mind of the desire realm until they finally arrive again at the meditative absorption of cessation. In this way, the meditative absorption of crossing in one leap consists of progressing by way of alternating distinct meditative equipoises and a certain type of subsequent attainment (the state of mind of the desire realm) in disparate ways.

6c) The nature of the culminating training of the path of familiarization
One speaks of the culminating training of the path of familiarization since it is the clear realization subsequent to manifesting what has the characteristic of cultivating said lesser, medium, and great stages of crossing in one leap by mastering them.[479] Here, the lesser, medium, and great levels of lesser crossing in one leap are presented as the second, third, and fourth bhūmis, respectively; the lesser, medium, and great levels of medium crossing in one leap, as the fifth, sixth, and seventh bhūmis; and the lesser, medium, and great levels of crossing in one leap, as the eighth, ninth, and tenth bhūmis. Some also say that all these nine levels of lesser, medium, and great crossing in one leap are cultivated in their entirety on each one of the bhūmis.

7) The manner in which the conceptions that are factors to be relinquished through familiarization are relinquished

As for the manner in which the conceptions that are factors to be relinquished through familiarization are relinquished, the conceptions taught here are in terms of imputation alone. For in those whose minds are not altered by Buddhist philosophical systems, the mental clinging to the characteristics of the objects of the conceptions explained here does not arise. An example of such conceptions is the clinging mind of thinking, "For those to be guided who like the dharma in a brief form, the dharma was taught in a summarized manner."[480] The reason that the seeds of such conceptions cannot be eliminated merely through directly seeing the nature of phenomena lies not in the fact that these seeds are unable to obstruct the direct realization of the nature of phenomena on the path of seeing, but rather in the fact that imputational conceptions are not definite as factors to be relinquished through seeing. Examples of not all imputational conceptions being definite as factors to be relinquished through seeing are the conceptions of clinging to the lack of real existence that arise during the subsequent attainment of the impure bhūmis. Also, it is not by virtue of dividing the conceptions of clinging to imputations into imputational and innate ones that they are presented as two factors to be relinquished, but they are so presented by virtue of dividing them into manifest ones and those that retain a certain potency. Among these, the manifest conceptions of clinging to imputations obstruct the direct seeing of the nature of phenomena, while those that retain a certain potency do not obstruct this seeing. The manifest conceptions of clinging to imputations obstruct the direct seeing of the nature of phenomena because if the nature of phenomena is seen directly, it must be seen by way of having put an end to the manifest entertaining of the reference points of the clinging to the lack of real existence. As for those conceptions that retain a certain potency not obstructing the direct seeing of the reality of the nature of phenomena, their case is similar to the latencies of the innate clinging to real existence not obstructing the direct seeing of the lack of real existence. Therefore, the conceptions to be relinquished through familiarization that are explained here do not refer to the innnate clinging to real existence, but are explained as the manifest conceptions of clinging to characteristics during the subsequent attainments of the impure bhūmis.[481] This represents the explanation by matching the factors to be relinquished and their remedies in the context of the preparatory and actual stages of the path of familiarization.

Here, the following qualm may arise: "It is not justified to match the first two conceptions about apprehender and apprehended with the two preparatory stages of the paths of seeing and familiarization, respectively, as factors to be relinquished and their respective remedies. Nor is it tenable to match the latter two conceptions about apprehender and apprehended with the two uninterrupted paths of the paths of seeing and familiarization, respectively, as factors to be relinquished and their respective remedies. For the paths of preparation cannot perform the function of eradicating the seeds of these conceptions. However, in terms of suppressing these seeds, it is reasonable to match all four conceptions with the paths of preparation as factors to be relinquished and their respective remedies because the four conceptions and the paths of preparation have mutually exclusive modes of apprehension and thus do not coexist." Therefore, the following is explained. According to the manner in which the Yogācāras explain this, the remedy that relinquishes the first conceptions about the apprehender does not arise before the remedies for the second conceptions about the apprehended have arisen. For the four conceptions about apprehender and apprehended must be relinquished in a strictly progressive manner and one is not able to relinquish the conceptions about the apprehender without having relinquished the conceptions about the apprehended. According to the manner in which the Niḥsvabhāvavādins explain this, it is easy to relinquish the first two conceptions about apprehender and apprehended because they are conceptions about the antagonistic factors. The latter two conceptions about apprehender and apprehended are difficult to relinquish because they are conceptions about the remedial factors. Therefore, the paths of preparation of both the path of seeing and the path of familiarization are presented as the remedies that relinquish the first two conceptions about apprehender and apprehended because they, through having put an end to one portion of reference points (those in terms of real existence), operate by entailing the aspect of the lack of real existence. As *Bodhicaryāvatāra* IX.32ab says:

> Through familiarity with the latent tendencies of emptiness,
> The latent tendencies of entities will be relinquished.

As for the latter two conceptions about apprehender and apprehended, it is justified to match them with the uninterrupted paths of both the path of seeing and the path of familiarization as factors to be relinquished and their respective remedies because these uninterrupted paths entail the aspect of the freedom from reference points in which all reference points have been put to an end. As *Bodhicaryāvatāra* IX.32cd says:

> Through familiarity with "utter nonexistence"
> These too will be relinquished later on.[482]

As for eliminating the above qualm in this context, I declare that this explanation by the Niḥsvabhāvavādins is excellent, while the elimination of said qualm by the Yogācāras amounts to eliminating a qualm with another meaning. Also, though the Niḥsvabhāvavādins eliminate this qualm as explained, the gist of it is that the seeds of all four conceptions must be relinquished through the uninterrupted paths.

G) The six causes and the four conditions[483]

This has three parts:

1) The definitions of the causes
2) The definitions of the conditions
3) Removing disputes about these definitions

1) The definition of a cause in general is "that which produces the nature of a result" or "that which matures a subseqent other referent"; for example, a barley seed. The definition of a substantial cause is "that which is primary in producing the nature of a result." The commentary on the *Vinayavibhāga* says:

> "Causes" refers to primary internal causes. "Conditions" refers to the conditions that are external aids.

It is not definite that whatever is a cause is a substantial cause—for example, the eye sense faculty is a cause of the eye consciousness, but not its substantial cause.[484] This is also stated in *Pramāṇavārttika* II.164cd:

> This is established because what is not consciousness
> Is not a substantial [cause] of consciousness.

When classified, causes are sixfold. *Abhidharmakośa* II.49 says:

> Enabling cause, simultaneous,
> Of similar outcome, congruent,
> Omnipresent, and maturing—
> Causes are asserted to be sixfold.

The definition of an enabling cause is "that which produces something that is other than itself and has the nature of a result" (*Abhidharmakośa* II.50a).

The definition of a simultaneous cause is "that which produces the nature of a result by these two being mutually dependent" (*Abhidharmakośa* II.50b). As for the manners of being mutually dependent, these include being dependent by nature (the four elements); by virtue of congruent supports (mind and mental factors); and in terms of defining characteristics and their instances (*Abhidharmakośa* II.50cd).

The definition of a cause of similar outcome is "that which produces a result that resembles its cause" (*Abhidharmakośa* II.52a). When divided, it is twofold—contaminated and uncontaminated. The definition of a contaminated cause of similar outcome is "that which produces a similar result and is a factor to be relinquished through the path" (*Abhidharmakośa* II.52b). The factors to be relinquished are classified as being of five types (the four types to be relinquished through seeing the four realities and the one type to be relinquished through familiarization) and as pertaining to the nine levels of saṃsāric existence. How is "similar outcome" to be understood? A preceding factor to be relinquished through seeing, such as the suffering of the desire realm, produces a following factor to be relinquished through seeing. Contaminated causes of similar outcome produce results that are similar in both type and level. The definition of an uncontaminated cause of similar outcome is "that which produces something that is similar to its cause and is not a factor to be relinquished through the path" (*Abhidharmakośa* II.52cd). The nine levels of the path are the nine uncontaminated grounds (the six grounds of dhyāna and the first three formless absorptions). Since they can produce each other, their being of a similar level is not definite, but they are all similar in being of uncontaminated type.

The definition of a congruent cause is "that which arises from a mind with congruent support and produces the nature of a result" (*Abhidharmakośa* II.53cd). Congruent support means that, for example, an eye consciousness and all its accompanying mental factors are congruent in having the same support—the eye sense faculty.

The definition of an omnipresent cause is "that which, in dependence on preceding onmipresent factors, produces the subsequent natures of the flaws of its own respective level" (*Abhidharmakośa* II.54ab). Avalokitavrata's *Prajñāpradīpaṭīkā* says:

> The previously arisen omnipresent phenomena of one's own respective level are the omnipresent causes of the subsequent afflicted phenomena [of that very level].[485]

Thus, this cause refers to particular instances of afflicted phenomena and its result consists of subsequent afflicted phenomena because the *Abhidharmakośabhāṣya* says:

> This refers to the common cause of afflicted phenomena. Therefore, it is another [cause] that is separate from causes of similar outcome.[486]

It is called "omnipresent" because it focuses on all five above types of factors to be relinquished. As the *Viniścayasaṃgrahaṇī* says:

> Therefore, it is called "omnipresent" and "seizing all bases."[487]

"All" refers to all pleasant and unpleasant objects. In general, afflictive omnipresent causes are divided into eleven—the seven factors to be relinquished through seeing the reality of suffering (the five views, doubt, and the ignorance that is unmixed with other afflictions) and the four factors to be relinquished through seeing the reality of the origin of suffering (two views, doubt, and the ignorance that is congruently associated with other afflictions). Some say, "There is no certainty for omnipresent causes to be eleven in number because all minds and mental factors that are congruently associated with these eleven are omnipresent causes too." Desire, anger, and pride are not omnipresent causes because their respective objects are determined distinctly, that is, they arise by focusing on seeing a pleasant object and so forth, respectively. The factors to be relinquished through seeing the realities of cessation and the path are not omnipresent causes either because their respective objects are determined distinctly, that is, the direct wrong engagements focus only on uncontaminated phenomena and the juxtaposed wrong engagements focus only on the wrong engagements in cessation and the path. The factors to be relinquished through familiarization are not omnipresent causes either because their respective objects are determined distinctly. The reason applies for the following reasons. It was already explained that, among the four factors to be relinquished through familiarization, the three of desire, anger, and pride determine their respective objects distinctly. Therefore, also the ignorance that is congruently associated with these three determines its objects distinctly.

The definition of a maturing cause is "that which is a contaminated nonneutral phenomenon and produces the nature of a result" because *Abhidharmakośa* II.54cd says that only nonvirtues and contaminated virtues are maturing causes. Neutral phenomena and uncontaminated virtues are not maturing causes because they have little power and are not moisturized by craving, just as rotten seeds or fertile seeds that are not moisturized.

2) The definitions of the conditions

The definition of a condition in general is "that which produces the distinctive features of a result." When classified, conditions are fourfold. *Mūlamadhyamakakārikā* I.2 says:

> Conditions are fourfold:
> Causal, objective,
> Immediate, and dominant.
> There is no fifth condition.

The definition of a causal condition is "that which produces the distinctive features of a result together with its nature." The self-isolate of "causal condition" consists of the five causes other than the enabling cause (*Abhidharmakośa* II.61d).

The definition of an object condition is "that which produces the distinctive features of a result in the form of appearing as the cognitive aspect of a specific object," for example, blue.

The definition of an immediate condition is "a given preceding cognition that directly produces the distinctive features of the subsequent moment of this cognition." The *Pramāṇaviniścaya* says:

> This is known to be the preceding consciousness that serves as the cause for the adjacent cognition.[488]

This explains that, from an immediate condition, a direct result must be produced. The assertion that both cause and result here are cognitions is the system of the Mere Mentalists, while both Vaibhāṣikas and Sautrāntikas hold that there is the production of matter from immediate conditions. Some say, "The moment of consciousness of being about to enter the meditative absorption of cessation is the immediate condition for the moment of consciousness of rising from this meditative absorption." However, this is not the case because the ālaya-consciousness and so forth arise in between said two moments. The self-isolate of the immediate condition consists of all minds and mental factors (*Abhidharmakośā* II.62ab). Some claim, "The minds and mental factors that exist in the mind stream of the last moment, that is, when becoming an arhat, are not immediate conditions."[489] However, *Pramāṇavārttika* II.45ab and II.41ab hold that these are immediate conditions:

> What is contradictory in that the last mind
> Connects with another mind?
> If such a propelling factor exists,
> It would exist later in such a way too.

The definition of a dominant condition is "that which is able to produce the distinctive features of a result independently" because *Abhidharmakośa* II.62d says that "enabling causes" are explained to be dominant conditions.

3) Removing disputes about these definitions

Some say, "At the time when the nature of a vase is produced by clay, are its distinctive features produced or not? If they are, it follows that the clay is a condition with regard to the vase. If they are not produced, it follows that the nature and the distinctive features of the vase are not one because they have the property of being mutually exclusive in that they are substances that arise or do not arise from clay, respectively." Since the distinctive features of the vase are produced at that point, the second flaw does not apply. The first consequnce is accepted because—as stated above—*Abhidharmakośa* II.61d and II.62d explain that causes and conditions are coextensive and one in nature. This general topic of causes and conditions was compiled from the excellent explanations of Shang Tsebongwa Chökyi Lama.[490]

6) The serial training[491]

You may wonder, "How is it that one progresses through the serial training in a sequential manner?" It is primarily through the view (in terms of the nature of the lack of entity), which consists of the factor of becoming familiar with the aspects of the three knowledges and represents the continuum whose type consists of training in the first two among the four trainings. This is why one speaks here about the "serial training of realizing the nature of the lack of entity." By virtue of the serial training being preceded by both the complete training in all aspects and the culminating training, it is also not unsuitable to present it as the special path of the two latter trainings. What is the main function of this training? Its function is to manifest special qualities, which refers to the yoga of clearly bringing forth the qualities of the dharmakāya after having fully completed the accumulation of merit that consists of engaging in skillful means (the six pāramitās and the six recollections) during subsequent attainment. What are said qualities of the dharmakāya? They refer to its ability to display, from the perspective of others, the appearances of the rūpakāyas. The cause for being able to display these appearances is omniscient and loving wisdom. The causes for bringing forth this wisdom in a very clear manner are the six pāramitās—to train well in the six pāramitās, in due order, during the subsequent attainment of the ten bhūmis makes one progress higher and higher through these ten bhūmis. When embraced by the activity of prajñāpāramitā, the completion of the four latter among the ten pāramitās (means, aspiration prayers, power, and wisdom) is implicitly established too because these four are the aids that are congruently associated with prajñāpāramitā. As for the boundary line of prajñāpāramitā being completed, it is said that, in general, it is completed from the sixth bhūmi onward, but this is said with the intention of this bhūmi being identified as the boundary line that is the beginning of the arising of prajñāpāramitā.

In brief, one practices this yoga here by welding the last serial training (realizing the nature of the lack of entity) during meditative equipoise and the six first serial trainings (the six pāramitās) during subsequent attainment into an inseparable union. The manner in which one practices in this way is that one, based on the six recollections, relies on the three jewels, takes giving and ethics as the basis of the six pāramitās, and takes one's supreme meditation deity as witness. How does recollection take place through these six? When analyzed through discriminating prajñā, one does not mentally engage in the characteristics of these six—they are aspects of the freedom from reference points that is free from mental engagement. For example, in actual fact, the lack of recollection of the deity is the supreme recollection of the deity.[492] For what is presented as recollection in this context is to recollect the cognitive aspect of realizing the basic nature of the deity, whereas to recollect the focal object that appears as a deity on the level of the seeming is not the recollection that actually fulfills this function in this context here. Therefore, the sūtras say that mental nonengagement is virtue and mental engagement is nonvirtue. This kind of mental nonengagement is also what is intended here, but it is not something like the stopping of any thoughts in terms of experience and recollection (as a subcategory of mental factors) in the system of a Chinese master who boasted about the Madhyamaka view.[493] In brief, it is from the perspective of the sixth consciousness itself becoming without any characteristics that it is clearly manifest as the actuality of mental nonengagement. However, the explanation nowadays that being free from apprehending generalities—as the kind of cognition that impairs the sixth consciousness—is the view of Mahāmudrā free from mental engagement is nothing but the occurrence of a dharma famine. The manner in which the position of said Chinese master and the Mahāmudrā free from mental engagement do not accord should be understood from my other works.[494] In any case, any kind of recollection that entails characteristics is not what is meant here because this is the context of putting an end to reification.

You may wonder, "But if the six recollections are identified from the perspective of the view, what is the difference from the view of realizing the nature of the lack of entity?" The latter represents the view that pervades the common basis of the training, while the former is the view that pervades what is uncommon in this training. In addition, the latter represents the view of meditative equipoise, while the former is the view of subsequent attainment. Or the latter is to be accomplished and the former is what accomplishes it.[495] How does it accomplish this? During subsequent attainment, it is the very mental nonengagement free from reference points during meditative equipoise that is recollected in the form of becoming familiar with mind lacking any recollection in terms of the focal objects and aspects of the freedom from reference points.

"Still, how can it be that, among the six pāramitās, prajñā is presented as conduct and not as the view?" Prajñā is indeed presented as the view, but the meaning of its being presented as conduct is as follows. It is impossible for bodhisattvas to perform any activities in terms of the triad of agent, object, and action without them being embraced by prajñā during each and every phase of both meditative equipoise and subsequent attainment. Therefore, the intention behind presenting prajñā in terms of engaging in conduct is by referring to the prajñā of subsequent attainment.

You may wonder, "During which phases of the path does one cultivate this training?" Āryavimuktisena explains that it exists during the three phases that consist of the path of accumulation, the path of preparation, and the paths of seeing and familiarization being taken as one. Haribhadra skips the path of accumulation and holds that this training exists during the three phases that consist of the paths of preparation, seeing, and familiarization, respectively.[496] As for engaging in each one of the thirteen elements of the serial training, the sūtras say:

> Bodhisattvas exert themselves in the serial activity, the serial training, and the serial practice.[497]

The *Vṛtti* says that "activity" is said for the sake of identifying the generation of bodhicitta; "training" refers to the factors conducive to penetration; and "practice" refers to the realizations of the paths of seeing and familiarization. That these three are put forth is in order to understand clear realization to be gradual.[498] Therefore, the assertion that the serial training lasts from the path of accumulation up through the end of the continuum is justified.

7) The instantaneous training[499]

This has two parts:

1) Nature
2) Divisions

1) The nature of the instantaneous training is the final yoga of bodhisattvas that cultivates a single last moment of training after having attained stability in the actuality of the three knowledges. You may wonder, "What is the gauge of having attained stability and what is the manner of instantaneously becoming familiar?" To answer the first question, when mastery over a single

quality of the buddhabhūmi is gained, one is able to master all such qualities of concordant type because all other such qualities are included completely in a single quality of this kind. "How can they all be included in it?" The reason for this is that all these qualities are inseparable as the nature of phenomena—Mahāmudrā. If mastery is gained over a single quality that has the nature of the two knowledges being inseparably one, mastery over the others is gained too. Though these actual qualities are the distinctive features of a buddha alone, their approximately concordant forms exist also on the special path of the tenth bhūmi because on this path the 108 conceptions that obscure these qualities have already been relinquished. This is also established through scripture because AA V.35cd–36 says:

> All the consummate qualities that accomplish
> The happiness of beings in all aspects,
>
> Just like rivers [feeding] into the great ocean,
> Sustain these mahāsattvas,
> Who are embellished with the desired fruition,
> From all sides.

"But if bodhisattvas have the qualities of a buddha (such as the ten powers), are these qualities then not the uncommon distinctive features of their being a buddha?" As just explained, speaking of these qualities as the unique features of a buddha is in terms of such qualities being fully qualified. As for the approximately concordant forms of these qualities, they are even seen on certain levels other than the special path of the tenth bhūmi, that is, on the eighth and ninth bhūmis. For the passage in the sūtras that pertains to AA I.69d and explains the purifications of the ninth bhūmi identifies these qualities as the ten powers and so on.[500]

"What are the qualities to be mastered through this instantaneous training?" They are twofold. The first set refers to attaining the not yet matured uncontaminated types of realization (from generosity up through the excellent minor marks), although, on the special path of the end of the continuum, they are not yet free from the stains that are the impregnations of negative tendencies. The second set refers to attaining, on the buddhabhūmi, the matured uncontaminated types of realization (such as the ten powers) that are free from said stains. "What is the meaning of 'matured' and 'nonmatured'?" Haribhadra explains that the former means not arising as the nature of the bright qualities due to not being free from the stains that are the impregnations of negative tendencies, while the latter is the opposite of that. According to the intention of Buddhaśrījñāna, "nonmatured" refers to the uncontaminated realizations up through the seventh bhūmi because they entail being dependent on effort. He takes the realization that is attained at the end of the continuum to be similar in type to these realizations. "Matured" refers to the uncontaminated realizations from the eighth bhūmi onward because they do not depend on effort. This is also clear in *Uttaratantra* I.141:

> The stains related to the seven bhūmis
> Resemble the stains of the enclosure of the womb.
> Similar to an embryo delivered from this enclosure,
> Nonconceptual wisdom possesses maturation.

Dharmamitra's *Prasphuṭapadā* holds:

> Before the arising of the path of seeing, all the many phenomena that consist of apprehender and apprehended are nonmatured. The true nature of these phenomena is uncontaminated. The realizations of noble ones are matured, which are twofold—the supramundane matured [realizations] from the first up through the seventh bhūmis and the inconceivable and spontaneously present matured [realizations] on the buddhabhūmi. The phenomena on these [bhūmis] are [referred to as] matured because they are matured in that they differ from the phases before [them].[501]

In brief, the meaning of being "nonmatured" here refers to those who are obscured by the stains that obscure the uncontaminated and unconditioned having attained only a little bit of the power of the uncontaminated phenomena that eliminate these stains. Since the actual uncontaminated power is the dharmadhātu, in terms of its self-solate it is explained as being unconditioned, and since the function of this power is to relinquish obscurations, it is explained as being conditioned. To be "matured" is the opposite of the above. However, in terms of its self-isolate this is also presented as unconditioned, while the maturation that consists of the obscurations having been relinquished through the function of the dharmadhātu's power is presented as conditioned.

To answer the second question above ("What is the manner of instantaneously becoming familiar?"), it means to familiarize, on the special path of the tenth bhūmi, with all phenomena of saṃsāra and nirvāṇa lacking characteristics as well as apprehender and apprehended being nondual. On this, the great translator Ngog quotes *Mahāyānasūtrālaṃkāra* XX.21cd:

> This fourfold fruition
> Is based on the four bhūmis.[502]

Accordingly, he explains that, after having gradually become familiar with these four in due order from the seventh through the tenth bhūmis, on the special path of the tenth bhūmi four instants arise in a sequential manner. The former two of these instants are explained as cause and result, respectively, and the same goes for the latter two. Also, the former two and the latter two instants are causes and results, respectively. This is also in accord with the *Ālokā*. Prajñākaramati and others say that these four instants are not like an enumeration of four individual moments, but divide the wisdom that arises as having the nature of a single instant into four isolates. Some Tibetan masters say, "This training consists of two instants—from the perspective of an instant of a cognition without characteristics, nonmaturation is experienced, and from the perspective of an instant of a cognition of nonduality, maturation is experienced." Those who are capable of analyzing should scrutinize this.

Others say, "It follows that this instantaneous training and the culminating training of the uninterrupted path explained above are equivalent because they are the same training of clearly seeing the first instant of the knowledge of all aspects." These two are not established as the same training—the instantaneous training taught here is presented from the point of view of accomplishing qualities, while the culminating training of the uninterrupted path is presented from the point of view of the ceasing of the obscurations of what makes one attain these qualities. Therefore, the first instant of the knowledge of all aspects is necessarily the direct result of the instantaneous training and the instantaneous training is necessarily the direct cause of its specific result. In the context of the complete training in all aspects, this very instantaneous training refers to familiarizing with each one of all these aspects for a long time. In the context of the culminating training, it means the most consummate realization that has arisen from such familiarizing. In the context of the serial training, it refers to a sequential such familiarizing that is very swift by virtue of having attained very great stability in this familiarizing. In the context of the instantaneous training, it represents the simultaneous familiarization with said aspects through being consummately familiar with them. This is taught through the examples of an arrow sequentially piercing the petals of a lotus and a person jumping over a wall.

As for the manner in which the instantaneous training operates, through its being distinguished by the relinquishment of the 108 conceptions to be relinquished through familiarization at the end of the continuum, at this point the ten pāramitās are mastered, by virtue of which manifesting one of them manifests all the others too. What is also manifested at this point are all the many instances of nondual wisdom that there are, which are distinguished by the relinquishment of the impregnations of negative tendencies of clinging to duality and so on through a single instance of nondual knowing.

2) As for the divisions of the instantaneous training, Haribhadra speaks of the instantaneous training being fourfold in terms of nonmaturation, maturation, lack of characteristics, and nonduality. Here, it is clear that "nonmaturation" is the opposite of and designated in dependence on "maturation." As for these designations, the first two aspects of the instantaneous training are presented in terms of the qualities to be attained, while the latter two are presented in terms of how the object to be realized and the time of its realization are instantaneous. Also, the latter two aspects are presented from the point of view of being familiar with the aspects of the three knowledges as being without arising, while the former two are presented from the point of view of being familiar with the power for the manifestation of the buddhadharmas. Āryavimuktisena explains the single section of the sūtras that teaches the instantaneous training by dividing it into four.

Here, it is reasonable that the fact of one single uncontaminated quality including all uncontaminated phenomena is explained by the first verse of Chapter Seven of the AA. The concordant example for this fact is given by the next verse. The following verse speaks about the fact that the matured uncontaminated knowledge includes all qualities of buddhahood. The last two verses teach the latter two among the four instants of the instantaneous training, which represent the manner in which what is included in the two former instants is realized. You may wonder, "But then the two latter instants are repetitious." They are not—the former two instants are referred to from the perspective of all mistakenness about the nature of seeming reality (emptiness) being terminated, while the latter two instants are referred to from the perspective of all mistakenness about ultimate reality being terminated.

8) The dharmakāya

A) The general presentation of the kāyas[503]

This has three parts:

1) The nature of just the dharmakāya in general
2) The natures of the different kāyas
3) The distinctions in terms of the kāyas being fully qualified or nominal and the manner in which knowable objects are seen

1) The nature of just the dharmakāya in general

The nature of the dharmakāya as such is the fruition of the two obscurations being relinquished completely and the two accumulations being perfected. You may wonder, "Which one among the five results is it?" It has distinct aspects of fruition. For from the perspective of having relinquished what was to be relinquished, it is presented as a result of freedom; from the perspective of having realized what was to be realized, as a result that concords with its cause; and, by virtue of the tathāgata heart primordially existing, as a dominated result. Therefore, to present it as a matured result is just nominal because the factors to present it as an actual matured result are not complete. In brief, the dharmkāya must be explained from the perspective of the three elements of relinquishment, realization, and powerful capacity not being distinct. Thus, through having practiced the two accumulations separately and in union, what is to be relinquished is relinquished, realization is produced, and the powerful capacity of these two—relinquishment and realization—promotes the welfare of others. It is in terms of these isolates that the dharmakāya per se is the basis for designating it as the svābhāvikakāya, the sāmbhogikakāya, and the nairmāṇikakāya. In terms of just its own isolate, it is explained as "dharmakāya," "svābhāvikakāya," "the kāya of the actual way of being," and "attainment—ultimate reality."

Haribhadra speaks about the actual way of being and the way of appearing of this kāya. The kāya in terms of the actual way of being is not something different than the dharmakāya itself because the *Vivṛti* explains that the latter has "the nature of the svābhāvikakāya."[504] Therefore, the kāya in terms of the way of appearing is presented as the three kāyas that are different from the svābhāvikakāya.[505] The justification for presenting it this way lies in the svābhāvikakāya's three different ways of appearing for buddhas, bodhisattvas, and ordinary sentient beings, just as the sky can appear red, green, or black. As for its two latter ways of appearing (for bodhisattvas and sentient beings), it is difficult to present them as the actual Tathāgata because they consist of the continua of the consciousnesses of those persons to whom they appear. As for the first way of appearing, it is the very buddha wisdom that appears for the svābhāvikakāya itself as the nature of the dharmakāya because the fact of a mind stream being endowed with the powerful capacity of this wisdom to promote the welfare of sentient beings in the manner of being an appearance for others is able to point out that this mind stream represents being a buddha. Therefore, this wisdom is not separate or different from the svābhāvikakāya. You may wonder, "Though it is not different, how is it divided in terms of isolates?" This is done from the perspective of this wisdom not being other than the svābhāvikakāya itself and from the perspective of this wisdom appearing to itself, with the latter representing the dharmakāya. In the great tantra collections, this latter one is explained as "wisdom kāya." These two kāyas (svābhāvikakāya and dharmakāya) are of one taste as the essence that is the nature of phenomena. For both are nothing other than suchness free from reference points and these two nondual kāyas nevertheless have the capacity to, from the perspective of others, produce the appearances of the sāmbhogikakāya and the nairmāṇikakāya. These two appearances that are put forth through the power of said capacity are presented as the seeming bearers of the nature of phenomena because Haribhadra's *Vivṛti* says, ". . . by way of giving rise to appearances with specific purposes for the seeming [reality] of yogins, . . ."[506]

As for the nature of the dharmakāya in specific[507] being wisdom, it is the ultimate knowledge that represents *the change of* all *states*[508] of stains having been completely relinquished. Some proponents of inferior philosophical systems say, "The ālaya-consciousness exists on the buddhabhūmi, and "having relinquished it" just means *the change* through having relinquished its stains—the impregnations *of* negative *states*—so that the ālaya-consciousness has *changed* into mirrorlike nondual wisdom." Though this is invalidated through infinite scriptures and reasonings, I will not elaborate on these here.[509] Suffice it to say that such explanations are nothing but self-invented.

"If wisdom is identified as above, how is it divided?" It is fivefold—the four wisdoms clearly stated in *Mahāyānasūtrālaṃkāra* IX.67–76 and, by implication, the dharmadhātu wisdom. Among these, the dharmadhātu wisdom is the essence of all kāyas—the svābhāvikakāya, the basic element of all wisdoms, the wisdom of the nature of phenomena—whose nature it is to be free from all factors to be free from and to be endowed with all qualities (some explain this wisdom from the point of view of negation alone, but this is mistaken). This very wisdom is divided into four in terms of its distinct functions. Mirrorlike wisdom refers to the aspects of a tathāgata's own uncommon dharmas appearing within luminous dharmadhātu wisdom through the power of the ālaya-consciousness having become pure. The wisdom of equality refers to being endowed with great love and compassion in an equal way for all beings by virtue of the afflicted mind having become completely pure. Discriminating wisdom refers to having become a treasury of samādhis and dhāraṇīs that are unobstructed with regard to all knowable objects by virtue of the flux of the mental consciousness having been terminated. All-accomplishing wisdom refers to having attained the power to creatively manifest as and transform into favorable circumstances in accordance with the respective objects of enlightened activity in infinite realms of sentient beings by virtue of being free from the five sense consciousnesses.[510] Among these four, the first two are primarily the knowledges that perform activities from a buddha's own perspective, while the latter two are primarily the knowledges that perform activities from the perspective of others. Through the power of a buddha's knowledge through aspiration (see AA VIII.8), the kāyas of the two latter wisdoms (sāmbhogikakāya and nairmāṇikakāya) appear. From the perspective of others (those to be guided), these kāyas are conceived as being endowed with three distinctive features—the characteristics of minds and mental factors are complete since they appear as the duality of apprehender and apprehended; they perform activities, such as teaching the dharma; and they entail the change of state of the latent tendencies of dualistic appearance.[511] If you wonder to which among these four wisdoms the twenty-one sets of uncontaminated wisdom in AA VIII.2–6 correspond, this can be explained by correlating each one of the former to the latter, but it is not the case that each one of these twenty-one sets is not included in the nature of each one of these four wisdoms.[512]

2) The natures of the different kāyas

This has four parts:

a) The division into two kāyas
b) The division into three kāyas
c) The division into four kāyas
d) Haribhadra's *Ālokā* and *Vivṛti* on the AA teaching three or four kāyas513

2a) The division into two kāyas

This refers to the ultimate and the seeming kāyas being different because *Uttaratantra* III.1ab says:

> One's own welfare and the welfare of others are the ultimate kāya
> And the seeming kāya that is supported by it, [respectively].

2b) The division into three kāyas

This is stated in *Uttaratantra* I.8cd:

> One's own welfare is by virtue of the first three qualities,
> And the welfare of others, by virtue of the latter three.

From among the triad of the svābhāvikakāya, the sāmbhogikakāya, and the nairmāṇikakāya, the latter two each have their actual way of being and way of appearing. In this context here, these latter two kāyas are primarily explained from the perspective of their way of appearing, but the ones that actually fulfill this function must be taken as the sāmbhogikakāya and the nairmāṇikakāya in terms of their actual way of being because the svābhāvikakāya possesses these two kāyas, which do not represent the same self-isolate as the svābhāvikakāya. As for the svābhāvikakāya, *Uttaratantra* II.45–46 says that it has five characteristics:

It is unconditioned, indivisible,
Free from the two extremes,
And liberated from the three obscurations—
Afflictive, cognitive, and those of meditative absorption.

By virtue of being stainless, nonconceptual,
The object of yogins,
And the nature of the dharmadhātu,
It is pure luminosity.

Uttaratantra II.47–48 says that it has five qualities:

The wonderful form of svābhāvika is endowed with
The qualities of being unfathomable, incalculable,
Inconceivable, and unequaled,
As well as the attainment of supreme purity.

By virtue of being vast, not enumerable,
Not the sphere of dialecticians,
An absolute unity, and the elimination of latent tendencies,
It is, in due order, unfathomable and so on.

When the presentation of three kāyas is accepted, the dharmakāya is nothing other than the svābhāvikakāya because it is difficult to present the twenty-one sets of uncontaminated wisdom described in AA VIII.2–6 as anything other than the dharmadhātu operating in the mind stream that consists of these sets of wisdom. The dharmadhātu in this context is identified as having the nature of the nondual wisdom that consists of the twofold knowledge of suchness and variety. For in terms of the dharmadhātu being presented as both the cause that produces the buddha qualities and the result that is produced, this is the context of presenting it as the actuality of the produced result that is taught here. Therefore, it is the position of Haribhadra to present the dharmadhātu as the svābhāvikakāya in terms of merely its nature of being said cause, while the intention of Āryavimuktisena is to hold that the svābhāvikakāya refers to both wisdoms (the knowledges of suchness and variety) that are produced through this cause.

With regard to Āryavimuktisena's intention, some people have the following doubt: "These two wisdoms are not the svābhāvikakāya because these two wisdoms are explained as the qualities of the svābhāvikakāya." There is no flaw for the following reasons. This is not contradictory because through identifying its qualities, one is able to understand also the kāya that is endowed with these qualities. Also, from a certain point of view, the twenty sets of wisdom and the two wisdoms of knowing suchness and variety are not other in substance than the svābhāvikakāya that possesses them. In this context, the remaining two kāyas in terms of the actual way of being also must be identified as this very kāya because one does not find any other kāya as which they could be identified. In brief, this description by Āryavimuktisena of all buddhakāyas being included in three presents the first one as the actual way of being and the latter two as the way of appearing. "But as what are the sāmbhogikakāya and the nairmāṇikakāya in terms of the actual way of being identified?" They are the opposites of what appear as what are not the actual kāyas of the Buddha that are established as being endowed with five and four distinctive features, respectively.[514]

2c) The division into four kāyas
This has two parts:
  a) The manner of dividing
  b) Answers to disputes

2ca) Haribhadra speaks about "the kāyas in terms of the actual way of being," with the svābhāvikakāya being the nature of phenomena that is endowed with realization—wisdom—and the dharmakāya being the wisdom that is connected to the nature of phenomena. "The kāyas in terms of the way of appearing" are the sāmbhogikakāya and the nairmāṇikakāya, which entail appearances that are suitable to appear from the perspective of others. The nature of phenomena that is endowed with twofold purity is the element of all aspects of wisdom being experienced from the perspective of self-awareness. The corresponding two kāyas consist of the knowledge of luminous wisdom that is distinguished by being free from adventitious stains, which is the nature of being free from attachment and obstruction (that is, afflictive and cognitive obscurations), respectively. The difference between the first two kāyas is that the svābhāvikakāya represents the true nature of the sāmbhogikakāya and the nairmāṇikakāya, while the dharmakāya functions as the dominant condition of the sāmbhogikakāya and the nairmāṇikakāya. They are also distinct in that the svābhāvikakāya represents meditative equipoise's own nature, while the dharmakāya promotes the welfare of others.

The defining characteristic of the third kāya—the sāmbhogikakāya—is buddhahood being endowed with the five certainties. It is instantiated by the blazing splendor of the major and minor marks. There is an explanation about the sāmbhogikakāya being twofold in terms of being greater and lesser,[515] but all these sāmbhogikakāyas are one in terms of substance. For if all dharmakāyas (their supports) are one in substance, all sāmbhogikakāyas (which are supported by the former) must be of one substance too. The fourth kāya—the nairmāṇikakāya—is the special rūpakāya that promotes the welfare of others through the twelve deeds of a buddha since these are the distinct features of the activity of the sāmbhogikakāya that engage the desire realm. These deeds are described in *Uttaratantra* II.54–56.

2cb) The answers to disputes have two parts:
1) Explaining the system of asserting three kāyas to be stainless
2) Explaining the approach of asserting four kāyas to be flawless

2cb1) Explaining the system of asserting three kāyas to be stainless has three parts:
a) Stating our own assertion
b) Putting forth the qualms of others about it
c) Showing that these qualms do not apply

2cb1a) Our own assertion is that the buddhakāyas are three—one in terms of the actual way of being and two in terms of the way of appearing.

2cb1b) Others say, "It follows that all-accomplishing wisdom and discriminating wisdom that are included in the buddhabhūmi are not included in the buddhakāyas because they are not included in any of said three kāyas. The entailment is yours and the reason applies because these two wisdoms are neither one of the two rūpakāyas and thus are not included in the mind streams of others. They are not the svābhāvikakāya either because it is the wisdom kāya that is endowed with the three distinctive features."

2cb1c) As for the three distinctive features asserted by these others, they say, "Said two wisdoms are explained as the uncontaminated dharmakāya because of yogins performing activities (such as teaching the dharma) on the level of the seeming; because of the fundamental change of state (the distinctive feature of relinquishment); and because of entailing mind and mental factors (the distinctive feature of nature). Thus, one cannot present these two wisdoms as the svābhāvikakāya." This statement entails the following flaws. From the perspective of progressing from above, the first two reasons in it are uncertain—if the svābhāvikakāya does not accomplish the welfare of sentient beings, how could it be buddhahood? If it does accomplish the welfare of others, how could it accomplish it in any other way than through producing the appearances of the two rūpakāyas on the level of the seeming? Also, if the svābhāvikakāya is not distinguished through the feature of the change of state, how could it be pure of adventitious stains? As for the wisdom of having changed state (the svābhāvikakāya), in terms of its aspect of not having changed before, it is a nonimplicative negation, and in terms of its aspect of having changed later, it is an implicative negation. From the perspective of progressing from below, the latter two reasons do not apply. If there is any flux of mind and mental factors on the level of a tathāgata, it follows that the eight consciousnesses have not undergone their change of state. It also follows that, on said level, there are mental states of apprehending distinctive features and what possesses such features and, in that case, it follows that conceptions exist on this level. Furthermore, it was already taught above that the svābhāvikakāya is not established as not being the change of state.

Some say, "The svābhāvikakāya and the dharmakāya are not the same because Maitreya describes them in distinct passages in the AA (verses VIII.1 and VIII.2–11, respectively)." However, Maitreya made this division into distinct passages by thinking about the actual svābhāvikakāya and its qualities, respectively. Otherwise, if the dharmakāya is presented from the point of view of being conditioned and so on, this directly contradicts the teachings of its "being unconditioned and spontaneously present." Some think, "It is not reasonable that nothing but the essence of the nature of phenomena is a kāya." As far as I am concerned, this does not mean that this kāya is claimed to be nothing but the nature of phenomena devoid of the nature of wisdom. Therefore, by taking this position, Dölpopa Sherab Gyaltsen identifies "the svābhāvikakāya of the sage" in AA VIII.1c as the svābhāvikakāya. If one wonders, he says, what the enumeration of "the uncontaminated dharmas" in VIII.1b consist of, they are identified in VIII.2–6. In brief, it appears that he did not explain the meaning of these five verses as the twenty-one sets of uncontaminated wisdom, but coined the conventional expression "the explanation of each one of the 140 uncontaminated dharmas."[516]

2cb2) Explaining the approach of asserting four kāyas to be flawless

a) Stating our own assertion

b) Putting forth the qualms of others about it

c) Showing that these qualms do not apply

2cb2a) Our own assertion with regard to four kāyas is that the kāya in terms of the actual way of being is twofold by virtue of being divided as the nature of phenomena and what bears this nature, while the kāya in terms of the way of appearing is divided into sāmbhogikakāya and nairmāṇikakāya.

2cb2b) Some say, "This is wrong because only three kāyas are taught in the brief introduction in AA I.17 (svābhāvikakāya, sambhogakāya, and nairmāṇikakāya) and, in general, the pāramitāyāna explains no kāyas other than three."

2cb2c) In general, it is not that the dharmakāya is not taught in the AA—it is in fact taught explicitly in VIII.40c:

> The enlightened activity of the dharmakāya . . .[517]

"But if you say that it is taught in this way (that is, after the other three kāyas), would it not rather have to be taught right after the svābhāvikakāya?" It appears that the above is added after the discussion of the three kāyas for the sake of understanding the necessity of realization—the wisdom dharmakāya—functioning as the dominant condition when a buddha's svābhāvikakāya, sāmbhogikakāya, nairmāṇikakāya, and so on engage in enlightened activity for the welfare of others. Therefore, if the twenty-one sets of uncontaminated wisdom were not something separate from the three kāyas, it would follow that these twenty-one sets exist primordially. If that is accepted, it follows that these twenty-one sets of wisdom are not something that did not exist before and have then been clearly manifested. Since such consequences are not acceptable, the dharmakāya (as consisting of said twenty-one sets of wisdom) is separate from the svābhāvikakāya. It is also not suitable to present the dharmakāya as the sāmbhogikakāya or the nairmāṇikakāya because it is not suitable to appear to sentient beings.

"So which of these two positions—there being three or four kāyas—do you take?" There is no contradiction in listening to both—"wisdom kāya" and "dharmakāya" just represent different isolates, but refer to a single specifically characterized phenomenon without any difference in nature.[518]

2d) Haribhadra's *Ālokā* and *Vivṛti* on the AA teaching three or four kāyas[519]

In the dispute as to whether the AA teaches three or four kāyas, both Haribhadra's *Ālokā* and *Vivṛti* first refer to Āryavimuktisena's comments in his *Vṛtti*[520] as exemplifying the position of those who assert three kāyas (svābhāvikakāya, sāmbhogikakāya, and nairmāṇikakāya). According to the *Vivṛti* (interspersed with the comments by JNS), these people take AA VIII.1 literally and claim that precisely the uncontaminated supramundane dharmas mentioned in it are the distinctive features of the svābhāvikakāya. They explain that the svābhāvikakāya itself (the basis of these features) has the defining characteristic of being the nature of these uncontaminated wisdoms—the fact of their not arising or not being established from their own side. The fact that the svābhāvikakāya does not give up these uncontaminated wisdom dharmas is expressed as "dharmatākāya," but this is stated here in abbreviated form as "dharmakāya" (as in AA VIII.6d) through the elision of the Sanskrit particle *-tā* that forms abstract nouns. Thus it expresses the connection of the svābhāvikakāya being both the nature of phenomena and a kāya.[521] This is followed by the rhetorical question, "What are said wisdom dharmas, which are uncontaminated by virtue of having the characteristic of being of the dharmakāya's nature?" As an answer to this, the above people say that these wisdom dharmas are listed in AA VIII.2–6, whereas a dharmakāya separate from the svābhāvikakāya is not taught.[522]

Those others who assert four kāyas reply the following. The feature of the function of buddhahood is that seeming buddhas display as kāyas by way of giving rise to certain appearances with specific purposes for the yogic perceptions of ordinary beings and noble ones. The feature of its relinquishment is the fundamental change in terms of the states of the adventitious stains having become pure, which means abiding in the remainder—the ultimate mind of a buddha. The feature of its nature is to teach the dharma and so on through making these kāyas appear in the mind streams of others (those to be guided) from the perspective of these others. The performance of functions such as these and the knowledge on which they are based—the vajra minds and mental factors of the nonduality of apprehender and apprehended—must undoubtedly be accepted as being existent on the buddhabhūmi also by those who assert three kāyas, but then the question is how they are included in the three kāyas? It is difficult for those who assert three kāyas to answer this question, so they do not give any reply to it.[523] Instead, some of them adduce AA I.17:

> As svābhāvika[kāya], sambhoga[kāya],
> And also as nairmāṇika[kāya], which is other,
> The dharmakāya, together with its activity,
> Is proclaimed to be fourfold.

This is taken by them to mean that there are only three kāyas because this verse does not use the word "dharmakāya" immediately after the word "svābhāvikakāya." However, those who assert four kāyas reply that this verse is phrased in such a way by virtue of the force of demonstrating the purpose already taught above (linking the dharmakāya with enlightened activity); from the perspective of facilitating the prosody of this verse; and because of matching enlightened activity with the agent of buddha wisdom alone. Therefore, it is not contradictory to all the statements about four kāyas that are also made in other quarters, that is, the mantrayāna.[524]

3) The distinctions in terms of the kāyas being fully qualified or nominal and the manner in which knowable objects are seen

This has two parts:

a) The distinctions in terms of the kāyas being fully qualified or nominal
b) The manner in which knowable objects are seen

3a) The distinctions in terms of the kāyas being fully qualified or nominal

The conventional term "nominal buddhahood" does not apply to the svābhāvikakāya. As for the sāmbhogikakāya and the nairmāṇikakāya, they have the nature of actual buddhahood because they attract the children of the Buddha and are the actual kāyas of the mirrorlike wisdom and the all-accomplishing wisdom, respectively. For *Mahāyānasūtrālaṃkāra* IX.69cd and 74cd explain this clearly by matching the sāmbhogikakāya and the nairmāṇikakāya with these wisdoms:

> Because sambhoga-buddhahood
> Arises as this reflection of wisdom.[525]
> . . .
> Through infinite and inconceivable various forms,
> It accomplishes the welfare of sentient beings.

Some object, "The sāmbhogikakāya and the nairmāṇikakāya are absolutely not the buddhahood that fulfills this function." This is mistaken because it directly contradicts the system of presenting the actual kāya of the actual way of being as three kāyas. Also, according to this objection, it would follow that the three kāyas in terms of the actual way of being are not inseparable. Therefore, the two rūpakāyas in terms of the way of appearing are not buddhahood because they are kāyas on the level of the seeming and because they consist of appearances for others, that is, those to be guided. The seeming kāyas that appear for beings such as noble bodhisattvas in the form of the blazing major and minor marks and the like are not of any other substance than the cognitions of these bodhisattvas to whom they appear in this way because they are invariably observed together, just like the appearance of blue for a sense consciousness for which blue appears. The two seeming rūpakāyas do not exist as the sāmbhogikakāya and the nairmāṇikakāya of actual buddhahood. For if they existed in this way, they would have to be unsuitable to appear as certain aspects on the level of the seeming for others (such as bodhisattvas), but they obviously do appear as such aspects. Thus, such appearances are nothing other than their experiencers' own cognitive aspects. Some people raise concerns about this, saying, "If the rūpakāyas are nothing other than the cognitions that appear in the form of these rūpakāyas, what is the cause that casts these appearances? If they appear without a cause, everything could arise from everything, so you must explain this." If this is considered within the Sautrāntika system, there is such a concern. However, to explain this in terms of their perspective, though there is no substantially established cause here that casts the appearance of an aspect, it is not contradictory for an aspect to appear. For except for solely the appearance of an aspect, any cause that casts it is not observed as something suitable to appear. As *Pramāṇavārttika* III.335cd says:

> The appearance as blue is seen,
> [But] there is no separate external referent.

Thus, the sāmbhogikakāya and the nairmāṇikakāya of a buddha that actually fulfill this function are not any kind of physical form and such because the Buddha said in the *Vajracchedikāprajñāpāramitāsūtra*:

> Those who see me by way of form
> And those who follow me by way of sound
> Have engaged in the wrong approach—
> Such persons do not see me.
>
> The buddhas are seen by way of the dharma—
> The guides are dharmakāya indeed.[526]

The gist of this is that, for the arising of the intermittent appearances of the rūpakāyas, there are no other referents that cast their aspects. However, this is not contradictory because they appear in these forms by virtue of the awakening of the latent tendencies of such appearances, which is based on the immediate conditions of the cognitions for which they appear in these ways. This is also established through scriptures because *Pramāṇavārttika* III.336 says:

> Here, certain [later] ones are the awakening
> Of the latent tendencies of certain [former] ones.
> Therefore, it is certain that mind [entails such] aspects,
> But it does not depend on external referents.

"So what are these latent tendencies?" They represent the element that consists of dualistic appearances. "And what are the conditions that awaken them?" They are the merits and[527] aspiration prayers of those to be guided because AA VIII.9 says:

> Once the cause has come to maturity,
> For whomever and whenever,
> It will unfold as beneficial
> Activity to them.

Thus, the two kāyas that are appearances for others represent the enlightened activity that exists in the realms of sentient beings as its recipients. In brief, it is the object condition which consists of the wisdom possessed by the svābhāvikakāya that appears as the three kāyas (dharmakāya, sāmbhogikakāya, and nairmāṇikakāya) for the cognitions through which buddhas, bodhisattvas, and ordinary beings, in due order, delimit this object condition.

Some think, "If the rūpakāyas that are appearances for others are not buddhahood, it follows that the three piṭakas and so on are not the words of the Buddha," and, "If the two rūpakāyas that are appearances for others possess wisdom, it follows that they are buddhahood. If they do not possess wisdom, this contradicts the wisdom of the sāmbhogikakāya functioning as a support. If the buddhanairmāṇikakāya has no wisdom, this contradicts its being the nairmāṇikakāya of a buddha." To answer the first concern, in general, the words of the Buddha are twofold. Among these, the Buddha's words that exist for the objects that are their recipients consist of certain elements in the mind streams of those to be guided—it is the various cognizances which consist of their mental continua appearing as the names, sentences, and so on of the genuine dharma. This is what is labeled as "the words of the Buddha." As for the Buddha's words that exist for the agent, they are nothing other than the nature of the dharmakāya because nobody else except a buddha who truly fulfills this function possesses the words of a buddha. Consequently, it is not the case that the words of the Buddha that appear nowadays are not the words of the Buddha.

To answer the second concern above, buddha wisdom exists in everything that is a rūpakāya of a buddha because it is the very wisdom kāya itself that appears as the kāyas of a buddha to different beings to be guided. It is established that wisdom exists in these appearances because what is not that wisdom is not connected to these appearances. However, it was already explained above that, when these appearances of rūpakāyas appear based on said wisdom, it is not the case that this wisdom casts their aspects by way of existing as any kind of external referent, such as form. Though wisdom exists in what appears as the two rūpakāyas, it is established that what appears as the rūpakāyas is not actual buddhahood because the appearance-aspect in these appearances is displayed as looking like sentient beings, while the basis of said appearances is established as buddhahood.

Here, some say, "Then it follows that the rūpakāyas that appear for the eye consciousnesses of those to be guided are noble buddhas because they are persons with mind streams that consist of the knowledge of all aspects." In the objects that are observed as rūpakāyas, the wisdom kāya exists in a nondual manner, and it is in terms of this fact that one speaks of the dharmakāya existing in the rūpakāyas. However, from the perspective of the appearance-aspects that appear to the cognitions of the sentient beings who observe these objects, it is not said that the dharmakāya exists in the rūpakāyas. Thus, one must understand well the distinctions between the basis of appearance (true actuality), the locations of appearances (the cognitions of those to be guided), the manner in which they appear (the aspects of objects), and so on. Consequently, though whatever is a sāmbhogikakāya or a nairmāṇikakāya must possess wisdom in its continuum, the two rūpakāyas that are the appearance-aspects that appear to the eye consciousnesses of sentient beings are the mere sāmbhogikakāya and nairmāṇikakāya, but not the actual sāmbhogikakāya and nairmāṇikakāya. Therefore, if one mistakes the appearance-aspect that consists of an aspect of the basis of appearance appearing toward and within the cognitions of those to be guided as being an appearance-aspect that, through these very cognitions, appears again outside of cognition as the aspect of an outer referent, it is difficult to explain that wisdom exists in such an appearance-aspect.

In brief since whatever appears for the cognitions of sentient beings is mistaken, it is not suitable as buddhahood because unmistaken supports (the kāyas) and what is supported by them (the wisdoms) do not appear to sentient beings. This meaning represents the general Buddhist approach because Dharmakīrti says the following in his *Saṃtānāntarasiddhi*. The appearance-aspects that appear at the time of two debaters appearing to each other consist of certain parts of the cognitions of those for whom they appear. Therefore, though these appearance-aspects are not different in substance from the cognitions for which they appear, the two streams of cognition are proved to be other in substance. Through the supernatural knowledge of knowing what is going on in the minds of others, one presumes knowing the minds of others, but in terms of what is actually happening, the actual object that is known through supernatural knowledge is not anything other than one's own cognition. Therefore, the mind streams of persons are different. "But then what is the manner in which the minds of others are known?" It refers to the fact of hidden objects appearing directly to yogins who have attained the power of a very lucid mind, but this still means that a cognition of knowing the mind of another person appears as this very cognition's aspect that just reflects the mind of the other person.[528]

3b) The manner in which knowable objects are seen

Bhāvaviveka, Śāntarakṣita, his followers, and others explain that, though buddha wisdom cognizes the appearances of the correct seeming by way of their appearing to this wisdom just as they are, this wisdom does not become mistaken. Asaṅga, Dignāga, and others hold that all consciousnesses of dualistic appearances appear under the sway of ignorance and thus do not appear to budda wisdom—wisdom only perceives the ultimate.[529] Great ones such as Candrakīrti assert that, in terms of the Tathāgatas' own appearances, no seeming appearances emerge for them, but from the perspective of others (those to be guided), these tathāgatas display cognizing seeming appearances. However, here one must follow the bodhisattva Asaṅga because his position is the one that is related to this context of explaining the works of Maitreya. Therefore, though master Vinītadeva follows this system of Asaṅga and yet says that there is mistakenness during the subsequent attainment of buddhas, this is a case of not identifying the position of said system as it is. In this system, it is difficult to explain that buddhas have both meditative equipoise and subsequent attainment. Also, if dualistic appearances still emerge after the latent tendencies of the mistakenness of dualistic appearances have been eradicated, it follows that the minds of buddhas are not stable in terms of relinquishment. For example, if strands of falling hair continue to appear after the disease of blurred vision has been cured, it is very difficult to speak of this disease having been removed.

The gist of this is as follows. If you wonder how buddhas cognize what is to be cognized, it is the cognition of the true reality of any phenomena that must be presented as the cognition of all that is to be cognized. This is just like presenting "cognizing the true reality of the sixteen aspects of the four realities" as "cognizing the actuality of the four realities." As for the nature of this manner of cognizing, the direct cognition or perception of the fundamental nature of all cognizable objects as the freedom from reference points is the wisdom of knowing suchness, while the direct cognition or perception of the possible extent of the fundamental nature of each one of these cognizable objects is the wisdom of knowing variety. Thus, the appearance-aspects that appear to sentient beings, which represent the bearers of the nature of phenomena and the ways in which distinct cognizable objects appear to these beings, do not have to appear to buddhas for the following reasons. Since they are appearance-aspects that represent nonexistents which nevertheless appear under the sway of mistakenness, they are not present within the fundamental nature of buddhahood. Also, deceiving referents do not appear to valid perception. If they did, it would follow that the cognition of a buddha is just seeming valid perception. If that is accepted, this contradicts the statement in all sūtras and tantras that buddhas always cognize all phenomena in a direct manner. Again, others say, "A buddha's own appearances in meditative equipoise pertain solely to direct perception, but during subsequent attainment and for the appearances of others, they appear as seeming direct perception." However, this is simply their own fabrication because there is no scriptural basis for this anywhere.

In brief, though seeming reality does not appear for buddhas, this is not contradictory to their cognizing all cognizable objects. Their cognition is one that truly fulfills this function because it distinctly cognizes, without mixing them, both the mistaken and unmistaken manners of the actual way of being and the way of appearing of the seeming. Still, what is assessed through a buddha's cognizing the way of appearing of the seeming is nothing other than this buddha's very own self-awareness. It is with this point in mind that glorious Dharmakīrti's *Pramāṇavārttika* II.32 says:

> Whoever cognizes the true reality
> Of what is to be adopted and to be rejected, including the means,
> Is asserted as a valid cognizer,
> But not a cognizer of everything.

Therefore, all deceiving phenomena of the seeming are appearances of entities that are created by ignorance alone, but such appearances do not emerge for buddhas. For if they did, this would mean that what is mistaken appears for buddhas. Thus since the philosophical systems that claim that the seeming appears for buddhas are false, some find themselves in the need to make statements such as, "What is mistaken appears to buddhas, but buddhas are not mistaken." However, other than what appears to a mistaken consciousness, what could what is mistaken be? "So what is the entity that is independently cognized by buddhas themselves?" They solely cognize the nature of ultimate reality, that is, the perfect nature—the true end free from meditative equipoise and subsequent attainment.

About this, some have the following concern: "If the seeming does not appear to buddha wisdom, it follows that they are not omniscient." To explain how this concern does not invalidate what was said above, there is nothing in the mahāyāna scriptures of definitive meaning that proves that seeming appearances emerge for buddha wisdom. For the followers of the mahāyāna explain the following. In general since all aspects of the seeming are unreal, from the perspective of the yoga of yogins who are engaged in what is truly real there is absolutely no seeing of anything as being mistaken and, in particular, there are absolutely no external entities. Therefore, if what does not exist at the time of being a sentient being appears as existent at the time of being a buddha, what could be more unreasonable than that? Especially, no matter whether you take the Yogācāra-Mādhyamikas who engage in vast yogas or the Mādhyamikas who engage in common consensus and fearlessly propound the profound,[530] in any system of anybody among them, there is not even a single word in their scriptures that seeming appearances appear to buddhas. In addition, there are invalidations of scripturally unsupported claims such as the above. For verse 17 of Nāgārjuna's *Mahāyānaviṃśikā* says:

> Just as dream experiences
> Do not appear upon being examined,
> Upon awakening from the sleep of the darkness of ignorance,
> Saṃsāra is unobservable.[531]

Mahāyānasūtrālaṃkāra XIX.53 says:

> With true reality being obscured, for childish beings,
> What is not true reality appears everywhere.
> Having eliminated this, for bodhisattvas,
> True reality appears everywhere.

Also, Nāgārjuna says:

> For example, under the sway of being asleep,
> [People] may see a son,
> A wife, a palace, an abode, and so forth.
> Upon awakening, they do not see [them anymore].
>
> Likewise, seeming cognitions,
> Once one's eyes of insight are opened
> And one has parted from the sleep of ignorance,
> Are not seen at the time of being awake.
>
> For example, in the middle of the night's darkness,
> Unreal evil spirits may be seen.
> Once the sun shines and one's eyes are open,
> They will not appear.
>
> Likewise, when the learned overcome
> The latent tendencies of ignorance without exception
> Through the sun of knowing true reality,
> They do not behold the objects of minds and mental factors.[532]

Furthermore, there is the following invalidation through reasoning. If any aspects of the seeming were to emerge for the cognition of buddhas as their own appearances, the question is whether these aspects exist as having the nature of the very cognition to which they appear as such aspects, or whether they are something else. As for the first possibility, the question is whether these aspects exist or do not exist as something that is other in substance than what casts these aspects. In the first case, by virtue of accepting the existence of apprehender and apprehended being other in substance, one has moved outside of the mahāyāna system. In the second case, it would follow that all the various appearances of seeming reality (such as the six types of beings and the two obscurations) are buddha wisdom. For what appear as said appearances for buddha wisdom are the actual buddha wisdom, while any cause that casts these aspects and is other in substance is unobservable. As for the second possibility above, if the cognitive aspect that appears for cognition itself is not self-awareness, this contradicts the following statement by the guardian of the teachings Dharmakīrti. He said that, through the reasoning of establishing mind as having two facets (subject and object), the second facet is established as mind, at which point it is also established as self-awareness.[533] Therefore, our assertion shall be formulated as a probative argument. Whatever is a cognizable object that appears under the sway of ignorance does necessarily not appear to buddha wisdom, just as in the example of falling strands of hair not appearing for those who are free from blurred vision. The same applies for all the various appearances of seeming reality. This is a reason of observing a larger category that is contradictory to the predicate to be negated.[534] In brief, within the scope of what appears to others, a buddha's mere cognizing the appearances of the seeming is justified, but it is not the case that these appearances are cognized by way of appearing as direct objects for buddha wisdom.

Here, some raise the following dispute: "If buddha wisdom cognizes the seeming within the scope of what appears to others, it follows that it must cognize the seeming directly. For it is cognized by said wisdom and it is not suitable for any other cognitional mode to exist on this level because inferential cognition that assesses hidden objects does not exist on said level. Also, if the seeming is cognized by this wisdom, it becomes its directly assessed object." The first reason is uncertain because all presentations from the perspective of either direct perception or inferential cognition in terms of a cognition cognizing a cognizable object and so on refer to sentient beings, while what is cognized on the buddhabhūmi is an inconceivable object. Therefore, it does not have to be engaged through such limited ways of cognizing cognizable objects. The second reason is uncertain too because also the innate clinging to identity is a directly assessed object of the mode of apprehension of buddha wisdom, but it is not observed to appear for direct perception. In addition, even if this wisdom cognizes object generalities and so on, they need not be cognized directly by it. For this wisdom cognizes object generalities and so on in the manner of their being appearances for others, just as a wakening consciousness, at its own time, realizes the way of appearing of objects in a dream.

B) Enlightened activity[535]

The enlightened activity of the dharmakāya (the primordial Heart free from stains) engages all sentient beings and does not depend on the triad of completion, maturation, and purification. Nevertheless, the enlightened activity of the dharmakāya that displays in such a way as if someone had newly become a buddha through the power of having temporarily performed said triad takes all the infinite numbers of sentient beings as its object conditions, with the knowledge of the dharmakāya being the immediate condition and also the dominant cause of this enlightened activity. Yet it is only from the perspective of the dharmakāya's nature and function, respectively, that it is presented as the immediate cause and the dominant cause—in actual fact, the enlightened activity of accomplishing the welfare of others occurs in an uninterrupted and spontaneous manner until saṃsāra is emptied. As for the nature of this activity, it is nice to present it as the nature of a buddha's knowledge, loving-kindness, and power—fundamental awareness (*rig pa*). Therefore, this enlightened activity is twofold—the enlightened activity that exists in terms of its agent and the enlightened activity that exists in terms of its recipients or objects. The first one is nothing other than the uncontaminated wisdom—the dharmakāya—that is presented in AA VIII.2–6 in twenty-one sets. The second one is the dominant condition that consists of the power of a tathāgata's compassion and blessings and is instrumental in increasing sentient beings' roots of virtue that are conducive to merit and conducive to liberation. That such increases take place in sentient beings is taken to be enlightened activity because said increases represent the very traces of enlightened activity. You may wonder, "In which manner does enlightened activity operate?" It operates in three ways by establishing those to be guided in the support of the path, the path itself, and the fruition of the path.[536] Since this is clearly discussed in Asaṅga's *Ratnagotravibhāgavyākhyā* and elsewhere, this much elaboration shall suffice here.[537]

Appendix II: Charts

Chart 22: The 173 aspects of the complete training in all aspects

A) The twenty-seven aspects of the knowledge of entities

See the twenty-seven aspects of the four realities in the knowledge of entities (Chart 5 in Volume One).

B) The thirty-six aspects of the knowledge of the path

See the thirty-six aspects of the four realities in the knowledge of the path (Chart 5 in Volume One).

C) The 110 aspects of the knowledge of all aspects

1) The thirty-seven aspects in common with the knowledge of entities[538]

a) the path of examining entities:
(1)–(4) the four foundations of mindfulness
b) the path that arises from effort:
(5)–(8) the four correct efforts
c) the path of training in samādhi:
(9)–(12) the four limbs of miraculous powers
d) the path of preparing for clear realization:
(13)–(17) the five faculties
e) the path of connecting with clear realization:
(18)–(22) the five powers
f) the path of clearly realizing the realities:
(23)–(29) the seven branches of enlightenment
g) the path that is conducive to pure final deliverance:
(30)–(37) the eightfold path of the noble ones

2) The thirty-four aspects in common with the knowledge of the path

a) the path of the remedies:
(1)–(3) the three samādhis of emptiness, wishlessness, and signlessness
b) the path of manifesting:
(4)–(6) the first three of the eight liberations[539]
c) the path of blissfully abiding amidst visible phenomena:
(5)–(11) the five remaining liberations
d) the supramundane path:
(12)–(20) the nine meditative absorptions of progressive abiding[540]
e) the path of relinquishment:
(21)–(24) the four readinesses of the path of seeing
f) the path of buddhahood:
(25)–(34) the ten pāramitās

3) The uncommon thirty-nine aspects of the knowledge of all aspects

a) the ten powers (1)–(10)[541]
b) the four fearlessnesses (11)–14)
c) the four discriminating awarenesses (15)–(18)
d) the eighteen unique qualities (19)–(36)
e) suchness (37)
f) self-arising omniscient wisdom (38)
g) buddhahood (39)

Chart 23: The different models of the sequence of the samādhis of the preparatory lion's sport and the actual crossing in one leap on the path of familiarization

1) According to the *Prajñāpāramitāsūtra in Eighteen Thousand Lines*, the *Vṛtti*, and the *Ālokā*

preparatory lion's sport[542]

1 – 2 – 3 – 4 – 5 – 6 – 7 – 8 – 9 – 8 – 7 – 6 – 5 – 4 – 3 – 2 – 1 →

actual crossing in one leap

1 – 2 – 3 – 4 – 5 – 6 – 7 – 8 – 9 – 1 – 9 – 2 – 9 –3 – 9 – 4 – 9 – 5 – 9 – 6 – 9 – 7 – 9 – 8 – 9 – 8 – 0 – 9 – 0 – 8 – 0 – 7 – 0 – 6 – 0 – 5 – 0 – 4 – 0 – 3 – 0 – 2 – 0 – 1 – 0

2) According to the *Vivṛti*

1 – 2 – 3 – 4 – 5 – 6 – 7 – 8 – 9 – 8 – 7 – 6 – 5 – 4 – 3 – 2 – 1 →
1 – 9 – 2 – 9 –3 – 9 – 4 – 9 – 5 – 9 – 6 – 9 – 7 – 9 – 8 – 9 – 8 – 0 →
9 – 0 – 8 – 0 – 7 – 0 – 6 – 0 – 5 – 0 – 4 – 0 – 3 – 0 – 2 – 0 – 1 – 0

3) According to the *Sārottama* and *Marmakaumudi*

preparatory lion's sport (uncertain for *Marmakaumudi*)

1 – 2 – 3 – 4 – 5 – 6 – 7 – 8 – 9 – 8 – 7 – 6 – 5 – 4 – 3 – 2 – 1 →

actual crossing in one leap

1. ascending	1 – 2 – 3 – 4 – 5 – 6 – 7 – 8 – 9 →
2. ascending	1 – 9 – 2 – 9 –3 – 9 – 4 – 9 – 5 – 9 – 6 – 9 – 7 – 9 – 8 – 9 – 0 →
descending	9 – 0 – 8 – 0 – 7 – 0 – 6 – 0 – 5 – 0 – 4 – 0 – 3 – 0 – 2 – 0 – 1 – 0

4) According to the *Śuddhamatī*

crossing in one leap

1. ascending	1 – 2 – 3 – 4 – 5 – 6 – 7 – 8 – 9 →
2. ascending	1 – 9 – 2 – 9 –3 – 9 – 4 – 9 – 5 – 9 – 6 – 9 – 7 – 9 – 8 – 9 – 8 – 9 – 0 →
descending	9 – 0 – 8 – 0 – 7 – 0 – 6 – 0 – 5 – 0 – 4 – 0 – 3 – 0 – 2 – 0 – 1 – 0

5) According to JNS

preparatory lion's sport

1 – 2 – 3 – 4 – 5 – 6 – 7 – 8 – 9 – 8 – 7 – 6 – 5 – 4 – 3 – 2 – 1 →

actual crossing in one leap

lesser	1 – 2 – 3 – 4 – 5 – 6 – 7 – 8 – 9 →
medium	1 – 9 – 2 – 9 –3 – 9 – 4 – 9 – 5 – 9 – 6 – 9 – 7 – 9 – 8 – 9 – 8 – 0 – 8 – 9[543] – 7 – 9 – 6 – 9 – 5 – 9 – 4 – 9 – 3 – 9 – 2 – 9 – 1 – 9 – 0 →
great	1 – 0 – 2 – 0 –3 – 0 – 4 – 0 – 5 – 0 – 6 – 0 – 7 – 0 – 8 – 0 – 9 – 0 – 9 – 0 – 8 – 0 – 7 – 0 – 6 – 0 – 5 – 0 – 4 – 0 – 3 – 0 – 2 – 0 – 1 – 0

6) According to CE

preparatory lion's sport

1 – 2 – 3 – 4 – 5 – 6 – 7 – 8 – 9 – 8 – 7 – 6 – 5 – 4 – 3 – 2 – 1 →

actual crossing in one leap

lesser	1 – 2 – 3 – 4 – 5 – 6 – 7 – 8 – 9 – 8 – 7 – 6 – 5 – 4 – 3 – 2 – 1 →
medium	1 – 9 – 2 – 9 –3 – 9 – 4 – 9 – 5 – 9 – 6 – 9 – 7 – 9 – 8 – 9 – 8 – 0 →
great	9 – 0 – 8 – 0 – 7 – 0 – 6 – 0 – 5 – 0 – 4 – 0 – 3 – 0 – 2 – 0 – 1 – 0 (– 1 – 0 – 2 – 0 –3 – 0 – 4 – 0 – 5 – 0 – 6 – 0 – 7 – 0 – 8 – 0 – 9 – 0)

7) According to LN

preparatory lion's sport
1 – 2 – 3 – 4 – 5 – 6 – 7 – 8 – 9 – 8 – 7 – 6 – 5 – 4 – 3 – 2 – 1[544] →

actual crossing in one leap

plain crossing in one leap	1 – 2 – 3 – 4 – 5 – 6 – 7 – 8 – 9 →
special crossing in one leap	1 – 9 – 2 – 9 –3 – 9 – 4 – 9 – 5 – 9 – 6 – 9 – 7 – 9 – 8 – 9 – 8 – 0 →
very special crossing in one leap	8 – 0 – 7 – 0 – 6 – 0 – 5 – 0 – 4 – 0 – 3 – 0 – 2 – 0 – 1 – 0

Vivṛti:
preparatory lion's sport
1 – 2 – 3 – 4 – 5 – 6 – 7 – 8 – 9 – 8 – 7 – 6 – 5 – 4 – 3 – 2 – 1 →
actual crossing in one leap

plain crossing in one leap	1 – 2 – 3 – 4 – 5 – 6 – 7 – 8 – 9 – 8 – 7 – 6 – 5 – 4 – 3 – 2 – 1 →
special crossing in one leap	1 – 9 – 2 – 9 –3 – 9 – 4 – 9 – 5 – 9 – 6 – 9 – 7 – 9 – 8 – 9 – 8 – 0 –9 – 0 →
very special crossing in one leap	8 – 0 – 7 – 0 – 6 – 0 – 5 – 0 – 4 – 0 – 3 – 0 – 2 – 0 – 1 – 0

8) According to YT

preparatory lion's sport
1 – 2 – 3 – 4 – 5 – 6 – 7 – 8 – 9 – 8 – 7 – 6 – 5 – 4 – 3 – 2 – 1 →
actual crossing in one leap

lesser	Haribhadra	1 – 2 – 3 – 4 – 5 – 6 – 7 – 8 – 9 – 8 – 7 – 6 – 5 – 4 – 3 – 2 – 1 →
	sūtras and other comm.	1 – 2 – 3 – 4 – 5 – 6 – 7 – 8 – 9 →
medium	2 Vimuktisenas; Haribhadra	1 – 9 – 2 – 9 –3 – 9 – 4 – 9 – 5 – 9 – 6 – 9 – 7 – 9 – 8 – 9 – 8 – 0 – 9 – 0 →
	Śuddhamatī	1 – 9 – 2 – 9 –3 – 9 – 4 – 9 – 5 – 9 – 6 – 9 – 7 – 9 – 8 – 9 – 8 – 9 – 0[545] →
	acc. to sūtras in 100,000 & 25,000 lines (plus revised edition); *Sārottama*; *Marmakaumudi*	1 – 9 – 2 – 9 –3 – 9 – 4 – 9 – 5 – 9 – 6 – 9 – 7 – 9 – 8 – 9 – 0 →
great		8 – 0 – 7 – 0 – 6 – 0 – 5 – 0 – 4 – 0 – 3 – 0 – 2 – 0 – 1 – 0

9) According to RT

preparatory lion's sport
eight liberations in progressive and reverse orders →
1 – 2 – 3 – 4 – 5 – 6 – 7 – 8 – 9 – 8 – 7 – 6 – 5 – 4 – 3 – 2 – 1 →
examination of dependent origination in progressive and reverse orders[546] →

actual crossing in one leap
lesser 1 – 2 – 3 – 4 – 5 – 6 – 7 – 8 – 9 →
medium 1 – 9 – 2 – 9 –3 – 9 – 4 – 9 – 5 – 9 – 6 – 9 – 7 – 9 – 8 – 9 – 8 – 0 →
great 9 – 0 – 8 – 0 – 7 – 0 – 6 – 0 – 5 – 0 – 4 – 0 – 3 – 0 – 2 – 0 – 1 – 0

Vivṛti:
preparatory lion's sport
1 – 2 – 3 – 4 – 5 – 6 – 7 – 8 – 9 – 8 – 7 – 6 – 5 – 4 – 3 – 2 – 1 →

actual crossing in one leap
lesser 1 – 2 – 3 – 4 – 5 – 6 – 7 – 8 – 9
medium 1 – 9 – 2 – 9 –3 – 9 – 4 – 9 – 5 – 9 – 6 – 9 – 7 – 9 – 8 – 9 – 8 →
great 0 – 9 – 0 – 8 – 0 – 7 – 0 – 6 – 0 – 5 – 0 – 4 – 0 – 3 – 0 – 2 – 0 – 1 – 0[547]

10) According to LSSP/PSD

preparatory lion's sport
1 – 2 – 3 – 4 – 5 – 6 – 7 – 8 – 9 – 8 – 7 – 6 – 5 – 4 – 3 – 2 – 1 →

actual crossing in one leap
ascending
not alternating with cessation 1 – 2 – 3 – 4 – 5 – 6 – 7 – 8 – 9 →
alternating with cessation:
sūtra in 18,000 lines 1 – 9 – 2 – 9 – 3 – 9 – 4 – 9 – 5 – 9 – 6 – 9 – 7 – 9 – 8 – 9 – 8 – 0 →
revised 25,000 lines 1 – 9 – 2 – 9 – 3 – 9 – 4 – 9 – 5 – 9 – 6 – 9 – 7 – 9 – 8 – 9 – 0 →
descending 9 – 0 – 8 – 0 – 7 – 0 – 6 – 0 – 5 – 0 – 4 – 0 – 3 – 0 – 2 – 0 – 1 – 0

11) According to PK

preparatory lion's sport

1 – 2 – 3 – 4 – 5 – 6 – 7 – 8 – 9 – 8 – 7 – 6 – 5 – 4 – 3 – 2 – 1 →

actual crossing in one leap

1 – 9 – 2 – 9 –3 – 9 – 4 – 9 – 5 – 9 – 6 – 9 – 7 – 9 – 8 – 9 →
8 – 0 – 9 – 0 – 8 – 0 – 7 – 0 – 6 – 0 – 5 – 0 – 4 – 0 – 3 – 0 – 2 – 0 – 1 –
0 – 1 – 0 – 2 – 0 –3 – 0 – 4 – 0 – 5 – 0 – 6 – 0 – 7 – 0 – 8 – 0 – 9 – 0

Chart 24: The six causes, four conditions, and five results

Causes

Cause in general: That which produces the nature of a result

Substantial cause: That which is primary in producing the nature of a result (or that which primarily produces the continuum of its own substance as its specific result)

Cooperative cause: That which primarily produces something that is not the continuum of its own substance as its specific result

The six causes

(1) *Enabling cause:* That which produces something that is other than itself and has the nature of a result

(2) *Simultaneous cause:* That which produces the nature of a result by these two being mutually dependent

(3) *Cause of similar outcome:* That which produces a result that resembles its cause

- *contaminated cause of similar outcome:* That which produces a similar result and is a factor to be relinquished through the path
- *uncontaminated cause of similar outcome:* That which produces something that is similar to its cause and is not a factor to be relinquished through the path

(4) *Congruent cause:* That which arises from a mind with congruent support and produces the nature of a result

(5) *Omnipresent cause:* That which, in dependence on preceding onmi-present factors, produces a subsequent nature of the flaws of its own respective level

(6) *Maturing cause:* That which is a contaminated nonneutral phenomenon and produces the nature of a result

Conditions

Condition in general: That which produces the distinctive features of a result

The four conditions

(1) *Causal condition:* That which produces the distinctive features of a result together with its nature
(2) *Object condition:* That which produces the distinctive features of a result as an object's specific aspect of appearing
(3) *Immediate condition:* A given preceding consciousness that directly produces the subsequent moment of this consciousness
(4) *Dominant condition:* That which is able to produce the distinctive features of a result independently

Results

Result in general: That which is to be produced

The five results

(1) *Matured result:* A nonobscuring and neutral phenomenon that is included in the continuum of a sentient being and arises from a maturing cause
(2) *Dominated result:* A phenomenon that either arises at present or later from entities or conditioned phenomena which are merely not obstructing it
(3) *Result that concords with the cause:* A phenomenon that arises from either a cause of similar outcome or an omnipresent cause and is similar in type with them
(4) *Result produced by persons:* A phenomenon that arises through the power of its specific causes
(5) *Result of freedom:* The extinction or relinquishment of the factors to be relinquished through prajñā[548]

Relationships between the six causes and the five results

enabling cause	→	dominated result
simultaneous cause congruent cause	→	result produced by persons
cause of similar outcome omnipresent cause	→	result concordant with the cause
maturing cause	→	matured result

Chart 25: The change of state of the eight consciousnesses into the four (five) wisdoms and the three (four) kāyas

According to Yogācāra

<table>
<tr><th colspan="2">Consciousness</th><th>Wisdom</th><th>Kāya</th><th>Bhūmi of change of state</th></tr>
<tr><td>1</td><td>eye consciousness</td><td rowspan="5">all-accomplishing wisdom</td><td rowspan="5">nairmāṇikakāya</td><td rowspan="5">1</td></tr>
<tr><td>2</td><td>ear consciousness</td></tr>
<tr><td>3</td><td>nose consciousness</td></tr>
<tr><td>4</td><td>tongue consciousness</td></tr>
<tr><td>5</td><td>body consciousness</td></tr>
<tr><td>6</td><td>mental consciousness</td><td>discriminating wisdom</td><td rowspan="2">sāmboghikakāya</td><td rowspan="2">8</td></tr>
<tr><td>7</td><td>afflicted mind</td><td>wisdom of equality</td></tr>
<tr><td>8</td><td>ālaya-consciousness</td><td>mirrorlike wisdom</td><td>dharmakāya</td><td>10</td></tr>
<tr><td></td><td></td><td colspan="2">D H A R M A D H Ā T U</td><td></td></tr>
</table>

According to the Third Karmapa

<table>
<tr><th colspan="2">Consciousness</th><th>Wisdom</th><th>Kāya</th><th>Bhūmi of change of state</th></tr>
<tr><td>1</td><td>eye consciousness</td><td rowspan="6">all-accomplishing wisdom</td><td rowspan="7">nairmāṇikakāya</td><td rowspan="6">1</td></tr>
<tr><td>2</td><td>ear consciousness</td></tr>
<tr><td>3</td><td>nose consciousness</td></tr>
<tr><td>4</td><td>tongue consciousness</td></tr>
<tr><td>5</td><td>body consciousness</td></tr>
<tr><td>6A</td><td>nonconceptual mental consciousness</td></tr>
<tr><td>6B</td><td>conceptual mental consciousness</td><td rowspan="2">discriminating wisdom</td><td rowspan="3">8</td></tr>
<tr><td>7A</td><td>immediate mind</td><td rowspan="2">sāmboghikakāya</td></tr>
<tr><td>7B</td><td>afflicted mind</td><td>wisdom of equality</td></tr>
<tr><td>8</td><td>ālaya-consciousness</td><td>mirrorlike wisdom</td><td>dharmakāya</td><td>10</td></tr>
<tr><td></td><td></td><td>dharmadhātu (wisdom)</td><td>svābhāvikakāya</td><td></td></tr>
</table>

According to JNS and CE

<table>
<tr><th></th><th>Consciousness</th><th>Wisdom</th><th>Kāya</th><th>Bhūmi of change of state</th></tr>
<tr><td>1</td><td>eye consciousness</td><td rowspan="5">all-accomplishing wisdom</td><td rowspan="5">nairmāṇikakāya</td><td rowspan="5">8</td></tr>
<tr><td>2</td><td>ear consciousness</td></tr>
<tr><td>3</td><td>nose consciousness</td></tr>
<tr><td>4</td><td>tongue consciousness</td></tr>
<tr><td>5</td><td>body consciousness</td></tr>
<tr><td>6</td><td>mental consciousness</td><td>discriminating wisdom</td><td rowspan="2">not specifically assigned</td><td>9–10</td></tr>
<tr><td>7</td><td>afflicted mind</td><td>wisdom of equality</td><td>8</td></tr>
<tr><td>8</td><td>ālaya-consciousness</td><td>mirrorlike wisdom</td><td>sāmbhogikakāya</td><td>10</td></tr>
<tr><td></td><td></td><td>dharmadhātu wisdom
ālaya-wisdom</td><td>svābhāvikakāya
dharmakāya</td><td></td></tr>
</table>

According to TOK[549]

<table>
<tr><th></th><th>Consciousness</th><th>Wisdom</th><th>Kāya</th><th>Bhūmi of change of state</th></tr>
<tr><td>1</td><td>eye consciousness</td><td rowspan="5">all-accomplishing wisdom</td><td rowspan="5">nairmāṇikakāya</td><td rowspan="5">8</td></tr>
<tr><td>2</td><td>ear consciousness</td></tr>
<tr><td>3</td><td>nose consciousness</td></tr>
<tr><td>4</td><td>tongue consciousness</td></tr>
<tr><td>5</td><td>body consciousness</td></tr>
<tr><td>6</td><td>mental consciousness</td><td>discriminating wisdom</td><td rowspan="2">sāmboghikakāya</td><td>9</td></tr>
<tr><td>7</td><td>afflicted mind</td><td>wisdom of equality</td><td>8</td></tr>
<tr><td>8</td><td>ālaya-consciousness:
luminous aspect
empty aspect</td><td>mirrorlike wisdom
dharmadhātu wisdom</td><td>dharmakāya</td><td>10</td></tr>
</table>

Chart 26: Overview of the eight topics and the seventy points of the AA

1. The knowledge of all aspects
(10 points)

(1) *generating bodhicitta* (the motivational ground of bodhisattvas)
(2) *the instructions* (applying this motivation)
(3) *the factors conducive to penetration* (the path of preparation as the first major result of this application)
(4) *the disposition* (the dharmadhātu as the underlying ground of all practice)
(5)–(6) *the focal objects and the aim of practice* (all phenomena/the three greatnesses)

the nature of practice
- (7) *armorlike practice*
- (8) *the practice of ninefold engagement*
- (9) *the practice of the seventeen equipments*
- (10) *the practice of final deliverance*

2. The knowledge of the path
(11 points)

(2) the knowledge of the path of śrāvakas
(3) *the knowledge of the path of pratyekabuddhas*

the knowledge of the path of bodhisattvas
- (1) *its causes*
- (4) *the path of seeing*
- the path of familiarization
  - (5) *its function* (sixfold benefit)
  - the contaminated path of familiarization (subsequent attainment)
    - (6) *aspiration*
    - (7) *praise, eulogy, and laudation*
    - (8) *dedication*
    - (9) *rejoicing*
  - the uncontaminated path of familiarization (meditative equipoise)
    - (10) *accomplishment* (the uninterrupted paths of bhūmis 2–10)
    - (11) *utter purity* (the paths of liberation of bhūmis 2–10)

3. The knowledge of entities
(9 points)

the knowledge of entities of bodhisattvas consists of

(1) *not dwelling in saṃsāra* (by virtue of prajñā)

(2) *not dwelling in peace* (—inferior forms of nirvāṇa—by virtue of compassion)

(4) *being close* (to fruitional prajñāpāramitā) *due to skill in means*

(6) *being the remedy* (for the knowledge of entities of śrāvakas and pratyekabuddhas; due to realizing the emptiness of all phenomena)

(7) *the training* (nonreferential meditative equipoise that stops clinging to any characteristics)

(8) *the equality* of this training (in order to eliminate obstacles)

(9) its fruition—*the paths of seeing of śrāvakas, pratyekabuddhas* (implicitly), *and bodhisattvas* (explicitly)

the knowledge of entities of śrāvakas and pratyekabuddhas is

(3) *distant* (from fruitional prajñāpāramitā) *due to lack of means*

(5) *the antagonistic factor* (of the knowledge of entities of bodhisattvas; due to clinging to real existence)

4. The complete training in all aspects
(11 points)

(1) *the aspects* (the cognitive aspects that are the 173 aspects of all three knowledges)
(2) *the trainings* (the nature of this training consisting of the five natural and the fifteen situational trainings)

the preliminary factors of the actual training
(3) its fourteen *qualities*
(4) its forty-six *flaws*
(5) its *defining characteristics*
(6) *the factors conducive to liberation* (the first temporary result of this training—the path of accumulation)

the actual training
(7) *the factors conducive to penetration* (the path of preparation)
(8) *the irreversible learners* (the signs of irreversibility on the paths of preparation, seeing, and familiarization)
(9) *training in the equality of saṃsāra and nirvāṇa*
(10) *training in pure realms*
(11) *tenfold training in skill in means*

5. The culminating training
(8 points)

the culminating training of the path of preparation
(1) *the signs* (of the level of heat during the waking state and in dreams)
(2) *the increase* (in merit on the level of peak)
(3) *the stability* (of not regressing into the paths of śrāvakas or pratyekabuddhas on the level of poised readiness)
(4) *the continuous abiding of the mind* (the immeasurable two accumulations on the level of the supreme dharma)

(5) *the culminating training of the path of seeing* (the imputational conceptions about apprehender and apprehended; the causes of enlightenment; its nature; and the manner of familiarizing with it)
(6) *the culminating training of the path of familiarization* (crossing in one leap; the innate conceptions about the apprehender and the apprehended; limitless qualities)
(7) *the culminating training of the* final *uninterrupted path* of the path of familiarization (the vajralike samādhi)
(8) sixteen *mistaken notions* (about the two realities being contradictory—the factors to be relinquished during the vajralike samādhi)

6. The serial training
(13 points)

(1)–(6) *the six pāramitās* (conduct or the consummate training)

the *six recollections* (the union of view and conduct or the consummate way of thinking) *of*

(7)–(9) *the three jewels*
(10) *ethics*
(11) *giving* (the two bases of the six pāramitās)
(12) *deities* (witnesses on the path)

(13) *training in realizing the nature of the lack of entity* (wisdom and the general view for (1)–(13))

7. The instantaneous training
(4 points)

(1) *training in terms of nonmaturation* (being in the process of overcoming the most subtle stains—the impregnations of negative tendencies that obscure the infinite uncontaminated phenomena of wisdom)
(2) *training in terms of maturation* (wisdom overcoming even the most subtle stains in a single instant)
(3) *training in terms of the lack of characteristics* (realizing all phenomena as dreamlike)
(4) *training in terms of nonduality* (no longer seeing phenomena as the duality of apprehender and apprehended)

8. The dharmakāya
(4 points)

(1) the *svābhāvikakāya* (the twofold purity of the dharmadhātu being primordially pure and also pure of all adventitious stains, which includes the twenty-one sets of uncontaminated qualities)
(2) the *sāmbhogikakāya* (the thirty-two major and the eighty minor marks, including their causes on the path)
(3) the *nairmāṇikakāya* (various benefits being performed through various physical forms for various beings until the end of saṃsāra)
(4) *enlightened activity* (twenty-seven aspects of effortlessly and nonconceptually establishing beings in the support of the path, the path, and the fruition)

Appendix III: The Third Karmapa's Synopsis of the Eight Chapters of Prajñāpāramitā[550]

Oṃ svasti siddhaṃ hūṃ

Paying homage respectfully at the feet
Of the guru and Mañjughoṣa,
I shall write down some brief notes
As a summary of prajñāpāramitā.

Part 1: The eight topics

{90} This has four parts:

1) Identifying the three knowledges (the objects)
2) Identifying the four trainings (the means)
3) Identifying the dharmakāya (the fruition)
4) The boundary lines of these eight clear realizations

1. Identifying the three knowledges (the objects)

This has two parts:

1) The three knowledges as such
2) The three knowledges as taught in the first three chapters of the AA

1.1. The three knowledges as such

This has three parts:

1) Definitions
2) The meanings of the terms that are the definienda
3) Divisions of the instances

1.1.1. Definitions

The knowledge of entities

The definition of **the knowledge of entities**: the realization that all entities are without arising.

This has three parts:

a) The entities to be known
b) The minds that know them
c) The manner in which these minds know these bases

a) The entities to be known are all phenomena of saṃsāra and nirvāṇa, which are summarized in the four realities in their sixteen aspects. Among them, the realities of suffering and its origin constitute saṃsāra, and the realities of cessation and the path constitute nirvāṇa. {91} The reality of suffering is what is to be known like a disease. The reality of the origin of suffering is to be relinquished like the cause of this disease. The reality of cessation is to be attained like the state of being without disease. The reality of the path is to be relied on in one's mind stream like an excellent medicine. Tīrthikas and ordinary beings whose minds are not altered through study and reflection do not understand this.

The reality of suffering consists of our own present contaminated skandhas as the results that are produced through being formed by the karma and the afflictions of past lives. Thus, they are the skandhas that are seized by the three sufferings and made up of various unclean phenomena. Not understanding this, we cling to them as being real as something permanent, clean, happy, a self, and what is mine. Since these kinds of clinging to their being real are afflictive obscurations, as their remedies śrāvakas and pratyekabuddhas study and reflect on their respective piṭakas and thus create the notions of these skandhas being impermanent and so on. They understand that permanence and cleanness do not even exist on the mere level of the seeming and put an end to any previous clinging to their real existence.

The reality of the origin of suffering consists of these very contaminated skandhas that make up the causes and conditions which produce the entirety of the karmas, afflictions, sufferings, and contaminated skandhas of following lives. Not understanding this, tīrthikas and so on cling to them as being real as either the causes of what is permanent, clean, happy, a self, and what is mine, or as not being the causes of suffering and so on. {92} These kinds of clinging to the skandhas as being real are also afflictive obscurations. Therefore, as their remedies, through study and reflection, śrāvakas and pratyekabuddhas understand that something permanent, clean, happy, a self, and what is mine do not even exist on the level of the seeming, and that what is impermanent and unclean represents the causes of the karmas and afflictions of following lifetimes and the causes for all bodies. Through this, they relinquish them.

The reality of cessation exists on the level of the seeming as what is to be attained (like being without disease) and refers to being empty of a personal self and so on. Tīrthikas and so on do not understand this kind of attainment or, even if they understand it, they cling to it as being real as something to be attained that is permanent, single, a self, and what is mine. These kinds of clinging to real existence are also afflictive obscurations. Therefore, as their remedies, through study and reflection, śrāvakas and so on understand that a permanent and independent personal self and so on do not even exist on the level of the seeming. It is in this way that they render the reality of cessation into that which is to be attained like the state of being without disease.

As for the reality of the path, tīrthikas do not understand that it is to be relied on like an excellent medicine or, even if they understand it, they cling to it as being real in the sense of there definitely being some permanent, single, and independent reality of the path to be relied on in their own mind streams. These kinds of clinging to real existence are also afflictive obscurations. Therefore, as their remedies, through study and reflection, śrāvakas and so on understand that a personal self that is permanent, single, independent, and so on does not even exist on the level of the seeming and that it is just an impermanent succession of moments. It is in this way that they render the path into something to rely on in their mind streams. {93}

b) The minds that know these bases are the mental states of studying, reflecting, and meditating that range from the level of a beginner up through buddha wisdom.

c) As for the manner in which these minds know these bases, the śrāvakas realize that the phenomena of saṃsāra and nirvāṇa (or the four realities in their sixteen aspects) are empty of any agent (such as a self, Cha,[551] or Īśvara), which thus does not even exist on the level of the seeming. They also realize that a permanent, single, and independent self that represents a nature of its own (such as a primal cosmic substance or a conscious individual)[552] does not even exist on the level of the seeming either. Thus, all coarse appearances (the outer world and the bodies of beings) and what appear as various pleasant and unpleasant objects (such as forms, sounds, smells, tastes, and tangible objects) are held to be delusive, just like reflections in a mirror or objects in a dream, while the single and partless minute particles that build up these coarse appearances are said to be ultimately real. As for consciousness, what appears as its uninterrupted continuum since beginningless saṃsāra until now (or from a being's birth until death) is equally held to be delusive. The single and partless instants that make up these momentary continua of consciousness (which represent the simultaneous ceasing of the last one and the arising of the next one, just like the ascending and descending beams of a scale) are held to be ultimately real.

Therefore, entities (all phenomena of saṃsāra and nirvāṇa) are asserted as ultimate, {94} while a permanent, single, and independent self does not even exist on the level of the seeming. As for the identity of phenomena, it consists of the outer apprehended (partless minute particles) and partless inner apprehenders. What knows all this through study, reflection, and meditation is the knowledge of entities of the śrāvakas. In addition to this, the knowledge of entities of the pratyekabuddhas is what realizes, through study, reflection, and meditation, that outer apprehended objects (minute particles) are not really established ultimately either, but still clings to the partless moments of the inner apprehender as being absolutely real. In addition, the mahāyāna knowledge of entities is what realizes, through study, reflection, and meditation, that partless moments of inner apprehenders too are actually without nature and free from reference points. In these ways, the three kinds of the knowledge of entities are identified.

The knowledge of the path

The definition of **the knowledge of the path**: the realization that all paths are without arising.

This has three parts:

a) The paths to be realized
b) The mind that realizes them
c) The manner in which this mind realizes these paths

a) The paths to be known are the very three knowledges of entities of śrāvakas, pratyekabuddhas, and the mahāyāna explained above—based on these three knowledges of entities one proceeds from saṃsāra to nirvāṇa. These three paths are complete within the mind stream of a single mahāyāna person in the manner of the lower being incorporated in the higher. {95} In this way, from the perspective of bodhisattvas realizing that all phenomena of saṃsāra and nirvāṇa (the four realities) are empty of a permanent, single, and independent personal self, the knowledge of the path resembles the knowledge of entities of śrāvakas. From the perspective of their additionally realizing that outer apprehended objects (minute particles) are without nature, this knowledge resembles the knowledge of entities of pratyekabuddhas. From the perspective of their additionally realizing that inner apprehenders are without nature too, it represents the mahāyāna's own knowledge of entities. When these three manners of realization are considered within the mind stream of a single person, they just represent three different divisions in terms of the isolates of a mind that has a single nature, but they are not different in substance.

b) The mind that realizes these represents the knowledge of entities of bodhisattvas themselves.

c) As for the manner in which this mind realizes these paths, the above three knowledges of entities within the single mind stream of a bodhisattva are the path that progresses from saṃsāra to nirvāṇa. Therefore, they are also called "path." From the perspective of this very path automatically knowing that it itself is actually without nature and free from reference points, it is called "the knowledge of the path." Śrāvakas and pratyekabuddhas do not have this knowledge of the path. For though they have the kinds of knowledge of entities that realize entities (the two realities) and the path in the sense of all phenomena of saṃsāra and nirvāṇa being empty of a personal identity and also [being empty] of half of a phenomenal identity, respectively, {96} these knowledges of entities do not realize on their own that they themselves are without nature. Therefore, the knowledge of the path exists only in the mahāyāna.

The knowledge of all aspects

The definition of **the knowledge of all aspects**: the realization that all aspects are without arising.

This has three parts:

a) The aspects to be realized
b) The mind that realizes them
c) The manner in which this mind realizes these aspects

a) The aspects to be realized are the set of the sixteen aspects (such as impermanence) that exist in the four realities (the entities) and the set of the sixteen moments of wisdom that are the aspects which exist in the mahāyāna's knowledge of the path, or on its path of seeing. These aspects are twofold—the aspect of the ultimate fundamental nature and the aspects of the nature of the seeming. The first one refers to the fact that the above two sets of sixteen aspects actually abide free from reference points, which is merely labeled by the name "aspect." The aspects of the nature of the seeming consist of the sixteen aspects of the four realities and the sixteen moments of the knowledge of the path on the path of seeing. The first have been explained above, and the latter refer to the sixteen moments of the minds that are the subjects of the objects which consist of the four realities, with four such moments (dharma readiness, dharma cognition, subsequent readiness, and subsequent cognition) with regard to each reality.

To identify the four momentary wisdoms that are the subjects of the reality of suffering, {97} "the readiness for the dharma cognition of the reality of suffering" is the mind of realizing that the first aspect of this reality (suffering) is actually without nature and free from reference points. "The wisdom that is the dharma cognition of the reality of suffering" is taught from the perspective of realizing that the reality of suffering is neither established as permanent nor, in actual fact, as impermanent. "The readiness for the subsequent cognition of the reality of suffering" is taught from the perspective of realizing that the reality of suffering is empty of an agent (such as a self, Cha, or Īśvara) since such an agent does not even exist on the level of the seeming, and that, in actual fact, even these skandhas—(the contaminated results that are empty of such an agent) are free from reference points. "The wisdom that is the subsequent cognition of the reality of suffering" is taught from the perspective of realizing that a permanent, single, and independent personal self does not exist in these skandhas that are contaminated results even on the level of the seeming and that what appear as phenomenal identities (collections of minute particles and moments of consciousness) are, in actual fact, without nature and free from reference points.

As for the four momentary wisdoms that are the subjects of the reality of the origin of suffering, "the readiness for the dharma cognition of the reality of the origin of suffering" is the mind of realizing that these present contaminated skandhas, on the level of the seeming, {98} are the causes of the karmas and afflictions of following lifetimes, and, actually, are not established as such causes, but are free from reference points. "The wisdom that is the dharma cognition of the reality of the origin of suffering" is the mind of realizing that all the karmas and afflictions of following lifetimes originate in dependence on these present contaminated skandhas, while they are actually not established as either originating or nonoriginating, but are free from reference points. "The readiness for the subsequent cognition of the reality of the origin of suffering" is the mind of realizing that all the suffering of following lifetimes (such as karma and afflictions) arises in dependence on these present contaminated skandhas, while it is actually not established as either arising or nonarising, but is free from reference points. "The wisdom that is the subsequent cognition of the reality of the origin of suffering" is the mind of realizing that these present contaminated skandhas are the conditions for producing the contaminated skandhas (such as suffering, karma, and afflictions) of following lifetimes, while they are actually not established as either being or not being conditions, but are free from reference points.

As for the four momentary wisdoms that are the subjects of the reality of cessation, "the readiness for the dharma cognition of the reality of cessation" is the mind of realizing that, in nirvāṇa (the uncontaminated purified skandhas), karma and afflictions (the causes of suffering) are ceased and thus relinquished, through which the reality, or the skandhas, of suffering (their results) is ceased and relinquished too, {99} while neither of them are actually established as either being or not being ceased, but are free from reference points. "The wisdom that is the dharma cognition of the reality of cessation" is the mind of realizing that, in the uncontaminated purified skandhas, karma and afflictions (the causes of suffering) are at peace and thus relinquished, through which the reality of suffering (their results) is at peace and relinquished too, while neither of them are actually established as either being or not being at peace, but are free from reference points. "The readiness for the subsequent cognition of the reality of cessation" is the mind of realizing that these uncontaminated purified skandhas, through the reality of the origin of suffering (the cause) and the reality of suffering (its result) including their latent tendencies being relinquished, are true happiness, excellent, and real, while they are actually not established as either being or not being excellent, but are free from reference points. "The wisdom that is the subsequent cognition of the reality of cessation" is the mind of realizing that these uncontaminated purified skandhas, through the stains of the reality of the origin of suffering (the cause) and the reality of suffering (its result) including their latent tendencies being relinquished, are the definite liberation from the three realms of saṃsāra and thus are the final deliverance into the level of nirvāṇa, while they are actually not established as either being or not being final deliverance, but are free from reference points.

As for the four momentary wisdoms that are the subjects of the reality of the path, "the readiness for the dharma cognition of the reality of the path" is the mind of realizing that the path (the six pāramitās or the three trainings) is to be relied on in one's mind stream like an excellent medicine, {100} while it is actually not established as something to be relied on in one's mind stream, but is free from reference points. "The wisdom that is the dharma cognition of the reality of the path" is the mind of realizing that the six pāramitās or the three trainings are appropriate to be relied on in one's mind stream, while they are actually not established as something appropriate to be relied on in one's mind stream, but are free from reference points.[553] "The readiness for the subsequent cognition of the reality of the path" is the mind of realizing that the six pāramitās or the three trainings are to be accomplished by oneself, while they are actually not established as either being or not being something to be accomplished, but are free from the reference points of existing or not existing as something to be relied on and accomplished in one's own mind stream. "The wisdom that is the subsequent cognition of the reality of the path" is the mind of realizing that the six pāramitās or the three trainings, through relying on and practicing them in one's own mind stream, are the paths and bhūmis that are conducive to the final deliverance from the sufferings of the three realms of saṃsāra and make one attain nirvāṇa, while they are actually not established as either being or not being what is conducive to final deliverance, but are free from reference points.

These sixteen aspects of wisdom here are just divisions of wisdom (the subject) in dependence on the four realities (the objects). On the other hand, the sixteenfold division into readinesses and cognitions by way of both (a) the subjects of these objects and (b) the wisdoms that are the subjects of these subjects is the system of the Mere Mentalists, which should be understood from elsewhere.[554] {101} Since the above presentation is the system of the

Mādhyamikas, it is described here so that beginners can understand it easily. Therefore, the aspects to be known or realized are all phenomena of saṃsāra and nirvāṇa, such as the two sets of sixteen aspects that are naturally included in subject and object.

b) The mind that realizes these aspects is nothing but the mahāyāna knowledge of the path explained before.

c) As for the manner in which this mind realizes these aspects, "the knowledge of all aspects" is the mind that is this very mahāyāna knowledge of the path (which realizes the three paths to be without nature) realizing that the aspects of this knowledge of the path that were explained above are actually not established as any nature whatsoever and are free from reference points.

1.1.2. The meanings of the terms that are the definienda

The knowledge of entities bears this name because it knows that entities—the four realities as the genuine nature of all phenomena of saṃsāra and nirvāṇa—are without arising. The knowledge of the path bears this name because it knows that the three paths of śrāvakas, pratyekabuddhas, and the mahāyāna are without arising. The knowledge of all aspects bears this name because it knows that the phenomena of saṃsāra and nirvāṇa that consist of the subjects—{102} mere appearing aspects—are actually without arising and free from reference points.

1.1.3. Divisions of the three knowledges

This has five parts:

a) The basis of the division consists of the three knowledges as such.

b) The nature of the division consists of the knowledge of entities, the knowledge of the path, and the knowledge of all aspects.

c) As for the reason for them being divided into three, since there are three objects (the four focal objects that are the four realities, the three paths, and the aspects), they are referred to as the three states of mind which realize that these three objects are without arising.

d) As for the meaning of the division, the three knowledges are of the same nature in terms of their general type, but different isolates. Thus, one speaks of "the knowledge of entities" from the perspective of a mahāyāna person realizing through studying, reflecting, and meditating that the four realities (or the true nature of saṃsāra and nirvāṇa) are actually not established as any nature whatsoever and are free from reference points. One speaks of "the knowledge of the path" from the perspective of realizing that this very knowledge of entities is the path to progress to the buddhabhūmi and therefore is actually without nature and free from reference points. One speaks of "the knowledge of all aspects" from the perspective of realizing that this very knowledge of the path (the mere aspects that are the phenomena of saṃsāra and nirvāṇa as explained above) is actually without nature and is free from reference points. Therefore, when taken as the general type of the three knowledges, these three knowledges {103} exist from the path of accumulation of beginners up through buddhahood. As for the distinct particulars of this general type, the knowledge of entities of śrāvakas and pratyekabuddhas exists in the mind streams of śrāvakas and pratyekabuddhas; the knowledge of the path of bodhisattvas exists in the mind streams of bodhisattvas; and the knowledge of all aspects of buddhas exists in the mind streams of buddhas. Thus, it is by virtue of their being connected to the mind streams of different persons that one speaks of three particular knowledges. The details will be explained below in the next section on these three knowledges as ascertained in the first three chapters of the AA.

e) The definite number of three knowledges is in terms of their three objects, as explained under (c).

This briefly identifies the general isolate of the three knowledges as such.

1.2. The three knowledges as taught in the first three chapters of the AA

1.2.1. The knowledge of all aspects

Identifying it through definitions

The definition of **the knowledge of all aspects as such:**[555] the special yoga of realizing that all aspects are without arising.

The definition of **the knowledge of all aspects that knows suchness**: the direct realization of the ultimate true nature of all aspects of knowable objects. {104}

The definition of **the knowledge of all aspects that knows variety**: the direct realization of all the aspects whose nature it is to be causes and results.

In the first definition, "special" refers to the distinctive features of ultimate enlightened activity, realization, and relinquishment that make this knowledge special. Therefore, the knowledge of all aspects that is explained here in the first chapter of the AA exists as being associated with the mind streams of buddhas alone, but not in any others.

The manner of these definitions eliminating what is discordant in type

The knowledge of all aspects is established to be the knowledge of all aspects of a buddha alone through the phrase "realizing that all are without arising" in the above first definition excluding everything that is not prajñāpāramitā; the phrase "all aspects" eliminating the possibility of it being any of the remaining seven topics of the AA; and "special" excluding its being any of the approximately concordant forms of the knowledge of all aspects up through the end of the continuum. In the second definition, "direct realization of the ultimate true nature" excludes that it is the knowledge of all aspects that knows variety.

1.2.2. The knowledge of the path

Identifying its self-isolate through definitions

The definition of **the knowledge of the path as such**: the special realization of the three paths being unobservable.

The definition of **the knowledge of the path that knows suchness**: the realization of the true nature that is the nonexistence of the three appearances of the three paths.

The definition of **the knowledge of the path that knows variety**: the realization that the three paths, just like illusions, appear yet are without nature.

In the first definition, "special" refers to the following distinctive features—{105} the two mental states of realizing that the three paths as the objects and the three paths as the subjects are without nature (with these two mental states being of the same nature, just as what is produced and what is impermanent); the prajñā which knows the nature of phenomena—their being without nature; and the skill in means for the welfare of sentient beings that is motivated by great compassion.

The manner of these definitions eliminating what is discordant in type

The knowledge of the path is established as such through the phrase "realization as being unobservable" in the above first definition excluding, in general, everything that is not prajñāpāramitā; "path" eliminating the possibility of it being any of the other seven topics of the AA; and "special" excluding its being the knowledge of the path of buddhas or ordinary beings. Therefore, this knowledge of the path exists in the mind streams of bodhisattvas from the path of seeing up through the end of the continuum, but not in others. In the second definition, the phrase "the realization of the true nature that is the nonexistence of the aspects"[556] eliminates this being the knowledge of the path that knows variety. In the third definition, the phrase "the realization that they, just like illusions, appear yet are without nature" eliminates this being the knowledge of the path that knows suchness.

Some may say, "The phrase 'realization of the three paths' in the first definition is not able to exclude the knowledge of the path being the four trainings or the dharmakāya because these also focus on the path." From the perspective of focusing on the path as such, the four trainings and the dharmakāya are not to be excluded because it is precisely because of this that they are the knowledge of the path. Rather, the above phrase is able to exclude focusing on the mere path as such from the perspective of the other two knowledges focusing on all entities and all aspects, respectively. One should know that analogous disputes about the knowledge of all aspects and the knowledge of entities are answered in respectively corresponding ways.

1.2.3. The knowledge of entities

Identifying its self-isolate through definitions

{106} The definition of **the knowledge of entities as such**: the special realization that all bases are without arising.

The definition of **the knowledge of entities that is an antagonistic factor**: the realization, which entails clinging to characteristics, that all bases are without a self.

The definition of **the knowledge of entities that is its remedial factor**: the remedy for the clinging to characteristics within said realization.[557]

In the first definition, "special" refers to the distinctive feature of being free from the seeds of ignorance about a self. The other two definitions are qualified through either representing a factor to be relinquished by bodhisattvas or its remedy. Therefore, the actual[558] knowledge of entities exists in the mind streams of śrāvakas and pratyekabuddhas, while the third one exists in bodhisattvas.

The manner of these definitions eliminating what is discordant in type

The knowledge of entities is established as such through the phrase "the realization that all are without a self" in the above first definition excluding, in general, everything that is not prajñāpāramitā, and "all bases" excluding its being any of the other seven topics of the AA. In the second definition, the phrase "which entails clinging to characteristics" excludes this being the remedial knowledge of entities of bodhisattvas and thus establishes it as being the knowledge of entities of śrāvakas and pratyekabuddhas (which is the antagonistic factor of the remedial knowledge of entities). In the third definition, "remedy" eliminates this being the knowledge of entities of śrāvakas and pratyekabuddhas (which is said antagonistic factor) and thus establishes it as the mahāyāna knowledge of entities. Therefore, the knowledge of entities that is an antagonistic factor exists only in the mind streams of śrāvakas and pratyekabuddhas, while the knowledge of entities that is its remedy exists solely in mahāyāna mind streams. {107}

2. Identifying the four trainings (the means)

2.1. The complete training in all aspects

Identifying its self-isolate through definitions

The definition of **the complete training in all aspects**: familiarizing with the three knowledges in a combined manner. The knowledge of entities is the mental state of a[559] mahāyāna person realizing, through ascertaining by way of studying, reflecting, and meditating, that all phenomena of saṃsāra and nirvāṇa within the four realities (the entities) are without arising. Since this very realization is also the path, from the perspective of this very path realizing that it itself is without nature, it is called "the knowledge of the path." From the perspective of this very knowledge of the path (or this very knowledge of entities) realizing that the entirety of the various aspects (such as impermanence) that exist in the four realities (the entities) and the entirety of the various aspects (such as the subsequent readinesses and cognitions) that exist in this very path are without nature, it is the knowledge of all aspects. Therefore, the complete training in all aspects consists of bodhisattvas knowing during meditative equipoise that all these three knowledges are actually without nature and are free from reference points, and their realizing during subsequent attainment that, on the level of the seeming, these knowledges appear yet are without nature, just like illusions.

The definition of **the complete training in all aspects during meditative equipoise**: familiarizing with the three knowledges of suchness in a combined manner. {108} The manner of familiarizing in a combined manner is as explained just above. "The knowledge of suchness" refers to the knowledge that the very three knowledges of the meditative equipoises during which entities, the path, and the aspects are realized to be without arising are actually without nature and are free from reference points.

The definition of **the complete training in all aspects during subsequent attainment**: familiarizing with the three knowledges of variety in a combined manner. The manner of familiarizing in a combined manner is as before. "The knowledge of variety" is the wisdom during subsequent attainment, which is the mental state of a mahāyāna person realizing that the sixteen aspects (such as impermanence) of the four realities (the entities) appear yet are without nature, just like illusions. Since this very realization is also the path, from the perspective of this very path realizing that itself, just like an illusion, appears yet is without nature, it is the knowledge of the path during subsequent attainment. From the perspective of this very knowledge of the path (or this very knowledge of entities) automatically knowing that the entirety of the various aspects (such as impermanence) that exist in the four realities (the entities) and the entirety of the various aspects (such as the subsequent readinesses and cognitions) that exist in this very path (or in the nature of the knowledge of the path) appear yet are without nature, just like illusions, it is the knowledge of all aspects. Therefore, within the mind stream of a bodhisattva, the knowledge of entities, the knowledge of the path, and the knowledge of all aspects (which depend on the three objects that are entities, the path, and the aspects, respectively) are of a single inseparable nature in terms of their substance, but are three different isolates. {109} Thus, what is designated by the above expression "familiarizing with the three knowledges of variety in a combined manner" is nothing but familiarizing more and more with the three knowledges in the mind stream of a single person during subsequent attainment in a manner that is without clinging due to knowing that these knowledges are actually without nature and are free from reference points, while they, on the level of the seeming, appear yet are without nature, just like illusions. The preceding two definitions should be understood in analogous ways.

The manner of these definitions eliminating what is discordant in type

The complete training in all aspects is established as such through the phrase "the three knowledges" in the above definitions excluding, in general, everything that is not prajñāpāramitā; "in a combined manner" excluding separately; and "familiarizing" excluding its being the dharmakāya. In the second definition, the phrase "suchness" excludes this being the familiarization with the three knowledges during subsequent attainment. In the third definition, "variety" eliminates this being the familiarization with the three knowledges during meditative equipoise.

2.2. The culminating training

Identifying its self-isolate through definitions

The definition of **the culminating training as such**: familiarizing with the three knowledges in the manner of gaining mastery over them. The manner of familiarizing with the three knowledges corresponds to the one in the context of the complete training in all aspects. As for "the manner of gaining mastery over them," before, in the context of the complete training in all aspects, during meditative equipoise, one familiarized with the three knowledges actually being without nature and free from reference points, and, during subsequent attainment, one familiarized with these three knowledges appearing yet being without nature, just like illusions. Accordingly, through having done so, the phase in one's mind stream during which the lesser clear illumination of this being so arises within one's samādhi is called "attaining the culminating training" or "attaining realization." {110} "Familiarizing with the three knowledges in the manner of gaining mastery over them" means to further familiarize with this training as before in order that this lesser clear illumination does not decline, but increases more and more into the great clear illumination of realizing that the three knowledges are without nature.

The definition of **the culminating training during meditative equipoise**: familiarizing with the three knowledges of suchness in the manner of gaining mastery over them. The manner of familiarizing and so on is as above. "The knowledge of suchness" refers to the knowledge of entities (which realizes entities to be without arising), the knowledge of the path (which realizes the path to be without arising), and the knowledge of all aspects (which realizes the aspects to be without arising) during meditative equipoise. "Familiarizing with the three knowledges of suchness in the manner of gaining mastery over them" means to familiarize with these three knowledges in order to first attain the lesser clear illumination during the samādhi of realizing that they are actually without nature and are free from reference points and then to enhance this illumination more and more.

The definition of **the culminating training during subsequent attainment**: familiarizing with the three knowledges of variety in the manner of gaining mastery over them. The manner of familiarizing and so on is as above. As for "the knowledge of variety," the knowledge of entities during subsequent attainment is the realization of a mahāyāna person during subsequent attainment that the four realities (the entities) appear yet are without nature, just like illusions. Since this very realization is also the path, from the perspective of this very path realizing that it itself is actually without nature, but, on the level of the seeming, appears yet is without nature, just like an illusion, {111} it is the knowledge of the path during subsequent attainment. It is the knowledge of all aspects from the perspective of realizing that the entirety of the various aspects (such as impermanence) that exist in the knowledge of entities (or in its bases—the four realities) and the entirety of the various aspects (such as the subsequent readinesses and cognitions) that exist in this very path (or in the knowledge of the path) are actually without nature and are free from reference points, while they, on the level of the seeming, appear yet are without nature, just like illusions. Therefore, within the mind stream of a single person, the knowledge of entities, the knowledge of the path, and the knowledge of all aspects (which depend on the three objects that are entities, the path, and the aspects, respectively) are of a single nature in terms of their substance, but are three different isolates. "Familiarizing with the three knowledges of variety in the manner of gaining mastery over them" means to familiarize with these knowledges, though not depending on entities, paths, and aspects during the phase of such subsequent attainment, in order to first attain the lesser clear illumination of the samādhi of realizing that the three knowledges are actually without nature and are free from reference points, while, on the level of the seeming, they appear yet are without nature, just like illusions, and then to enhance this illumination more and more.

The manner of these definitions eliminating what is discordant in type

The culminating training is established as such through the phrase "the three knowledges" in the above definitions excluding, in general, everything that is not prajñāpāramitā; "familiarizing" excluding everything that is not a training; and "in the manner of gaining mastery over them" excluding the isolates of the other three trainings. In the second definition, "knowledge of suchness" excludes this being the familiarization with the three knowledges during subsequent attainment. In the third definition, "knowledge of variety" eliminates this being the familiarization with the three knowledges during meditative equipoise.

2.3. The serial training

Identifying its self-isolate through definitions

{112} The definition of **the serial training as such**: familiarizing with the three knowledges in a sequential manner. As for the way of familiarizing in a sequential manner, the knowledge of entities is the mental state of a mahāyāna person realizing that all phenomena of saṃsāra and nirvāṇa (which consist of the four realities—the entities) are without nature through ascertaining by way of study, reflection, and so on that they are actually without nature, but, on the level of the seeming, are like illusions. The knowledge of the path is to realize that these bases are without nature through first ascertaining them to be without nature and then familiarizing with that. When this very knowledge of the path realizes, on the level of the seeming, that it is without nature through its having ascertained that it itself is without nature and then having familiarized with that, it realizes that the entirety of the various aspects (such as impermanence) that exist in the four realities (the bases of the knowledge of entities or of the knowledge of the path) and the entirety of the various aspects of wisdom (such as the subsequent readinesses and cognitions) that exist in this very path (or the knowledge of the path) are actually without nature and are free from reference points, while, on the level of the seeming, they are just like illusions. This is the knowledge of all aspects. Then, it is realized that this very knowledge too is actually without nature, while it, on the level of the seeming, is just like an illusion. The serial training means to familiarize with all this in order to be increasingly familiar with it.

At the time of the complete training in all aspects, bodhisattvas ascertain through study and reflection that the three knowledges are without nature and then familiarizes with that. By virtue of this, at the time of the culminating training, through the prajñā that arises from mundane meditation, {113} they first attain the lesser clear illumination of the samādhi of realizing that the three knowledges are without nature and then enhance this samādhi of realizing that more and more. This is the purpose of the culminating training. Then, through familiarizing with this in order to gain mastery over the realization that the three knowledges are actually without nature, while, on the level of the seeming, they are just like illusions, bodhisattvas reach the phase of the realization of the serial training first arising in their mind streams. This happens right when a clear illumination that is even greater than before arises in the samādhi of realizing that the three knowledges are without nature. Then, in order to enhance the clear illumination in that samādhi even further, bodhisattvas familiarize with the three knowledges in a sequential manner as explained above.

The definition of **the serial training during meditative equipoise**: familiarizing with the three knowledges of suchness in a sequential manner. "The three knowledges of suchness" refers to the three knowledges of realizing that entities, the path, and the aspects during meditative equipoise are without arising.

The definition of **the serial training during subsequent attainment**: familiarizing with the three knowledges of variety in a sequential manner. "The knowledges of variety" are the three knowledges by way of realizing that entities, the path, and the aspects during subsequent attainment appear yet are without nature, just like illusions.

The manner of these definitions eliminating what is discordant in type

The serial training is established as such through the phrase "familiarizing with the three knowledges" in the above definitions excluding, in general, everything that is not a training in prajñāpāramitā, and "familiarizing in a sequential manner" excluding the isolates of the other three trainings. {114}

2.4. The instantaneous training

Identifying its self-isolate through definitions

The definition of **the instantaneous training as such**: familiarizing with the three knowledges in an instant in the final phase of the path. Here, "familiarizing with the three knowledges" corresponds in part to the familiarization in the context of the complete training in all aspects. The "final familiarization" is the phase of familiarizing after having perfected all the previous trainings. In brief, it is called "the vajralike samādhi."

The definition of **the instantaneous training during meditative equipoise**: familiarizing with the three knowledges of suchness in an instant.

The definition of **the instantaneous training during subsequent attainment**: familiarizing with the three knowledges of variety in an instant.

The manner of these definitions eliminating what is discordant in type

The instantaneous training is established as such through the phrase "familiarizing with the three knowledges in an instant" in the above definitions excluding, in general, everything that is not the instantaneous training, while the phrases "final familiarization" and "in an instant" exclude the isolates of the other three trainings.

3. Identifying the dharmakāya (the fruition)

Identifying its self-isolate through a definition

{115} The definition of **the dharmakāya**: the final maturation of the three knowledges. This is its identification by way of a general summary without differentiating it in terms of the various assertions of distinct Buddhist philosophical systems.

The manner of this definition eliminating what is discordant in type

The dharmakāya is established as such through the phrase "the three knowledges" excluding, in general, everything that is not prajñāpāramitā; "three" excluding the three knowledges being separate, such as the knowledges of entities of śrāvakas or pratyekabuddhas; and "final maturation" excluding its having a common locus with the three knowledges in the mind streams of learners on the path. Thus, it is established as the three knowledges that exist in the mind streams of buddhas alone.

The eight topics or eight clear realizations of the AA summarize everything that is to be ascertained by the large, medium, and brief prajñāpāramitā sūtras.

4. The boundary lines of these eight clear realizations

The boundary lines of the three knowledges

The three knowledges as such exist from the path of accumulation of beginners up through the buddhabhūmi. However, among the three knowledges that are discussed in the first three chapters of the AA, the knowledge of all aspects exists only on the buddhabhūmi (and not anywhere below up through the end of the continuum) because it is the ultimate knowledge of the dharmakāya.

The knowledge of the path exists on both the paths of seeing and familiarization of bodhisattvas, but nowhere else. This knowledge of the path does not exist on the buddhabhūmi {116} because it needs to be enhanced further and further, whereas there is nothing to be enhanced for buddhas since they already finished such enhancement. This knowledge of the path does not exist in ordinary beings either because it is the direct realization of this knowledge of the path being without nature, which ordinary beings do not have.

The knowledge of entities exists on the three paths of seeing, familiarization, and nonlearning of śrāvakas and pratyekabuddhas as well as on the paths of seeing and familiarization of bodhisattvas, but nowhere else. As for the two kinds of the knowledge of entities that are an antagonistic factor and its remedy, respectively, neither of them exists in buddhas. For the knowledge of entities that is an antagonistic factor is equivalent to the clinging to characteristics, whereas buddhas have relinquished the clinging to characteristics, including the impregnations of negative tendencies. Nor does the knowledge of entities that is its remedy exist in buddhas because it is the remedy for the clinging to characteristics. There is no need to rely on such a remedy at this level due to there being absolutely no clinging to characteristics (the factor to be relinquished) on it, just as there is no need to rely on any medicine for wind, gall, or phlegm diseases if all such diseases are already completely cured. The knowledge of entities does not exist in childish beings either because it is the direct realization that all bases are without a self, which childish beings do not have.

The boundary lines of the four trainings

The complete training in all aspects exists from the path of accumulation up through the end of the continuum because it is taught that there are fourteen[560] situational trainings (from the training of difficult realization that entails great hardships and takes a long time up through the completely pure training). As the sūtras say:

> Bodhisattvas who have newly entered the yāna {117} abandon this prajñāpāramitā upon hearing about it and thus accumulate the karma of falling into what is wrong. They are the ones who become fully perfect buddhas only through great hardships.[561]

The culminating training exists from the level of heat of the path of preparation up through the end of the continuum. On this level of heat, AA V.1cd says:

> The signs of the training of having reached culmination
> Are asserted as twelvefold.

Also, this training does not exist between the end of the continuum and buddhahood because AA V.37–38 speaks of the uninterrupted samādhi there.

As for the boundary lines of the serial training, according to Āryavimuktisena it exists from the path of accumulation up through the end of the continuum. With regard to the serial training, the sūtras speak of the serial activity, the serial training, and the serial practice, which are the paths of knowing the paths of seeing and familiarization.[562] Directly commenting on this, the *Vṛtti* explains that "serial activity" is said for the sake of knowing the path of accumulation; "serial training," for the sake of knowing the path of preparation; and "serial practice," for the sake of knowing the paths of seeing and familiarization. Thus, the serial clear realization ranges from the level of a beginner up through finally reaching the knowledge of all aspects.[563] According to Haribhadra, {118} the serial training exists on the three paths of preparation, seeing, and familiarization, but not on the path of accumulation because the latter lacks the cause of the serial training, which is the culminating training.[564]

The instantaneous training exists only at the end of the continuum because the final fruition (the dharmakāya) is attained in the immediately subsequent moment. The reason here is established through the sūtras saying that the dharmakāya is fully realized in the next moment after this training and AA I.4cd saying:

> Full realization in a single instant,
> And the dharmakāya . . .
> The boundary lines of the dharmakāya

It exists solely on the buddhabhūmi (the mahāyāna path of nonlearning) since AA IX.1c speaks of it as "maturation" and AA IX.2c says, "the fruition (the dharmakāya and enlightened activity)." The ultimate dharmakāya explained here does not exist on any levels below the buddhabhūmi up to the end of the continuum because its direct cause—the instantaneous training—does not exist on these levels. {119}

Part 2: The seventy points

1. The ten points of the knowledge of all aspects

These can be summarized into two—(a) the path of the knowledge of all aspects and (b) the nature of this path.

a) The path of the knowledge of all aspects[565]

This path is twofold—the path of accumulation and the path of preparation (the branches conducive to penetration). The former refers to the time span from first generating bodhicitta up through listening to the instructions through study and reflection.

1) The definition of **the generation of bodhicitta**: being focused on the welfare of others and enlightenment, which is congruently associated with the wishful striving for these two. Therefore, motivated by the wishful striving to attain unsurpassable enlightenment by focusing on the welfare of others, one takes the bodhisattva vows and then {120} keeps all the bodhisattva precepts. The details should be known from elsewhere.

2) The definition of **the instructions**: that which teaches bodhisattvas to focus on all phenomena through their being endowed with means. Such instructions pertain to those persons who are endowed with a fully qualified spiritual friend, the generation of bodhicitta, the mahāyāna disposition, and the wish to listen to these instructions. The instructions, which also include the manner in which to make them a living experience, teach, "Understand that the nature of all phenomena of saṃsāra and nirvāṇa (or all entities to be adopted and to be rejected) are actually emptiness free from reference points, while, on the level of the seeming, they appear yet are without nature, just like illusions. Motivated by great compassion (the means), for the welfare of all sentient beings practice the three trainings (or the six pāramitās in such a manner that all of them are complete within any one of them)."

3) The definition of **the branches conducive to penetration**: the special mundane wisdom. Being divided into the four levels of heat, peak, poised readiness, and the supreme dharma, the distinctive features that make it special are as follows. It focuses on the aspects (such as impermanence) that exist in the four realities (its four focal objects) as actually being without nature. By virtue of the awareness that is the mahāyāna disposition (the cause), it possesses the qualities of the realizations of all three yānas in the manner of the lower being incorporated in the higher. Its distinctive feature of being mentored lies in being mentored externally by a spiritual friend who teaches the three mindsets (not being cowed, afraid of, or terrified by emptiness) and being mentored internally {121} by being skilled in means. During meditative equipoise, this wisdom is associated with the complete set of the four conceptions in terms of what is to be put to an end. During subsequent attainment, it is associated with the factors to be relinquished that are the four conceptions in terms of what is to be accomplished. These mahāyāna branches conducive to penetration are far more distinguished than those of śrāvakas and pratyekabuddhas because the latter do not possess the above distinctive features.

b) The nature of the path (practice) is fourfold—the foundation of practice, the focal object, the aim, and practice's own nature.

4) The definition of **the foundation of practice**: the dharmadhātu that serves as the basis for practice. This refers to the naturally pure and reference-point-free mind streams of all persons in whom the yoga of the level of heat of the culminating training has arisen and of those beyond.

5) The definition of **the focal objects**: any phenomena that are to be realized as certain aspects through the prajñā of practice. All phenomena of saṃsāra and nirvāṇa are to be realized through the meditative equipoise of the person who is the practitioner as actually being without nature and free from reference points. During subsequent attainment, they are to be realized as appearing yet being without nature, just like illusions.

6) The definition of **the aim**: the final aim to be strived for through practice. This is what the person who is the practitioner takes as the fruition of practice to be strived for—the three greatnesses or the three kāyas.

Practice's own nature is fourfold.

7) The definition of **the armorlike practice**: {122) mustering armorlike vigor for the six pāramitās. This means to don the great mental armor of thinking, "For the welfare of all sentient beings and for the sake of the three greatnesses (or the three kāyas), I practice in such a manner that all of the six pāramitās are complete within any one of them."

8) The definition of **the practice of engagement**: mustering the vigor of application for great enlightenment. This means mustering vigor for practicing the six pāramitās in such a manner that all of them are complete within any one of them for the sake of attaining the consummate relinquishment and realization of the mahāyāna.

9) The definition of **the practice of the equipments**: mustering vigor for directly giving rise to the temporary great enlightenment. This means mustering vigor for practicing the six pāramitās as before for the sake of the consummate relinquishment and realization of the path of seeing and beyond arising in one's mind stream.

10) The definition of **the practice of final deliverance**: mustering vigor for directly giving rise to the final great enlightenment. This means mustering vigor for practicing the six pāramitās as before for the sake of giving rise to the dharmakāya at the end of the continuum of the ten bhūmis in one's last existence.

The divisions and boundary lines of these should be known from elsewhere.

2. The eleven points of the knowledge of the path

{123} These can be summarized into two—(a) the branches of the knowledge of the path and (b) the knowledge of the path as the result of these branches.

a) 1) The definition of **the branches of the knowledge of the path**: the freedom from obstacles and the completeness of favorable conditions, which make it suitable for the result—the knowledge of the path—to arise in the mind stream. For example, when the gods of the desire and form realms listen to the Buddha teaching prajñāpāramitā, their pride that is based on their bodies radiating light as a karmic maturation is an obstacle for the arising of the knowledge of the path in their mind streams. Seeing this, the Buddha outshines their karmically caused light through his natural light, thus eclipsing them like sunlight does moonlight. Through this, the gods are made to give up their pride and are rendered suitable for the arising of the knowledge of the path in their mind streams.

b) The knowledge of the path as the result is threefold—the knowledges of the path of (a) śrāvakas, (b) pratyekabuddhas, and (c) bodhisattvas.

ba) 2) The definition of **the knowledge of the path of śrāvakas**: the direct knowledge of the four realities together with their sixteen aspects, such as impermanence (the entities), through the principle of personal identitylessness. This is the direct realization that in entities (all phenomena of saṃsāra and nirvāṇa that are included in the four realities together with their sixteen aspects), {124} a personal self (such as a permanent, single, and independent spirit, or a self that is a creating agent, such as Cha or Īśvara) does not even exist on the level of the seeming. Śrāvakas directly realize that all pleasant and unpleasant appearances and all that appears as a continuum of consciousness are seeming delusive appearances; that consciousness is a coarse continuum of moments; and that the building blocks of coarse matter are minute partless particles.

bb) 3) The definition of **the knowledge of the path of pratyekabuddhas**: the direct knowledge of the above focal objects in the manner of not observing the apprehended by virtue of the latter being distinguished as being without nature. In addition to the above manner of realization of the śrāvakas, pratyekabuddhas realize that outer minute particles are without nature.

bc) The knowledge of the path of bodhisattvas is twofold—the perfect paths of (a) seeing and (b) familiarization.

bca) 4) The definition of **the path of seeing**: directly and newly seeing that the aspects (such as impermanence) that exist in the four realities are without nature, which functions as the support for progressing to liberation. Up through the supreme mundane dharma, first one familiarizes, through ascertainment by way of study and reflection, with all phenomena of saṃsāra and nirvāṇa that are included in the four realities as being without nature. Through this, on the path of seeing, the basic nature of the four realities is directly and newly seen to be emptiness free from reference points. The above definition refers to the first moment of that. {125}

bcb) The path of familiarization is twofold—(a) the function of the path of familiarization and (b) the path of familiarization that possesses this function.
bcba) 5) The definition of **the function of the path of familiarization**: the distinctive feature of the qualities that arise from familiarization. These are the qualities that arise based on familiarizing more and more with the true nature of the four realities that has already been seen on the path of seeing.
bcbb) The path of familiarization that possesses this function is twofold—contaminated and uncontaminated. The first one is threefold—aspiration, dedication, and rejoicing. The first one of these is twofold—the actual aspiration and its benefit.

6) The definition of **the path of familiarization as aspiration**: the certainty that the mother is endowed with qualities. This is the thought that mother prajñāpāramitā, through being made a living experience by way of the triad of studying, reflecting and meditating, is certain to be the source of all temporary and ultimate qualities.

The benefit of aspiration is threefold—praise, eulogy, and laudation.

7) The definition of **the benefit of aspiration (praise, eulogy, and laudation)**: the proclamation of the merit of aspiration by genuine beings in order to create enthusiasm in the meditator. If one cultivates a vast aspiration for the mother for one's own welfare, one receives the nine degrees of great, medium, and lesser praises by genuine beings (buddhas and bodhisattvas). If one cultivates this aspiration for the welfare of both oneself and others, one additionally receives the nine degrees of great, medium, and lesser eulogies by these beings. If one cultivates this aspiration for the mother solely for the sake of others, without considering oneself at all, {126} in addition to said praises and eulogies one receives the nine degrees of great, medium, and lesser laudations.

8) The definition of **the path of familiarization as dedication**: in a nonreferential manner, turning all virtuous roots into the great enlightenment for the welfare of all sentient beings. This is the dedication that is embraced by nonreferential prajñā, thinking, "May all the many virtuous roots that there are in the beginning, the middle, and the end, which have been accumulated in the three times and are connected to the mind streams of myself and others, be the causes for myself and all infinite sentient beings attaining unsurpassable buddhahood."

9) The definition of **the path of familiarization as rejoicing**: familiarizing with the special mind of delighting in all virtuous roots in a nonreferential manner. This is the cultivation of limitless joy that is without attachment, hatred, or envy by virtue of being embraced by nonreferential prajñā and considers all the virtuous roots in the mind streams of oneself and others throughout the three times to be most excellent.

The uncontaminated path of familiarization is twofold.

10) The definition of **the path of familiarization as accomplishment**: familiarizing with directly seeing all phenomena as the dharmadhātu. This means to familiarize more and more with what has already been seen on the path of seeing—that all phenomena of saṃsāra and nirvāṇa included in the four realities are actually without nature and are free from reference points.

11) The definition of **the pure path of familiarization**: {127} the remedial means to purify the obscurations. This refers to the obscurations being relinquished through realizing the nature of phenomena—emptiness—in meditative equipoise.

3. The nine points of the knowledge of entities

These nine points are (1) not abiding in the extremes of either saṃsāra or nirvāṇa by virtue of prajñā and compassion; (2) abiding in these two extremes by virtue of lacking compassion, despite realizing all phenomena to be empty of one-and-a-half of the two kinds of identity;[566] (3) the hīnayāna knowledge of entities being distant from the fruitional mother by virtue of its not being the means or the cause for buddhahood; (4) the mahāyāna knowledge of entities being close to the fruitional mother by virtue of its being the means or the cause for buddhahood; (5) the hīnayāna knowledge of entities being an antagonistic factor of the mahāyāna one; (6) the mahāyāna knowledge of entities being the remedy for the clinging to characteristics of the hīnayāna one; (7) the training in equality in terms of the subject; (8) the training in equality in terms of the object;[567] and (9) the path of seeing of the knowledge of entities of bodhisattvas.

These can be summarized into three—(a) the nature of the knowledge of entities, (b) the trainings, and (c) the path of seeing. The first one is also threefold—(a) natures, (b) capacities, and (c) functions.

aa) Natures

1) The definition of **the mahāyāna knowledge of entities**: not abiding in the extremes of either saṃsāra or nirvāṇa by virtue of prajñā and compassion. Through being endowed with the prajñā of knowing that the aspects of all phenomena of saṃsāra and nirvāṇa included in the four realities (the entities) are actually without nature and are free from reference points, one attains nirvāṇa and thus does not abide in saṃsāric existence. {128} Through being endowed with the great compassion that embraces all sentient beings who do not know this, one is skilled in means and thus promotes the welfare of sentient beings through various enlightened activities until saṃsāra is emptied.

2) The definition of **the hīnayāna knowledge of entities**: through being endowed with the prajñā of knowing that all phenomena of saṃsāra and

nirvāṇa included in the four realities are without a permanent, single, and independent personal self and without phenomenal identity in the sense of apprehended objects (minute particles) being without nature, one attains nirvāṇa and thus does not abide in saṃsāra. Through lacking the great compassion that embraces all sentient beings and the prajñā of realizing the equality of saṃsāra and nirvāṇa, one clings to saṃsāra as being real as the extreme that is to be absolutely rejected and thus falls into nirvāṇa as the extreme of extinction.

ab) Capacities

3) The definition of **the capacity of the hīnayāna knowledge of entities**: not attaining the fruitional nondual mother prajñāpāramitā by virtue of being distant from her. The reason for this is that this knowledge of entities is not the cause of the fruitional nondual mother prajñāpāramitā by virtue of its clinging to saṃsāra and nirvāṇa as being real as different phenomena, by virtue of its clinging to them as what is to be rejected and to be adopted, respectively, and by virtue of its lacking the skill in means that is motivated by great compassion.

4) The definition of **the capacity of the mahāyāna knowledge of entities**: swiftly attaining the fruitional nondual mother prajñāpāramitā by virtue of being close to her.[568] The reason for this is that this knowledge of entities is the means or the cause of the fruitional mother by virtue of its being endowed with the prajñā of realizing saṃsāra and nirvāṇa as equality as well as {129} with the skill in means that is motivated by great compassion.

ac) Functions

5) The definition of **the function of the hīnayāna knowledge of entities**: an antagonistic factor or factor to be relinquished through the mahāyāna knowledge of entities. The reason for this is that it entails clinging to the three phenomena[569] as being real.

6) The definition of **the function of the mahāyāna knowledge of entities**: the remedy for this.[570] The reason for this is that it is free from any clinging to characteristics since the three phenomena are realized as equality.

b) Trainings

7) The definition of **the training in equality in terms of the subject**: familiarizing with the realization that all phenomena of saṃsāra and nirvāṇa included in the four realities (the entities) are actually without nature and are free from reference points.

8) The definition of **the training in equality in terms of the object**: the realization that the focal object (the fruition to be attained or adopted) and the mind that makes itself attain or adopt what it focuses on are actually equality in that they are not established as any nature whatsoever.

c) The path of seeing

9) The definition of **the path of seeing of the knowledge of entities of bodhi-sattvas:** that which provides the opportunity for liberation through directly and newly seeing that all bases are without nature. The paths of seeing of śrāvakas and pratyekabuddhas are to be understood implicitly as the opposite of this. {130}

One should understand that both the subject that trains and the training in equality in terms of the object represent the training in the mahāyāna knowledge of entities.

4. The twelve points of the complete training in all aspects[571]

These can be summarized into two—teaching the progression of familiarization (a) in general and (b) in particular. The first one is fourfold—(a) aspects, (b) persons, (c) the nature of the divisions of the training, and (d) preliminary dharmas.

aa) 1) The definition of **the aspects (the objects of the training)**: the aspects of impermanence, identitylessness, and so on that exist in the four realities (the entities).

ab) 2) The definition of **the persons who familiarize**: the fortunate who engage in dharma activities with regard to mother prajñāpāramitā through training their mind streams in the presence of buddhas. They are the fortunate who, by virtue of having gathered the accumulations in the presence of buddhas for limitless eons, at present make mother prajñāpāramitā their living experience through studying, reflecting, and meditating.

ac) 3) The definition of **the nature of the division of the training**: {131} familiarizing with the realization that all bases are without nature. Having realized that all phenomena of saṃsāra and nirvāṇa included in the four realities (the entities) are actually without nature and are free from reference points, one familiarizes with this through meditative equipoise. During subsequent attainment, through knowing that these phenomena appear yet are without nature, just like illusions, one practices the pāramitās (such as generosity) without any clinging.

ad) The preliminary dharmas are fourfold.

4) The definition of **the qualities**: the fruitions of the actual cultivation of the training that one is to cultivate. These qualities arise from the training that is their cause and represent the attainment of the three fruitions (or three greatnesses) by virtue of mahāyāna followers having practiced the six pāramitās.

5) The definition of **the faults**: any phenomena that function as obstacles to engaging in the dharma of the mother. Evil māras may magically appear in the disguises of one's parents, friends, preceptors, masters, and so on, approaching

the bodhisattvas who study, reflect, and meditate on mother prajñāpāramitā. They make them abandon the dharma of the mahāyāna, saying, "What is the point of your writing, reading, studying, explaining, and meditating on prajñāpāramitā? You just suffer through giving away limitless heads, legs, arms, and so on, so give rise to the attitude of the śrāvakas!" Through this, bodhisattvas may stray into mistaken paths, such as the hīnayāna. Also, the māras may teach them mistaken dharmas that are corruptions of the mahāyāna and say, "Practice these dharmas and you will attain unsurpassable enlightenment without needing any great hardships or a long time." {132}

6) The definition of **the defining characteristics**: that which defines the trainings as being the causes and being distinguished. The mahāyāna trainings (such as the complete training in all aspects) are the uncommon causes of buddhahood and thus more distinguished than the trainings of śrāvakas.

7) The definition of **the mahāyāna factors conducive to liberation**: beginners practicing generosity and such in the manner of means and prajñā being unified. This means that a mahāyāna person, after having given rise to bodhicitta, practices the pāramitās through being embraced by nonreferentiality (that is, without clinging) and subsequently dedicates such practice as the cause for perfect enlightenment for the sake of all sentient beings.

b) The progression of familiarization in particular is threefold—(a) the phases of familiarization (the factors conducive to penetration), (b) the persons, and (c) the actual progression of familiarization.

ba) 8) The definition of **the mahāyāna factors conducive to penetration**: practicing through the consummate attitude and application by focusing on all sentient beings, which is done by way of the engagement through aspiration. From the phase of lesser heat onward, one is motivated by the consummate attitude of practicing the six pāramitās for the welfare of all sentient beings, and from the phase of peak onward, one engages in the consummate application of actually practicing these pāramitās.

bb) 9) The definition of **the persons who familiarize**: bodhisattvas in the mahāyāna who do not fall back into the hīnayāna, with a minimum of four of them representing a complete mahāyāna saṃgha. In fact, with there being absolutely no way for these mahāyāna persons {133} to fall back into the hīnayāna, any number—even a single one—of these mahāyāna followers being engaged in familiarization is sufficient to represent the mahāyāna saṃgha.

bc) The actual progression of familiarization is threefold.

10) The definition of **the training in the equality of existence and peace**: through familiarizing with the realization that afflicted phenomena and purified phenomena are as nonexistent as dream objects once the consciousness that perceived them wakes up, the conceptions of clinging to these two as being something to be rejected and adopted, respectively, are relinquished.

Through study, reflection, and meditation, one understands that all phenomena of saṃsāra and nirvāṇa are actually without nature (emptiness free from reference points) and are just like dreams, illusions, and reflections that appear on the level of the seeming. Through this, one relinquishes all clinging to real existence in terms of saṃsāra being real as something to be rejected; nirvāṇa, as something to be adopted; and the path, as something to be relied on in one's mind stream. In this way, one familiarizes with all phenomena of saṃsāra and nirvāṇa being equality as (or within) the dharmadhātu.

11) The definition of **the training in pure realms**: upon seeing impure realms, to engage in virtue and make aspiration prayers as the remedies for these realms, thus creating pure realms. Upon seeing grounds with alkaline earth, gorges, thorns, or grounds covered with filth and sentient beings with short lifespans, many diseases, little prajñā, or without aspiration for the dharma, bodhisattvas make vast aspiration prayers, such as, "If I engage in virtue, may the realm in which I become a fully perfect buddha be one in which the ground is of gold studded with many patterns of blue beryl, or of blue beryl studded with many patterns of gold, as even as the palm of a hand, as soft as Kancalidi, and so on. {134} May those to be guided by me (the buddha in this realm) be endowed with consummate lifespans, physical forms, prajñā, and possessions, and solely aspire for and enjoy the mahāyāna."

12) The definition of **the training in skill in means**: the familiarization with the three doors to liberation and so on that is distinguished by the subject that consists of prajñā and compassion. As for the phenomena of saṃsāra and nirvāṇa that are included in the four realities (the entities), the fact that they themselves or their distinct specific causes are not established is the door to liberation that is emptiness.[572] The fact that their nature is not established is the door to liberation that is signlessness. The fact that results are not established is the door to liberation that is wishlessness. Actually, all these phenomena are emptiness free from reference points, while, from the perspective of the seeming without examination and analysis, these various appearances of saṃsāra and nirvāṇa as being different and so on are delusive appearances, just like dreams and illusions. Therefore, through the prajñā of the persons who familiarize with these phenomena as being illusions understanding this, they themselves do not abide in saṃsāra. Their skill in means of being motivated by the great compassion that embraces all sentient beings who do not understand this is to practice the six pāramitās for the welfare of others without any attachment. Thus, this training here means to never be without this kind of meditative equipoise and subsequent attainment.

5. The seven points of the culminating training[573]

{135} These can be summarized into three—the culminating trainings of the paths of (a) preparation, (b) seeing, and (c) familiarization. The first one is fourfold.

a) 1) The definition of **the culmination of heat as illustrated by its signs**: being congruently associated with the samādhi of having attained the clear illumination of mastery over the three knowledges. This means that, through having familiarized in a combined manner with the three knowledges as actually being without nature and free from reference points, one first attains the lesser clear illumination of the samādhi in which the wisdom that arises from familiarizing with this samādhi realizes the three knowledges to be without nature.

2) The definition of **the culmination of peak as illustrated by increase**: being congruently associated with the samādhi in which this clear illumination expands. This means that, through making efforts in familiarizing with the fact that this clear illumination in the previous samādhi is without nature, during meditative equipoise the clear illumination of the samādhi in which the three knowledges are realized to be without nature becomes stronger than before, and, during subsequent attainment, the clinging to real existence becomes weaker.

3) The definition of **the culmination of poised readiness as illustrated by stability**: being congruently associated with the samādhi of engaging in a part of emptiness. Through the power of having familiarized with the clear illumination in the previous samādhi, its clear illumination becomes even stronger. Thus, during meditative equipoise, {136} there is no arising of fear of the three knowledges being without nature, and, during subsequent attainment, there is no arising of fear of the three knowledges being illusionlike. Therefore, this is the attainment of poised readiness for emptiness—the profound nature of phenomena.

4) The definition of **the culmination of the supreme dharma as illustrated by the mind settling**: being congruently associated with the samādhi of the imminence of the path of seeing. Through the power of having familiarized with the clear illumination in the previous samādhi in which the three knowledges are realized to be without nature, its clear illumination becomes even stronger than that. Thus, the arising of the path of seeing—which directly realizes that all phenomena of saṃsāra and nirvāṇa included in the three times and the four realities are without nature (which was not realized in this manner before)—is not interrupted by any other moment.

b) 5) The definition of **the culmination of the path of seeing**: that which constitutes both the attainment of mastery over the thirty-six pāramitās, which are completely pure of the three spheres, and the remedy for the four conceptions that are factors to be relinquished through seeing. Up through the level of the supreme dharma, the six pāramitās were practiced free from attachment in such a manner that all are complete in each one of them. By virtue of this, one knows that all phenomena are without nature, and, through the power of having familiarized with the prajñā that realizes this, this realization is attained clearly. At that point, there is no longer any effort of practicing the six pāramitās in such a manner that all are complete in each one of them, but this happens spontaneously. Also, this is the remedy for the four conceptions of clinging to the real existence of what appear as various kinds of apprehender and apprehended (such as saṃsāra and nirvāṇa, or what is to be adopted and to be rejected); clinging to the absolutely real existence of the consciousness that clings to saṃsāra and nirvāṇa as being different and appears as various kinds of appearances; clinging to the absolutely real existence of a personal self as being permanent, single, independent, clean, and so on; and {137} clinging to the absolutely real existence of phenomenal identities—mere imputed individuals being impermanent and such.

c) 6) The definition of **the culmination of the path of familiarization**: that which constitutes both the attainment of mastery over meditative absorptions and the remedy for the four conceptions that are factors to be relinquished through familiarization. Through having cultivated more and more the samādhis of the nine meditative absorptions on the path of familiarization (such as on the second bhūmi) before, one has become greatly familiar with the realization that all phenomena are without nature, and, during subsequent attainment, one has become familiar with all phenomena being illusionlike. Through the power of never separating from this kind of meditative equipoise and subsequent attainment, the conceptions to be relinquished on each level of the path of familiarization become thinned out more and more. Therefore, during the culminating training of the path of familiarization, one is becoming free from these conceptions to be relinquished and nonconceptual wisdom is unfolding more and more. Through this, at the point of the final culmination of familiarization, one is free from said conceptions to be relinquished and nonconceptual wisdom has unfolded. Thus, through gaining mastery over the samādhis of the nine meditative absorptions, these occur without any effort and spontaneously.

7) The definition of **the uninterrupted culmination**: the mastery over the three knowledges in which buddhahood is imminent. The power of the realization of the three knowledges being without nature expands up through the tenth bhūmi. Through this, at the end of the continuum of the ten bhūmis, the realization that the three knowledges are without nature and free from reference points is attained for the first time in a manner that is without the distinction into meditative equipoise and subsequent attainment and

occurs spontaneously. {138} Thus, the attainment of buddhahood in the next moment is not interrupted by any other moments.

6. The serial training

These can be summarized into two—(a) the nature of the path (the practice of the six pāramitās) and (b) eliminating obstacles to the path.

a) 1)–6) The definition of **the serial training in practicing the six pāramitās**: practicing generosity, maintaining ethics, cultivating patience, mustering vigor, practicing dhyāna, and cultivating prajñā without observing the three spheres. When practicing these six, such as generosity, there are no things to be given, no recipients, {139} and no giver (such as a self or me). In brief, any entities such as someone who practices the six pāramitās (a self or me); the six pāramitās as what are to be practiced; the benefits that are aimed at through this practice; and its focal objects are not established as any nature whatsoever and thus are free from reference points. However, from the perspective of the seeming without examination and analysis, they exist in an illusionlike manner—appearing yet being without nature. Thus, this training here means to practice the pāramitās in an attachment-free manner for the sake of oneself and others attaining buddhahood for the welfare of those sentient beings who do not realize this.

b) Eliminating obstacles to the path is fourfold, the first being (a) the threefold relinquishment of clinging to the supports of the path—abandoning clinging to the real existence of the three jewels.

ba) 7)–9) The definition of **the recollection of the three jewels as the objects of refuge**: in the manner of there being no recollection ultimately, familiarizing with the recollection of the jewel of the Buddha; the dharmas that are explained as virtuous, nonvirtuous, and neutral; and the jewel of the saṃgha of irreversible noble bodhisattvas. Actually, the three jewels as the objects of refuge are not established as any nature whatsoever. Through understanding this, on the level of the seeming and in an attachment-free manner one recollects the Buddha as the teacher, the dharma as the path, and the irreversible saṃgha as the aids for progressing on the path.

As for apprehending the causal Buddha as the teacher, one takes the previous Buddha Śākyamuni as the object of one's trust, thinking that it is impossible for him to deceive one, that he never does anything false, and that one therefore shall practice in accordance with his words. As for taking the fruitional buddha as the teacher who is an object of refuge, {140} one thinks that one, upon having attained the buddhakāya with its consummate enlightened activity, will promote the welfare of all sentient beings.

As for taking the dharma as the path, in terms of the causal dharma one thinks that one shall study and explain all the dharmas of the piṭakas taught by Buddha Śākyamuni before; practice all the virtues to be practiced that are explained in them; relinquish all the nonvirtues that are to be relinquished; and rest in equanimity with regard to what is neutral, or transforms it into virtue. Then, one acts accordingly. In terms of taking the fruitional dharma as the path, based on the above one relinquishes all one's nonvirtues and evils; practices all virtues to be practiced; and rests in equanimity with regard to what is neutral, or turns it into virtue. In brief, this means to never be without the practice of the six pāramitās or the three trainings.

As for the jewel of the saṃgha, in terms of the causal saṃgha one thinks that one will practice the path just as former bodhisattvas (such as Mañjuśrī) have practiced it, thus taking them as objects of one's trust. In terms of the fruitional saṃgha, through oneself being endowed with the three mahāyāna trainings or the two sets of qualities in terms of awareness and liberation, one absolutely never falls back into the hīnayāna.

bb) The relinquishment of clinging to the bases of the path is twofold.

10) The definition of **the recollection of ethics**: maintaining ethics in the manner of there being no recollection ultimately.

11) The definition of **the recollection of giving**: practicing generosity in the manner of there being no recollection ultimately. Actually, any entities such as someone who maintains ethics (a self or me); the ethics to be maintained; {141} maintaining it; sentient beings at whom maintaining these ethics is aimed; and its focal objects (such as buddhas) are without nature. The same goes for generosity—all entities such as someone who gives (a self or me), something to be given, and a recipient are without nature. Through being embraced by the prajñā of knowing this, on the level of the seeming ethics and generosity are practiced in an attachment-free manner.

bc) The relinquishment of clinging to the witness of the path refers to **the recollection of the deity**.

12) Its definition: in the manner of there being no recollection ultimately, familiarizing with the recollection of deities and bodhisattvas in the realms of desire and form. This refers to familiarizing with recollection by thinking, "Ultimately, any entities such as someone to be worried about (a self or me), someone who worries (the bodhisattvas), and their worrying are not established as any nature whatsoever. Through knowing that, on the level of the seeming, if I do not practice in an attachment-free manner the relinquishment of all the nonvirtues to be relinquished by bodhisattvas, the deities and bodhisattvas in the desire and form realms (such as the buddhas there) will be

worried and I will be ashamed. Since they see me directly and are present as witnesses at all times, I shall absolutely not commit any nonvirtues."

bd) The cause of the purity of the path is **the serial training in familiarizing with the nature of the lack of entity**.

13) Its definition: the sequential familiarization with the realization that all phenomena (such as form) have the nature of the lack of entity. Through studying, reflecting, and so on, one realizes that all phenomena of saṃsāra and nirvāṇa are ultimately not established as the nature of any entities, such as saṃsāra and nirvāṇa, something to be adopted and to be rejected, or pleasant and unpleasant objects. {142} In this way, through the knowledge of entities, one familiarizes with outer objects being without nature; through the knowledge of the path, one familiarizes with the inner subjects being without nature; through the knowledge of all aspects, one familiarizes with their aspects being without nature too; and through the trainings (such as the complete training in all aspects), one familiarizes with the realization that also the three knowledges themselves are without nature.

7. The four points of the instantaneous training

These can be summarized into two—(a) the two instants of manifesting the qualities and (b) the two instants of realizing what is to be known.

a) 1) The definition of **the instantaneous training in terms of nonmaturation**: through the single moment of wisdom at the end of the continuum, manifesting all nonmatured uncontaminated dharmas in a combined manner in one single instant. The manifestation of all uncontaminated dharmas of not yet completely pure relinquishment and realization in a combined manner means that all these dharmas of not yet completely pure relinquishment and realization are rendered into pure relinquishment and realization through the instantaneous wisdom at the end of the continuum. {143}

2) The definition of **the instantaneous training in terms of maturation**: through the single moment of wisdom at the end of the continuum, manifesting all uncontaminated dharmas of the phase of maturation in one single instant. This means that the single wisdom at the end of the continuum realizes in a single instant that uncontaminated wisdom—in terms of both subject and object—is pure as the dharmadhātu.

b) 3) The definition of **the instantaneous training in terms of the lack of characteristics**: in one single instant and through the single moment of wisdom at the end of the continuum, realizing that all afflicted and purified phenomena lack any characteristics of aspects. This means that the single instant of wisdom at the end of the continuum realizes in one single instant that afflicted phenomena are not established as the characteristics of saṃsāra and what is to be rejected, and that purified phenomena are not established as the characteristics of nirvāṇa and what is to be adopted, but that they are emptiness free from reference points.

4) The definition of **the instantaneous training in terms of nonduality**: bodhisattvas at the end of the continuum realizing in one instant the true nature of nonduality as being the dhātu of all phenomena. In the single instant of the wisdom of bodhisattvas at the end of the continuum, all conceptions of clinging to duality (such as the dualistic appearances of saṃsāra and nirvāṇa, the dualistic appearances of self and others, and the dualistic appearances of apprehender and apprehended) including their latent tendencies are relinquished. Thus, all phenomena are realized as equality in that they are the dharmadhātu. In the mind stream of a bodhisattva at the end of the continuum, these instants of wisdom are of an inseparable nature in terms of their substance. {144} They are four by virtue of being divided through isolates in terms of their manners of realization, but they are not four different substantial entities.

8. The dharmakāya

The four points of the dharmakāya are the svābhāvikakāya, the sāmbhogikakāya, the nairmāṇikakāya, and enlightened activity. These can be summarized into two—(a) the ultimate kāya and (b) the seeming kāyas.

a) 1) The definition of **the svābhāvikakāya**: the nature of phenomena (nonarising) that has the nature of the wisdom and the relinquishment of a buddha. This refers to the buddha wisdom that knows suchness and variety, which is actually without nature and free from reference points. This is what the *Prāsaṅgika Mādhyamikas call "dharmakāya."

b) The seeming kāyas are discussed in three parts—(a) the rūpakāyas (the supported), (b) the dharmakāya (the support),[574] and (c) enlightened activity.

ba) The rūpakāyas are twofold.

2) The definition of **the sāmbhogikakāya**: the kāya which has the nature of the blazing major and minor marks, appears to bodhisattvas who dwell on the bhūmis as their object, and teaches solely the mahāyāna dharma. It is endowed with the five certainties of being embellished by the thirty-two major and the eighty minor marks; being solely surrounded by retinues of bodhisattvas who dwell on the bhūmis; dwelling in the place that is the pure realm of Richly Adorned Akaniṣṭha; turning solely the dharma wheel of the mahāyāna dharma; and remaining for as long as saṃsāra is not emptied. {145}

3) The definition of **the nairmāṇikakāya**: the buddhakāya that accomplishes higher realms and definite excellence for ordinary beings and noble ones in pure and impure realms. It promotes the welfare of sentient beings

through various emanations—supreme emanations (such as the king of Śākyas); artistic emanations (such as Viśvakarma);[575] and incarnate emanations (such as deer). As the *Mahāyānasūtrālaṃkāra* says:

Through artistry, incarnation, great enlightenment,
And always demonstrating nirvāṇa,
The nirmāṇakāya of the Buddha
Is the great means for liberation.[576]

bb) The definition of **the dharmakāya** was explained above. Its function is to serve as the dominant condition of the rūpakāyas and thus promote the welfare of sentient beings until saṃsāra is emptied.

bc) 4) The definition of **enlightened activity**: based on the dharmakāya, establishing those to be guided in the support of the path, the path, and the fruition of the path. This means to mature those to be guided who are not yet matured, liberate those who are matured, and make those who are liberated reach the final point of buddhahood.

Through having composed a summary
Of the detailed explanations that teach the mother of the
victors— {146}
This brief elucidating synopsis—
May the welfare of beings be accomplished.

This was composed by the dharma lord and great paṇḍita Rangjung Dorje.

Maṅgalaṃ bhavantu.

Appendix IV: The Third Karmapa's Stanzas That Express Realization[577]

I pay homage to noble Mañjuśrī Kumārabhūta.

I pay homage to the Tathāgata
Who taught dependent origination
To be free from the extremes
Of existence, nonexistence, and both existence and nonexistence.[578]

Once the vivid arising
Of all phenomena is completely pure,
Cessation is not observable,
Just as in an entity that never arose.

Once mind and mental factors
Have become unobservable,
How could it be tenable that the natures
Of form and so on appear?

Nonappearing and unseen,
Where do phenomena arise?
If the primordially pure nature of phenomena
Is conceived as arising and ceasing,
It is like tying a knot into space.

Childish beings are mistaken
About the actuality that is like this,
Just as being happy and suffering while dreaming,
Thus clinging to self and mine.

The world is imagined by your own imagination.
Imagination is not real as imagination.
Imagination is not what is past, nor is it what is in the future,
And in which middle could there be imagination?

What could be the place of an imagination
Arising outside of the three times?

The victorious Buddha said,
"Temporarily, from name and form,[579]
The āyatanas arise, and from these, contact,
Craving, grasping, and becoming."

Ultimately, they are pure.[580]
If you wonder why, this is because
The Omniscient One did not see arising and ceasing.
Once there is no stirring
Of false imagination's formations,
What becomes of consciousness?

This omnipresent formation,
From where does it arise?
What is its creator?
This is very profound indeed.

This ālaya-consciousness,
Including its appropriating part,
Just like water, gold, and space,
Is primordially pure and luminous.[581]

Since it is without coming [and going],[582] being different, or one,
It is the actuality of dependent origination.
Through not realizing precisely this,
Suffering and its origin are produced.

In order to realize cessation and the path,
Correctly rely on the two realities.
Starting with the application of mindfulness
All the way up through buddhahood,
This is very profound indeed.

Since sentient beings are unobservable,
How could compassion observe them?
Therefore since this [compassion] is boundless,
The children of the victors give rise to bodhicitta.

Since the body is devoid of the body,
Form is like foam spraying up.
Because feelings are void,
Understand them to be like bubbles.

Since they are like a mirage, a banana tree, and an illusion,
Discrimination, formation, and consciousness
Are primordially pure.[583]
Therefore, mind and phenomena will be realized.[584]

By virtue of this, the dharmas of the [four]
Correct efforts are manifested.
Based on them, the very profound [four]
Limbs of miraculous powers are attained.[585]

Confidence, mindfulness, vigor,
Samādhi, and prajñā are the five faculties,
Which are the support for turning into the five powers.
Through realizing that the apprehended is void,

Where could the apprehender abide?[586]
This is just like seeing the horns of a rabbit.
Nevertheless, in an illusory manner,
They are to abide in sentient beings.

Through the seven branches of enlightenment,
And all phenomena to be relinquished through seeing
Being viewed as utterly void, one is liberated.
Therefore, one should train in this through the correct view.

Through realizing this view of the freedom from extremes,
Excellent right thought,
Speech, livelihood, aims of actions,
Effort, mindfulness, and samādhi [come about].

What make you attain these supreme [aspects] of the path of the noble ones
Are emptiness, signlessness, and wishlessness,
Which are the doors to samādhi.

Generosity, ethics, patience,
Vigor, and dhyāna, these five,
Through practicing by abiding in this actuality,
Will receive the name pāramitā.

This is prajñāpāramitā—
Being nonreferential and skilled in means.
Being infinite, just like space,
This is the supreme powerful armor.

Just like the sky, aspiration prayers become limitless.
Based on that, wisdom is boundless [too],
And from this arise all buddhadharmas,
Such as samādhis, dhāraṇīs, fearlessnesses,
Perfectly discriminating awarenesses,
And the eighteen unique [qualities].

This is the mahāyāna—
The relinquishment of [saṃsāric] existence and peace.
It is not [taught] in order to be afraid of it.
Whoever does not engage in it,
Through what would [their practice] become pāramitā?

These words that manifested through confidence
In the sons of the victors,
Mañjughoṣa, Avalokita, and Ajita,
Were written by the one called "Rangjung Dorje"
In the place [named] Lhadeng.[587]

It may well be that this contains mistakes—
May they not turn into flaws that obscure.
[But] if there is a little bit of virtue in it,
May it become the basis for the liberation of all beings.

Appendix V: The Definitions of the Eight Topics and the Seventy Points of the AA according to JG, JNS, CE, STT, SLG/PK, and LSSP/PSD

JG[588]

The definition of **the knowledge of all aspects**: the wisdom that lacks the stains of all obscurations and directly realizes all aspects of suchness and variety in a momentary manner.

It is classified as:

(1) The knowledge of all aspects of suchness: the wisdom of directly realizing the nature of phenomena, that is, all stains being at peace.

(2) The knowledge of all aspects of variety consists of:

(a) the wisdom of directly realizing all aspects of knowable objects (all natures, causes, and results of phenomena without exception)

(b) the final wisdom of directly realizing the ten points of the knowledge of all aspects in terms of its primary causes and results.

Boundary lines: in its actual form, only on the buddhabhūmi; in its approximately concordant forms, on the four last paths of bodhisattvas and also in śrāvakas and pratyekabuddhas.

The definition of **the knowledge of the path**: primarily the clear realization of noble bodhisattvas of the three paths being without nature ultimately, and, through being embraced by this realization, directly realizing said paths and promoting the welfare of others on the level of the seeming without manifesting the true end through not completing the triad of completion, maturation, and purification.

It is classified as:

(1) The knowledge of the path of the final deliverance of the three yānas: by way of not observing the three paths ultimately, directly knowing and realizing them on the level of the seeming, thus promoting the welfare of those with the three dispositions of śrāvakas, pratyekabuddhas, and bodhisattvas and not manifesting the true end as above.

(2) The knowledge of the path of realizing the three paths as being unarisen has the character of being inseparable from the wisdom of the knowledge of all aspects that exists in the mind streams of buddhas.

Boundary lines: from the mahāyāna path of seeing up through the end of the continuum.

The definition of **the knowledge of entities**: the knowledge that directly realizes all bases as being primarily empty of a personal identity and is embraced by this realization.
It is classified as:
(1) The knowledges of entities that are antagonistic factors: the direct realizations of all entities being primarily empty of either a personal identity or the apprehended aspect of phenomenal identity and being embraced by these respective realizations.
(2) The knowledge of entities that is the remedy of the former: the direct realization of phenomenal identitylessness in a fully complete manner.

Boundary lines: in its fully qualified form (1), from the paths of seeing of śrāvakas and pratyekabuddhas onward; in its fully qualified form (2), from the mahāyāna path of seeing onward; in its approximately concordant forms (1) and (2), on the paths of accumulation and preparation of śrāvakas, pratyekabuddhas, and bodhisattvas, respectively.

The definition of **the complete training in all aspects**: the yoga of bodhisattvas familiarizing with the aspects of the three knowledges in a combined manner in order to gain mastery over these aspects after having understood them through study and reflection.
It is classified as:
(1) 173 in accordance with the number of all aspects of the three knowledges
(2) The five natural and the fifteen situational trainings.

Boundary lines: from the lesser path of accumulation up through the end of the continuum.

The definition of **the culminating training**: the yoga of bodhisattvas that is the consummate familiarization with the three knowledges in a combined manner, which is based on the preceding complete training in all aspects on the great path of accumulation.
It is classified as sevenfold—the culminating trainings on:
(1)–(4) the four levels of the path of preparation
(5) the path of seeing
(6) the path of familiarization
(7) the uninterrupted path.

Boundary lines: from the level of heat of the path of preparation up through the end of the continuum.

The definition of **the serial training**

According to Āryavimuktisena: the yoga of sequentially training in the thirteen dharmas as the object of training. *Boundary lines*: from the path of accumulation up through the end of the continuum.

According to Haribhadra: the yoga of bodhisattvas that is based on the culminating clear realization and consists of familiarizing with the aspects of the three knowledges by way of going through them in due order as they are realized individually and in combination in order to gain stability in them. *Boundary lines*: from right after the culminating training (on the path of preparation) up through the moment before the end of the continuum.

It is classified as thirteenfold.

The definition of **the instantaneous training**

According to Āryavimuktisena: the final yoga of realization in the manner of realizing the two uncontaminated dharmas.

According to Haribhadra: the final yoga of bodhisattvas that arises by virtue of the power of the serial training.

It is classified as fourfold by way of the isolates of its four distinct characteristics, though it is of a single nature.

Boundary lines: solely at the end of the continuum.

The definition of **the dharmakāya**: the final fruition or maturation of the four trainings—the kāya that is endowed with many branches of uncontaminated dharmas.

It is classified as the three or four kāyas plus its enlightened activity.

Boundary lines: solely on the buddhabhūmi.

JNS[589]

The definitions of the eight topics

The definition of **the knowledge of all aspects**: the direct realization that all aspects are primordial peace.

The definition of **the knowledge of the path**: the direct realization of bodhisattvas, who have entered what is flawless, that the three paths which they generated in their mind streams are primordial peace.

The definition of **the knowledge of entities**: the direct realization that all bases are primordial peace without abiding in existence or peace, which at the same time is the remedy for apprehending characteristics with respect to the triad of knowable objects, the path, and the fruition.

The definition of **the complete training in all aspects**: familiarizing with the triad of entities, the path, and the aspects being without nature in order to gain mastery over the three knowledges for the welfare of others.

The definition of **the culminating training**: familiarizing with the triad of entities, the path, and the aspects being without nature in order to attain the dharmakāya for the welfare of others, which is the most consummate familiarity [resulting] from the power of having cultivated the complete training in all aspects.

The definition of **the serial training**: familiarizing with the triad of entities, the path, and the aspects being without nature in order to ultimately attain the dharmakāya for the welfare of others and to temporarily attain the instantaneous [training].

The definition of **the instantaneous training**: familiarizing with the triad of entities, the path, and the aspects being without nature in order to reach the consummation [resulting] from the power of having cultivated the serial [training] and to attain the dharmakāya for the welfare of others.

The definition of **the dharmakāya**: the accomplishment of the perfect fruition by virtue of having cultivated the four trainings that take the three knowledges as their objects.[590]

CE[591]

The definitions of the eight topics

The definition of **the knowledge of all aspects**: the wisdom that directly realizes all phenomena to be without arising and represents the final two welfares. *Boundary lines*: in its fully qualified form, solely on the buddhabhūmi; in its approximately concordant forms, on the paths of the noble ones below the buddhabhūmi (with the wisdoms of suchness and variety respectively existing from the first and eighth bhūmis onward).

The definition of **the knowledge of the path**: that which realizes the three paths to be primordially without arising and serves as the remedy for the cognitive obscurations. *Boundary lines*: from the first bhūmi onward.

The definition of **the knowledge of entities**: that which serves as the remedy for the afflictive obscurations through realizing personal identitylessness. *Boundary lines*: the knowledge of entities that represents factors to be relinquished, from the paths of seeing of śrāvakas and pratyekabuddhas onward; the one that is their remedy, from the first bodhisattvabhūmi onward.

The definition of **the complete training in all aspects**: the familiarization with the triad of entities, the path, and the aspects being without nature in order to realize the three knowledges. *Boundary lines*: from the path of accumulation up through the end of the continuum.

The definition of **the culminating training**: the highest form of the familiarization with the triad of entities, the path, and the aspects being without nature. *Boundary lines*: from the level of heat of the path of preparation up through the end of the continuum.

The definition of **the serial training**: the sequential familiarization in order to gain stability in the culminating training. *Boundary lines*: from the level of heat up through the moment just before the end of the continuum.

The definition of **the instantaneous training**: the simultaneous familiarization by virtue of having gained stability in familiarizing with the three knowledges in a combined manner. *Boundary lines*: only at the end of the continuum.

The definition of **the dharmakāya**: the final fruition of the four trainings. *Boundary lines*: solely on the buddhabhūmi.

STT[592]

The definitions of the eight topics

The definition of **the knowledge of all aspects**: the special yoga of realizing that all aspects are without arising. *Boundary lines*: only on the buddhabhūmi.

The definition of **the knowledge of the path**: the special realization of the three paths being unobservable. *Boundary lines*: on the paths of seeing and familiarization of bodhisattvas.

The definition of **the knowledge of entities**: the special realization that all bases are without arising. *Boundary lines*: on the three paths of seeing, familiarization, and nonlearning of śrāvakas and pratyekabuddhas as well as on the paths of seeing and familiarization of bodhisattvas.

The definition of **the complete training in all aspects**: familiarizing with the three knowledges in a combined manner. *Boundary lines*: from the path of accumulation up through the end of the continuum.

The definition of **the culminating training**: familiarizing with the three knowledges in the manner of gaining mastery over them. *Boundary lines*: from the level of heat of the path of preparation up through the end of the continuum.

The definition of **the serial training**: familiarizing with the three knowledges in a sequential manner. *Boundary lines*: Āryavimuktisena—from the path of accumulation up through the end of the continuum; Haribhadra—on the three paths of preparation, seeing, and familiarization.

The definition of **the instantaneous training**: familiarizing with the three knowledges in an instant in the final phase of the path. *Boundary lines*: only at the end of the continuum.

The definition of **the dharmakāya**: the final maturation of the three knowledges. *Boundary lines*: solely on the buddhabhūmi.

The definitions of the seventy points

1. The ten points of the knowledge of all aspects

1) The definition of **the generation of bodhicitta**: being focused on the welfare of others and enlightenment, which is congruently associated with the wishful striving for these two.

2) The definition of **the instructions**: that which teaches bodhisattvas to focus on all phenomena through their being endowed with means.

3) The definition of **the branches conducive to penetration**: the special mundane wisdom.

4) The definition of **the foundation of practice**: the dharmadhātu that serves as the basis for practice.

5) The definition of **the focal objects**: any phenomena that are to be realized as certain aspects through the prajñā of practice.

6) The definition of **the aim**: the final aim to be strived for through practice.

7) The definition of **the armorlike practice**: mustering armorlike vigor for the six pāramitās.

8) The definition of **the practice of engagement**: mustering the vigor of application for great enlightenment.

9) The definition of **the practice of the equipments**: mustering vigor for directly giving rise to the temporary great enlightenment.

10) The definition of **the practice of final deliverance**: mustering vigor for directly giving rise to the final great enlightenment.

2. The eleven points of the knowledge of the path

1) The definition of **the branches of the knowledge of the path**: the freedom from obstacles and the completeness of favorable conditions, which make it suitable for the result—the knowledge of the path—to arise in the mind stream.

2) The definition of **the knowledge of the path of śrāvakas**: the direct knowledge of the four realities together with their sixteen aspects (the entities), such as impermanence, through the principle of personal identitylessness.

3) The definition of **the knowledge of the path of pratyekabuddhas**: the direct knowledge of the above focal objects in the manner of not observing the apprehended by virtue of the latter being distinguished as being without nature.

4) The definition of **the path of seeing of bodhisattvas**: directly and newly seeing that the aspects (such as impermanence) that exist in the four realities are without nature, which functions as the support for progressing to liberation.

5) The definition of **the function of the path of familiarization**: the distinctive feature of the qualities that arise from familiarization.

6) The definition of **the path of familiarization as aspiration**: the certainty that the mother is endowed with qualities.

7) The definition of **the benefit of aspiration (praise, eulogy, and laudation)**: the proclamation of the merit of aspiration by genuine beings in order to create enthusiasm in those who familiarize [with such aspiration].

8) The definition of **the path of familiarization as dedication**: in a nonreferential manner, turning all roots of virtue into the great enlightenment for the welfare of all sentient beings.

9) The definition of **the path of familiarization as rejoicing**: familiarizing with the special mind of delighting in all roots of virtue in a nonreferential manner.

10) The definition of **the path of familiarization as accomplishment**: familiarizing with directly seeing all phenomena as the dharmadhātu.

11) The definition of **the pure path of familiarization**: the remedial means to purify the obscurations.

3. The nine points of the knowledge of entities

1) The definition of **the mahāyāna knowledge of entities**: by virtue of prajñā and compassion, not abiding in the extremes of either saṃsāra or nirvāṇa.

2) The definition of **the hīnayāna knowledge of entities**: through being endowed with the prajñā of knowing that all phenomena of saṃsāra and nirvāṇa included in the four realities are without a permanent, single, and independent personal self and without phenomenal identity in the sense of apprehended objects (minute particles) being without nature, one attains nirvāṇa and thus does not abide in saṃsāra, but through lacking the great compassion that embraces all sentient beings and the prajñā of realizing the equality of saṃsāra and nirvāṇa, one clings to saṃsāra as being real as the extreme that is to be absolutely rejected and thus falls into nirvāṇa as the extreme of extinction.

3) The definition of **the capacity of the hīnayāna knowledge of entities**: not attaining the fruitional nondual mother prajñāpāramitā by virtue of being distant from her.

4) The definition of **the capacity of the mahāyāna knowledge of entities**: swiftly attaining the fruitional nondual mother prajñāpāramitā by virtue of being close to her.

5) The definition of **the function of the hīnayāna knowledge of entities**: an antagonistic factor or factor to be relinquished through the mahāyāna knowledge of entities.

6) The definition of **the function of the mahāyāna knowledge of entities**: the remedy for this.

7) The definition of **the training in equality in terms of the subject**: familiarizing with the realization that all phenomena of saṃsāra and nirvāṇa included in the four realities (the entities) are actually without nature and free from reference points.

8) The definition of **the training in equality in terms of the object**: the realization that the focal object (the fruition to be attained or adopted) and the mind that makes itself attain or adopt what it focuses on are actually equality in that they are not established as any nature whatsoever.[593]

9) The definition of **the path of seeing of the knowledge of entities of bodhisattvas**: that which provides the opportunity for liberation through directly and newly seeing that all bases are without nature.

4. The twelve points of the complete training in all aspects[594]

1) The definition of **the aspects (the objects of the training)**: the aspects of impermanence, identitylessness, and so on that exist in the four realities (the entities).

2) The definition of **the persons who familiarize**: the fortunate who engage in dharma activities with regard to mother prajñāpāramitā through training their mind streams in the presence of buddhas.

3) The definition of **the nature of the division of the training**: familiarizing with the realization that all bases are without nature.

4) The definition of **the qualities**: the fruitions of the actual cultivation of the trainings that one is to cultivate.

5) The definition of **the faults**: any phenomena that function as obstacles to engaging in the dharma of the mother.

6) The definition of **the defining characteristics**: that which defines the trainings as being the causes and as being distinguished.

7) The definition of **the mahāyāna factors conducive to liberation**: beginners practicing generosity and such in the manner of means and prajñā being unified.

8) The definition of **the mahāyāna factors conducive to penetration**: practicing through the consummate attitude and application by focusing on all sentient beings, which is done by way of the engagement through aspiration.

9) The definition of **the persons who familiarize**: bodhisattvas in the mahāyāna who do not fall back into the hīnayāna, with a minimum of four of them representing a complete mahāyāna saṃgha.

10) The definition of **the training in the equality of existence and peace**: through familiarizing with the realization that afflicted and purified phenomena are as nonexistent as dream objects once the consciousness that perceived them wakes up, the conceptions of clinging to these two as being something to be rejected and adopted, respectively, are relinquished.

11) The definition of **the training in pure realms**: upon seeing impure realms, to engage in virtue and make aspiration prayers as the remedies for these realms, thus creating pure realms.

12) The definition of **the training in skill in means**: the familiarization with the three doors to liberation and so on that is distinguished by the subject that consists of prajñā and compassion.

5. The seven points of the culminating training[595]

1) The definition of **the culmination of heat as illustrated by its signs**: being congruently associated with the samādhi of having attained the clear illumination of mastery over the three knowledges.

2) The definition of **the culmination of peak as illustrated by increase:** being congruently associated with the samādhi in which this clear illumination expands.

3) The definition of **the culmination of poised readiness as illustrated by stability:** being congruently associated with the samādhi of engaging in a part [of emptiness].

4) The definition of **the culmination of the supreme dharma as illustrated by the mind settling:** being congruently associated with the samādhi of the imminence [of the path of seeing].

5) The definition of **the culmination of the path of seeing:** that which constitutes both the attainment of mastery over the thirty-six pāramitās, which are completely pure of the three spheres, and the remedy for the four conceptions that are factors to be relinquished through seeing.

6) The definition of **the culmination of the path of familiarization:** that which constitutes both the attainment of mastery over meditative absorptions and the remedy for the four conceptions that are factors to be relinquished through familiarization.

7) The definition of **the uninterrupted culmination:** the mastery over the three knowledges in which buddhahood is imminent.

6. The thirteen points of the serial training

1)–6) The definition of **the serial training in practicing the six pāramitās:** practicing generosity, maintaining ethics, cultivating patience, mustering vigor, practicing dhyāna, and cultivating prajñā without observing the three spheres.

7)–9) The definition of **the recollection of the three jewels as the objects of refuge:** in the manner of there being no recollection ultimately, familiarizing with the recollection of the jewel of the Buddha; the dharmas that are explained as virtuous, nonvirtuous, and neutral; and the jewel of the saṃgha of irreversible noble bodhisattvas.

10) The definition of **the recollection of ethics:** maintaining ethics in the manner of there being no recollection ultimately.

11) The definition of **the recollection of giving:** practicing generosity in the manner of there being no recollection ultimately.

12) The definition of **the recollection of the deity:** in the manner of there being no recollection ultimately, familiarizing with the recollection of deities and bodhisattvas in the realms of desire and form.

13) The definition of **the serial training in familiarizing with the nature of the lack of entity:** the sequential familiarization with the realization that all phenomena (such as form) have the nature of the lack of entity.

7. The four points of the instantaneous training

1) The definition of **the instantaneous training in terms of nonmaturation**: through the single moment of wisdom at the end of the continuum, manifesting all nonmatured uncontaminated dharmas in a combined manner in one single instant.

2) The definition of **the instantaneous training in terms of maturation**: through the single moment of wisdom at the end of the continuum, manifesting all uncontaminated dharmas of the phase of maturation in one single instant.

3) The definition of **the instantaneous training in terms of the lack of characteristics**: in one single instant and through the single moment of wisdom at the end of the continuum, realizing that all afflicted and purified phenomena lack any characteristics of aspects.

4) The definition of **the instantaneous training in terms of nonduality**: bodhisattvas at the end of the continuum realizing in one instant the true nature of nonduality as being the dhātu of all phenomena.

8. The four points of the dharmakāya

1) The definition of **the svābhāvikakāya**: the nature of phenomena (nonarising) that has the nature of the wisdom and the relinquishment of a buddha.

2) The definition of **the sāmbhogikakāya**: [the kāya] which has the nature of the blazing major and minor marks, appears to bodhisattvas who dwell on the bhūmis as their object, and teaches solely the mahāyāna dharma.

3) The definition of **the nairmāṇikakāya**: the buddhakāya that accomplishes higher realms and definite excellence for ordinary beings and noble ones in pure and impure realms.

4) The definition of **enlightened activity**: based on the dharmakāya, establishing those to be guided in the support of the path, the path, and the fruition of the path.

SLG/PK[596]

The definitions of the eight topics

The definition of **the knowledge of all aspects**: the actual causes that make one attain the knowledge of all aspects.

The definition of **the knowledge of the path**: the nonconceptual wisdom (including its branches) of knowing the path(s).

The definition of **the knowledge of entities**: the nonconceptual wisdom (including its branches) of knowing entities.

The definition of **the complete training in all aspects**: the training that is the support which consists of the yoga making one attain the three knowledges.

The definition of **the culminating training**: the training that is the first fruition of the training which makes one attain the three knowledges.

The definition of **the serial training**: the training of progressively training in the objects that are the means to finalize the first two yoga trainings which make one attain the three knowledges.

The definition of **the instantaneous training**: the training of attaining the highest degree of the three yoga trainings which make one attain the knowledge of all aspects.

The definition of **the dharmakāya**: the final fruition of having cultivated the four trainings.

The definitions of the seventy points

1. The ten points of the knowledge of all aspects

1) The definition of **the generation of bodhicitta**: the generation of mind as emptiness with a heart of compassion.

2) The definition of **the instructions**: the instructions on the activities to attain what is to be strived for when generating the mindset in the mahāyāna.

3) The definition of **the branches conducive to penetration**: the dharmas that are distinguished by being a bodhisattva's factors conducive to penetration.

4) The definition of **the disposition**: the dhātu's capacity to produce the dharmas of the noble ones.

5) The definition of **the focal objects**: the bases of bodhisattvas realizing the phenomena that they did not realize before, which are the objects that include both antagonistic factors and remedies.

6) The definition of **the aim**: the triad of great compassion (the welfare of others), great relinquishment (one's own welfare), and great wisdom.

7) The definition of **the armorlike practice**: the training in what is to be engaged, that is, the activity of cultivating the six pāramitās as each others' branches.

8) The definition of **the practice of engagement**: the activity that makes one attain the knowledge of all aspects.

9) The definition of **the practice of the equipments**: the activity of finalizing the engagement in the mahāyāna.

10) The definition of **the practice of final deliverance**: the final practice.

These can be summarized in four points—the person who is the practitioner (1)–(4); the focal object of practice (5); the aim of practice (6); and the nature of practice (7)–(10).

2. The eleven points of the knowledge of the path

1) The definition of **the support for the arising of the knowledge of the path**: the essence of the support (being free from obstacles) being endowed with four distinctive features—the dominant condition (generating bodhicitta); the causal condition (being endowed with the disposition); the nature of not rejecting saṃsāra; and the function of accomplishing the benefit of others.

2) **The path of the śrāvakas**—its nature consists of their paths of the noble ones, while its preparation consists of their paths of accumulation and preparation.[597]

3) **The path of the pratyekabuddhas**—its nature consists of the three features of fruition (attaining enlightenment by themselves without the need for others teaching them); nature (relinquishment of the conceptions about the apprehended, but not those about the apprehender); and support (the disposition of a pratyekabuddha), while its preparation consists of the four factors conducive to penetration.

4) The nature of **the path of seeing of the mahāyāna** consists of its sixteen moments such as the dharma readiness of suffering.

5) **The function of the path of familiarization** is sixfold—pacifying; bowing down; being victorious over the afflictions; being invulnerable to attacks; attaining enlightenment; and becoming objects of worship.

6) The definition of **the path of familiarization as aspiration**: the preparatory stage of the uncontaminated path of familiarization, which is associated with the mental factors of ascertaining, through the power of valid cognition, the qualities of the uncontaminated dharmas when engaging in familiarizing with them.

7) The definition of **praise, eulogy, and glorification**: that which produces enthusiasm for familiarizing with the uncontaminated dharmas.

8) The definition of **the path of familiarization as dedication**: dedicating the roots of virtue of the three times (which are free from any characteristics or

being focal objects) for the sake of great enlightenment while being endowed with the prajñā of realizing emptiness.

9) The definition of **the path of familiarization as rejoicing**: the experience and delight of rejoicing in the virtues of oneself and others (all seeming and ultimate subjects) in the three times.

10) The definition of **the path of familiarization as accomplishment**: the path of familiarization of realizing the other-dependent nature as being illusionlike through revealing it (the wisdom of subsequent attainment).

11) The definition of **the pure path of familiarization**: the path of familiarization of realizing the perfect nature as being spacelike through revealing it (the wisdom of meditative equipoise).

These can be summarized in five points—the person who is the practitioner (1); the path of śrāvakas (2) and the path of pratyekabuddhas (3), both of which are to be known by the practitioner; the path of seeing (4); and the path of familiarization (5)–(11).

3. The nine points of the knowledge of entities

1) **The knowledge of entities of not abiding in existence or peace** means to neither abide in saṃsāra through realizing the flaws of existence, such as impermanence (which also exists in śrāvakas and pratyekabuddhas) nor to abide in nirvāṇa through great compassion.[598]

2) **The knowledge of entities of śrāvakas and pratyekabuddhas** is the opposite of the above.

3) **The knowledge of entities that is distant from the mother due to not being the means** is the knowledge of entities of śrāvakas and pratyekabuddhas—though they possess the realization of the actuality of the other-dependent nature (such as impermanence), they lack the realization of the perfect nature being spacelike and thus focus on characteristics.

4) **The knowledge of entities that is not distant from the mother due to being the means** refers to lacking what is not the means—clinging to the reality of (a) the imaginary nature that consists of the names and characteristics which are the means for revealing the perfect nature and (b) dualistic appearances.

5) **The knowledge of entities that represents antagonistic factors** consists of the threefold clinging to the characteristics of knowable objects, conduct, and the fruition.

6) **The knowledge of entities that is a remedy** is fourfold—putting an end to clinging to knowable objects; lacking conceit about conduct; knowing phenomena to be of the same nature; and demonstrating this knowledge to be profound.

7) **The trainings in the knowledge of entities** are the ten specific characteristics of the training—the fourfold stopping of clinging to objects (form and so on; their impermanence and so on; their being incomplete or complete;

detachment from them); the threefold nature of the trainings (being unchanging; not being an agent; and what is hard to do); their twofold performing of activity (producing the fruition and seizing the benefit); and what is to be realized (which is illustrated through examples).

8) **The equality of these trainings** is the general characteristic of realizing the fourfold equality that is common to all the above features of the training—realizing that the four kinds of conceit in terms of clinging, characteristics, reference points, and realization are not observable as true reality.

9) The distinctive features of the natures of **the paths of seeing** of śrāvakas, pratyekabuddhas, and bodhisattvas are explained through their respective sixteen moments.

These can be summarized in five points—the distinctive features of compassion (1)–(2); prajñā (3)–(4); remedy (5)–(6); training (7)–(8); and the path (9).

4. The eleven points of the complete training in all aspects

1) **The aspects** consist of the twenty-seven aspects of the knowledge of entities, the thirty-six aspects of the knowledge of the path, and the 110 aspects of the knowledge of all aspects.

2) **The trainings** consist of the persons who train and the twentyfold nature of the training.

3) **The qualities** are twentyfold.

4) **The faults** are forty-six.

5) **The fruition and the defining characteristics** consist of four—the characteristics of knowledge, distinctiveness, and activity, and the nature that is defined.

6) **The factors conducive to liberation** consist of the mahāyāna path of accumulation that is more distinguished than those of śrāvakas and pratyekabuddhas by virtue of its defining characteristics of prajñā and means—being skilled in correct practice through generosity and so on arising in one's mind stream by way of the aspect of the prajñā of focusing on the lack of characteristics.

7) **The factors conducive to penetration** consist of ten aspects that cover the twelve levels of the path of preparation.

8) **The irreversible learners** are the bodhisattvas who are endowed with the signs of irreversibility and respectively dwell on the factors conducive to penetration, the path of seeing, and the path of familiarization.

9) **The familiarization with the equality of existence and peace of the irreversible nonlearners** refers to equality because they do not display in either saṃsāra or nirvāṇa, and it refers to nonlearning because there is neither anything to be learned nor a learner.

10) **The training in pure realms** means that, through having familiarized with the equality of both saṃsāra and nirvāṇa, one becomes a buddha in a buddha realm.

11) **The training in skill in means** consists of the tenfold training in going beyond hindrances and so on.

These can be summarized in four points—instances in terms of the training's objects, nature, fruition, and hindrances (1)–(4); its defining characteristics (5); its time of attainment in terms of engaging in the training (6) and fully completing it (7); and the power of the training that is attained through familiarization, which is in terms of the divisions of its supports (8) and the actual powers within these supports (9)–(11).

5. The seven points of the culminating training[599]

1)–4) **The signs of the culminating trainings of heat, peak, poised readiness, and the supreme dharma** are twelve, sixteen, two, and two, respectively.

5) **The culminating training of the path of seeing** is fivefold in terms of its factors to be relinquished; the power to produce its fruition; the nature of its fruition; the nature of the path of seeing; and its function.

6) **The culminating training of the path of familiarization** is threefold in terms of its support (the path of familiarization); its factors to be relinquished (the four conceptions); and what it supports (the qualities).

7) **The uninterrupted culminating training**, in its nature, is samādhi, which has the distinctive features of all favorable conditions being complete and being free from antagonistic obstacles.

6. The thirteen points of the serial training

The serial training is thirteenfold in terms of first training in the nature of the lack of entity; then, in the six recollections; and thereafter, in the six pāramitās.

7. The four points of the instantaneous training

The instantaneous trainings in terms of nonmaturation, maturation, the lack of characteristics, and nonduality take place on the seventh, eighth, ninth, and tenth bhūmis, respectively.

8. The five points of the dharmakāya

1) The definition of **the svābhāvikakāya**: the kāya of being free from both natural and adventitious stains.

2) The definition of **the dharmakāya**: the collection of the dharmas that make one a buddha.

3) The definition of **the sāmbhogikakāya**: the kāya that is adorned with the major and minor marks that are brought about through hundreds of forms of merit.

4) The definition of **the nairmāṇikakāya**: the rūpakāya that is the natural outflow of the sāmbhogikakāya.

5) The definition of **enlightened activity**: the welfare of others that is promoted for as long as saṃsāra exists.

LSSP/PSD and LNG[600]

The definition of **prajñāpāramitā**: the knowledge of directly realizing the nature of phenomena free from reference points, which has gone, or makes one go, to the nonabiding nirvāṇa. *Boundary lines*: the fully qualified one, on the three paths of the noble ones of the mahāyāna; the nominal one, from the paths of accumulation and preparation onward.

LNG:

The definition of **natural prajñāpāramitā**: the elements that are the objects of the knowledge that directly realizes all phenomena as being free from reference points (equivalent to ground prajñāpāramitā). *Boundary lines*: on all three paths of the noble ones of the mahāyāna.

The definition of **scriptural prajñāpāramitā**: the words of the Buddha and the treatises that are the cognizances which appear as the assemblies of the names, words, and letters that teach by taking the prajñāpāramitās of ground, path, and/or fruition as their main subject matters. *Boundary lines*: before the path is entered up through the buddhabhūmi.

The definition of the **prajñāpāramitā of the path**: the knowledge that directly realizes that all phenomena are free from reference points and causes one to proceed to the nonabiding nirvāṇa. *Boundary lines*: the fully qualified one, during the meditative equipoises of the noble ones of the mahāyāna; the approximately concordant one, on the paths of accumulation and preparation.

The definition of the **fruitional prajñāpāramitā**: the knowledge that has arrived at the nonabiding nirvāṇa and is the highest final level of directly realizing that all phenomena are free from reference points. *Boundary lines*: solely in buddhas.

The definitions of the eight topics

The definition of **the knowledge of all aspects**: the direct knowledge of all aspects of suchness and variety without exception in one single moment. *Boundary lines*: solely on the buddhabhūmi.

The definition of **the knowledge of the path**: the path of training which realizes that the three paths are without nature and which manifests the true end through completion, maturation, and purification. *Boundary lines*: the path of accumulation up through the path of nonlearning.[601]

The definition of **the knowledge of entities**: the limited knowledge that realizes that all bases are empty of a personal self. *Boundary lines*: the path of accumulation up through the path of nonlearning.[602]

The definition of **the complete training in all aspects**: the yoga of bodhisattvas in which they familiarize with the three types of nonarising in a combined manner in order to attain mastery over realizing the three knowledges. *Boundary lines*: the lesser path of accumulation up through the end of the continuum of the ten bhūmis.

The definition of **the culminating training**: the yoga of bodhisattvas in which they have gained mastery over familiarizing with the three types of nonarising in a combined manner based on the complete training in all aspects. *Boundary lines*: the level of heat up through the end of the continuum.

The definition of **the serial training**: the yoga of bodhisattvas in which they sequentially familiarize with the aspects of the three knowledges in order to stabilize the realization [that consists] of the simultaneous arising of the cognitive aspects of the three knowledges. *Boundary lines*: the path of accumulation up through the end of the continuum.[603]

The definition of **the instantaneous training**: the yoga of bodhisattvas that is the final [stage] of the sequential familiarization with the three knowledges. *Boundary lines*: solely at the end of the continuum.

The definition of **the dharmakāya**: the final fruition of having cultivated the trainings that is endowed with a multitude of uncontaminated branches. *Boundary lines*: solely on the buddhabhūmi.

The definitions of the seventy points

1. The ten points of the knowledge of all aspects

1) The definition of **the generation of bodhicitta**: the mind that is congruently associated with the desire for perfect enlightenment for the sake of others.[604] *Boundary lines*: the generation of bodhicitta that arises through aspiration, on the level of engagement through aspiration; the one that is the pure superior intention, on the first seven bhūmis; the one that is maturation, on the three pure bhūmis; and the one of [all] obscurations having been relinquished,[605] on the buddhhabhūmi.

2) The definition of **the instructions**: the means of expression that unmistakenly instruct in the means to attain what is to be strived for when generating the mindset of the mahāyāna. *Boundary lines*: from the level of a beginner up through the buddhabhūmi.[606]

3) The definition of **the mahāyāna branches conducive to penetration**: the clear realizations that arise after the mahāyāna path of accumulation and consist of the level of engagement through aspiration. *Boundary lines*: solely on the path of preparation.

4) The definition of **the disposition**: the dhātu that is discussed here and acts as the fundamental basis for practice.[607] *Boundary lines*: by way of the phenomena for which it is the foundation, from heat up through the end of the continuum.

5) The definition of **the focal objects**: what serve as the knowable objects of those who practice.[608]

6) The definition of **the aim**: the final fruition in terms of which [bodhi]-sattvas will engage in the practice. *Boundary lines*: solely on the buddhabhūmi.

The general definition of **practice**: the activity of accomplishing the two welfares for the sake of unsurpassable enlightenment, which is based on the generation of the mindset of the mahāyāna.[609]

7) The definition of **the armorlike practice**: making the pāramitās a living experience through completely including all six in each one of them. *Boundary lines*: the path of accumulation up through the end of the continuum.

8) The definition of **the practice of engagement**: the activity of engaging in the mahāyāna primarily through what arises from meditation. *Boundary lines*: heat up through the end of the continuum.[610]

9) The definition of **the practice of the equipments**: the direct deliverance into great enlightenment. *Boundary lines*: the first fifteen equipments, on the supreme dharma of the path of preparation; the two equipments of the bhūmis and the remedies, on the paths of seeing and familiarization.[611]

10) The definition of **the practice of final deliverance**: that which undoubtedly delivers into the final points of deliverance. *Boundary lines*: on the special path of the tenth bhūmi.

2. The eleven points of the knowledge of the path

1) The definition of **the four branches of the knowledge of the path**: the basis that is suitable for the arising of the knowledge of the path (overcoming pride), the certain or uncertain object for its arising, the nature (not rejecting saṃsāra), and the function (attracting others as a retinue and so on).[612]

2) The definition of **the path of the śrāvakas**: the limited knowledge that realizes merely personal identitylessness.[613]

3) The definition of **the path of the pratyekabuddhas**: the limited knowledge that realizes one-and-a-half of the two [types of] identitylessness.[614]

4) The definition of **the path of seeing of the mahāyāna**: the supramundane wisdom that realizes the two [types of] identitylessness before the uncontaminated path of familiarization arises.[615]

5) The definition of **the function of the path of familiarization**: the benefit that is the result of the path of familiarization.

6) The definition of **the path of familiarization as aspiration**: the contaminated path of familiarization that, in the manner of being certain, apprehends the fact that the mother is endowed with qualities, just as it is. *Boundary lines*: the aspiration in terms of one's own welfare, from the second up through the seventh bhūmis; the aspiration in terms of the welfare of oneself and others, on the eighth bhūmi;[616] and the aspiration in terms of the welfare of others, on the tenth bhūmi.

7) The definition of **the triad of praise, eulogy, and glorification**: either the aspect of the buddhas and higher bodhisattvas being delighted with the bodhisattvas who cultivate the three aspirations, or the aspect of [the former] expressing the qualities of the [latter] dwelling in the ultimate. *Boundary lines*: from the second up through the tenth bhūmis.

8) The definition of **the path of familiarization as dedication**: the contaminated path of familiarization that turns virtues into the branches of perfect enlightenment for the sake of others. *Boundary lines*: from the second up through the tenth bhūmis.

9) The definition of **the path of familiarization as rejoicing**: the contaminated path of familiarization of delighting in the virtues of oneself and others. *Boundary lines*: from the second up through the tenth bhūmis.

10) The definition of **the path of familiarization as accomplishment**: the uncontaminated path[617] of familiarization that is the cause for final realization.

11) The definition of **the pure path of familiarization**: the uncontaminated path[618] of familiarization of the mahāyāna that is the cause for final relinquishment.[619]

3. The nine points of the knowledge of entities

1) The definition of **the knowledge of entities of not abiding in [saṃsāric] existence through prajñā**: the knowledge that puts an end to the troubles of [saṃsāric] existence through the prajñā of realizing the lack of any nature.

2) The definition of **the knowledge of entities of not abiding in peace through compassion**: the knowledge that puts an end to the trouble of peace through the force of the special generation of bodhicitta.

3) The definition of **the knowledge of entities that is distant due to not being the means**: the knowledge of entities that is constrained by clinging to characteristics with respect to the triad of knowable objects, the path, and the fruition, and thus is not able to function as the remedy for this [clinging].

4) The definition of **the knowledge of entities that is not distant due to the means**: the knowledge that entails special means and prajñā.

5) The definition of **[the knowledge of entities that is] an antagonistic factor**: the knowledge of entities that exists as a factor to be relinquished by bodhisattvas since it is constrained by the clinging of mistakenly engaging in the fundamental nature of entities.

6) The definition of **the knowledge of entities that is a remedy**: the knowledge that is able to function as a remedy for the clinging to characteristics with respect to entities since it realizes that they are without nature.

7) The definition of **the trainings in the knowledge of entities**: the path of familiarization by putting an end to the clinging to entities (such as form),

which implicitly covers the trainings of śrāvakas and pratyekabuddhas. *Boundary lines*: from the path of accumulation up through the tenth bhūmi.

8) The definition of **the equality of these trainings**: the aspect of cultivating the trainings in the knowledge of entities that puts an end to conceit about subject and object.

9) The definition of **the path of seeing**: newly seeing the realities free from the thirty-two superimpositions, which implicitly covers the hīnayāna paths of seeing.

4. The eleven points of the complete training in all aspects

1) The definition of **the aspects**: the distinct objective or cognitive features that serve as the factors to familiarize with through the trainings.

2) The definition of **the trainings**: the yogas of bodhisattvas in which they familiarize with the three knowledges in a combined manner in order to gain mastery over them. *Boundary lines*: from the path of accumulation up through the tenth bhūmi.

3) The definition of **the qualities**: what is to be attained temporarily and ultimately through cultivating the trainings. *Boundary lines*: from heat onward.[620]

4) The definition of **the faults**: the activities of māras that disrupt the arising of the trainings and their becoming special.[621]

5) The definition of **the defining characteristics**: the knowledges that define the nature or the capacity of the trainings. *Boundary lines*: from the path of accumulation up through the tenth bhūmi.

6) The definition of **the factors conducive to liberation**: the path that consists of the phase of not having the nature of the faculties of purified phenomena and furthers the distinctive features of freedom.

7) The definition of **the factors conducive to penetration**: the wisdom of the engagement through aspiration that entails the special aspect of focusing on sentient beings and represents the principal [wisdom] that arises from meditation.

8) The definition of **irreversible [learners]**: the bodhisattvas who possess the signs of the certainty of not falling into either [saṃsāric] existence or peace. *Boundary lines*: from the path of preparation up through the path of familiarization.

9) The definition of **the training in the equality of existence and peace**: the training of realizing, and then familiarizing with, both saṃsāra and nirvāṇa as being without nature. *Boundary lines*: from the path of preparation onward.[622]

10) The definition of **the training in pure realms**: the training that frees one's own twofold realm (container and content) from flaws. *Boundary lines*: from the path of preparation onward.[623]

11) The definition of **the training in skill in means**: the training in knowing whether or not it is the right time to manifest the ten objects of skill in means. *Boundary lines*: from the path of preparation onward.[624]

5. The eight points of the culminating training

1) The definition of **the signs**: that which consists of the heat [of the path of preparation] and defines the highest level of familiarization in a combined manner.

2) The definition of **increase**: that which consists of the peak of the path of preparation and represents the factor that is the increase of the highest level of familiarization in a combined manner.

3) The definition of **stability**: that which consists of the poised readiness [of the path of preparation] and represents the culmination of attaining stability in the respectively appropriate realization of the three knowledges and in not abandoning the welfare of sentient beings.

4) The definition of **the abiding of the mind**: that which consists of the supreme dharma [of the path of preparation] and represents the culmination of the mind one-pointedly abiding in the actuality of rejoicing in the generation of bodhicitta of the four [types of] bodhisattvas.

5) The definition of **the culmination of the path of seeing**: the highest level of familiarization in a combined manner that functions as the specific remedy for the conceptions that are factors to be relinquished through seeing.

6) The definition of **the culmination of the path of familiarization**: the highest level of familiarization in a combined manner that functions as the specific remedy for the conceptions that are factors to be relinquished through familiarization.

7) The definition of **the uninterrupted culmination**: the highest level of familiarization in a combined manner that serves as the direct cause for the knowledge of all aspects.

8) The definition of **wrong practice**: the ignorance of apprehending the two realities as contradictory.

6. The thirteen points of the serial training

1)–6) The definition of **the serial training in generosity**: the sequential familiarization with generosity (the same applies to the other five pāramitās).

7) The definition of **the serial training in the recollection of the Buddha**: not observing the qualities of the Tathāgata ultimately and sequentially recollecting them, just as they are, on the level of seeming [reality].

8) The definition of **the serial training in the recollection of the dharma**: not observing virtuous, nonvirtuous, and neutral dharmas ultimately and sequentially recollecting them, just as they are, on the level of seeming [reality].

9) The definition of **the serial training in the recollection of the saṃgha**: not observing the assemblies of irreversible learners ultimately and sequentially recollecting them, just as they are, on the level of seeming [reality].

10) The definition of **the serial training in the recollection of ethics**: not observing the three [sets of] vows ultimately and sequentially recollecting them, just as they are, on the level of seeming [reality].

11) The definition of **the serial training in the recollection of giving**: not observing the generosities of dharma and material things ultimately and sequentially recollecting them, just as they are, on the level of seeming [reality].

12) The definition of **the serial training in the recollection of the deity**: not observing the noble ones who are born as deities ultimately and sequentially recollecting them, just as they are, on the level of seeming [reality].

13) The definition of **the serial training in the nature of the lack of entity**: the realization of, and sequential familiarization with, all phenomena being without nature ultimately.[625]

7. The four points of the instantaneous training

1) The definition of **the instantaneous training in terms of nonmaturation**: the realization of all nonmatured dharmas in one single instant.

2) The definition of **the instantaneous training in terms of maturation**: the realization of all matured dharmas in one single instant.

3) The definition of **the instantaneous training in terms of the lack of characteristics**: the realization in one single instant that all phenomena lack characteristics.

4) The definition of **the instantaneous training in terms of nonduality**: the realization in one single instant that all phenomena are nondual.[626]

8. The four points of the dharmakāya

1) The definition of **the svābhāvikakāya**: the naturally pure dhātu being also pure of all adventitious stains without exception.[627]

2) The definition of **the sāmbhogikakāya**: the rūpakāya that, among those to be guided, appears only for bodhisattvas and serves as the dominant condition for the nairmāṇikakāya.

3) The definition of **the nairmāṇikakāya**: the kāya that arises by virtue of the sāmbhogikakāya as its dominant condition and guides many pure and impure beings.

4) The definition of **the dharmakāya**: the ultimate wisdom that is the complete change of state of buddhahood.

The definition of **enlightened activity**: the completely immaculate qualities that arise from the dharmakāya, which functions as their dominant condition.[628]

Appendix VI: TOK's Presentation of the Paths, Bhūmis, and Fruitions in the Causal Yāna of Characteristics

A) The presentation of paths and bhūmis[629]

This has two parts:

1) The presentation [of the natures] of the paths
2) The presentation of the natures of the bhūmis

1. The presentation of the natures of the paths

This has five parts:

1) The nature of the path
2) The classificational enumerations
3) The hermeneutical etymology of the meaning of the term
4) The difference between actual and nominal [paths]
5) The detailed explanations of each one of the five paths

1.1. The nature of the path

> **The nature of the path is that which, once one has entered it,**
> **Serves as a stepping stone for progressing towards more superior states.**

The nature of the path on which one is to progress **is that which, once one has entered it, serves as a stepping stone for progressing towards more superior** mundane or supramundane **states.** {465} Some present the definition of the path as "the virtuous actions that serve as the causes for liberation" or "what is able to relinquish the factors to be relinquished." These [definitions] are not tenable because it follows [from them] that the bhūmis or the factors that are the remedies are also the path. Also the assertion of some others that the isolate of path is "what causes progressing" is not tenable because what causes progressing on the path (which is something like a stepping stone on which one is to progress) applies to the agent, that is, the person [who progresses on it].

1.2. The classificational enumerations

> **The classifications are many, such as [in terms of] the three yānas or being contaminated and uncontaminated,**
> **But the general outline of all of them consists of the five paths.**

In general, **the classifications** of paths are limitless—the three paths **of the three yānas**; the two paths to higher states and liberation, or to higher realms and definite excellence, or mundane and supramundane paths, respectively; and the two paths that are **contaminated and uncontaminated.** The word **such as** includes a fourfold [classification of] paths, such as [the path of] preparation;[630] [another] fourfold classification of paths in terms of being swift, slow, difficult, and easy; the two paths of learning and nonlearning; and the two paths of meditative equipoise and subsequent attainment. There **are many** different contextual categories of classification such as these, **but the** most well-known **general outline of all** supramundane paths is known as **the five paths** of accumulation, preparation, seeing, familiarization, and nonlearning.

1.3. The hermeneutical etymology of the meaning of the term

> **The hermeneutical etymology is that something is a path because it is the basis for progressing.**

The hermeneutical etymology that comes from the [Sanskrit] term *panthā*[631] (path), which derives from the root *path*[632] (to go), is as follows. **Something is** called **a "path" because it is** a stepping stone for progressing or **the basis for progressing.** Since it is that on which the persons who have entered this path are to progress, it is that on which such progression takes place. The *[Prajñāpāramitā]saṃcayagāthā* says:

> By traveling in it, all sentient beings pass beyond misery.[633]

Accordingly, one proceeds towards nirvāṇa through that in which one travels, that is, in dependence on that. Therefore, from the point of view of being similar to a vehicle or a carrier, [the path] is also called *yāna*. {466}

1.4. The difference between actual and nominal paths

> **Śrāvakas and pratyekabuddhas entail proceeding, so their paths are actual and their results are nominal.**

The mahāyāna is final, with its path being nominal and its result actual.
Those [paths] which join one with actual clear realization are nominal.

Since [the paths] of **śrāvakas and pratyekabuddhas entail proceeding** towards something higher, **their paths are** fully qualified [as paths] **and their results are nominal.** Since [the path] of **the mahāyāna is** the **final** relinquishment and realization, **its path is nominal and its result** is fully qualified. Furthermore, master Jñānamitra says:

> Since [the paths of] accumulation and preparation are mundane, they are not the reality of the path. Rather, they are the retinue of the [actual] path because they cause it to arise.[634]

Accordingly, some masters, such as Dré Sherab Bar assert the following:

> Since [the paths of] accumulation and preparation are conceptual and contaminated, they are not the actual path. However, [here,] the cause [of the actual path] is labeled as the path.

Thus since the two [paths of] accumulation and preparation, which will be explained [below], **join one with** the **actual clear realization** of the path of seeing, they certainly must be called "**nominal** paths." However, the *Ratnakūṭa* says that although they are conceptual, nonconceptuality arises from correct conception. It [illustrates this] through the example that fire arises from rubbing two wooden sticks [against each other]. [Furthermore, said two paths] are explained to be contaminated since they are connected to [contaminated mental] seeds. This refers to their being connected to the ālaya [consciousness] that is endowed with these paths, whereas the factor that is the path [itself] is uncontaminated. Therefore, in these [sources], also [the paths of accumulation and preparation] are paths that are fully qualified as such.

1.5. The detailed explanations of each one of the five paths

This has five parts:

1) The path of accumulation
2) The path of preparation
3) The path of seeing
4) The path of familiarization
5) The path of completion

1.5.1. The path of accumulation

This has eight parts:

1) Presenting its definition
2) Identifying its instances
3) Classification
4) Determining its nature
5) The features of relinquishment and realization
6) Stating its qualities
7) Its function
8) Teaching its hermeneutical etymology

1.5.1.1. Presenting its definition

> **The path of accumulation consists of the virtuous actions that are conducive to liberation.**

The nature or definition[635] of **the path of accumulation** is "that which is a basis for progressing towards nirvāṇa {467} and **consists of the virtuous actions that are conducive to liberation.**"

1.5.1.2. Identifying its instances

> **Its instances are the efforts in studying, meditating, and so on.**

The instances of this path **are** the remedies that mature the mind stream, that is, **the efforts in studying,** reflecting, and **meditating** from the time of having generated bodhicitta until the arising of the wisdom of heat.

1.5.1.3. Classification

> **The cultivations of the foundations of mindfulness, the correct efforts,**
> **And the limbs of miraculous powers are its lesser, medium, and great [levels].**
> **Or it is classified as fourfold, such as the level of beginners.**

There is a threefold [classification of the path of accumulation] as lesser, medium, and great. **The cultivation of the** four **foundations of mindfulness** represents the **lesser** path of accumulation, during which it is not certain that one enters the path of preparation. The cultivation of **the** four **correct efforts** represents the **medium** path of accumulation, during which the time of entering the path of preparation is certain. The cultivation of **the** four **limbs of**

miraculous powers represents the **great** path of accumulation, during which it is certain that [the level of] heat of the path of preparation arises. **Or it** can be **classified as fourfold—the level of beginners,** the level of confidence, what is conducive to liberation, and the armorlike practice.

1.5.1.4. Determining its nature

> **It has three features—arising, relying, and what it focuses on.**

This path **has three features**—(1) the [psychophysical] supports in which it **arises,** (2) the grounds on which it **relies,** and (3) the objects **on which it focuses.** (1) It is asserted that the path of accumulation arises only in men and women of the three continents, but not in other beings, neuters, and hermaphrodites. (2) When one makes efforts in yoga from time to time, one relies on the six grounds of dhyāna or on one-pointed reflection [within the mental frame] of the desire realm. The other virtuous actions that serve as causes [for progressing], that is, the ethics of ordinary sentient beings, rely on the grounds of the desire [realm]. (3) One focuses on the ethics of ordinary sentient beings, that is, on [proper] engaging and rejecting in terms of body and speech. Through making efforts in yoga from time to time, repulsiveness and such are the focuses of purifying one's conduct. The focuses of the foundations of mindfulness are to focus on the body and so on. {468} Other virtuous actions that serve as causes are to focus on the words and meanings of the Buddha's words.

1.5.1.5. The features of relinquishment and realization

> **The coarse factors are relinquished and identitylessness is**
> **realized as an object generality.**

The very **coarse factors** to be relinquished that produce suffering in saṃsāra **are relinquished** through the invalidating remedy. Through the three prajñās [of studying, reflecting, and meditating], the two **identitylessnesses are realized** in the form of **object generalities.**

1.5.1.6. Stating its qualities

> **On the basis of the disposition, mind, and conduct, one possesses**
> **five attributes.**
> **One attains the visions, supernatural knowledges, and the**
> **samādhi of the stream of dharma.**

You may wonder, "What kind of featuring qualities do bodhisattvas on the path of accumulation possess?" **The disposition** of the mahāyāna is awakened [in them], they generate the twofold **mind** of enlightenment, **and** they train in the six pāramitās as their **conduct. On the basis of** these, they moreover **possess five attributes.** (1) They rely on the ethics of ordinary sentient beings. (2) They control the gates of their senses. (3) They are aware of the amount of food [that they eat]. (4) Not sleeping during the first and the last third of the night, they make efforts in yoga. (5) They delight in remaining in alertness.

(1) The first one of these [attributes] does not mean that they lack the ethics or vows of dhyāna, but that they mainly rely on any one of the seven sets of prātimokṣa [vows] of the mahāyāna.

(2) The general presentation of the second [attribute] is to control the gates of the senses through the powerful mindfulness of devoted application and constant application. Based on that, that profundity and prajñā are primary means that the engagement in all objects of the five sense faculties is embraced by prajñāpāramitā. That vastness and means are primary refers to engaging in everything for the welfare of others and actualizing the sphere of bodhisattvas—purified aspiration prayers.

(3) Through being aware of what is allowed and forbidden with regard to food and other such things that are offered out of devotion, they know [the proper] quantities. Therefore, they eat and so on with the intention that it is in order to nurture the countless kinds of organisms that live within their bodies, and {469} in order that their [psychophysical] supports for practicing the dharma remain for a long time.

(4) Since they are endowed with mindfulness during the first and the last third [of the night], they relinquish attachment to hustle and bustle. Thus, they make efforts in the yogas that purify the obscurations, such as familiarizing with repulsiveness and the immeasurables.

(5) In all that they engage in or avoid (such as what is to be adopted and rejected in terms of their three doors), they should never be free from the guard of alertness. Thus, they delight in remaining in alertness with regard to performing what is suitable and relinquishing what is not suitable.

Furthermore, those on the path of accumulation attain the qualities of this stage, that is, **the** [five] **visions** and **the** five **supernatural knowledges.** The final special result [of the path of accumulation] is to attain **the samādhi of the stream of dharma.** This means that one, while not moving from this samādhi, enters the ocean of the buddha realms of the ten directions and comes to hear the genuine dharma from the mouths of this ocean of buddhas. As the *Mahāyānasūtrālaṃkāra* says:

Then, within the stream of dharma,
Vast instructions are received
From the buddhas in order to attain
Vast calm abiding and wisdom.[636]

1.5.1.7. Its function

During its lesser, medium, and great [levels], one mentally engages in the four or two realities
And turns away from the four mistakennesses or reification.
One relinquishes antagonistic factors, and generates and increases virtuous dharmas.
The eight conceptions are relinquished and one-pointed samādhi is performed.

When explained according to their order, the functions **during the lesser, medium, and great** [levels of the path of accumulation] are as follows. On the lesser path of accumulation, the function of the four foundations of mindfulness is that the śrāvakas **mentally engage in the four realities** of the noble ones and **turn** their minds **away from the four mistakennesses.** The followers of the mahāyāna mentally engage in the **two** realities and turn their minds away from all **reification.** On the medium path of accumulation, the function of the four correct efforts is that the first two correct efforts **relinquish antagonistic factors, and** the latter two correct efforts **generate and increase virtuous dharmas.** {470} On the great path of accumulation, the function of the four limbs of miraculous powers is to **relinquish the eight** mistaken mundane **conceptions** (such as the conception of desire) **and** to **perform** mastery over **samādhi** in which the mind is **one-pointed.**

1.5.1.8. Teaching its hermeneutical etymology

The hermeneutical etymology is that it is the path of gathering the accumulation of virtue for being a suitable vessel,
Is conducive to liberation, and [represents] confidence and invalidation.

The hermeneutical etymology or the meaning of the term is **that it is the path of gathering** a vast **accumulation of virtue** in order to make one a **suitable vessel** for the arising of the realization of heat [on the path of preparation]. Therefore, it is called "the path of accumulation." It also has the following names. Since one mentally engages in it in a way that **is conducive**

to liberation (that is, nirvāṇa), it is "the roots of virtue that are conducive to liberation." Since one's aspiration for the three jewels and emptiness is powerful, it is the level of **confidence**. It is [also] "the **invalidating** remedy" since the śrāvakas regard the appropriating skandhas as defects (just as a disease or an abscess and so on) and the followers of the mahāyāna regard them to be without nature.

1.5.2. The path of preparation

This has eight parts:

1) Presenting its definition
2) Identifying its instances
3) Classification
4) Determining its nature
5) The features of relinquishment and realization
6) Stating its qualities
7) Its function
8) Teaching its hermeneutical etymology

1.5.2.1. Presenting its definition

> **The path of preparation is the phase of clearly realizing the ultimate.**

The nature of **the path of preparation** is "that which **is** a stepping stone for liberation and consists of **the phase of clearly realizing the ultimate.**"

1.5.2.2. Identifying its instances

> **It is the prajñā that arises from mundane meditation.**

The instances of this path are the relinquishing remedy, that is, **the prajñā that arises from mundane meditation** from the time when the wisdom of heat has arisen until the arising of the path of seeing. {471}

1.5.2.3. Classification

> **There are many classifications, [such as in terms of its] nature, that is, engagement through aspiration and so on.**
> **However, the arising of the heat of wisdom, the peak of shakable roots of virtue,**
> **The attainment of the poised readiness for the profound, and the supreme of mundane dharmas are its four [levels].**

During two of these, respectively, the five faculties and powers are cultivated.

As for the classifications of this path, it can be classified through its **nature, that is,** it can be classified as the level of **engagement through aspiration**, the contaminated path of familiarization, what is conducive to penetration, the practice of engagement, **and so on.**

It can also be classified as two in terms of the classification of accumulation and preparation—[the level] that is both accumulation and preparation and [the level] that is not accumulation, but preparation. The first one of these is the continuity of the path of accumulation that [continues to] exist on the path of preparation. Since the latter one prepares one for the four realities or the two identitylessnesses, it represents preparation, but is not the actual path of accumulation. Therefore, it is [the level] that is not accumulation.

When classified in terms of lesser and great, it can be classified as the lesser, medium, and great path of preparation. The lesser one means that there is no certainty about the time when the path of seeing arises. The medium one refers to this being certain. The great one means that the path of seeing will arise in this lifetime.

Thus, **there are many** categories of **classification. However**, it is the [fourfold] classification through the manners of realization that is most well-known. (1) Just as heat occurs as a foreshadow of the arising of fire through rubbing wooden sticks [against each other, the first level of the path of preparation is called] **heat** because it is the foreshadow of **the arising of** the firelike nonconceptual **wisdom** of the path of seeing. (2) Since [the second level] is **the peak** (that is, the supreme or highest [point]) **of shakable roots of virtue,**[637] [it is called] "peak." The [Sanskrit] equivalent of peak is *mūrdha*,[638] which also means "brief." Thus, it is also said to be something brief or a peak since it does not remain for a long time. (3) Through being unswaying, one **attains the poised readiness for the profound** dharma in a way that is approximately concordant with the path that sees reality. Thus since one is not afraid of emptiness, [this is called] poised readiness. (4) Though there is no cause of similar outcome [in the fourth level that gives rise to the path of seeing], it is still able to induce the path of the noble ones.[639] Therefore, it is **the supreme** among **mundane dharmas**, and is thus [called] the supreme mundane dharma. It functions as the dominant condition for the uncontaminated path of seeing. The *Abhisamayālaṃkāra* says:

> Lesser, medium, and great degrees
> Of heat and so on are more distinguished.[640]

{472} Thus, some followers of the mahāyāna assert that all four[641] [levels of the path of preparation] are threefold, that is, that its classification is twelvefold [altogether]. Accordingly, [their description is as follows].

[During] heat, one meditates by focusing on the dharmas of the four realities through personally experienced wisdom. Through doing so, [there arise] the samādhi (calm abiding) and the prajñā (superior insight), plus the primary minds and mental factors that are congruently associated with these aids, of attaining the lesser [degree of the] clear illumination that consists of the realization that, other than being the inner apprehender (mere mental discourse), something apprehended that consists of outer referents is without nature. [The level of] heat is presented as lesser, medium, and great from the point of view of whether this clear illumination of emptiness and identitylessness [appears] sometimes, most of the time, or even more often and in a clearer way than that. The wisdom of heat is called "the arising of the lesser path of seeing" since a little bit of what was not seen before is seen. In comparison with [the levels of] peak and so on, it is an experience of the most inferior clear [illumination] of emptiness and identitylessness.

[During] peak, through constantly making efforts as before, [there arise] the samādhi and the prajñā, plus their congruently associated aids, of attaining the medium [degree of] clear illumination. This consists of the expanding and increasing, even more than before, of the very illumination that is the realization of the apprehended being without nature. [The level of peak] is [classified as] lesser, medium, and great from the point of view of whether one is aware of this realization of identitylessness sometimes, most of the time, or more often and in a clearer way than that even in one's dreams.

[During] poised readiness, through meditating as before, all that appears as [outer] referents appears as nothing but mind. Therefore, [there arises] the samādhi and prajñā, plus their congruently associated factors, of attaining the great [degree of the] clear illumination. This consists of the relinquishment of the distraction of the apprehended and the attainment of the lesser [degree of the] clear illumination that represents the realization of the apprehender being without nature too. [The level of poised readiness] is [divided into] lesser, medium, and great based on whether one is sometimes fearless of emptiness, most of the time fearless, or always fearless.

[During] the supreme dharma, through meditating as before, immediately after this [level], the path of seeing arises and then one will realize that the apprehender is without nature. {473} Therefore, in terms of the mundane paths, [this level is the samādhi and the prajñā, plus their congruently associated factors, of] attaining the great [degree of the] clear ilumination that the apprehender is without nature. In terms of the supramundane paths, it is the samādhi and the prajñā, plus their congruently associated factors, of attaining the medium [degree] of this [illumination]. The lesser, medium, and great [supreme dharma] represent the realizations that consist of the inferior, medium, and great clear [illumination] that the apprehender is without nature.

Both the higher and the lower abhidharma agree in making the [above] division into the three lesser, [medium,] and great [degrees of] these [four levels of] penetration only for [the level of] poised readiness, but not for the other [three].

As for the nature of the mental [cognitive] aspects of these [four levels], in comparison with the nonconceptual wisdom of the path of seeing, it is conceptual. [However,] in comparison with the ordinary conceptions that apprehend terms and referents, [the nature of these four levels] is nonconceptual direct pereception because it is explained that they represent the clear illumination of the apprehended being without nature.

During two of these four [levels], **respectively, the five faculties and** the five **powers are cultivated.** During the two [levels of] heat and peak, one cultivates the [five] faculties, and during the two [levels of] poised readiness and the supreme dharma, the five powers.

1.5.2.4. Determining its nature

> **It has the distinctive features of that in which it arises, on which it relies, and what it focuses on.**

The determination of the nature of this path has three parts—(1) the [psychophysical] supports **in which it arises**, (2) the grounds **on which it relies**, and (3) the objects **on which it focuses.**

(1) It [can] arise in men and women of the three continents and in the six classes of gods of the desire realm. Once the path of accumulation has been generated in one's mind stream in a former state as a human, [the path of preparation] will arise in one's rebirth as any kind of god in the resire realm. In some [teachings] of the uncommon mahāyāna, there are also explanations that it [can] arise in particular animals, such as nāgas.

(2) As for the grounds on which it relies, the path of preparation of the śrāvakas relies on the six grounds of dhyāna—(1) the not ineffective preparatory stage of the first dhyāna, (2) the ordinary actual [first dhyāna], (3) the special [actual first dhyāna], and (4)–(6) the remaining three actual dhyānas. Here, those who have not previously become free from attachment rely on the [above] preparatory stage of [the first] dhyāna, while those who have become free from attachment with regard to the desire [realm] rely on the actual [dhyānas].

The pratyekabuddhas who practice in groups {474} rely on any one of the six grounds of dhyāna, while the rhinolike ones rely on the actual fourth dhyāna.

As for bodhisattvas, the Vaibhāṣikas say [in the *Abhidharmakośa*]:

> The teacher and the rhinos, up through enlightenment,
> Rely on the last dhyāna and accomplish all in one . . .[642]

Thus, they assert that bodhisattvas rely on the fourth dhyāna. There is also the assertion by some followers of the mahāyāna that [bodhisattvas] rely on any one of the actual four dhyānas.

(3) As for the objects on which [the path of preparation] focuses, the Sautrāntikas say that, [during] the three [levels of] heat, peak, and poised readiness, one focuses on the apprehended being without nature, and [during] the supreme dharma, one focuses on the apprehender being without nature. As for the realization of the apprehended being without nature, its lesser [degree] is the attainment of the illumination that is heat; its medium [degree], the increase of this illumination, which is peak; and its great [degree], the stable realization that is poised readiness.

Some followers of the mahāyāna assert that, through heat [and peak], one realizes that the apprehended is without nature. Through poised readiness and the supreme dharma, one realizes that the apprehender is without nature. Here, the realization that the apprehended within the class of afflicted phenomena is without nature is heat. The realization that the apprehended within the class of purified phenomena is [without nature] is peak. As for the realizations that the apprehender is without nature, poised readiness is the realization that the apprehender which involves the support of a substantially existent person is without nature. The supreme dharma is the realization that the apprehender which involves the support of an imputedly existent individual is [without nature]. This accords with the *Abhisamayālaṃkāra* saying:

> The conceptions about the apprehended are twofold
> In terms of entities and their remedies,
> Each of which is subdivided into nine
> Based on ignorance, skandhas, and so on.
>
> Likewise, those about the apprehender are asserted as twofold,
> Based on substance and imputation
> In terms of the nature of an independent self and so on,
> And what is based on the skandhas and so on.[643]

You may wonder, "To which [category of] mental states do these [four] penetrations belong?" They consist primarily of the self-awareness with which one has familiarized oneself through the three prajñās [of studying, reflecting, and meditating], just as in the example of the self-awareness of being familiar with desire and so on. {475}

1.5.2.5. The features of relinquishment and realization

> **The imputational obscurations are relinquished through**
> **suppressing them.**
> **Through realization, one engages in the principle of the two**
> **identitylessnesses.**

The imputational afflictive and cognitive **obscurations are relinquished** in the manner of **suppressing them.** In terms of the realities, one realizes that one half of phenomenal identity—the apprehended—is without nature.

Also, some followers of the mahāyāna assert that the realizations through the paths of preparation of the three yānas are as follows. The śrāvakas realize through heat and peak that the apprehended [aspect] of personal identity is without nature. Through poised readiness and supreme dharma, they realize [the same for] the apprehending [aspect] of personal identity. The pratyekabuddhas realize through heat and peak, respectively, that the apprehended [aspects] of personal identity and phenomenal identity are without nature. Through poised readiness and the supreme dharma, respectively, they realize [the same for] the apprehending [aspects] of each of these two identities. Bodhisattvas realize through [both] heat and peak that the apprehended [aspects] of both personal and phenomenal identity are without nature. Through [both] poised readiness and supreme dharma, they **realize** [the same for] the apprehending [aspects] **of the two identities.**

Noble Nāgārjuna does not assert any difference in the realization of identitylessness between the paths of preparation of all three yānas, only [some] differences in the means and the clear or unclear [illumination] of the respective focal objects of the four penetrations. The prajñāpāramitā sūtras [say] that also those who train in the path of the śrāvakas should train in this pāramitā of prajñā.[644] The *[Prajñāpāramitā]saṃcayagāthā* says:

> As for those who think, "I shall become a śrāvaka of the Sugata"
> And those who wish to become pratyekabuddhas or, likewise,
> dharma kings
> Without relying on this poised readiness, they cannot attain [their
> respective goals].[645]

Thus, this is the intention of what is described in the intermediate and large discourses [of these sūtras].

1.5.2.6. Stating its qualities

> **It is endowed with the qualities of not being severed, not falling, and so on.**

The *Mahāyānasūtrālaṃkāra* says:

> In those who attain peak, the roots [of virtue] are not severed.
> Those who attain poised readiness do not fall into the lower realms and so on.[646]

The *Ratnameghasūtra* {476} says that one is liberated from the degenerations of ordinary beings and **endowed with the qualities of** samādhis, dhāraṇīs, liberations, supernatural knowledges, **and so on**. The mother [sūtras] and the *[Abhisamay]ālaṃkāra* say that those with sharp faculties attain the signs of being irreversible from perfect enlightenment.

1.5.2.7. Its function

> **It relinquishes clinging to identity and generates the realization of the first [bhūmi].**

The prajñā that originates from mundane meditation (said four factors conducive to penetration) **relinquishes** the fourfold mistakenness[647] of **clinging to** personal and phenomenal **identities and generates the realization of** the path of seeing, that is, **the first** bhūmi.

1.5.2.8. Teaching its hermeneutical etymology

> **The hermeneutical etymologies are what is conducive to penetration, engagement through aspiration,**
> **And preparing for the direct realization of the ultimate.**

Since the firelike nonconceptual wisdom of the path of seeing overcomes and penetrates all mistaken conceptions of ordinary beings at their root, the actual penetration refers to the path of seeing. Since [the path of preparation] is conducive to that, it is called "**what is conducive to penetration.**" Since one engages in the poised readiness for the nature of phenomena through the power of aspiring for it, [this path is called] "the level of **engagement through**

aspiration." Through cutting through the conceptions of apprehender and apprehended in one's own mind stream, the prajñā that arises from mundane meditation **prepares for** the first supramundane bhūmi (the path of seeing), which is **the direct realization of the ultimate** dharmadhātu. Since this is the path on which [such happens], it is [called] "the path of preparation." These **are the hermeneutical etymologies.** In a [more] general sense, engagement through aspiration is explained as [referring to] both [the paths of] accumulation and preparation.

1.5.3. The path of seeing

This has eight parts:

1) Presenting its definition
2) Identifying its instances
3) Classification
4) Determining its nature
5) The features of relinquishment and realization
6) Stating its qualities
7) Its function
8) Teaching its hermeneutical etymology

1.5.3.1. Presenting its definition

> **The path of seeing newly sees true reality.**

{477} It is a basis for progressing towards nirvāṇa and consists of the phase of **newly** and clearly realizing **true reality.**

1.5.3.2. Identifying its instances

> **It is that which is associated with the congruent factors of**
> **supra[mundane] calmness and superior [insight].**

The instances of the path of seeing are the remedies that relinquish certain factors, that is, the direct seeing of the true nature of phenomena—the four realities being without any identity. **It is associated with the congruent factors of supra**mundane **calm** abiding **and superior** insight.

1.5.3.3. Classification

> **In its own nature, it is indivisible.**
> **One mainly trains in the seven branches of enlightenment.**

When [this path] is classified through its supports, that is, the persons [in whom it arises], it is twofold in terms of approachers and abiders. When classified through the yānas, there are the three paths of seeing of śrāvakas, pratyekabuddhas, and bodhisattvas. When classified through its nature, it can be classified into sixteen moments and so on, but [all of] these are made in adaptation to the śrāvakas. Since the **own nature** of the path of seeing consists of a single moment, **it is indivisible.** On this path, **one trains in the seven branches of enlightenment**, such as correct mindfulness.

1.5.3.4. Determining its nature

This has two parts:

1) The presentation of the way in which the factors to be relinquished through seeing are relinquished
2) The presentation of the way in which the path of seeing arises

1.5.3.4.1. The presentation of the way in which the factors to be relinquished through seeing are relinquished

> **It is asserted that the factors to be relinquished through seeing**
> **(Eighty-eight, ninety-four, 112[648] and so on)**
> **Are relinquished through concurrence with ceasing or arising, or through the arising of nondual wisdom.**

The determination of the nature of this path has three parts:

1) The definition of the factors to be relinquished
2) Classification of the factors to be relinquished
3) The way in which the factors to be relinquished are relinquished

1.5.3.4.1.1. The definition of the factors to be relinquished

In general, the definition of mere affliction is "that which greatly agitates the mind stream." In particular, the definition of **the factors to be relinquished through seeing** is "that which greatly agitates the mind stream through imputation."

1.5.3.4.1.2. Classification of the factors to be relinquished

This has two parts:

1) The classification of their nature
2) The classification of the way of relinquishment

1.5.3.4.1.2.1. The classification of their nature

This is twofold—primary afflictions and secondary afflictions. If the primary afflictions have been relinquished, {478} the secondary afflictions are automatically relinquished. Therefore, [only] the first are explained [here]. They are the six of desire, anger, pride, ignorance, doubt, and view. View is fivefold—the views about a real personality, the views about extremes, wrong views, the views to hold a view as paramount, and the views to hold ethics and spiritual discipline as paramount.

1.5.3.4.1.2.2. The classification of the way of relinquishment

[This classification] is twofold in terms of the factors to be relinquished through seeing and the factors to be relinquished through familiarization, [but this section deals only with] the first [factors to be relinquished]. In the system of the Vaibhāṣikas, these are asserted as **eighty-eight**. The *Abhidharmakośa* says:

> They are ten, seven, seven, and eight,
> Excluding three or two views, respectively.
> Suffering and so on in the desire [realm]
> Are relinquished through seeing in due order.[649]

The *Viniścayasaṃgrahaṇī*[650] explains **ninety-four** factors to be relinquished through seeing. The *Abhidharmasamuccaya*[651] explains that, in the desire realm, there are ten [factors to be relinquished through seeing], that is, the [above] five afflictions and the five that make up view. Since these [ten] engage in the four realities [of the noble ones], there are forty [altogether]. In the two higher realms, there is no anger. Thus, there are nine [factors to be relinquished through seeing] in each [of these two realms]. Since these [factors too] engage in the four realities, there are four times nine, that is, thirty-six in each [realm]. The two sets of these sum up to seventy-two, which makes a total of **112**.

It may be said, "However, if there is no form [in the formless realm], the fourfold[652] [view of] holding ethics and spiritual conduct as paramount that apprehends physical and verbal conducts as the causes for becoming pure and liberated is not tenable. Therefore, the factors to be relinquished through seeing are 108." This is not[653] the case. For in the [formless realm], though there is indeed no apprehending of physical and verbal conducts as the causes for becoming pure and liberated, there exists the apprehension that one's view is the cause for one's own liberation, which is a concern in the form of holding ethics and spiritual discipline as paramount. "If it were like this, would this not represent [the view of] holding a view as paramount?" No, it would not be [this view]—the aspect of holding a view as paramount is to apprehend it as being paramount, primary, and such, whereas the aspect of holding ethics and spiritual discipline as paramount is to apprehend [the process of] becoming pure and liberated. Therefore, their modes of apprehension are dissimilar.

It may be said, "[The realities of] suffering and its origin are contained in the three realms, but [the realities of] the uncontaminated cessation and path are not contained in them. Therefore, it is not tenable to present 'the cessations and paths of each of the three realms.'" {479} There is no mistake in this for the following reasons. The *Viniścayasaṃgrahaṇī* explains that this is [presented] in terms of the three realms. Since the suffering [of the desire realm] and its origin (the factors [of the desire realm] to be relinquished) are something within the desire realm, the cessation of this suffering including its causes is labeled as "the cessation of the desire realm." The means to manifest this [cessation] are labeled as "the path of the desire realm." The cessations and paths of the two higher realms are labeled in the same way. It may be objected, "However, it is contradictory that the *Abhidharmasamuccaya* explains 112 factors to be relinquished through seeing and the *Viniścayasaṃgrahaṇī*, ninety-four." Here, some [scholars] say that these represent the systems of the Yogacārās and the Sautrāntikas, respectively. However since these [two] presentations [actually] are a more subtle and a more coarse one, it is better to explain them as representing the intentions of different sūtras.

1.5.3.4.1.3. The way in which the factors to be relinquished are relinquished
The śrāvakas **assert that** the [factors to be relinquished through seeing] **are relinquished through** a path **concurrent with ceasing.**[654] The *Abhidharmakośa* [says]:

> Through the path concurrent with ceasing,
> Its obscurations are relinquished.[655]

The common yāna [slightly] changes the reading of this [verse]:

> Through the path concurrent with arising,
> Its obscurations are relinquished.

Thus, it asserts that [said factors to be relinquished through seeing] are relinquished through the remedy that is a path concurrent with **arising.**

The uncommon mahāyāna says that, ultimately, factors to be relinquished and their remedies are not established. Therefore, both [their] arising and ceasing are **not** tenable. This accords with the *Abhisamayālaṃkāra* saying:

> There is nothing to be removed in this
> And not the slightest to be added.[656]

The *Bodhicaryāvatāra* says:

> When phenomena are empty in this way,
> What is there to gain and what to lose?[657]

Even if this is examined on [the level of] the seeming, it is not asserted that the remedies relinquish the factors to be relinquished for the following reason. When the factors to be relinquished exist, the remedies do not exist, and once the remedies have arisen, the factors to be relinquished have ceased. Therefore, there is no meeting of nonsimultaneous phenomena. From the perspective of a mental state that does not examine [this], **the arising of wisdom** is labeled with the conventional expression "the factors to be relinquished have been relinquished," just as in the case of the [two] beams of a scale rising up and sinking down [simultaneously]. {480}

1.5.3.4.2. The presentation of the way in which the path of seeing arises

> **It has four distinctive features: arising, relying, manner of realization, and moments.**

The way in which the path of seeing arises has four parts:

1) The [psychophysical] supports in which it arises
2) The grounds on which it relies
3) The manners of realization
4) [The issue] of in how many moments it arises

1.5.3.4.2.1. The [psychophysical] supports in which it arises

It [can] **arise** in men and women of the three continents and in gods of the desire realm since they are of sharp faculties and possess the Buddha's scriptures, while their weariness [of saṃsāra] is great. It does not arise in [beings of] the three lower realms since they are obscured by great obscurations of karmic maturation, and also not in [beings of the continent of] Uttarakuru and the two higher realms since they lack weariness.

1.5.3.4.2.2. The grounds on which it relies

The path of seeing of the śrāvakas **relies** on any of the six grounds of dhyāna. Here, if one has not previously become free from attachment, one relies on the preparatory stage of the first dhyāna. If one has [such freedom from attachment], one relies on the actual dhyānas. One does not rely on the grounds of the desire [realm] since the path of seeing is accompanied by the congruent factors of calm abiding and superior insight, whereas calm abiding is weak and distraction is predominant on the grounds of the desire [realm]. One also does not rely on the formless [absorptions] since their superior insight is minor.

If one makes efforts in the preparatory stages of the second dhyāna and so on, it is certainly possible that [the path of seeing] can be developed [on the basis of these]. However, it is difficult to develop [it] since their calm abiding is minor. It may be objected, "In this case, the same is true for the preparatory stage of the first dhyāna." It is not the same for the following reason. The arising of the path of seeing must rely on the state of mind of an actual dhyāna. However, if one does not attain [any of these] actual [dhyānas], just the preparatory stage of the first [dhyāna] is easier [to cultivate than the one of the second dhyāna. Thus,] one does not rely on the preparatory stage of the second [dhyāna] since it is sufficient to rely on the actual first [dhyāna], which is easier than that.

The pratyekabuddhas who practice in groups rely on any of the six grounds of dhyāna, and the rhinolike ones rely on the actual fourth dhyāna. It may be objected [to the latter], "However, [there is] the explanation that the rhinolike ones, after they have died, are reborn in the desire realm only. This is then not reasonable because, [through relying on the fourth dhyāna,] they have relinquished the afflictions of the third dhyāna and below." There is no mistake in this since [such pratyekabuddhas] are not reborn through karma, but through aspiration prayers.

Bodhisattvas {481} rely on the very pure fourth dhyāna. They do not rely on the preparatory stages since they have attained the samādhi of the stream of dharma before.

1.5.3.4.2.3. The manners of realization

In the system of the common yāna, the śrāvakas **realize** that the objects [in question]—the four realities—lack any personal identity. Here, their focus is not on the realities that are [mere] presentations [in texts], but they focus on the specifically characterized phenomena that are called "the realities which are presented [in texts]." The pratyekabuddhas realize that the apprehended [aspects] of personal and phenomenal identitylessness are without nature. Bodhisattvas realize both identitylessnesses. In the uncommon system of the mahāyāna, the mother [sūtras] say:

> Also those who wish to train in the bhūmis of the śrāvakas should train in this pāramitā of prajñā.[658]

In following this and other such statements, noble Nāgārjuna and his spiritual heirs do not assert differences in the realizations of identitylessness by all three bearers of the disposition.

1.5.3.4.2.4. The issue of in how many moments it arises

This has two parts:

1) [The system of] the common yāna
2) The uncommon system

1.5.3.4.2.4.1. The system of the common yāna

The *Abhidharmakośa* says:

> From the supreme mundane dharma
> [Comes] the uncontaminated dharma readiness
>
> With regard to the suffering of the desire [realm].
> From that [comes] the dharma cognition with regard to this [suffering].
> Likewise, the subsequent readiness and cognition with regard to the remaining sufferings [follow].
> The same applies to the three [other] realities.[659]

Accordingly, the Vaibhāṣikas assert that, right after the supreme dharma [of the path of preparation], [there follow] four moments—the poised readiness for the dharma cognition with regard to the [reality of] suffering of the desire [realm], the dharma cognition with regard to this, then the poised readiness for the subsequent cognition with regard to the [reality of] suffering of the higher realms, and the subsequent cognition with regard to this. The same [pattern] applies to the three remaining realities. Thus, it is the uncontaminated prajñās of these sixteen **moments** that see the [four] realities. The *Abhidharmakośa* says:

> In due order, poised readinesses and cognitions
> Are the uninterrupted paths and the [paths] of liberation.
> Since the [first] fifteen moments among these
> See what has not been seen, they are the path of seeing.
> . . .
> In the sixteenth, one abides in its result.[660]

{482} Accordingly, the eight poised readinesses are the uninterrupted paths since they sever the attainment that consists of the factors to be relinquished through seeing. The eight cognitions are the paths of liberation since they experience the attainment of the freedom [from these factors to be relinquished]. Their [first] fifteen moments are the actual path of seeing, while the sixteenth is its result and has a continuum. Therefore, it represents [the beginning of] the path of familiarization.

In the Madhyamaka system of the mahāyāna, within seeing the nature of phenomena in its omnipresence, there are no divisions in terms of any [subsequent] new seeing that is of a different type [than the earlier seeing]. From this perspective, the path of seeing is presented as being [a single] moment. However, in terms of the manner in which it cuts through superimpositions and its manner of enhancement, it has sixteen moments. Here, the four dharma readinesses are the uninterrupted paths that relinquish the factors to be relinquished through seeing, that is, the sufferings contained in the levels of [all] three realms. The four dharma cognitions are the paths of liberation on which these [factors] have been relinquished. The four subsequent readinesses are the uninterrupted paths that cut through the superimpositions of apprehending these [dharma readinesses and dharma cognitions] as some [factors] that are not the causes for the future qualities of noble ones. The four subsequent cognitions are the paths of liberation on which these [superimpositions] have been relinquished.

[Haribhadra's] *Aṣṭasāhasrikāprajñāpāramitāvyākhyā*[661] says that it is a single moment in terms of the result, that is, clear realization. However, through eliminating wrong ideas about each one of the [four] realities, it has sixteen moments. The *Mumimatālaṃkāra* says that the dharma poised readiness with regard to suffering is the path of seeing that fully qualifies as such, and that the other [moments] are nominal. Others assert that, through the different degrees of [beings'] faculties, any number of moments from one to sixteen that is individually suitable may arise. Through the intention of the *Abhidharmasamuccaya*, it is clear that the sixteen moments arise in due order in an uninterrupted way since anything else would be contradictory to the difference between approacher and abider, the boundary lines between [different] faculties, and so on.

Here, [the term] "moment" [is understood as the time that it takes] to complete the activity of a certain path. This is what is referred to as a moment. Thus, it refers to a moment [as the time that it takes to] complete an activity.

1.5.3.4.2.4.2. The uncommon system

It is taught, "In actual fact, bodhisattvas attain poised readiness for the dharma of nonarising." {483} Therefore, it is not asserted that, ultimately, the path of seeing arises. A sūtra says:

> Nonarising is the single reality.
> Some call this "four realities."
> Once one abides in the heart of enlightenment, not even a single
>   reality
> Is seen to be established, so how could four?

The *Yuktiṣaṣṭikā* says:

> Right upon dharma cognition,
> If there were a distinction in it,

Then those unlearned people
Who think that even very subtle entities
Arise through something
Would not see the actuality of origination through conditions.[662]

You may wonder, "So what is the point of the explanations in the sūtras that the path of seeing arises as one single moment, sixteen [moments], and so on?" These [explanations were given] with the intention to take care of the realists. Here, the basis of this intention is dependent origination. The purpose is to introduce those who cling to entities [into dependent origination]. The invalidation of the explicit statement is stated in the *Mūlamadhyamakakārikā*:

Not from themselves, not from something other,
Not from both, and not without a cause—
At any place and any time,
All entities lack arising.[663]

Thus, [also the arising of the path of seeing] is refuted through the negation of arising in the four possible ways. Furthermore, if one analyzes in how many moments the path of seeing arises, one also has to analyze in how many [moments] it ceases. Thus, this becomes extremely absurd. As the *Mūlamadhyamakakārikā* says:

If you think, "I see
Origin and cessation,"
Origin and cessation
Are seen through stupidity.[664]

You may wonder, "Is this arising in dependence not an arising?" The *Anavatapta[nāgarāja]paripṛccha[sūtra]* says:

What arises in dependence does not arise.
It does not have the nature of arising.
What depends on conditions is emptiness.
Those who know emptiness are conscientious.

[In his *Śūnyatāsaptati*,] noble Nāgārjuna says:

"In dependence on that, this originates."
This way of talking of the world is not negated.

> What is dependent origination is without nature. {484}
> So how could one be certain about its existence?[665]

and [in his *Mūlamadhyamakakārikā*]:

> Because there is no phenomenon
> That is not dependent origination,
> Therefore, there is no phenomenon
> That is not emptiness.[666]

Since there are extensive other statements like these, all phenomena are without arising.

1.5.3.5. The features of relinquishment and realization

> **Suchness is realized directly and variety, as it is appropriate.**

The seeds of the factors to be relinquished through seeing are relinquished at their root. The actuality of the **suchness** of the nature of phenomena **is realized directly and** also the actuality of the **variety** of the bearers of this nature is realized **as it is appropriate.** This corresponds to what the *Mahāyānasūtrālaṃkāra* says:

> They directly perceive the dharmadhātu
> Free from the characteristic of duality.[667]

1.5.3.6. Stating its qualities

> **There is freedom from the five fears and the qualities are twelve hundred.**

Those on the path of seeing are **free from the five fears**, such as [the fear of] the lower realms.[668] They attain the powers that arise during subsequent attainment, that is, **the twelve** times **hundred qualities**, such as attaining one hundred samādhis and so on. However since they still have the factor of an innate "me" and self, they [also] have the innate latencies for the afflictions that arise from this. Therefore, it is asserted that they lack any reification of anything whatsoever, but still may have momentary scares, such as a person who is scared of a pile of snow. Likewise, when they are distracted, they even have subtle imputational factors of being frightened of falling into saṃsāra or of wishing to be famous. However, these [emotions] are not as massive as in ordinary beings because they return to instantaneous mindfulness and thus do not have to rely on any remedies.

In brief, it is taught, "Once the path of seeing is attained, conceptions [still] arise, but they are terminated and mastered through wisdom in the second moment. Therefore, from then onwards, one progresses on the path through the impetus [of this] without needing any efforts. This is similar to the progressive flight of an arrow through the impetus [caused by] one's fingers." {485}

1.5.3.7. Its function

> **One is released from [saṃsāric] existence and subdues the ground of nirvāṇa.**

The factors to be relinquished [here] (the imputational afflictions) are all relinquished and the causes that cast one into saṃsāra are terminated. Therefore, **one is released from [saṃsāric] existence and subdues the ground of** the total relinquishment of saṃsāra, that is, **nirvāṇa.**

1.5.3.8. Teaching its hermeneutical etymology

> **The hermeneutical etymologies are uncontaminated virtue, relinquishing remedy,**
> **First generation, and the direct seeing of the freedom from reference points.**

[Since this path] serves as the remedy for contaminated entities, it is called "**uncontaminated virtue.**" Since it relinquishes the afflictions that are factors to be relinquished through seeing at their root, it is [called] "**relinquishing remedy.**" Since it is the beginning of the dharmas of noble ones, it is also [called] "the **first generation** of the supramundane mind." Since it is the path of **directly seeing** the reality of the noble ones that was never seen before (the nature of phenomena **free from reference points**), it is called "the path of seeing." These are the meanings of its hermeneutical etymologies.

You may wonder, "However, how does it differ from the realization during the path of preparation before?" The realization of the path of seeing consists of directly seeing the specifically characterized nature of phenomena [as such], whereas the realization of the path of preparation consists of realizing a mere fraction of the nature of phenomena that is partially concordant with said [actual nature of phenomena].

1.5.4. The path of familiarization

This has eight parts:

1) Presenting its definition
2) Identifying its instances
3) Classification
4) Determining its nature
5) The features of relinquishment and realization
6) Stating its qualities
7) Its function
8) Teaching its hermeneutical etymology

1.5.4.1. Presenting its definition

> **The path of familiarization is the phase of becoming familiar with what is special.**

The definition of **the path of familiarization is** "that which is a stepping stone for liberation and consists of **the phase of** having to **become familiar with special** samādhis."

1.5.4.2. Identifying its instances

> **One makes one's mind stream accustomed to what has been directly realized.**

The instances of this path are the remedies that relinquish everything. {486} This means that **one makes one's mind stream accustomed to**, and familiarizes with, this very actuality of the nature of phenomena **that has been directly realized** through the path of seeing.

1.5.4.3. Classification

This has two parts:

1) The mundane path of familiarization
2) The supramundane path of familiarization

1.5.4.3.1. The mundane path of familiarization

> **The contaminated path of familiarization is to be understood from what was explained above.**

The contaminated mundane **path of familiarization** is pointed out through **what was explained above** in the chapter that explicates the brahmayāna[669] and **is to be understood from** there. It is not described here.

1.5.4.3.2. The supramundane path of familiarization

> **The uncontaminated path beyond [requires] the supports of śrāvakas, pratyekabuddhas, and bodhisattvas.**
> **It [consists of] four paths: preparation, uninterrupted,**
> **Liberation, and special. Its nature is lesser, medium, and great.**
> **The classification [through] familiarity in equipoise and attainment is twofold.**
> **One has to train in the eightfold path of the noble ones.**

When **the path of familiarization** with the **uncontaminated** [state] **beyond** misery [(nirvāṇa)] is classified, [there] are five [ways of classifying it]—(1) classification through its [psychophysical] **supports**, (2) classification through the factors to be relinquished, (3) classification through the paths, (4) classification through its nature, and (5) classification through familiarization.

(1) The first is threefold—the paths of familiarization **of śrāvakas, pratyekabuddhas, and bodhisattvas.**

(2) The classification through the factors to be relinquished means that the number of remedies corresponds to the 144 factors to be relinquished through familiarization.

(3) The classification through the **paths** is **four**fold—the path of **preparation**, the **uninterrupted** path, the path of liberation, **and** the **special** path.

(4) The classification through **its nature** is threefold—the **lesser, medium, and great** path of familiarization.

(5) **The classification through familiarization is twofold**, that is, familiarizing **through** meditative **equipoise and** subsequent **attainment.**

During the phase [of the path of familiarization], **one has to train in the eightfold path of the noble ones**, such as correct view.

1.5.4.4. Determining its nature

> **The 414 factors to be relinquished through familiarization are relinquished through their remedies.**
> **It has the distinctive features of support, ground, and focus.**

The teaching on the nature of this path {487} has two parts:

1) The way in which the factors to be relinquished through familiarization are relinquished
2) The way in which the path of familiarization arises

1.5.4.4.1. The way in which the factors to be relinquished through familiarization are relinquished

This has three parts:

1) The definition of the factors to be relinquished through familiarization
2) Their classification
3) The way in which they are relinquished through their remedies

(1) The definition of **the factors to be relinquished through familiarization** is "that which greatly agitates the mind through the innate [clinging to] identity."

(2) Their classification is as follows. [In the mahāyāna, there are] six innate afflictions in the desire realm. Since there is no anger in the two higher realms, there are five [innate afflictions] in each one of their eight levels (the first dhyāna and so on), that is, forty altogether. Through adding these to the above [six of the desire realm, there are] forty-six. They are [each] divided into great, medium, and lesser [degrees], and these [degrees] are again each [subdivided] into the greater of the great and so on. Since [the forty-six mentioned are thus divided into] nine each, the grand total of [the afflictive factors to be relinquished through familiarization] is **414**.

(3) The way in which they **are relinquished through their remedies** is to be understood in the same way as it was explained for the path of seeing.

1.5.4.4.2. The way in which the path of familiarization arises

[This path] **has the three features** of (1) the [psychophysical] **supports** in which it arises, (2) the **grounds** on which it relies, and (3) the objects on which it **focuses.**

(1) It [can] arise in men and women of the three continents and in the gods (except for those without discrimination and those on the Peak of Existence) because these are meritorious [psychophysical] supports. [As for other beings,] obscurations are predominant in the three lower realms and Uttarakuru, as well as in neuters and hermaphrodites. The [gods] without discrimination do not have a clear mind, and those on the Peak of Existence do not regard the higher realms [below them] as peaceful. Therefore, [the path of familiarization] does not arise in them.

(2) The path of familiarization of the śrāvakas [can] rely on nine [grounds]—the four actual dhyānas, the preparatory stage of the first dhyāna, its actual special [form], and the three formless resultant states. The reasons why they do not rely on other [grounds] are as follows. The mind of the desire realm is not workable, while the mind of the Peak of Existence is not clear. Since the preparatory stages of [both] the three remaining dhyānas and the [other] three formless [absorptions] entail efforts to attain something higher, their calm abiding is weak, and calm abiding and superior insight do not become united through their power. Therefore, [śrāvakas] do not rely on [any of] them.

As for the path of familiarization of the pratyekabuddhas, {488} those who practice in groups rely on any of the six [grounds of] dhyāna, and the rhino-like ones rely on the actual fourth dhyāna.

The path of familiarization of bodhisattvas relies on the very pure fourth dhyāna. However, as for the levels of their rebirths, through karma and aspiration prayers, they are only born in the two realms of desire and form, but not in the formless [realm]. When they train their proficiency in samādhi, that is, when they engage in such absorptions as the lion's sport and crossing in one leap, they [also use] the formless absorptions and [the meditative absorption of] cessation.

(3) As for the objects on which [the path of familiarization] focuses, in the common yāna, after the path of seeing, one familiarizes oneself with calm abiding and superior insight that are associated with their congruent factors and focus on the true nature of the four realities. In the uncommon mahāyāna, one familiarizes oneself in such a way that the nature of phenomena which was realized on the path of seeing and the wisdom [that realized it] become connected with all phenomena.

1.5.4.5. The features of relinquishment and realization

> **One mainly relinquishes the cognitive obscurations and clearly realizes the nature of phenomena.**

[In general,] the remaining fetters that one was not able to relinquish through the path of seeing are the factors to be relinquished through familiarization that are gradually relinquished. In particular, the followers of the mahāyāna **mainly** and foremost **relinquish the cognitive obscurations.** As it is said in *the Mahāyānasūtrālaṃkāra*:

> After the afflictions to be relinquished through seeing
> Have all been completely relinquished,
> In order to relinquish the cognitive obscurations,
> One applies oneself to familiarization.[670]

Haribhadra says [in his *Aṣṭasāhasrikāprajñāpāramitāvyākhyā*]:

> Because one focuses on what is not different from the entity that was perceived through the path of seeing as explained . . .[671]

Accordingly, [the path of familiarization] is approximately concordant with the path of seeing, that is, the direct **realization** of **the nature of phenomena.** [Such relinquishment and realization] are essentially [the results] of the supramundane path of familiarization, whereas the mundane path [of familiarization] produces its results within saṃsāra. Therefore, it is [even] inferior to the path of seeing.

1.5.4.6. Stating its qualities

> **Special qualities increase further.**

{489} What consists of the clear realizations subsequent [to the path of seeing] and the **special qualities** of the ten bhūmis **increase further** and further.

1.5.4.7. Its function

> **It frees from latent obscurations and makes one gradually progress through the ten bhūmis.**

Through relinquishing the factors to be relinquished—all innate and **latent** afflictive and cognitive **obscurations**—at their root, **it makes the** supramundane **ten bhūmis** manifest. Up through the seventh bhūmi, there is [still] a danger for those with the most inferior faculties to regress to some inferior form of enlightenment. Therefore, these are the impure bhūmis. Since one does not regress [in this way] from the eighth bhūmi onward, the [remaining bhūmis] are the pure ones.

1.5.4.8. Teaching its hermeneutical etymology

> **The hermeneutical etymology is to make oneself familiar with realization.**

The hermeneutical etymology is as follows. Since it is the path of **making oneself familiar with** familiarizing with the true reality that was **realized** on the path of seeing, it is called "the path of familiarization." Since it is uncontaminated, it is called "uncontaminated roots of virtue." Since it is the remedy that relinquishes through familiarization, it is also [called] "relinquishing remedy."

1.5.5. The path of completion

This has eight parts:

1) Presenting its definition
2) Identifying its instances
3) Classification
4) Determining its nature
5) The features of relinquishment and realization

6) Stating its qualities
7) Its function
8) Teaching its hermeneutical etymology

1.5.5.1. Presenting its definition

> **The path of completion is the clear realization of the final object of familiarization.**

The definition of **the path of completion** is "that which **is** the basis for actualizing nirvāṇa and consists of the phase of **clearly realizing the final object of familiarization.**"

1.5.5.2. Identifying its instances

> **Its instances are the vajra samādhi at the end of the continuum, All-Illumination, and so on.**

The **instances** of this path—the remedy that fully completes relinquishment—**are** the following. **The end of the continuum** of the ten bhūmis—**the vajra**like **samādhi**—relinquishes even the [most subtle] afflictive [obscurations], which are as if they dwell {490} deep under one's skin and within one's marrow, and the most subtle cognitive obscurations. Thereafter, one dwells on the eleventh [bhūmi, called] **All-Illumination** (the buddhabhūmi).

1.5.5.3. Classification

> **It is classified through the three yānas, the two paths, the three levels, and so on.**
> **The ten dharmas of nonlearning consist of the uncontaminated five skandhas.**

Its **classification through the yānas** is **three**fold—the paths of nonlearning of śrāvakas, pratyekabuddhas, and bodhisattvas. It can [also] be classified [in terms of] **the two paths** (the uninterrupted path and [the path] of liberation), **the three levels** ([the level of] the dharmas of nonlearning, the level of realizing what had to be done, and [the level] of [all] obscurations having been relinquished),[672] **and so on.** Furthermore, both the knowledge that the termination of the afflictions [indeed] represents [their] termination and the knowledge that no further arising of suffering [indeed] means no further arising [of suffering] are also distinctive features of the path of nonlearning.

During these phases, there exist **the ten dharmas of nonlearning**—(1)-(8) the final eightfold path of the noble ones (from the correct view of nonlearning up through the correct samādhi of nonlearning), (9) the perfect mind of nonlearning that is utterly liberated, and (10) the perfect prajñā of nonlearning that is utterly liberated. These ten dharmas of nonlearning are [presented] in terms of **the five uncontaminated skandhas**—(1) the skandha of ethics (the perfect speech, aims of action, and livelihood of nonlearning), (2) the skandha of samādhi (the samādhi and mindfulness [of nonlearning]), (3) the skandha of prajñā (the view, thought, and vigor [of nonlearning]), (4) the skandha of liberation (the mind that is utterly liberated), and (5) the skandha of the vision of the wisdom of liberation (the prajñā of liberation).

1.5.5.4. Determining its nature

> **Its nature [refers to] in what [it arises], on which [it relies], and on what it focuses.**

The determination of the **nature** of this path has three parts—(1) the [psychophysical] supports **in which** it arises, (2) the grounds **on which** it relies, and (3) the objects **on which it focuses.** (1)-(2) In the system of the śrāvakas, the first and the second [point] are the same as in the [corresponding] explanation on the supramundane path of familiarization that was given before. {491} In the system of the common mahāyāna, it is asserted that [the path of nonlearning] arises in the [psychophysical] support of a human body, and especially in the [psychophysical] support of a bodhisattva within the brahman or royal caste in the central country of Jambudvīpa. It arises from the ground that is the vajralike samādhi [which is based on] the fourth dhyāna. The system of the uncommon mahāyāna asserts that [the physical] support [of this path] is a bodhisattva on the tenth bhūmi and that it arises from the dominant condition of the vajralike samādhi [that is based on] the highest form of the utterly pure fourth dhyāna. (3) As for the objects on which [this path] focuses, in the system of the common yāna, through the vajralike samādhi, it focuses on the objects that consist of the four realities, the reality of cessation, or the ten dharmas of nonlearning. In the system of the uncommon mahāyāna, it focuses on the nonabiding nirvāṇa.

1.5.5.5. The features of relinquishment and realization

> **All obstacles are relinquished, and suchness and variety are realized.**

The features of relinquishment and realization of this path are as follows. The **obstacles** for the respective [type of] liberation **are relinquished** without exception. One realizes that the actuality of **suchness**—the nature of phenomena—is pure of all the respective factors to be relinquished. The actuality of **variety is realized** as it is described in the *Abhidharmakośa*:

> Arhats, rhinos, and the teacher, respectively,
> See a dichilio[cosm], a tri[chiliocosm], and countless [cosms].[673]

1.5.5.6. Stating its qualities

> **[It has] common and special inconceivable qualities.**

Limitless **qualities** are attained—the **common** are "arhathood," "termination of contamination," "lack of afflictions," and so on, while the **special** are the powers, the fearlessnesses, the unique [qualities], the knowledge of all aspects, and so on.

1.5.5.7. Its function

> **It manifests the kāyas and wisdoms without exception.**

Its function is that **it** directly **manifests the** three **kāyas and** the four **wisdoms.**

1.5.5.8. Teaching its hermeneutical etymology

> **The hermeneutical etymologies are uncontaminated roots of virtue, the remedy for [saṃsāric] existence,** {492}
> **And having reached the end of progressing and what had to be learned.**

Since [this path] is free from all contaminations, it is called "**uncontaminated roots of virtue.**" Since it causes relinquished afflictions to not arise again, it is [called] "**the remedy for [saṃsāric] existence.**" Since one has **progressed** to the point of completion at which the factors to be relinquished have been relinquished and what is to be known is known, it is [called] "the path of completion." Since one **has reached the end of what had to be learned,** it is also called "the path of nonlearning."

You may wonder, "So why is this called 'path'?" Through the vajralike samādhi, there is something to be relinquished that is to be relinquished in the earlier moment as well as something to be attained that is to be attained in the later moment. Therefore, it is called "the path of completion." On this, in the system of the common yāna, the *Abhidharmakośa* says:

> Because they have power over the attainment
> Of higher and higher states, such as nirvāṇa,
> They are the faculties of making one know everything,
> Knowing everything, and likewise being endowed with knowing everything.[674]

Therefore, [some] say, "That which masters the path of seeing (the faculty of making one know everything unknown) exists on the path of preparation. That which masters the path of familiarization (the faculty of knowing everything) exists on the path of seeing. That which masters the path of completion (the faculty of being endowed with knowing everything) exists on the path of familiarization." However, in the uncommon mahāyāna, the conventional terms of these faculties are not used.

2. Teaching the presentation of the bhūmis

This has three parts:

1) Presenting the bhūmis as twofold
2) Teaching the differences between these two
3) Detailed explanation of the buddhabhūmis

2.1. Presenting the bhūmis as twofold

This has two parts:

1) Brief introduction
2) Detailed explanation

2.1.1. Brief introduction

> **In general, bhūmis are twofold—those of being free from attachment and those of buddhahood.**

The bases that are the supports for the collection of the qualities of noble ones are the **bhūmis. In general**, they **are** presented as **twofold**, called "**the** bhūmis **of being free from** desirous **attachment**" **and** "**the** bhūmis of fully perfect **buddhahood.**" Other names for these [two] are "the bhūmis of śrāvakas and pratyekabuddhas" and "the bhūmis of bodhisattvas," or "the bhūmis of the hīnayāna" and "the bhūmis of the mahāyāna." {493}

2.1.2. Detailed explanation

This has two parts:

1) The bhūmis free from attachment
2) The buddhabhūmis

2.1.2.1. The bhūmis free from attachment

> **They are the bhūmis of the disposition, the eighth, seeing, diminishment, freedom, realization, śrāvakas, and pratyekabuddhas.**

"The bhūmis of freedom from desire" refers primarily to the familiarization with personal identitylessness and the four realities of the noble ones, that is, to the eight bhūmis of the hīnayāna. **They are** called "**the bhūmi of the disposition, the eighth** [bhūmi], [the bhūmis of] **seeing, diminishment, freedom** from desire, **realizing** what had to be done, **śrāvakas, and pratyekabuddhas.**" Therefore, a "mighty lord of the eight bhūmis" has power over these.

Here, at the beginning [of this list], the bhūmi of seeing what is pure is added, and the [bhūmi of] pratyekabuddhas is not counted [separately], as will be explained [below]. According to this way of explaining the eight bhūmis, they are as follows. (1) The first one—"the bhūmi of seeing what is pure"—is the path of accumulation of the śrāvakas because it is the virtue that is conducive to liberation (what is solely pure is liberation, and focusing on it is virtue). (2) The bhūmi of the disposition consists of [the levels of] great poised readiness and the supreme dharma of the path of preparation. For on [the levels of] heat, peak, and below, it is possible to turn to the mahāyāna, and on [the levels of] medium poised readiness and below, it is possible to turn to [the yāna of] the pratyekabuddhas. However, once one has attained [the levels of] great poised readiness and above, one does not turn to other yānas, but one's disposition is definite as the one of a śrāvaka or a pratyekabuddha, [respectively]. (3) The eighth bhūmi refers to approaching stream-enterers (the approachers toward the first fruition [of the śrāvaka path], which is the eighth [bhūmi] when counted backward from arhathood). (4) The bhūmi of seeing is the [actual] fruition of a stream-enterer because one directly sees the [sixteen] aspects of the four realities. (5) The bhūmi of diminishment is the fruition of a [once-]returner because the afflictions of the desire [realm] have been relinquished for the most part. (6) The bhūmi of freedom from desire is the fruition of a nonreturner because one is free from desire for the desire [realm]. (7) The bhūmi of realizing what had to be done is the fruition that is arhathood—{494} it is the path of the direct realization of the four realities. (8) The bhūmi of śrāvakas is either [regarded as] the bhūmi that is the basis for this classification or it is [taken as including] the remaining three approachers (such as approaching [once-]returners). For the other clear realizations of the śrāvakas are taught by the other names [above], and thus this general name is understood as [referring to these] particular ones [of their realizations].

The bhūmi of the pratyekabuddhas is as follows. One wishes that oneself alone will become enlightened [through] the thirty-seven dharmas concordant with enlightenment. Through such a generation of the mindset [of pratyekabuddhas], one gathers the accumulations (such as pleasing the buddhas) for one hundred eons. At the time of one's last rebirth in a realm without buddhas and śrāvakas, one manifests enlightenment through one's own power without depending on other masters. Here, this [bhūmi] is not counted as [a part of] the classification of [the eight hīnayāna] bhūmis.

2.1.2.2. The buddhabhūmis

> **It is said that these are the ten bodhisattvabhūmis of the mahāyāna.**

"The bhūmis of a fully perfect buddha" refers to the familiarization with the two identitylessnesses and [the cultivation of] the samādhi of emptiness—the nature of all phenomena. **These are the ten bhūmis of the mahāyāna**, that is, the ten bhūmis from "Supreme Joy" up through "Dharma Cloud" that are discussed below. As it says in the *Ratnāvalī*:

> Just as the eight bhūmis of the śrāvakas are explained
> In the yāna of the śrāvakas,
> Likewise, in the mahāyāna,
> The ten bodhisattvabhūmis are.[675]

In [the chapter on] supreme immutability,[676] these buddhabhūmis are explained to have a twofold subdivision—"the tathāgatabhūmis" and "the buddhabhūmi." In its intention, this corresponds to the explanation in some treatises that the ten supramundane bhūmis are the bodhisattva[bhūmis] and the eleventh, the buddhabhūmi.

2.2. Teaching the differences between these two

> **They possess differences in terms of miraculous powers, supernatural knowledges, realization, familiarization,**
> **Seeing, language, teaching the dharma, promoting welfare, and nirvāṇa.**

You may wonder, "What are the differences between these two [types of] bhūmis?" **They possess** many kinds of **differences.** (1) In terms of the bhūmis, {495} there are two [types of] **miraculous powers**—partial and minor miraculous powers on the bhūmis free from attachment and full-fledged miraculous powers on the buddhabhūmis. (2) Likewise, there are two [types of] **supernatural knowledges**—the five supernatural knowledges other than that of the termination of contamination on the former [bhūmis] and the six supernatural knowledges including the supernatural knowledge of the termination of contamination (that is, all seeds of afflictions) on the latter. (3) There are also two [types of the] **realization** of identitylessness—on the former [bhūmis], [there is the realization of the] mere [fact] that the imputation of a person onto the continuum of the five appropriating skandhas lacks any identity. On the latter, [there is] the realization that all imputations as a person and its phenomena lack any identity. (4) There are two manners of the path of **familiarization** too—on the former [bhūmis], it consists of the familiarization with the four realities of the noble ones and, on the latter, the familiarization with all phenomena as being without any real nature, that is, the samādhi of emptiness. (5) There are also two ways of **seeing**—through the former [bhūmis], one sees a countable number of hidden actualities and, through the latter ones, one sees the number of all limitless actualities. (6) There are two [different aspects in terms of] **language, teaching the dharma**, and **promoting** the **welfare** [of beings] as well—the former [bhūmis] work with the languages of a minor number of sentient beings, teach the dharma to them, and promote their welfare. The latter have the character of [doing the same for] a limitless number of sentient beings. (7) There are also two **nirvāṇas**. Since the former [bhūmis] do not relinquish all latent tendencies of the obscurations without exception, [their nirvāṇa] has some remainder of the skandhas. Since the latter relinquish said [latent tendencies] without exception, [their nirvāṇa] is without any remainder of the skandhas.

2.3. Detailed explanation of the buddhabhūmis

This has six parts:

1) The nature of a bhūmi
2) Instances
3) Hermeneutical etymology
4) Classifications
5) Special [explanation]
6) The reason why the bhūmis are definitely ten

2.3.1. The nature of a bhūmi

> **The nature of a bhūmi is to be the basis for special qualities.**

The nature of a bhūmi is the prajñā in the mind stream of a bodhisattva (from the first generation of bodhicitta up through full enlightenment) {496} that realizes identitylessness and is accompanied by the congruent factor of samādhi. This serves as **the** support or **basis for** the progressive further arising of **special qualities.**

2.3.2. Instances

> **The instances consist of the means and prajñā in the mind streams of learners.**

Its **instances consist of** the knowledges **in the mind streams of learning** bodhisattvas, that is, their [respective] wisdoms and their congruently associated factors that are seized by special **means** and function as the support for special qualities.

2.3.3. Hermeneutical etymology

> **The hermeneutical etymologies are support, attainment, freedom, and further progression.**

You may wonder, "Why are they called bhūmis?" The *Mahāyānasūtrālaṃkāra* says:

> Because of delighting in various accomplishments of virtue,
> [Bodhisattvas] dwell [on them] always and everywhere.
> Therefore, the bodhisattvabhūmis
> Are asserted as abodes.[677]

Accordingly, just like the great earth, they function as the bases, abodes, or **supports** for all qualities. Therefore, they are called "bhūmis." Alternatively, the *Mahāyānasūtrālaṃkāra* states:

> Since [bodhisattvas] apply themselves to ascend higher and higher
> On these immeasurable [abodes]
> For the sake of innumerable beings becoming fearless,
> They are asserted as bhūmis.[678]

The [Sanskrit] equivalent for ground is *bhūmi*. Through the certainties [that derive from] eliding or adding [certain] syllables, the general hermeneutical etymologies of "ground" are as follows. *Bhū*, [when interpreted as] *bhūta*, [means] "element"—just like the great element [earth], [the bhūmis] function as supports for the assemblies of qualities. *Mi*, [when interpreted as] *amita*, [means] "immeasurable"—they are **attained** through immeasurable hardships. Or *bhū* [can be interpreted as] *abhaya*, [which means] "fearless"—once the bhūmis are attained, one is **free** from the five fears and so on. Furthermore, *bhū* [can be understood as] *bhūya*, [which means] "higher and higher." Thus, by relying on the [respective] lower ones, [the bhūmis] function as supports for **progressing further** and increasingly higher. For all these reasons, they are called "bhūmis." In brief since they, similar to the ground of the earth, function as supports for qualities, they are designated as "bhūmis." These **are the** general **hermeneutical etymologies** of "bhūmi."

2.3.4. Classifications

> **The classifications [are in terms of] beings and noble ones, the**
> **four ways of attainment (aspiration, engagement,**
> **Realization, {497} and accomplishment), the ways of**
> **accomplishment (nonaccomplishment and accomplishment),**
> **And pride (much, subtle, and no pride).**

When the bhūmis are **classified** in merely a common way, [there are] four [ways to do this]:

1) The classification in terms of **beings and noble ones**
2) The classification in terms of the ways of attainment
3) The classification in terms of the ways of accomplishment
4) The classification in terms of pride

1) The first [classification] has two parts:

a) The bhūmis of ordinary worldly beings
b) The supramundane bhūmis

1a) The definition of the first is "that which functions as the support for the qualities of engaging in the attributes of the noble ones." Their instances are suitably classified as two—the bhūmi of beginners and the bhūmi of engagement through aspiration. The first one consists of the phase of the path of accumulation, which starts with the awakening of the disposition for the mahāyāna and the first generation of bodhicitta since this represents the maturation of one's immature mind stream. The latter one is the phase of the path of preparation since it represents a mere cultivation of aspiring for the actuality of emptiness.

1b) The definition of a supramundane bhūmi is "that which functions as the support for the special qualities of the noble ones." Its instances consist of the phases from the path of seeing up through the path of completion. For these [paths] are what make one familiar with, and accustomed to, the samādhi of the uncontaminated wisdom of true reality that is directly realized on the first bhūmi.

2) The classification in terms of **the ways of attainment** is fourfold. The engagement through mainly cultivating aspiration for the dharmas is called "the bhūmi that is attained through **aspiration**." The **engagement** in the ten dharma activities as one wishes is "the bhūmi that is attained through conduct." The direct realization of the nature of phenomena on the first bhūmi and above is "the bhūmi that is attained through **realization**." In particular, on the eighth bhūmi and above, there is effortless and spontaneous engagement. Therefore, this is "the bhūmi that is attained [through] **accomplishment**." For the *Mahāyānasūtrālaṃkāra* says:

> The attainment of the bhūmis is fourfold
> Because of engagement in aspiration and conduct,
> Realization, and through
> Accomplishment of the bhūmis.[679]

3) There is a fourfold classification in terms of the ways of **accomplishment**. The phases of [the paths of] accumulation and preparation (the bhūmi of engagement through aspiration) are called "**nonaccomplishment**." {498} The phases of [the paths of] seeing and meditation (the bhūmis of pure superior intention) are [called] "**accomplishment**." [The latter bhūmis of] accomplishment are also classified as [two]. From the perspective of entailing efforts from the first up through the seventh [bhūmi], they are [called] "nonaccomplishment." Since there is no effort on the eighth [bhūmi] and above, they are [called] "accomplishment." The above text says:

> All bhūmis should be known
> As nonaccomplishment and accomplishment.
> Those of accomplishment are again asserted
> As nonaccomplishment and accomplishment.[680]

4) There is a threefold classification in terms of **pride**—the bhūmi of engagement through aspiration [involves] **much** pride; the seven impure bhūmis, **subtle** pride; and the three pure bhūmis, **no pride.** The above text says:

They are asserted as [involving] much pride,
Subtle pride, and no pride.[681]

2.3.5. The special explanation of the bhūmis of the uncommon mahāyāna

This has six parts:

1) The natures and the hermeneutical etymologies of the names
2) The purifications and where one transits to
3) The practices and persons
4) The three trainings and the [five] skandhas
5) The purities, relinquishments, and realizations
6) The distinctive features in terms of qualities and birth

2.3.5.1. The natures and the hermeneutical etymologies of the names

Supreme Joy, The Stainless One, The Illuminating One, The Radiating One,
Difficult to Master, The Facing One, Gone Afar, The Immovable,
The Excellent One, and Dharma Cloud.

These are the names of the first through the tenth bhūmis. Their hermeneutical etymologies are as follows. (1) Since one sees the actuality of the nature of phenomena that was not seen before, supreme joy arises upon seeing that one is close to one's own welfare (supreme enlightenment) and that the welfare of others (the vast welfare of sentient beings) will be accomplished. Therefore, the first bhūmi is designated as "**Supreme Joy**."

(2) Since it is free from the stains of corrupted ethics and mental engagement in the hīnayāna, the second one is [called] "**The Stainless One**."

(3) Through the power of samādhi, one searches for limitless dharmas and shines the great light of dharma on others. Therefore, the third one is "**The Illuminating One**."

(4) Since the fire of the prajñā of the [thirty-seven] factors concordant with enlightenment {499} burns the two obscurations, the fourth one is "**The Radiating One**."

(5) When one matures sentient beings, by virtue of the afflictions due to the wrong practices of others the realms of sentient beings and one's own mind are difficult to master. Since the mastery over both is accomplished, the fifth one is [called] "**Difficult to Master**."

(6) Based on the pāramitā of prajñā, one faces the equality of [saṃsāric] existence and nirvāṇa. Thus, the sixth one is "**The Facing One**."

(7) Since one is close to attaining the path of single progress (the eighth bhūmi), one is connected with it and has reached the end of the training that entails effort. Therefore, the seventh one is [called] "**Gone Afar.**"

(8) The eighth one is not moved by the two discriminations of making efforts toward what has characteristics and what lacks characteristics. Therefore, it is "**The Immovable One.**"

(9) Since the fine insight of the four discriminating awarenesses has been attained, the ninth one is [called] "**The Excellent One.**"

(10) The cloudlike gates of samādhis and dhāraṇīs pervade the immeasurable spacelike dharmas that have been attained on the ninth bhūmi and below from the buddhas. Therefore, the tenth one is [called] "**Dharma Cloud.**"

2.3.5.2. The purifications and where one transits to

> **Through the sequence of the purifications, there is transition.**

(1) The first bhūmi [is attained] **through** ten **purifications**, such as the unwavering intention with regard to all bases. (2) Likewise, the second bhūmi [is attained] through eight purifications, such as ethics and repaying [the good] that has been done [to oneself]. (3) The third bhūmi [is attained] through five purifications, such as never being satisfied with what one has attained. (4) The fourth bhūmi [is attained] through ten purifications, such as abiding in solitude. (5) The fifth bhūmi [is attained] through ten purifications, such as relinquishing close relations with householders for the sake of gain and so on. (6) The sixth bhūmi [is attained] through twelve purifications, that is, training in the six dharmas that are to be perfected (such as generosity) and in the six dharmas that are to be relinquished (such as desiring the [states of] śrāvakas and pratyekabuddhas). (7) The seventh bhūmi [is attained] through twenty or forty purifications, that is, through relinquishing twenty factors such as apprehending a self and thus relying on the twenty opposite dharmas such as knowing the three doors to liberation. (8) The eighth bhūmi [is attained] through eight purifications, such as knowing the engagements of all sentient beings just as they are. {500} (9) The ninth bhūmi [is attained] through twelve purifications, such as infinite aspiration prayers. (10) The tenth bhūmi is attained through ten purifications, such as the very fine discrimination through the mental state of examining [all] the limitless knowable objects up through the ninth bhūmi. As the *Abhisamayālaṃkāra* says:

> Through tenfold purification,
> The first bhūmi is attained.
> Intention, beneficial things . . .[682]

As for the manner of **transiting** [from one bhūmi to the next], the first up through the tenth bhūmis constitute [the very phases of] the respective bhūmis for as long as their specific purifications have not been completed. Once these [purifications] have been completed, this marks the transition to the [next] higher [bhūmi]. The *Aṣṭasāhasrikā[prajñāpāramitā]vyākhyā* says:

> One should understand that, for as long as the dharmas that consist of the purifications of any one bhūmi have not been completed, it is [still this] bhūmi. Once they have been completed, this is another bhūmi.[683]

2.3.5.3. The practices and persons

> **The ten pāramitās (such as generosity) are mainly performed on their respective bhūmis.**
> **[The persons] consist of [those with] pure view, ethics, meditative equipoise, lack of pride,**
> **Mental attainment, purification, maturation, and full completion and bestowed empowerment.**

Bodhisattvas who abide on the first bhūmi **mainly** practice the pāramitā of **generosity** and **perform** the remaining pāramitās as its retinue. Those who abide on the tenth [bhūmi] mainly practice the pāramitā of wisdom and perform the remaining ones as its retinue. Thus, from [the first one] up through [the tenth one,] **the ten pāramitās** are matched with the ten **bhūmis** in due order. The ten pāramitās correspond to the list in the *Madhyāntavibhāga*:

> Generosity, ethics, patience, vigor,
> Dhyāna, prajñā, means,
> Power, aspiration prayers, and wisdom—
> These are the ten pāramitās.
> . . .
> Distinct and nondistinct [practice]
> Are to be understood with regard to the ten bhūmis.[684]

(1) Thus since those who abide on the first bhūmi realize that the dharmadhātu is empty of the two identities, they are called "the persons with the **pure view**." {501} (2) Likewise, on the second bhūmi, since they are not affected by even the most subtle downfalls, they are "[the persons with] pure **ethics**." (3) On the third bhūmi, since they attain limitless dhyānas and samādhis, they are

"[the persons who] rest in **meditative equipoise**." (4) On the fourth bhūmi, since they lack clinging, they are "[the persons who] **lack pride** with regard to differences between phenomena." (5) On the fifth bhūmi, since they attain the equality of mind, they are "[the persons who] lack pride with regard to differences between mind streams." (6) On the sixth bhūmi, since they are naturally pure, they are "[the persons who] lack pride with regard to differences between afflicted and purified phenomena." (7) On the seventh bhūmi, since they abide in the lack of characteristics, they are "[the persons who] **attained** the **mind** of cultivating the factors concordant with enlightenment in each moment." (8) Since they are effortless on the eighth bhūmi, they are "[the persons with] equanimity and purification." (9) On the ninth bhūmi, since they attain mastery over the four discriminating awarenesses, they are "[the persons who are] skilled in the **maturation** of sentient beings." (10) On the tenth bhūmi, since they attain great supernatural knowledge, they are "[the persons who are] very powerful, **fully complete** the body of the doors of samādhis and dhāraṇīs, display emanations (such as those who dwell in Tuṣita), **and** obtain the **empowerment** that is **bestowed** by all buddhas."

2.3.5.4. The three trainings and the [five] skandhas

> **The three trainings [occur] on six [bhūmis], and the results are accomplished on four.**
> **After the nature of phenomena has been realized, the five skandhas are gradually purified.**

On the first bhūmi, one trains in the causes for **the** pure **three trainings**. On the second one, one trains in the training of ethics; on the third one, in the training of mind; **on** the fourth, fifth, and **six**th, in due order, one trains in the prajñās of knowing the factors concordant with enlightenment, the realities, and dependent origination. Through this, their **results are accomplished** [on the last four bhūmis]—on the seventh bhūmi, wisdom without characteristics; on the eighth one, effortless wisdom; on the ninth one, the maturation of sentient beings; and on the tenth one, the supports of samādhis and dhāraṇīs. {502}

After the nature of phenomena has been directly **realized** on the first bhūmi, **the** [five pure] **skandhas are gradually purified**—on the second one, the skandha of ethics; on the third one, the skandha of samādhi; on the fourth, fifth, and sixth, the skandha of prajñā; on the seventh one and above, the [skandha] of the liberation from the obscurations of the four results [above]; on the buddhabhūmi, one is liberated even from the obscurations that obstruct knowable objects and has completely purified the skandha of the vision of the wisdom of liberation.

2.3.5.5. The purities, relinquishments, and realizations

> **They possess the three causes, the roots of virtue become increasingly pure,**
> **The cognitive obscurations are gradually relinquished, and the ten kinds of wisdom are accomplished.**

During many eons, [bodhisattvas] venerate the three jewels, mature sentient beings, and dedicate the roots of virtue for enlightenment. Through **these three causes, the roots of virtue** from the first up through the tenth bhūmis **become** completely **pure**. The differences between the bhūmis in terms of more or less excellent purity should be known according to the *Daśabhūmikasūtra*, in which this is matched with examples.

The differences in terms of relinquishment and realization between those who abide on the bhūmis are as follows. On the path of seeing, the 112 [afflicted] factors to be relinquished through seeing are relinquished and, on the path of familiarization, said factors to be relinquished through familiarization. However, when [these two paths] are presented as the ten bhūmis, on each one of the ten bhūmis their respective antagonistic factors (the **cognitive obscurations** that consist of [certain forms of] ignorance) **are gradually relinquished** through the distinct wisdoms of realizing [ten different aspects of] the dharmadhātu. According to the *Daśabhūmikasūtra*, [bodhisattvas on the first bhūmi] have relinquished the five fears:

> Right upon attaining the bhūmis, they are free from the five fears in terms of
> Losing their livelihood, death, lack of praise, lower realms, and retinue.
> They are free from these fears and do not have any form of anxiety.
> If you wonder why, they do not have any basis of an identity.[685]

According to the *Uttaratantra*, they also relinquished the four rivers of suffering:

> The root of the suffering of death, sickness,
> And aging, is removed by the noble ones.
> [Suffering] arises from the power of karma and afflictions,
> [But] they lack it, because they lack these.[686]

{503} Thus, in these and other ways, they are liberated from inconceivably [many kinds of] fears. [Here,] it is to be implicitly understood that, subsequently, this [freedom] gradually increases from the first up through the tenth bhūmis. Although they are liberated from said four sufferings, they display themselves as if they were not liberated [from them], which represents their deliberate rebirths within [saṃsāric] existence. As the above text says:

> Due to their nature of compassion,
> They display birth, death, sickness, and aging.
> [But] they are beyond birth and so on
> Because they see true reality.[687]

The realizations [on the ten bhūmis] are that, during the meditative equipoises of all ten bhūmis, the mode of being of the ultimate nature of phenomena, just as it is, is realized to be the freedom from [all] extremes of reference points, just like space. During their subsequent attainments, the mode of being of the entire variety of the seeming bearers of this nature is realized to be appearing and yet without nature, just like an illusion. Thus, other than [seeing] the reality of the nature of phenomena that is first seen on the path of seeing, there are no dissimilar other types of realization that see something new [later]. However, when [this seeing] is related to the differences between the ten bhūmis, it can be classified as the [corresponding] ten realizations of the certainty of having eliminated [certain] superimpositions that are attained subsequent to the relinquishment of the respective factors to be relinquished [on these bhūmis].

Here, the *Mahāyānasūtrālaṃkāra* and the *Madhyāntavibhāga* state the following. (1) On the first bhūmi, since one realizes that the dharmadhātu pervades all knowable objects, the nature of phenomena is realized as the actuality of omnipresence. (2) Likewise, on the second [bhūmi], since one sees it as natural luminosity, the nature of phenomena is [realized as] the highest actuality among phenomena. (3) On the third one, the dharma that is taught is [realized as] the actuality that is the natural outflow of realization. (4) On the fourth one, [the nature of phenomena] is [realized as] the actuality of the lack of clinging to anything whatsoever as what is mine. (5) On the fifth one, it is [realized as] the actuality that, as the pure dhātu, the mind streams of oneself and others are not different. (6) On the sixth one, it is [realized as] the actuality of neither having been afflicted nor newly being pure since the stains are adventitious and [the nature of phenomena] is naturally pure. (7) On the seventh one, it is [realized as] the actuality of there being no difference between the characteristics of the dharmas, such as the sūtras. (8) On the eighth one, since the poised readiness for the dharma of nonarising is attained, {504} [the nature of phenomena is realized as] the actuality of there being neither any decrease of afflicted phenomena nor any increase of purified phenomena. Or it is [realized as] the actuality of mastery over nonconceptuality since the afflicted mind has undergone its change of state, and of mastery over pure realms since the sense consciousnesses have undergone their change of state. (9) On the ninth one, [the nature of phenomena is realized as] the actuality of mastery over the wisdom that consists of the [four] discriminating awarenesses since the mental consciousness has undergone its change of state. (10) On the tenth one, it is realized as the actuality of the matrix of mastery over enlightened activity since the welfare of sentient beings is promoted by creating emanations just as one pleases. Since there are ten nonafflictive cognitive obscurations as the factors to be relinquished [by the ten bhūmis, respectively], it is in terms of their being the remedies that relinquish these [factors] that they are realized as the ten bhūmis. Therefore, they are presented as exactly **ten** [kinds of] **wisdom**.

As for the ten different isolates of what is realized during the subsequent attainments [of the ten bhūmis as mentioned above], there is no difference [between the ten bhūmis] as far as the sheer realization from the perspective of meditative equipoise is concerned. During the meditative equipoise of the first bhūmi, nonconceptual wisdom realizes the actualities of all ten isolates [above] (such as the nature of phenomena being omnipresent) in their entirety. The same applies for the second up through the tenth [bhūmis]. However, during the [respective] subsequent attainments [of the ten bhūmis], [this realization] appears as [ten] different [types of] certainty. On the first bhūmi, it appears as the certainty of having realized the nature of phenomena as the actuality of omnipresence. On the second one, it appears as the certainty of having realized it as the highest actuality, and so on. In this way, through these ten certainties, the [corresponding ten] cognitive obscurations are relinquished.

2.3.5.6. The distinctive features in terms of qualities and birth

On the first [bhūmi], one attains twelve times one hundred
qualities,
And on the tenth one, as many as an inexpressible [number of]
particles.
Starting with the eighth bhūmi, the ten masteries over one's
lifespan and so on are attained,
And on the tenth one, one attains being bestowed with the
empowerment of great light rays.

[Bodhisattvas may be] reborn through the influence of karma, aspiration, samādhi, and mastery.
Those who dwell on the bhūmis are reborn through maturation as cakravartins and so on.

On the first bhūmi, **one attains twelve times one hundred qualities** because they arise in every moment. These [qualities] {505} appear in the chapter of the bodhisattva Hayagrīva in the *Daśabhūmikasūtra*. [Here,] they are formulated as a mnemonic verse:

(1) One attains one hundred samādhis and (2) enters them.
(3) One sees one hundred buddhas and (4) knows their blessings.
(5) One shakes one hundred worldly realms and (6) travels to one hundred [pure] realms.
(7) One illuminates one hundred such [realms] and (8) matures one hundred beings.
(9) One lives for one hundred eons and engages in them from beginning to end.
(10) One opens one hundred doors of dharma, (11) displays one hundred bodies,
And (12) displays a retinue of one hundred bodhisattvas
Who perfectly surround each one of these bodies.

On the second bhūmi, these [twelve] qualities are multiplied one thousand times; on the third one, one hundred thousand times; on the fourth one, one billion times; on the fifth one, ten billion times; on the sixth one, one trillion times; and on the seventh one, one hundred sixtillion times. On the eighth one, they are equal to the number of minutest particles in one hundred thousand trichiliocosms. On the ninth one, they equal the number of one million countless trichiliocosms. **On the tenth one**, one attains [a number] that is equal to the minutest **particles** of the most **inexpressible** [number] of inexpressible [numbers of] buddha realms and even more than that.

It is taught that, on **the eighth bhūmi, the ten masteries are attained**. These ten are described in the *Dharmasaṃgītisūtra*:

You may wonder, "What are the ten masteries of bodhisattvas?" The ten masteries are (1) mastery over **lifespan**, (2) mind, (3) necessities, (4) karma, (5) birth, (6) creative willpower, (7) aspiration prayers, (8) miraculous powers, (9) wisdom, and (10) dharma.

(1) One lives as many eons as one wishes. {506} (2) In each moment, one is able to rest in, and rise from, meditative equipoise in infinite samādhis. (3) Through one's mere thoughts [of them], one is able to fill the world with all kinds of food and riches. (4) One engages in all fields of arts, crafts, and karma just as one pleases. (5) One is born as any god, human being, and so on that one wishes [to be]. (6) One transforms all things as one pleases, such as transforming the whole ground of the earth into all kinds of gems, which are then suitable to be enjoyed by sentient beings once they see them. (7) One fulfills one's aspiration prayers in just the way that one has made them, such as filling the whole universe with buddhas. (8) One is able to create emanations as one wishes, such as fitting infinite realms within the space of the tip of a hair. (9) One knows the knowable objects that one wishes to know. (10) One is skilled in presenting the names of all dharmas.

In general, the bare attainment of the ten masteries exists [already] during the seven impure bhūmis. However, the consummate forms of the ten masteries exist only on the three pure bhūmis, while the utterly pure ten masteries exist on the buddhabhūmi. The initial attainment of these ten masteries on the eighth bhūmi corresponds to their description in the sūtras. However, once one attains [the level on] the tenth bhūmi on which one is prevented [from reaching enlightenment] by just a single birth, the capacities of the ten masteries are perfected, that is, they are attained in a fully complete manner. Therefore, this is the intention behind the statement that they are attained on the tenth bhūmi, [which is found] in the summary of [the chapter on] supreme immutability in the *Kālacakra[tantra]*.

On the tenth bhūmi, one also attains **being bestowed with the** special **empowerment**. The *Mahāyānasūtrālaṃkāra* says:

> With the empowerment of great light rays bestowed by all buddhas,
> They possess total mastery over the dharma,
> Know the aspects of displaying the maṇḍala of a buddha's retinue,
> And, through applying the precepts, strive to administer
> punishment and reward.[688]

Furthermore since the sūtra collections describe limitless qualities of each bhūmi, {507} they cannot be presented in a way that is definite in each and every aspect.

You may wonder, "How do **those who dwell on the bhūmis** take rebirths?" In general, bodhisattvas [can be reborn in] two [ways]—(1) rebirth through influence and (2) rebirth through maturation.

(1) **Rebirth through influence** is fourfold—(a) rebirth through **karma**, (b) rebirth through **aspiration** prayers, (c) rebirth through **samādhi**, and (d) rebirth through **mastery**. The first one [applies to] bodhisattvas who dwell on [the level of] engagement through aspiration;[689] the second one, to bodhisattvas who abide on the bhūmis and take rebirths as animals and so on for the welfare of others; the third one, to bodhisattvas who abide in the form realm and take rebirths in the desire realm, while not moving out of their samādhis; and the fourth one, to bodhisattvas who take rebirths for the welfare of others in such a way that they create emanations.

(2) As for **rebirth through maturation**, it is explained that those bodhisattvas who dwell on the first bhūmi are mostly reborn **as cakravartin** kings who wield power over Jambudvīpa. Likewise, those on the second [bhūmi] take births as cakravartins who rule over [all] four continents; those on the third one, as Śakra, who rules over The Thirty-three; those on the fourth one, as the ruler of the gods in Free from Combat; those on the fifth one, as the ruler of the gods in Tuṣita; those on the sixth one, as the ruler of the gods in Enjoying Emanations; those on the seventh one, as the ruler of the gods in Power [over Others' Emanations]; those on the eighth one, as Brahmā, the lord of a chiliocosm; those on the ninth one, as the ruler over the worlds of a dichiliocosm; and those bodhisattvas who dwell on the tenth bhūmi, as Maheśvara, the ruler over the [five] pure abodes.

2.3.6. The reason why the number of the bhūmis is definitely ten

> **The meditative equipoises are alike, but due to the differences in**
> **the subsequently attained certainties**
> **And purifications, the number of the bhūmis is definitely ten.**

In general, during **the meditative equipoises** of the ten bhūmis, there is no difference with regard to nonreferential compassion and the realization that all phenomena are emptiness. **However, due to the differences in** there being **the** [certainties about] the ten dissimilar isolates of the dharmadhātu, {508} the ten pāramitās, **and** the **purifications** during **subsequent attainment**, they are divided into **ten bhūmis** and **the number** of these **is definite.**

It may be said, "What is to be analyzed in this context of the presentation of bhūmis and paths is [the question] at which stage śrāvakas and pratyekabuddhas enter the bhūmis and paths of the mahāyāna." Since there appears to be no clear explanation of this point in the majority of the sūtras and tantras, I quote the explanation in the *Vairocanābhisaṃbodhitantra*:

> [On] the bhūmi of engagement through aspiration,
> One cultivates the three states of mind.

Then, through the six pāramitās
And the four means of attraction,
This bhūmi of aspiration becomes unequalled.

Accordingly, on the bhūmi of engagement through aspiration, one cultivates the three states of mind of entering, abiding, and rising.[690] Through great compassion, the mind that rises from [this cultivation] engages in the six pāramitās and the four means of attraction. Thus, this very statement that [śrāvakas and pratyekabuddhas] enter the path of the mahāyāna starting with [the level of] engagement through aspiration is to be taken as the definitive meaning.

B) Determining the fruitions[691]

This has two parts:

1) The general explanation of nirvāṇa, the result of the three yānas
2) The special explanation of buddhahood, the result of the mahāyāna

1. The general explanation of nirvāṇa, the result of the three yānas

The result to be attained through the three yānas is nirvāṇa.
The natural nirvāṇa is the suchness of phenomena.
As for the nirvāṇa of cessation, the nominal one is attained during the engagement through aspiration
And the ultimate one, by virtue of seeing and familiarization,
Consisting of the incomplete of learners and the complete of nonlearners.
The nonabiding nirvāṇa does not fall into the extremes of [saṃsāric] existence and peace.

The result to be attained through all **three yānas is nirvāṇa.** {592} When explained in a general way, [there are] three [types]—(1) **the natural nirvāṇa,** (2) the nirvāṇa of cessation, and (3) the nonabiding nirvāṇa.

(1) The *Mūlamadhyamakakārikā* says:

What is expressible has come to an end,
Because the sphere of mind has come to an end.
The unarisen and unceasing
Nature of phenomena equals nirvāṇa.[692]

Accordingly, this **is the suchness of phenomena** that is completely pure by nature.

(2) **The nirvāṇa of cessation** is twofold. (a) On the **nominal one**, the *Abhidharmasamuccaya* says:

> "How is this in a terminological sense?" It is the cessation by virtue of the seeds having been weakened through mundane paths. Therefore, the Bhagavān declared this to be nirvāṇa as one of its enumerations by virtue of being a branch of it.[693]

Accordingly, this refers to the nominal [kinds of] cessation that are attained **during the engagement through aspiration.** (b) **The ultimate** cessations are the cessations that **are attained** through the paths of **seeing and familiarization**. The above text says:

> "How is it in the ultimate sense?" It is the cessation by virtue of the complete eradication of the seeds through the prajñā of noble ones.[694]

These are again twofold—(a) **the not** fully **complete** and (b) the fully complete. (ba) The above text says:

> "What are the [cessations that are] not fully complete?" They are the cessations of learners—what constitutes the result of a stream-enterer, what constitutes the result of a once-returner, or what constitutes the result of a nonreturner.[695]

Accordingly, [the not fully complete cessations] are all the cessations **of learners.** (bb) As for **the** fully **complete**, the above text says:

> "What are the [cessations that are] fully complete?" They are the cessations of nonlearners—what constitute the results of arhathood.[696]

Accordingly, [the fully complete] are all the cessations **of nonlearners.** These [cessations] exist as two [types], that is, [the nirvāṇas] with remainder and without remainder in accordance with the gradual progressions of the respective yānas.

(3) **The nonabiding nirvāṇa** is the nirvāṇa that, through the power of the prajñā and the compassion of buddhas and bodhisattvas, **does not fall into the** two **extremes of [saṃsāric] existence and peace.** {593}

2. The special explanation of buddhahood, the result of the mahāyāna

This has three parts:

1) The nature of buddhahood
2) The meaning of this term
3) The way in which the enlightened activity of the kāyas is accomplished

2.1. The nature of buddhahood

It is that which possesses the three greatnesses . . .

The nature of the final result—completely perfect buddhahood—**is that which possesses** the defining characteristics of **the three greatnesses**. The kāya that is utterly pure of the two obscurations together with their latent tendencies is great relinquishment. The wisdom that lucidly views the entire maṇḍala of knowable objects without exception is great realization. The permanent, all-encompassing, and spontaneously present promotion of the welfare of beings through the force of the [first two greatnesses] is great mind. The *Abhisamayālaṃkāra* says:

> This aim of the self-arisen ones,
> By virtue of the three greatnesses, should be known as threefold—
> The mind of the highest state of all sentient beings,
> Relinquishment, and realization.[697]

2.2. The meaning of this term

And awakening and unfolding like a lotus.

You may wonder, "Why is this called 'buddhahood'?" It is called "buddhahood" because it is the **awakening** from sleeplike ignorance **and** thus mind's **unfolding** toward the two knowable objects.[698] As it is said:

> Because they awaken from the sleep of ignorance
> And because their minds unfold toward knowable objects,
> Buddhas awaken and unfold like a lotus.[699]

2.3. The way in which the enlightened activity of the kāyas is accomplished

This has three parts:

1) Teaching the connection in terms of what is accomplished from which causes
2) Explaining the distinctive features of how this is accomplished in certain places
3) Detailed explanation of the results that are accomplished

2.3.1. Teaching the connection in terms of what is accomplished from which causes

> **Through completing the accumulation of merit through bodhicitta,**
> **The result of maturation—the rūpakāyas—is accomplished.**
> **The result of freedom through the accumulation of wisdom is the dharmakāya.**

Through being endowed with the intention of **bodhicitta**, its application—the vast two accumulations that consist of the six pāramitās—is **completed.** Due to this, the two kāyas are obtained. For the sake of **the accumulation of merit,** {594} one practices the benefit of sentient beings, due to which **the result of maturation—the rūpakāyas—is accomplished.** For the sake of **the accumulation of wisdom,** one cultivates nonconceptual samādhi, which leads to the accomplishment of **the result of freedom** from stains, that is, **the dharmakāya.** As the *Ratnāvalī* says:

> This rūpakāya of the Buddha
> Originates from the accumulation of merit.
> The dharmakāya, in brief,
> O king, originates from the accumulation of wisdom.[700]

2.3.2. Explaining the distinctive features of how this is accomplished in certain places

> **In the great Akaniṣṭha, based on the support of the sāmbhogikakāya,**
> **The dharmakāya is manifested. In a trichiliocosm,**
> **Nairmāṇikakāyas simultaneously demonstrate the way of becoming enlightened.**
> **Being the completion of the two welfares, the two kāyas represent support and supported.**

What is ultimately nonexistent does not appear, and what appears does so because it exists.
Therefore, this is liberation because one acts as one pleases.

You may wonder, "In which place is this buddhahood accomplished?" **In the great Akaniṣṭha**[701] that is completely beyond the three realms, **the dharmakāya is manifested based on the support of the sāmbhogikakāya. In** the one billion four-continent worlds of **a trichiliocosm, nairmāṇikakāyas simultaneously demonstrate the way of becoming** fully **enlightened.** The *Laṅkāvatārasūtra* says:

In the lovely place of Akaniṣṭha
That has left behind all pure realms,
The perfect Buddha became the Buddha.
A single emanation became the Buddha here.

The presentation of the kāyas as threefold represents a definite number for which [the Buddha] saw a necessity—the two rūpakāyas are **the** most excellent **welfares** of oneself and others, while the dharmakāya is their support. Maitreya said [in his *Mahāyānasūtrālaṃkāra*]:

Through the three kāyas, the welfare of oneself and others
As well as the support for these are taught.[702]

Various other [sources] explain that the dharmakāya is the ultimate [kāya] and one's own welfare, while both rūpakāyas represent the seeming [kāyas] and the welfare of others. As for the latter [two], the sāmbhogikakāya appears from the perspective of pure beings to be guided, while the nairmāṇikakāya appears from the perspective of impure beings to be guided. {595} The first one of these [three] is the support for the latter two. [Thus,] in due order, **the two** [(dharmakāya and rūpakāyas)] **are support and supported.**

Since **what is ultimately nonexistent**—the entirety of adventitious stains and obscurations—has been relinquished, it **does not appear** [any more], while **what exists** in an ever unchanging way—the entirety of the dharmadhātu—**appears** directly. **Therefore, this is** the enjoyment of uncontaminated affluence as one pleases. As the *Mahāyānasūtrālaṃkāra* says:

What does not exist and what exists are to be known
As what does not appear and what appears, respectively.
This change of state is liberation
Because one acts as one pleases.[703]

2.3.3. Detailed explanation of the results that are accomplished

This has four parts:

1) The explanation of the kāyas (the support)
2) [The explanation of] the wisdoms (the supported)
3) [The explanation of] the qualities of freedom and maturation
4) [The explanation of] the enlightened activity that is performed

2.3.3.1. The explanation of the kāyas (the support)

This has two parts:

1) Their definitions and so on
2) Their distinctive features

2.3.3.1.1. Their definitions and so on

This has four parts:

1) The dharmakāya
2) The sāmbhogikakāya
3) The nairmāṇikakāya
4) The supplementary topic of the intention of the *Uttaratantra*

2.3.3.1.1.1. The dharmakāya

This has two parts:

1) Meaning of the term and definition
2) Its classification as different kāyas

2.3.3.1.1.1.1. Meaning of the term and definition

> **The dharmadhātu endowed with all uncontaminated qualities,**
> **The nature of phenomena endowed with twofold purity, is the kāya that is the support.**
> **It has the eight defining characteristics of being equal, profound,**
> **Permanent, single, truly real, pure, luminous, and connected to perfection.**

Adducing a quotation from the *Ratnāvalīṭīkā* in the *Saṃskṛtāsaṃskṛtaviniścaya*, the hermeneutical etymology of the dharmakāya corresponds to the following:

The dharmakāya is the kāya of **the nature of phenomena** (dharmatākāya). It is [called] "body" for the following reasons: since it is the "body" of all dharmas, it does not go beyond the nature that is the suchness of all beings. [Furthermore,] it is the **kāya that is the support** of all mundane and supramundane qualities.[704]

Thus, this term is explained in the manner of the [syllable] -tā in dharmatākāya being elided.[705] The definition [of the dharmakāya] is as follows. It is **the** very **dharmadhātu** that is pure by nature, **endowed with all uncontaminated qualities**, and, after having become free from all adventitious stains as well, has the very nature of being **endowed with twofold purity.** {596} This is the svābhāvikakāya or dharmakāya. As the *Abhisamayālaṃkāra* says:

> Those who have attained purity in every respect
> And the uncontaminated dharmas,
> Theirs is the svābhāvikakāya of the sage,
> Which bears the characteristic of the nature of these.[706]

The *Mahāyānasaṃgraha* says:

> First, the svābhāvikakāya is the dharmakāya of the tathāgatas since it is the basis of mastery over all dharmas.[707]

When differentiated through isolates, **it has the eight defining characteristics of being equal, profound, permanent, single, truly real, pure, luminous, and connected to perfect** enjoyment. (1) It is equal because there is no difference between the dharmakāyas of all buddhas. (2) It is profound because it is free from all reference points and therefore difficult to realize. (3) It is permanent because it is unconditioned and therefore lacks the three times, arising, and ceasing. (4) It is single because dhātu and wisdom are not different and therefore inseparable. (5) It is truly real because it is beyond the extremes of superimposition and denial and therefore is unmistaken. (6) It is pure because it is free from the stains of the three obscurations.[708] (7) It is luminous because it is through nonconceptuality that it is observed as this very nonconceptuality. (8) It is connected to perfect enjoyment because it serves as the support for the perfect enjoyment that has the character of vast qualities.

2.3.3.1.1.1.2. Its classification as different kāyas

> **Some present consummate relinquishment as the**
> **svābhāvika[kāya]**
> **And consummate realization as the dharmakāya.**

Its nature is indifferentiable, but in **some** exegetical approaches there is also the following **presentation**: "After both afflictive and cognitive obscurations together with their latent tendencies have been uprooted on the paths, they are [completely] overcome right at the end of the vajralike samādhi. This **consummate relinquishment** is **the svābhāvika**kāya. The wisdom of knowing what is to be known—suchness and variety—{597} directly sees and realizes the defining characteristics of all phenomena, just as they are. This **consummate realization is the dharmakāya.**" Such is the case since these two are object and subject, respectively. The svābhāvikakāya is what bears the defining characteristic of natural purity in the sense that the nature of all phenomena is emptiness free from all reference points. The dharmakāya is what bears the defining characteristic of pure wisdom that sees [the nature of phenomena] in this way.

2.3.3.1.1.2. The sāmbhogikakāya

This has two parts:
1) Meaning of the term and definition
2) Classification

2.3.3.1.1.2.1. Meaning of the term and definition

> **In Richly Adorned, the sāmbhogikakāya is adorned with the major and minor marks**
> **And continuously enjoys the noble ones and the mahāyāna.**
> **It has the eight defining characteristics of retinue, realm, body, characteristics, dharma,**
> **Performance, spontaneous presence, and lack of nature.**

The meaning of the term "**sāmbhogikakāya**" follows the *Abhisamayālaṃkāra* saying:

> [Since it] enjoys the mahāyāna,
> It is held to be the sāmbhogikakāya.[709]

Thus, it is [called that way] since it is the support for perfectly enjoying the dharma of realization of the mahāyāna or since it teaches the dharma of the mahāyāna in order for it to be perfectly enjoyed. Its definition is "the kāya that is **adorned with the major and minor marks in** Great **Richly Adorned** Akaniṣṭha **and**, together with **the noble** children of the victors, **continuously enjoys** solely the dharma of **the mahāyāna.**" The *Abhisamayālaṃkāra* says:

> Since this [kāya] of the sage, whose character lies in
> The thirty-two major marks and the eighty minor marks,
> Enjoys the mahāyāna,
> It is held to be the sāmbhogikakāya.[710]

When differentiated through isolates, **it has the eight characteristics of retinue, realm, body, characteristics, dharma, performance, spontaneous presence, and lack of nature.** (1) Its retinue together with which it enjoys [the dharma] consists exclusively of bodhisattvas who dwell on the ten bhūmis. (2) The [pure] realm in which it enjoys [the dharma] is Richly Adorned Akaniṣṭha. (3) The bodies that enjoy are those of Vairocana and so on. {598} (4) The characteristics that it possesses are the thirty-two major and the eighty minor marks. (5) The dharma that it fully enjoys is solely the mahāyāna. (6) The enlightened activity that it performs consists of the prophecies for the children of the victors and so on. (7) Spontaneous presence means that its performance [of enlightened activity] and so on happen effortlessly and spontaneously, just as in the case of a wish-fulfilling jewel. (8) Its lack of nature means that it appears as various [phenomena] (such as said kāyas), but cannot be identified [as said phenomena], just like a rainbow.

When this is explained as the five certainties, (1) the certainty of place refers to Akaniṣṭha. (2) The certainty of nature refers to being adorned with the major and minor marks. (3) The certainty of time means that it abides permanently, that is, until saṃsāra is empty. (4) The certainty of retinue refers to bodhisattvas on the ten bhūmis. (5) The certainty of dharma means that it proclaims nothing but the dharma of the mahāyāna.

2.3.3.1.1.2.2. Classification

> **It is classified as twofold—greater and lesser, or actual and nominal.**
> **[There are] the three assertions of its being one, different, and lesser and greater.**

When classified on the mere conventional level, **it** can be **classified as twofold**. [The body] that appears in Richly Adorned [Akaniṣṭha] is the **great** sāmbhogikakāya **and** the one that resides in the Akaniṣṭha that is a pure abode [in the form realm] is the **lesser** one. **Or** the **actual** [sāmbhogikakāya] is the actual way of being **and** the **nominal** one, the way of appearing. In general, some scholars **assert** that all buddhas have just **one** and the same sāmbhogikakāya and that there is absolutely no second one. Similar to the assertions of the tīrthikas, some [others] say that the sāmbhogikakāyas of buddhas are definitely **different**. [Some say] that there are two [kinds of] sāmbhogikakāyas, that is, **lesser and greater.** From among these **three** [positions], the explanatory approaches of the first one and the last one are excellent since the *Mahāyānasūtrālaṃkāra* says:

In the undefiled dhātu
Buddhas are neither one nor many
Since they have no body, just like space,
And yet accord with their previous bodies.[711]

Since it is thus explained that there are no specifically characterized bodies, there is no need to draw parallels to material things. {599}

This kāya appears, but lacks any nature, just like a reflection in a mirror. In this way, it appears to bodhisattvas on the ten bhūmis and serves as the support of [the attainment of their] dharmakāyas. Since it is a self-appearance of cognition, what appears as [its parts] (from the eyes up through the body) does not constitute [the five āyatanas] from the eye āyatana up through the body āyatana. Since permanence in terms of a continuum is not possible with what is obstructive either, it is beyond what is obstructive. [King] Indrabhūti states in his *Jñānasiddhi* that if one asserts kāyas that are not wisdom, since [ordinary] bodies possess the feature of perishing, the same would follow for wisdom too. As he says [in this text]:

If one says, "The wisdom of buddhas
Possesses bodies and limbs,"
It will perish after one has passed into nirvāṇa.
Since bodies have the feature of perishing,
Wisdom would perish too.
Therefore, it is not reasonable
That the wisdom kāyas of buddhas perish.[712]

Thus, [this kāya] is presented as twofold—consisting of what appears for buddhas themselves and what appears for bodhisattvas.

2.3.3.1.1.3. The nairmāṇikakāya

This has two parts:
1) Meaning of the term and definition
2) Classification

2.3.3.1.1.3.1. Meaning of the term and definition

The nairmāṇikakāya promotes the welfare of beings
Through various emanations for as long as saṃsāra lasts.
It has the eight [characteristics] of support, cause, realm, time, nature, engagement, maturation, and liberation.

The meaning of the term "**nairmāṇikakāya**" is that it is definitely changed into something else [at some point] because it is a body that has the nature of being emanated. For master Daśabālaśrīmitra explains:

> Emanation means being an emanation and the kāya that is established through that is the nairmāṇikakāya.[713]

Its definition [is "the kāya that **promotes the welfare of beings through various emanations for as long as saṃsāra lasts.**"][714]

When differentiated through isolates, **it has the eight** defining characteristics **of support, cause, realm, time, nature**, causing **engagement**, causing **maturation, and** causing **liberation.** (1) Its support is the dharmakāya—[it appears] while [the latter] is unmoving.[715] (2) Its cause refers to its arising from great compassion, that is, the wish to benefit all beings. {600} (3) The realms [in which it appears] are all kinds of pure and impure [realms]. (4) The time [of its activity] lasts for as long as saṃsāra [exists]. (5) Its nature consists of the forms of the three emanations of artistry, incarnation, and enlightenment. (6) To cause engagement means that it causes ordinary worldly people to strive for, and engage in, [one of] the three types of nirvāṇa, as is individually appropriate. (7) To cause maturation means that it causes the maturation of the accumulations of those who have entered the path. (8) To cause liberation means that it, for those who are matured through what is virtuous, causes liberation from the bondage of [saṃsāric] existence.

2.3.3.1.1.3.2. Classification

> **Artistic, incarnate, and supreme nairmāṇikakāyas demonstrate the deeds.**

[Nairmāṇikakāyas] are classified as three—(1) **artistic** nairmāṇikakāyas, (2) **incarnate** nairmāṇikakāyas, and (3) **supreme nairmāṇikakāyas.** Through demonstrating nirvāṇa when the right time has come, they connect those to be guided with liberation. For the *Mahāyānasūtrālaṃkāra* says:

> Through artistry, incarnation, and great enlightenment
> And always demonstrating nirvāṇa,
> The nirmāṇakāya of the Buddha
> Is the great means for liberation.[716]

Nairmāṇikakāyas of artistry are those that demonstrate such [deeds] as playing sitar for the sake of guiding gandharvas. Incarnate nairmāṇikakāyas are those that display as rabbits, deer, and so on. Supreme nairmāṇikakāyas of great enlightenment are those that show themselves as [buddhas] such as [Buddha] Śākyamuni. [All of] them **demonstrate** [activivities] such as **the** twelve **deeds.** The first two are the nairmāṇikakāyas that are not fully mature, while the latter is the fully mature nairmāṇikakāya. As for the difference between being and not being fully mature, it is explained that they are or are not mature in the sense of being dissimilar in terms of supreme actions, but not just in terms of mere maturation.

2.3.3.1.1.4. Teaching the intention of the *Uttaratantra* as a supplementary topic

> **The *Uttaratantra* says that the nature consists of purity, self,**
> **bliss, and permanence**
> **And that the three kāyas have five defining characteristics each.**

The *Mahāyānottaratantra* **says that the nature** of said kāyas **consists of** the pāramitās of supreme **purity, self, bliss, and permanence and** {601} **that** all **three kāyas have five defining characteristics each.**

Mind as such, which is pure by nature, was the support of latent tendencies before, but at the time of buddhahood it does not function as a support of latent tendencies. Therefore, it is endowed with twofold purity. This is the pāramitā of supreme purity.

From the moment of [mind] being conceptual, it has the nature of being affected by latent tendencies. Within that, [mind as such] has never come under the power of anything other, that is, conceptions. Therefore, it is the supreme self. That is since all conceptions about the reference points of [both] self and no-self are at peace, this is the pāramitā of the supreme self.

From the eighth bhūmi onward, conceptions that appear as terms and their referents cease. However, the appearances of container and contents that emerge within the nonconceptual [sphere of] appearances are the most subtle suffering, that is, the skandhas that have a mental nature. [At the time of buddhahood,] these [skandhas], including their cause (the ground of the latent tendencies of ignorance), have ceased and therefore the entirety of suffering, including its causes, has ceased. Therefore, this is the pāramitā of supreme bliss.

That there is no decrease of saṃsāra and no increase of nirvāṇa is the equality of [saṃsāric] existence and peace. Since the familiarization with this has reached its end, the nature of the equality of saṃsāra and nirvāṇa has been found and it is primordially impossible for this to change for as long as space exists. Therefore, this is the pāramitā of supreme permanence.

That in which these four pāramitās are complete is the buddhakāya. Thus, they are complete in any kāya of the actual mode of being.

[Also, the three kāyas] possess five defining characteristics each. The five of the dharmakāya are that it is (1) unconditioned, (2) not analyzable as two, (3) unmistaken, (4) pure of obscurations, and (5) naturally luminous.[717]

The five of the sāmbhogikakāya are that (1)–(3) its verbal expressions, its physical appearance, and its activity are continuous, (4) its activity is spontaneously present, and (5) it displays many activities of the three kāyas, but is free from the nature of these [activities].[718]

The five of the nairmāṇikakāya are that it (1) demonstrates the path of peace, (2) matures those to be guided, (3) gives the prophecies, (4) displays the forms that guide [sentient beings and represent the uninterrupted] stream of all kinds of enlightened activities, and (5) appears for the cognizance of others.[719]

[Thus, the *Uttaratantra*] explains that the two rūpakāyas represent buddhahood, {602} while the *Suvarṇaprabhāsasūtra* explains that they do not. Some [other sources] say that buddhahood does not exist. The scholars who know the essential point [here] assert that these [explanations] represent the expedient meaning, the definitive meaning, and the final definitive meaning, respectively.

2.3.3.1.2. The explanation of the distinctive features of the three kāyas

This has three parts:

1) The distinctive feature of equality
2) The distinctive feature of permanence
3) The distinctive feature of appearance

2.3.3.1.2.1. The distinctive feature of equality

> **They are equal in terms of support, intention, and enlightened activity.**

From among the three distinctive features of the three kāyas, the feature of equality is as follows.

The dharmakāyas of all buddhas **are equal** since their **support**—the dharmadhātu—is not different. The sāmbhogikakāyas of all buddhas are equal since their **intention** is not different. The nairmāṇikakāyas of all buddhas are equal since they serve as a common **enlightened activity**. As the *Mahāyānasūtrālaṃkāra* says:

> They are asserted to be equal in terms of
> Support, intention, and activity.[720]

2.3.3.1.2.2. The distinctive feature of permanence

> **They are permanent in terms of nature, continuity, and an uninterrupted series.**

The distinctive feature of permanence is as follows. The dharmakāya is **permanent in terms of nature** since its essential character is the ultimate freedom from arising and ceasing. The sāmbhogikakāya is permanent in terms of its being the flow of a **continuity** since the enjoyment of dharma is continuous. The nairmāṇikakāya is permanent in terms of being **an uninterrupted series** of performing activity. For even after [certain of its manifestations] have disappeared [at certain points], [others] are displayed again and again. Thus, [certain continua] of similar type become discontinued, but [others] arise [instead] without delay. Thus, the above text says:

> In terms of nature, in terms of continuity,
> And in terms of an uninterrupted series, they are permanent.[721]

2.3.3.1.2.3. The distinctive feature of appearance

> **They appear by virtue of being pure of cognitive, afflictive, and karmic obscurations, respectively.**

The distinctive feature of appearance is as follows. The dharmakāya **appears by virtue of** the dharmadhātu's **being pure of cognitive** obscurations. The sāmbhogikakāya appears by virtue of [the dharmadhātu's] being pure of **afflictive** obscurations. {603} The nairmāṇikakāya appears by virtue of [the dharmadhātu's] being pure of **karmic obscurations.** Furthermore, one should understand that the two rūpakāyas are the kāyas that arise by virtue of the coming together of three [factors]—they are established due to the blessings of [a buddha's] dharmakāya, [the respective spheres of] appearance of those to be guided, and the previous aspiration prayers [of said buddha].

2.3.3.2. The explanation of the wisdoms (the supported)

This has five parts:

1) Detailed classification
2) The meanings of the terms and their natures
3) The causes through which they are accomplished
4) The ways of changing state
5) Matching them with the kāyas and their manner of knowing

2.3.3.2.1. Detailed classification

> **The supported is wisdom in its five modes of uncontaminated knowing.**

What is connected with these kāyas in such a way that it is **supported** [by them] **is wisdom**. When it is classified in terms of **its modes of uncontaminated knowing**, it is **fivefold**. (1) The suchness that is endowed with twofold purity is called "dharmadhātu wisdom." It is the basis and support for all [following] wisdoms. (2) The knowledge of all phenomena without exception through a single wisdom is mirrorlike wisdom. (3) The knowledge that all knowable objects are equality in that they are without nature is the wisdom of equality. (4) The knowledge of the entire range of phenomena without mixing them up is discriminating wisdom. (5) The knowledge of the activities to guide those who are to be guided is all-accomplishing wisdom.

2.3.3.2.2. The meanings of the terms and their natures

This has five parts:

1) The explanation of the meaning of dharmadhātu
2) [The explanation of the meaning of] mirrorlike
3) [The explanation of the meaning of] equality
4) [The explanation of the meaning of] discriminating
5) [The explanation of the meaning of] all-accomplishing

2.3.3.2.2.1. The explanation of the meaning of dharmadhātu

> **The dharmadhātu is nondual, free from the three, and nonconceptual.**

According to the *Nighaṇṭa*, the meaning of this term is as follows:

> *Dharmadhātuviśuddha* means the completely pure dharmadhātu. It serves as the cause and expanse for the arising and originating of the dharmas of the noble ones (such as the powers and fearlessnesses). Therefore, within the dharmadhātu (that is, suchness), the adventitious afflictive obscurations and cognitive obscurations (which are like clouds) are translucent and purified. Since it is similar to the pure expanse of the sky, it is called "the completely pure expanse of dharmas."[722]

Its nature is as follows. {604} It is without arising in the beginning, abiding in the middle, and ceasing in the end. Dhātu and awareness cannot be differentiated [from each other] as something different. It does **not** exist as an object for the **dual** extreme of superimposition and denial and it is **free from the three** obscurations. It is by nature free from tainting stains and does **not** exist as an object of **conceptions. The** completely pure **dharmadhātu** is the suchness of all phenomena and their unmistaken nature. It represents the cause that generates all qualities of the noble ones and is the essential character of all tathāgatas. The *Uttaratantra* says:

> Without beginning, middle, and end, indifferentiable,
> Nondual, free from the three, stainless, and nonconceptual—
> This is the nature of the dharmadhātu, which is seen
> By yogins in meditative equipoise who strive for it.[723]

2.3.3.2.2.2. The explanation of the meaning of mirrorlike

> **Without clinging, all knowable objects appear, just like in a mirror.**

According to the *Nighaṇṭa*, the meaning of this term is as follows:

> *Ādarśajñāna* means mirrorlike wisdom. Since it focuses on the completely pure dharmadhātu, it is free from all conceptions of apprehender and apprehended. This refers to the change of state of the ālaya-consciousness, through which the reflections of all phenomena appear [as clearly in it] as anything whatsoever [can] appear in a polished mirror. Thus, it is called "mirrorlike wisdom."

Its nature is as follows. Through being **without clinging** to what is mine, it clearly and always knows all objects, **just like** reflections **in a mirror.** Therefore, it is not ignorant about the entirety of **knowable objects** and does not depend on the appearance of any aspects of objects. As the *Mahāyānasūtrālaṃkāra* says:

> Mirrorlike wisdom is without what is mine,
> Unconfined, ever present,
> Not ignorant about the entirety of knowable objects,
> Yet never directed toward them.[724]

2.3.3.2.2.3. The explanation of the meaning of equality

Pure cultivation represents the equality of [saṃsāric] existence and peace.

As for the meaning of this term, the above text says:

> *Samatājñāna* means the wisdom of equality. {605} When the utterly pure familiarization with the actuality of true reality is clearly realized for the first time on the first bhūmi, no distinction is made between oneself and others and they are realized to be an equality. Through purification on the following higher bhūmis, on the buddhabhūmi this [eventually] becomes the nonabiding nirvāṇa. At this time, the afflicted mind has undergone a transition and changed state as wisdom. This is called "[the wisdom of] equality."

Its nature is as follows. Due to the familiarity with, and the **purity** of, the **cultivation** of the equality of oneself and others on the paths of learning, the nonabiding nirvāṇa is attained. At this point, **[saṃsāric] existence and peace** are realized as being **equality.** As [the *Mahāyānasūtrālaṃkāra*] says:

> The wisdom of equality toward sentient beings
> Is held to be stainless by virtue of pure cultivation.
> To reside in nonabiding peace
> Is asserted to be the wisdom of equality.[725]

2.3.3.2.2.4. The explanation of the meaning of discriminating

The discrimination of the entire variety represents the doors of samādhi and dhāraṇī.

As for the meaning of this term, the above text says:

> *Pratyavekṣājñāna* means discriminating wisdom. Through the change of state of the mental consciousness, [this wisdom] serves as the basis for all dhāraṇīs, samādhis, dhyānas, and meditative absorptions. It represents the operating of the wisdom that is unobstructed with regard to all knowable objects, pours down the great rain of dharma, cuts through all kinds of doubt, and serves as the cause for [buddhas] displaying their kāyas in the colors of precious substances (such as blue beryl). This is called "discriminating wisdom."

Its nature is to effortlessly engage in the unmistaken distinction and **discrimination** of the general and specific characteristics **of the entire variety** of knowable objects and to be endowed with limitless **doors of samādhi and dhāraṇī.** As [the *Mahāyānasūtrālaṃkāra*] says:

> Discriminating wisdom
> Is always unimpeded toward all knowable objects.
> It is just like a treasury
> Of dhāraṇīs and samādhis.[726]

2.3.3.2.2.5. The explanation of the meaning of all-accomplishing

> **The play of the skill in infinite means is all-accomplishing.**

As for the meaning of this term, {606} the above text says:

> *Krityānuṣṭhānajñāna* means all-accomplishing wisdom. Through the change of state of the consciousnesses of the five sense faculties (such as the eye), [this wisdom] serves as the basis for promoting the welfare of many sentient beings in all worldly realms through various infinite means. This is called "all-accomplishing wisdom."

Its nature is the knowledge of **accomplishing** the welfare of sentient beings through the manifold **play of skill in means** in order to mature those to be guided in limitless worldly realms. As [the *Mahāyānasūtrālaṃkāra*] says:

> All-accomplishing wisdom
> Accomplishes the welfare of all sentient beings
> In all realms through various
> Immeasurable and inconceivable emanations.[727]

2.3.3.2.3. The causes through which they are accomplished

> **They arise from relinquishment (such as listening), retaining the dharma,**
> **Cultivating equality, teaching the dharma, and accomplishing welfare.**

The wisdom of the dharmadhātu is accomplished through what entails all aspects of vast **relinquishment (such as** the maturation of the latent tendencies for **listening)**. The *Mahāyānasaṃgraha* says:

The small, medium, and great latent tendencies for listening are to be regarded as the seeds of the dharmakāya.[728]

As the *Mahāyānasūtrālaṃkāra* says:

Wherever the seeds of the afflictive and cognitive obscurations,
ever present since primordial time,
Are destroyed through all kinds of very extensive relinquishments,
Buddhahood is attained as the change of state endowed with the
supreme qualities of the pure dharmas,
Which is obtained through the path of utterly pure wisdom that is
nonconceptual and very vast in scope.[729]

Likewise, mirrorlike wisdom **arises from** listening to a lot of the genuine **dharma** and **retaining** it. The wisdom of equality [comes] from **cultivating** the **equality** of oneself and others. Discriminating wisdom [originates] from lucidly **teaching the** perfect **dharma**. All-accomplishing wisdom [comes] from **accomplishing** the **welfare** of others. {607} As the *Mahāyānasūtrālaṃkāra* says:

Due to retaining, due to equanimity,
Due to elucidating the perfect dharma,
And due to accomplishing activities,
The four wisdoms arise.[730]

2.3.3.2.4. The ways of changing state

The change of state of the empty and luminous [aspects] of the
ālaya, the afflicted mind,
The mental consciousness, and the five sense doors represents
the nature of the uncontaminated.

The change of state of the aspect of **emptiness of the ālaya** is called "dharmadhātu wisdom." The change of state of its **luminous** aspect is [called] "mirrorlike wisdom." The change of state of **the afflicted mind** is [called] "the wisdom of equality." The change of state of **the mental consciousness** is [called] "discriminating wisdom," **and** the change of state of the consciousnesses of **the five sense doors** is [called] "all-accomplishing wisdom." As master Candragomī says:

What is the ālaya-consciousness
Becomes mirrorlike wisdom.

This is asserted by some
As the nature of the dharmadhātu.

The change of state of the afflicted mind
Is to be designated as the wisdom of equality.
Discriminating wisdom
Is the one of the mental consciousness.

Since the consciousnesses of the five sense faculties
Fully apprehend all referents,
Nothing less than accomplishing everything
For the welfare of all sentient beings is attained.

[In the following,] the meaning of change of state is [explained]. As it is said:

The seed of existence is consciousness.[731]

Alternatively, [the *Abhidharmakośa*] gives the following definition of the dhātu of consciousness:

Contaminated consciousness
Is the dhātu of consciousness and the support for birth.[732]

Once the [consciousness that is described in these two quotations] has been let go of, the continuum of this type of consciousness undergoes a transition into **the nature of uncontaminated** wisdom. This is like iron transforming into gold through [an alchemistic elixir] that turns it into gold.

2.3.3.2.5. Matching them with the kāyas and their manner of knowing

Two each are included in two kāyas and the all-accomplishing one, in the nairmāṇikakāya.
Since it is beyond mind, it is free from the reference points of existence and nonexistence.
The way of knowing the nature of phenomena without appearance
And dependent origination as the mere way of appearance {608} **is inconceivable.**

The *Buddhabhūmisūtra* says that the five wisdoms **are included in** the three kāyas—**two** among the five wisdoms (dharmadhātu and mirrorlike [wisdom]) are included in the dharmakāya; **two** (the [wisdom of] equality and discriminating [wisdom]), in the sāmbhogikakāya; **and the all-accomplishing one, in the nairmāṇikakāya.**

As for [the question] whether wisdom exists on the buddhabhūmi or not and the manner in which wisdom knows, there were quite a number of people in India and Tibet who mostly spoke about this through conceptual imputations. Whatever their number may have been, ultimately speaking since this very buddha wisdom **is beyond** the sphere of **mind, it is free from all reference points** of extremes (such as **existence, nonexistence**, being, or nonbeing). Also the *Suvikrāntavikrāminparipṛcchasūtra* says that wisdom is free from existence, nonexistence, and both.

The manner in which this wisdom knows knowable objects is as follows. **The** ultimate **nature of phenomena** is known in a manner of being **without appearance**. As the *Satyadvayavibhāga* of the Madhyamaka [tradition] says:

> The omniscient one directly sees
> Everything as being devoid of any imputed nature
> And arising in dependence,
> Being nothing but how it appears.[733]

Accordingly, the seeming [reality] that is not conceptually imputed by followers of philosophical systems—the **mere** appearance of **dependently originating** causes and results—is known in a **way** [that entails] **appearance.** [Wisdom] also knows that [and how] certain superimposed aspects appear in the respective minds [that superimpose them]. Thus, this is like knowing, through the supernatural knowledge of knowing the minds of others, that, from the perspective of the person in whom this dream is happening, a dream is happening. Therefore since **the way of knowing** knowable objects is beyond the sphere of dialecticians, it **is inconceivable** for ordinary worldly people. As the *Laṅkāvatārasūtra* says:

> Personally experienced wisdom
> Is not the sphere of dialecticians.[734]

The *Pramāṇavārttika* says:

> This analysis of the characteristics of identifying
> [Phenomena] such as form and mind in such a way
> Is in terms of those with impure minds,
> But the realization of yogins is inconceivable.[735]

When one refers to this in terms of the seeming, [it is as follows.] If one designates mind and mental factors {609} as wisdom, such a wisdom does not exist because it constitutes the termination of all mistakenness. [However,] when one considers that [wisdom] knows all knowable objects without exception, it exists because the kāyas of the change of state have been found.

2.3.3.3. The explanation of the qualities of freedom and maturation

This has two parts:

1) Brief introduction
2) Detailed explanation

2.3.3.3.1. Brief introduction

> **When the limitless qualities are summarized, they are twofold in terms of freedom and maturation.**

When all **the limitless** and immeasurable **qualities** of perfect buddhas **are** briefly **summarized, they are** included in **two** sets. [The first one is] the final welfare of oneself, which is [referred to as] the thirty-two qualities that primordially and inseparably exist in the ultimate dharmakāya and are classified as the result that is the mere **freedom** from stains. [The second one is] the final welfare of others, which is referred to as the thirty-two qualities of maturation that exist in the seeming rūpakāyas and are accomplished through being developed in a progressive manner. The *Uttaratantra* says:

> One's own welfare and the welfare of others are the ultimate kāya
> And the seeming kāya that is supported by it, respectively.
> The results of freedom and maturation
> Are these qualities that are classified as sixty-four.[736]

2.3.3.3.2. Detailed explanation

This has two parts:

1) The qualities of freedom
2) The qualities of maturation

2.3.3.3.2.1. The qualities of freedom

This has two parts:

1) The thirty-two [qualities] as per the intention of the *Uttaratantra*
2) The twenty-one uncontaminated [sets of qualities] as per the intention of the *Abhisamayālaṃkāra*

2.3.3.3.2.1.1. The thirty-two [qualities] as per the intention of the *Uttaratantra*

This has two parts:
1) Connection through a brief introduction
2) Detailed commentary on their meaning

2.3.3.3..2.1.1.1. Connection through a brief introduction

The ultimate qualities of freedom are thirty-two.

2.3.3.3.2.1.1.2. Detailed commentary on their meaning

This has three parts:
1) The ten powers
2) The four fearlessnesses
3) The eighteen unique [qualities]

2.3.3.3.2.1.1.2.1. The ten powers

What is the case, maturation, faculties, constitutions,
inclinations, what leads everywhere,
Afflicted {610} and purified phenomena, recollection, birth and
death, and the termination of contamination—
The ten powers of knowing these overcome the obscurations.
They resemble a vajra.

The single power of the wisdom of a tathāgata is classified as tenfold through the objects that it knows.

(1) Through the previous generation of bodhicitta and the commitment to vows having been firm, [the power of] knowing **what is the case** (such as that the [karmic] maturation of virtuous actions is to obtain what is pleasant) and what is not the case (such as that the maturation [of such actions] could be something unpleasant) [is accomplished].

(2) Likewise, through having taught about actions and their results, [the power of] knowing the results of individual actions that were committed—the **maturation** of actions that is experienced individually—[is accomplished].

(3) Through having taught the dharma in accordance with the faculties [of individual beings], [the power of] knowing their higher and lower **faculties** (such as confidence) [is accomplished].

(4) Through having treated [beings] in accordance with their constitutions, [the power of] knowing their various **constitutions** (such as the different dispositions of the three yānas) [is accomplished].

(5) Through having treated [beings] in accordance with their inclinations, [the power of] knowing their various **inclinations** (such as the inclinations for contaminated or uncontaminated phenomena) [is accomplished].

(6) Due to being familiar with all yānas, [the power of] knowing the paths **that lead everywhere** in saṃsāra and nirvāṇa [is accomplished].

(7) Through having sincerely devoted oneself to samādhis, [the power of] knowing the modes of **afflicted and purified phenomena** (such as dhyānas and liberations) [is accomplished].

(8) Since virtuous actions have not become wasted, [the power of] **recollecting** the former states [of existence of beings is accomplished]. {611}

(9) Due to [causes] such as the superior intention toward sentient beings, [the power of] knowing the [manners of their] **deaths**, transitions, **and** [re] **births** through the divine eye [is accomplished].

(10) Through teaching the dharma for the sake of terminating contaminations, **the power of knowing** peace—**the termination of contamination**—is accomplished.

Thus since these **ten** powers **overcome the obscurations** (such as ignorance) and are never again dismantled by any obscurations, **they resemble a vajra.**

2.3.3.3.2.1.1.2.2. The four fearlessnesses

> **Enlightenment, termination of contamination, prophecy, and**
> **the path of final deliverance**
> **Represent the fearlessnesses about teaching the two welfares.**
> **They resemble a lion.**

(1) Since the fearlessness of being fully **enlightened** with regard to all phenomena means to know and realize all phenomena, there is no point in it that could be disputed by anyone—even the most powerful person—in the world by saying, "It is not like this." This is consummate realization.

(2) Since the fearlessness of the **termination of contamination** is the termination of all contamination such as desire, there is no point in those who proclaim it in this way that could be disputed. This is consummate relinquishment.

(3) Since the fearlessness of giving **prophecies** about obstructing phenomena means to directly see [all] obstructing factors (such as attachment to sense pleasures and liberation), there is no point in teaching them as such that could be disputed.

(4) Since the fearlessness of teaching **the path of final deliverance** means that [buddhas] directly see that liberation is attained through the dharmas

concordant with enlightenment and never through something else, there is no point in teaching them in this way that could be disputed by anyone. {612}

The first **two** [fearlessnesses] represent the [consummate] **welfare** of oneself and the latter two, the consummate welfare of others. **The fearlessness** and intrepidness **to teach** the dharma in the middle of retinues through these four **resemble** [those of] **a lion.**

2.3.3.3.2.1.1.2.3. The eighteen unique [qualities]

> **The six that consist of conduct and realization as well as the three of activity and knowledge**
> **Are the eighteen [qualities] that are unique compared to others. They resemble space.**

The exclusive distinctive features of buddhas **are the eighteen [qualities] that are unique compared to others**, such as śrāvakas and pratyekabuddhas—(a) **the six that consist of conduct**, (b) the six that consist of **realization**, (c) **the three** that consist of **activity**, **and** (d) the three that consist of **knowledge. They resemble space**, which is [unique in the sense of] not being mingled with the other four elements—it is the unconditioned element that represents the lack of anything that possesses a form which is manifest for others.

(a) As for the [qualities] that consist of conduct, arhats [still] have the [six flaws of] mistaken [physical conduct] (such as walking together with a mad elephant); pointless chatter (such as laughter and verbal abuse); deterioration of already attained mindfulness; not abiding in meditative equipoise during subsequent attainment; discriminating notions that [saṃsāric] existence and peace are different; and dwelling in indifference without examining those to be guided. On the contrary, the six unique conducts [of buddhas] are that (1) the physical conduct of tathāgatas is without any mistakenness (such as crushing snakes with the heels of their shoes). (2) Their verbal conduct is without any pointless chatter (such as speaking words that are not meaningful). (3) Since their mental conduct is without afflictions, they recollect their actions and words a long time back. Therefore, they are without any deterioration of mindfulness. (4) Since they engage in the entirety of meditative equipoise and subsequent attainment with the full knowledge of doing so, there is no time when they are {613} not in meditative equipoise. (5) Since their realization of the equality of [saṃsāric] existence and peace is complete, they lack discriminating notions of saṃsāra and nirvāṇa being different. (6) Though it is possible that those to be guided, while being examined [by the buddhas], become lost in what is meaningless, [buddhas] never dwell in indifference without examining them.

(b) As for the six that consist of realization since arhats have remaining cognitive obscurations, they have the weakness of not having attained the six qualities such as striving. On the contrary since tathāgatas have relinquished all cognitive obscurations, they lack any deterioration in the sense of not having attained the six unique realizations—(7)–(9) the three faculties of vigor, mindfulness, and prajñā, (10) striving (their matrix), (11) liberation (their result), and (12) the vision of the wisdom of liberation.

As for the ways of listing these [six qualities, there are various] intentions in different sūtras. Thus, this category in the prajñā[pāramitā sūtras] speaks of [(11) and (12) as] the two [qualities] of samādhi and liberation. Other [sūtras] state them to be samādhi and the vision of liberation. In *Uttaratantra* [III.12cd], based on the *Ratnādārikāparipṛcchasūtra*, the two [qualities] of liberation and [its] vision are described. [As in the above list,] when samādhi is not counted [among these six realizations], the intention is that it is included in [the fourth one among the above six qualities of conduct, that is,] lacking a mind that is not in meditative equipoise.

(c) The three that consist of activity correspond to the *Uttaratantra* saying:

> Actions are preceded by wisdom.[737]

The actions of the three doors of arhats are sometimes virtuous and sometimes neutral. {614} On the contrary, the three unique enlightened activities [of buddhas] are exclusively virtuous for the following reasons. Since all enlightened activities of tathāgatas—their activities of (13) body, (14) speech, and (15) mind—are motivated by wisdom, they are preceded by wisdom as their causal motivation. Since they flow simultaneously with wisdom, they follow wisdom as the motivation at the time [of engaging in them].

(d) As for the three that consist of knowledge, the wisdom of arhats entails attachment since it does not realize [its objects] through just the slightest effort, and it entails obstruction since it does not realize everything. On the contrary since tathāgatas realize all knowable objects through just the slightest effort, they are not attached or obstructed with regard to any entities that arise in (16) the past, (17) the future, and (18) the present, and have attained the unobscured vision of wishless wisdom. This is unique wisdom.

To count the eighteen unique [qualities] as the lack of pointless chatter and so on is the system of the Sautrāntikas and those above them from among the four [Buddhist] philosophical systems. The *Abhidharmakośa* says:

> The unique buddha qualities
> Are eighteen, such as the powers.[738]

The *Bhāṣya* [on this] explains the list of the eighteen that consist of the ten powers, the four fearlessnesses, the three unique foundations of mindfulness,[739] and great compassion as representing the system of the Vaibhāṣikas.

2.3.3.3.2.1.2.2. The twenty-one uncontaminated sets [of qualities] as per the intention of the *Abhisamayālaṃkāra*

> **In detail, they are the twenty-one uncontaminated sets—**
> **The factors concordant with enlightenment, the immeasurables, the liberations,**
> **The meditative absorptions, the totalities, the [āyatanas of] overpowering, dispassion,**
> **The knowledge through aspiration, the supernatural knowledges, the discriminating awarenesses,**
> **The four purities in all respects, the masteries, the powers, the four fearlessnesses,**
> **[The ways of] nothing to hide, the foundations of mindfulness, lack of forgetfulness, latent tendencies being overcome,**
> **Great Compassion, the unique [qualities], and the knowledge of all [aspects].**

In detail, the qualities of the ultimate dharmakāya {615} **are** described as **the twenty-one uncontaminated sets** in the [last] chapter of the *Abhisamayālaṃkāra* that teaches the fruition—the dharmakāya.

(1) The first set consists of **the** [thirty-seven] **factors concordant with enlightenment** (from the [four] foundations of mindfulness up through the eightfold path of noble ones) that are contained within a tathāgata's very own kāya. They are not like [said factors] during the time as a sentient being, which are not clearly manifest, since the factors of freedom and power are not fully perfected. [These here] are fully perfected, free from stains, and represent the uncontaminated wisdom that consists of the dharmadhātu. The same applies for all the [following] sets of uncontaminated wisdom.

(2) **The immeasurables** (such as love) cause other beings to be born in the four pure states [of Brahmā].

(3) **The** eight **liberations** are as follows. [First,] one looks at outer forms with the notion that inner consciousness possesses form, and then one looks at outer forms with the notion that inner [consciousness] is not something that possesses form. These are called "the two liberations when what does not possess form looks at form." The liberation of [particular notions of] beauty is called "perfectly abiding by having manifested the nature of being pleasant through the body." The [next] four are called "the Āyatanas of Space,

Consciousness, Nothing Whatsoever, and Neither Discrimination Nor Nondiscrimination." The [last] one is called "the cessation of discriminations and feelings."

(4) The fourth set consists of **the** nine **meditative absorptions** of progressive abiding, which are called "the meditative absorptions that are the four dhyānas of the form realm, the four meditative absorptions of the formless realm, and the meditative absorption of cessation."

(5) The fifth [set] consists of the ten types of totality which are called "**the totalities** of earth, water, fire, wind, blue, yellow, red, white, infinite space, and infinite consciousness."

(6) The sixth set consists of the eight āyatanas of **overpowering**. The [first] two are described as "with the notion that inner consciousness possesses form, {616} looking at outer forms and [seeing] each one of all their outer aspects as the aspects of small or big, respectively, thus overpowering their [remaining aspects]." The next two mean that "one looks at outer forms with the notion that inner [consciousness] is formless and [sees] them as the aspects of small or big, respectively, thus outshining their [remaining aspects]." The next four types are described as "with solely the notion that inner [consciousness] is formless, seeing [all aspects of outer forms as] blue, yellow, red, and white, respectively, thus outshining their [remaining aspects]." In brief, through [buddhas] having attained the power to stop the appearances that appear to [beings] with equal [perceptional] propensities as the four elements and the four colors, their samādhi causes [said appearances] to not appear [in these ways] and causes all objects to appear only, solely, and totally as gold and such.

(7) **Dispassion** is what is called "the samādhi that uproots the continuum of the enemies that are the afflictions contained in the mind streams of others."

(8) **The knowledge through aspiration** is said to be as follows. "True reality is free from all characteristics of reference points and does not go beyond such a nature, but those to be guided regard it as representing the characteristics of reference points. Since [buddhas] have accomplished [their former] aspiration prayers to overcome the desire and so on [of those to be guided] and to eliminate their doubts, the wisdom of tathāgatas engages in the welfare of beings for as long as saṃsāra lasts and their knowledge interacts with sentient beings even during the entire time of [their] being liberated [from saṃsāra]."[740]

(9) As for **the** six **supernatural knowledges**, the divine eye is to see all the forms in which all the various close and distant [beings] are reborn after their present bodies have passed away. The divine ear is to hear and understand all the various sounds, languages, and designations. The knowledge of [all] particulars of mind is to know all the more or less predominant thoughts and latencies of sentient beings. The [supernatural] knowledge of the body's

miraculous powers refers to knowing how to blaze [with fire], [display] many, few, good, or bad [bodies], walk on water, and sink into the earth. {617} The recollection of former states means to remember, starting with the present bodies [of beings], in which places they dwelled in former lifetimes and the accounts of whatever actions they committed. The knowledge of the termination of contamination means that, while being conscious of the progression of when certain afflictions to be relinquished through seeing and familiarization have been relinquished and certain [others] have not [yet] been relinquished, [buddhas] know that they have attained the wisdom [of knowing] that [said factors] are exhausted and do not arise [again].

(10) As for **the** four **discriminating awarenesses**, the discriminating awareness of dharma is to teach the eighty-four thousand doors of dharma as the various remedial means in accordance with the different ways of thinking of sentient beings. The discriminating awareness of meaning is to know the meanings that are expressed by the words and statements about the general characteristics of phenomena (impermanence, suffering, emptiness, and identitylessness) and their ultimate characteristic (their lack of arising and ceasing). The discriminating awareness of semantics is to not be ignorant about all beings' designations, languages, and their meanings. The discriminating awareness of self-confidence is to be unobstructed in teaching the dharma and cutting through doubts.

(11) **The four purities** are referred to as "completely pure [psychophysical] support, focal object, mind, and wisdom."

(12) As explained before, **the** ten **masteries** are the masteries over lifespan, mind, necessities, karma, birth, creative willpower, aspiration prayers, miraculous powers, wisdom, and dharma. The first three of these are the results of generosity; [the masteries over] karma and birth, those of ethics; [the mastery over] creative willpower, the one of patience; [the mastery over] aspiration prayers, the one of vigor; [the mastery over] miraculous powers, the one of dhyāna; and the last two, those of prajñā. During the phases of training, they are partially concordant with the actual [masteries], while [the latter exist] only on the buddhabhūmi.

(13) The thirteenth [set] consists of **the** ten **powers**.

(14) The fourteenth [set] consists of **the four fearlessnesses**.

(15) The physical, verbal, and mental conducts of tathāgatas are completely pure of mistakenness. In the nature of buddhas, {618} there is no shame or anxiety in the sense of being concerned that others might come to know their mistaken conducts. Therefore, they do not think, "I should hide something so that it does not become evident." This represents their three [ways] of **nothing to hide** [in their physical, verbal, and mental conducts].

(16) The three types of **the foundation of mindfulness** are as follows. "When tathāgatas teach the dharma, they are absolutely free from attachment to those who want to listen with respect, anger toward those who do not want to listen, and the arising of both attachment and aversion equally toward those who sometimes have respect and sometimes do not have respect. Thus, while being endowed with mindfulness, they rest in equanimity."

(17) The nature [of buddhas] is to **lack forgetfulness**. "Without ever missing the time to promote the welfare of sentient beings, they show in any form that is suitable to guide particular [beings]. Therefore, [they have] the characteristic of it being impossible for their activity in a particular situation to be untimely."

(18) Since they have relinquished the seeds that have the nature of the latencies of afflictive and cognitive obscurations, their **latent tendencies** are perfectly **overcome**.

(19) **Great compassion** for all beings is "the intention to benefit all beings."

(20) The twentieth [set] consists of the eighteen **unique** buddha qualities that are unique to them when compared to the lesser noble ones below them.

(21) **The knowledge** of all aspects is the knowledge of all aspects that represents the fruitional knowledges of all aspects, which is explained as the nature of the dharmakāya that is liberated from all factors to be relinquished.

2.3.3.3.2.2. The explanation of the qualities of maturation

This has two parts:

1) Brief introduction
2) Detailed explanation

2.3.3.3.2.2.1. Brief introduction

> **The two types of rūpakāyas are like the moon in the sky and in water—**
> **They appear, but are not established. These are the qualities of maturation.**

From among **the two rūpakāyas**, the sāmbhogikakāya **is like the moon** that appears **in the sky and** the nairmāṇikakāya [is like] the moon that is a [reflection of the] moon **in water**. Thus, under the influence of [taking care of] those to be guided, **they appear** in all kinds of forms, {619} **but are not established** as the natures of these [appearances]. **The** actual **qualities of maturation are** the thirty-two excellent major marks. The eighty minor marks and [the sixty aspects of] melodious voice [are discussed] as ancillary topics below.

2.3.3.3.2.2.2. Detailed explanation

> **They are adorned with the major and minor marks of a great being—**
> **The thirty-two such as even [soles] marked with wheels**
> **And the eighty such as copper-colored, glossy, and prominent [nails].**
> **They are [also] endowed with the sixty aspects of Brahmā's melodious voice.**

The thirty-two [major marks are as follows]. (1) Since the tathāgatas have been firm in their commitments before, their soles are level and **even**. (2) Through having practiced generosity, their palms and soles are **marked with wheels**. (3) Since they did not despise others, their heels are broad and their ankles do not protrude. (4) Because they have protected other sentient beings from fear, their fingers are long. (5) Since they did not create schisms within the retinues of others through slandering, their fingers and toes are joined by webs. (6) Through having provided various garments, the skin of their hands and feet is soft and supple. (7) Through having supplied vast amounts of foods and drinks, seven places of their bodies (the two palms, the two soles, the two shoulders, and the nape of the neck) have convex surfaces. (8) Because they have retained the dharma taught by the buddhas, their calves are fleshy and tapering like the calves of an antelope, which refers to those of a śarabha, and eight-legged lion, or a deer.[741] {620} (9) Since they have guarded secret words and abandoned sexual intercourse, their secret parts are withdrawn in a sheath, just as with elephants. (10) Through having gradually performed vast virtues, their upper bodies are massive, like the one of a lion. (11) Through having performed virtues in a perfect manner, the flesh between their shoulders is compact without any concavities [above and below the clavicles]. (12) Because they have provided others with fearlessness, their shoulder joints are evenly rounded. (13) Since they delighted in acting for others, their palms are soft, round, and even, that is, without any highs and lows. (14) Since they made efforts for the welfare of sentient beings, their arms are so long that they reach to their knees without bending down. (15) Through having engaged in an insatiable manner in the ten virtues, their bodies are completely pure of stains and endowed with an aura of light that is an arm span wide. (16) Because they have given medicine and so on to the diseased, the color of their throats is stainless and its shape is curved like a conch shell. (17) Since they have first trained in virtuous actions and perfected them later, their jaws are like those of the king of wild animals. (18) Since they [always] have adopted an equal intention towards sentient beings, they have forty teeth

(an equal number of twenty each in the upper and the lower [jaws]), which are well arranged, {621} pure of stains, and of equal size. (19) Through having guarded the actions of their three doors, their eyeteeth are perfectly white. (20) Through having spoken the truth, their tongues are infinitely long and inconceivable. (21) Since they supplied many [kinds of] tastes, [all] foods taste wonderful to their tongues. (22) Because they have spoken gentle and pleasing words, their self-arisen speech is as mellifluous as the sound of the kalāpin [bird] and the melodious voice of Brahmā. (23) Through being endowed with love and having protected everybody, their exquisite eyes are as blue as an utpala [flower]. (24) Since their intentions are without deceit and hypocrisy, their eyelashes are glossy and untangled, like those of a chief bull. (25) Since they have praised those who are praiseworthy, their beautiful and stainless faces possess the white ūrṇā hair with thirty-two strands at the spot between the eyebrows. (26) Through respect for their gurus, they are endowed with an uṣṇīṣa, their bodies being upright and immovable. (27) Through having been efficient in searching for the dharma, their skin is pure, delicate, and has a goldlike hue. (28) Since they have relinquished hustle and bustle, their body hairs are fine and soft, with one growing from each pore. (29) Since they retained the instructions in a way that is concordant with them, {622} the tips of their body hairs point upwards and curl to the right. (30) Through their loving-kindness for everybody and through having abandoned weapons, their hair is stainless and as blue as a dark-blue sapphire. (31) Because they have connected themselves and all others to samādhi, their bodies are as well proportioned as the maṇḍala of a perfect nyagrodha tree. (32) The ever excellent and incomparable Buddha, the great ṛṣi, is endowed with a body that is firm and has the power of Nārāyaṇa.[742]
The minor marks are as they are described in the *Abhisamayālaṃkāra*:

> The sage's nails are (1) copper-colored,
> (2) Glossy, and (3) prominent. His fingers and toes[743] are
> (4) Rounded, (5) compact, and (6) tapering.
> His veins (7) do not protrude and (8) are free from knots.
>
> (9) His ankles do not protrude and (10) his feet are equal [in size].
> He walks with the stride of (11) a lion, (12) an elephant,
> (13) A goose, and (14) a lordly bull, and walks (15) by keeping to the right [side],
> (16) Elegantly, and (17) upright. The limbs of his body are (18) well rounded,

(19) Smooth, (20) slender,
(21) Clean, (22) soft, and (23) pure.
(24) His genitals are fully developed
And (25) his figure is beautiful and stately.

(26) His steps are even and (27) his eyes {623}
Are pure. His body is (28) beautifully youthful,
(29) Not sunken, (30) with full [flesh],
And (31) very firm.

(32) His limbs are well proportioned
And (33) his vision is unobscured and pure.
His belly is (34) round, (35) smooth, (36) unmarred,
And (37) slender. His navel is (38) deep

And (39) winds to the right.
(40) He is beautiful to behold from all sides,
(41) His conduct is clean,
And (42) his body is free from black moles.

(43) His hands are as soft as cotton wool
And the lines on his palms arc (44) glossy, (45) deep, and (46) extensive.
(47) His face is not too long
And (48) his lips are red like a bimba berry.

His tongue is (49) supple, (50) slender,
And (51) red. His voice is (52) like thunder,
(53) Sweet, and gentle. His eyeteeth are (54) round,
(55) Sharp, (56) white, (57) equal [in size],

And (58) tapering. His nose is (59) prominent
And (60) supremely pure.
His eyes are (61) wide, (62) with well-developed eyelashes,
And (63) like the petals of a lotus.

His eyebrows are (64) elongated, (65) smooth,
And (66) shiny, and (67) their hairs are of equal length.
His arms are (68) long and muscular, and his ears
Are (69) equal and (70) completely unimpaired.

His forehead is (71) well shaped
And (72) broad, and (73) his head is large.
His hair is (74) as black as a black bee,
(75) Thick, (76) smooth, (77) not shaggy,

(78) Not unruly, and (79) has a fragrant smell
That captivates the minds of people.
[His hands and feet] are ornamented with (80) endless knots,
(81) Auspicious [signs], and (82) swastikas.
These are held to be the minor marks of a buddha.[744]

[For some] among these [minor marks, further explanations are provided here]. (3) Prominent nails means that they are not sunken. (9) The ankle joints do not protrude widely. (10) Both feet are of equal length and width. (11) [Buddhas] walk with the stride of a lion because they outshine the beings above the earth, such as humans. (12) [They have] the stride of an elephant since they outshine the beings beneath the earth, such as nāgas. (13) [The have] the stride of a goose or a garuḍa since they outshine the sentient beings who move through the sky and the beings on earth. (14) [They have] the stride of a chief bull since they lead their retinues. (24) Since their entire genitals are prominent and distinct, they are fully developed. (37) Since their bellies are wide and beautiful, they are even. (38) The cavity of their navel is deep and (39) its lines wind to the right. (47) Their mouth does not have the flaw of being excessively large. (53) Their vocal chords are not very long. (64) Since their two eyebrows join, they are long. (71) Since their forehead is appropriately large and not protuberant, it is well shaped. (78) Their hair parts equally [to both sides]. (80)–(82) The endless knots and the rims of the wheels on their hands and feet {625} are surrounded by seven-layered endless patterns of auspiciousness and square patterns in the shape of swastikas. The other [minor marks] are easy to understand.

You may wonder, "What kind of entity is the nature of these [major and minor marks]?" [There are] different systems of making assertions about them. According to the factions of the śrāvakas, they are something that has the nature of minutest particles, that is, they have the nature of the matter of outer referents. This means they [belong to] the āyatana of form. According to the Vijñaptivādins, their nature is samādhi associated with the congruent factor of prajñā. Since it is declared that their function is to produce an appearance for those to be guided, they are something that appears to others [than the buddhas], that is, the mere cognizances of those to be guided. However, conventionally speaking, a presentation of something like what has form as in the āyatanas is necessary here. Accordingly, in the Madhyamaka that concords with Yogācāra, they consist of the ways in which [beings] believe in what appears as the correct seeming. As [the *Uttaratantra*] explains:

Ordinary beings do not understand
That this is an appearance in their own minds.
Still, there is a purpose for them
To see the image of the [Buddha].[745]

The sixty aspects of Brahmā's melodious voice can be found in the *Tathāgataguhyasūtra*[746] and are explained in detail by Abhayā[karagupta] in his treatise *Munimatālaṃkāra*. [Here,] the meaning of this [explanation] is summarized in mnemonic verses:

(1) Supple, (2) gentle, (3) pleasant, (4) appealing,
(5) Pure, (6) stainless, (7) utterly clear,
(8) Sounding nicely and well, (9) worthy to listen to,
(10) Not harmful, (11) well sounding, (12) disciplined, (13) not rough,

(14) Not rude, (15) very disciplined, (16) sweet to the ears,
(17) Satisfying the body, (18) satisfying the mind,
(19) Delighting the heart, (20) producing joy and happiness,
(21) Completely without distress, (22) understandable by all, {626}

(23) Cognizable, (24) completely clear,
(25) Pleasing, (26) very pleasing,
(27) Making everything known, (28) causing understanding,
(29) Appropriate, (30) connected, (31) lacking the flaw of repetitiousness,

(32) Having the force of a lion's roar,
(33) Trumpeting [like] an elephant, (34) thundering,
(35) [Being like] the sound of the lord of nāgas, (36) the songs of gandharvas,
And (37) the melody of the kalāpin [bird],

(38) Resounding [like] the melodious voice of Brahmā,
(39) Sounding [like] the tuneful voice of the cīvaṃcīva [bird],[747]
(40) As pleasant as the melodious speech of the lord of gods,[748]
(41) [Being like] the sound of a drum, (42) not arrogant, (43) not low,

(44) Emulating all sounds, (45) no parts of words being slurred or
(46) incomplete,
(47) Not timid, (48) not weak, (49) very joyful, (50) pervasive,
(51) Fully realizing, (52) continuous, (53) ongoing,
(54) Perfecting all sounds,

(55) Satisfying all sense faculties, (56) not abusive,
(57) Unchanging, (58) not hasty, (59) resounding in all surroundings,
And (60) being endowed with the supreme of all aspects.

2.3.3.4. The explanation of the enlightened activity that is performed

This has two parts:
1) The detailed explanation of the seven points of activity
2) Their summary in two [points]

2.3.3.4.1. The detailed explanation of the seven points of activity

Enlightened activity is spontaneously present, without bias,
Blended into one, {627} **uninterrupted, [has] various means,**
Accords with karmic dispositions, and protects.

The **enlightened activity** of perfect buddhas is as follows. (1) They lack even the slightest characteristics of conception and effort in terms of "I should do such and such." Still, through the force of their prior generation of bodhicitta and vast aspiration prayers, the welfare of inconceivably [many] beings to be guided comes about in exact correspondence with each of their individual constitutions, intentions, and latencies in an effortless and spontaneous way through limitless miraculous displays of body, speech, and mind. This is similar to a wish-fulfilling jewel that is without effort and yet radiates light or the great drum of the gods, which does not have conceptions and yet teaches the four synopses of the dharma.[749]

(2) Without any bias of shining or not shining, the orb of the sun simultaneously shines on all containers of clear and unclear water in a way that individually matches them. Likewise, **without** the slightest **bias** in terms of "I shine on this one, but not on that one," a buddha's activities of body, speech, and mind shine simultaneously on those to be guided in ways that match their individual superior or inferior karmic dispositions.

(3) Blending together, the infinite rays of the sun engage in a single activity like opening a lotus. Likewise, the wisdoms and enlightened activities of all buddhas engage in guiding each sentient being by **blending into one**.

(4) Within the dhātu of unconditioned space, conditioned entities arise and perish in an uninterrupted manner. Likewise, after having become a completely perfect buddha within the uncontaminated dhātu, enlightened activity deals with those to be guided when the right time has come and does not deal with them when it has not come yet. {628} In such a way, the activities of a buddha are always **uninterrupted**.

(5) The welfare of those to be guided is promoted in limitless realms of the ten directions for as long as saṃsāra lasts. [This is accomplished] through **various means** as it is suitable, such as [demonstrating] full enlightenment for certain [beings], turning the wheel of dharma for certain [others], and demonstrating nirvāṇa for some [others].

(6) Due to differences in the heights of mountains, the rays of the [rising] sun shine on them in due order. Likewise, also the enlightened activity of a buddha deals with the beings to be guided, who have superior, medium, and inferior **karmic dispositions**, in gradual ways that individually **accord with** them.

(7) The welfare of sentient beings is promoted through five ways of **protecting** them. That is, merely through seeing a buddha, they are protected from harm, the lower realms, that which is not the means [for liberation], the sufferings of the three realms, and inferior yānas.

2.3.3.4.2. Their summary in two points

> **It establishes those to be guided in the supports of the paths (higher states),**
> **The actual paths, and their completions. Therefore, in brief,**
> **It is contained in the two [aspects] of being effortless and uninterrupted.**

The nature of the enlightened activity of the victors is the uninterrupted display of whatever guides whomever, which is equal to space. Its function is that **it**, through the three boundless miraculous displays [of body, speech, and mind], **establishes those to be guided in the supports of the paths (higher states**—the yānas of gods and pure states), **the actual paths** of accumulation, preparation, and so on, **and their completions** (the fruitions of the three yānas). **Therefore, in brief, it is contained in the two** [aspects] **of being effortless and uninterrupted.** This corresponds to [the description of] the first [aspect] in the *Uttaratantra*:

> Since they lack conceptions as to {629}
> For whom, whereby, how,
> And when [they perform] guiding activities,
> [The activities] of the sages are always effortless.[750]

The latter [aspect] is also described in this text:

> Because of setting out for the sake of others,
> Because of seeing sentient beings and oneself as equal,
> And because of what is to be done not being completed,
> There is no end of activity.[751]

Appendix VII: Short Biographies of the Third, Seventh, and Eighth Karmapas and the Fifth Shamarpa

The Third Karmapa, Rangjung Dorje

The Third Karmapa was born on January 27, 1284 into a family of Nyingma tantric practitioners in the area of Mangyül Tingri Langkor[752] in Tsang, Central Tibet. His father was Dönba Chöbal[753] and his mother Jomo Yangdren.[754] From the age of three onward, he would sit on rocks or other seats and teach his playmates. He also proclaimed himself to be the Karmapa. At the age of five, he visited the Second Karmapa's main disciple and lineage holder, the great Drugpa Kagyü siddha Urgyenpa Rinchen Bal[755] (1230–1309), who had already had a dream about his arrival. He tested the young Karmapa, who then reported details of the meeting between Rinchen Bal and the Second Karmapa, Karma Pakshi. Rinchen Bal returned all the Karmapa's possessions, including the Black Crown, bestowed the lay vows upon him, and gave him the name Rangjung Dorje, which had been Karma Pakshi's secret name. Thereafter, he began offering the Karmapa empowerments and instructions. At seven, Rangjung Dorje was ordained as a novice by Tropuwa Künden Sherab,[756] with whom he also studied the vinaya. Two years later, he arrived at the Karmapas' main seat in Tsurpu,[757] where, over the next nine years, he received the entire transmissions of both the Kagyü and Nyingma lineages from his principal tutor, the great siddha Nyenré Gendün Boom,[758] as well as other teachers, such as Lopön Sherab Bal,[759] Gyagom Yeshe Ö,[760] and Namtsowa Mikyö Dorje.[761] After a retreat on the slopes of Mount Everest at age eighteen, Rangjung Dorje received full monastic ordination from Shönu Jangchub[762] and Gendün Rinchen.[763]

In the following years, he studied extensively with many great masters of all Tibetan traditions, thus gaining mastery of most of the Buddhist transmissions from India to Tibet. This included studying Madhyamaka, Yogācāra, the five texts of Maitreya, abhidharma, and pramāṇa at the famous Kadampa monastic college of Sangpu[764] with Śākya Shönu[765] (then abbot of its "lower" monastic seat) and Lodrö Tsungmé (mid-thirteenth to mid-fourteenth century); detailed expositions and empowerments of the Kālacakratantra and many other "old" and "new" tantras from Nyedowa Kunga Döndrub[766] (born 1268) and Tsültrim Rinchen;[767] teachings on medicine from Lama Baré;[768] and the *Vima Nyingtig*[769] as well as the Six Dharmas of Niguma from the most eminent exponent of Dzogchen at the time, Rigdzin Kumārarāja (1266–1343), the main teacher of the great Nyingma master Longchen Rabjampa (1308–1368). With the latter, Rangjung Dorje also shared a mutual teacher-student relationship.

Throughout his life, the Third Karmapa spent considerable time in solitary meditation retreats but also traveled throughout Tibet, giving teachings and often acting as a mediator in local conflicts. He also had many visions of great masters of the past and deities. During a retreat in his early twenties at Karma Yangön,[770] he experienced such a significant encounter with Vimalamitra and Padmasambhava, both melting into a point between his eyebrows. At this moment, he realized all the Dzogchen tantras of the Nyingma lineage. Thereafter, he wrote several volumes on Dzogchen, the most important being the *Karma Nyingtig*,[771] thus unifying the teachings of the Kagyü Mahāmudrā and the Nyingma Dzogchen. Through this and the teachings he had received mainly from Rigdzin Kumārarāja, the Karmapa became both a tertön ("treasure-revealer") and a lineage holder in the Nyingma Dzogchen tradition. In 1310, he met with the famous Sakya master Yagdön Sangyé Bal[772] (1348–1414). Thereafter, he stayed in retreat on the slopes of Mt. Everest and at the hermitage of Gampo Sanglung[773] in Tagpo.[774] Altogether, he stayed for three years in Tagpo and Kongbo,[775] teaching, meditating, founding hermitages, and visiting holy places. In 1318, at the hermitage of Tsurpu Gung,[776] he had visions of the outer and inner spheres of the Kālacakra teachings, upon which he composed a treatise on a revised system of astrology, which is transmitted to this day as the Tsurpu tradition of Tibetan astrology. In the same year, he founded the hermitage of Upper Dechen[777] in the Tsurpu Valley, where he also wrote several of his most famous treatises, such as *The Profound Inner Reality* and *The Distinction between Consciousness and Wisdom*.

Rangjung Dorje is reported to have met Dölpopa once between 1320 and 1324 and prophesied that the latter would come to realize an especially sublime view unlike his present one.[778] It was soon after that Dölpopa formulated his system of "other-emptiness." In 1324, Rangjung Dorje returned for one year to Kongbo, teaching and establishing several monasteries and retreat facilities. While staying at Gogtreng[779] in Kongbo—a place where Padmasambhava had meditated—he composed his autocommentary on *The Profound Inner Reality* in 1325. In 1326, the Karmapa quelled a feud between the Central Tibetan kingdom of Tsal and the Khampas. He proceeded to eastern Tibet, restored Karma Gön,[780] and had an iron bridge built over the Sogchu[781] River in 1328.

Continuing the relationship of the Mongol imperial court with the Second Karmapa, Rangjung Dorje was invited to China by the emperor Toq Temür of the Yüan dynasty in 1331. He entered China in 1332, to learn that the emperor had just died. His nephew and successor, Irinjibal (a.k.a. Ratnaśrī), urged the Karmapa to continue his journey, but he also died soon after Rangjung Dorje's arrival at the court in Ta'i-tu. The Karmapa assisted in the complex matters of installing the next emperor, Togan Temür—Irinjibal's elder brother, and bestowed many teachings upon him. Having promised the emperor to return in two years, Rangjung Dorje left the court for Tibet in 1334. He visited Wu-t'ai-shan (the holy mountain of Mañjuśrī)[782] and several places in Kham on the way, arriving in Tsurpu late in 1335. Upon being reinvited to the Mongol court, the Karmapa departed from Tsurpu in August 1336 and arrived in Beijing in 1337. During the eighth Tibetan month of that year (August-September), he prophesied a severe earthquake, making the emperor and his court camp on an open plain, thus saving many people. During the last two years of his life at the court, Rangjung Dorje functioned as spiritual and political advisor to the emperor, taught the dharma, and established some monasteries. In the summer of 1338, at a meeting of Mongol officials, he announced, "I, a yogin, am like a cloud. May all who wish to grasp the meaning of my teachings do so swiftly." On June 21 in 1339, Rangjung Dorje passed away, and it is said that his image appeared in the full moon that night.

As for the Karmapa's scriptural legacy, besides the texts mentioned, further important works that are still available are his autocommentary on *The Profound Inner Reality*, the *Aspiration Prayer of Mahāmudrā*,[783] an *Instruction Manual on Uniting with Connate Mahāmudrā*,[784] *Pointing Out the Three Kāyas*,[785] *The Nonduality of Prāṇa and Mind*,[786] a commentary on the *Hevajratantra*, commentaries on Saraha's three cycles of Dohā, Tilopa's *Ganges Mahāmudrā*, and the Six Dharmas of Nāropa, several texts on the Cakrasaṃvaratantra, the Kālacakratantra, and Cutting Through (gcod), *The Treatise on Pointing Out the Tathāgata Heart*, his commentary on Nāgārjuna's *Dharmadhātustava*, and the *Synopsis of the Eight Chapters of Prajñāpāramitā*.

Rangjung Dorje's main disciples were Gyalwa Yungdönba[787] (1284–1365), who was his successor as a lineage holder; the First Shamarpa, Tragpa Sengé[788] (1283–1349); and Yagdön Sangyé Bal.

The Seventh Karmapa, Chötra Gyatso

Born to a family of tantric practitioners in Chilha[789] in northern Tibet, the Seventh Karmapa (1454–1506) was heard to say "Ama-la" (mother) while he was still in his mother's womb. At birth, he spoke the Sanskrit syllables AḤ HŪṂ, and at five months of age, he said, "There is nothing in the world but emptiness. People may think there is real existence, but they are wrong. For me, there is neither birth nor death."

When he was nine months of age, his parents took him to the First Goshir Gyaltsap, Baljor Töndrub[790] (1427–1489), who recognized and enthroned him as the Seventh Karmapa in accordance with the instruction letter of the Sixth Karmapa. At four, he received a series of empowerments, and at eight, the lay ordination and the bodhisattva vows from Gyaltsab Rinpoche. During the following three years, the basic Kagyü teachings were transmitted to him by Gyaltsab Rinpoche, Pengar Jampel Sangpo[791] (who also ordained him as a novice), and the Second Tai Situ, Dashi Namgyal[792] (1450–1497), at Karma Gön in East Tibet, one of the three main seats of the Karma Kagyü lineage. Thereafter the Karmapa traveled to northeastern Tibet, ended local feuds between Buddhists and Bönpos, taught the dharma, and continued his training. Displaying great erudition at an early age, he joined teachings at monastic colleges with the senior scholars, and at Surmang Monastery, he composed several texts. In 1471, he entered a meditation retreat for seven years.

Subsequently, the Karmapa stayed for a while at his main seat in Tsurpu, where he restored the large buddha statue commissioned by the Second Karmapa and established a famous large monastic college. When he visited the local ruler of a province in southern Tibet, he met the First Karma Trinlépa. After having taught the latter for five months, he installed him as the abbot of Chökor Lhunpo[793] Monastery, where he had established a monastic college. Eventually, Chötra Gyatso's reputation as a scholar spread to India and China, so that he received offerings from the abbot of Bodhgayā and was visited by Indian paṇḍitas such as Rāhulakīlaya and Śīlasāgara. He also received an invitation from the Chinese emperor. In 1498, he recognized the Third Tai Situ, Dashi Baljor[794] (1498–1541). At Rinpung[795] in Central Tibet, he taught monks from many different Tibetan Buddhist schools, among them Śākya Chogden, whom he declared to be his equal.

In general, Chötra Gyatso dedicated much of his life to retreat, but also founded several monastic colleges, settled political disputes, worked to protect animals from being killed, and initiated iron bridge constructions. He authored many texts on both sūtras and tantras, such as JG and his famous commentary on Dignāga's and Dharmakīrti's works on pramāṇa, the four-volume *Ocean of*

Texts on Reasoning. When he dictated the latter text, himself being renowned as an incarnation of Dharmakīrti, he did not rely on any written texts, but composed and quoted everything from memory. When he paused his dictation, he would resume it later at the exact point he had left off.

The day before his passing away, the Karmapa provided details of his next incarnation and passed on the lineage to Tai Situ. Besides the latter, his foremost students included the Second Gyaltsab Rinpoche, Dashi Namgyal[796] (c. 1490–1518); the Fourth Shamarpa, Chökyi Tragpa Yeshé Balsangpo[797] (1453–1524); the First Sangyé Nyenpa Rinpoche, Dashi Baljor (1457–1519); Tagpo Rabjampa Chögyal Denpa[798] (1449–1524); Śākya Chogden; and Karma Trinlépa.

The Eighth Karmapa, Mikyö Dorje

The Eighth Karmapa (1507–1554) was born in a village called Satam[799] in the region of Ngomchu[800] in eastern Tibet into a family of yogins. At birth, he is said to have uttered, "I am the Karmapa." His rebirth was confirmed by the Third Tai Situ, who took him to the main eastern Karma Kagyü seat of Karma Gön when he was three months old. The Karmapa was formally enthroned at age six by the Second Goshir Gyaltsab. He studied with Dülmo Dashi Öser[801] (b. 1474); Tagpo Dashi Namgyal[802] (1512–1587); the First Karma Trinlépa, Choglé Namgyal (1456–1539); and the First Sangyé Nyenpa Rinpoche. The latter was a great siddha and had been selected by the Seventh Karmapa as the principal teacher of the Eighth. After Sangyé Nyenpa had ordained Mikyö Dorje as a novice in 1516, until 1519 he bestowed all the major transmissions of the Kagyü lineage to him. At age twenty-one, the Karmapa received full ordination as a monk from Khenchen Chödrub Sengé[803] and Karma Trinlépa. The Second Pawo Rinpoche, Tsugla Trengwa (1504–1566), reports that, during this occasion, Chödrub Sengé exhorted the Karmapa to uphold the *Shentong* approach.[804] Thereafter, Mikyö Dorje studied both the sūtrayāna and the tantrayāna with Karma Trinlépa for three years, such as the five works of Maitreya, the major texts on valid cognition, higher and lower abhidharma, vinaya, the *Mūlamadhyamakakārikā*, the *Madhyamakāvatāra*, and the *Hevajratantra*. This included extensive teachings on the AA and its commentaries, which resulted in the composition of JNS (completed in 1529).

Even at a young age, the Eighth Karmapa did not remain constantly at his main seat in Tsurpu, but traveled throughout Tibet with his large monastic camp, giving teachings and help to all who asked for it, often also mediating political conflicts. In addition, he taught extensively at the great Karma Kagyü monastic college (shédra) of Tagpo Legshé Ling.[805] Throughout his life, he received several invitations to teach at the Chinese and Mongol courts. However, for various reasons, he declined every time.

Mikyö Dorje was both an exceptional meditation master and a prolific scholar, composing over thirty volumes, many of which were written during his extensive travels. Even to this day, together with the Seventh Karmapa's *Ocean of Texts on Reasoning*, the Eighth Karmapa's commentaries on the four other major subjects of the Tibetan monastic colleges (vinaya, abhidharma, prajñāpāramitā, and Madhyamaka) represent the backbone of sūtrayāna studies in the Karma Kagyü School. Equally famed are his extensive writings on Mahāmudrā and vajrayāna topics, such as his *Pointing Out the Three Kāyas*[806] and his large commentary on Drikungpa Jigden Sumgön's[807] (1143–1217) *Single Intention of the Genuine Dharma*.[808] He also composed many sādhanas and practice liturgies (such as the *Four-Session Guru Yoga*,[809] a central practice of the Karma Kagyü School) and compiled the famous *Ocean of Kagyü Dohās*.[810] In addition, Mikyö Dorje excelled as a painter (inspiring the Karma Gadri style of thangka painting),[811] poet, and sculptor. Once, at Tsurpu, he made a small marble statue of himself and left an impression of his fingers in a leftover piece of marble by squeezing it like soft clay.[812] When consecrating the statue in the midst of many followers, he asked it whether it looked like him and the statue replied, "Sure I do!"

Shortly before his death, the Eighth Karmapa pacified an outbreak of leprosy in southern Tibet, soon after which he started to show signs of the disease himself and eventually passed away. His main disciples were the Fifth Shamarpa; the Second Pawo Rinpoche; the Third Gyaltsab, Tragpa Baljor (1519–1549);[813] and the Fourth Situpa, Chökyi Kocha (1542–1585).[814]

The Fifth Shamarpa, Göncho Yenla

The Fifth Shamarpa (1525–1583) was born in Ganden Kangsar[815] in the southern Tibetan province of Gongbo.[816] As soon as he was born, he looked at his mother and smiled at her. At the age of two, he was recognized and enthroned by the Eighth Karmapa. At the age of four, the young Shamarpa had learned reading and writing without effort and already knew several major texts on Tibetan grammar and Buddhism, such as Aśvaghoṣa's *Fifty Stanzas on the Guru* and the Third Karmapa's *Profound Inner Reality*.[817] When he was eight, he received the vows of an upāsaka[818] from the Eighth Karmapa, who gave him the name Göncho Bang[819] and his red crown. He continued to obtain many empowerments, reading transmissions, and instructions from the Karmapa (such as the Six Dharmas of Nāropa, the Six Dharmas of Niguma, and Mahāmudrā) and completed his education with him at the age of twelve. Thereafter, he was instructed by the Second Pawo Rinpoche, thus obtaining the entire transmission of the Kagyü lineage. In 1539, he received his novice vows and became formally installed at his main seat, Yangbachen,[820] by the Eighth Karmapa. He continued to receive many profound teachings and spent time in meditation retreats at Tsurpu, with his realization increasing greatly. In 1542, he was fully ordained as a monk by the Karmapa, Pawo Rinpoche, and Śākya Gyatso.[821] Besides these three, Göncho Yenla also studied with the tertön Shigbo Lingpa Kargyi Wangchug Dsal[822] (1524–1583), Kunga Chösang,[823] the Jonang master Dzamtang Gyalwa Sengé[824] (1509–1580), and Dalung Namgyal Tragba[825] (1469–1530?). After the Eighth Karmapa had passed away in 1554, he became the supreme holder of the Kagyü lineage until 1561, when he enthroned the Ninth Karmapa, Wangchug Dorje[826] (1556–1603) and passed on all the transmissions to him.

Göncho Yenla was not only very erudite in both the sūtras and the tantras but also a highly accomplished meditation master. His collected works in eight volumes include texts on the seven-point mind training; a general presentation of the tantras; instructions on the Six Dharmas of Nāropa and the Six Applications of the Kālacakratantra; a brief interlinear commentary, a more detailed explanation, and a general synopsis on the Third Karmapa's *Profound Inner Reality*; interlinear commentaries on the latter's *Pointing Out the Tathāgata Heart* and *Distinction between Consciousness and Wisdom*; several teachings on Mahāmudrā, such as a commentary on Tilopa's *Ganges Mahāmudrā*[827] and texts on the Drikung "Fivefold Mahāmudrā"; a glossary of Buddhist terminology; and various sādhanas.

Besides the Ninth Karmapa, the Fifth Shamarpa's numerous illustrious disciples from different Kagyü, Nyingma, and Sakya schools included the

Fourth Gyaltsab Rinpoche, Tragpa Töndrub[828] (1550–1617); the Fifth Situpa, Chökyi Gyaltsen[829] (1562–1632); the Third Pawo Rinpoche, Tsugla Gyatso[830] (1567–1633); Kyabda Drubcho Wangpo[831] (1563–1618; abbot of Legshé Ling and reincarnation of the Drugpa Kagyü siddha Gyalwa Götsangpa);[832] Sönam Gyatso[833] (the main teacher at Legshé Ling); Karma Trinlé Lhundrub (main teacher at another Kagyü college, called Sungrab Ling);[834] the head of the Drikung Kagyü, Chögyal Püntso[835] (1547–1602); the head of the Daglung Kagyü, Kunga Dashi[836] (1536–1599/1605); Namka Dashi[837] (founder of the Karma Gadri painting style); Yenpa Lodé[838] (1536–1597; a reincarnation of the great tertön Pema Lingpa);[839] and the Sakya master Dsedong Dagchen Kunga Legbé Jungné.[840]

Appendix VIII: The Abhisamayālaṃkāra

Abhisamayālaṃkāranāmaprajñāpāramitopadeśaśāstra

The Treatise on the Pith Instructions on Prajñāpāramitā, Called The Ornament of Clear Realization

She is the one who, through the all-knowledge, guides the śrāvakas who search for peace to utter peace.
She is the one who, through the knowledge of the path, makes those who promote the benefit of beings accomplish the welfare of the world.
Being united with her, the sages proclaim this variety endowed with all aspects.
I pay homage to this mother of the Buddha with his assemblies of śrāvakas and bodhisattvas.

So that the path of the knowledge of all aspects
That is explained here by the teacher,
Though not experienced by others,
Will be seen by the intelligent, [I.1]

And that, having committed to memory the meaning of the sūtras,
Which has the character of the ten dharma practices,
They may realize them in an easy way
Is the purpose of this undertaking. [I.2]

Prajñāpāramitā is proclaimed
By way of the eight topics.
The knowledge of all aspects, the knowledge of the path,
Then the all-knowledge, [I.3]

The full realization of all aspects,
The attainment of culmination, the serial one,
The full realization in a single instant,
And the dharmakāya—these are the eight. [I.4]

Generating bodhicitta, the instructions,
The four branches of penetration,
The foundation of practice,
Whose nature is the dharmadhātu, [I.5]

The focal object, the aim,
The activities of [donning] the armor and engaging,
The equipments, and final deliverance
Represent the knowledge of all aspects of the sage. [I.6]

Eclipsing and so on,
The paths of disciples and rhinos,
The path of seeing, which is of great benefit
By virtue of the qualities in this [life] and others, [I.7]

As well as function, aspiration,
Praise, eulogy, and laudation,
Dedication and rejoicing
(Both unsurpassable mental engagements), [I.8]

Accomplishment, and utter purity
(The path of familiarization)
Describe the knowledge of the path
Of skillful bodhisattvas. [I.9]

Not dwelling in existence through prajñā,
Not dwelling in peace through compassion,
Being distant due to lacking the means,
Not being distant due to the means, [I.10]

Antagonistic and remedial factors,
Training, its equality,
And the paths of seeing of śrāvakas and so on
Are asserted as the all-knowledge. [I.11]

Aspects, trainings,
Their qualities, flaws, and characteristics,
The factors conducive to liberation and penetration,
The assembly of irreversible learners, [I.12]

The equality of existence and peace,
And unsurpassably pure lands
Make up the full realization of all aspects,
Which includes skill in means. [I.13]

Its sign, increase,
Stability, continuous abiding of the mind,
The four conceptions'
Four kinds of remedy [I.14]

On the paths called "seeing"
And "familiarization," respectively,
The uninterrupted samādhi,
And mistaken notions [I.15]

Represent the culminating clear realization.
The serial [training] is thirteenfold.
The full realization in a single instant
Is fourfold by way of characteristics. [I.16]

As svābhāvika[kāya], sambhoga[kāya],
And also as nairmāṇika[kāya], which is other,
The dharmakāya, together with its activity,
Is proclaimed to be fourfold. [I.17]

The knowledge of all aspects

The generation of bodhicitta is, for the welfare of others,
The desire for completely perfect enlightenment.
Briefly and in detail, this and that
Are expressed according to the sūtras. [I.18]

Earth, gold, moon, fire,
Treasure, jewel mine, ocean,
Vajra, mountain, medicine, friend,
Wish-fulfilling gem, sun, song, [I.19]

King, treasure-vault, highway,
Vehicle, fountain,
Pleasant melody, river, and cloud—
Through [being like] these, it is twenty-twofold. [I.20]

Practice, the realities,
The three jewels (such as the Buddha),
Nonclinging, being completely untiring,
Fully embracing the path, [I.21]

The five visions,
The six qualities of supernatural knowledge,
The path of seeing and the one called "familiarization"—
The instructions on these should be known as tenfold. [I.22]

Those of duller and sharper faculties,
Those who attain through confidence and seeing, those from family to family,
Those with a single interval, in the intermediate [state], after being born,
With effort, without effort, who progress to Akaniṣṭha, [I.23]

Three leapers, those who progress to the highest peak of existence,
Those who overcame attachment to form,
[Attain] peace amidst visible phenomena, are a bodily witness,
And the rhinos—these are twenty. [I.24]

By virtue of focal objects, aspects,
Causes, and being mentored,
Based on being associated
With the four conceptions in due order, [I.25]

Compared to śrāvakas and rhinolike ones,
A protecting bodhisattva's
Lesser, medium, and great degrees
Of heat and so on are more distinguished. [I.26]

The focal objects are impermanence and so on,
Which are the substrates of the realities.
Their aspects are to refrain from clinging and so on,
The cause for attaining all three yānas. [I.27]

[The further ones] are the rising and falling of form and so on,
Nonabiding, abiding, imputations, and being inexpressible.
Not abiding in form and so on
Is their lack of nature by virtue of being such. [I.28]

These two having a common nature,
There is no abiding in their being impermanent and such.
Their being empty of being that
Is their common nature. [I.29]

There is no grasping at phenomena.
Not seeing the characteristics of these,
Prajñā investigates
In terms of all being unobservable. [I.30]

Form and so on are without nature,
Their nature being their nonbeing.
They are without arising and without final deliverance,
Are purity, and without characteristics. [I.31]

Not dwelling on their characteristics,
There is no aspiration and no discrimination.
Samādhi, its function,
Prophecy, termination of conceit, [I.32]

The common nature of the three,
And the nonconceptuality of samādhi—
These are the lesser, medium, and great degrees
Of the factors conducive to penetration. [I.33]

The conceptions about the apprehended are twofold
In terms of entities and their remedies,
Each of which is subdivided into nine
Based on ignorance, skandhas, and so on. [I.34]

Likewise, those about the apprehender are asserted as twofold,
Based on substance and imputation
In terms of the nature of an independent self and so on,
And what is based on the skandhas and so on. [I.35]

The mind not being intimidated and such,
Those who teach the lack of nature and so on,
And abandoning the antagonistic factors of these
Means being mentored in every way. [I.36]

The foundation for the six dharmas of realization,
Both remedy and relinquishment,
The complete consumption of these,
Prajñā with compassion, [I.37]

What is not in common with the disciples,
The progression of the welfare of others,
And the effortless operation of wisdom
Are called "the disposition." [I.38]

Because the dharmadhātu is indivisible,
Divisions of the disposition are not tenable.
But by virtue of the divisions of the phenomena founded on it,
Its divisions are expressed. [I.39]

The focal object is all phenomena.
They are virtuous and so on,
Those called mundane realizations,
Those asserted to be supramundane, [I.40]

Contaminated and uncontaminated phenomena,
Those that are conditioned and unconditioned,

Phenomena in common with the disciples,
And the uncommon ones of the sage. [I.41]

This aim of the self-arisen ones,
By virtue of the three greatnesses, should be known as threefold—
The mind of the highest state of all sentient beings,
Relinquishment, and realization. [I.42]

Armorlike practice is explained accordingly
Through six sets of six
By combining each one
Of the six, such as generosity. [I.43]

Dhyānas and formless states, generosity and such,
Path, love and so forth,
Not having anything as a focal object,
Purity of the three spheres, [I.44]

Aim, the six supernatural knowledges,
And the principle of the knowledge of all aspects—
One should know that the practice of engagement refers to these,
Which means mounting the mahāyāna. [I.45]

Loving-kindness, the six such as generosity,
Calm abiding with superior insight,
The path of union,
Skill in means, [I.46]

Wisdom, merit,
The path, dhāraṇī, the ten bhūmis,
And the remedies—these should be known
As the progression of the practice of the equipments. [I.47]

Through tenfold purification
The first bhūmi is attained.
Intention, beneficial things,
An equal mind toward sentient beings, [I.48]

Giving away, serving friends,
Searching for the genuine dharma as focal object,
A constant mindset of leaving,
Longing for the buddhakāya, [I.49]

Teaching the dharma, and true speech,
Which is asserted to be the tenth.
Through not observing any nature
These are to be understood as purifications. [I.50]

Ethics, gratitude, patience,
Utter joy, great compassion,
Respectful service, listening to the guru with reverence,
And the eighth, vigor for generosity and such. [I.51]

Insatiable desire to study,
Giving the dharma without expecting any reward,
Purification of the buddha realm,
Not being weary of saṃsāra, [I.52]

And shame and embarrassment
Represent the fivefold lack of conceit.
Dwelling in forests, having little desire, being content,
Resorting to strict abstinence, [I.53]

Not abandoning the training,
Despising sense pleasures,
Turning away, renouncing all there is,
Being uncowed, and disregard. [I.54]

Intimacy, jealousy in terms of families,
Places that invite crowds,
Praising oneself, disparaging others,
The ten paths of nonvirtuous actions, [I.55]

Conceit and arrogance, mistakenness,
Deficient states of mind, and tolerance for afflictions—
If these ten are relinquished,
The fifth bhūmi is attained. [I.56]

Through generosity, ethics, patience, vigor,
Dhyāna, and prajñā being perfected,
The mind of longing for the disciples and the rhinos
And being afraid are relinquished, [I.57]

One is uncowed by beggars,
Not sad even when one has given away everything,
And not rejecting beggars even when poor.
Through these the sixth bhūmi is attained. [I.58]

Clinging to a self, sentient being,
Soul, person, extinction, and permanence;
With regard to characteristics, causes, skandhas,
Dhātus, āyatanas, [I.59]

And the three realms, dwelling on,
Being attached to, and one's mind being cowed by them;

Clinging to views about the three jewels
And ethics as being such, [I.60]

Disputing emptiness,
And opposing it—
Those in whom these twenty flaws are removed
Attain the seventh bhūmi. [I.61]

Knowing the three doors to liberation,
Being pure of the three spheres,
Compassion, no conceit,
Knowing the equality of phenomena and the single principle, [I.62]

Knowing nonarising and poised readiness,
The single flow of dharmas,
Overcoming conceptions,
Relinquishing discriminations, views, and afflictions, [I.63]

Familiarizing with calm abiding,
Being skilled in superior insight,
A tamed mind, wisdom
Unobstructed in all respects, [I.64]

Not being a ground for attachment,
Going all at once to other realms as one pleases,
And displaying one's own being everywhere—
These are the twenty. [I.65]

Knowing the minds of all sentient beings,
Playing with supernatural knowledges,
Manifesting a superb buddha realm,
Tending to the buddhas in scrutiny, [I.66]

Knowing the faculties, purifying
The realm of a victor, dwelling in illusionlikeness,
And assuming existence at will—
These are said to be the eight activities. [I.67]

Infinite aspiration prayers,
Knowing the languages of gods and so on,
Streamlike eloquent presence,
Supreme descent into a womb, [I.68]

Excellency of family, descent, lineage,
Retinue, birth,
Renunciation, bodhi trees,
And perfection of qualities. [I.69]

Having passed beyond nine levels,
This dwelling on the buddhabhūmi
By virtue of wisdom should be known
As the tenth bodhisattvabhūmi. [I.70]

One should know the eight kinds of remedies
On the paths of seeing and repeated exercise
In order to pacify the eight conceptions
About the apprehended and the apprehender. [I.71]

Final deliverance in terms of the aim, equality,
The welfare of sentient beings, effortlessness,
And being beyond extremes,
Final deliverance characterized by attainment, [I.72]

Final deliverance in terms of the knowledge of all aspects,
And the one that has the path as its sphere.
One should know that the practice of final deliverance
Consists of these eight kinds. [I.73]

This is the first chapter, on the knowledge of all aspects, in *The Treatise on the Pith Instructions on Prajñāpāramitā, Called* The Ornament of Clear Realization.

The knowledge of the path

Eclipsing the gods through light
So as to make them suitable,
Definite object, pervasiveness,
Nature, and its activity. [II.1]

Within the scope of the knowledge of the path,
Through not observing the aspects
Of the four realities of the noble ones
This path of the śrāvakas is to be understood. [II.2]

Since form and so on are empty,
By virtue of their emptinesses being undifferentiable
This represents heat. Through not observing them
This is asserted as having gone to the peak. [II.3]

The poised readinesses [arise] through preventing
Any abiding in them by way of being permanent and so on.
Starting with the ten bhūmis,
Through the detailed teachings on nonabiding [II.4]

The supreme dharma is explained
On the path of the noble śrāvakas.
For what reason is that? Because the Buddha,
Upon realization, did not see any phenomena. [II.5]

They do not need instructions by others
Since they realize the self-arisen by themselves.
This expresses the profundity
Of the wisdom of the rhinos. [II.6]

In certain ones who wish to hear
Certain topics in certain ways,
Even without words, these very topics
Will appear in them accordingly. [II.7]

Through the conceptions about apprehended referents being relinquished,
Through the apprehender not being relinquished,
And through the foundation, the path of the rhinos
Should be understood to be encompassed. [II.8]

The aspect of pointing out that imputations
Do not contradict the nature of phenomena
Represents heat. Peak is distinguished by
Form and so on being without decrease and so on. [II.9]

Since form and so on are not apprehended
By virtue of the emptiness of the internal and so on,
This is poised readiness. The supreme dharma consists
Of the aspects of form and so on being without arising and so on. [II.10]

Through four moments of readiness and cognition
For each one of the realities,
The path of seeing and its benefit
Are explained within the knowledge of the path. [II.11]

Suchness and buddhahood
Not being accepted as synonyms
Because of their not existing as mutual support and supported,
Greatness, no valid cognition, [II.12]

No measure, no extremes,
Ascertaining the form and such
Of one who dwells in it to be buddhahood,
Nothing to be adopted or to be discarded and so on, [II.13]

Love and so on, emptiness,
Attaining buddhahood,

Laying hold of all that is purified,
Eliminating all fears and diseases, [II.14]

The grasping at nirvāṇa being at peace,
Being protected and so on by the buddhas,
Beginning with not killing sentient beings,
Oneself abiding in the principle of the knowledge of all aspects [II.15]

And establishing sentient beings [in it],
As well as dedicating generosity and such
For perfect enlightenment
Are the moments of the knowledge of the path. [II.16]

Being disciplined in every respect, bowing down
In all respects, victory over the afflictions,
Being invulnerable to attacks,
Enlightenment, and the foundation for worship. [II.17]

Aspiration is to be understood as threefold
In terms of one's own welfare, the welfare of oneself and others,
And the welfare of others, each one of them
Being regarded as threefold— [II.18]

Lesser, medium, and great.
Dividing these into the lesser of the lesser and so on
Makes them threefold too.
Thus, it is asserted as twenty-sevenfold. [II.19]

Praise, eulogy, and laudation
On the levels of aspiration
For prajñāpāramitā
Are considered through a triad of nines. [II.20]

As for special dedication,
Its function is supreme.
It has the aspect of nonreferentiality
And the characteristic of unmistakenness. [II.21]

It is free, the sphere of mindfulness about the nature
Of the abundance of merit of the buddhas,
Endowed with means, without characteristics,
Entails rejoicing by the buddhas, [II.22]

And is not included in the three realms.
The three other aspects of dedication
Lie in its character of producing great merit
To lesser, medium, and great degrees. [II.23]

Through both means and nonobservation,
One rejoices in roots of virtue.
The mental engagement in rejoicing
Is stated here to be familiarization. [II.24]

Its nature, supremacy,
Nonformation of anything,
Procuring without observing
Phenomena, and the great goal. [II.25]

Attending to the buddhas, generosity and such,
As well as skill in means
Are the causes for aspiration in this case.
The causes for being destitute of the dharma are [II.26]

Being under the power of māras,
Not aspiring for the profound nature of dharmas,
Clinging to the skandhas and so on,
And being seized by bad friends. [II.27]

The purity of the fruition is nothing but
The purity of form and such since these two
Are not different and are indivisible.
It is in this sense that purity is proclaimed. [II.28]

The purities of disciples, rhinos, and the children of the victors
Are due to their having relinquished
Afflictive, cognitive, and [the obscurations] of the three paths,
But the Buddha's [purity] is utterly so in all aspects. [II.29]

Purity is the path that consists
Of the lesser of the lesser remedies and so on
For the greater of the great degrees of the stains and so on
On the nine levels. [II.30]

Through removing qualms about this,
It is asserted that the path's
Equality of what verifies and what is to be verified
Is the remedy for the three realms. [II.31]

This is the second chapter, on the knowledge of the path, in *The Treatise on the Pith Instructions on Prajñāpāramitā, Called* The Ornament of Clear Realization.

The knowledge of entities

Not abiding on the near or the far shore,
Nor in between these two,
By virtue of understanding the times as equality,
She is asserted as prajñāpāramitā. [III.1]

Through lack of means she is distant
Because characteristics are observed.
Through skill in means
Her proper closeness is proclaimed. [III.2]

The antagonistic factors are discriminating notions about engaging
In the skandhas (such as form) being emptiness,
The phenomena included in the three times,
And the factors of enlightenment (such as generosity). [III.3]

No clinging to "me" with regard to generosity and such
And enjoining others to this
Stop the extreme of attachment.
Thus, attachment to the victors and so on is subtle. [III.4]

Since the path of dharma is free by nature,
This is its profundity.
The knowledge of phenomena being of a single nature
Is the relinquishment of attachment. [III.5]

By virtue of rejecting what is seen and such,
She is said to be difficult to realize.
Since she is not known as form and such,
She is asserted to be inconceivable. [III.6]

Thus, within the scope of the all-knowledge,
This entire division of
Antagonistic factors and remedies
Should be known as it was explained. [III.7]

The trainings that stop engaging in
Form and so on, their impermanence and so on,
Their being incomplete or complete,
And detachment from them, [III.8]

The trainings in terms of no change, no agent,
The three kinds of what is hard to do,
Wishing for fruitfulness,
Since fruitions are attained according to destiny, [III.9]

Being independent of others,
And what makes seven kinds of appearance understood.
The fourfold lack of conceit about form and such
Is asserted to be its equality. [III.10]

Within the scope of the all-knowledge, the path of seeing
Has the character of momentary readinesses and cognitions,
[Such as] dharma cognition and subsequent cognition,
With regard to the realities of suffering and so on. [III.11]

Form being neither permanent nor impermanent,
Beyond extremes, pure,
Neither arising nor ceasing and so on,
Like space, without contagion, [III.12]

Free from grasping,
Inexpressible through a nature of its own,
With its meaning thus being impossible
To convey to others through expressions, [III.13]

Not serving as a focal object,
Being utterly pure, no diseases arising,
The unpleasant realms being extinct,
Nonconceptuality with regard to manifesting the fruition, [III.14]

No connection with characteristics,
And no arising of any consciousness
With regard to both entities and names—
These are the moments of the all-knowledge. [III.15]

The three [knowledges] are this one,
Then this one, and next this one.
This announces the conclusion
Of these three topics. [III.16]

This is the third chapter, on the all-knowledge, in *The Treatise on the Pith Instructions on Prajñāpāramitā, Called* The Ornament of Clear Realization.

The complete training in all aspects

The specific instances of cognizing entities
Represent the defining characteristic of "aspects."
By virtue of the three kinds of omniscience,
They are asserted as three kinds. [IV.1]

Beginning with the aspect of nonexistence
Up through the aspect of immovability,
Four for each one of the realities
And fifteen of them for the path are taught. [IV.2]

In terms of the cause, the path, suffering,
And cessation, in due order,
They are said to be eight, seven,
Five, and sixteen. [IV.3]

Starting with the foundations of mindfulness
And ending with the aspects of buddhahood,
In approximate concordance with the reality of the path,
And distinguished through the threefold omniscience [IV.4]

Of disciples, bodhisattvas,
And buddhas, in due order,
They are asserted as thirty-seven,
Thirty-four, and thirty-nine. [IV.5]

Those who lived up to their duties toward the buddhas,
Planted roots of virtue in relation to them,
And are protected by spiritual friends
Are the vessels for listening to her. [IV.6]

Since they attended to the buddhas, asked them,
And engaged in generosity, ethics, and so on,
These genuine beings are held to be the vessels
For taking her up, retaining her, and so on. [IV.7]

Because of not abiding in form and so on,
Because of having stopped involvement in them,
Because of their suchness being profound,
Because of their being difficult to fathom, [IV.8]

Because of their being immeasurable,
Because of realization being slow and full of hardships,
Because of the prophecy, irreversibility,
Final deliverance, no obstructions, [IV.9]

Being close to enlightenment, swift,
The welfare of others, without increase and decrease,
Not seeing dharmas or nondharmas and so on,
Not seeing the inconceivability of form and so on, [IV.10]

Because of not conceiving the characteristics
Or the being of form and such,

Bestowing precious fruitions,
Purity, and a set period of time. [IV.11]

The qualities are fourteenfold,
Such as vanquishing the power of māras.
The flaws are to be known
As four sets of ten plus six. [IV.12]

What defines should be known
As the defining characteristic, which is threefold
(Knowledge, distinctiveness, and activity),
And what is defined is the nature. [IV.13]

The Tathāgata appearing,
The world having the character of not being perishable,
The conduct of the minds of sentient beings,
Their being concentrated and moving outside, [IV.14]

The aspect of inexhaustibility,
Being endowed with attachment and so on, vast,
Great, immeasurable,
Consciousness being indemonstrable, [IV.15]

Mind being invisible,
Consciousnesses being discerned as coming forth and so on,
Knowing these as aspects
Of suchness, and furthermore [IV.16]

The sage realizing suchness
And communicating it to others—
These make up the defining characteristic of knowledge
In the context of the all-knowledge. [IV.17]

Emptiness, signlessness,
Relinquishment of desires,
No arising, no ceasing, and so on,
The nature of phenomena being unperturbed, [IV.18]

Nonformation, nonconceptualization,
Distinction, and nonexistence of defining characteristics—
These are asserted as the defining characteristic of knowledge
In the context of the knowledge of the path. [IV.19]

Abiding through relying
On one's own dharma, to be honored,
To be respected, to be pleased,
To be worshipped, lacking an agent, [IV.20]

Being the knowledge that engages everywhere,
Showing what is invisible,
The world's aspect of emptiness,
The one who indicates, makes known, makes visible, [IV.21]

And shows inconceivability and peace,
As well as the cessation of the world and discriminations—
These are said to be the defining characteristic of knowledge
In terms of the principle of the knowledge of all aspects. [IV.22]

The defining characteristic of distinctiveness
Is explained by way of the sixteen moments
That have the realities as their sphere and are distinguished
Through the distinctive features of inconceivability and so on. [IV.23]

Being inconceivable, being incomparable,
Transcending all measure and calculation,
Incorporating all noble ones, being what the wise know,
The knowledge not in common, [IV.24]

Swift knowledge, lacking decline and increase,
Engaging, being completely accomplished,
Focusing, foundation,
Completeness, being held, [IV.25]

And lacking any relishing are to be known
As the sixteen distinctive features
Through which this special path
Is distinguished from other paths. [IV.26]

Representing benefit, happiness, protection,
The refuge and place of rest for humans,
An aid and an island,
Acting as the leader, [IV.27]

Being spontaneously present, having the character of not manifesting
The fruition through the three yānas,
And, lastly, the activity of being a resource—
These represent the defining characteristic of activity. [IV.28]

Being devoid of afflictions, signs, characteristics,
And antagonistic factors and remedies,
Hard to be done, devoted in an exclusive manner,
Aim, nonobservation, [IV.29]

Refraining from clinging,
What is discerned as the focal object,

Being antagonistic, unobstructed,
Without ground, without going and arising, [IV.30]

And not observing suchness—
This sixteenfold nature
Is defined as something like a definiendum,
And thus is held to be the fourth defining characteristic. [IV.31]

Being skilled in the full accomplishment
Of signlessness, generosity, and so on,
Within this complete realization of all aspects,
Are asserted as the factors conducive to liberation. [IV.32]

They are fivefold—the confidence of focusing on the Buddha and so on,
The vigor whose sphere consists of generosity and so on,
The mindfulness of the consummate intention,
Nonconceptual samādhi, [IV.33]

And the prajñā of knowing
Phenomena in all aspects.
It is held that perfect enlightenment is easy to realize
By those who are sharp, and hard to realize by the dull. [IV.34]

The focal object of heat here
Is praised as being all sentient beings.
This is described as ten aspects,
Such as an equal mind towards them. [IV.35]

Through oneself turning away from evil
And abiding in generosity and so on,
One establishes others in these two,
Praises them, and makes them conform, [IV.36]

Which represent reaching the peak. Likewise, poised readiness
Is the knowledge of the realities within oneself and others.
The supreme dharma is likewise to be understood
Through maturing sentient beings and so on. [IV.37]

Starting from the branches of penetration
Up through the paths of seeing and repeated exercise,
The bodhisattvas who dwell on these
Are the irreversible assembly here. [IV.38]

By virtue of speaking of twenty kinds of signs,
Such as turning away from form and so on,
[There are] the characteristics of irreversibility
Of those who dwell on the branches of penetration. [IV.39]

Turning away from form and so on,
Termination of doubt and unfavorable states,
Oneself abiding in virtue
And establishing others in it, [IV.40]

Generosity and so on that are based on others,
No indecisiveness even about profound actuality,
The body being loving and so on,
Not being associated with fivefold obscuration, [IV.41]

Overcoming all latencies,
Mindfulness and alertness,
Clean robes and so on,
The body not being infested with parasites, [IV.42]

Mind being without crookedness, assuming
Abstinence, lacking greed and so on,
Proceeding by being endowed with the nature of phenomena,
Searching for the hells for the welfare of the world, [IV.43]

Others being unable to lead one astray,
Realizing, "This is māra,"
When māra teaches another path,
And the conduct that pleases the buddhas— [IV.44]

By virtue of these twenty signs,
Those who dwell on heat, peak,
Poised readiness, and the supreme dharma
Do not turn away from perfect enlightenment. [IV.45]

The sixteen moments of readiness
And cognition on the path of seeing
Should be known as the characteristics
Of irreversible bodhisattvas. [IV.46]

Turning away from discriminating notions of form and so on,
Firmness of mind, turning away
From both the inferior yānas,
Dissolution of the branches of the dhyānas and so on, [IV.47]

Lightness of body and mind,
Skill in means in using what is desirable,
Constantly pure conduct,
Purity of livelihood, [IV.48]

With regard to the skandhas and so on, obstacles,
The accumulations, the battle

Of the faculties and so on, and greed and so on,
Stopping to dwell on [IV.49]

Connecting and being occupied with them,
Observing not the least phenomenon,
Certainty about one's own bhūmi
And dwelling on the triple bhūmi, [IV.50]

As well as renouncing one's life for the sake of the dharma—
These sixteen moments
Are the signs of irreversibility
Of the intelligent who dwell on the path of seeing. [IV.51]

The path of familiarization is profound
And such profundity is in terms of emptiness and so on.
This profundity is the state of being liberated
From the extremes of superimposition and denial. [IV.52]

The path of familiarization consists of the repeated
Reflections, verifications, and absorptions
During the branches of penetration,
The path of seeing, and the path of familiarization itself. [IV.53]

Because it is an uninterrupted continuum,
It is treated as ninefold
Through its lesser, medium, and great degrees
Being further divided into lesser and so on. [IV.54]

The descriptions as countless and so on
Do not hold out in terms of the ultimate.
In terms of the seeming, the sage asserted
Them to be the true natural outflows of compassion. [IV.55]

In the inexpressible entity
Decrease and increase are not tenable.
Through the progression called "familiarization,"
What could decrease and what could be obtained? [IV.56]

In the same way as enlightenment
This [path] accomplishes the desired goal.
Enlightenment has the defining characteristic of suchness,
Which is also asserted as the defining characteristic of this. [IV.57]

Enlightenment through an earlier mind
Is not reasonable, nor is it through a later one.
In accordance with the example of an oil lamp,
The eightfold nature of phenomena is profound. [IV.58]

Its profundity lies in arising, ceasing,
Suchness, what is to be cognized,
Cognition, engagement, nonduality,
And skill in means. [IV.59]

Since phenomena are dreamlike,
[Saṃsāric] existence and peace are not conceptualized.
The refutations of the qualms about karma
Not existing and so on are just as explained. [IV.60]

The world of sentient beings is impure,
And so is the world that is the environment.
By virtue of accomplishing the purity of those,
The purity of a buddha realm [appears]. [IV.61]

As for the object and this training,
Overcoming the hordes of enemies,
Not abiding, hitting just as [intended],
Uncommon characteristic, [IV.62]

Not becoming attached, not observing,
Having terminated characteristics and aspiration prayers,
The sign of this, and being unlimited
Represent the tenfold skill in means. [IV.63]

This is the fourth chapter, on the complete realization of all aspects, in *The Treatise on the Pith Instructions on Prajñāpāramitā, Called* The Ornament of Clear Realization.

The culminating training

Even in dreams, all phenomena
Are regarded as dreamlike and so on—
The signs of the training of having reached culmination
Are asserted as twelvefold. [V.1]

By comparing it in many ways,
Such as the virtue of worshipping as many buddhas
As there are beings in Jambudvīpa,
Increase is sixteenfold. [V.2]

The unsurpassable perfection
Of the dharmas of the three omnisciences
And the nonabandonment of the welfare of sentient beings
Are described as "stability." [V.3]

By using the examples of a four-continent world,
A chiliocosm, a dichiliocosm, and a trichiliocosm,
This samādhi is expressed
Through the abundance of merit. [V.4]

One should know that the two conceptions about the apprehended—
In terms of engagement and withdrawal—
Are ninefold each and that their character
Is [to apprehend] objects not as they are. [V.5]

The two conceptions about substantially and imputedly existent sentient beings
Are asserted as the ones about the apprehender.
Divided by ordinary beings and noble ones,
Each one of them is ninefold. [V.6]

If apprehended referents do not exist like that,
Can these two be asserted as the apprehenders of anything?
Thus, their characteristic is the emptiness
Of a nature of an apprehender. [V.7]

Nature, disposition,
Perfect accomplishment of the path,
Unmistakenness about the focal object of consciousness,
Antagonistic factors and remedies, [V.8]

One's own realization, agent,
Its activity, and the result of activity—
Being based on the factors of engaging in these,
Conceptions are asserted as ninefold. [V.9]

Realizations being deficient
Due to falling into existence or peace,
Lacking being mentored,
The aspects of the path being incomplete, [V.10]

Progressing by virtue of another condition,
Turning away from the aim,
Being limited, variety,
Being ignorant about abiding and engaging, [V.11]

And subsequent pursuing—
The conceptions about these are ninefold,
Being based on the factors of withdrawal
As they arise in the minds of śrāvakas and so on. [V.12]

The first about the apprehender should be known
In terms of seizing and discarding,
Mental engagement,
Adhering to the three realms, [V.13]

Abiding, clinging,
Imputing phenomenal entities,
Attachment, remedy,
And impairment of proceeding as one wishes. [V.14]

No final deliverance according to the aim,
Identifying the path as not being the path,
Ceasing and arising,
Being conjoined and not being conjoined with entities, [V.15]

Abiding, destroying the disposition,
The absence of striving and the cause,
And observing opposing forces
Are the other conceptions about the apprehender. [V.16]

Pointing out the enlightenment of others,
Entrusting the cause for this,
And the cause for its uninterrupted attainment
With its characteristic of an abundance of merit. [V.17]

The wisdom of the termination and the nonarising
Of the stains is called "enlightenment,"
But these two should be understood, in due order,
By virtue of the lack of termination and the lack of arising. [V.18]

In the nature without cessation,
Through the path called "seeing,"
What could be terminated that is born by conception
And what nonarising could be attained? [V.19]

That phenomena exist and, at the same time,
The cognitive obscurations of the teacher
Are terminated—this claim by others
I consider as amazing. [V.20]

There is nothing to be removed in this
And not the slightest to be added.
Actual reality is to be seen as it really is—
Whoever sees actual reality is liberated. [V.21]

That in which generosity and so on
Are mutually combined with each other

And which consists of poised readiness
In one single moment is the path of seeing here. [V.22]

Then, after having been absorbed
In the samādhi of the lion's sport,
Dependent origination is examined
In its progressive and reverse orders. [V.23]

After the twofold progressing and returning through
The nine absorptions, including cessation,
The intermittent consciousness belonging to the desire [realm],
Which is not in meditative equipoise, is assumed. [V.24]

Through crossing over one, two,
Three, four, five, six, seven, and eight,
The meditative absorption of crossing in one leap consists of
Proceeding up through cessation in disparate ways. [V.25]

With regard to being concise, detailed, not mentored
Through not being protected by the buddhas,
Lacking the qualities of the three times,
And the threefold excellent path— [V.26]

These first conceptions about the apprehended
Have the aspects of the training as their sphere.
It is asserted that the second ones have the engagements
Of minds and mental factors as their objects. [V.27]

These conceptions about the nonarising of the mind,
Not mentally engaging in the heart of enlightenment,
Mentally engaging in the hīnayāna,
Not mentally engaging in perfect enlightenment, [V.28]

Familiarizing, not familiarizing,
The opposites of these,
And not being in accord with true reality
Should be known as those on the path of familiarization. [V.29]

The first ones about the apprehender are to be known
In terms of having imputed sentient beings as their sphere,
Imputed phenomena, not being empty,
Attachment, and the character of discrimination. [V.30]

They are further proclaimed with regard to
The formation of entities, the three yānas,
The impurity of offerings,
And disordered conduct. [V.31]

Having imputed sentient beings and the cause of these
As their objects, the other nine kinds [of conceptions]
That are associated with the path of familiarization
Are its antagonistic factors by virtue of being overcome through it. [V.32]

In terms of ignorance about the three obscurations
Of the three omnisciences, respectively,
The path of peace, being conjoined with
Or disjoined from suchness and so on, [V.33]

Being unequal, suffering and so on,
The nature of the afflictions,
And nonduality, these conceptions
Are asserted as the last ones. [V.34]

When these pestilences have become extinguished,
It is like breathing freely again after a long time.
All the consummate qualities that accomplish
The happiness of beings in all aspects, [V.35]

Just like rivers [feeding] into the great ocean,
Sustain these mahāsattvas,
Who are embellished with the desired fruition,
From all sides. [V.36]

It is compared to the virtues of having established
The people in a trichiliocosm
In the consummate realizations of disciples and rhinos
And on the flawless [bhūmi] of bodhisattvas. [V.37]

Through such an abundance of merit
This uninterrupted samādhi
Immediately before attaining buddhahood
Is the knowledge of all aspects. [V.38]

The lack of entity is asserted as the focal object of this,
Mindfulness as its dominant factor,
And peacefulness as its aspect. In this regard,
Those who talk a lot dispute [V.39]

About the justification of the focal object,
The identification of the nature of this,
The wisdom of the knowledge of all aspects,
The ultimate and the seeming, [V.40]

The training, the three jewels,
The means, the realization of the sage,

Mistakenness, the path,
Remedies and antagonistic factors, [V.41]

Defining characteristic, and familiarization.
Those people's utterances about these sixteen
Are asserted as the wrong ideas
About the knowledge of all aspects. [V.42]

This is the fifth chapter, on the culminating training, in *The Treatise on the Pith Instructions on Prajñāpāramitā, Called* The Ornament of Clear Realization.

The serial training

By way of generosity up through prajñā,
The recollections of the Buddha and so forth,
And the nature of the lack of entity,
The serial activity is asserted. [VI.1]

This is the sixth chapter, on the serial training, in *The Treatise on the Pith Instructions on Prajñāpāramitā, Called* The Ornament of Clear Realization.

The instantaneous training

By virtue of each one, such as generosity,
Including all that is uncontaminated,
The sage's realization in a single instant
Is to be understood. [VII.1]

Just as a waterwheel driven by a person
Through just a single spot to step on
Turns simultaneously in its entirety,
So does wisdom in a single instant. [VII.2]

When abiding in the state of the true nature
Of all matured spotless phenomena,
At that point, prajñāpāramitā is born—
The wisdom in one single instant. [VII.3]

Through abiding in phenomena being dreamlike
By way of having engaged in generosity and such,
The lack of characteristics of phenomena
Is discovered in one single instant. [VII.4]

With not even a dream and the seeing of it
Being perceived in a dualistic fashion,

The true reality that is the nonduality of phenomena
Is seen in one single instant. [VII.5]

This is the seventh chapter, on the instantaneous training, in *The Treatise on the Pith Instructions on Prajñāpāramitā, Called* The Ornament of Clear Realization.

The dharmakāya

Those who have attained purity in every respect
And the uncontaminated dharmas,
Theirs is the svābhāvikakāya of the sage,
Which bears the characteristic of the nature of these. [VIII.1]

The factors concordant with enlightenment, the immeasurables,
The liberations, the ninefold
Progressive meditative absorptions,
The ten totalities, [VIII.2]

The āyatanas of overpowering,
Divided into eight kinds,
Dispassion, knowledge through aspiration,
The supernatural knowledges, the discriminating awarenesses, [VIII.3]

The four purities in all respects,
The ten masteries, the ten powers,
The four fearlessnesses,
The three ways of nothing to hide, [VIII.4]

The threefold foundation of mindfulness,
The true nature of being without forgetfulness,
The latent tendencies being overcome,
Great compassion for beings, [VIII.5]

The eighteen qualities that are said
To be unique to a sage,
And the knowledge of all aspects—
The dharmakāya is described as these. [VIII.6]

The dispassion of śrāvakas means avoiding
The afflictions of people upon being seen [by them].
The dispassion of the victor refers to extinguishing
The stream of their afflictions in villages and so on. [VIII.7]

The Buddha's knowledge through aspiration
Is held to be effortless, free from attachment,

Unobstructed, remaining forever,
And solving all questions. [VIII.8]

Once the cause has come to maturity,
For whomever and whenever,
It will unfold as beneficial
Activity to them. [VIII.9]

Though the god of rain may send rainfalls,
An unsuitable seed will not grow.
Likewise, though buddhas come forth,
The unsuitable will not come to enjoy any good. [VIII.10]

By virtue of the vastness of activity like that,
Buddhahood is described as "all-pervading."
By virtue of being inexhaustible,
It is also declared to be "permanent." [VIII.11]

Since this [kāya] of the sage, whose character lies in
The thirty-two major marks and the eighty minor marks,
Enjoys the mahāyāna,
It is held to be the sāmbhogikakāya. [VIII.12]

It is marked with wheels on hands and feet, and has tortoiselike feet.
Fingers and toes are joined by webs,
Hands and feet are soft and supple,
The body has seven convex surfaces, [VIII.13]

Long fingers, broad heels, and is tall and straight.
It has nonprotruding ankles, body hairs that point upward,
Antelopelike calves, long and beautiful arms,
And is the supreme of those whose sexual organ is covered by a sheath. [VIII.14]

The skin has a golden hue and is delicate.
It has well-grown body hairs, each one single by itself and curling to the right,
The face is adorned with the ūrṇā hair, and the upper body is lionlike.
It has evenly rounded shoulders, with compact flesh in between, [VIII.15]

And even unpleasant tastes appear as the most delicious tastes for it.
Its figure has symmetrical proportions like a nyagrodha [tree],
It has an uṣṇīṣa on the head, a large and beautiful tongue,
A melodious voice like Brahmā, jaws like a lion, [VIII.16]

Very white teeth of equal size, well arranged,
And in a complete set of forty,

Dark-blue eyes, and eyelashes like those of a magnificent heifer.
These are the thirty-two marks. [VIII.17]

As for the causes that accomplish
These respective marks,
Through completing them
These marks will be possessed in full. [VIII.18]

Escorting the gurus and so on,
Firmness with regard to vows,
Relying on the means of attraction,
Providing magnificent things, [VIII.19]

Liberating those to be killed,
Undertaking and increasing virtue,
And so on—these are the causes that accomplish
These marks according to the sūtras. [VIII.20]

The sage's nails are copper-colored,
Glossy, and prominent. His fingers and toes are
Rounded, compact, and tapering.
His veins do not protrude and are free from knots. [VIII.21]

His ankles do not protrude and his feet are equal [in size].
He walks with the stride of a lion, an elephant,
A goose, and a lordly bull, and walks by keeping to thc right [side],
Elegantly, and upright. The limbs of his body are well rounded, [VIII.22]

Smooth, slender,
Clean, soft, and pure.
His genitals are fully developed
And his figure is beautiful and stately. [VIII.23]

His steps are even and his eyes
Are pure. His body is beautifully youthful,
Not sunken, with full [flesh],
And very firm. [VIII.24]

His limbs are well proportioned
And his vision is unobscured and pure.
His belly is round, smooth, unmarred,
And slender. His navel is deep [VIII.25]

And winds to the right.
He is beautiful to behold from all sides,
His conduct is clean,
And his body is free from black moles. [VIII.26]

His hands are as soft as cotton wool
And the lines on his palms are glossy, deep, and extensive.
His face is not too long
And his lips are red like a bimba berry. [VIII.27]

His tongue is supple, slender,
And red. His voice is like thunder,
Sweet, and gentle. His eyeteeth are round,
Sharp, white, equal [in size], [VIII.28]

And tapering. His nose is prominent
And supremely pure.
His eyes are wide, with well-developed eyelashes,
And like the petals of a lotus. [VIII.29]

His eyebrows are elongated, smooth,
And shiny, and their hairs are of equal length.
His arms are long and muscular, and his ears
Are equal and completely unimpaired. [VIII.30]

His forehead is well shaped
And broad, and his head is large.
His hair is as black as a black bee,
Thick, smooth, not shaggy, [VIII.31]

Not unruly, and has a fragrant smell
That captivates the minds of people.
[His hands and feet show] endless knots and swastikas.
These are held to be the minor marks of a buddha. [VIII.32]

The perpetual nairmāṇikakāya of the sage
Is the one through which various benefits
For the world are performed equally
Until the end of existence. [VIII.33]

Likewise, it is held that its activity
Is perpetual until the end of saṃsāra.
The activity of pacifying beings,
Establishing them in the fourfold means of attraction, [VIII.34]

Realizing afflicted phenomena
And purified phenomena,
The true nature of the welfare of sentient beings,
The six pāramitās, [VIII.35]

The buddha path, emptiness
Of a nature, the termination of duality,

Symbols, nonobservation,
Maturing living beings, [VIII.36]

The bodhisattva path,
Putting an end to clinging,
Attaining enlightenment, pure
Buddha realms, definitiveness, [VIII.37]

The immeasurable welfare of sentient beings,
The qualities of attending to buddhas and so on,
The branches of enlightenment, actions
Being never lost, seeing reality, [VIII.38]

Relinquishing mistakenness,
The manner of its nonsubstantiality,
Purification, the accumulations,
Conditioned and unconditioned phenomena [VIII.39]

Being understood as nondifferent,
And establishing in nirvāṇa—
The enlightened activity of the dharmakāya
Is held to be twenty-sevenfold. [VIII.40]

This is the eighth chapter, on the dharmakāya, in *The Treatise on the Pith Instructions on Prajñāpāramitā, Called* The Ornament of Clear Realization.

The characteristic, the training in it,
Its highest degrees, its progression,
Its final conclusion, and its maturation—
This is another summary in six points. [IX.1]

The threefold object (the cause),
The fourfold training,
And the fruition (the dharmakāya and enlightened activity)—
This is another summary in three points. [IX.2]

This completes *The Treatise on the Pith Instructions on Prajñāpāramitā, Called* The Ornament of Clear Realization, composed by Lord Maitreyanātha.

Glossary: English–Sanskrit–Tibetan

English	Sanskrit	Tibetan
abider in a fruition	phalastha	’bras gnas
adventitious stains	āgantukamala	glo bur gyi dri ma
afflicted phenomenon	saṃkleśa	kun nas nyon mongs pa
afflictive obscuration	kleśāvaraṇa	nyon mongs pa’i sgrib pa
ālaya-wisdom	—	kun gzhi’i ye shes
all-knowledge	sarvajñatā	thams cad shes pa nyid
analytical cessation	pratisaṃkyhānirodha	so sor brtags pa’i ’gog pa
appearing object	—	snang yul
approach of virtuous effort	śrāmaṇya	dge sbyor gyi tshul
approacher	pratipannaka	zhugs pa
Aspectarian	sākāravādin	rnam bcas pa
āyatana of overpowering	abhibhāyatana	zil gyis gnon gyi skye mched
basic element	dhātu	khams
bodhicitta of application	bodhiprasthānacitta	’jug pa’i byang chub kyi sems
bodhicitta of aspiration	bodhipraṇidhicitta	smon pa’i byang chub kyi sems
causal condition	hetupratyaya	rgyu rkyen
cause of similar outcome	sabhāgahetu	skal mnyam gyi rgyu
(fundamental) change of state	āśrayaparivṛtti	gnas yongs su gyur pa
clinging to real existence	*satyagrahaṇa	bden ’dzin

cognitive aspect	jñānākāra	shes pa'i rnam pa
cognitive obscuration	jñeyāvaraṇa	shes bya'i sgrib pa
cognizance	vijñapti	rnam par rig pa
complete training in all aspects	—	rnam rdzogs sbyor ba
conceived form	vikalpitarūpa	rnam par brtags pa'i gzugs
conditioned (phenomenon)	saṃskṛta	'dus byas
contaminant	anuśaya	phra rgyas
contaminated	sāsrava	zag bcas
crossing in one leap	avaskandha, viṣkandha, vyutkrānta	thod rgal
culminating training	—	rtse mo'i sbyor ba
dharma cognition	dharmajñāna	chos shes
dharma readiness	dharmakṣānti	chos bzod
dharmas concordant with enlightenment	bodhipakṣadharma	byang chub phyogs chos
disposition	gotra	rigs
distancing remedy	dūrībhāvapratipakṣa	thag sring ba'i gnyen po
distinctive feature of the six āyatanas	ṣadāyatanaviśeṣa	skye mched drug gi khyad par
dominant condition	adhipatipratyaya	bdag rkyen
door to liberation	vimokṣadvāra	rnam par thar pa'i sgo
eight liberations	aṣṭavimokṣa	rnam thar brgyad
elimination-of-other	anyāpoha	gzhan sel
emptiness endowed with the supreme of all aspects	sarvākāravaropetā-śūnyatā	rnam kun mchog ldan gyi stong pa nyid
emptiness in the sense of extinction	—	chad pa'i stong pa nyid
engagement through aspiration	adhimukticaryā	mos pas spyod pa
entity	bhāva/vastu	dngos po

factors conducive to liberation	mokṣabhāgīya	thar pa cha mthun
factors conducive to penetration	nirvedhabhāgīya	nges 'byed cha mthun
False Aspectarian	*alīkākāravādin	rnam brdzun pa
false imagination	abhūtaparikalpa	yang dag ma yin kun rtog
form of the nature of phenomena	dharmatārūpa	chos nyid kyi gzugs
foundation of mindfulness	smṛtyupasthāna	dran pa nye bar bzhag pa
four realities of the noble ones	caturāryasatya	'phags pa'i bden pa bzhi
freedom from reference points	niṣprapañca	spros bral
fruition of virtuous effort	śrāmaṇyaphala	dge sbyor tshul gyi 'bras bu
generally characterized (phenomenon)	sāmānyalakṣaṇa	spyi mtshan
ground of the latent tendencies of ignorance	avidyāvāsanābhūmi	ma rig bag chags kyi sa
heterologous set	vipakṣa	mi mthun phyogs
homologous set	sapakṣa	mthun phyogs
identitylessness	nairātmya	bdag med
imaginary (nature)	parikalpita(svabhāva)	kun brtags (kyi rang bzhin)
imaginary form	parikalpitarūpa	kun tu brtags pa'i gzugs
immediate condition	samanantarapratyaya	de ma thag rkyen
implicative negation	paryudāsapratiṣedha	ma yin dgag
impregnations of negative tendencies	dauṣṭhulya	gnas ngan len pa
imputedly existent	prajñaptisat	btags yod
innate	sahaja	lhan skyes
instance-isolate	—	gzhi ldog
instantaneous training	kṣanikaprayoga	skad cig ma'i sbyor ba

invalidating remedy	vidūṣaṇapratipakṣa	rnam par sun 'byin pa'i gnyen po
invariable co-observation	sahopalambhaniyama	lhan cig dmigs par nges pa
isolate	vyatireka	ldog pa
karma, volitional	cetanākarma	sems pa'i las
karma, volitioned	cetayitvā karma	bsam pa'i las
knowledge of all aspects	sarvākārajñatā	rnam kun mkhyen pa nyid
knowledge of entities	vastujñāna	gzhi shes pa
knowledge of the path	mārgajñatā	lam shes pa nyid
knowledge of termination and nonarising	kṣayānutpattijñāna	zad pa dang mi skye ba shes pa
lack of nature	niḥsvabhāva	ngo bo nyid/rang bzhin med pa
latent tendencies for listening	śrutavāsanā	thos pa'i bag chags
latent tendency	vāsanā	bag chags
lineage of profound view	—	zab mo lta rgyud
lineage of vast activity	—	rgya chen spyod rgyud
lion's sport	siṃhavijṛmbhita	seng ge'i rnam bsgyings
meaning-isolate	—	don ldog
meditative absorption of cessation	nirodhasamāpatti	'gog pa'i snyoms 'jug
meditative absorption without discrimination	asaṃjñisamāpatti	'du shes med pa'i snyoms 'jug
meditative absorptions of progressive abiding	anupūrvavihāra-samāpatti	mthar gnas kyi snyoms 'jug
meditative equipoise	samāhita	mnyam bzhag
mental nonengagement	amanasikāra	yid la mi byed pa
mental state	buddhi	blo
mentation	manas	yid
mere cognizance	vijñaptimātra	rnam rig tsam

Mere Mentalist	—	sems tsam pa
mere mind/Mere Mentalism	cittamātra	sems tsam
mind as such	cittatvam, cittam eva	sems nyid
natural outflow	niṣyanda	rgyu mthun pa
naturally abiding disposition	prakṛtisthagotra	rang bzhin gnas rigs
negative entailment	vyatirekavyāpti	ldog khyab
nominal ultimate	paryāyaparamārtha	rnam grangs pa'i don dam
nonafflicted ignorance	akliṣṭāvidyā	nyon mongs can ma yin pa'i ma rig pa
nonanalytical cessation	apratisaṃkyhānirodha	so sor brtags min 'gog pa
Non-Aspectarian	nirākāravādin	rnam med pa
nonentity	abhāva/avastu	dngos med
nonimplicative negation	prasajyapratiṣedha	med dgag
nonnominal ultimate	aparyāyaparamārtha	rnam grangs ma yin pa'i don dam
nonobservation	anupalabdhi, anupalambha	mi dmigs pa
nonreferential	anupalambha, anālambana	mi dmigs pa, dmigs med
nonreturner	anāgāmin	phyir mi 'ong ba
object condition	ālambanapratyaya	dmigs rkyen
object generality	arthasāmānya	don spyi
(once-)returner	(sakṛd)āgāmin	(lan gcig) phyir 'ong ba
other-dependent (nature)	paratantra(svabhāva)	gzhan dbang (gi rang bzhin)
path of accumulation	sambhāramārga	tshogs lam
path of familiarization	bhāvanāmārga	sgom lam
path of liberation	vimuktimārga	rnam grol lam
path of nonlearning	aśaikṣamārga	mi slob pa'i lam
path of preparation	prayogamārga	sbyor lam

path of seeing	darśanamārga	mthong lam
perceptual valid cognition	pratyakṣapramāṇa	mngon sum tshad ma
perfect (nature)	pariniṣpanna-(svabhāva)	yongs grub (kyi rang bzhin)
perfect form	pariniṣpannarūpa	yongs su grub pa'i gzugs
personal identitylessness	pudgalanairātmya	gang zag gi bdag med
personally experienced (wisdom)	pratyātmavedanīya (jñāna) (svapratyātmāryajñāna)	so so rang rig (pa'i ye shes)
phenomenal identitylessness	dharmanairātmya	chos kyi bdag med
positive entailment	anvayavyāpti	rjes khyab
preparatory stage	sāmantaka	nyer bsdogs
purified phenomenon	vyavadāna	rnam par byang ba
Real Aspectarian	*satyākāravādin	rnam bden pa
realist	vastusatpadārthavādin	dngos po (yod pa)r smra ba
reason that operates through the power of entities	vastubalapravṛttam liṅgam	dngos po stobs zhugs kyi rtags
reference point	prapañca	spros pa
referent	artha	don
referent aspect	arthākāra	don gyi rnam pa
referent object	—	zhen yul
reification	bhāvagrāha	dngos 'dzin
relinquishing remedy	prahāṇapratipakṣa	spong ba'i gnyen po
repetitive cognition	—	bcad shes
result of freedom	visaṃyogaphala	bral ba'i 'bras bu
result that concords with its cause	niṣyandaphala	rgyu mthun gyi 'bras bu
result through personal effort	puruṣakāraphala	skyes bu byed pa'i 'bras bu
seeming (reality)	saṃvṛti(satya)	kun rdzob (bden pa)

self-aware(ness)	svasaṃvedana, svasaṃvitti	rang rig
self-isolate	—	rang ldog
serial training	—	mthar gyis pa'i sbyor ba
slight exiting	—	nud chung
specifically characterized (phenomenon)	svalakṣaṇa	rang mtshan
sphere	gocara	spyod yul
stream-enterer	srotāpanna	rgyun zhugs pa
subject property	pakṣadharmatā/-tva	phyogs chos
subsequent attainment	pṛṣṭhalabdha	rjes thob
subsequent cognition	anvayajñāna	rjes shes
subsequent readiness	anvayakṣānti	rjes bzod
substantial cause	upādānakāraṇa	nyer len gyi rgyu
substantially existent	dravyasat	rdzas yod
superior intention	adhyāśaya	lhag pa'i bsam pa
sustaining remedy	ādhārapratipakṣa	gzhi'i gnyen po
term generality	śabdasāmānya	sgra spyi
three natures	trisvabhāva	ngo bo nyid/rang bzhin gsum
three spheres	trimaṇḍala	'khor gsum
totality	kṛtsna	zad par
true end	bhūtakoṭi	yang dag pa'i mtha'
true reality	tattva	de (kho na) nyid
ultimate (reality)	paramārtha(satya)	don dam (bden pa)
unconditioned (phenomenon)	asaṃskṛta	'dus ma byas
uncontaminated	anāsrava	zag med
unfolding disposition	paripuṣṭagotra	rgyas 'gyur gyi rigs
uninterrupted path	ānantaryamārga	bar chad med lam
valid cognition	pramāṇa	tshad ma

views about a real personality	satkāyadṛṣṭi	'jig tshogs la lta ba
wisdom of knowing suchness	yathāvatjñāna	ji lta ba mkhyen pa'i ye shes
wisdom of knowing variety	yāvatjñāna	ji snyed mkhyen pa'i ye shes
yogic valid perception	yogipratyakṣapramāṇa	rnal 'byor mngon sum tshad ma

Glossary: Tibetan–Sanskrit–English

Tibetan	Sanskrit	English
kun brtags kyi gzugs	parikalpitarūpa	imaginary form
kun brtags (kyi rang bzhin)	parikalpita(svabhāva)	imaginary (nature)
kun nas nyon mongs pa	saṃkleśa	afflicted phenomenon
kun rdzob (bden pa)	saṃvṛti(satya)	seeming (reality)
kun gzhi'i ye shes	—	ālaya-wisdom
skad cig ma'i sbyor ba	kṣanikaprayoga	instantaneous training
skal mnyam gyi rgyu	sabhāgahetu	cause of similar outcome
skye mched drug gi khyad par	ṣadāyatanaviśeṣa	distinctive feature of the six āyatanas
skyes bu byed pa'i 'bras bu	puruṣakāraphala	result through personal effort
khams	dhātu	basic element
'khor gsum	trimaṇḍala	three spheres
gang zag gi bdag med	pudgalanairātmya	personal identitylessness
glo bur gyi dri ma	āgantukamala	adventitious stains
dge sbyor gyi tshul	śrāmaṇya	approach of virtuous effort
dge sbyor gyi tshul gyi 'bras bu	śrāmaṇyaphala	fruition of virtuous effort
'gog pa'i snyoms 'jug	nirodhasamāpatti	meditative absorption of cessation
rgya chen spyod rgyud	—	lineage of vast activity
rgyas 'gyur gyi rigs	paripuṣṭagotra	unfolding disposition
rgyu rkyen	hetupratyaya	causal condition

rgyu mthun	niṣyanda	natural outflow
rgyu mthun gyi 'bras bu	niṣyandaphala	result that concords with its cause
rgyun zhugs pa	srotāpanna	stream-enterer
sgom lam	bhāvanāmārga	path of familiarization
sgra spyi	śabdasāmānya	term generality
nges 'byed cha mthun	nirvedhabhāgīya	factors conducive to penetration
ngo bo nyid med pa	niḥsvabhāva	lack of nature
dngos po	bhāva/vastu	entity
dngos po stobs zhugs kyi rtags	vastubalapravṛttam liṅgam	reason that operates through the power of entities
dngos po (yod pa)r smra ba	vastusatpadārthavādin	realist
dngos med	abhāva/avastu	nonentity
dngos 'dzin	bhāvagrāha	reification
mngon sum tshad ma	pratyakṣapramāṇa	perceptual valid cognition
bcad shes	—	repetitive cognition
chad pa'i stong pa nyid	—	emptiness in the sense of extinction
chos kyi bdag med	dharmanairātmya	phenomenal identitylessness
chos nyid kyi gzugs	dharmatārūpa	form of the nature of phenomena
chos bzod	dharmakṣānti	dharma readiness
chos shes	dharmajñāna	dharma cognition
ji snyed mkhyen pa'i ye shes	yāvatjñāna	wisdom of knowing variety
ji lta ba mkhyen pa'i ye shes	yathāvatjñāna	wisdom of knowing suchness
'jig tshogs la lta ba	satkāyadṛṣṭi	views about a real personality

'jug pa'i byang chub kyi sems	bodhiprasthānacitta	bodhicitta of application
rjes khyab	anvayavyāpti	positive entailment
rjes thob	pṛṣṭhalabdha	subsequent attainment
rjes bzod	anvayakṣānti	subsequent readiness
rjes shes	anvayajñāna	subsequent cognition
nyer bsdogs	sāmantaka	preparatory stage
nyer len gyi rgyu	upādānakāraṇa	substantial cause
nyon mongs pa'i sgrib pa	kleśāvaraṇa	afflictive obscuration
mnyam bzhag	samāhita	meditative equipoise
btags yod	prajñaptisat	imputedly existent
thag sring ba'i gnyen po	dūrībhāvapratipakṣa	distancing remedy
thams cad shes pa nyid	sarvajñatā	all-knowledge
thar pa cha mthun	mokṣabhāgīya	factors conducive to liberation
thod rgal	avaskandha, viṣkandha, vyutkrānta	crossing in one leap
thos pa'i bag chags	śrutavāsanā	latent tendencies for listening
mthar gyis pa'i sbyor ba	—	serial training
mthar gnas kyi snyoms 'jug	anupūrvavihāra-samāpatti	meditative absorptions of progressive abiding
mthun phyogs	pakṣa	homologous set
mthong lam	darśanamārga	path of seeing
de (kho na) nyid	tattva	true reality
de ma thag rkyen	samanantarapratyaya	immediate condition
don	artha	referent
don gyi rnam pa	arthākāra	referent aspect
don dam (bden pa)	paramārtha(satya)	ultimate (reality)
don ldog	—	meaning-isolate
don spyi	arthasāmānya	object generality
dran pa nye bar bzhag pa	smṛtyupasthāna	foundation of mindfulness

bdag rkyen	adhipatipratyaya	dominant condition
bden 'dzin	*satyagrahaṇa	clinging to real existence
'du shes med pa'i snyoms 'jug	asaṃjñisamāpatti	meditative absorption without discrimination
'dus byas	saṃskṛta	conditioned (phenomenon)
'dus ma byas	asaṃskṛta	unconditioned (phenomenon)
ldog khyab	vyatirekavyāpti	negative entailment
ldog pa	vyatireka	isolate
nud chung	—	slight exiting
gnas ngan len pa	dauṣṭhulya	impregnations of negative tendencies
gnas yongs su gyur pa	āśrayaparivṛtti	(fundamental) change of state
rnam kun mkhyen pa nyid	sarvākārajñatā	knowledge of all aspects
rnam kun mchog ldan gyi stong pa nyid	sarvākāravaropetā-śūnyatā	emptiness endowed with the supreme of all aspects
rnam grangs pa'i don dam	paryāyaparamārtha	nominal ultimate
rnam grangs ma yin pa'i don dam	aparyāyaparamārtha	nonnominal ultimate
rnam grol lam	vimuktimārga	path of liberation
rnam bcas pa	sākāravādin	Aspectarian
rnam thar brgyad	aṣṭavimokṣa	eight liberations
rnam bden pa	*satyākāravādin	Real Aspectarian
rnam par brtags pa'i gzugs	vikalpitarūpa	conceived form
rnam par thar pa'i sgo	vimokṣadvāra	door to liberation
rnam par byang ba	vyavadāna	purified phenomenon
rnam par mi rtog pa'i ye shes	nirvikalpajñāna	nonconceptual wisdom
rnam par rig pa	vijñapti	cognizance
rnam par sun 'byin pa'i gnyen po	vidūṣaṇapratipakṣa	invalidating remedy

rnam med pa	nirākāravādin	Non-Aspectarian
rnam rdzogs sbyor ba	—	complete training in all aspects
rnam brdzun pa	*alīkākāravādin	False Aspectarian
rnam rig tsam	vijñaptimātra	mere cognizance
rnal 'byor mngon sum tshad ma	yogipratyakṣapramāṇa	yogic valid perception
snang yul	—	appearing object
spong ba'i gnyen po	prahāṇapratipakṣa	relinquishing remedy
spyi mtshan	sāmānyalakṣaṇa	generally characterized (phenomenon)
spyod yul	gocara	sphere
spros pa	prapañca	reference point
spros bral	niṣprapañca	freedom from reference points
phyir mi 'ong ba	anāgāmin	nonreturner
(lan gcig) phyir 'ong ba	(sakṛd)āgāmin	(once-)returner
phyogs chos	pakṣadharmatā/-tva	subject property
phra rgyas	anuśaya	contaminant
'phags pa'i bden pa bzhi	caturāryasatya	four realities of the noble ones
bag chags	vāsanā	latent tendency
bar chad med lam	ānantaryamārga	uninterrupted path
byang chub phyogs chos	bodhipakṣadharma	dharmas concordant with enlightenment
bral ba'i 'bras bu	visaṃyogaphala	result of freedom
blo	buddhi	mental state
'bras gnas	phalastha	abider in a fruition
sbyor lam	prayogamārga	path of preparation
ma rig bag chags kyi sa	avidyāvāsanābhūmi	ground of the latent tendencies of ignorance
mi mthun phyogs	vipakṣa	heterologous set

mi dmigs pa	anupalabdhi, anupalambha	nonobservation, nonreferential
mi slob lam	aśaikṣamārga	path of nonlearning
med dgag	prasajyapratiṣedha	nonimplicative negation
mos pas spyod pa	adhimukticaryā	engagement through aspiration
dmigs rkyen	ālambanapratyaya	object condition
dmigs med	anupalambha, anālambana	nonreferential
smon pa'i byang chub kyi sems	bodhipraṇidhicitta	bodhicitta of aspiration
rtse mo'i sbyor ba	—	culminating training
tshad ma	pramāṇa	valid cognition
tshogs lam	sambhāramārga	path of accumulation
zhugs pa	pratipannaka	approacher
zhen yul	—	referent object
gzhan dbang (gi rang bzhin)	paratantra(svabhāva)	other-dependent (nature)
gzhan sel	anyāpoha	elimination-of-other
gzhi ldog	—	instance-isolate
gzhi shes pa	vastujñāna	knowledge of entities
gzhi'i gnyen po	ādhārapratipakṣa	sustaining remedy
zag bcas	sāsrava	contaminated
zag med	anāsrava	uncontaminated
zad pa dang mi skye ba shes pa	kṣayānutpattijñāna	knowledge of termination and nonarising
zad par	kṛtsna	totality
zab mo lta rgyud	—	lineage of profound view
zil gyis gnon gyi skye mched	abhibhāyatana	āyatana of overpowering
yang dag pa'i mtha'	bhūtakoṭi	true end
yang dag ma yin kun rtog	abhūtaparikalpa	false imagination

yid	manas	mentation
yid la mi byed pa	amanasikāra	mental nonengagement
yongs grub (kyi rang bzhin)	pariniṣpanna-(svabhāva)	perfect (nature)
yongs su grub pa'i gzugs	pariniṣpannarūpa	perfect form
rang ldog	—	self-isolate
rang mtshan	svalakṣaṇa	specifically characterized (phenomenon)
rang bzhin gnas rigs	prakṛtisthagotra	naturally abiding disposition
rang bzhin med pa	niḥsvabhāva	lack of nature
rang bzhin gsum	trisvabhāva	three natures
rang rig	svasaṃvedana, svasaṃvitti	self-aware(ness)
rigs	gotra	disposition
lam shes pa nyid	mārgajñatā	knowledge of the path
shes pa'i rnam pa	jñānākāra	cognitive aspect
shes bya'i sgrib pa	jñeyāvaraṇa	cognitive obscuration
seng ge'i rnam bsgyings	siṃhavijṛmbhita	lion's sport
sems nyid	cittatvam, cittam eva	mind as such
sems pa'i las	cetanākarma	volitional karma
sems tsam	cittamātra	mere mind, Mere Mentalism
sems tsam pa	—	Mere Mentalist
so so rang rig (pa'i ye shes)	pratyātmavedanīya (jñāna) (svapratyātmāryajñāna)	personally experienced (wisdom)
so sor brtags pa'i 'gog pa	pratisaṃkyhānirodha	analytical cessation
so sor brtags min 'gog pa	apratisaṃkyhānirodha	nonanalytical cessation
bsam pa'i las	cetayitvā karma	volitioned karma
lhag pa'i bsam pa	adhyāśaya	superior intention
lhan skyes	sahaja	innate
lhan cig dmigs par nges pa	sahopalambhaniyama	invariable co-observation

Bibliography

Canonical Texts

Abhayākaragupta. *Aṣṭasāhasrikāprajñāpāramitāvṛttimarmakaumudī.* (Shes rab kyi pha rol tu phyin pa brgyad stong pa'i 'grel pa gnad kyi zla 'od). P5202. D3805.

——. *Munimatālaṃkāra.* (Thub pa'i dgongs rgyan). P5299. D3903.

Anonymous. *Vivṛtagūḍhārthapiṇḍavyākhyā.* (Don gsang ba rnam par phye ba bsdus te bshad pa). P5553. D4052.

Āryavimuktisena. *Pañcaviṃśatisāhasrikāprajñāpāramitopadeśaśāstrābhisamayālaṃkāravṛtti.* (Shes rab kyi pha rol tu phyin pa stong phrag nyi shu brgya pa'i man ngag gi bstan bcos mngon par rtogs pa'i rgyan gyi 'grel pa; a.k.a. Nyi khri snang ba). Sanskrit edition of the first chapter by C. Pensa. Rome: Istituto Italiano per il Medio ed Estremo Oriente, 1967. P5185. D3787.

Asaṅga. *Abhidharmasamuccaya.* (Chos mngon pa kun las btus pa). P5550. D4049. English translations (from the French by W. Rāhula) by S. Boin-Webb, Fremont: Asian Humanities Press, 2000; and Migme Chodron, Pleasant Bay, Canada: Gampo Abbey, 2001.

——. *Bodhisattvabhūmi.* (Byang chub sems dpa'i sa). P5538. D4037.

——. *Mahāyānasaṃgraha.* (Theg chen bsdus pa). P5549. D4048.

——. *Ratnagotravibhāgavyākhyā* or *Mahāyānottaratantraśāstravyākhyā.* (Theg pa chen po'i rgyud bla ma'i bstan bcos rnam par bshad pa). Sanskrit ed. by E. H. Johnston, Patna: Bihar Research Society, 1950. P5526.

——. *Viniścayasaṃgrahaṇī.* (Rnam par gtan la dbab pa bsdu ba). P5539. D4038.

——. *Yogācarābhūmi.* (Rnal 'byor spyod pa'i sa). P5536. D4035.

Atiśa. *Prajñāpāramitāpiṇḍārthapradīpa.* (Shes rab kyi pha rol tu phyin pa'i don bsdus sgron ma). P5201. D3804.

Bhadanta Vimuktisena. *Pañcaviṃśatisāhasrikāprajñāpāramitopadeśaśāstrābhisamayālaṃkāra-vārttika.* (Shes rab kyi pha rol tu phyin pa stong phrag nyi shu brgya pa'i man ngag gi bstan bcos mngon par rtogs pa'i rgyan gyi rnam 'grel). P5186. D3788.

Buddhaśrījñāna (eighth-ninth centuries). *Saṃcayagāthāpañjikā.* (Bsdus pa tshig su bcad pa'i dka' 'grel). P5196. D3798.

Buddhaśrījñāna (twelfth-thirteenth centuries). *Abhisamayālaṃkārabhagavatīprajñāpāramitopa-deśaśāstrāvṛttiprajñāpradīpāvalīnāma.* (Bcom ldan 'das ma shes rab kyi pha rol tu phyin pa'i man ngag gi bstan bcos mngon par rtogs pa'i rgyan gyi 'grel pa shes rab sgron me phreng ba zhes bya ba). P5196. D3800.

Daṃṣṭrāsena. *Śatasāhasrikāprajñāpāramitābṛhaṭṭīkā.* (Shes rab kyi pha rol tu phyin pa 'bum pa'i rgya cher 'grel pa). P5205. D3807.

Dharmakīrtiśrī. *Prajñāpāramitopadeśaśāstrābhisamayālaṃkāravṛttidurbodhālokānāmaṭīkā.* (Shes rab kyi pha rol tu phyin pa'i man ngag gi bstan bcos mngon par rtogs pa'i rgyan gyi 'grel pa rtogs par dka' ba'i snang ba zhes bya ba ba'i 'grel bshad). P5192. D3794.

Dharmamitra. *Abhisamayālaṃkārakārikāprajñāpāramitopadeśaśāstraṭīkāprasphuṭapadānāma.* (Shes rab kyi pha rol tu phyin pa'i man ngag gi bstan bcos mngon par rtogs pa'i rgyan gyi tshig le'ur byas pa'i 'grel bshad tshig rab tu gsal ba zhes bya ba). P5194. D3796.

Dharmaśrī. *Prajñāpāramitākośatāla.* (Shes rab kyi pha rol tu phyin pa'i mdzod kyi lde mig). P5204. D3806.

——. *Śatasāhasrikāvivaraṇa.* (Stong phrag brgya pa'i rnam par bshad pa). P5203. D3802.

Dignāga. *Prajñāpāramitārthasaṃgrahakārikā* or *Prajñāpāramitāpiṇḍārtha.* (Shes rab kyi pha rol tu phyin ma bsdus pa'i tshig le'ur byas pa; a.k.a. Sher phyin bsdus don/brgyad stong don bsdu). Sanskrit edition by E. Frauwallner, *WZKS* 3 (1959): 140–44. P5207. D3809.

Haribhadra. *Abhisamayālaṃkāranāmaprajñāpāramitopadeśaśāstravivṛti.* (Shes rab kyi pha rol tu phyin pa'i man ngag gi bstan bcos mngon par rtogs pa'i rgyan ces bya ba'i 'grel pa; abbr. 'Grel pa don gsal). Sanskrit edition by R. Tripāṭhī, Sarnath, India: Tibetan Institute for Higher Buddhist Studies, 1977. P5191. D3793.

——. *Aṣṭasāhasrikāprajñāpāramitāvyākhyānābhisamayālaṃkārālokā.* (Shes rab kyi pha rol tu phyin pa brgyad stong pa'i bshad pa mngon par rtogs pa'i rgyan gyi snang ba). Sanskrit editions by U. Wogihara, Tokyo, 1932–35 and P. L. Vaidya, Darbhanga: Mithila Institute, 1960. P5189. D3791.

——. *Bhagavatīratnaguṇasaṃcayagāthāpañjikāsubodhinīnāma.* (Bcom ldan 'das yon tan rin po che sdus pa'i tshig su pa'i dka' 'grel). P5190. D3792.

——. *Pañcaviṃśatisāhasrikāprajñāpāramitā.* (Shes rab kyi pha rol tu phyin pa nyi khri lnga stong pa; abbr. Mdo le brgyad ma). P5188. D3790.

Kumāraśrībhadra. *Prajñāpāramitāpiṇḍārtha.* (Shes rab kyi pha rol tu phyin pa'i don bsdus pa). P5195. D3797.

Maitreya. *Abhisamayālaṃkāra.* (Mngon rtogs rgyan). Sanskrit editions by T. Stcherbatsky and E. Obermiller, Bibliotheca Buddhica 23, Leningrad, 1929; G. Tucci, Baroda, 1932; U. Wogihara, Tokyo, 1932–35; K. Kajiyoshi in *Hannya-kyō no kenkyu*, 1944, pp. 275–320. P5148. D3786.

——. *Dharmadharmatāvibhāga.* (Chos dang chos nyid rnam par 'byed pa). P5523. D4022.

——. *Madhyāntavibhāga.* (Dbus dang mtha' rnam par 'byed pa). P5522. D4021.

——. *Mahāyānasūtrālaṃkāra.* (Theg pa chen po'i mdo sde rgyan). P5221. D4020.

——. *Ratnagotravibhāgamahāyānottaratantraśāstra.* (Theg pa chen po'i rgyud bla ma). Sanskrit edition by E. H. Johnston, Patna, India: The Bihar Research Society, 1950. P5525. D4024.

Prajñākaramati. *Abhisamayālaṃkāravṛittipiṇḍārtha.* (Mngon par rtogs pa'i rgyan gyi 'grel pa'i bsdus don). P5193. D3795.

Ratnākaraśānti. *Aṣṭāsāhasrikāprajñāpāramitāpañjikāsārottamānāma.* (Shes rab kyi pha rol tu phyin pa brgyad stong pa'i dka' grel snying po'i mchog ces bya ba). Sanskrit edition by P. S. Jaini, Patna, India: Kashi Prasad Jayaswal Research Institute, 1979. P5200. D3803.

——. *Abhisamayālaṃkārakārikāvṛittiśuddhamatīnāma.* (Mngon par rtogs pa'i rgyan gyi 'grel pa'i tshig le'ur byas pa'i 'grel pa dag ldan zhes bya ba). P5199. D3801.

Ratnakīrti. *Abhisamayālaṃkāravṛittikīrtikalānāma*. (Mngon par rtogs pa'i rgyan gyi 'grel pa grags pa'i cha zhes bya ba). P5197. D3799.

Smṛtijñānakīrti. *Prajñāpāramitāmātṛikāśatasāhasrikābṛhacchāsanapañcaviṃśatisāhasrikā-madhyaśāsanāṣṭādaśa-sāhasrikālaghuśāsanāṣṭasamānārthaśāsana*. (Yum shes rab kyi pha rol tu phyin pa brgyas par bstan 'bum dang 'bring du bstan pa nyi khri lnga stong dang bsdus te bstan pa khri brgyad stong pa rnams mthun par don brgyad kyi bstan pa). P5187. D3789.

Sthiramati. *Madhyāntavibhāgaṭīkā*. (Dbus dang mtha' rnam par 'byed pa'i 'grel bshad). P5534. D4032.

——. *Sūtrālaṃkāravṛttibhāṣya*. (Mdo sde rgyan gyi 'grel bshad). P5531. D4034.

Vasubandhu. *Abhidharmakośa*. (Chos mngon pa mdzod). P5590. D4089.

——. *Abhidharmakośabhāṣya*. (Chos mngon pa mdzod kyi bshad pa). P5591. D4090. French translation by La Vallée Poussin, Paris 1923–31. English translations (from the French) by Leo Pruden (see below in Modern Works under his name); and Gelong Lodrö Sangpo, Pleasant Bay, Canada: Gampo Abbey, 2000–2006.

——. *Dharmadharmatāvibhāgavṛtti*. (Chos dang chos nyid rnam par 'byed pa'i 'grel pa). P5529. D4028.

——. *Madhyāntavibhāgabhāṣya*. (Dbus mtha' rnam 'byed kyi 'grel pa). P5528. D4027.

——. *Mahāyānasūtrālaṃkārabhāṣya*. (Theg pa chen po'i mdo sde rgyan gyi 'grel pa). P5527. D4026.

——. *Śatasāhasrikāpañcaviṃśatisāhasrikāṣṭādaśasāhasrikāprajñāpāramitābṛhaṭṭīkā*. (Sher phyin 'bum pa dang nyi khri lnga stong pa dang khri brgyad stong pa'i rgya cher 'grel pa; abbr. Yum gsum gnod 'joms). P5206. D3808.

——. *Vyākhyāyukti*. (Rnam bshad rigs pa). P5562. D4061.

Tibetan Treatises

Bdud 'joms 'jigs bral ye shes rdo rje. 1991. *The Nyingma School of Tibetan Buddhism*. 2 vols. Trans. Gyurme Dorje and M. Kapstein. Boston: Wisdom Publications.

Blo gros mtshungs med. 1999. *Theg pa chen po'i rgyud bla ma'i bstan bcos kyi nges don gsal bar byed pa'i rin po che'i sgron me*. In *Sa skya pa'i mkhas pa rnams kyi gsung skor*, vol. 3. Kathmandu: Sa skya rgyal yongs gsung rab slob gnyer khang, 239–565.

Bu ston rin chen grub. 1931. *History of Buddhism*. Trans. E. Obermiller. Heidelberg: Otto Harrassowitz.

——. 2001. *Shes rab kyi pha rol tu phyin pa'i man ngag gi bstan bcos mngon par rtogs pa'i rgyan ces bya ba'i 'grel pa'i rgya cher bshad pa lung gi snye ma*. 2 vols. Sarnath, India: Kargyud Relief and Protection Committee, Central Institute of Higher Tibetan Studies.

Chos grags rgya mtsho (Karmapa VII). 1985. *Tshad ma legs par bshad pa thams cad kyi chu bo yongs su 'du ba rigs pa'i gzhung lugs kyi rgya mtsho*. 4 vols. Rumtek (Sikkim, India): Karma Thupten Chosphel.

——. n.d. *Shes rab kyi pha rol tu phyin pa'i man ngag gi bstan bcos mngon rtogs rgyan gyi 'grel bshad tham cad kyi legs par bshad pa kun las btus pa 'jig rten gsum gyi sgron me*. Unpublished Nithartha *international* File (jigsumsgronmeK7).

Chos kyi 'byung gnas (Situpa VIII). 1988. *Sde dge'i bka' 'gyur dkar chag*. Chengdu, China: Si khron mi rigs dpe skrun khang.

——. 1999. *Kun mkhyen chos 'byung gnas kyi gsung rgyun dri ma med pa blo gsal bung ba'i dga' ston dge 'dun nyi shu'i rnam bzhag*. Mundgod, India: Drepung Gomang Library.

Chos kyi 'byung gnas (Situpa VIII) and 'Be lo Tshe dbang kun khyab. 1972. *Sgrub brgyud karma kaṃ tshang brgyud pa rin po che'i rnam par thar pa rab 'byams nor bu zla ba chu shel gyi phreng ba*. 2 vols. New Delhi: Gyaltsan and Kesang Legshay.

Chos kyi grags pa. 1982. *Chos 'khor dvogs gcod*. In *Shes rab snying po'i rnam bshad chos 'khor dvogs gcod bzhugs*. Sarnath, India: Kargyud Relief and Protection Committee, Central Institute of Higher Tibetan Learning, 37–56.

Chos kyi rgyal mtshan, Se ra rje btsun pa. 1989. *Bstan bcos mngon par rtogs pa'i rgyan 'grel dang bcas pa'i rnam bshad rnam pa gnyis kyi dka' ba'i gnas gsal bar byed pa legs bshad skal bzang klu dbang gi rol mtsho*. 2 vols. Zi ling: Mtsho sngon mi rigs par khang.

——. 1999. *Rgyan 'grel spyi don rol mtsho*. 2 vols. Mundgod, India: Library of Gaden Jangtse Monastery.

——. 2004. *Kar lan klu sgrub dgongs rgyan*. Sarnath, India: Vajra Vidya Institute.

Dbu ma gzhan stong skor bstan bcos phyogs bsdus deb dang po. 1990. Rumtek (Sikkim, India): Karma Shri Nalanda Institute.

Dkon mchog yan lag (Shamarpa V). 2006. *A Concise Elucidation of the* Abhisamayālaṃkāra. (*Mngon rtogs rgyan gyi 'grel pa nyung ngu rnam gsal*. In *Mngon rtogs rgyan gyi 'grel pa nyung ngu rnam gsal dang mngon rtogs rgyan rtsa 'grel gyi sbyor ṭīk*). Seattle: Nitartha *international* Publications. Also *Mngon rtogs rgyan gyi 'grel pa nyung ngu rnam gsal*. Sarnath, India: Vajra Vidya Institute, 2005. Also *dbu med* manuscript (same title), n.p., n.d.

Dngul chu thogs med bzang po dpal. 1979. *Theg pa chen po mdo sde rgyan gyi 'grel pa rin po che'i phreng ba*. Bir, India: Dzongsar Institute Library.

Dol po pa shes rab rgyal mtshan. 1998. *Ri chos nges don rgya mtsho*. Beijing: Mi rigs dpe skrun khang.

Dpa' bo gtsug lag phreng ba. 2003. *History of the Dharma, A Feast for the Learned* (*Dam pa'i chos kyi 'khor lo bsgyur ba rnams kyi byung ba gsal bar byed pa mkhas pa'i dga' ston*). 2 vols. Sarnath, India: Vajra Vidya Institute.

——. n.d. *Byang chub sems dpa'i spyod pa la 'jug pa'i rnam bshad theg chen chos kyi rgya mtsho zab rgyas mtha' yas pa'i snying po*. Rouffignac, France: Nehsang Samten Chöling.

Dpal sprul 'jigs med chos kyi dbang po. 1997. *Shes rab kyi pha rol tu phyin pa'i man ngag gi bstan bcos mngon par rtogs pa'i rgyan ces bya ba'i spyi don dang 'bru 'grel*. Beijing: Mi rigs dpe skrun khang.

——. 2003. *Sher phyin skabs dge 'dun nyi shu'i zur bkol*. In *Dpal sprul 'jigs med chos kyi dbang po'i gsung 'bum*, vol. 5. Chengdu, China: Si khron mi rigs dpe skrun khang, 419–21.

Dul mo bkra shis 'od zer. 2006. *Theg pa chen po'i rgyud bla ma'i 'grel pa gsal ba nyi ma'i snying po*. In *Dpal rgyal dbang ka rma pa sku phreng gsum pa rang byung rdo rje'i gsung 'bum*, vol. ja. Lhasa: Dpal brtsegs bod yig dpe rnying zhib 'jug khang, 126–262.

Gnyal zhig 'jam dpal rdo rje. n.d. *Mngon par rtogs pa'i rgyan gyi 'grel pa theg pa chen po la 'jug pa*. *Dbu med* manuscript at LTWA, Dharamsala.

Go bo rab 'byams pa bsod nams seng ge. 1968. *Sher phyin mngon rtogs gyi mtshon byed kyi yan lag rgyas par bshad pa sbas don rab gsal*. Dehradun, India: Sakya Centre.

——. 1979. *Shes rab kyi pha rol tu phyin pa'i man ngag gi bstan bcos mngon rtogs rgyan gyi gzhung snga phyi'i 'brel dang dka' gnas la dpyad pa sbas don zab mo'i gter gyi kha 'byed.* In *Go bo rab 'byams pa bsod nams seng ge'i bka' 'bum*, vol. 7. Dehradun: Sakya College, 1–453.

'Gos lo tsā ba gzhon nu dpal. 1996. *The Blue Annals.* Trans. G. N. Roerich. Delhi: Motilal Banarsidass.

——. 2003a. *Deb ther sngon po.* 2 vols. Sarnath, India: Vajra Vidya Institute.

——. 2003b. *Theg pa chen po'i rgyud bla ma'i bstan bcos kyi 'grel bshad de kho na nyid rab tu gsal ba'i me long.* Ed. Klaus-Dieter Mathes. Nepal Research Centre Publications 24. Stuttgart: Franz Steiner Verlag.

G.yag ston sangs rgyas dpal. 1994. *Mngon rtogs rgyan dang 'grel pa don gsal rtsa 'grel gyi dgos don stsol ba rin chen bsam 'phel dbang gi rgyal po.* Beijing: Mi rigs dpe skrun khang.

Gzhan phan chos kyi snang ba (a.k.a. Mkhan po gzhan dga'). 1978. *Phar phyin 'grel mchan gzhan phan snang ba.* In *G'zun* [sic!] *chen bcu gsum gyi mchan 'grel*, vol. 1. Dehradun, India: Khochhen Tulku, 77–393.

——. *Sher phyin mchan 'grel yan lag.* 1987. In *Mkhan po gzhan phan chos kyi snang ba'i gzhung chen bcu gsum*, vol. 3. New Delhi: Konchog Lhadrepa, 71–75.

'Ju mi pham rgya mtsho. 1975. *Bde gshegs snying po stong thun chen mo seng ge'i nga ro.* In *Collected Writings of 'Jam-mgon 'Ju Mi-pham-rgya-mtsho*, vol. pa. Ed. Sonam T. Kazi. Gangtok: 282–304.

——. 1984. *Mngon rtogs rgyan gyi mchan 'grel pun da ri ka'i do shel.* In *Collected Writings of 'Jam-mgon 'Ju Mi-pham-rgya-mtsho*, vol. 4. Paro, Bhutan: Lama Ngodrup and Sherab Drimay, 1–347.

——. 1990. *Mkhas pa'i tshul la 'jug pa'i sgo zhes bya ba'i bstan bcos.* Chengdu, China: Si khron mi rigs dpe skrun khang.

——. c. 1990a. *Collected Works (gsung 'bum).* Sde dge dgon chen edition. Kathmandu: Dilgo Khyentse Rinpoche.

——. c. 1990b. *Chos dang chos nyid rnam par 'byed pa'i tshig le'ur byas pa'i 'grel pa ye shes snang ba rnam 'byed.* In *Collected Works* (*gsung 'bum*), vol. pa. Kathmandu: Dilgo Khyentse Rinpoche, 1–51.

——. c. 1990c. *Dbus dang mtha' rnam par 'byed pa'i 'grel pa 'od zer phreng ba.* In *Collected Works*, vol. pa. Kathmandu: Dilgo Khyentse Rinpoche, 660–784.

Ka rma phrin las pa phyogs las rnam rgyal. 2006a. *Mngon rtogs rgyan rtsa 'grel gyi sbyor ṭīk 'jig rten gsum sgron la 'jug pa.* In *Mngon rtogs rgyan gyi 'grel pa nyung ngu rnam gsal dang mngon rtogs rgyan rtsa 'grel gyi sbyor ṭīk.* Seattle: Nitartha *international* Publications, 287–708. Also Vajra Vidya Institute, Sarnath, India, 2004, and blockprint n.p., n.d.

——. 2006b. *Zab mo nang don gyi rnam bshad snying po gsal bar byed pa'i nyin byed 'od kyi phreng ba.* In *Collected Works of Rangjung Dorje*, vol. tram: 1–553.

Khra 'gu rin po che. 1999. *Sher phyin gyi 'grel pa.* Unpublished Nitartha *international* file (TH00__1.E1).

Kong sprul blo gros mtha' yas. 1982. *The Treasury of Knowledge* (*Theg pa'i sgo kun las btus pa gsung rab rin po che'i mdzod bslab pa gsum legs par ston pa'i bstan bcos shes bya kun khyab*; includes its autocommentary, *Shes bya kun la khyab pa'i gzhung lugs nyung ngu'i tshig gis rnam par 'grol ba legs bshad yongs 'du shes bya mtha' yas pa'i rgya mtsho*; abbr. *Shes bya kun khyab mdzod*). 3 vols. Beijing: Mi rigs dpe skrun khang.

——. 1990a. *Rnam par shes pa dang ye shes 'byed pa'i bstan bcos kyi tshig don go gsal du 'grel pa rang byung dgongs pa'i rgyan*. In *Dbu ma gzhan stong skor bstan bcos phyogs bsdus deb dang po*. Rumtek (Sikkim, India): Karma Shri Nalanda Institute, 63–129. Also as Rumtek blockprint, n.d.

——. 1990b. *De bzhin gshegs pa'i snying po bstan pa'i bstan bcos kyi rnam 'grel rang byung dgongs gsal*. In *Dbu ma gzhan stong skor bstan bcos phyogs bsdus deb dang po*. Rumtek (Sikkim, India): Karma Shri Nalanda Institute, 130–90. Also as Rumtek blockprint, n.d.

——. 2005a. *Rnal 'byor bla na med pa'i rgyud sde rgya mtsho'i snying po bsdus pa zab mo nang don nyung ngu'i tshig gis rnam par 'grol ba zab don snang byed*. Seattle: Nitartha *international* Publications. Also as Rumtek blockprint, n.d.

——. 2005b. *Theg pa chen po rgyud bla ma'i bstan bcos snying po'i don mngon sum lam gyi bshad srol dang sbyar ba'i rnam par 'grel ba phyir mi ldog pa seng ge nga ro*. Seattle: Nitartha *international* Publications. Also as Rumtek blockprint, n.d.

Krang dbyi sun et al. 1993. *Bod rgya tshig mdzod chen mo*. 2 vols. Beijing: Mi rigs dpe skrun khang.

Mdo sngags bstan pa'i nyi ma. 1986. *Sher phyin mngon par rtogs pa'i rgyan gyi tshig don rnam par bshad pa ma pham zhal lung*. Sarnath, India: Nyingma Students Welfare Committee, Central Institute of Higher Tibetan Studies.

——. n.d. *Stong thun gnad kyi zin thun*. Photocopy of a digital file from Shechen Monastery, Kathmandu, Nepal.

Mi bskyod rdo rje (Karmapa VIII). 1990. *The Lamp That Excellently Elucidates the System of the Proponents of Shentong Madhyamaka* (*Dbu ma gzhan stong smra ba'i srol legs par phye ba'i sgron me*). In *Dbu ma gzhan stong skor bstan bcos phyogs bsdus deb dang po*. Rumtek (Sikkim, India): Karma Shri Nalanda Institute, 13–47.

——. 1996. *Dbu ma la 'jug pa'i rnam bshad dpal ldan dus gsum mkhyen pa'i zhal lung dvags brgyud grub pa'i shing rta*. Seattle: Nitartha *international* Publications.

——. 2003. *The Noble One's Resting at Ease*. (*Shes rab kyi pha rol tu phyin pa'i lung chos mtha' dag gi bdud rtsi'i snying por gyur pa gang la ldan pa'i gzhi rje btsun mchog tu dgyes par ngal gso'i yongs 'dus brtol gyi ljon pa rgyas pa*). 2 vols. Seattle: Nitartha *international* Publications. Also blockprint (same title), 2 vols. Rumtek: Karma Shri Nalanda Institute, n.d. Also *Phar phyin. Dpal mnyam med 'gro mgon bka' brgyud pa'i gsung rab phyogs bsgrigs legs bshad kun 'dus dri med lung rigs gan mdzod las pod bco lnga pa*. Zi ling: Mtsho sngon mi rigs par khang, 2001.

——. 2004. *Theg pa chen po pha rol tu phyin pa'i spang gnyen gyi khrid*. In *Dpal rgyal ba ka rma pa sku 'phreng brgyad pa mi bskyod rdo rje'i gsung 'bum*, vol. dza. Ed. Karma bde legs. Lhasa: 513–22.

Ngag dbang kun dga' dbang phyug. 1987. *Shes rab kyi pha rol tu phyin pa'i man ngag gi bstan bcos mngon par rtogs pa'i rgyan 'grel pa dang bcas pa'i tshig don snying po gsal ba'i me long*. Bir: Dzongsar Institute Library.

Ngag dbang yon tan bzang po. 2000. *Jo nang chos 'byung dang rje jo nang chen po'i ring lugs*. Beijing: Mi rigs dpe skrun khang.

Nus ldan rdo rje. n.d. *Mkhas pa'i tshul la 'jug pa'i sgo'i mchan 'grel legs bshad snang ba'i 'od zer*. n.p.

Nya dbon kun dga' dpal. 1978. *Bstan bcos mngon par rtogs pa'i rgyan 'grel ba dang bcas pa'i rgyas 'grel bshad sbyar yid kyi mun sel*. New Delhi: Ngawang Zopa.

Padma dkar po. 1974. *Sher phyin gyi lung la 'jug pa'i sgo*. In *Kun mkhyen pad ma dkar po'i gsung 'bum*, vol. ja. Darjeeling: Kargyud Sungrab Nyamso Khang, 403–79.

——. 1982. *Shes rab snying po'i rnam bshad klu sgrub kyi dgongs pa gsal bar bstan pa*. In *Shes rab snying po'i rnam bshad chos 'khor dvogs gcod bzhugs*. Sarnath, India: Kargyud Relief and Protection Committee, Central Institute of Higher Tibetan Learning, 1–36. Also in *Rgyal dbang 'brug pa kun mkhyen pad ma dkar po'i gsung gzhung 'grel skor*, vol. 3. Thimpu, Bhutan: Āchārya Shedup Tenzin and Lama Dhondup Tharchen, 1991, 53–78.

——. 1991. *Mngon par rtogs pa'i rgyan gyi 'grel pa rje btsun byams pa'i gzhal lung*. In *Rgyal dbang 'brug pa kun mkhyen pad ma dkar po'i gsung gzhung 'grel skor*, vol. 3. Thimpu, Bhutan: Āchārya Shedup Tenzin and Lama Dhondup Tharchen, 157–496.

Padmavajra, rdzogs chen mkhan po. n.d. *Sher phyin mngon rtogs rgyan gyi spyi don byams mgon dgongs pa'i gsal byed bla ma brgyud pa'i zhal lung*. n.p.

Rang byung rdo rje (Karmapa III). 2004a. *Mngon rtogs rgyan gyi sa bcad snang byed sgron me*. In *Mngon rtogs rgyan gyi sa bcad snang byed sgron me dang skabs brgyad kyi stong thun dang dbu ma chos dbyings bstod pa'i rnam bshad*. Sarnath, India: Vajra Vidya Institute, 1–88. Also in *Collected Works*, vol. cha: 377–425.

——. 2004b. *Shes rab kyi pha rol tu phyin pa skabs brgyad kyi stong thun*. In *Mngon rtogs rgyan gyi sa bcad snang byed sgron me dang skabs brgyad kyi stong thun dang dbu ma chos dbyings bstod pa'i rnam bshad*. Sarnath, India: Vajra Vidya Institute, 89–146. Also in *Collected Works*, vol. cha: 426–87.

——. 2006a. *Collected Works*. (*Dpal rgyal dbang ka rma pa sku phreng gsum pa rang byung rdo rje'i gsung 'bum*). 11 vols. Lhasa: Dpal brtsegs bod yig dpe rnying zhib 'jug khang.

——. 2006b. *Chos dang chos nyid rnam par 'byed pa'i bstan bcos kyi rnam par bshad pa'i rgyan*. In *Collected Works*, vol. cha: 488–613.

——. 2006c. *Rtogs pa brjod pa'i tshig bcad*. In *Collected Works*, vol. ca: 89–92.

——. n.d. *Zab mo nang gi don gsal bar byed pa'i 'grel pa*. Rumtek (Sikkim), India.

Rnam rgyal grags pa. n.d. *Rigs lam gsal byed*. www.dharmadownload.net/pages/english/Texts/texts_0027.htm.

Rngog lo tsā ba blo ldan shes rab. 1993a. *Shes rab kyi pha rol tu phyin pa'i man ngag gi bstan bcos kyi don bdus pa (lo tsa ba'i bsdus don/ṭīk chung)*. Dharamsala: LTWA.

——. 1993b. *Theg chen rgyud bla ma'i don bsdus pa*. Dharamsala: LTWA.

Rong ston shes bya kun rig. 1971. *Shes rab kyi pha rol tu phyin pa'i man ngag gi bstan bcos mngon par rtogs pa'i rgyan gyi 'grel pa dang bcas pa'i dka' ba'i gnas rnam par 'byed pa zab don gnad kyi zla 'od*. Gangtok (Sikkim, India): Sherab Gyaltsen.

——. 1988. *Shes rab kyi pha rol tu phyin pa'i man ngag gi bstan bcos mngon par rtogs pa'i rgyan gyi 'grel pa'i rnam bshad tshig don rab tu gsal ba*. Ed. David P. Jackson and S. Onoda (see under Modern Works below).

——. 1997. *Theg pa chen po rgyud bla ma'i bstan bcos rtsa 'grel bzhugs so*. Chengdu, China: Si khron mi rigs dpe skrun khang.

Sa bzang ma ti paṇ chen blo gros rgyal mtshan. 1977. *Dam pa'i chos mngon pa kun las btus pa'i 'grel pa zhes bya ba rab gsal snang ba*. Gangtok (Sikkim, India): Gon po Tseten.

——. 1999. *Theg pa chen po'i rgyud bla ma'i bstan bcos kyi rnam par bshad pa nges don rab gsal snang ba*. In *Sa skya pa'i mkhas pa rnams kyi gsung skor*, vol. 4. Kathmandu: Sa skya rgyal yongs gsung rab slob gnyer khang, 1–520.

Śākya mchog ldan. 1975. *Dbu ma'i 'byung tshul rnam par bshad pa'i gtam yid bzhin lhun po.* In *The Complete Works (gsuṅ 'bum) of gSer-mdog Paṇ-chen Śākya-mchog-ldan*, vol. 4. Ed. Kunzang Tobgey. Thimpu, Bhutan: 209–48.

——. 1988a. *'Dzam gling sangs rgyas bstan pa'i rgyan mchog yongs rdzogs gnas lngar mkhyen pa'i paṇḍita chen po gser mdog paṇ chen shākya mchog ldan gyi gsung 'bum legs bshad gser gyi bdud rtsi* (*Collected Works*). 24 vols. New Delhi: Ngawang Tobgyal.

——. 1988b. *Byams chos lnga'i nges don rab tu gsal ba zhes bya ba'i bstan bcos.* In *Collected Works*, vol. da: 1–38.

——. 1988c. *Byams chos lnga'i lam gyi rim pa gsal bar byed pa'i bstan bcos rin chen sgrom gyi sgo 'byed.* In *Collected Works*, vol. da: 39–156.

——. 1988d. *Shes rab kyi pha rol tu phyin pa'i man ngag gi bstan bcos mngon par rtogs pa'i rgyan 'grel pa dka' ba'i gnas rnam par bshad nas nang gzhan gyi grub pa'i mtha' rnam par dbye ba lung rigs kyi rol mtsho.* In *Collected Works*, vols. ka: 9–565 and kha: 1–470.

——. 1988e. *Shes rab kyi pha rol tu phyin pa'i mdo dang mngon par rtogs pa'i rgyan 'grel pa dang bcas pa'i lus dang yan lag rgyas par bshad pa lung don rgya mtsho.* In *Collected Works*, vol. ga: 1–162.

——. 1988f. *Mngon par rtogs pa'i rgyan 'grel pa dang bcas pa'i spyi'i don nyer mkho bsdus pa lung chos rgya mtsho'i snying po.* In *Collected Works*, vol. ga: 163–562.

——. 1988g. *Mngon par rtogs pa'i rgyan 'grel pa don gsal ba dang bcas pa'i rnam par bshad pa shing rta'i srol gnyis gcig tu bsdus pa'i lam po che.* In *Collected Works*, vol. na: 1–319.

——. 1988h. *Shes rab kyi pha rol tu phyin pa'i man ngag gi bstan bcos mngon par rtogs pa'i rgyan 'grel pa dang bcas pa'i snga phyi'i 'brel rnam par btsal zhing dngos bstan gyi dka' ba'i gnas la legs par bshad pa'i dpung tshogs rnam par bkod pa bzhed tshul rba rlabs kyi phreng ba.* In *Collected Works*, vol. da: 157–587.

——. 1988i. *Dge 'dun nyi shu'i mtha' rnam par dpyad pa'i thal 'gyur ngag gi dbang po'i mdzes rgyan.* In *Collected Works*, vol. pa: 1–111.

——. 2000. *Three Texts on Madhyamaka.* Trans. Iaroslav Komarovski. Dharamsala: LTWA.

Sgam po pa. 1990. *The Jewel Ornament of Liberation.* (*Thar pa rin po che'i rgyan*). Chengdu, China: Si khron mi rigs dpe skrun khang. Trans. H. Guenther. London, 1959; reprint, Berkeley: Shambhala, 1971.

Tāranātha. 1980. *History of Buddhism in India.* Trans. Lama Chimpa and Alaka Chattopadhyaya. Calcutta: Bagchi.

Thub bstan brtson 'grus phun tshogs (a.k.a. Dzogchen Khenpo Tsöndrü). 1985?. *Shing rta'i srol 'byed bshad mdo 'grel tshul sogs sher phyin 'chad pa'i sngon 'gro.* In *Thub bstan brtson 'grus phun tshogs kyi gsung 'bum*, vol. 1. Mysoorie, India: Nyingma Monastery, Mkhan-po Padma-śes-rab, 239–66. Trans. Adam Pearcey, *A Preliminary to the Explanation of the Prajñaparamita - Founders of Traditions, Explanatory Sutras, Ways of Commenting, etc.* http://www.lotsawa-house.org/prajnaparamitaprelim.html.

——. 1996. *Bstan bcos chen po mngon rtogs rgyan gyi lus rnam bzhag gi 'grel pa 'jigs med chos kyi dbang po'i zhal lung.* Mysoorie, India: Snga 'gyur mtho slob mdo sngags rig pa'i 'byung gnas gling gi dpe mdzod khang (at Namdroling's Ngagyur Nyingma Institute). Trans. Adam Pearcey, *The Words of Jikmé Chökyi Wangpo: A Commentary Presenting the Subject Matter of the Great Treatise, the Abhisamayalankara.* http://www.lotsawahouse.org/70points.html.

Thub bstan kun bzang, spom ra dge bshes, ed. 1999. *Grub mtha' dang don bdun cu.* Bylakuppe: Se ra smad dpe mdzod khang.

Thub bstan phrin las. 1997. *Shes rab kyi pha rol tu phyin pa'i man ngag gi bstan bcos mngon par rtogs pa'i rgyan gyi dka' 'grel legs bshad lung gi rgya mtsho*. Beijing: Mi rigs dpe skrun khang.

Tsong kha pa. 1985. *Shes rab kyi pha rol tu phyin pa'i man ngag gi bstan bcos mngon par rtogs pa'i rgyan 'grel pa dang bcas pa'i rgya cher bshad pa'i legs bshad gser phreng*. In *Collected Works*, vols. tsa and tsha. Dharamsala: Bod gzhung shes rig dpar khang. Also in *Legs bshad gser gyi phreng ba zhes bya ba bzhugs so*. Taipei, Taiwan: The Corporate Body of the Buddha Educational Foundation, 2000, 1–1112.

Ye shes dbang phyug, spom ra dge bshes. 1999. *Grub mtha' mkhas pa'i yid 'phrog dang don bdun cu*. Bylakuppe: Ser smad dpe mdzod khang.

Zur mang padma rnam rgyal. n.d. *Dri lan tshes pa'i zla ba*. n.p.

Modern Works

Amano, Koei Hirofusa. 1964. "The Buddhakāya Theory of Haribhadra." *Shūkyō Kenkyū (Journal of Religious Studies)* 37 (4) [no. 179]: 27–57.

——. 1965. "The Doctrine of the Twofold-Truth in Haribhadra." *JIBS* 13 (2): 619–24.

——. 1969. "On the Composite Purpose of the *Abhisamayālaṃkāra-kārikā-śāstra*—Haribhadra's Way of Explaining." *JIBS* 17 (2): 59–69.

——. 1975. *A Study on the Abhisamayālaṃkārakārikāśāstravṛtti*. Tokyo: Japan Science Press.

——. 1983. "Late Prajñā Philosophy." In *Prajñā Philosophy, Lectures in Mahāyāna Buddhism*, vol. 2. Tokyo: Shunjūsha, 194–223.

——. 2000. *Abhisamayālaṃkāra-kārikā-śāstra-vivṛti*. Haribhadra's Commentary on the *Abhisamayālaṃkārakārikā-śāstra* edited for the first time from a Sanskrit Manuscript. Kyoto: Heirakuji-Shoten.

——. 2005. *Index to the Abhisamayālaṃkāra-kārikā-śāstra-vivṛti: Tibetan-Sanskrit*. Kyoto: Heirakuji-Shoten.

Anacker, Stefan. 1978. "The Meditational Therapy of the *Madhyāntavibhāgabhāṣya*." In *Mahāyāna Buddhist Meditation: Theory and Practice*, ed. Minoru Kiyota. Honolulu: University of Hawai'i Press, 83–113.

——. 1986. *Seven Works of Vasubandhu*. Delhi: Motilal Banarsidass.

——. 1992. "An Unravelling of the *Dharma-Dharmatā-Vibhāga-Vṛtti* of Vasubandhu." *AS* 46 (1): 26–36.

Apple, James Boyd. 2001. "Twenty Varieties of the *Saṃgha*: Tsong kha pa's Soteriological Exegesis." Ph.D. diss., University of Wisconsin.

——. 2003. "Twenty Varieties of the Saṃgha: A Typology of Noble Beings (Ārya) in Indo-Tibetan Scholasticism (Part I)." *JIP* 31: 503–92.

——. 2004. "Twenty Varieties of the Saṃgha: A Typology of Noble Beings (Ārya) in Indo-Tibetan Scholasticism (Part II)." *JIP* 32: 211–79.

——. 2008. *Stairway to Nirvāṇa: A Study of the Twenty* Saṃghas *Based on the Works of Tsong kha pa*. Albany: State University of New York Press.

Arnold, Dan. 2003. "Verses on Nonconceptual Awareness: A Close Reading of *Mahāyānasaṃgraha* 8.2-13." *Indian International Journal of Buddhist Studies* 4: 19–49.

——. 2005. "Is *Svasaṃvitti* Transcendental? A Tentative Reconstruction Following Śāntarakṣita." *Asian Philosophy* 15 (1): 77–111.

Bareau, André. 1955. *Les sectes bouddhiques du Petit Véhicule*. Saigon: École française d'Extrême-Orient.

Bastian, E. W. 1980. "Mahayana Buddhist Religious Practice and the Perfection of Wisdom according to the *Abhisamayālaṃkāra* and the *Pañcaviṃśatisāhasrikā Prajñāpāramitā*. The Interpretation of the First Two Topics by Haribhadra, Rgyal-tshab dar ma rin chen, and Rje btsun chos kyi rgyal mtshan." Ph.D. diss., University of Michigan.

Beautrix, Pierre. 1970. *Bibliographie de la Littérature Prajñāpāramitā*. Bruxelles: Publications de l'Institut Belge des Hautes Études Bouddhiques.

Berzin, Alex. 2006a. "Ridding Oneself of the Two Sets of Obscurations in Sutra and Highest Tantra According to Nyingma and Sakya." http://www.berzinarchives.com/web/en/archives/advanced/tantra/level3_intermediate_theory/eliminating_2_sets_obscurations.html.

——. 2006b. "The Five Pathway Minds (Five Paths): Advanced Presentation." http://www.berzinarchives.com/web/en/archives/sutra/level4_deepening_understanding_path/path/five_pathway_minds_five_paths/five_pathway_minds_five_paths_advan.html.

Bhuti, Tsewang, trans. 2000. "Klong rdol bla ma's List of 108 dharmas of Prajñāpāramitā and the Commentary." *TJ* 25 (3): 48–68.

Bokar, Rinpoche. 1994. *Profound Wisdom of the Heart Sutra*. San Francisco: Clear Point Press.

Boquist, Åke. 1993. *Trisvabhāva. A Study of the Development of the Three-nature-theory in Yogācāra Buddhism*. Lund Studies in African and Asian Religions 8. Lund: Department of History of Religions, University of Lund.

Broido, Michael M. 1984. "Abhiprāya and Implication in Tibetan Linguistics." *JIP* 12: 1–33.

——. 1988. "Veridical and Delusive Cognition: Tsongkhapa on the Two *Satyas*." *JIP* 16: 29–63.

——. 1989. "The Jo-nang-pas on Madhyamaka: A Sketch." *TJ* 14 (1): 86–91.

Brown, Brian E. 1991. *The Buddha Nature*. Delhi: Motilal Banarsidass.

Brunnhölzl, Karl, trans. and ann. 2001. *A Commentary on the Perfection of Knowledge: The Noble One Resting at Ease*. Mt. Allison, Canada: Nitartha Institute.

——. 2002. *The Presentation of Grounds, Paths, and Results in the Causal Vehicle of Characteristics in The Treasury of Knowledge* (*Shes bya kun khyab mdzod*, ch. 9.1 and 10.1). Mt. Allison, Canada: Nitartha Institute.

——. 2004. *The Center of the Sunlit Sky*. Ithaca: Snow Lion Publications.

——. 2007a. *Straight from the Heart*. Ithaca: Snow Lion Publications.

——. 2007b. *In Praise of Dharmadhātu*. Ithaca: Snow Lion Publications.

——. 2009. *Luminous Heart*. Ithaca: Snow Lion Publications.

Bühnemann, Gudrun. 1980. *Der Allwissende Buddha. Ein Beweis und seine Probleme. Ratnakīrti's Sarvajñāsiddhi, übersetzt und kommentiert*. Wiener Studien zur Tibetologie und Buddhismuskunde 4. Wien: Arbeitskreis für tibetische und buddhistische Studien, Universität Wien.

Burchardi, Anne. 2002. "Toward an Understanding of *Tathāgatagarbha* Interpretation in Tibet with Special Reference to the *Ratnagotravibhāga*." In *Religion and Secular Culture in Tibet*, ed. Henk Blezer. Tibetan Studies 2: Proceedings of the Ninth Seminar of the International Association for Tibetan Studies, Leiden 2000. Leiden: E. J. Brill, 59–77.

——. 2007. "The Diversity of the *gzhan stong* Madhyamaka Tradition." *Journal of the International Association for Tibetan Studies*, no. 3. www.thdl.org.

Buswell, Robert E. 1992. "The Path to Perdition: The Wholesome Roots and Their Eradication." In *Paths to Liberation: The Mārga and Its Transformations in Buddhist Thought*, ed. Robert Buswell and Robert Gimello. Honolulu: University of Hawai'i Press, 107–34.

——. 1997. "The Aids to Penetration (*Nirvedha-bhāgīya*) according to the Vaibhāṣika School." *JIP* 25: 589–611.

Buswell, Robert E., and Robert M. Gimello, eds. 1992. *Paths to Liberation: The Mārga and Its Transformations in Buddhist Thought*. Honolulu: University of Hawai'i Press.

Cabezón, José I. 1990. "The Canonization of Philosophy and the Rhetoric of Siddhānta in Tibetan Buddhism." In *Buddha Nature*, ed. P. Griffiths. Tokyo: Kenkyusha Printing Co., 7–26.

Cabezón, José I., and Geshe Lobsang Dargyay. 2007. *Freedom from Extremes: Gorampa's "Distinguishing the Views" and the Polemics of Emptiness*. Boston: Wisdom Publications.

Cha, John Younghan. 1996. "A Study of the *Dharmadharmatāvibhāga*: An Analysis of the Religious Philosophy of the Yogācāra, together with an Annotated Translation of Vasubandhu's Commentary." Ph.D. diss., Northwestern University.

Chakrabarti, Arindam. 1990. "On the Purported Inseparability of Blue and the Awareness of Blue: An Examination of Sahopalambhaniyama." In *Mind Only School and Buddhist Logic*, ed. Doboom Tulku. Delhi: Tibet House and Aditya Prakashan, 17–36.

Collier, Nicholson Thomson. 1998. "Ornamenting Intentions: Intention and Implication in Buddhist Hermeneutics." Ph.D. diss., University of Chicago.

Conze, Edward. 1947. "On Omniscience and the Goal." *The Middle Way* 22 (3): 62–63.

——. 1952. "The Composition of the Aṣṭasāhasrika Prajñaparamita." *Bulletin of the School of Oriental and African Studies* 14 (2): 251–62.

——. 1953. "The Ontology of the *Prajñāpāramitā*." *PEW* 3 (2): 117–30.

——, trans. 1954a. *Abhisamayālaṃkāra*. Serie Orientale Roma 6. Rome: Istituto Italiano per il Medio ed Estremo Oriente.

——. 1954b. "Maitreya's Abhisamayālaṅkāra." *East and West* 5 (3): 192–97.

——, trans. 1954c. Typescripts of various short prajñāpāramitā sūtras (Library of Institut für Geschichte und Kultur Indiens und Tibets Hamburg), n.p.

——. 1955. *Selected Sayings from the Perfection of Wisdom*. London: The Buddhist Society.

——. 1957a. *Vajracchedikā Prajñāpāramitā*. Serie Orientale Roma 13. Rome: Istituto Italiano per il Medio ed Estremo Oriente.

——. 1957b. "Marginal Notes to the *Abhisamayālaṃkāra*." In *Liebenthal Festschrift*, ed. Kshitis Roy. Visvabharati: Santiniketan, 21-35.

——. 1958. *Buddhist Wisdom Books*. London: Allen and Unwin.

——. 1960a. *The Prajñāpāramitā Literature*. 's Gravenhage: Mouton and Co.

——. 1960b. "The Development of *Prajñāpāramitā* Thought." *Bukkyo to Bunka (Buddhism and Culture)*, ed. Susumu Yamaguchi. Kyoto: 24–45.

——. 1961. "Abhisamayālaṃkāra (1)." *Encyclopedia of Buddhism*, fascicule I. Colombo: Government of Ceylon, 114–16.

——. 1962. *The Gilgit Manuscript of the Aṣṭadaśasāhasrikāprajñāpāramitā*. Serie Orientale Roma 26. Rome: Istituto Italiano per il Medio ed Estremo Oriente.

——. 1967a. *Thirty Years of Buddhist Studies*. Oxford: Bruno Cassirer.

——. 1967b. *Materials for a Dictionary of the Prajñāpāramitā Literature*. Tokyo: Suzuki Research Foundation.

——, trans. 1973. *The Perfection of Wisdom in Eight Thousand Lines & Its Verse Summary*. Bolinas: Four Seasons.

——, ed. and trans. 1974. *The Gilgit Manuscript of the Aṣṭādaśasāhasrukāprajñāpāramitā*. Serie Orientale Roma 46. Rome: Istituto Italiano per il Medio ed Estremo Oriente.

——, trans. 1975a. *The Large Sutra on Perfect Wisdom*. Berkeley: University of California Press.

——. 1975b. *Further Buddhist Studies*. Oxford: Bruno Cassirer.

——. 1978. "Notes on the text of the *Aṣṭasāhasrikā*." *Journal of the Royal Asiatic Society* 1: 14–20.

——, trans. 2002. *Perfect Wisdom. The Short Prajñāpāramitā Texts*. (Reprint; orig. publ. 1973 by Luzac, London). Buddhist Publishing Group: Totnes (UK).

Conze, Edward, I. B. Horner, David Snellgrove, and Arthur Waley, trans. and eds. 1999. *Buddhist Texts through the Ages*. New Delhi: Research Press.

Conze, Edward, and Iida Shotaro. 1968. "Maitreya's Questions in the Prajñāpāramitā." In *Mélanges d'Indianisme à la mémoire de Louis Renou*. Publications de l'Institut de Civilisation Indienne 28. Paris: 229–42.

Cox, Collett. 1992. "Attainment through Abandonment: The Sarvāstivādin Path of Removing Defilements." In *Paths to Liberation: The Mārga and Its Transformations in Buddhist Thought*, ed. Robert Buswell and Robert Gimello. Honolulu: University of Hawai'i Press, 63–105.

Dalai Lama, H. H. 1997. *The Gelug/Kagyü Tradition of Mahamudra*. Ithaca: Snow Lion Publications.

D'Amato, Mario. 2003. "Can All Beings Potentially Attain Awakening? *Gotra*-Theory in the *Mahāyānasūtrālaṃkāra*." *JIABS* 26 (1): 115–38.

——. 2007. "Trisvabhāva in the *Mahāyānasūtrālaṃkāra*." www.empty-universe.com/yogacara/trisvabhava_in_msa.pdf.

Dargyay, Lobsang. 1981. "The View of Bodhicitta in Tibetan Buddhism." In *The Bodhisattva Doctrine in Buddhism*, ed. Leslie Kawamura. Waterloo: Wilford Laurier University Press, 95–109.

——. 1990. "What is Non-Existent and What is Remanent in Śūnyatā." *JIP* 18: 81–91.

Davidson, Ronald M. 1985. "Buddhist Systems of Transformation: Asraya-parivrtti/-paravrtti among the Yogacara." Ph.D. diss., University of California.

——. 1989. "*Āśrayaparāvṛtti* and *Mahāyānābhidharma*: Some Problems and Perspectives." In *Amalā Prajñā: Aspects of Buddhist Studies*, ed. N. H. Samtani. Delhi: Sri Satguru Publications, 253–62.

Dayal, Har. 1970. *The Bodhisattva Doctrine in Buddhist Sanskrit Literature*. New Delhi: Motilal Banarsidass.

Della Santina, P. 1986. *Madhyamaka Schools in India: A Study of the Madhyamaka Philosophy and of the Division of the System into the Prāsaṅgika and Svātantrika Schools*. Delhi: Motilal Banarsidass.

Dessein, Bart, trans. 1999. *Saṃyuktābhidharmahṛidaya*. 3 vols. Delhi: Motilal Banarsidass.

Dewar, Tyler. 2008. *The Karmapa's Middle Way*. Ithaca: Snow Lion Publications.

Dreyfus, Georges B. J. 1997. "Tibetan Scholastic Education and the Role of Soteriology." *JIABS* 20 (1): 31–62.

——. 2003. *The Sound of Two Hands Clapping*. Berkeley: University of California Press.

——. 2005. "Where Do Commentarial Schools Come From? Reflections on the History of Tibetan Scholasticism." *JIABS* 28 (2): 273–98.

Dreyfus, Georges, and Christian Lindtner. 1989. "The Yogācāra Philosophy of Dignāga and Dharmakīrti." *Studies in Central and East Asian Religions* 2: 27–52.

Dreyfus, Georges B. J., and Sara L. McClintock, eds. 2003. *The Svātantrika-Prāsaṅgika Distinction*. Boston: Wisdom Publications.

Duckworth, Douglas S. 2005. "Buddha-Nature and a Dialectic of Presence and Absence in the Works of Mi-pham." Ph.D. diss., University of Virginia.

Dzigar Kongtrul. 2003. *The Ornament of Clear Realization: A Commentary on the Abhisamayālamkāra*. Ed. Michaela Haas. Roqueredonde: Rigpa Shedra.

Dzogchen Ponlop, Rinpoche. 2001–2003, 2007. *Commentary on* The Ornament of Clear Realization. *Introduction, Topic One, and Topics Two–Three*. Transcripts of oral teachings at Nitartha Institute, Mt. Allison, Sackville, Canada 2000–2002. 3 vols. Halifax: Nitartha Institute.

Eckel, Malcolm D. 1985. "Bhāvaviveka's Critique of Yogācāra Philosophy in Chapter XXV of the *Prajñāpradīpa*." In *Miscellanea Buddhica*, ed. Chr. Lindtner. Indiske Studier 5. Copenhagen: Akademisk Forlag, 24–75.

——. 1987. "Indian Commentaries on the Heart Sutra: The Politics of Interpretation." *JIABS* 10 (2): 69–79.

Édou, Jérôme. 1996. *Machig Labdrön and the Foundations of Chöd*. Ithaca: Snow Lion Publications.

Eimer, Helmut. 2006. *Buddhistische Begriffsreihen als Skizzen des Erlösungsweges*. Wiener Studien zur Tibetologie und Buddhismuskunde 65. Wien: Arbeitskreis für tibetische und buddhistische Studien, Universität Wien.

Fann, K. T. 1969. *Wittgenstein's Conception of Philosophy*. Berkeley: University of California Press.

Forman, Robert. 1989. "Paramārtha and Modern Constructivists." *PEW* 39: 393–418.

Frauwallner, Erich. 1951. "Amalavijñana und Alayavijñana." *Beiträge zur indischen Philologie und Altertumskunde. Walter Schubring zum 70. Geburtstag dargebracht von der deutschen Indologie*. Alt- und neu-indische Studien 7. Hamburg: Cram, DeGruyter, 148–59.

——. 1956. *Geschichte der indischen Philosophie*. 2 vols. Salzburg: Otto Müller Verlag.

——. 1963, 1964, 1971. "Abhidharma-Studien." I–III. *WZKS* 7: 20–36; 8: 59–99; 15: 69–121.

——. 1994. *Die Philosophie des Buddhismus*. Berlin: Akademic Verlag.

Freeman, Ch. E. 1991. "*Saṃvṛtti, Vyavahāra* and *Paramārtha* in the *Akṣayamatinirdeśa* and its Commentary by Vasubandhu." In *Buddhist Forum* II, ed. Tadeusz Skorupski. London: University of London, School of Oriental and African Studies, 97–114.

Friedmann, David. L. 1937. *Sthiramati: Madhyāntavibhāgaṭīkā: Analysis of the Middle Path and Extremes*. Utrecht: Utrecht University.

Fujita, Kōtatsu. 1975. "One Vehicle or Three?" *JIP* 3: 79–166.

Galloway, Brian. 1980. "A Yogācāra Analysis of the Mind, Based on the Vijñāna Section of Vasubandhu's *Pañcaskandhaprakaraṇa* with Guṇaprabha's Commentary." *JIABS* 3 (2): 7–20.

——. 1988. "Sudden Enlightenment in the *Abhisamayālaṃkāra*, the *Lalitavistara*, and the *Śikṣāsamucchaya*." *WZKS* 32: 141–47.

Garfield, Jay L. 2002. *Empty Words*. New York and Oxford: Oxford University Press.

Gedün Lodrö, Geshe, and Jeffrey Hopkins. 1998. *Calm Abiding and Special Insight*. Ithaca: Snow Lion Publications.

Gimello, Robert. 1976. "Apophatic and Kataphatic Discourse in Mahāyāna: A Chinese View." *PEW* 26 (2): 117–36.

Gómez, Luis O. 1977. "The Bodhisattva as Wonder-worker." In *Prajñāpāramitā and Related Systems*, ed. Lewis Lancaster. Berkeley: University of California, 221–61.

Gregory, Peter N., ed. 1987. *Sudden and Gradual*. Honolulu: University of Hawai'i Press.

Griffiths, Paul J. 1981. "Buddhist Hybrid English: Some Notes on Philology and Hermeneutics for Buddhologists." *JIABS* 4 (2): 17–32.

——. 1986. *On Being Mindless*. La Salle: Open Court.

——. 1990a. "Painting Space with Colors: Tathāgatagarbha in the *Mahāyānasūtrālaṃkāra*-Corpus IX.22–37." In *Buddha Nature*, ed. P. Griffiths. Tokyo: Kenkyusha Printing Co., 41–63.

——. 1990b. "Omniscience in the *Mahāyānasūtrālaṃkāra* and Its Commentaries." *Indo-Iranian Journal* 31: 85–120.

——. 1994a. *On Being Buddha*. Albany: State University of New York Press.

——. 1994b. "What Else Remains in Śūnyatā? An Investigation of Terms for Mental Imagery in the *Madhyāntavibhāga*-Corpus." *JIABS* 17 (1): 1–25.

Griffiths, Paul J., et al. 1989. *The Realm of Awakening*. Oxford: Oxford University Press.

Grosnick, William. 1981. "Nonorigination and Nirvāṇa in the Early Tathāgatagarbha Literature." *JIABS* 4 (2): 33–43.

Gupta, Rita. 2002. "Reflections on Professor G. Tucci's Remarks on Madhyānta-Vibhāgaṭīkā and Abhisamayālaṃkāra." In *Perspective of Buddhist Studies*, ed. Pranabananda Jash. New Delhi: Kaveri Books, 119–31.

Haas, Michaela. 2008. "Die tibetische Rezeption des *Abhisamayālaṃkāra* am Beispiel der ersten drei Kapitel in der Kommentierung von rDza dPal spruls sPyi don." Ph.D. diss., University of Bonn.

Habito, Ruben L. F. 1986. "The Notion of Dharmakāya: A Study in the Buddhist Absolute." *Journal of Dharma* 11 (4): 348–78.

Hakamaya, Noriaki. 1971. "Asvabhāva's Commentary on the *Mahāyānasūtrālamkāra* IX. 56–76." *JIBS* 20 (1): 473–65.

——. 1980. "The Realm of Enlightenment in *Vijñaptimātratā*: The Formulation of the 'Four Kinds of Pure Dharmas.'" *JIABS* 3 (1): 22–41.

Hall, Bruce C. 1986. "The Meaning of Vijñapti in Vasubandhu's Concept of Mind." *JIABS* 9 (1): 7–23.

Harding, Sarah, trans. and ed. 2003. *Machik's Complete Explanation*. Ithaca: Snow Lion Publications.

Harris, Ian Charles. 1991. *The Continuity of Madhyamaka and Yogācāra in Indian Mahāyāna Buddhism*. Leiden, Netherlands: E. J. Brill.

Harrison, Paul. 1987. "Who Gets to Ride in the Great Vehicle? Self-Image and Identity Among the Followers of the Early Mahāyāna." *JIABS* 10 (1): 67-89.

——. 1992. "Is the *Dharma-kāya* the Real 'Phantom Body' of the Buddha?" *JIABS* 15 (1): 44–95.

Hattori, Masaaki. 1982. "The Dream Example in Vijñānavāda Treatises." In *Indological and Buddhist Studies. Volume in Honour of Professor J. W. de Jong on his Sixtieth Birthday*, ed. L. A. Hercus et al. Canberra: Faculty of Asian Studies, 235–41.

Hirabayashi, Jay, and Shotaro Iida. 1977. "Another Look at the Mādhyamika versus Yogācāra Controversy Concerning Existence and Non-existence." In *Prajñāpāramitā and Related Systems*, ed. Lewis Lancaster. Berkeley: University of California, 341–60.

Hiriyanna, M. 1932. *Outlines of Indian Philosophy*. London: George Allen and Unwin.

Hixon, Lex. 1993. *The Mother of the Buddhas*. Wheaton: Quest Books.

Hookham, S. K. 1991. *The Buddha Within*. Albany: State University of New York Press.

Hopkins, Jeffrey. 1992. "A Tibetan Perspective on the Nature of Spiritual Experience." In *Paths to Liberation: The Mārga and Its Transformations in Buddhist Thought*, ed. Robert Buswell and Robert Gimello. Honolulu: University of Hawai'i Press, 225–67.

——. 1996. *Meditation on Emptiness*. Boston: Wisdom Publications.

——, trans. and introd. 2006. *Mountain Doctrine*. Ithaca: Snow Lion Publications.

——, trans. and ann. 2007. *The Essence of Other-Emptiness*. Ithaca: Snow Lion Publications.

Hurvitz, Leon. 1977. "The Abhidharma on the 'Four Aids to Penetration.'" In *Buddhist Thought and Asian Civilization*, ed. Leslie Kawamura and Keith Scott. Emeryville: Dharma Publishing, 59–104.

Inagaki, Hisao. 1977. "Haribhadra's Quotations from Jñānagarbha's *Anantamukha-nirhāradhāraṇīṭīkā*." In *Buddhist Thought and Asian Civilization*, ed. Leslie Kawamura and Keith Scott. Emeryville: Dharma Publishing, 132–44.

Isoda, H. 1970. "A Study of *Cittotpāda* in the *Abhisamayālaṃkāra*." *JIBS* 19 (1): 71–76.

——. 1971. "A Study on the *Nirvedha-bhāgīya* in the *Abhisamayālaṃkāra*." *JIBS* 20 (2): 541–48.

Iwata, Takashi. 1984. "One interpretation of the saṃvedana inference of Dharmakīrti." *JIBS* 33 (1): 397–94.

Jackson, David P. 1985. "Madhyamaka Studies among the Early Sa-skya-pas." *TJ* 10 (2): 20–34.

Jackson, David P., and S. Onoda, eds. 1988. *Rong-ston on the Prajñāpāramitā Philosophy of the Abhisamayālamkāra: His Sub-commentary on Haribhadra's 'Sphuṭārtha.'* Kyoto: Nagata Bunshodo.

Jackson, Roger R. 1990. "Luminous Mind Among the Logicians—An Analysis of *Pramāṇavārttika* II.205–211." In *Buddha Nature*, ed. P. Griffiths. Tokyo: Kenkyusha Printing Co., 95–123

——. 2001. "The dGe ldan-bKa' brgyud Tradition of Mahāmudrā: *How Much dGe ldan? How Much bKa' brgyud?*" In *Changing Minds*, ed. Guy Newland. Ithaca: Snow Lion Publications, 155–91.

Jaini, Padmanabh S. 1972. "The *Ālokā* of Haribhadra and the *Sāratamā* of Ratnākaraśānti: A Comparative Study of the Two Commentaries of the *Aṣṭasāhasrikā*." *Bulletin of the School of Oriental and African Studies* 35: 271–84.

———. 1979. *Sāratamā, a Pañjikā on the Aṣṭa-sāhasrikā Prajñāpāramitā Sūtra by Ācārya Ratnākaraśānti*. Tibetan-Sanskrit Works Series 18. Patna, India: Kashi Prasad Jayaswal Research Institute.

———. 1992. "On the Ignorance of the Arhat." In *Paths to Liberation: The Mārga and Its Transformations in Buddhist Thought*, ed. Robert Buswell and Robert Gimello. Honolulu: University of Hawai'i Press, 135–45.

Jampa Thaye (David Stott). 1994. *An Introduction to the Cycle of Texts Belonging to the Madhyamaka Empty-of-Other System*. Bristol: Ganesha Press.

Jamspal, L., et al., trans. 2004. *The Universal Vehicle Discourse Literature (Mahāyānasūtrālaṁkāra)*. Editor-in-chief Robert A. F. Thurman. Treasury of the Buddhist Sciences. New York: American Institute of Buddhist Studies, Columbia University.

Kajiyama, Yuichi. 1982. "On the Meanings of the Words Bodhisattva and Mahāsattva in Prajñāpāramitā Literature." In *Indological and Buddhist Studies. Volume in Honour of Professor J. W. de Jong on his Sixtieth Birthday*, ed. L. A. Hercus et al. Canberra: Faculty of Asian Studies, 253–70.

Kano, Kazuo. 2006. "rNgog Blo-ldan Shes-rab's Summary of the *Ratnagotravibhāga*." Ph.D. diss., University of Hamburg.

Kaplan, Stephen. 1990. "A Holographic Alternative to a Traditional Yogācāra Simile: An Analysis of Vasubandhu's Trisvabhāva Doctrine." *The Eastern Buddhist* 23: 56–78.

Kapstein, Matthew. 1992. "The Illusion of Spiritual Progress: Remarks on Indo-Tibetan Buddhist Soteriology." In *Paths to Liberation: The Mārga and Its Transformations in Buddhist Thought*, ed. Robert Buswell and Robert Gimello. Honolulu: University of Hawai'i Press, 193–224.

———. 1997. "From Kun-mkhyen Dol-po-pa to 'Ba'-mda' dge legs: Three Jo-nang-pa Masters on the Interpretation of the Prajñāpāramitā." In *Tibetan Studies*, ed. Ernst Steinkellner et al. Proceedings of the Seventh Seminar of the International Association for Tibetan Studies, Graz 1995, vol. 1. Wien: Verlag der Österreichischen Akademie der Wissenschaften, 457–75.

———. 2000a. "We Are All Gzhan stong pas." *Journal of Buddhist Ethics* 7: 105–25.

———. 2000b. "What Is 'Tibetan Scholasticism'? Three Ways of Thought." In M. Kapstein, *The Tibetan Assimilation of Buddhism*. Oxford: Oxford University Press, 85–120.

Katsura, Shoryu. 1976. "A Synopsis of the *Prajñāpāramitopadeśa* of Ratnākaraśānti." *JIBS* 25 (1): 487–84.

Kawamura, Leslie, ed. 1981. *The Bodhisattva Doctrine in Buddhism*. Waterloo: Wilford Laurier University Press.

———. 1993. "Āśrayaparivṛtti in the Dharma-dharmatā-vibhāga." In *Studies in Original Buddhism and Mahayana Buddhism in Commemoration of late Professsor Dr. Fumimaro Watanabe*, ed. E. Mayeda, vol. 1. Kyoto: Nagata Bunshodo, 73–90.

Kawasaki, Shinjo. 1985. "*Sarvajña* and *Sarvākārajña* in the *Mahāprajñā-pāramitā-upadeśa-śāstra*." In *Various Problems in Buddhist Thought*. Tokyo: Shunjūsha, 355–72.

Keenan, John P. 1980. "A Study of the *Buddhabhūmyupadeśa*: The Doctrinal Development of the Notion of Wisdom in Yogācāra Thought." Ph.D. diss., University of Wisconsin.

———. 1982. "Original Purity and the Focus of Early Yogācāra." *JIABS* 5 (1): 7–18.

———. 1989. "Asaṅga's Understanding of Mādhyamika." *JIABS* 12 (1): 93–107.

——. 1997. *Dharmapāla's Yogācāra Critique of Bhāvaviveka's* [sic!] *Mādhyamika Explanation of Emptiness*. Studies in Asian Thought and Religion 20. Lewiston/Queenston/Lampeter: The Edwin Mellen Press.

——. 2002. *The Interpretation of the Buddha Land*. Berkeley: Numata Center for Buddhist Translation and Research.

King, Richard. 1994. "Early Yogācāra and Its Relationship with the Madhyamaka School." *PEW* 44 (4): 659–83.

——. 1998. "Vijñaptimātratā and the Abhidharma Context of Early Yogācāra." *Asian Philosophy* 8 (1): 5–18.

Klein, Anne C. 1992. "Mental Concentration and the Unconditioned: A Buddhist Case for Unmediated Experience." In *Paths to Liberation: The Mārga and Its Transformations in Buddhist Thought*, ed. Robert Buswell and Robert Gimello. Honolulu: University of Hawai'i Press, 269–308.

Kobayashi, Mamoru. 1981. "On Ratnākaraśānti's Commentaries on the *Abhisamayālaṃkāra*." *JIBS* 30 (1): 132–33.

Komarovski, Iaroslav, trans. 2000. *Three Texts on Madhyamaka*. Dharamsala, India: LTWA.

Kongtrul Lodrö Tayé, Jamgön. 1995. *Buddhist Ethics*. Translated by the International Translation Committee of Kalu Rinpoché. Ithaca: Snow Lion Publications.

Konow, Sten. 1941. *The First Two Chapters of the Daśasāhasrikā-Prajñāpāramitā*. Oslo.

Kritzer, Robert. 1999. *Rebirth and Causation in the Yogācāra Abhidharma*. Wiener Studien zur Tibetologie und Buddhismuskunde 44. Wien: Arbeitskreis für tibetische und buddhistische Studien, Universität Wien.

——. 2005. *Vasubandhu and the Yogācārabhūmi: Yogācāra Elements in the Abhidharmakośabhāṣya*. Tokyo: The International Institute for Buddhist Studies.

Kunst, Arnold. 1977. "Some Aspects of the Ekayāna." In *Prajñāpāramitā and Related Systems*, ed. Lewis Lancaster. Berkeley: University of California, 313–26.

Lamotte, Étienne. 1949–76. *Le Traité de la Grande Vertue de Sagesse*. 4 vols. Louvain: Institut Orientaliste. English translation by Migme Chodron, Pleasant Bay: Gampo Abbey (Canada), 2007.

——. 1998. *Śūraṃgamasamādhisūtra: The Concentration of Heroic Progress*. Trans. S. Boin-Webb. London: Curzon Press.

Lancaster, Lewis, ed. 1977. *Prajñāpāramitā and Related Systems*. Berkeley Buddhist Studies Series 1. Berkeley: University of California.

Lati Rinbochay, Denma Lochö Rinbochay, L. Zahler, and J. Hopkins. 1983. *Meditative States in Tibetan Buddhism*. London: Wisdom Publications.

La Vallée Poussin, Louis de. 1928–1948. *Vijñaptimātratāsiddhi: La Siddhi de Hiuan-tsang*. Paris: P. Geuthner.

Lethcoe, Nancy R. 1976. "Some Notes on the Relationship between the *Abhisamayālaṅkāra*, the Revised *Pañcaviṃśatisāhasrikā*, and the Chinese Translations of the Unrevised *Pañcaviṃśatisāhasrikā*." *JAOS* 96 (4): 499–511.

Lévi, Sylvain. 1932. *Un système de philosophie bouddhique. Matériaux pour l'étude du système Vijñaptimātra*. Paris: H. Champion.

Levinson, Jules B. 1994. "The Metaphors of Liberation: A Study of Grounds and Paths According to the Middle Way School." Ph.D. diss., University of Virginia.

——. 1996. "The Metaphors of Liberation." In *Tibetan Literature: Studies in Genre*, ed. J. Cabezón and R. Jackson. Ithaca: Snow Lion Publications, 261–77.

Limaye, Surekha Vijay, trans. 1992. *Mahāyānasūtrālaṃkāra*. Delhi: Sri Satguru Publications.

Lindtner, Christian. 1982. *Nāgārjuniana*. Indiske Studier 4. Copenhagen: Akademisk Forlag.

——. 1985. "A Treatise on Buddhist Idealism." In *Miscellanea Buddhica*, ed. Chr. Lindtner. Indiske Studier 5. Copenhagen: Akademisk Forlag, 109–221.

——. 1986. "Bhavya's Critique of Yogācāra in the *Madhyamakaratnapradīpa*, Chapter IV." In *Buddhist Logic and Epistemology*, ed. B.K. Matilal and R.D. Evans. Dordrecht: D. Reidel, 239–63.

——. 1992. "The *Laṅkāvatārasūtra* in Early Indian Madhyamaka Literature." *AS* 46 (1): 244–79.

——. 1997. "*Cittamātra* in Indian Mahāyāna until Kamalaśīla." *WZKS* 41: 159–206.

Lipman, Kennard. 1980. "Nītārtha, Neyārtha, and Tathāgatagarbha in Tibet." *JIP* 8: 87–95.

——. 1982. "Cittamātra and Its Madhyamaka Critique." *PEW* 32: 295–308.

Lochö Rinbochay, Denma, and Jeffrey Hopkins. n.d. "Grounds and Paths: Lectures by Denma Lochö Rinbochay on Gön-chok-jik-may-wang-bo's *A Presentation of the Grounds and Paths: An Ornament Beautifying the Three Vehicles*." University of Virginia. Unpublished Transcript.

Lopez, Donald S., Jr. 1987. *A Study of Svātantrika*. Ithaca: Snow Lion Publications.

——. 1988a. *The Heart Sūtra Explained*. Albany: State University of New York Press.

——. 1988b. "On the Interpretation of the Mahāyāna Sūtras." In *Buddhist Hermeneutics*, ed. Donald Lopez. Honolulu: University of Hawai'i Press, 47–70.

——. 1992. "Paths Terminable and Interminable." In *Paths to Liberation: The Mārga and Its Transformations in Buddhist Thought*, ed. Robert Buswell and Robert Gimello. Honolulu: University of Hawai'i Press, 147–92.

——. 1996. *Elaborations on Emptiness*. Princeton: Princeton University Press.

Lusthaus, Dan. 2002. *Buddhist Phenomenology. A Philosophical Investigation of Yogācāra Buddhism and the* Ch'eng Wei-shih lun. London: RoutledgeCurzon.

Makransky, John J. 1989. "Controversy over Dharmakāya in India and Tibet: A Reappraisal of its Basis, *Abhisamayālaṃkāra* Chapter 8." *JIABS* 12 (2): 45–78.

——. 1990. "Controversy over Dharmakāya in Indo-Tibetan Buddhism: A Historical-Critical Analysis of *Abhisamayālaṃkāra* Chapter 8 and its Commentaries in Relation to the *Large Prajñāpāramitā Sūtra* and the Yogācāra Tradition." Ph.D. diss., University of Wisconsin.

——. 1992. "Proposal of a Modern Solution to an Ancient Problem: Literary-Historical Evidence that the *Abhisamayālaṃkāra* Teaches Three Buddha Kāyas." *JIP* 20 (2): 149–90.

——. 1997. *Buddhahood Embodied*. Albany: State University of New York Press.

Mano, Ryūkai. 1967. "Gotra in Haribhadra's Theory." *JIBS* 40 (2): 972–64.

——. 1968. "Tathāgata in Haribhadra's Commentary." *Indogakku Bukkyōgaku kenkyū* 16 (1): 975–69.

——. 1970. "On the Three Jñātas." *JIBS* 43 (2): 21–26.

——. 1972. *A Study of the Abhisamayālaṃkāra*. Tokyo: Sankibō Buddhist Book Store.

——. 1975. *Bonbun Hassenju Hanya-shaku Sakuin-Genkanshōgonron no Kenkyū*. [Index to the *Ālokā*]. Tokyo: Sankibō Buddhist Book Store.

Mathes, Klaus-Dieter. 1996. *Unterscheidung der Gegebenheiten von ihrem wahren Wesen (Dharmadharmatāvibhāga)*. Swisttal-Odendorf, Germany: Indica et Tibetica Verlag.

——. 1998. "Vordergründige und höchste Wahrheit im *gźan stoṅ*-Madhyamaka." *Annäherung an das Fremde*. XXVI. Deutscher Orientalistentag vom 25. bis 29.9.1995 in Leipzig. Ed. H. Preissler and H. Stein. *Zeitschrift der Deutschen Morgenländischen Gesellschaft* 11: 457–68.

——. 2000. "Tāranātha's Presentation of *trisvabhāva* in the *gŹan stoṅ sñiṅ po*." *JIABS* 23 (2): 195–223.

——. 2002. "'Gos Lo tsâ ba gZhon nu dpal's Extensive Commentary on and Study of the *Ratnagotravibhāgavyākhyā*." In *Religion and Secular Culture in Tibet*, ed. Henk Blezer. Tibetan Studies 2: Proceedings of the Ninth Seminar of the International Association for Tibetan Studies, Leiden 2000, vol. 2/2. Leiden: E. J. Brill, 79–96.

——. 2004. "Tāranātha's 'Twenty-One Differences with regard to the Profound Meaning'–Comparing the Views of the Two gŹan stoṅ Masters Dol po pa and Śākya mchog ldan." *JIABS* 27 (2): 285–328.

——. 2006. "Blending the Sūtras with the Tantras: The Influence of Maitrīpa and his Circle on the Foundation of *Sūtra Mahāmudrā* in the Kagyu Schools." In *Buddhist Literature and Praxis: Studies in its Formative Period 900–1400*, ed. Ronald M. Davidson and Christian K. Wedemeyer. Proceedings of the Tenth Seminar of the International Association for Tibetan Studies, Oxford 2003, vol. 4. Leiden: Brill, 201–27.

——. 2007. "The Ontological Status of the Dependent (*paratantra*) in the *Saṃdhinirmocanasūtra* and the *Vyākhyāyukti*." In *Indica and Tibetica. Festschrift für Michael Hahn zum 65. Geburtstag von Freunden und Schülern überreicht*, ed. Konrad Klaus and Jens-Uwe Hartmann. Wiener Studien zur Tibetologie und Buddhismuskunde 66. Wien: Arbeitskreis für tibetische und buddhistische Studien, Universität Wien, 323–40.

——. 2008. *The Direct Path to the Buddha Within: Gö Lotsāwa's Mahāmudrā Interpretation of the Ratnagotravibhāga*. Boston: Wisdom Publications.

May, Jacques. 1971. "La philosophie bouddhique idéaliste." *AS* 25: 265–323.

Meinert, Carmen. 2003. "Structural Analysis of the *Bsam gtan mig sgron*: A Comparison of the Fourfold Correct Practice in the *Āryāvikalpapraveśanāmadhāraṇī* and the Contents of the Four Main Chapters of the *Bsam gtan mig sgron*." *JIABS* 26 (1): 175–95.

Mimaki, Katsumi. 1992. "The Intellectual Sequence of Ratnākaraśānti, Jñānaśrīmitra, and Ratnakīrti." *AS* 46 (1): 297–306.

Nagao, Gadjin M. 1964. *Madhyāntavibhāga-bhāṣya*. Tokyo: Suzuki Research Foundation.

——. 1991. *Mādhyamika and Yogācāra: A Study of Mahāyāna Philosophy*. Trans. L. Kawamura. Albany: State University of New York Press.

——. 1994. *An Index to Asaṅga's Mahāyānasaṃgraha*. 2 vols. Tokyo: International Institute for Buddhist Studies.

Nagasawa, Jitsudo. 1962. "Kamalaśīla's Theory of the Yogācāra." *JIBS* 10 (1): 364–71.

Narima, J. K. 1992 . *Literary History of Sanskrit Buddhism*. (Reprint; orig. publ. 1919). Delhi: Motilal Banarsidass.

Naughton, Alex. 1989. "The Buddhist Path to Omniscience." Ph.D. diss., University of Wisconsin.

Ngari Panchen Pema Wangyi Gyalpo.1996. *Perfect Conduct: Ascertaining the Three Vows*. Boston: Wisdom Publications.

Nguyen, Cuong Tu. 1990. "Sthiramati's Interpretation of Buddhology and Soteriology." Ph.D. diss., Harvard University.

Nishio, Kyoo, ed. 1982. *The Buddhabhūmi-sūtra and the Buddhabhūmi-vyākhyāna of Śīlabhadra*. Tokyo: Kokusho Kankokai.

Obermiller, Eugene. 1933a. "Doctrine of Prajñāpāramitā as Exposed in the *Abhisamayālaṃkāra* of Maitreya." *Acta Orientalia* 11: 1–133, 334–54.

——. 1933b. "A Study of the Twenty Aspects of *Śūnyatā* (Based on Haribhadra's *Abhisamayālaṃkarālokā* and the *Pañcaviṃśatisāhasrikā*)." *Indian Historical Quarterly* 9 (1): 170–87.

——. 1933c, 1936, 1943. *Analysis of the Abhisamayālaṃkāra*. London: Luzac.

——. 1934. "The Term *Śūnyatā* and its Different Interpretations." *Journal of the Greater Indian Society* 1: 105–17, 123–35.

——. 1988. *Nirvāṇa in Tibetan Buddhism*. Ed. Harcharan Singh Sobti. Delhi: Motilal Banarsidass.

——. 1991. *Prajñāpāramitā in Tibetan Buddhism*. Ed. Harcharan Singh Sobti. Delhi: Motilal Banarsidass.

Olson, Robert F. 1974. "Candrakīrti's Critique of Vijñānavāda." *PEW* 24 (1): 405–11.

Padmakara Translation Group, trans. 2005. *The Adornment of the Middle Way: Shantarakshita's Madhyamakalankara with Commentary by Jamgön Mipham*. Boston: Shambhala.

Palden Sherab, Khenpo. 1993. *Ceaseless Echoes of the Great Silence*. Boca Raton: Sky Dancer Press.

Pandeya, Ramchandra. 1999. *Madhyānta-vibhāga-śāstra. Containing the Kārikā-s of Maitreya, Bhāṣya of Vasubandhu and Ṭīkā by Sthiramati*. Delhi: Motilal Banarsidass.

Paul, Diana. 1979. "The Concept of Tathāgatagarbha in the *Śrīmālādevī Sūtra* (Sheng-man Ching)." *JAOS* 99 (2): 191–203.

——. 1984. *Philosophy of Mind in Sixth-Century China: Paramārtha's "Evolution of Consciousness."* Stanford: Stanford University Press.

Pensa, Corrado. 1967. *L'Abhisamayālaṃkāravṛtti di Ārya-Vimuktisena*. Serie Orientale Roma 37. Rome: Istituto Italiano per il Medio ed Estremo Oriente.

Pettit, John Whitney. 1999. *Mipham's Beacon of Certainty*. Boston: Wisdom Publications.

Pezzali, A. 1981. "Bodhisattva et Prajñāpāramitā, L'Essence du Madhyamaka." *Indologica Taurinensia* 8–9: 307–12.

Pfandt, Peter. 1986. *Mahāyāna Texts Translated into Western Languages*. Köln: Brill.

Potter, Karl H. 1991. *Presuppositions of India's Philosophies*. Delhi: Motilal Banarsidass.

——, ed. 1996. *Encyclopedia of Indian Philosophies. Vol. 7. Abhidharma Buddhism to 150 A.D.* Delhi: Motilal Banarsidass.

——, ed. 1999. *Encyclopedia of Indian Philosophies. Vol. 8. Buddhist Philosophy from 100 to 350 A.D.* Delhi: Motilal Banarsidass.

——, ed. 2003. *Encyclopedia of Indian Philosophies. Vol. 9. Buddhist Philosophy from 350 to 600 A.D.* Delhi: Motilal Banarsidass.

Powell, James K. 1998. "The Great Debate in Mahāyāna Buddhism: The Nature of Consciousness." Ph.D. diss., University of Wisconsin.

Powers, John. 1992. *Two Commentaries on the Saṃdhinirmocana-Sūtra by Asaṅga and Jñānagarbha.* Lewiston/Queenston/Lampeter: The Edwin Mellen Press.

Prasad, H. S., introd. and ed. 1991.*The Uttaratantra of Maitreya. E. H. Johnston's Sanskrit Text and E. Obermiller's English Translation.* Delhi: Sri Satguru Publications.

Prince, A. F., and Wong Mou-lam, trans. 1990. *The Diamond Sutra and the Sutra of Hui-Neng.* Boston: Shambhala.

Pruden, Leo M., trans. 1991. *Abhidharmakośabhāṣyam.* 4 vols. (English translation of the French translation by Louis de La Vallée Poussin, 1923-31). Berkeley: Asian Humanities Press.

Qing, Fa. 2001. "The Development of *Prajñā* in Buddhism from Early Buddhism to the *Prajñāpāramitā* System: With Special Reference to the Sarvāstivāda Tradition." Ph.D. diss., University of Calgary.

Rabten, Geshe. 1983. *Echoes of Voidness.* Trans. Stephen Batchelor. London: Wisdom Publications.

Rahula, Walpola. 1971. *Le Compendium de la Super-Doctrine Philosophie.* Paris: École française d'Extrême-Orient.

Rawlinson, Andrew. 1977. "The Position of the *Aṣṭāsāhasrikā Prajñāpāramitā* in the Development of Early Mahāyāna." In *Prajñāpāramitā and Related Systems*, ed. Lewis Lancaster. Berkeley: University of California, 3–34.

——. 1983. "The Ambiguity of the Buddha-nature Concept in India and China." In *Early Ch'an in China and Tibet*, ed. W. Lai and Lewis Lancaster. Berkeley: Asian Humanties Press, 259–79,

Reigle, David. 1997. "The 'Virtually Unknown' Benedictive Middle in Classical Sanskrit: Two Occurrences in the Buddhist *Abhisamayālaṃkāra." Indo-Iranian Journal* 40 (2): 119–23.

Ringu Tulku. 1981. "The Mahayana Concept of Dharani." In *Teachings at Tushita*, ed. Glenn H. Mullin and Nicholas Ribush. New Delhi: Mahayana Publications, 134–37.

Ruegg, David Seyfort. 1963. "The Jo naṅ pas: A School of Buddhist Ontologists according to the *Grub tha' śel gyi me loṅ." JAOS* 83: 73–91.

——. 1968/69. "Ārya and Bhadant Vimuktisena on the Gotra Theory of the Prajñāpāramitā." In *Festschrift für E. Frauwallner. WZKS* 12–13: 303–17.

——. 1969. *La théorie du tathāgatagarbha et du gotra.* Publications de l'École Française d'Extrême-Orient 70. Paris: École Française d'Extrême-Orient .

——. 1976. "The Meanings of the Term Gotra and the Textual History of the *Ratnagotravibhāga.*" *Bulletin of the School of Oriental and African Studies* 39: 341–63.

——. 1977. "The Gotra, Ekayāna and Tathāgatagarbha Theories of the Prajñāpāramitā according to Dharmamitra and Abhayākaragupta." In *Prajñāpāramitā and Related Systems*, ed. Lewis Lancaster. Berkeley: University of California, 283–312.

——. 1981. *The Literature of the Madhyamaka School of Philosophy in India.* Wiesbaden: Otto Harrassowitz.

——. 1985. "Purport, Implicature and Presupposition: Sanskrit *Abhiprāya* and Tibetan *dgoṅs pa/ dgoṅs gzhi* as Hermeneutical Concepts." *JIP* 13: 309–25.

——. 1988. "A Kar ma bka' brgyud Work on the Lineages and Traditions of the Indo-Tibetan Dbu Ma (Madhyamaka)." In *Orientalia Iosephi Tucci Memoriae Dicata*, ed. G. Gnoli and L. Lanciotti. Rome: Istituto Italiano per il Medio ed Estremo Oriente, 1249–80.

——. 1989. *Buddha-nature, Mind and the Problem of Gradualism in a Comparative Perspective*. London: School of Oriental and African Studies.

——. 1995. "Some Reflections on the Place of Philosophy in the Study of Buddhism." *JIABS* 18 (2): 145–81.

——. 2000. *Three Studies in the History of Indian and Tibetan Madhyamaka Philosophy*. Studies in Indian and Tibetan Madhyamaka Thought, Part 1. Wiener Studien zur Tibetologie und Buddhismuskunde 50. Wien: Arbeitskreis für tibetische und buddhistische Studien, Universität Wien.

Sakuma, S. Hidenori. 1994. "The Classification of the Dharmakāya Chapter of the *Abhisamayālaṃkāra* by Indian Commentators: The threefold and the fourfold Buddhakāya Theories." *JIP* 22: 259–97.

Samtani, Narayan H. 2002. *Gathering the Meanings: The Arthaviniścaya Sūtra and its Commentary Nibandhana*. Berkeley: Dharma Publishing.

Samten, Jampa. 1997. "Notes on the Late Twelfth or Early Thirteenth Century Commentary on the Abhisamayālaṃkāra: A Preliminary Report of a Critical Edition." In *Tibetan Studies*, ed. Ernst Steinkellner et al. Proceedings of the Seventh Seminar of the International Association for Tibetan Studies, Graz 1995, vol. 2. Wien: Verlag der Österreichischen Akademie der Wissenschaften, 831–41.

Sangharakshita. 1993. *Wisdom Beyond Words: The Buddhist Vision of Ultimate Reality*. Birmingham: Windhorse Publications.

Schmithausen, Lambert. 1969a. *Der Nirvāṇa-Abschnitt in der* Viniścayasaṃgrahaṇī *der* Yogācārabhūmiḥ. Veröffentlichungen der Kommission für Sprachen und Kulturen Süd- und Ostasiens 8. Österreichische Akademie der Wissenschaften, philosophisch-historische Klasse, Sitzungsberichte, 264. Band, 2. Abhandlung. Wien: Hermann Böhlaus.

——. 1969b. "Zur Literaturgeschichte der älteren Yogācāra-Schule." *Zeitschrift der Deutschen Morgenländischen Gesellschaft*, Supplementa I: 811–23.

——. 1973a. "Spirituelle Praxis und Philosophische Theorie im Buddhismus." *Zeitschrift für Missionswissenschaft und Religionswissenschaft* 57 (3): 161–86.

——. 1973b. "Zu D. Seyfort Rueggs Buch 'La théorie du tathāgatagarbha et du gotra' (Besprechungsaufsatz)." *WZKS* 22: 123–60.

——. 1977. "Textgeschichtliche Beobachtungen zum 1. Kapitel der *Aṣṭasāhasrikā Prajñāpāramitā*." In *Prajñāpāramitā and Related Systems*, ed. Lewis Lancaster. Berkeley: University of California, 35–80.

——. 1981. "On Some Aspects of Descriptions of Theories of 'Liberating Insight' and 'Enlightenment.'" In *Studien zum Jainismus und Buddhismus: Gedenkschrift für L. Alsdorf*, ed. K. Bruhn and A. Wezler. Alt- und neu-Indische Studien 23. Wiesbaden: Franz Steiner Verlag, 199–250.

——. 1983. "The Darśanamārga Section of the *Abhidharmasamuccaya* and its Interpretation by Tibetan Commentators (with Special Reference to Bu ston Rin chen grub)." In *Contributions on Tibetan and Buddhist Religion and Philosophy*, ed. Ernst Steinkellner and Helmut Tauscher. Proceedings of the Csoma de Körös Symposium held at Velm-Vienna, 13-19 September 1981, vol. 2. Wiener Studien zur Tibetologie und Buddhismuskunde 11. Wien: Arbeitskreis für tibetische und buddhistische Studien, Universität Wien, 259-74.

——. 1984. "On the Vijñaptimātra Passage in *Saṃdhinirmocanasūtra* VIII.7." *Acta Indologica* 7: 433–55.

——. 1987. *Ālayavijñāna: On the Origin and the Early Development of a Central Concept of Yogācāra Philosophy*. 2 vols. Tokyo: International Buddhist Institute for Buddhist Studies.

——. 1992. "A Note on Vasubandhu and the *Laṅkāvatārasūtra*." *AS* 46 (1): 392–97.

——. 2000. "On Three *Yogācārabhūmi* Passages Mentioning the Three *Svabhāvas* or *Lakṣaṇas*." In *Wisdom, Compassion, and the Search for Understanding*, ed. J. Silk. Honolulu: University of Hawai'i Press, 245–63.

——. 2001. "Zwei charakteristische Lehren der Yogācāras." In *Buddhismus in Geschichte und Gegenwart* 5. Universität Hamburg: 5–14.

Sharma, Ramesh Kumar. 1985. "Dharmakīrti on the Existence of Other Minds." *JIP* 13: 55–71.

Shastri, Yajneshwar S. 1989. *Mahāyānasūtrālaṃkāra of Asaṅga. A Study in Vijñānavāda Buddhism*. Delhi: Sri Satguru Publications.

Shih, Heng-Ching. 1988. "The Significance of Tathāgatagarbha: A Positive Expression of Śūnyatā." *Philosophical Revue* (Taiwan) 11: 227–46.

Smith, E. Gene. 2001. *Among Tibetan Texts: History and Literature of the Himalayan Plateau*. Boston: Wisdom Publications.

Snellgrove, David. 1987. *Indo-Tibetan Buddhism*. Boston: Shambhala .

Soeng, Mu. 2010. *The Heart of the Universe: Exploring the Heart Sutra*. Boston: Wisdom Publications.

Sparham, Gareth. 1987. "Background Material for the First of the Seventy Topics in Maitreyanātha's Abhisamayālaṃkāra." *JIABS* 10 (2): 139–58.

——. 1989. "A Study of Haribhadra's *Abhisamayālaṃkārālokā-prajñāpāramitā-vyākhyā*." Ph.D. diss., University of British Columbia.

——. 1992. "Indian Altruism: A Study of the Terms *bodhicitta* and *cittotpāda*." *JIABS* 15 (2): 224–41.

——. 1993. *Ocean of Eloquence: Tsongkhapa's Commentary on the Yogācāra Doctrine of Mind*. Albany: State University of New York Press.

——. 1996. "A Note on Gnyal zhig 'Jam pa'i rdo rje, the Author of a Handwritten Sher Phyin Commentary from about 1200." *TJ* 21 (1): 19–29.

——. 2001. "Demons on the Mother: *Objections to the Perfect Wisdom Sūtras in Tibet*." In *Changing Minds*, ed. Guy Newland. Ithaca: Snow Lion Publications, 193–214.

——, trans. 2006. *Abhisamayālaṃkara with Vṛtti and Ālokā*. Vol. One: First Abhisamaya. Fremont: Jain Publishing Co.

——, trans. 2008a. *Abhisamayālaṃkara with Vṛtti and Ālokā*. Vol. Two: Second and Third Abhisamaya. Fremont: Jain Publishing Co.

——, trans. 2008b. *Golden Garland of Eloquence*. Vol. One: First Abhisamaya. Fremont: Jain Publishing Co.

——, trans. 2008c. *Golden Garland of Eloquence*. Vol. Two: Second and Third Abhisamaya. Fremont: Jain Publishing Co.

——, trans. 2009. *Abhisamayālaṃkara with Vṛtti and Ālokā*. Vol. Three: Fourth Abhisamaya. Fremont: Jain Publishing Co.

——, trans. 2010. *Golden Garland of Eloquence*. Vol. Three: Fourth Abhisamaya. Fremont: Jain Publishing Co.

Sponberg, Alan. 1979. "Dynamic Liberation in Yogacara Buddhism." *JIABS* 2 (1): 44–64.

——. 1981. "The Trisvabhāva Doctrine in India and China." *Bukkyō Bunka Kenkyujo Kiyo* 21: 97–119.

Stanley, Richard. 1988. "A Study of the Madhyāntavibhāga-bhāṣya-ṭīkā." Ph.D. diss., Australian National University, Canberra.

Stcherbatsky, Theodore. 1992. *Abhisamayālankāra-Prajñāpāramitā-Upadeśa-Šāstra. Introduction, Sanscrit Text, and Tibetan Translation*. (Reprint; originally published in 1929 in Leningrad, Bibliotheca Buddhica 23). New Delhi: Motilal Banarsidass.

Stearns, Cyrus. 1995. "Dol-po-pa Shes-rab rgyal-mtshan and the Genesis of the *gzhan stong* Position in Tibet." *AS* 49 (4): 829–52.

——. 1999. *The Buddha from Dolpo*. Albany: State University of New York Press.

Steinkellner, Ernst, et al., eds. 1997. *Tibetan Studies*. Proceedings of the Seventh Seminar of the International Association for Tibetan Studies, Graz 1995. Wien: Verlag der Österreichischen Akademie der Wissenschaften.

Sutton, Florin Giripescu. 1991. *Existence and Enlightenment in the* Laṅkāvatāra-sūtra*: A Study in the Ontology and Epistemology of the Yogācāra-School of Mahāyāna-Buddhism*. Albany: State University of New York Press.

Suzuki, Daisetz Teitaro. 1968. *On Indian Mahayana Buddhism*. New York: Harper.

——. 1979. *The Laṅkāvatārasūtra*. Boulder: Prajñā Press.

——. 1998. *Studies in the Lankavatara Sutra*. (Reprint; originally published in 1930). Delhi: Munshiram Manoharlal Publishers.

Takasaki, Jikido. 1966a. *A Study on the Ratnagotravibhāga*. Serie Orientale Roma 33. Rome: Istituto Italiano per il Medio ed Estremo Oriente.

——. 1966b. "Dharmatā, Dharmadhātu, Dharmakāya, and Buddhadhātu—Structure of the Ultimate Value in Mahāyāna Buddhism." *JIBS* 14 (2): 919–903.

——. 1971. "The *Tathāgatagarbha* Theory in the *Mahāparinirvāṇa-sūtra*." *JIBS* 19 (2): 1024–1015.

Takeuchi, Shoko. 1977. "Phenomena and Reality in Vijñaptimātra Thought. On the Usages of the Suffix 'tā' in Maitreya's Treatises." In *Buddhist Thought and Asian Civilization*, ed. Leslie Kawamura and Keith Scott. Emeryville: Dharma Publishing, 254–67.

Tarthang Tulku. 1977. *Lineage of Diamond Light*. Crystal Mirror Series 5. Emeryville: Dharma Publications.

Tenpa Gyaltsen, Āchārya Lama. 2007. *Commentary on* The Ornament of Clear Realization. *Topics Four and Five–Eight*. Transcripts of oral teachings at Nitartha Institute, Mt. Allison, Sackville, and Duncan, Canada 2003–2004. 2 vols. Halifax: Nitartha Institute.

Thich Nhat Hanh. 1988. *The Heart of Understanding: Commentaries on the Prajñāpāramitā Heart Sūtra*. Berkeley: Parallax Press.

——. 1992. *The Diamond That Cuts Through Illusion*. Berkeley: Parallax Press.

Thrangu Rinpoche. 2004. *The Ornament of Clear Realization*. Auckland: Zhyisil Chokyi Ghatsal Charitable Trust Publications.

Thurman, Robert A. F. 1976. *The Holy Teaching of Vimalakīrti*. University Park: Pennsylvania State University Press.

Tillemans, Tom J. F., and Toru Tomabechi. 1995. "Le *Dbu ma'i byuṅ tshul* de Śākya mchog ldan." *AS* 49 (4): 891–918.

Tola, Fernando, and Carmen Dragonetti. 1982. "Dignāga's *Ālambanaparīkṣāvṛtti*." *JIP* 10: 105–34.

——. 1983. "The *Trisvabhāvakārikā* of Vasubandhu." *JIP* 11: 225–66.

——. 2004. *Being as Consciousness. Yogācāra Philosophy of Buddhism*. Delhi: Motilal Banarsidass.

Trungpa, Chögyam. 1999. *Glimpses of Space*. Halifax: Vajradhatu Publications.

Tsonawa, L.N. 1985. *Indian Buddhist Pandits*. Dharamsala: LTWA.

Tucci, Giuseppe. 1930. *On Some Aspects of the Doctrines of Maitreya[nātha] and Asanga*. Calcutta: University of Calcutta.

——. 1932. *The Commentaries on the Prajñāpāramitās*. Vol. 1: *The Abhisamayālamkārālokā of Haribhadra*. Gaekwad's Oriental Series 62. Baroda: Oriental Institute.

——. 1971a. "Ratnākaraśānti on Āśraya-Parāvṛtti." In *Opera Minora*, vol. 2. Rome: Rome University, 529–32.

——. 1971b. "Minor Sanskrit Texts on the Prajñā-Pāramitā: The *Prajñāpāramitāpiṇḍārthaṃ* of Dignāga." In *Opera Minora*, vol. 2. Rome: Rome University, 429–52.

——. 1986. *Minor Buddhist Texts*. (Reprint; originally published as Serie Orientale Roma 9 in 1956/58). Delhi: Motilal Banarsidass.

Ueda, Yoshifumi. 1967. "Two Main Streams of Thought in Yogācāra Philosophy." *PEW* 17: 155–65.

Waldron, William. 1994–1995. "How Innovative is the Ālayavijñāna?" *JIP* 22 (3): 199–258 and 23 (1): 9–51.

——. 2003. *The Buddhist Unconscious*. London: RoutledgeCurzon.

Walleser, Martin. 1914. *Prajñāpāramitā, Die Vollkommenheit des Erkennens*. Göttingen: Vandenhoeck und Ruprecht.

Walshe, Maurice, trans. 1995. *The Long Discourses of the Buddha*. Boston: Wisdom Publications.

Wangchuk, Dorji. 2007. *The Resolve to Become a Buddha: A Study of the Bodhicitta Concept in Indo-Tibetan Buddhism*. Tokyo: International Institute for Buddhist Studies.

Watanabe, Shogo. 1994. "A Comparative Study of the '*Pañcaviṃśatisāhasrikā Prajñāpāramitā*.'" *JAOS* 114 (3): 386–96.

Wayman, Alex. 1957. "Contributions Regarding the Thirty-Two Characteristics of the Great Person." In *Liebenthal Festschrift*, ed. Kshitis Roy. Visvabharati: Santiniketan, 243-60.

——. 1961. "The Mirror-Like Knowledge in Mahāyāna Buddhist Literature." *AS* 25: 353–63.

——. 1979. "Yogācāra and the Buddhist Logicians." *JIABS* 2 (1): 65–78.

——. 1980. "The Sixteen Aspects of the Four Noble Truths and Their Opposites." *JIABS* 3 (2): 67–76.

——. 1989. "Doctrinal Affiliations of the Buddhist Master Asaṅga." In *Amalā Prajñā: Aspects of Buddhist Studies*, ed. N. H. Samtani. Delhi: Sri Satguru Publications, 201–21.

Williams, Paul. 1983. "On Rang Rig." In *Contributions on Tibetan and Buddhist Religion and Philosophy*, ed. Ernst Steinkellner and Helmut Tauscher. Proceedings of the Csoma de Körös Symposium held at Velm-Vienna, Austria, 13-19 September 1981, vol. 2. Wiener Studien zur Tibetologie und Buddhismuskunde 11. Wien: Arbeitskreis für tibetische und buddhistische Studien, Universität Wien, 321–32.

——. 1998. *The Reflexive Nature of Awareness*. Surrey: Curzon Press.

Willis, Janice Dean. 1979. *On Knowing Reality: The* Tattvārtha *Chapter of Asaṅga's* Bodhisattvabhūmi. New York: Columbia University Press.

Wilson, Joe B. 2001. "Gung thang and Sa bzang Ma ti Paṇ chen on the Meaning of 'Foundational Consciousness' (ālaya, kun gzhi)." In *Changing Minds*, ed. Guy Newland. Ithaca: Snow Lion Publications, 215-31.

Xing, Guang. 2002. "The Evolution of the Concept of the Buddha from Early Buddhism to the Formulation of the Trikāya Theory." Ph.D. diss., University of London.

Yamabe, Nobuyoshi. 1997. "The Idea of *Dhātu-vāda* in Yogacara [sic!] and *Tathāgata-garbha* Texts." In *Pruning the Bodhi Tree*, ed. J. Hubbard and P. L. Swanson. Honolulu: University of Hawai'i Press, 193–204 and 208–19.

Yao, Zhihua. 2003. "Knowing That One Knows: The Buddhist Doctrine of Self-Cognition." Ph.D. diss., Boston University.

Yeh, Ah-yueh. 1967. "The Theory of the Three Natures in the Madhyānta-vibhāga-bhāṣya." *Transactions of the International Conference of Orientalists in Japan* 12. Tokyo: Tōhō Gakkai, 107–8.

Zacchetti, Stefano. 2005. *In Praise of the Light*. Bibliotheca Philologica et Philosophica Buddhica 8. Tokyo: International Research Institute for Advanced Buddhology, Soka University.

Zahler, Leah J. 1994. "The Concentrations and Formless Absorptions in Mahāyāna Buddhism: Ge-luk Tibetan Interpretations." Ph.D. diss., University of Virginia.

Zimmermann, Michael. 2002. *A Buddha Within: The Tathāgatagarbhasūtra. The Earliest Exposition of the Buddha Nature Teaching in India.* Bibliotheca Philologica et Philosophica Buddhica 6. Tokyo: International Research Institute for Advanced Buddhology, Soka University.

Notes

1 The image here alludes to this river being considered as very holy by Hindus—even its mere sight is said to wash away all one's negative deeds (it rises on the summit of Mount Amarakaṇṭaka in Madhya Pradesh in Central India and, after a westerly course of about eight hundred miles, ends in the Gulf of Cambay below the city of Bharuch).

2 Tib. dkon mchog yan lag.

3 Note that Appendices I and II in both volumes respectively form unities, with the numbering of their topics and charts in Volume One continuing in Volume Two for the sake of being able to refer to them in an unambiguous manner.

4 Note though that JNS (Appendices I5A2 and I5F6) says the following about the conceptions to be relinquished on the path of familiarization: "The instances of the innate clinging to real existence are exclusively factors to be relinquished through familiarization and they do not occur in the mind streams of mahāyāna noble ones because these have directly realized that all phenomena lack real existence. 'But then it follows that the innate clinging to real existence represents a factor to be relinquished through seeing.' This does not follow because to render the innate clinging to real existence into something that does not arise anymore depends exclusively on the path of familiarization. Therefore, though said clinging has not been relinquished on the path of seeing, it does not become manifest on the path of familiarization." "It is not by virtue of dividing the conceptions of clinging to imputations into imputational and innate ones that they are presented as two factors to be relinquished, but they are presented in this way by virtue of dividing them into manifest ones and those that retain a certain potency. Among these, the manifest conceptions of clinging to imputations obstruct the direct seeing of the nature of phenomena, while those that retain a certain potency do not obstruct this seeing. The manifest conceptions of clinging to imputations obstruct the direct seeing of the nature of phenomena because if the nature of phenomena is seen directly, it must be seen by way of having put an end even to the manifest entertaining of the reference points that consist of the clinging to the lack of real existence. As for those conceptions that retain a certain potency not obstructing the direct seeing of the reality of the nature of phenomena, their case is similar to the latencies of the innate clinging to real existence not obstructing the direct seeing of the lack of real existence. Therefore, the conceptions to be relinquished through familiarization that are explained here do not refer to the innnate clinging to real existence, but are explained as the manifest conceptions of clinging to characteristics during the subsequent attainments of the impure bhūmis."

5 For overviews and definitions of all eight topics and seventy points of the AA, see Chart 26 and Appendix V.

6 Here, "training" is generally understood as the union of calm abiding and superior insight that realizes all subjects and objects as well as the three knowledges to be empty of any reality. "Familiarizing in a combined manner" refers to familiarizing with all 173 aspects of the three knowledges together. STT (p. 107) says on this that the mahāyāna knowledge of entities is

the realization of all phenomena of saṃsāra and nirvāṇa within the four realities (the entities) being without arising. Since this very realization is also the path, from the perspective of this very path realizing that itself is without nature, it is called "the knowledge of the path." From the perspective of this very knowledge of the path realizing that the entirety of the various aspects (such as impermanence) that exist in the four realities (the entities) and the entirety of the various aspects (such as the subsequent readinesses and cognitions) that exist in this very path are without nature, it is the knowledge of all aspects. Therefore, the complete training in all aspects consists of bodhisattvas knowing during meditative equipoise that all these three knowledges are actually without nature and free from reference points, and their realizing during subsequent attainment that, on the level of the seeming, these knowledges appear yet are without nature, just like illusions.

7 For details, see below and Chart 22.

8 For more details on the four remedies, see Appendix I1H3ad1 and Chart 20 in Volume I as well as JNS on V.22.

9 According to CZ (pp. 312–430), the complete training in all aspects covers Without Basis (Chapter Thirty-eight) up through Demonstration of the Development of Skill in Means (Chapter Fifty-four).

10 In both occurrences of this term in this paragraph, CE just has *gang zag med*, but JNS (vol. 2, p. 10) both times says *gang zag gi bdag med.*

11 For more details on these focal objects and aspects, see Appendix I4A.

12 JNS (vol. 2, p. 12) says that "entities" are the focal objects, that is, all knowable objects which are presented as the four realities and so on. As for "knowing" them, the aspects that are the distinct features of the specific instances of mind delimiting these directly perceived objects represent the defining characteristics of "the aspects of the training." When classified since there are three kinds of focal object of omniscient wisdom, also the knowledges that know them are asserted to be of three kinds. Thus, these aspects (which are aspects of consciousness) are not without basis, but are presented on the basis of the aspects of the three knowledges. In general, there are many different ways of commenting on this verse since the two Vimuktisenas, the Kashmiri Dharmaśrī (author of the *Śatasāhasrikāvivaraṇa*), Dharmamitra, and Dharmakīrtiśrī have dissimilar positions. Both the *Ālokā* (D3791, fol. 176a.3–4) and the *Vivṛti* (D3793, fol. 104b.3–4) explain that "aspects" refers to the specific instances of the wisdoms that focus on the nature of the remedial dharmas (such as impermanence) for the antagonistic factors (such as clinging to permanence) and thus are not without basis.

13 CZ, p. 312.

14 CE has the common misspelling *rtog pa* for *rtogs pa* as in all other commentaries.

15 Commenting on the *Vivṛti*, JNS (vol. 2, pp. 13–14 and 25–27) says that, in order to eliminate concerns about the aspects of the four realities as taught in the prajñāpāramitā sūtras not being in accord with the sixteen as explained in the abhidharma, Haribhadra matches the two sets. JNS explains the meaning of most among the above twenty-seven aspects in *italics* in ways that differ from CE—(2) phenomena not being observable; (3) being free from self and mine; (4) being empty of any personal or phenomenal identity; (5) not being suitable as either a produced basis or an established fruition; (7) expressions that entail examination and analysis appropriating karma, which leads to the skandhas, but all of this not existing as such; (8) the four name skandhas (mainly feelings) as the conditions for rebirth not existing as such; (9) cessation being merely something to be manifested by virtue of suffering having ceased, but not being established as something to be attained by having gone anywhere; (10) with the afflictions being primordial peace, they are not established as something to be removed or relinquished again;

(11) the collection of qualities that consist of the supremacy of the nature of phenomena being free from becoming exhausted; and (12) there being no purity to be attained through anything in what is primordially without arising. As for the fifteen aspects of the reality of the path, they are classified as three sets—(a) the four aspects of focusing during the uncontaminated path of the meditative equipoise that serves as the remedy for the afflictive obscurations of śrāvakas and pratyekabuddhas in common; (b) the eleven aspects of focusing on the remedies for the cognitive obscurations specific to the pratyekabuddhas (the conceptions about the apprehended) during (ba) contaminated subsequent attainment and (bb) uncontaminated meditative equipoise. The four aspects under (a) are (13) being the remedy for the clinging that there is an agent who attains the fruition, while there is none; (14) being the remedy for a cognizer that is invalidated through valid cognition; (15) being the remedy for clinging to superior and inferior; and (16) rendering the obscurations into something that has the property of not arising, that is, knowing that the obscurations are the factors to be relinquished. The five aspects under (ba) are (17) the nature of the cognitive obscurations that are the conceptions about the apprehended being dreamlike in lacking a nature in terms of specific characteristics (thus, when analyzed through reasoning, they are free from all reference points); (18) their nonarising, just as the sound of an echo; (19) their not being existent, just as the form of an optical illusion or a shadow, which implies primordial nonceasing; (20) their not being established in the first place, just as water isn't in a mirage; and (21) their being natural nirvāṇa, that is, being naturally at peace like the characteristics of an illusion. The six aspects under (bb) are (23) these cognitive obscurations being not observable as either purified phenomena to be adopted or as someone who is purified (the support of such phenomena); (25) overcoming all conceit about any reference points, such as form; (26) overcoming all agitation of observing a mind stream in which one's own realization is relished; and (27) overcoming conceptions about the dharmadhātu deteriorating. For further presentations of the aspects of the four realities, see CE above (2.3.1.2.1.1.2.1.1.2.1.2. The lesser instruction on the four realities) and on IV.3 as well as Charts 4–5 in Volume One.

16 CE follows the default Tibetan phrasing of putting "innate" before "imputational" in this pair, but in terms of the meaning, the order is the reverse since the former obscurations are always presented as coarser and relinquished before the latter (also, the following presentation would not make any sense in the reverse order).

17 In a more general sense, these two obscurations are usually presented as the equivalents of afflictive and cognitive obscurations, respectively.

18 For more details, see Appendices I4B and I5A (esp. I5A2) in Volume One. Note that the above is just a very brief and moreover not entirely identical digest of JNS's more detailed presentations of the conceptions that are the cognitive obscurations. Compare also MPZL (p. 39), which says, "In general, conceptions are definitely threefold—imputational ones, innate ones, and their subtle latencies. Therefore, the first are relinquished through the path of seeing; the second, through the nine levels of the path of familiarization; and the third, through the vajralike samādhi. In particular, as for the conceptions that cling to substantial existence, their imputational parts are relinquished through the path of seeing. Their innate seminal parts are relinquished through the seventh bhūmi, which completes the relinquishment of the afflictive obscurations. Their latencies, which represent cognitive obscurations, are relinquished through the three pure bhūmis. [In this way,] one is free from the [absurd] consequence that the four conceptions of the practice of the equipment of the remedies on the path of familiarization and the culminating training of the path of familiarization are incomplete. For those who assert that the conceptions of clinging to substantial existence have been relinquished on the first bhūmi, it appears difficult to explain the practice of the equipment of the remedies on the path of familiarization and the culminating training of the path of familiarization because [AA I.14cd–15ab] says:

> The four conceptions'
> Four kinds of remedy

On the paths called "seeing"
And "familiarization," respectively . . ."

19 CZ, p. 313.

20 Note that, in the following four paragraphs, the words in " " represent the sixteen aspects of the four realities as in the abhidharma.

21 JNS (vol. 2, pp. 28–34) says that it is reasonable to explain the aspects of the knowledge of the path after the ones of the knowledge of entities. For after bodhisattvas have cultivated the remedies for the afflictive obscurations and the cognitive obscurations that are the conceptions about the apprehended, they must familiarize themselves with phenomenal identitylessness as the remedy for the cognitive obscurations that are the conceptions about the apprehender. Still, one may wonder what the point is in matching the thirty-six cognitive aspects of the knowledge of the path—all of which are realizations of phenomenal identitylessness—with the sixteen cognitive aspects of the four realities as found in the abhidharma (as the *Ālokā* and the *Vivṛti* do). This is done in order to understand that the latter are included in the former in the manner of the lower being incorporated in the higher. This in turn is for the sake of understanding that the knowledge of the path of bodhisattvas is able to take care of disciples with all three dispositions (śrāvakas, pratyekabuddhas, and bodhisattvas). In addition, said thirty-six aspects are matched with the sixteen in order to eliminate the qualms of some people that the four realities in thirty-six aspects discord with those in sixteen aspects and thus do not represent the true dharma. (The purpose of explicitly matching the sixteen aspects found in the abhidharma with the twenty-seven cognitive aspects of the knowledge of entities is implied through the latter being explained in the sūtras as being aspects of phenomenal identitylessness, but not as aspects of personal identitylessness. Thus, through matching these twenty-seven with the sixteen of the abhidharma, there is no need to explicitly explain the former as aspects of personal identitylessness because it is automatically understood that the realizations of the latter are included in the former in the manner of the lower being incorporated in the higher.) As for the different order of the four realities in AA IV.3, it is due to their being presented in terms of causes and results, with the origin of suffering and the path being the causes for afflicted phenomena (suffering) and purified phenomena (cessation), respectively. Also since the origin of suffering is what is to be relinquished, it is taught here by way of the factors to be relinquished and their remedies. Since the path is what is to be relied upon in the mind stream, it is taught by way of theses and their justifications. Since suffering is what is to be understood, it is taught by way of its general and specific characteristics. Since cessation is what is to be manifested, it is taught by way of possessing twofold purity. In detail (as far as JNS differs from CE), as for the origin of suffering, (1) desire is the liking of contaminated objects and the result of this cause is the striving for these objects. The remedy here is being free from desire since one needs to put an end to desire as the cause in order to put an end to its result. (2) Or the cause for actually engaging in desire is the preceding striving to engage in it. Through not dwelling in this, the result (desire) is put to an end because its cause (striving) has ceased. (3) To excessively delight in objects agitates the mind stream. Therefore, to put an end to this, one realizes the dhātu in which all reference points and characteristics are at peace. These three put the "causes" of saṃsāra to an end. (4)–(6) To make desire unobservable, hatred nonexistent, and ignorance vanish are the remedies for the "origin" of saṃsāric beings. (7) The afflictions are produced by (false) imagination. Thus, through gradually rendering the afflictions nonexistent, this imagination is also put to an end. (8) The clinging to the transitory collection of the five skandhas as a sentient being is put to an end through realizing that the true end is the lack of a sentient being. As for the reality of the path, (9) being immeasurable is the nature of the "path" of bodhisattvas because its emphasis lies on promoting the welfare of immeasurably many sentient beings by virtue of relinquishing antagonistic factors—it is the path of opening up the opportunity of the state of true reality for all sentient beings. (11) Not being different is the nature of "appropriateness," because it is the subsiding of

all kinds of characteristics in all phenomena. (12) Since the clinging to inferiority or superiority is naturally pure, it refers to the appropriateness of realizing it as the single principle of emptiness. (13) The justification for nonconceptuality is the "accomplishment" of overcoming conceptions about needing to manifest the nature of phenomena, which is what is to be realized. (14) The justification for being unassessable is the valid cognition that establishes the essence of the nature of phenomena. (15) The justification for lacking attachment is being "conducive to deliverance" through not clinging to flaws and qualities as being inferior or superior, respectively. As for the reality of suffering, (16) it is "impermanent" right upon its nature being established, but it does not depend on any other causes for its perishing. (17) "Suffering" refers to lacking excessive attachment since all-pervasive conditionedness has the nature of suffering. (18)–(19) Through realizing the basic nature of "being empty" and "identityless," all stains of any identity (such as a nonempty agent) are eliminated. These four are the specific characteristics of suffering as well as the aspects of the reasonings that establish personal identitylessness. (20) Not to be established as any characteristics is the general characteristic of suffering as well as the aspect of the reasoning that establishes phenomenal identitylessness. As for the reason why "empty" and "identityless" are only taught as aspects of the reality of suffering despite being aspects of the other three realities too, Sthirapāla says, "Impermanence and suffering are presented as distinctive features of being empty and identityless. For entities are impermanent since they are emptiness. If they were not emptiness, it would follow that they are permanent entities. Through not understanding what is identityless, just as it is, all formations that look like something with an identity are suffering. If there were any identity, it would follow that all formations that look like something with an identity are happiness." The aspects of the reality of cessation are explained by matching them with the first sixteen emptinesses found in the prajñāpāramitā sūtras—the first three put an end to the stains that are entities; the following eight, to the stains of clinging; the next one means being devoid of conceptions about an agent; and the last four eliminate the stains of mistakenness. (24) The emptiness of emptiness refers to emptiness being the remedy for viewing emptiness as being emptiness (or being the remedy for all views or identities imputed by others, including those about emptiness). (25) The emptiness of the great means that even all-pervasive form is not established as an entity. (26) The emptiness of the ultimate refers to its not being established as a remedy ultimately. (27)–(28) The emptinesses of conditioned and unconditioned phenomena mean that these phenomena respectively depend on their counterpart and thus are not established independently. (29) As for the emptiness of what is beyond extremes, by virtue of being one taste, the cause for delimiting extremes—the middle—is not established either. (30) The emptiness of what is without beginning and end means being empty of these two since not even viewing these as two ends is established. (31) The emptiness of what is not rejected refers to the dharmas of realization being empty of being such dharmas because they are to be left behind like a raft. (32) By virtue of the agents that are imputed by others (such as the tīrthikas) having ceased, one speaks of the aspect of the emptiness of the primordial nature since it is realized that all phenomena are unobservable. By virtue of the mistakenness about objects (imaginary knowable objects); the mistakenness about characteristics (general and specific characteristics); and the mistakenness about time (such as earlier, later, and in between) having ceased, there are the aspects of wisdom realizing that (33) all phenomena are emptiness because all imputed phenomena are mistaken; that (34) they are empty of specific characteristics because general characteristics are not substantially established and specific characteristics are empty of a nature; and that (35) the three times are unobservable because none of them abides. (36) Through having put an end to the clinging to the basic nature of phenomena as being a nature, the aspect of final deliverance is the wisdom of realizing that this basic nature does not exist as an entity through its own nature and that it is empty of any other nature. Earlier Tibetans assert the sixteen factors that are to be put to an end through these aspects of the sixteen emptinesses as "referent aspects" and the remedial sixteen emptinesses that put them to an end as "cognitive aspects." The final position of Āryavimuktisena,

Haribhadra, Abhayākaragupta, Ratnākaraśānti, and others on this must be presented as follows. The factors to be put to an end are the sixteen antagonistic factors; the conducive factors that cease them are the remedial wisdoms—the sixteen cognitive aspects of the corresponding emptinesses; and the cessations that consist of these remedies having relinquished said factors to be relinquished are the sixteen emptinesses that are revealed as the outcome of this process.

22 CZ, p. 315.

23 JNS (vol. 2, p. 36) says that the aspects of the knowledge of all aspects are of the single nature of nonconceptual wisdom. However, there is no flaw to divide them into three sets since the clear realizations of all noble persons are included in the knowledge of all aspects. Here, the aspects of the knowledge of all aspects are taught as if contained in the mind streams of śrāvakas and bodhisattvas. There is no flaw in this. For these aspects being first taught by way of progressively giving rise to them in the mind stream through their manner of familiarizing with their focal objects and so on is for the sake of easily realizing what is to be manifested on the buddhabhūmi through further familiarization with the continuum of these types of focal objects and aspects in the manner of the lower being incorporated in the higher. Also, to present the aspects of the knowledge of entities and the path by way of practicing the path (as stated above in CE) does not amount to being a repetition of the fifteen aspects of the reality of the path as discussed above in the context of the twenty-seven aspects of the knowledge of entities. For above, the reality of the path was taught by way of its defining characteristics, whereas the path as taught here is explained by way of its instances.

24 JNS (vol. 2, p. 37) explains the distinction between "common" and "uncommon" here. The aspects of the knowledge of all aspects taught here represent the division into the threefold omniscience that is approximately concordant with the reality of the path of the four kinds of noble ones. The first of these two realities of the path (the aspects in common with the knowledges of entities and the path) are taught as being "in common" with the intention that they are not the reality of the path of the buddhabhūmi that actually fulfills this function, while the third one (the uncommon aspects of the knowledge of all aspects) is taught to be "uncommon" with the intention that it is this actual reality of the path of the buddhabhūmi. Though the former two are not this reality of the path that actually fulfills this function, it is not that they are not suitable as aspects of the knowledge of all aspects because the knowledge of all aspects entails the knowledges of all aspects that exist in whichever other persons. However, on the other hand, it is mistaken to explain that the buddhabhūmi's own dharmas concordant with enlightenment, the three doors to liberation, and so on are in common with śrāvakas, pratyekabuddhas, and bodhisattvas because these dharmas that represent the qualities of the greatness of the kāya of the tathāgatas are unique to the mind streams of buddhas and thus do not exist in the mind streams of anybody else. For the dharmas concordant with enlightenment and so on of the śrāvakas and so on are completely different from those of buddhas in terms of their focal objects and aspects. For more details on all the following explanations of the 110 aspects of the knowledge of all aspects, see Appendix I4C.

25 This can also be understood as "purifying samādhi."

26 Usually, as also JNS explains, the last two flaws are not applying the respective antidotes for dullness and agitation when they arise and still applying their antidotes when they have already ceased and the mind is settled.

27 In other words, the five powers are the same as the five faculties—these are called "powers" once they cannot be overcome by their respective opposites. JNS (vol. 2, p. 49) adds that these five are called "faculties" and "powers" respectively because they perform different distinct functions.

28 As with the four realities of the noble ones and as being obvious from the overall progression here, it is not so much that the eightfold path itself is noble, but "noble" refers to the persons

who are actually able to practice and realize it—if at all, ordinary beings can only practice a likeness of it. As Kapstein 1992 (p. 224) says: "Note, too, that popular literature on Buddhism in the West has almost universally failed to observe that, from the standpoint of the Abhidharma tradition, the eightfold path represents not an elementary guide to the Buddhist life but the practice of only the most advanced disciples." In terms of the mahāyāna path, JNS (vol. 2, p. 55) adds that this eightfold path exists from the second moment of the first bhūmi up through buddhahood.

29 CE has "thought" (*rtog pa*), which is emended here (*rtogs pa*) in accordance with what is said about view at the beginning of this paragraph.

30 In this outline, CE mistakenly switches path (b) with path (e).

31 Commenting on the *Vivṛti*, JNS (vol. 2, p. 58) says that the door of emptiness is the remedy for the five wrong views; the door of signlessness, for the conceptions that are tainted through these views; and the door of wishlessness, for any aspirations for the three realms. Rongtön's brief text on how to familiarize with the three doors to liberation according to the mahāyāna (*rnam thar sgo gsum sgom tshul theg chen lam bzang*) says that Haribhadra, in explaining the practice of familiarizing with these three doors, describes how they can be matched with familiarizing with the sixteen aspects of the four realities. According to the mahāyāna, emptiness is related to the ground (or basis); signlessness, to the path; and wishlessness, to the fruition. In due order, the three conceptions that block these three doors are to take the ground as real; to take the the path as having real characteristics; and to consider the result as something to be wished for. It is in order to eliminate these three ideas that one cultivates the samādhis of the three doors. In this context, (1) "ground" refers to the skandhas, dhātus, and āyatanas, with connate ignorance about them functioning as the fundamental cause of saṃsāra. As *Śūnyatāsaptati* 65ab says:

> Conceptions about actual reality
> Are said to be ignorance by the Teacher.

In order to overcome this ground of saṃsāra, one must ascertain the emptiness of said ground and then familiarize with that emptiness. Through relinquishing clinging to the ground as being real, the door of emptiness will be opened. (2) However, when one familiarizes with emptiness and takes this familiarization to have any real characteristics, that will only serve to bind one. As AA I.27c says:

> Their aspects are to refrain from clinging and so on.

Since one must put an end to any clinging towards the four realities, even attachment to the path is to be avoided. Therefore, one must cultivate the path lacking any real characteristics or signs, which will open the door to signlessness. (3) AA III.10cd says:

> The fourfold lack of conceit about form and such
> Is asserted to be its equality.

Thus, one should not entertain any form of conceit, which means that one must abandon not only the hope that there is some fruition to be attained through any other means, but even the hope of attaining any fruition through realizing emptiness. Through this, the door to wishlessness will be opened. It is in this way that the explanation of the knowledge of the path consisting of these three doors must be related to the mahāyāna approach.

32 In addition to the first way of looking, JNS (vol. 2, p. 64) explains the latter two notions as follows (according to the commentary of the *Abhidharmasamuccaya*). (b) Beautiful forms are connected to ugly ones and vice versa in that what is known as beautiful is, for example, nothing but the skin, which is just one of the thirty-six impure bodily substances. On the reverse side, it is nothing but such impure substances that are regarded as beautiful. (c) Through mixing the

forms of these three vases, one familiarizes with their being of one taste in being nothing but ugly. In the *Sūtra of Dharma Omnipresence* [not contained in the *Kangyur*], all eight liberations of bodhisattvas are explained as wisdoms of resting in meditative equipoise with regard to all phenomena.

33 Commenting on the *Vivṛti*, JNS (vol. 2, p. 64) says that liberations (4)–(7) have the nature of the path of abiding in accordance with liberation—the nonabiding nirvāṇa. Liberation (8) has the nature of abiding in peace—reference points and characteristics having subsided. According to PSD (pp. 284–85), the difference between the regular four formless absorptions and the absorption of cessation versus these five as said five liberations is that they are presented as the former by virtue of being balanced with regard to their focal objects that consist of the great elements of the body or primary minds and mental factors. They are presented as liberations from the point of view of being liberated from the fetters of their own respective levels and not being mixed with them.

34 Commenting on the *Vivṛti*, JNS (vol. 2, p. 72) says that these four readinesses have the characteristic of being purified phenomena because they are the uninterrupted paths of the path of seeing that consist of realizing the four realities and because they lack afflictions.

35 "As above" refers to the physical supports mentioned under 2c from the perspective of the mahāyāna. Generally speaking, as JNS (vol. 2, pp. 58 and 67) says, in both the hīnayāna and the mahāyāna abhidharma, the physical supports for the meditative absorption of cessation are those under 2c. More specifically, in terms of the hināyāna presentation in the *Abhidharmakośa*, JNS (vol. 2, p. 61) says that the first three and the last one of the eight liberations arise only in the men and women on the three continents (i.e., except Uttarakuru). See Appendix I4C2b–c at the respective beginnings of the sections "Higher abhidharma" and "Lower abhidharma."

36 JNS (vol. 2, pp. 346–47) quotes an unidentified sūtra on this, saying that if bodhisattvas were to rest longer in this meditative absorption, their bodhisattva conduct would deteriorate.

37 Note that JNS (vol. 2, p. 70) explicitly says that the true intention of the AA and its commentaries with regard to the meditative absorption of cessation here is as presented in the Yogācāra system and gives the reasons why it cannot be explained according to the Madhyamaka system alone (see Appendix I4C2d). Also, in terms of the meditative absorption of cessation of nonlearners, JNS does not speak of the seven consciousnesses having ceased within ālaya-wisdom, but within mirrorlike wisdom (see, however, Appendix I1E1 on the disposition in Volume One, in which JNS uses the term "ālaya-wisdom" several times). For more details on the meditative absorption of cessation, see Appendices I4C2c–d and I5F2.

38 Tibetan *khams* can mean "element," "constitution," "realm," and so on. Usually this power is explained as knowing the different mental constitutions of sentient beings that enable them to travel different spiritual paths.

39 CE has *sngon du gyur pa* (emended to *mngon du gyur pa*).

40 The following comments from JNS on the *Vivṛti* (vol. 2, pp. 73–79) differ from or supplement CE. The first four sets (3a–3d) represent the division of qualities, while the next three (3e–3g) make up the nature of wisdom. Specifically, (4) buddhas know which worldly realms are or are not suitable to be purified. (7) The two obscurations of the dhyānas and formless absorptions are (a) the afflictions that obscure them as the notion of not having attained them, and (b) the afflictions intrinsic to the respective absorptions, once they are attained. (8) "Past states" are glossed as being familiar with hīnayāna or mahāyāna virtues from before. (15) refers to the individual specifications of all phenomena (definienda); (16) is the awareness of all general and specific characteristics of all phenomena (defining characteristics); and (17) refers to knowing all the different languages of all countries (since the certainty about the instances that function as the bases for definienda and defining characteristics depends on terms). Thus, (18) is the

self-confidence of not being afraid to speak because one knows all presentations of all phenomena's definienda, defining characteristics, and instances. (19)–(20) A buddha's body and speech are without mistakenness and useless chatter triggered by the three poisons. (21) Mindfulness means not forgetting their realization. (23) Buddhas lack discriminations in terms of dualistic appearances being different. Wisdom precedes and follows the enlightened activities of (31) the body (miraculous powers, radiating light, and so on); (32) speech (teaching the dharma, giving prophecies, and so on); and (33) mind (knowing all that can be known and blessing those to be guided). (34)–(36) In each one of the three times, wisdom operates without attachment (by virtue of having relinquished the afflictive obscurations) and without obstruction (by virtue of having relinquished the cognitive obscurations). All Buddhist schools up through the Vijñānavādins agree that buddhas know all phenomena of the seeming, but Mādhyamikas do not. Unlike the mahāyāna, *Abhidharmakośa* VII.28ab says that the eighteen unique qualities of buddhas include all their qualities, which consist of the ten powers, the four fearlessnesses, the three applications of mindfulness, and great compassion. (37) The true nature of the tathāgatas as explained by all buddhas in the three times is the wisdom of great nirvāṇa. (38) Mastery over all phenomena by virtue of the nature of phenomena is the play of self-arising wisdom because it does not need to depend on any other masteries. (39) Having fully perfected all aspects of the uncommon qualities of a buddha, the two obscurations (including their latent tendencies) have been excellently purified and wisdom is realized. As for the question of what the difference between the aspects of "self-arising" and "buddhahood" is, the *Vṛtti* (D3787, fol. 127b.4–5) explains the former one as being the aspect that is the mastery over the divisions of the aspects (such as the powers), the suchness that is their nature, and all phenomena, while the latter is the aspect that is the aim. According to Dharmamitra, when the wisdom of the knowledge of all aspects is attained through having focused on suchness, it is presented as self-arisen in terms of its power of mastering all entities. In terms of distinctly knowing all the various aspects of this wisdom, it is presented as the aspect of buddhahood. Finally, JNS summarizes the 173 aspects of the three knowledges as follows. The twenty-seven aspects of the knowledge of entities in the mind streams of śrāvakas are uncontaminated because they are taught as the kind of remedy that serves to deliberately relinquish the afflictions. The same twenty-seven aspects in the mind streams of bodhisattvas are contaminated because they represent the knowledge of entities that is not cultivated as the remedy for the afflictions for one's own sake. The thirty-six aspects of the knowledge of the path in bodhisattvas are solely contaminated because, for the sake of others, they do not relinquish a certain portion of their afflictions in a deliberate manner. The full completion of all the uncontaminated qualities of the 110 aspects of the knowledge of all aspects is unique to the buddhas. They are nothing but uncontaminated because buddhas relinquished the afflictive and cognitive obscurations including their latent tendencies in all respects and thus attained mastery over all phenomena. However, this does not refer to the thirty-seven aspects among these 110 that exist in the mind streams of śrāvakas and the thirty-four that exist in bodhisattvas because they are not the aspects that are the uncommon qualities of the buddhas. The full completion of all 173 aspects is buddhahood, while the training in these aspects on the paths of learning represents the complete training in all aspects (see also Chart 22).

41 Commenting on the *Vivṛti*, JNS (vol. 2, pp. 80–81) says that suitable vessels for prajñāpāramitā are those who listen to her as above, retain her through the prajñā that arises from reflection, and properly engage in her mentally through the prajñā that arises from meditation. These people (1) accumulate and train in the roots of virtue in general with regard to past and present buddhas and, in particular, (2) please them through services and honors in terms of body, speech, and mind. (3) They ask the buddhas about all the doubts in their own minds, (4) practice the ten pāramitās, and (5) are blessed by the buddhas as their spiritual friends. Through having familiarized themselves with causes (1)–(4), they are respectively able to listen to, retain, not forget the meaning of, and properly engage mentally in the texts of the mother who is characterized by all the aspects

explained before. (5) represents the all-encompassing cause that equally pertains to all four results in terms of being a proper vessel (listening, retaining, and so on).

42 CZ, p. 318.

43 In the context of the culminating training, "training" is understood as the yoga of the union of calm abiding and superior insight of bodhisattvas that is embraced by prajñā and familiarizes with all the above-mentioned 173 aspects of the three knowledges.

44 The remaining four are once-returner, nonreturner, śrāvaka arhat, and pratyekabuddha arhat.

45 JNS (vol. 2, pp. 83–85) first explains these twenty aspects of training in accordance with Trolungba Lodrö Jungné (whose commentary differs somewhat from Haribhadra's) by way of a fivefold classification in terms of (a) the objects of training, (b) the trainees, (c) the means to complete familiarization, (d) the results, and (e) the time. (a) The objects of training—the three doors to liberation—are as follows. (1) Focusing on the door to liberation that is emptiness is the training in nonabiding because of naturally not abiding in all phenomena. (2) Focusing on signlessness is the training in not involving oneself in signs because of having stopped conceit about being involved in emptiness. Focusing on wishlessness consists of (3) the training in profundity because of the suchness of the door of signlessness being profound by virtue of not [JNS has no negative here] being really established; (4) the training in what is difficult to fathom because of the true nature of the bearers of this nature that are free from signs being difficult to fathom; and (5) the training in what is immeasurable because of the final measure of these natures of phenomena being immeasurable. Through this manner of threefold focusing on the object that is wishlessness, the three extremes of wishing for the three knowledges are put to an end. (b) As for the trainees (the persons who are the supports of the training), (6) those who lack the proper karmic disposition do not swiftly realize the above three actualities (3)–(5). They are impaired vessels for the teachings of prajñāpāramitā because when they hear these three profound actualities in their above order, they become intimidated, afraid, and terrified. Thus, they have to realize them during other occasions through long-lasting efforts and with great hardships. However since they will indeed realize enlightenment if they make great efforts, this is the training of those who are afraid of emptiness. (7) Those who possess the proper karmic disposition are unimpaired supports and are endowed with their own welfare. Through having undergone great purification and training, they are not afraid of said profound actualities and thus mentally engage in the mother even in their dreams. Thus since the buddhas prophesy that these persons will become enlightened within the timespan of one or two buddhas having come to the world in uninterrupted succession, this is the training of obtaining the prophecy. (8) Even if such is not prophesied in one's present situation, it will be prophesied in another lifetime, and one thus trains in irreversibility from enlightenment at any time. (9) The training in final deliverance is like a person crossing some waste lands. (10) For that, one trains in the manner of being unobstructed by the four māras (skandhas, afflictions, death, and devaputramāra—clinging to meditative experiences) and the two levels (the paths of śrāvakas and pratyekabuddhas). (11) The training that is close to the full completion of the qualities of great enlightenment is like springtime [LN (vol. 2, p. 152) quotes *Prajñāpāramitāsaṃcayagāthā* X.7 on this example]. (12) The training that is swift in manifesting the result to be attained by oneself is like a pregnant woman who is about to give birth swiftly [LN: *Saṃcayagāthā* X.8]. (13) Those who are endowed with the welfare of others are the bodhisattvas who are endowed with their own welfare and train in turning the wheel of dharma out of compassion for the welfare of others through the four means of attracting those to be guided (generosity, pleasant words, beneficial activity, and consistency in words and deeds). (c) The trainings in completing the familiarization with the actuality of prajñāpāramitā are (14) the training in realizing that there is no increase and no decrease because of seeing that there is no increase and no decrease of any qualities or flaws

whatsoever in true reality [LN: *Saṃcayagāthā* X.9ab]; (15) the training in being free from views because of not seeing any defining characteristics—such as dharmas or nondharmas; (16) the training in putting an end to the aspect of inconceivability because of not seeing any imputations of the form of the nature of phenomena and so on being inconceivable; and (17) [same as in CE]. (d) The results of these are (18) the training in bestowing precious fruitions [same as in CE] and (19) the training in purifying the stains of the flaws. (e) The set period of time is (20) the training in going all the way through to the end [same as in CE]. JNS continues by reporting Dölpopa's position on IV.8–11, who says that presenting all these trainings as being definitely twenty in number contradicts the sūtras. Instead, it is justified to teach these verses by way of nine sets of meaning—lines IV.8ab teach the single training found in the sūtras; IV.8cd–9a, that prajñāpāramitā (that with which one is to familiarize) is profound, difficult to fathom, and immeasurable; IV.9b, the shortcomings of teaching her to those who are not proper verssels; IV.9cd up through "the welfare of others," the benefit when proper vessels practice her; "without increase . . ." up through IV.10c, the gauge of full perfection; IV.10d–11ab, the signs of engaging in the six pāramitās; IV.11c, that prajñāpāramitā bestows the precious buddhadharmas; "purity," that prajñāpāramitā is the sum of all purity; and "a set period of time," the set periods for the progressive stages of the dharma activities related to prajñāpāramitā. On the other hand, Haribhadra's commentaries present the definite number of twenty—five natural and fifteen situational—trainings (as in CE), which is also followed by the earlier Buddhaśrījñāna. However, Āryavimuktisena, Ratnākaraśānti, Prajñākaramati, Kumāraśrībhadra, and the later Buddhaśrījñāna all have their own distinct ways of classifying and summarizing the trainings. Commenting on the *Vivṛti*, JNS (vol. 2, pp. 85–87) explains the five natural trainings as the realizations of (1) not abiding in clinging by virtue of all phenomena not being established through a nature of their own; (2) not being involved in the characteristics of clinging to them as having a nature of their own; (3) these phenomena being naturally profound by virtue of suchness since they do not exist yet appear; (4) this being difficult to fathom through consciousness; and (5) not being measurable by mind. The fifteen situational trainings consist of those of (6) some beings of inferior karmic disposition being afraid of hearing about prajñāpāramitā; (7) beings of highest disposition not being afraid of either the words or the meaning; (8) correctly retaining the basic nature of suchness—ultimate reality; (9) relinquishing impeding phenomena that obstruct the accomplishment of great enlightenment and thus being delivered from all fetters; (10) not falling prey to obstructions because of always familiarizing with the dharma; (11) the foundation for newly and directly attaining the uncontaminated suchness of the tathāgatas; (12) accomplishment of the ultimate fruition—the dharmakāya; (13) turning the wheel of dharma for those to be guided; (14) not seeing any increase or decrease in the profound actualities; (15) not observing any virtue, nonvirtue, and so on in the desire, form, and formless realms; (16) not even being conceited about the aspect of the inconceivability of the form and so on of the perfect nature; (17) not conceiving appearing or labeled forms, their characteristics, or their nature; (18) directly seeing the first fruition of a stream-enterer and so on; (19) by virtue of the three characteristics (the imaginary, other-dependent, and perfect), forms being accordingly pure in three ways of being empty; and (20) not giving up one's efforts for accomplishing enlightenment—not only during some months or years, but innumerable eons. As for the difference between natural and situational trainings, Dré Sherab Bar says that the first five are the natural trainings because bodhisattvas engage in them throughout all situations. The others are situational because bodhisattvas engage in them from the level of a beginner up through the tenth bhūmi, respectively. The last training of a set period of time is also called "the training in means" because one does not give up one's efforts by having defined a set period of time. BT (p. 508) says that the reason for this training being named this way is that it represents the means for the arising of the path. As for the boundary lines, BT says that the first five trainings are natural because they are the ones which one must mainly cultivate throughout the entire mahāyāna path of learning and are the trainings of realizing the fundamental nature of objects. As for the situational trainings, (6) refers to the lesser path of accumulation; (7)–(10) represent the four levels of the path of preparation; (11) is the path of seeing; (12) exists from the second up through the seventh bhūmis; (13)–(17) pertain to the eighth bhūmi; (18)–(19) refer to the ninth and tenth bhūmis, respectively; and (20) exists up through the seventh bhūmi. The ways in which LN (vol. 2, pp. 151–57), YT (pp. 413–16), PBG (pp. 546–48), and NSML (pp. 410–11) differ in terms of these boundary lines are as follows. All agree that (6) refers to the path of accumulation of bodhisattvas with dull faculties. In addition, LN says that (12) exists from the seventh bhūmi onward and (19) up through the end of the continuum. Both LN and PBG agree that (18) exists primarily on the ninth bhūmi, but also all the time before. YT says that (7)–(10) exist from the path of accumulation up through the seventh bhūmi; (12), from the first up through the seventh bhūmis; (13)–(19), on the three pure bhūmis; and (20), on the path of accumulation. NSML says that (20) pertains to all bodhisattvas who are ordinary beings.

46 CZ, p. 319.

47 JNS (vol. 2, p. 87) adds another reason for these qualities being taught—seeing which qualities arise from cultivating the training in an unmistaken way.

48 According to JNS (vol. 2, p. 89), these boundary lines are explained by Dharmamitra, while Kumāraśrībhadra matches the fourteen qualities, in due order, with the four levels of the path of preparation and the ten bhūmis.

49 CZ, p. 326.

50 JNS (vol. 2, pp. 88–90) comments on these fourteen qualities as per the *Vivṛti* as follows. (1) When engaging in the mother, to attain the quality of vanquishing the power of māras (the attachment to sense pleasures, whose nature is an obstacle to such engagement) means being blessed by the buddhas. (2) To be considered and known by the minds of all buddhas means being considered by their nonconceptual wisdom. (3) To be directly seen by all buddhas means being seen through their pure wisdom eyes. (4) Being close to attaining perfect enlightenment means the cause for that. (5) To never be born in the unpleasant realms until reaching the level of irreversibility—the great welfare—means the great benefit of oneself and others merging with liberation. (6) To take birth in special good countries through having examined the ones in which one is never separated from the buddhas means working with the teachings in a genuine realm. (7) Not to be separated from the completion of all uncontaminated phenomena means completing the accumulation of the remedies and thus putting an end to the collection of the factors to be relinquished. (8) Those beings who are not afraid to speak gradually becoming perfect buddhas means that they proclaim or turn the wheel of the dharma of the knowledge of all aspects. (9) The bodhisattvas' familiarization with the profound never being divided through false imagination in any respect means that all buddhas act as aids for their accomplishing enlightenment. (10) Uncommon roots of virtue arising based on prajñāpāramitā means the production of vast special roots of virtue. (11) To practice in accordance with the vow of not giving up one's efforts for enlightenment means that bodhisattvas practice through rejoicing in the words of their initial vow to give rise to bodhicitta. (12) To be able to make other beings seize vast fruitions means connecting them with the profound mahāyāna dharma that they desire, just as they wish. (13) To accomplish the welfare of sentient beings temporarily through riches and so on means promoting the welfare of being in all respects. (14) Definite attainment of the training in accomplishing the excellencies of others in all lifetimes means attaining prajñāpāramitā in her complete entirety. These fourteen qualities arise in bodhisattvas who delight in practicing the above-mentioned twenty aspects of unmistaken training. In each of them, JNS says, the first phrase up to "means" is Haribhadra's condensation of the respective sūtra passages, while the parts after "means" represent his actual commentary on them (some people say that the former are the results and the latter the causes, but that is wrong).

51 CZ, p. 328.

52 According to this calculation, the year 2009 CE is the 461st in the next five-hundred-year period of mainly practicing ethics. JNS (vol. 2, p. 90) says that the timespan of the Buddha's teachings lasting for five thousand years is given, for example, in the *Bṛhaṭṭīkā* (D3808, fol. 208a.2–208b.1; this passage also presents the above division). However, the *Bhadrakalpikāsūtra* says that the essence of the teachings of the Buddha remains for one thousand years, while a facsimile of the genuine dharma will remain for five thousand years.

53 XI.2cd (D13, fol.7b.4; Conze 1973, p. 35).

54 The sūtra in twenty-five thousand lines (D9; ACIP SHES PHYIN NYI KHRI KHA@341a.7) says, "yawning, laughing, and fooling around with each other" (CZ, p. 332, translates the latter as "while sneering at one another"). Please note that the page numbers of those sūtras that are referenced in ACIP files in this volume should also be referenced in those very same ACIP files in Volume One. Due to a regrettable systemic mistake, the page references of those sūtras in Volume One (in particular, of all the prajñāpāramitā sūtras) are indicated as pertaining to the Derge *Kangyur*.

55 Note that, in terms of both contents and numbering, the forty-six flaws as presented in CE sometimes differ from other commentaries and also from JNS's comments on the *Vivṛti* (vol. 2, pp. 93–96), but the above numbers are explicitly stated in this way in CE. JNS presents said flaws in three main groups. (A) The twenty flaws of being close to the adverse conditions that depend on oneself consist of the following. (a) The two in terms of self-confidence are (1) very slow self-confidence that must be attained through great hardships and (2) very swift self-confidence without any reason. (b) The three flaws of the impregnations of negative tendencies (while copying the prajñāpāramitā and so on) are in terms of (3) body (as above); (4) mind (distracting conceptions of characteristics); and (5) speech (performing recitations and so on for the wrong reasons, that is, not being beneficial for accomplishing the two kinds of welfare). The seven flaws that are causes for giving up the mahāyāna are (6) fixating on reasons for rising from one's seat and leaving without any taste of the mother; (7) through engaging in the sūtras of śrāvakas and pratyekabuddhas, regressing from seizing the cause for the knowledge of all aspects; (8) regressing from it because of engaging in the sūtras of śrāvakas and pratyekabuddhas for the sake of savoring the excellencies of gain and honor; (9) regressing from seizing the supreme mahāyāna in every respect; (10) regressing from the mother as the permanent aim; (11) regressing from the true connection between cause and result by taking the causes and results of the unsurpassable mahāyāna dharma as not being supreme and those of the hīnayāna as being supreme; and (12) regressing from the unexcelled qualities of the dharmakāya. (c) The eight flaws of falling under the sway of distractions are (13) arising of a greatly agitated mind of conceptual self-confidence about the many aspects of objects such as form; (14) after having realized the mother, still clinging to writing her letters; (15) clinging to the mother as being a nonentity that is empty of performing a function; (16)–(17) are the same as (15)–(16) in CE; (18) mentally engaging in certain locations as well as various men and women in villages and cities by giving rise to thoughts of attachment and aversion; (19) savoring gain (alms), services, honors, and verses of praise through delighting in them and being full of proud conceit; and (20) searching for the skill in means of bodhisattvas in the sūtras of śrāvakas, which are deceiving since they are not the path to great enlightenment. (B) The twenty-three flaws of incomplete favorable conditions that depend on either oneself or others consist of different ways of the relationship between teacher and student deteriorating and thus failing to give rise to the path in the mind stream. (a) In the *Vivṛti*, the fourteen faults that happen due to the connection between master and student are explained through always stating the listener first and the one who explains second. However, the incompatibilities under each flaw may very well happen in a reversed way too—there is no certainty of either one only applying to the listener and not the teacher. In the sūtras, all these flaws here are attributed to the one who explains, with the reverse applying to the listener. Their relationship may deteriorate due to (21) the listener having intense striving, while

the one who explains is slothful; (22) differing objects of striving (the genuine dharma or what is not the dharma); (23) the listener having great desire for honor and gain but pretending to have little, while the teacher has great desire and does not pretend to have little; (24) the listener possessing the qualities of abstinence and the teacher not possessing them; (25) the listener's nature being virtuous and the teacher's not being so; (26) the listener liking to give, while the teacher is stingy; (27) the listener making offerings, while the teacher does not accept them; (28) the listener understanding through concise statements, while the teacher only understands through elaborations; (29) the listener having supernatural knowledge of the dharma, while the teacher lacks it; (30) the listener being endowed with the six pāramitās, while the teacher lacks them; (31) the listener being skilled in the means to practice the path according to the explanations, while the teacher is skilled in what is not these means; (32) the listener having attained dhāraṇī, while the teacher lacks it; (33) the listener wishing to write the letters of the mother, while the teacher does not; and (34) the listener being free from striving for sense pleasures, while the teacher is not. (b) The two faults that depend only on oneself are (35) turning away from being born in the unpleasant realms for the welfare of others; and (36) delighting in going to the pleasant realms through mentally engaging in one's own welfare. (c) The seven faults that depend on both the one who explains and the listener are (37) the teacher liking to make efforts in solitude, while the listener likes company; (38) the teacher providing no opportunity for the student who wishes to make a connection; (39) the teacher making efforts in proclaiming the dharma for the sake of even just a little bit of material goods, while the listener does not want to give any; (40) the teacher going to places that are life-threatening, while the listener goes to those that are not; (41) the teacher going to places of famine, while the listener does not; (42) the teacher going to places that are haunted by robbers and so on, while the listener does not; and (43) the teacher looking at the households of relatives and friends for the sake of alms, while the listener is unhappy about such distractions. (C) The three flaws of adverse conditions that depend on others are (44) the actuality of the mother to be planted within one's own mind stream being disconnected from this mind stream's rigidity through the influence of māras; (45) engaging in practicing a fabricated path taught by māras; and (46) small-minded persons developing a liking for fake objects of respect in the disguise of śrāmaṇas magically created by māras. It is explained that such fake spiritual friends created by māras, who deceive those with misplaced confidence, may follow them up through the seventh bhūmi. Since all these flaws are nothing but the māras of what is appropriated through one's own inner thinking appearing as if outside, all the Buddha's statements about the numerous activities of māras are simply elaborations on the activities of māras that are taught here. Thus, one should make efforts to relinquish the activities of māras in every respect. As for the remedies to eliminate these flaws, one needs to make efforts in the causes for rendering one's activities of writing down the profound prajñāpāramitā, requesting teachings, understanding them, and properly mentally engaging in them impenetrable by the actions of māras. For those who are endowed with such causes are protected, guarded, and sheltered by the buddhas and bodhisattvas of the ten directions.

56 A simple example for an exclusion of nonpossession (Tib. *mi ldan rnam gcod*) would be the statement, "Susan definitely is a good cook," excluding that she does not possess the feature of being a good cook. An example for an exclusion of possession by others (Tib. *gzhan ldan rnam gcod*) would be, "Only Susan is a good cook," excluding that others too possess the feature of being a good cook.

57 JNS (vol. 2, pp. 96–103) says that, in general, all phenomena are determined through the triad of defining characteristics (or definition), definiendum, and instances. However, the mind that determines such is also nothing but a conceptual imputation. As for defining characteristics, what is specifically characterized consists of any entities that are distinct in terms of time, place, and nature. Definitions or the defining characteristics of something specific must be free from the three flaws of underinclusion, overinclusion, and impossibility in order to distinctly

define it (in other words, a definition may not be too narrow or too broad and should not define something that does not exist). For example, "what is hot and burning" is the defining characteristic of the definiendum "fire," which is instantiated by "a sandalwood fire." What is generally characterized are notions such as "knowable object" or "impermanence," which apply to what is not distinct in terms of time and place. In particular, the above-mentioned twenty aspects (AA IV.8–11) are the instances of the culminating training, based on which the special conventional term "mahāyāna training" is defined. Thus, these are its defining characteristics in terms of their being the agents that define it (Dölpopa says that to explain the defining characteristics stated in AA IV.13 as the ones of the training contradicts both the sūtras and Maitreya—all three define nothing but the dharmadhātu wisdom that is free from adventitious stains). AA IV.13 speaks about (1)–(3) the defining characteristics of the mahāyāna training and (4) the instances of its nature. Among these, (1) the definition of the characteristic of the knowledge of the mahāyāna training is "that which is a characteristic of the mahāyāna training and primarily accomplishes the excellent realization of the dharmakāya in the future." It is threefold in terms of such training in the knowledge of entities, the knowledge of the path, and the knowledge of all aspects, which respectively accomplish the realizations that entities, the path, and all aspects are nonarising. The instances of these three, in due order, are (a) a bodhisattva's sixteen yogas of realizing that entities are nonarising (such as the mother being the one who gives birth to the tathāgatas in AA IV.14–17); (b) the sixteen yogas of realizing the basic nature of the path (such as the three doors to liberation in IV.18–19); and (c) the sixteen yogas of realizing the basic nature of all aspects (such as the tathāgatas honoring the mother in IV.20–22). (2) The definition of the characteristic of the distinctiveness of the mahāyāna training is "the features that make the mahāyāna training more distinguished than the hīnayāna training." Its instances are the bodhisattvas' sixteen yogas that belong to the type of realization that realizes phenomenal identitylessness (such as being inconceivable in IV.23–26). These instances pertain to the training in the knowledge of the path and the training in the knowledge of all aspects, but there is no division into two here in terms of defining characteristics and definienda. (3) The definition of the characteristic of the activity of the mahāyāna training is "that which makes one accomplish excellent enlightened activity for the welfare of others in the future." It is threefold in terms of the three knowledges. In due order, the three definitions of these are the types of realization that, once buddhahood is attained, (a) accomplish the three activities of benefit, bliss, and protection for those to be guided; (b) accomplish the seven activities of refuge and so on; and (c) function as the dominant condition for turning the wheel of dharma (IV.27–28). The instances of these three are the eleven yogas of bodhisattvas that accomplish these eleven activities. In this way, (1)–(3) the three defining characteristics of knowledge, distinctiveness, and activity of the mahāyāna training are presented in terms of their being the agents that define it. (4) These three defining characteristics may equally be presented in terms of being the objects to be defined. From that perspective, they are represented by AA IV.13d, with their sixteen instances consisting of the four natures such as "being devoid of afflictions" (IV.29ab); the five natures such as "hard to be done" (IV.29cd–30a); and the seven natures such as "focusing" (IV.30bd–31). Again, these sixteen instances of the nature of the mahāyāna training define what is suitable to be referred to through the conventional term "mahāyāna training"—they represent nothing but the above three characteristics of (1) the yogas of bodhisattvas realizing the basic nature of all entities, paths, and aspects; (2) the yogas of bodhisattvas realizing phenomenal identitylessness; and (3) the yogas of bodhisattvas accomplishing the activities of benefit, bliss, protection and so on. The purpose of giving this presentation of defining characteristics and what is defined is to realize the relationships between these two. In dependence on their names, their meanings are understood, and upon seeing their meanings, their names are remembered. The purpose of this is to facilitate engaging in what is to be adopted and discarding what is to be rejected. PSD (pp. 316–17) says that capacities (1) and (3) are inferred through their fruitions, such as knowing that a field has the capacity to produce a harvest when one sees this harvest being brought forth from this field. Likewise, seeing that the realization of the three knowledges and enlightened activity for the welfare of others originates from the mahāyāna training, one infers that this training possesses the capacities to produce them. (4) What is defined by characteristics (1)–(3) is the nature of this training, which in turn has sixteen isolates (AA IV.29–31).

58 The *Vivṛti* (D3793, fol. 110a.7) explicitly speaks of four defining characteristics here, with "the defining characteristic of the nature" being one of them since it is defined through the other three. Commenting on this, JNS (vol. 2, pp. 103–4) says that there is no other nature of defining characteristics here than the above-mentioned three characteristics of knowledge, distinctiveness, and activity. However, Haribhadra speaks of the nature as a defining characteristic in order to highlight that instances must be instances of a specific defining characteristic (in this case, the sixteen instances of "nature"). Otherwise, if the *Vivṛti* were taken literally here, it would directly contradict AA IV.13, which speaks of no more than three defining characteristics. Thus, Haribhadra first teaches characteristics (1)–(3) as the defining characteristics that define the definiendum "mahāyāna training" as the definiendum. Then, he indicates that the characteristic "nature" represents the defining characteristic that defines the instances of this definiendum as instances. Also, the instances under "nature" represent the bases or instances that are defined by characteristics (1)–(3). Thus, as for the word "and" in IV.13d [the Tibetan version of this line ends in *yang* ("also"), which renders Skt. *ca* ("and")], JNS says that it is acceptable to link it with verse IV.14 on the factors conducive to liberation. However, it is not unreasonable that most of the earlier Tibetan masters explain line IV.13d as serving to show that "nature" refers to both the instances and the definiendum of the training. The sixteenfold nature, which represents the instances of the mahāyāna training, is thus defined as its instances. Or they are presented as sixteen natures in the sense of being the defining characteristics that define the definiendum "mahāyāna training." However, they are not presented as the defining characteristics of the mahāyāna training as such because these are represented by characteristics (1)–(3).

59 On these views, see the commentary on IV.16b.

60 These sixty-two wrong views are, for example, described in the *Brahmajālasutta* (*Dīgha Nikāya* I.12–I.46; trans. in M. Walshe 1995, pp. 73–90; P1021, pp. 286.2.8ff.). The fourteen extremes listed here represent the fourteen "undecided" (Skt. *avyākṛta*, Tib. *lung du ma bstan pa*) questions that the Buddha refused to settle one way or another. As for the meaning of "undecided," JNS (vol. 2, pp. 108–9) explains that, when the Buddha was asked whether buddhas still exist after their death or not and so on, he did not decide the issue by answering that one of these possibilities is true. This means he did not give any of the following four types of "decided" answers. Among these, (1) "being decided in an absolutely affirming way" is exemplified by answering the question "Will all sentient beings die?" by saying, "They will die." (2) "Being decided by discriminating" is exemplified by answering the question "Do all sentient beings take rebirth?" by saying, "If they possess afflictions, they will take rebirth, and if they are without afflictions, they will not." (3) "Being decided by asking a counterquestion" means to, for example, respond to the question "Are human beings special?" by saying, "Depending on whom do you ask." (4) "Being decided by dropping the issue" is exemplified by answering the question "Is the personal self the same as or different from the skandhas?" by either remaining silent or asking, "Is the complexion of the child of a barren woman light or dark?" In brief, the reason for the above fourteen questions not being decided in any of the manners (1)–(4) is as follows. These questions were asked by certain people to be guided during the period of the first turning of the wheel of dharma. However, what these questions refer to needs to be decided as being very hidden objects by way of scriptural authority that is pure through the threefold analysis of not contradicting perception, inference, and other already so established scriptural authority. Thus, the reason why the Buddha did not give any decided answers on these very hidden objects when being asked by the above people during said period (such as the mendicant Vacchagotta) is that, even if he had given them a decided answer, they would still have needed to gain certainty

about his answer through such threefold analysis. Thus, the Buddha did not answer in any decided way because he knew that these fourteen questions came from people who were clinging to the five skandhas. In other words, even to demonstrate the very nonexistence of a self as the basis of these wrong views would not have any positive result in such questioners because they would not let go of their rigid grasping at such a self no matter what. Also, upon being asked by Ānanda about the reason for his silence later, the Buddha answered that such questions are just entirely baseless speculations, but not soteriologically relevant in the sense of being conducive to liberation from saṃsāric suffering—the Buddhist teachings are not interested in or concerned with the former, but only with the latter (for all the references to these questions in the Pāli canon, see Della Santina 1986, p. 15). As for the fourteen views underlying these questions, JNS (vol. 2, pp. 106–8) explains that, within the first three sets of four among them, the term "coming forth" refers to asserting the first one and the last two (Sāṃkhyas); "being withdrawn," asserting the second one and the last two (Lokāyatas or Cārvākas); "being scattered," asserting the first three (Nirgranthas or Jainas); and "being closed," asserting the last one (the Vātsīputrīyas asserting the person as being inexpressible as either the same as or different from the skandhas). As for the last two views, the Vaiśeṣikas view body and life-force as one, while the Sāṃkhyas view them as different (all these attributions to Indian schools come from the *Ālokā*). According to the words of scholars, the term "coming forth" (Skt. *unmiñjita* [lit. "opening one's eyes"]; Tib. *g.yo ba* [lit. "moving"]) means that the mind comes forth/opens up/moves by virtue of engaging in objects (such as the self and the world being permanent) in an affirmative manner. By virtue of the mind engaging in objects (such as the self and the world being impermanent) in a negating manner, it "withdraws" (Skt. *nimiñjita*, Tib. *'du ba*). It "scatters" by virtue of engaging in the objects of both possibilities in a manner that is both affirming and negating. It "contracts" by virtue of engaging objects through negating them—the views of neither. However, JNS adds, it needs to be greatly investigated in accord with the Sanskrit whether these explanations actually reflect the meanings of these terms or not.

61 This refers to the first four (starting with "being devoid of afflictions"; IV.29ab) among the sixteen instances of the nature of the training below, which characterize the knowledge of entities.

62 JNS (vol. 2, pp. 105–6 and 109) comments that the above are described as the defining characteristics of a buddha's sixteen wisdoms of directly realizing the fundamental nature of entities. However, implicitly, they teach the defining characteristics of the sixteen yogas of the bodhisattvas who focus on the phenomena that are entities. (1) They realize that the state of the Tathāgata appears based on this mother. (2) Right from the very beginning, the world (imputed entities such as the five skandhas) never existed. Since this applies through the power of entities, the "reality" of their being real as having never existed, which does not fit into the perspective of (ordinary) consciousness, is realized by bodhisattvas as having the character of not being perishable. (3) Through knowing that the conduct of the minds of sentient beings with its nature of utter ignorance is something to be relinquished, bodhisattvas reach the culmination of supreme relinquishment and thus know termination and nonarising. (4)–(5) Though all the minds of any sentient being that are concentrated inside (self-aware perception) or move outside (sense and mental perceptions) are presumed to be provisional valid cognitions, bodhisattvas consider them to be nonvalid cognitions because they arise from the cause that is false imagination. Thus, they know that these cognitions are established as the opposites of the cognitions of a person (a buddha) who represents (ultimate) valid cognition. (6) Thus, no consciousness of any sentient being whatsoever (be it collected inside or distracted outside) can bring any benefit or harm to the nature of phenomena that operates since the very beginning. Therefore, the primordial and profound nature of phenomena does not cease even when sentient beings and their consciousnesses have ceased. This is the aspect of inexhaustibility. (7)–(8) Bodhisattvas know that the minds of ordinary beings possess attachment and so on, meaning that they also possess other

afflictive fetters. (9) After even the consciousness that is liberated from attachment and so on has been eliminated, the genuine mind that engages true reality is vast. (10) Such a vast mind is great mind since it does not have any extent whatsoever. (11) The greatness of such a vast mind is ungraspable by saying, "Its assessable size is that much." (12) Since the consciousness of sentient beings is not observed through any nature of its own, it is indemonstrable. (13) Since the minds of sentient beings have never existed from the very beginning, sentient beings and their minds do not even appear as the objects of the five visions of the buddhas and are not seen by them. Therefore, mind is invisible. (14) Bodhisattvas know the consciousnesses of sentient beings that entertain the fourteen undecidable wrong views. (15) Once even the moving and proliferating states of mind that are other than the ones that focus on these four focal objects (coming forth and so on) are eliminated, bodhisattvas know the aspect that is the lucid manifest wisdom of suchness. (16) In brief, they know that the sage realizes the suchness of the two realities, just as it is, and communicates it to other sentient beings. These sixteen make up the defining characteristic of knowledge in terms of the knowledge of all entities because they define the conventional term "knowledge in terms of the knowledge of entities." Commenting on the *Vivṛti*, JNS (vol. 2, pp. 108–9) says that (1) indicates the agent who trains in the knowledge of entities. Among entities as the objects to be realized, (2) refers to the world in general not being perishable because it is primordially unestablished; (3)–(13) refer to the particulars to be realized in terms of sentient beings in general; and (14) indicates their undecided wrong views. (15) refers to the basis of realization (the nature of phenomena) and (16) to the fruition (wisdom). On (8), the *Ālokā* (D3791, fol. 204b.3–5) says, "Teaching the knowledge that mind is free from attachment and so on is as follows . . . As for these [states of mind] being 'naturally luminous,' if one examines through valid cognition the nature of the impure states of mind that have become so in the state of ordinary beings by virtue of the cause that is mistakenness, one realizes them to have the essential nature of being unarisen and so on. Through having merged with this [realization], by virtue of [mind's] capacity to not revert from [its state of] the remedies having arisen and to eliminate adventitious desire and so on, said [states of mind] are naturally luminous, and it is nothing but their nature to be utterly pure." As mentioned in the Introduction, this is virtually identical to how Dharmakīrti presents mind's naturally luminous nature in *Pramāṇavārttika* II.208cd–211ab.

63 CZ, p. 346.

64 This refers to the second five (starting with "hard to be done"; IV.29cd–30a) among the sixteen instances of the nature of the training, which characterize the knowledge of the path. JNS (vol. 2, pp. 111–12) comments that what is taught here are the sixteen yogas of tathāgatas that are the clear realizations of the basic nature of the path, which implicitly illustrate the sixteen yogas of bodhisattvas knowing the true nature of the path. These sixteen consist of the three wisdoms of realizing that (1) the nature of both the subject and the object of a tathāgata's knowledge are emptiness; (2) signlessness; and (3) characterized by the relinquishment of wishes; and the eight wisdoms of realizing that the characteristics of (4) no arising; (5) no ceasing; (6)–(7) no afflicted and no purified phenomena; (8) no entities; (9) the nature of nonentities; (10) no foundation or abiding; and (11) being spacelike are not established substantially. (12) Since this wisdom of the nature of phenomena does not go beyond the nature just explained, it is the immovable wisdom that cannot be confused or mixed up. (13) Since this wisdom cannot be taken as any one of the three times, it is nonformational. (14) This wisdom free from formation is the wisdom of not conceptualizing any nature or aspect of any phenomenon whatsoever. (15) Such nonconceptualization is the knowledge of demonstrating the distinction between the basic nature of the seeming (the object to be realized—not existing through a nature of its own—is not conceptualized in the sense of sheer nonexistence) and the basic nature of the ultimate (for the object to be realized is not empty of a nature of its own either). (16) Once this is demonstrated in such a way, this is the wisdom of realizing that the phenomena that appear as

characteristics from the perspective of those who just see this life lack any nature of their own. Commenting on the *Vivṛti*, JNS (vol. 2, p. 112) says that (1)–(11) are presented in terms of the true nature of the path; (12)–(14), in terms of the nature of phenomena being empty of the two kinds of identity; and (15)–(16), in terms of distinguishing the two realities, with the first one distinguishing the way things appear and the way they actually are, and the second one referring to either of these two ways lacking any substantial characteristics.

65 CZ, p. 351.

66 CE has "object" (*yul*), but, given the explanations in other commentaries, this is most probably a typo for "mother" (*yum*).

67 This refers to the last seven (starting with "focal object"; IV.30b–31) among the sixteen instances of the nature of the training below, which characterize the knowledge of all aspects. JNS (vol. 2, pp. 113–14) comments that the defining characteristics in terms of the training in the knowledge of all aspects that are taught here actually represent the clear realizations of a buddha directly seeing the defining characteristic of knowledge in relation to the knowledges of entities and the path. Illustrated by this, the sixteen yogas of bodhisattvas of realizing the same in approximate accordance with this buddha knowledge are taught too. (1) Since the ultimate wisdom of the knowledge of all aspects is the distinctive own dharma of those who are endowed with it, it dwells in the Tathāgata's own mind by relying on this very Tathāgata who is endowed with it. (2) Mother Prajñāpāramitā—Mahāmudrā—is honorable and to be attended; (3) respectable (an object of service); (4) the manners of display of buddhas and bodhisattvas serve as means to please her; and (5) she is to be worshipped. (6) Apart from just all phenomena plain and simple, there is no agent and thus neither any action, nor anything it would act upon or create. (7) This is the knowledge that engages the true nature of the knowledge of all aspects everywhere and knows this object, once it engages it. (8) The knowledge of the buddhas demonstrates the means for displaying or manifesting true reality (which was not seen, is not seen, and will not be seen by sentient beings in any respect) after it has become free from stains. (9) Buddhas realize the world as an aspect of emptiness; (10) indicate its mode of being; (11) teach the reasonings that produce the prajñā of certainty about these indications; 12) connect others with what is induced through these reasonings, or with directly seeing emptiness through the prajñā that is induced through these reasonings; and (13) show that it is inconceivable by those who see just this life and say things such as, "It is contradictory to be empty and yet to appear as perishing again." (14) Thus since this world has never existed in the first place, it is shown to be peace. (15)–(16) In brief, the entire world and all discriminations about it have already ceased right from the beginning. Commenting on the *Vivṛti*, JNS (vol. 2, pp. 114–15) says that (1) the feature of blissfully abiding (one's own welfare) refers to tathāgatas abiding through relying on the supreme object—the nature of phenomena, the vajra of supremely unchanging great bliss. In terms of the definitive meaning, with this foundation and the features founded on it not being different, there is no knowledge that is other than this basic nature of great bliss. (2)–(5) refer to venerating this mother of the victors—great bliss, Mahāmudrā—on the level of the seeming. (6) In terms of the definitive meaning, since this mother is without any formations, the most profound veneration of her is nonformation. (7) This mother or knowledge is also the wisdom of knowing suchness in that it is spacelike in being unattached and unobstructed with regard to the basic nature pervading everything in a way that is free from obscurations. (8) It is the wisdom of knowing variety in that it demonstrates to childish beings that exactly that which is not seen by genuine beings, but appears as if it were something (visible), is what appears as the mistaken variety of phenomena. (9) The power of the enlightened activity of the tathāgatas shows the world as an aspect of emptiness. (10) When they show this, they indicate that the world is emptiness in order to attract those who do not yet belong to their retinue, thus generating the prajñās of studying and reflecting. (11) In terms of maturing the beings they attracted in this way, they make the world known as emptiness, doing so in order to make these beings go

beyond the world. (12) In terms of liberating those whom they matured, they make the world visible as emptiness. (13)–(14) As the means for seeing this, they show that the basic nature of the four realities is inconceivable and that saṃsāra is peace because it never existed from the beginning. (15)–(16) To show this means to dwell in the cessation of the world and the cessation of discriminations.

68 CZ, p. 353.

69 JNS (vol. 2, pp. 117–18) comments that the following four sets of four distinctive knowledges, in due order, realize the true reality of the four realities of suffering, origin, path, and cessation (thus, unlike CE and most other commentaries, JNS switches the usual order of the last two realities and also interprets the *Vivṛti* in this way). The main feature that makes the knowledge on the mahāyāna path of seeing more distinguished than those of śrāvakas and pratyekabuddhas is that it realizes phenomenal identitylessness. In detail, the special knowledge of realizing the suchness of the reality of suffering consists of realizing the following four features of this very knowledge. (1) It is inconceivable in that thinking cannot engage it in a manner that penetrates it. (2) It is incomparable in that mundane knowledge cannot compare or compete with it. (3) It transcends measuring or not measuring objects and so on. (4) Its nature does not arise and cease, so it is completely beyond being calculable or not. To realize the suchness of the reality of the origin of suffering means to realize that (5) said knowledge incorporates all the uninterrupted causes and conditions for manifesting a great noble one. (6) Through being wise and skilled in this actuality, it trains well in all the essential points, and knows this actuality as it is. (7) It is not a common karmic disposition, but the knowledge of the supreme state. (8) It is swift in accomplishing one's needs. To realize the suchness of the reality of the path means to realize that (9) the power of this knowledge to swiftly accomplish its purposes never fluctuates between decline (being slow) and increase (being sharp). (10)–(11) It engages in all buddha qualities and, upon doing so, they are completely accomplished. (12) It attains mastery over focusing in all respects on what will be accomplished. To realize the suchness of the reality of cessation means to realize the following. (13) The distinctive feature of being skilled in the fact that this knowledge's own nature is prajñāpāramitā means to be supported by not being ignorant about the means to accomplish the proper outcome of any activity. (14) This training in means and prajñā purifies attachment and obstructions with regard to all extremes. (15) It also means to rely on a mentor who is skilled in purifying these. (16) It lacks relishing any nature or aspect of any phenomenon whatsoever because it lacks attachment and obstruction with regard to anything. Differing from and/or adding to CE and JNS's just-mentioned comments, JNS (vol. 2, pp. 118–20) comments on the *Vivṛti* as follows. The prajñā of the mahāyāna path of seeing is (1) inconceivable through the power of being embraced by buddhas, bodhisattvas, and the natural outflow of the dharmadhātu. (2) It is incomparable to any other kinds of prajñā and self-confidence. (5) It comprises all kinds of realizations of all noble persons. (7) It knows ultimate reality—the entity that is not the sphere of śrāvakas and pratyekabuddhas (JNS remarks that, here, Haribhadra explicitly refers to the nature of phenomena and ultimate reality as being an entity, wheras he never says that they are a nonentity). (9) In terms of all phenomena that are based on seeming and ultimate reality, there is no decline of their being clearly realized and no increase that is anything other than the termination of flaws [JNS has *nyes pa'i tshogs zab pa*, which is emended to . . . *zad pa*]. (10) The prajñā of the path of seeing engages in the six pāramitās through being pure of the three spheres. (11) Through applying themselves perfectly by way of the vigors of respectful and permanent application, bodhisattvas on this path accomplish the perfect accumulations of merit and wisdom of many eons in a single instant. (12) Focusing on all phenomena in a nonconceptual way refers to experiencing in a way that is free from aspects and natures. (13) The nature of the dharmadhātu is the foundation of the fruition to be strived for by bodhisattvas. (14) By virtue of the supports of substantial and cooperative causes and conditions for accomplishing this fruition, as well as through aspiration prayers,

the collection of causes for perfecting the pāramitās—the bhūmis of bodhisattvas and buddhas—are complete. (16) This prajñā does not relish or experience a nature of its own since it is without clinging. This implies that the paths of seeing of śrāvakas and pratyekabuddhas entail the opposites of the above sixteen characteristics.

70 CZ, p. 356.

71 Skt. *gati* (the Tibetan has *rten*—"support").

72 The sūtras say that this is because all phenomena never depart from being situated in their lack of arising and ceasing, coming and going, making efforts or not, and so on (CZ, p. 370).

73 JNS (vol. 2, pp. 121–22) glosses the eleven activities as follows—(1) liberating from saṃsāra; (2) establishing in nirvāṇa; (4) being the refuge of humans by virtue of the capacity of protection; (5) establishing them in the place of rest that is the supreme state; (6) warding off demons and opponents; (7) providing relief for the wretched; (8) leading inferior beings to be guided on the supreme path; (9) the functions of benefit, happiness, and protection not requiring any effort, but being natural or spontaneously present; (10) not manifesting the fruitions of the three yānas for one's own welfare; (11) being the agent of all these activities. Since the passages in the large, medium, and brief prajñāpāramitā sūtras on these eleven differ, there are several assertions, such as all of them being the activities of the knowledge of all aspects; all being the activities of bodhisattvas; the first two being the activities of bodhisattvas and the remaining nine being those of buddhas; or the opposite. However, it should be understood that being the characteristic of activity of the knowledge of the path alone does not entail not being suitable as the characteristic of activity of all the three knowledges. For it is taught that the knowledge of the path of bodhisattvas fully completes the causes, paths, and fruitions of all three yānas. Also, the special activities of the uncommon knowledges of the path and all aspects automatically accomplish the particular activities of the common knowledge of entities. Commenting on the *Vivṛti* (whose matching of the eleven activities with the three knowledges is followed by CE), JNS (vol. 2, pp. 122–23) says the following. (1) Benefit in the future means to merge with nirvāṇa. (2) The happiness in this life is due to not being harmed. (3) To accomplish the true nature of liberation is not a maturation of the origin of suffering since its nature is to be without suffering. (7) The nature of this activity is to be the support for realizing and attaining the welfare of oneself and others. (8) It arises as the nature of accomplishing the welfare of others. (10) means to not manifest the fruition of the final deliverance of the three yānas without having completed the accumulation of merit. (11) refers to accomplishing the kāya that demonstrates all dharmas of the knowledge of all aspects.

74 CZ, p. 367.

75 Unlike all other commentaries (and against a natural reading of lines IV.29ac), both CE and JNS take "devoid" (which is the first word of line IV.29c, but separated from "hard" by "and" in the Tibetan) to be connected with "hard to be done."

76 The Tibetan in both line IV.29c and in CE is *nges pa* ("certain," "definite").

77 See above under "the aim of practice" (the sixth point of the knowledge of all aspects).

78 JNS (vol. 2, pp. 124–25) does not match the sixteenfold characteristic of the nature with the three knowledges, but basically takes suchness, the ultimate, or the perfect nature as the nature of this training. This nature is (2) devoid of phenomena (such as signs and the bearers of signs) and (3) focal objects. It is devoid of (4) antagonistic factors, but if it is even devoid of reference points and anything that has been relinquished, it is also devoid of remedies. (5) Though the means for sentient beings to pass into nirvāṇa or to become enlightened are taught, it is impossible for sentient beings to become enlightened (see also Appendix I1E in Volume One).

Therefore, true reality is devoid of difficulties, such as accomplishing the path. (6) Since the dharmadhātu—the perfect nature—is definite as nothing but perfect buddhahood, true reality is devoid of the reference points of other yānas. (7) Because the aim is poised readiness for the perfect nature, it is devoid of the distractions of the other (two) characteristics (the imaginary and the other-dependent). (8) Since a nature is not observed, it is devoid of observation. (9) To refrain from clinging means being devoid of nature. (10) What is discerned as the ultimate focal object is devoid of seeming focal objects. (11) Since true reality is devoid of all mistakenness about true reality, it is antagonistic (to them). (12) Because the own nature of such being antagonistic is said to be a vajra, it is unobstructed. (13) This suchness is without any ground for saṃsāra and mistakenness to dwell on; (14) devoid of coming and going; and (15) devoid of arising—coming into existence newly. Though this is the context of these sixteen isolates in terms of the nature defining its above instances, here they are asserted as the fourth defining characteristic because they define something like a definiendum—the above defining characteristics of knowledge, distinctiveness, and activity of the three knowledges. Some Tibetan scholars say, "As for the defining characteristic of the nature, the meaning of the mother is to not differentiate distinct instances of the various defining characteristics of the nature in terms of each one of the three knowledges. Rather, the defining characteristic of the nature is taught through sixteen different ways of the sugata heart being devoid of reference points. It should be understood that this very heart functions as the foundation for all the defining characteristics of knowledge, distinctiveness, and activity." The Eighth Karmapa says that he rejoices in this statement, but since there are some points to be examined, that much shall suffice here. Commenting on the *Vivṛti* (whose matching the sixteen instances of nature with the three knowledges is followed by CE), JNS (vol. 2, pp. 125–26) says the following. (4) Antagonistic factors and remedies are respectively identified as desire and the lack of desire and so on. (5) Though ultimately nonexistent sentient beings cannot pass into nirvāṇa, bodhisattvas train in what is hard to be done—the activities of making these beings pass into nirvāṇa despite their nonexistence. (6) Bodhisattvas are devoted in an exclusive manner to the yāna that has the defining characteristic of not falling into other yānas. (7) The aim of buddhahood is the supreme object to be accomplished, which takes a long time. (8) Bodhisattvas do not observe any phenomena that represent something to be familiarized with or a familiarizer; (9) refrain from clinging to any entities; and (10) focus on the distinct features of the entities of which the all-knowledge and the knowledge of the path consist. (11) The nature of phenomena is antagonistic to the nature of what is mundane because it is taught as the opposite of the apprehender and apprehended of mundane accomplishment. (12) The realization of the lack of nature of what never existed (such as form) is unobstructed. (13) This is groundlessness, that is, emptiness because knowable objects and knowing are unobservable. (14) By virtue of suchness, there is no going. (15) Since there is no nature of form and so on, there is no arising. (16) Suchness—the nature of the triad of entities, nonentities, and both—is unobservable. This concludes the discussion of ninety-one defining characteristics in four sets—the forty-eight of knowledge, the sixteen of distinctiveness, the eleven of activity, and the sixteen of the nature. JNS concludes with a verse:

> The defining characteristic of knowledge is like being in the prime of one's youth;
> The defining characteristics of being distinguished is like being well-supported by companions;
> The defining characteristic of activity is like engaging in all kinds of bold and joyful sports—
> Thus, the defining characteristic of the nature—great bliss—will be experienced.

79 CZ, p. 372.

80 CE's explanation is based on the Tibetan term *thar pa cha mthun* ("concordant with a part of liberation") for the Sanskrit *mokṣabhāgīya*, which literally means "belonging or connected to liberation." That "belonging to" means "conducive" here is confirmed by Āryavimuktisena's

Vṛtti (D3787, fol. 145a.5), which glosses this term as follows. Liberation refers to the distinctive feature of freedom, and one speaks of "factors conducive to liberation" since they benefit or aid what belongs to (or is a part of) this liberation (as the *Abhidharmakośabhāṣya* on VI.20ab says, the same applies to "the factors conducive to penetration"). In general, Vaibhāṣika texts speak of three sets of roots of virtue—those associated with or conducive to merit, liberation, and penetration. The first are the virtuous actions of body, speech, and mind that produce the seeds which lead to rebirth as humans or gods. The second consist of the virtuous actions of body, speech, and mind (with mind being predominant) that are matured through consistent cultivation and perfected through the prajñās arising from study and reflection. According to the *Visuddhimagga*, these actions, which are based on the threefold lack of greed, hatred, and ignorance (such as generosity, keeping precepts, or studying the dharma), plant the seeds for the definite liberation from saṃsāra and eventually produce the attainment of nirvāṇa. In essence, this second kind of roots of virtue derives from the same types of meritorious actions as the first one. The difference lies in the underlying focus or outlook having shifted from wanting to attain a better rebirth within saṃsāra to striving for the unconditioned nirvāṇa. The third roots of virtue are the crucial points of an ordinary being becoming a noble one (they have already been discussed at length above).

81 JNS (vol. 2, pp. 127–28) says that this topic follows after the above defining characteristics of the three knowledges since a person who cuts through superimpositions with regard to these defining characteristics needs to give rise to the roots of virtue that are conducive to liberation, which are explained in six parts. (1) Their nature consists of the prajñā that arises from studying and reflecting as well as the virtuous actions that are motivated by that (*Abhidharmakośa* VI.25a). (2) Their definition is "the special prajñā that opens the gate to merging with the levels of liberation and omniscience and does not have the nature of the five faculties of the path of preparation." The definition of the path of accumulation is none other than that, which means that one gathers the accumulations since the prajñā of realizing identitylessness in the manner that an object generality (which does not have the nature of the levels of heat and above) eliminates obscurations that obstruct liberation. (3) Their division is into lesser, medium, and great. During these levels, in due order, one cultivates the four foundations of mindfulness, the four correct efforts, and the four limbs of miraculous powers. Or they can also be divided through the five faculties, such as confidence. (4) As for the meaning of the term, the reasons for speaking of "liberation" are twofold. On a temporary level, in terms of accomplishing the psychophysical support for the path, one is liberated from the psychophysical supports of the unpleasant realms. Ultimately, "liberation" means being liberated from all suffering. The roots of virtue in question here are "partial" since one merges with a part of this liberation. "Concordant" means not moving anywhere else other than liberation. (5) As for the boundary lines, "the factors conducive to merit" exist both in those who have entered the path and those who have not. "The factors conducive to liberation" exist from the path of accumulation onward. (6) As for the distinctive features of their causes, the persons in whom they arise are the men and women on the three continents (*Abhidharmakośa* VI.25b). The meditative grounds on which they are based are any among the six grounds of dhyāna, the four formless absorptions, and a mind of the desire realm (*Abhidharmakośa* VI.73ab asserts that the twenty-two factors that consist of the four foundations of mindfulness up through the five powers are based on these eleven types of meditative absorption). The causes from which the prajñā that is conducive to liberation arises are mainly studying and reflecting, but it is not that there is no such prajñā that arises from meditation because the *Abhidharmasamuccaya* states that the latter exists too. TOK (vol. 3, p. 470) explains: "[It] is the path of gathering a vast accumulation of virtue in order to make one a suitable vessel for the arising of the realization of heat [on the path of preparation]. Therefore, it is called 'the path of accumulation.' It also has the following names. Since one mentally engages in it in a way that is conducive to liberation (that is, nirvāṇa), it is 'the roots of virtue that are conducive to liberation.' Since one's aspiration for the three jewels and emptiness is powerful,

it is the level of confidence. It is [also] 'the invalidating remedy' since the śrāvakas regard the appropriating skandhas as defects (just as a disease or an abscess and so on) and the followers of the mahāyāna regard them to be without nature."

82 JNS (vol. 2, p. 129) says that, though it is realized that there are no signs, the nature of the path of accumulation, which is being skilled in the aspect of means that entails signs (completely and unmistakenly accomplishing generosity and the other pāramitās) is the preparation for the gradual realization of all the 173 aspects of the three knowledges. This is taught as "the factors conducive to liberation." Here, being skilled in means refers to the skill in the means to dwell in the nature of signlessness through putting an end to the mistakenness of signs with regard to what is signless. While there are no signs, through making effort in the virtues that entail signs (the causes), the respective manifestations of the results of virtue, genuine virtue, unconditioned virtue, and nonreferential virtue are all results that concord with their causes because they concord in type with the causes that are virtues.

83 CZ, p. 381.

84 JNS (vol. 2, pp. 130–32) says that IV.33–34 teaches the details of the skill in means mentioned in IV.32. In addition to CE, (1) includes focusing on the supreme ultimate cause and result. (3) is the mindfulness of excellent reflection on the meaning of what one has studied, just as it is. (5) is the prajñā of knowing the general and specific characteristics of phenomena in all their aspects. The reasons for buddhahood being easy or hard to realize, respectively, are that those of sharp faculties realize that these five factors of confidence and so on are without arising, while those of dull faculties still entertain clinging to their characteristics. According to the *Vivṛti*, this implies that those with medium and lesser skill in these five factors realize the enlightenments of pratyekabuddhas and śrāvakas, respectively.

85 CZ, p. 381.

86 JNS (vol. 2, pp. 133–35) says that all sentient beings are praised here as the focal objects of all four levels of the path of preparation because perfect buddhahood is accomplished by focusing on them. The individual cognitive aspects of such focusing have to be explained in terms of lesser, medium, and great with respect to each one of these four levels. Commenting on the *Vivṛti*, JNS (vol. 2, pp. 135–37) says that (a) the ten aspects of lesser, medium, and great heat are explained as familiarizing with a mind of equality through focusing on these beings and so on. From among these ten, (1)–(2) correspond to lesser heat; (3)–(5), to medium heat; and (6)–(10), to great heat. As for the latter, all sentient beings older than oneself are to be regarded as one's parents; all of equal age, as siblings; and all who are younger, as one's children. In sum, one should see all beings as being like friends who benefit one, companions on whom one can rely, and one's maternal and paternal relatives. In brief, through the first five aspects, one trains in bodhicitta toward all sentient beings in general, while the last five aspects represent the various ways in which one trains. Thus, parents and so on are not presented here as objects of attachment and aversion, but in terms of being objects for which love and compassion arises. (b) The four aspects of lesser peak consist of oneself turning away from nonvirtue; establishing others too in this; praising them for doing so; and making them conform to it. The four aspects of medium peak are oneself engaging in virtue (the pāramitās), with the remaining three being as above. The same goes for the four aspects of great peak in terms of oneself abiding in emptiness and so on. (c) The four aspects in each one of lesser, medium, and great poised readiness are the same in terms of oneself abiding in the four realities; deliberately abiding in the fruitions of stream-enterers and so on, but not manifesting the true end without having perfected the means; and abiding in the attainment of special flawless bodhicitta. Though the aspects of medium and great poised readiness are alike in terms of the manner in which the first bhūmi is manifested, the difference is that the aspects of the former refer to not manifesting the true end at an inappropriate time. (d) The four aspects in each one of the lesser, medium, and great supreme

dharma are the same in terms of maturing and liberating oneself and other sentient beings who possess the roots of virtue; generating special supernatural knowledge; and giving rise to and abiding in the wisdom of the knowledge of all aspects. According to JNS, this is the correct way of matching AA IV.35–37 with these aspects of the four levels of the path of preparation, whereas many earlier and later Tibetans explain this in mistaken ways. Some also say that the ten aspects of heat are the distinctive features of motivation, while the nine sets of aspects of peak, poised readiness, and supreme dharma are the distinctive features of application or training.

87 CZ, p. 385.

88 As mentioned before, this is how the respective purposes of the training in all aspects, the culminating training, and the serial training are described.

89 Lines 57cd. JNS (vol. 2, pp. 137–40) presents various opinions on whether and how the three paths of preparation, seeing, and familiarization are each taught six times over the first six chapters of the AA, and whether Āryavimuktisena's and Haribhadra's rebuttals of such concerns by others are correct or not. Though Ngog Lotsāwa is among those who criticize Haribhadra's way of rebutting, he agrees with the latter that there is no repetition of these three paths because the functions, focal objects, and aspects of each one of them are infinite and thus can be described as many distinctive features. Also, just repeating words does not amount to redundancy if the meaning is not repeated too. It is precisely for these reasons of there being no repetition in the first place that it is unreasonable to even try to eliminate concerns about repetition. As for JNS's own position on this, in Haribhadra's *Ālokā* and *Saṃcayagāthāpañjikā*, it is said that, in general, all three paths below the progression of familiarizing with the special knowledge of all aspects are just nominal, and, in particular, the wisdoms of the three pure bhūmis are labeled with the names of these three paths. This explanation is put forth in these texts as the system of those masters who explain the progression of the path in terms of clear realization per se. However, according to their position, the meaning of the paths that are taught in the chapters of the knowledge of all aspects and so on being presented as the pure bhūmis is in terms of the following. The three kinds of nonarising (with regard to entities, paths, and all aspects) are ascertained through studying and reflecting up through the seventh bhūmi. Then, they are made a living experience through the four trainings on the three pure bhūmis, and, finally, the fruition of the dharmakāya arises by virtue of that. In this context, the three Indian subcommentaries on Haribhadra's *Vivṛti* did not grasp his intention and mistakenly say that Āryavimuktisena and Haribhadra hold this to be the path per se, while these masters in fact assert it to be a shift in the path. However, through speaking about a shift in the path, they did not say that, respectively, the three knowledges and the four trainings are separate in terms of studying and reflecting on the one hand and making this a living experience on the other. According to the *Vivṛti*, the three paths of preparation, seeing, and familiarization taught in the first three chapters (which represent the three clear realizations of the three knowledges through familiarizing with all entities, paths, and aspects being without arising) refer to the realizations of the supramundane paths of seeing and familiarization being preceded by the realization of the mundane path of preparation. As for these three paths as taught in the chapters on the first three trainings, one should understand that they refer to the progressive arising of the lesser, medium, and great degrees of the uncontaminated wisdom that consist of the paths which are in every respect more special than the impure bhūmis by virtue of the distinctive feature of their being the phases of the increasing familiarization with the teachings in the chapters on the three knowledges that one has studied and reflected on before. In order to refute that these degrees of wisdom arise simultaneously, they were labeled with the conventional terms "the factors conducive to penetration," "path of seeing," and "path of familiarization," respectively, and discussed in this way in the chapters on the first three trainings. According to JNS, the three paths of preparation, seeing, and familiarization each being taught six times in the first six chapters of the AA is not repetitious or redundant. For in the first three chapters, they are taught from the perspective of the

view. In the latter three chapters, they are taught by way of this view being in union with the six pāramitās. In addition, there is no repetition within the first three chapters either because they respectively teach said three paths by way of the distinct isolates of the nonarising of entities, the path, and all aspects. Nor are the latter three chapters repetitious because they respectively teach the three paths by way of their distinct isolates in order to attain mastery; in terms of the modes of having attained such mastery; and in order to gain stability in this mastery.

90 JNS (vol. 2, pp. 144–45) explains that these signs are taught right after the path of preparation in this chapter because perfect enlightenment is certain upon attaining the path of preparation of the mahāyāna. This is similar to the first chapter, in which the foundation of practice (the disposition) is explained right after the path of preparation. PSD (p. 329) explains the meaning of irreversible as not turning away from what makes one attain buddhahood. The *Prasphuṭapadā* (D3796, fols. 71b.5–72a.1 and 72a.5–7) explains that, in general, "irreversible" is used in four different senses—being irreversible from attaining enlightenment (in a general sense), being irreversible from attaining the special enlightenment (of buddhahood), being irreversible from the supramundane bhūmis, and being irreversible from effortlessness. The first one exists, in common with noble śrāvakas, from the path of accumulation up through the level of poised readiness on the path of preparation. The second one exists starting with the level of heat of the mahāyāna path of preparation. The third one is the nature of the first bhūmi. The fourth one refers to the eighth bhūmi. Therefore, on the path of accumulation, there is no certainty of being irreversible from attaining the enlightenment of the special yāna and thus it is not called "irreversible." If one primarily takes the reason of (the disposition of a person's) own mind stream being certain, also the roots of virtue of the path of accumulation may be described as being irreversible. However, the mind streams of persons on the path of accumulation lack the qualities that instill trust in others in a way that accords with their own realizations. Also, though these realizations are certain as entities (in said mind streams), there are no easily identifiable signs that distinguish them. For these reasons, they do not serve as the bases for designating them with conventional terms and thus they are not described as "irreversible."

91 The Sanskrit (*liṅgam*) and Tibetan (*rtags*) words can mean both "sign" and "reason."

92 Interestingly, this is exactly what JNS does (see Appendix I4D).

93 The Tibetan has "sentient beings" instead of "world."

94 This is the highest level of rebirth as a god in the form realm (the uppermost level of the fourth dhyāna; see Chart 1 in Volume One).

95 See also Chart 12 in Volume One.

96 JNS (vol. 2, pp. 147–49) comments as follows—(2) termination of the doubts of taking true reality as not being true reality; (5) others to be guided who have been established in virtue in turn establishing yet others in generosity and so on; (10) possessing mindfulness of past objects and alertness about present objects; (11) cleanness of daily necessities (such as robes) by virtue of them being obtained without wrongdoing; (14) adopting the conduct of purifying the impregnations of the negative tendencies of body, speech, and mind; (16) proceeding towards enlightenment through not being in contradiction to the nature of phenomena. Commenting on the *Vivṛti*, JNS (vol. 2, pp. 149–53) says that (1) all phenomena, such as form, are the reverse of form and so on because they all lack a nature of their own. (2) Knowing the qualities of the three jewels, bodhisattvas attain yearning confidence in them, thus being without doubt as to whether these jewels are true refuges or not. (3) Through the power of their mind being grounded in virtue, they accomplish the path as desired and thus are not reborn in unfavorable existences. (5) They practice the six pāramitās through dedicating their own virtues to other beings by way of exchanging their own happiness with the sufferings of others. (8) Among the five obscurations as above, the first two obscure the training in ethics; the second two, the training in samādhi;

and the last one, the training in prajñā. The reasons for the pairs of drowsiness and torpor as well as agitation and regret (mind being agitated through attachment and remembering one's bad actions, respectively) each being counted as one are that, in the desire realm, the former pair obscures calm abiding and the latter superior insight (in turn, calm abiding and superior insight are the remedies for these respective obscurations). (9) Through familiarizing with the remedy that is emptiness, the manifest aspects of all latencies (such as ignorance) are gradually overcome in the manner of suppressing them. (10) Bodhisattvas are endowed with mindfulness and alertness through being in constant meditative equipoise by virtue of examining their minds. (11) Their entire way of living is pure, such as using their robes in ways that delight others through their purity. (12) The bodies of such bodhisattvas are free from parasites because the roots of virtue in their mind streams are way beyond the world. In other words, not only are these bodhisattvas not reborn in the unpleasant realms themselves, but their body, speech, and mind can never serve as the supports for other beings experiencing the unpleasant realms. (16) They progress on the path to buddhahood through not being in contradiction with the nature of phenomena by virtue of withdrawing all phenomena into abiding in being free from reference points and thus being endowed with prajñāpāramitā. Here, "withdrawing" refers to the realization of the actual and approximately concordant wisdom of prajñāpāramitā that all seeming phenomena are primordially not established because this withdraws or relinquishes the mind of clinging to these phenomena as being established. That seeming phenomena are not established as such phenomena is the true nature of the seeming, and to realize this means to "not be in contradiction with the nature of phenomena." The explanation by some that realizing the seeming as not being established means not being in contradiction with the true nature of the ultimate is wrong. For just not being in contradiction with the true nature of the seeming does not entail not being in contradiction with the true nature of the ultimate. Though the prajñā of realizing self-emptiness is not in contradiction with the true nature of the seeming, it is in contradiction with the true nature of the ultimate. For unlike the true nature of the seeming being realized as self-empty through this prajñā, the true nature of the ultimate is not suitable as being self-empty because it is not empty of a nature of its own. Otherwise, if the arising of the realization of not being in contradiction with the true nature of the seeming were the fully qualified realization of not being in contradiction with the true nature of the ultimate, all sentient beings would see true reality for precisely this reason. The reason applies because (a) the true nature of the seeming is not observable as anything other than mere appearances and because (b) these mere appearances are directly cognized even by those who do not see true reality. As for reason (a) applying, one may consider "the true nature of the seeming" as referring to what is temporarily able to perform a function or to emptiness. In the first case, reason (a) applies because, in this context of Madhyamaka here, apart from mere appearances, there is nothing else that is able to perform a function. In the second case, reason (b) also applies because it is taught that emptiness does not exist as something separate from form and so on. Thus, the emptiness of form and so on is mutually exclusive (or in contradiction) with the emptiness of the true nature of the ultimate. Some also say that to see form and such is the realization of not being in contradiction with the true nature of the seeming, while to see the emptiness of the seeming is the realization of not being in contradiction with the true nature of the ultimate. However, then it follows that one sees the true nature of the ultimate once one sees the true nature of the seeming. For according to this position, these two are the nature of phenomena and that which bears this nature, respectively, which means that they must be inseparable. Consequently, through seeing one, the other is seen too. If that is accepted, it represents a philosophical system that is outside the scope of *Svātantrika-Madhyamaka. Though there are infinite invalidations of such an assertion through scripture and reasoning, this will become too wordy. (18) By virtue of these bodhisattvas' nature of trusting their own realizations due to the valid cognition of threefold analysis and yogic valid perception, they are not confused. Thus, they cannot be led astray by teachers who are not buddhas, by what is not the path, or by any paths other than the one of the mahāyāna. (19) Since these bodhisattvas are skilled in knowing the means of the knowledge of all aspects (the cause for buddhahood), they do not fall under the sway of what is not the means—false paths in general and māra's deceptive teachings on certain views and meditations representing the meaning of the mother of the victors in particular.

97 CZ, pp. 388–89 (both CE and JNS have *gzugs las phyir mi ldog pa'i byang sems phyir mi ldog par rig par bya'o*, but the sūtras and all other sources agree on *phyir ldog pa* in the first case).

98 JNS (vol. 2, p. 154) comments that these are the signs of bodhisattvas being irreversible from the path of seeing.

99 In due order, these four signs are related to the readiness, the dharma cognition, the subsequent readiness, and the subsequent cognition of suffering. The same goes for the signs of the remaining three realities. JNS (vol. 2, p. 155) adds that (2) refers to bodhicitta being so firm that even the attempts of māras at reversing it cannot reverse it. (4) The meditative absorptions include the four dhyānas, the four formless absorptions, and the meditative absorption of cessation. Commenting on the *Vivṛti*, JNS (vol. 2, pp. 168–69) says the following. (1) Those who cling to phenomena examine and analyze phenomena (such as form) as being such and such, though these phenomena are nothing other than of the nature of emptiness as their specific characteristic. Bodhisattvas turn away from such examining. (2) Bodhicitta is firm by virtue of the blessings of the buddhas and so on. (3) Bodhisattvas turn away from lower yānas through having practiced the mahāyāna dharma that is more distinguished than inferior dharmas. (4) They terminate the branches of the dhyānas and so on through the power of having fully discriminated the basic nature of all phenomena and thus understanding how what is not an abode of liberation can be such an abode.

100 Skt. *brahmacārya*, Tib. *tshangs par spyod pa*. In particular, this refers to persons who have taken the five Buddhist lay vows, including celibacy.

101 V.13–15ab (this is one of the various ways in which the five wrong ways of livelihood are described; see Appendix I4C1g). JNS (vol. 2, pp. 155–56) adds the following comments. (5) Body and mind are very workable in terms of being weary of what one should be weary of and engaging in what one should engage in. (6) In order to attract those to be guided who have attachment as their retinue through practicing generosity and by way of material things, bodhisattvas physically and verbally enjoy desirable sense pleasures. However since any flux of their minds striving for objects has completely come to an end, such enjoyment is called "being skilled in means." They themselves regard desirable objects like poison, but through teaching the ways of relying on such desirable objects as medicines, they guide others through the causes that consist of the sense pleasures. Finally, through teaching those to be guided the means to regard desirable objects as poison, they render themselves and others untainted by the flaws of saṃsāra. (7) Though it seems as if bodhisattvas, through using desirable objects with skillful means, rely on them, they themselves do not regard these objects as anything whatsoever. Thus, they constantly dwell in pure conduct. (8) Bodhisattvas are also able to increase the roots of virtue of others who make offerings to them out of confidence in the qualities of these bodhisattvas. Based on this, they are able to purify the obscurations in their own mind streams and those of others. Thus, their livelihood is pure of wrongdoing. Commenting on the *Vivṛti*, JNS (vol. 2, p. 169) says that (5) bodhisattvas have relinquished suffering through being free from nonvirtue and thus go wherever they please. (7) Though bodhisattvas enjoy sense pleasures through skill in means, they are not attached to them because they see the flaws of these objects and thus do not try to own them as "theirs."

102 The Tibetan word *tshogs* in line IV.49b can mean both "accumulation" and "crowd" or "assembly." All other commentaries agree that it means the former here.

103 CE differs here in both numbering and meaning from other commentaries. According to most others and JNS (vol. 2, p. 156), the above four signs mean to respectively stop dwelling on connecting and being occupied with (9) the skandhas and so on; (10) the phenomena that are obstacles to clear realization; (11) the causes for enlightenment (the two accumulations) in a referential manner; and (12) talk and so on about the battle of the afflicted faculties and so on—their consciousnesses and objects. Here, "connecting" refers to the first moment of mental clinging. "Being occupied" is the clinging of being conscious of this moment through recollecting and determining it. "Dwelling on" is presented from the point of view of this clinging's own nature. "Respectively stopping" means stopping clinging's own nature and the manner of clinging, respectively. Commenting on the *Vivṛti*, JNS (vol. 2, pp. 169–70) says that bodhisattvas stop such connecting and so on with (9) the skandhas and so on by virtue of all phenomena abiding in emptiness; (10) the phenomena that obstruct realizing the path by virtue of having eliminated the antagonistic factors of the path of seeing to be relinquished; and (11) the accumulations of the causes (generosity and so on) that are the aspect of the means for enlightenment by virtue of understanding conceptions to be flaws because they are antagonistic to being free from reference points. As for (12), in order to relinquish apprehender and apprehended, the sūtras speak of "villages" as illustrating the sense faculties since the sense consciousnesses depend on them, just as people depend on a village. "Cities" illustrates the bases of the sense faculties—the elements. Just as cities are the supports of the conventional term "numbers," the elements are the supports of the faculties that derive from these elements. "Market towns" at business times illustrates the sense objects since they are the bases for consciousness engaging or rejecting them, just as such market towns are the bases for people to engage or reject certain things. As for the term "battle," its literal meaning refers to talk and so on about battles, while its ultimate meaning refers to the battle between the factors to be relinquished and their remedies. Here, bodhisattvas stop connecting and so on with either of these.

104 In addition to what CE says, JNS (vol. 2, p. 168) also glosses "the triple bhūmi" under (15) as having the character of the three knowledges (as does the *Vivṛti*). Commenting on the *Vivṛti*, JNS (pp. 170–72) says that (13) bodhisattvas disconnect from the antagonistic factors of the pāramitās by virtue of realizing the special qualities of the latter. (14) Since the nature of all phenomena consists of the three doors to liberation, from the perspective of the prajñā of realizing the basic nature of the seeming any general or specific characteristics of even the least thing that represents a phenomenon are unobservable. (15) Through the power of having eliminated the wrong cognitions that are nonvalid cognitions, bodhisattvas attain trust in their own realizations. Therefore, by virtue of the three knowledges and through being certain about the triple bhūmi, just as it is, which has the nature of the three kinds of noble persons of the three yānas seeing their respective realities, bodhisattvas realize that they abide on this triple bhūmi. (16) By virtue of the dharma that is the cause for the three knowledges eventually merging into the single knowledge of all aspects, they give up their life for its sake. As for how the sixteen moments of the path of seeing show as the signs of irreversibility from the perspective of others, once bodhisattvas have attained the wisdom of these sixteen moments in their meditative equipoise, through the power of having seen true reality their minds during subsequent attainment are pure in that they do not cling to apprehender and apprehended with regard to mundane appearances. The special ways of physical and verbal conduct that are the outflows of such a mind represent the correct reason that establishes the irreversibility of bodhisattvas with uncertain disposition on the path of seeing. For the result that accords with their meditative equipoise—their turning away from discriminating notions of form and so on—produces an inference from the perspective of others. Some may say, "But if there is no subsequent attainment of the path of seeing, how could the conduct during subsequent attainment become a sign?" Though there is no subsequent attainment of the path of seeing, it is not by virtue of a challenger who possesses the dharma vision of direct realization that the three modes are determined through valid cognition and the convention of irreversibility is established. Rather,

this happens through a defender who possesses the dharma vision of direct realization and formulates the probative argument, "Bodhisattvas of medium faculties with uncertain disposition on the path of seeing (the subject) are irreversible from perfect enlightenment because they are endowed with the realization that is capable of inducing special ways of physical and verbal conduct during subsequent attainment." When this is put forth, the convention of irreversibility is established in the mind stream of the challenger. It may be objected, "If one considers the time when this defender who possesses the dharma vision of direct realization could possibly formulate this probative argument—either in the state of meditative equipoise or during subsequent attainment—they are not able to do so in either case. For there can be no physical or verbal conduct during meditative equipoise and it is held that there is no subsequent attainment of the path of seeing." Under analysis, this is correct. However, in this case, such criticism does not apply because said defender who possesses the dharma vision of direct realization identifies a bodhisattva who has previously gone through the realization of the path of seeing and not only someone who is still dwelling on the path of seeing. Also, in terms of what is to be taken as the subject in question in the above probative argument, the defender does not take someone who dwells on the path of seeing alone, but merely bodhisattvas of medium faculties with uncertain disposition on the path of seeing in general. "But what is the purpose of people who possess the dharma vision proving each other to be irreversible?" There is the purpose of inferring each other's mind streams. "But if some people possess the dharma vision, there is no need for assessing each other's mind streams through probative arguments because they can do so directly through their supernatural knowledges." There is no absolute need for such inferences, but it is not contradictory to use probative arguments as a means to know each other's realizations because bodhisattvas operate in a way that accords with mundane behavior. "So what is the purpose then to operate in such a way?" That noble persons engage in conventions or actions on the seeming level of reality is only in terms of the need to guide other sentient beings, but it is impossible for them to slip into such conventions of others because they are always in accord with the ultimate that they realized in their meditative equipoise. Thus, it is in order to make those to be guided understand this that bodhisattvas explain the signs which appear from their own perspective in their meditative equipoise (the sixteen moments of cognition and readiness) by labeling them as the signs of subsequent attainment from the perspective of others because there is a special purpose for explaining them in this way. For in the mind streams of others to be guided, such as ordinary beings, the realizations in the meditative equipoise of such bodhisattvas cannot appear—what can appear to these beings is only the conduct of the latter during their subsequent attainment. Therefore, to explain that the appearances of such conduct (possessing the signs as taught here) represent an irreversible person on the path of seeing is an excellent incentive for those to be guided to produce roots of virtue themselves. If this were not explained in that way, but the actual meditative equipoise of these bodhisattvas were presented as the sign of their irreversibility since others cannot experience what exists in the mind streams of yogins on the path of seeing, how could these moments of personally experienced wisdom possibly serve as the characteristics that instill trust in those others who are to be guided? Consequently, the moments of cognition and readiness as such are not taught as the signs that give rise to trust in others.

105 CZ, p. 395.

106 As Cox 1992 (p. 75) points out, this threefold distinction in terms of relinquishment is already found in the earliest northern abhidharma texts.

107 For details, see Appendix I4E.

108 As it appears in CE, this passage is a combination of three passages, with the phrase "signlessness . . . cessation" being inserted from a later part of the sūtra in twenty-five thousand lines (see CZ, pp. 404 and 410). Moreover, CE adds "peace, suchness, the true end," between

"nirvāṇa" and "dharmas," which are found in Āryavimuktisena's *Vṛtti* (see below), but not in this list as it appears in the sūtra.

109 CZ, p. 405.

110 JNS (vol. 2, pp. 174–75) comments that the nature of the path of familiarization is profound. The dawning of clear realization in the mind stream through the progressive stages of relinquishment and realization is explained as "the buddha path." Through it appearing as if the stains that never existed in the profound nature of phenomena (what is to be clearly realized) are eliminated, it looks as if the nature of phenomena has become pure again. It is with this in mind that the learned ones describe this nature as "the conditioned nature of phenomena" and such. This nature of phenomena is profound emptiness and so on—Āryavimuktisena's *Vṛtti* (D3787, fol. 154a.1) speaks of its tenfold profundity (the three doors to liberation, nonformation, nonarising, freedom from desire, cessation, peace, suchness, and the true end) and the *Prajñāpāramitāsūtra in Eight Thousand Lines* (D12; ACIP SHES PHYIN BRGYAD STONG KA@188a.6–7; Conze 1973, p. 209) says that the dharmadhātu (the profound) should be understood as being divided into eleven in terms of the isolates that are the three doors to liberation, nonformation, nonorigination, nonarising, lack of entity, freedom from desire, cessation, nirvāṇa, and nonexistence. Here, profound has the meaning of "difficult to realize," which is intended to convey that it is not an object of consciousness. Superimposition and denial refer to superimposing that the dharmadhātu is consciousness and to denying that the dharmadhātu is the permanent activity of accomplishing what the noble ones wish for. Commenting on the *Vivṛti*, JNS (vol. 2, p. 175) says that the profound actuality of emptiness and so on does not exist as the nature of impure form and such. This profound actuality of emptiness and so on exists, while what is other than it (form and such) is empty in the sense of not existing, which means that, by nature, the stains do not exist. Though there are differences in terms of what is empty, of what it is empty, by virtue of what it is empty, and so on, in general, form and so on are not established as anything other than mere emptiness. If this is not realized, one falls into the extremes of superimposition and denial about emptiness and so on, while the true reality of being liberated from these extremes is the profundity of emptiness and so on. Thus, the path of familiarization is profound since it entails manifesting such profundity.

111 The sūtras, the AA, CE, and other commentaries all have "verifying" (Skt. *tulamana*, Tib. *'jal ba*), but JNS consistently uses "encountering" (Tib. *mjal ba*) in this context, which may just be a Tibetan typo, but to speak about directly encountering the profound nature of phenomena on the path of seeing makes perfect sense too. Thus, according to JNS (vol. 2, pp. 175–76), to practice the path through resting in meditative equipoise in the profound true reality that is to be reflected on, to be directly encountered, and to be absorbed in is called "the path of familiarization." Commenting on the *Vivṛti*, JNS (vol. 2, p. 176) says that it relates these three stages to the prajñās arising from study, reflection, and meditation, or the prajñās of the preparation, main part, and subsequent attainment of samādhi, respectively. Through these, in due order, one reflects on, verifies (encounters), and remains absorbed in the sixteen aspects of the four realities that are seen during the paths of preparation, seeing, and familiarization.

112 CZ, p. 405. JNS (vol. 2, p. 177) says that the path of familiarization entails an uninterrupted continuum in the manner of reflecting at the beginning, encountering in the middle, and realizing in the end. Thus, as an aside, this is what the *Hevajratantra* (Part 1, VIII.56) has in mind:

> Just as the stream of a river flows
> And the tip of an oil lamp [burns] continuously,
> Always, through the yoga of true reality,
> One rests in meditative equipoise day and night.

Considering this intention, the instruction manuals of Tibetan meditators say, "The meditation that is called 'the river stream yoga' happens when the realization of one taste (the third of the four yogas of Mahāmudrā) dawns. This is the one that actually fulfills this definition, while the path of familiarization is what conforms with it." Thus, here, it is this kind of continuum of the path of familiarization that is divided into nine degrees. On the *Vivṛti*, JNS (vol. 2, pp. 177–78) comments as follows. One may say here, "The ninefold division of the path of familiarization by virtue of bodhisattvas relinquishing the cognitive obscurations is not sufficiently refined because there are also afflictive obscurations that are factors to be relinquished through familiarization." There is no problem because the second omniscient one, Vasubandhu, says that the afflictions to be relinquished by bodhisattvas are the conceptions that are the cognitive obscurations [as mentioned before, I could not locate this phrase in Vasubandhu's works, but it is found in Asvabhāva's *Mahāyānasūtrālaṃkāraṭīkā* on VIII.1a (D4029, fol. 63a–b)]. Thus, the afflictive obscurations are relinquished as a matter of course during the relinquishment of the cognitive obscurations because these afflictive obscurations are not taught separately from the conceptions that are the cognitive obscurations. Basically, this is said with the intention that what obscures the attainment of omniscience is being ignorant about knowable objects. This ignorance about knowable objects is nothing other than false imagination, which is the producer of all primary and secondary afflictions. As for the manner of relinquishing these conceptions, just as very great darkness is eliminated by a little bit of light and a little bit of darkness needs to be eliminated by a strong light, the great, medium, and lesser degrees of such conceptions (and their respective subdivisions) are eliminated by lesser, medium, and great degrees of remedies. Therefore, in accordance with the number into which the remedies for these conceptions are divided by way of manifesting the aspects that are the defining characteristics of ultimate emptiness, the nine remedial phases with regard to the nine levels of saṃsāra (the desire realm, the four levels of the form realm, and the four levels of the formless realm) arise as an uninterrupted continuum. Thus, this is the path of familiarization.

113 CZ, p. 409.

114 Ibid., p. 410.

115 The Tibetan omits "true" (Skt. *bhūtāḥ*).

116 JNS (vol. 2, pp. 178–81) first presents how certain Tibetans, who are capable of critical analysis, explain that the instruction in the sūtras and IV.55 on the attainment of countless, immeasurable, and infinite virtues is not contradictory. This is so by virtue of the meaning of "countless" and so on being nothing other than the profound expanse of emptiness. What is taught as "countless" and so on is one as the true reality of ultimate emptiness and cannot be made different because it is inexpressible as different. The meaning of all phenomena being inexpressible like this is determined in the *Bodhisattvabhūmi* through four reasonings and three scriptural passages. The four reasonings are as follows. (1) All phenomena (from form up through the buddhadharmas), which serve as the bases of labeling, are nothing but labels either, while none of them exist as any entities that are real as they are labeled because they are not forms and so on by their very nature, and because there are no forms and so on apart from them either. The reason applies because if they existed as form and so on by their very nature, they have to be understood as forms and such merely by virtue of seeing them, even before having applied the terms "form" and so on. (2) If such phenomena were entities in the ways they are labeled, a single phenomenon would become many entities because many names apply to a single phenomenon. There is entailment because there is no difference between these many names in that one among them owns an entity, while the others do not own this entity. Therefore, no phenomenon exists as having the nature of a name. (3) So the question is whether phenomena, such as form, existed as the nature of form before they were given the name "form" or not. It may be replied that they did not exist as the nature of form before being labeled—the entities that are the bases of labeling arise first and then they are labeled with names, such as "form," as one pleases. But then, such entities that supposedly serve as the bases of the names through which they are labeled even before they are labeled by those names would be nonexistent and

inexpressible by their very nature. If this is accepted, they would not be suitable to be labeled with names later either because they are inexpressible. If this is accepted too, the fact that all phenomena are inexpressible and without nature is thereby well established. (4) Or it may be replied to the above question that the phenomena that serve as the bases of being labeled as form and so on exist as the nature of form and so on even before being labeled and are labeled later as the form and so on that consist of the words that label them. However, in this case, it would be suitable for a mind that uses the label "form" to arise merely by virtue of seeing the phenomenon that is the basis of being labeled as form, even before giving it a name. Therefore, ultimate phenomena are inexpressible, while the phenomena that consist of the variety of entities are mere names and imputations. Thus, "countless" means that the nature of phenomena cannot be counted as conditioned or unconditioned on the level of the seeming. "Immeasurable" and "infinite" refer to all phenomena—mistaken appearances in the three times—being unobservable because they have no measure. Teaching through such distinctions matches what the *Laṅkāvatārasūtra* (D107; ACIP MDO SDE CA@264a.2–3) says—the buddhas give names in order to counteract the world's ignorance that results from not giving names. Accordingly, though the actual way of being is being free from reference points, as a means to guide beings the buddhas teach as if there were reference points, which is the result of their compassion for sentient beings. Thus, they teach on these results that are the natural outflows of their causes through distinguishing them by calling them "countless" and so on. The *Prajñāpāramitāsūtra in Eighteen Thousand Lines* says, "What are described as 'countless,' 'immeasurable,' and 'infinite' teach the natural outflow of the Tathāgata's explanations." The second Buddha, Vasubandhu, says in his *Bṛhaṭṭīkā* (D3808, fol. 236b.6–7), "Numbers, measures, and so on exist in imaginary phenomena, but are absent in the expanse of emptiness. They are included in enumerations . . . This means that explanations in terms of the seeming are the natural outflow of great compassion." As for JNS's actual comments on IV.55 (vol. 2, pp. 181–82), lines IV.55ab are presented as the following objection: "Countless merit and so on, which are taught as the results of each one of the nine levels of the path of familiarization do not hold out in terms of the ultimate as specifically characterized objects (such as something countless) because even something countless and so on are nothing other than the nature of emptiness." The answer to this in lines IV.55cd is that, ultimately, something countless and so on do not hold out as anything other than emptiness. However, in terms of the seeming, out of their compassion for sentient beings, the sages asserted the arising of these twenty-seven results that are the natural outflows of their causes—the three degrees of each one of the nine levels of the path of familiarization. Commenting on the *Vivṛti*, JNS (vol. 2, pp. 182–83) continues that, just through the path of familiarization being described here to be manifold (such as countless), it is not the case that it is manifold and not definite as being ninefold. For the Buddha spoke of "countless" and so on in terms of both (a) the ultimate and (b) the seeming. (a) In their ultimate meaning, "countless" and so on stand for the nature of the dharmadhātu, in which one is to rest in meditative equipoise through the path of familiarization. In their meaning in terms of the seeming, these terms refer to the levels of the path of familiarization being definitely nine in number (the second through the tenth bhūmis), with each one of these nine levels being taught to produce countless, immeasurable, and infinite excellent virtues, just as a big heap of grain with nine corners is countless, immeasurable, and infinite. In sum, the question is whether the above objection is made in terms of the ultimate or the seeming. In the first case, since the entities of merit are infinite, they are countless; since they are countless, they cannot be assessed; and since they cannot be assessed, they are immeasurable. Through the nature of what is expressed by these terms, ultimately the path of familiarization connects with the single actuality of emptiness (which is described as having said characteristics) in the manner of repeated reflection and so on, with the profound nature of phenomena becoming liberated from superimposition and denial. However, when resting in meditative equipoise in this profound emptiness, there is no way that, based on isolates such as "countless," the nature of the path of familiarization—the dharmadhātu—could be divided into having any distinctive features (such as countless) that are substantial entities different from this dharmadhātu because all phenomena have the nature of not going beyond emptiness. The gist of this is that, ultimately, there are not more than nine progressive stages of realizing the profound nature of phenomena (the nature of the path that is explained as the ninefold path of familiarization) because it is taught that the descriptions of emptiness as being manifold, such as being countless, are nothing other than just the dharmadhātu—emptiness. "But if the nature of the path of familiarization is just the single nature of phenomena, it is not reasonable to divide the path of familiarization into nine either." Ultimately, one cannot but accept this. However, from a certain point of view, one cannot say that the division into nine is just as unjustified as the division into countless and so on. For "being countless" and so on are the distinctive features of the path of familiarization, but not the phenomenon that bears these features. Therefore, if one makes a division here, it is the path of familiarization itself (as that which bears these features) that must be divided. However, if one made a division in terms of its distinct features, such a division would become endless. In general, there are two kinds of making divisions—through grouping in general categories and through particular instances. In this context here, the first kind is applied because through using it, the latter is understood automatically. (b) In terms of speaking about "countless" and so on on the level of the seeming, through the buddhas teaching for childish beings that the ninefold nature of the path of familiarization arises as the great fruitions of countless merit and so on, out of their nonreferential great compassion they asserted the nature of the path of familiarization to be the fruition that is a natural outflow of the dharmadhātu.

117 CZ, p. 410.

118 The Tibetan simply has "path" (*lam*), while the Sanskrit is *vartmanā*.

119 JNS (vol. 2, p. 185) glosses "entity" as the path of familiarization, which is not established as or does not exist as an object of expression or a means of expression. In terms of the argument presented in IV.56, the first two lines represent the entailment by the reason; the third, the subject; and the fourth, the consequence. Commenting on the *Vivṛti*, the qualm reads, "The entity of the path of familiarization, which is asserted to be nothing other than the nature of phenomena, lacks any nature. Thus, in actual fact, it cannot be expressed as being the same as the nature of phenomena, other than it, both, or neither, and the realization of profound emptiness cannot be made more excellent through familiarizing with it again. Therefore, it is neither tenable to become free from antagonistic factors, nor that remedies arise and purified phenomena are obtained. If that is accepted, the path of familiarization does not perform the slightest function, which means that there is no point in giving any presentations of factors to be relinquished and remedies."

120 CZ, p. 410.

121 JNS (vol. 2, pp. 185–87) first presents how certain Tibetans, who are capable of critical analysis, comment on this verse. They say that, according to the sūtras (CZ, p. 411), "Bodhisattvas who are skilled in means do not think, 'Generosity and so on increase'—they think, 'Generosity and so on are mere names.'" When they engage in prajñāpāramitā in this way, they dedicate their generation of bodhicitta and all their virtues in conformity with unsurpassable enlightenment. Since such dedication is the nature of the path of familiarization, through such skill in means this path of familiarization of dedicating dreamlike virtues in conformity with enlightenment accomplishes and makes them attain the most supreme of all desired goals—unsurpassable enlightenment. The Buddha holds that the nature of this enlightenment is to have the defining characteristic of the suchness of all phenomena and that suchness too has the many defining characteristics of this enlightenment. This is well described in the *Vṛtti* (D3787, fols. 157b.6–158a.2), but Haribhadra reverses it. It is also the meaning of what Vasubandhu's *Bṛhaṭṭīkā* (D3808, fol. 237a.2–4) refers to as inexpressible emptiness: "By virtue

of being inexpressible, it is expressed as emptiness. Emptiness neither increases through bright dharmas nor decreases through black dharmas. You may wonder, 'But then, if the pāramitās and so on are also without increase and decrease, through which cause will the knowledge of all aspects become the fully perfect realization of unsurpassable completely perfect enlightenment?' It will become so through the power of dedicating with skill in means, which is taught through the last words of this sūtra passage: 'They dedicate in conformity with unsurpassable completely perfect enlightenment.'" On IV.57, JNS explains that great enlightenment is inexpressible and without increase or decrease, but still promotes the welfare of others. Likewise, though this path of familiarization is the profound nature of phenomena, it also accomplishes the desired goal of buddhahood through relinquishing the factors to be relinquished and so on. Thus, it is established that the path of familiarization is the nature of phenomena and yet is not something that does not perform activity. Therefore, lines IV.57ab answer the consequence in the above qualm by saying that, in terms of the seeming, the entailment is not certain. Lines IV.57cd indicate the answer that, ultimately, the consequence is accepted—just as enlightenment is the defining characteristic of suchness, this path of familiarization is also asserted to have the defining characteristic of suchness. Thus, ultimately, it can only be accepted that the path of familiarization is without activity or function. This acceptance on the ultimate level is not obvious in IV.57 itself, but the *Vivṛti* explains it as a supplement here. Commenting on the *Vivṛti*, JNS (vol. 2, pp. 187–88 and 197) first speaks about the entailment being uncertain in terms of the seeming by elaborating on the *Vivṛti's* following example. The beings to be guided focus on the dominant condition of primordially established buddhahood, which has the nature of the dharmakāya (and the other two kāyas) being of the essential character of the nonreferential wisdom of enlightenment since it abides as changeless suchness. It is merely through such focusing that their desired goal or function is accomplished by way of generating the mind of bodhicitta through the triad of completion, maturation, and purification, which is eventually suitable to appear as the special actualities of the rūpakāyas and the dharmakāya in accordance with these beings having gathered the accumulations of merit and wisdom, respectively. Just as in this example, through familiarizing with the actuality of the nature of phenomena by way of resting in it in meditative equipoise, in terms of the seeming, also this path of familiarization (which has the defining characteristic of suchness and clearly manifests reality through becoming free from adventitious stains) performs the desired activities of becoming free from stains, producing the remedies, and so on. For JNS's elaboration on the meaning of the above example of buddhahood performing activity, see Appendix I4F.

122 CZ, p. 411.

123 JNS (vol. 2, p. 199) formulates the objection as, "It follows that the mind of the path of familiarization is not the means to give rise to great enlightenment because it is not reasonable for this mind to be the means to give rise to enlightenment through either an earlier or a later one of its moments. The twofold reason does apply because any earlier and later moments of this mind do not meet. For at the time when an earlier moment of this mind exists, any later one has not yet arisen and thus does not exist, and at the time when a later one of its moments has arisen, any earlier ones have already ceased and thus do not exist." Commenting on the *Vivṛti*, JNS (vol. 2, pp. 199–201) first presents the threefold objection as negating the possibilities of enlightenment arising from (a) any isolated earlier or later moments of mind; (b) many simultaneous moments; and (c) many progressive moments together. Possibility (a) is impossible because the entire collection of causes for enlightenment, which is gathered over the path of learning, is never present in a complete manner, but there are only distinct single moments. (b) does not work since many simultaneous moments of mind are not possible in the single mind stream of a single being. (c) is not viable either because of the above reason of earlier and later moments not meeting and thus lacking any connection. JNS adds that some people present the objection here as it being unreasonable for the mind (the momentary stream of consciousness) to, by its

nature, turn into the nature of enlightenment. They claim that the buddhas and bodhisattvas answer this by saying that this momentary mind indeed becomes the nature of enlightenment. However, let alone such an answer, buddhas and bodhisattvas perfectly refute any possibility of attaining enlightenment without having eradicated mind, mentation, and consciousness.

124 CZ, p. 411.

125 Ibid., p. 412. JNS (vol. 2, p. 202) says that, just as the earlier and later moments of the flame of a lamp burn its wick in a joint manner, the signs of irreversibility of the path of familiarization—the eight aspects of the profound nature of phenomena—are declared to be the means for attaining enlightenment in dependence on the successive arising of their earlier and later moments. Commenting on the *Vivṛti*, JNS (vol. 2, pp. 203–6) elaborates that, in the first moment, the wick and the flame just meet at the same time, while there is no special intrinsic power in the flame to burn the wick. Thus, the first moment cannot burn the wick independently of the second moment. Likewise, the second moment does not possess any special power to burn the wick that is independent of the first moment either. If it had such independent power to burn the wick, it would follow that it has this function of burning the wick either all the time or never. Also, a second such moment that does not depend on the first moment would be something without a cause. As *Pramāṇavārttika* I.35 and *Pramāṇaviniścaya* II.59 say, if it arose without a cause, it would not be something that arises sometimes, but must be either permanently existent or permanently nonexistent. Even on the level of seeming reality, there is no such special power of the second moment that is independent of the first moment. Thus, there is no independent burning of the wick in either the first or the second moment without relying on the respectively other one. The burning of the wick occurs by virtue of the nature of dependent origination as mere conditions coming together, which only applies and satisfies as long as it is unexamined. Ultimately and under analysis, there is no flame as the cause that results in a burned wick because both of them as well as dependent origination per se are empty of a nature of their own in the first place. However, from the perspective of a mistaken consciousness that takes things at face value without analysis, the connection between preceding causes—the series of moments of a flame—and their following result—a burned wick—is conventionally established and observed in the world. Likewise, conventionally speaking, it is reasonable that, in dependence on preceding consciousnesses that appear as limited and feeble causes for accomplishing enlightenment (such as the foundations of mindfulness), later consciousnesses that appear as far more superior and powerful (such as practicing the path of familiarization) arise, which eventually lead to attaining enlightenment. In this way, the example of the oil lamp serves to make one understand the clear realization of the eightfold profundity of the nature of phenomena and the manner in which to familiarize with it.

126 JNS (vol. 2, pp. 206–8) comments as follows. (1) If seeming arising is examined, it is nonarising, and this nonarising is the ultimate that depends on this seeming itself. Those who assert that this is the ultimate that actually fulfills this function are the Niḥsvabhāvavādins, whereas the Great Mādhyamikas hold it to be the nominal ultimate. As for the ultimate sugata heart arising in a manner that is free from proliferations, within a mental state of examination and analysis not even a mere object generality (a conceptual elimination) of this manner of arising can possibly appear. Therefore since this kind of arising does not represent any kind of extreme, such as being permanent, impermanent, existing, or nonexisting, it is profound arising. (2) From the perspective of mistakenness on the level of the seeming, the manner of being mistaken about phenomena appearing is to mistake what is unarisen as having arisen. By virtue of being mistaken in this way, one does not examine whether this false arising through the power of what is unarisen is an arising in the first place. Thus, by being mistaken in this double manner, what seems to have arisen appears to cease. Through the continuity of such double mistakenness, thoughts such as "What has ceased has arisen again right now" occur in those who are tainted by ignorance. However, since it is impossible for any seeming phenomena to arise ultimately,

for something to cease is impossible too. Since the ultimate supreme nature remains unchanging, there is no ceasing and no discontinuity. Thus, this is profound ceasing. (3) The suchnesses of the two realities are different, and the triad of agent, object, and action through the power of entities exists in both of them. They are distinguished in terms of whether their respective modes of performing activity actually fulfill this function or not and in terms of being real or false. Nevertheless, since both suchnesses are of concordant type as far as mere emptiness goes, this is profound suchness. (4) What is to be cognized on the level of the seeming (all seeming phenomena) has no measure, is inconceivable, is to be cognized by consciousness, and cannot be assessed. As for the ultimate nature of phenomena, it has no measure, is inconceivable, is the object to be cognized by wisdom, and is beyond any assessment through measuring. However since perfect buddhas realize everything that is to be cognized within both realities, this is the profundity in terms of what is to be cognized. (5) Consciousness is a temporary appearance through the power of the condition of ignorance, while wisdom abides as the permanent nature that cannot be made different through any conditions. Thus, it is profound cognition. (6) Ultimate enlightenment does not change into something inferior or superior through engaging in certain ways of conduct. On the level of the seeming, however, through inferior or superior distinctive features of engaging in physical and verbal ways of conduct that are linked to corresponding motivations in the mind, it either seems as if there are adventitious stains or it seems as if these are eliminated. Thus, this is profound engagement. (7) Just as the true nature and the bearers of this nature in terms of the imputedly existent seeming do not exist as two, the true nature and the bearers of this nature in terms of the substantially existent ultimate do not exist as two either. In this way, since the true nature and the bearers of this nature in terms of each one of the two realities do not exist as two, this is profound nonduality. (8) The profound training in skill in means is that, from the perspective of the seeming, the buddhas display their search for the causes and conditions that are the means to become buddhas, as if they needed to be come buddhas newly. At the same time, they demonstrate that, ultimately, nothing but having been a buddha already right from the start is established as buddhahood. These are the eight profundities that are difficult to realize and are unfathomable. Commenting on the *Vivṛti*, JNS (vol. 2, pp. 208–10) says that (1) it is not that, through earlier or later moments of mind, its nature becomes enlightenment. Nor is it that great enlightenment is produced through negating that seeming phenomena have a nature because this is nothing but the nonexistence of merely having negated existence. So what is enlightenment? Through bodhisattvas familiarizing with the reality that they have seen, the triad of what is superimposed, what superimposes it, and the superimposing in terms of superimposing existence onto the adventitious stains that never existed in the first place becomes terminated. Through this, the actuality of perfect wisdom—the supreme actuality of enlightenment that exists right from the start—arises in a clearly manifest way. This is profound arising because it appears as if enlightenment arises again through the power of mutually dependent origination. (2) All phenomena lack any nature of arising in that they merely arise in dependence on conditions. In such a lack, arising and ceasing are not tenable, but in terms of presentations of the level of the seeming, one speaks of "ceasing" in dependence on "arising" on this level. (3) Bodhisattvas become familiar with suchness throughout all levels of the path of learning in such a way that they first reveal it in their meditative equipoise through wisdom and then familiarize with it further during subsequent attainment in a manner that concords with this perfect focal object. However, until the aspect of means is completed, they do not only rest in the meditative equipoise of suchness. Therefore, it is said that suchness is not manifested, which refers to the profundity of the manner of realizing it. (4) In order to relinquish the obscurations with regard to all phenomena that have the nature of suchness, bodhisattvas practice generosity and many other things. Through doing so, they gather the accumulations, which greatly enhances their power to relinquish these obscurations. This is the profound manner of the mind engaging in all that is to be cognized. (5) In terms of the nature of suchness, not seeing it as any reference point is the seeing that engages in the actual way of being. This is profound cognition. For though it applies in general to the cognitions of ordinary beings that nonexistence cannot be seen directly, the cognition of seeing reality means to have attained the dharma vision. This means that it is even possible for nonexistence to be seen since it is a very subtle object. (6) Though the nature of phenomena—emptiness—abides in lacking any engagement in any activity, through the gate of emptiness everything is possible. Thus, engaging in generosity and such is profound. (7) While abiding as the nature of nonduality (there being no seeming phenomenon as a second one that is other than the single ultimate nature of phenomena), on the level of the seeming all the means to accomplish seeming buddhahood are accomplished. This is profound nonduality. (8) Profundity in terms of skill in means refers to the following. Though sentient beings make efforts in completely gathering all the accumulations, these sentient beings do not attain the result of these efforts—buddhahood. "But if sentient beings do not become buddhas, it is pointless for them to make efforts in the means to accomplish it." The reason for sentient beings circling in saṃsāra is stated in *Pramāṇavārttika* II.191cd–192ab:

> As long as attachment to the self is not overcome,
> One is greatly tormented,
> And for that long, with a suffering [self] being superimposed,
> There is no abiding in the nature [of liberation].

Thus, in order to abide in the nature of great enlightenment, it is taught that the self must be put to an end. Also, though the one who clings to this self and to being a sentient being is not liberated or becoming a buddha, there is an intention behind practicing the path. One should trust what *Pramāṇavārttika* II.192cd says:

> Though there is no one who is liberated,
> Efforts are made in order to overcome wrong superimpositions.

The *Vivṛti* summarizes profundity by saying that mutually exclusive goals are accomplished through attaining inconceivable liberation. JNS comments on this that the manner in which all these eight points are profound is because it is hard to fathom that the goal of enlightenment is accomplished, in a manner of the two realities being mutually exclusive, through attaining the liberation or sphere that is inconceivable for consciousness.

127 CZ, p. 412.

128 See Appendix I4G.

129 JNS (vol. 2, p. 217) says that all phenomena lack a nature because they are dreamlike. They are not conceptualized and observed as some specifically characterized phenomena of existence or peace. Through not observing such, the interdependences of karma, causes, and results are terminated, and thus this means abiding in peace. Commenting on the *Vivṛti*, JNS (vol. 2, pp. 217–18) says that saṃsāra and purified phenomena (antagonistic factors and their remedies) are not established as different entities of their own and have the nature of mere reflections. Thus, they are realized to be equal in just appearing as if they were entities in a dream. Once the familiarity with this realization reaches its culmination, without moving away from this realization, it is permanent as nothing but the nature of the dharmakāya. As *Uttaratantra* I.38cd says:

> Since saṃsāra and nirvāṇa
> Are realized as equality, it is permanent.

Some meditators also assert that this passage here and AA IV.60ab mean the following. By familiarizing, through the power of meditation during the time of the path, with the connateness of saṃsāra and nirvāṇa as being equal and of one taste, this connateness' being of the same nature at the time of the ground results in the attainment of the fruition that is the permanent dharmatākāya.

130 CZ, p. 415.

131 The Tibetan has "answers" (*lan*).

132 CZ, p. 415. As mentioned in Appendix I4G, in CZ the second part of the answer here is included in the question, while the first part of the answer follows later. Commenting on the *Vivṛti*'s answer to the above objection, JNS (vol. 2, pp. 218–20) says that it also applies to realists (such as the śrāvakas) who assert ultimately existing outer objects. For they assert partless material particles and moments of consciousness that perish without needing any causes for their perishing other than their own arising. However, if they perish in this way, there is no time or chance for producing any karma either. These realists may say, "Ultimately, it is like that, but this does not contradict the production of karma in dependence on coarse continua in terms of the seeming because *Abhidharmakośa* IV.1a says:

> The various worlds arise from karma."

However, this equally establishes the position of the Mādhyamikas—ultimately, there is no killer, nobody to be killed, and no killing. Nevertheless, in terms of the seeming, this does not mean that killing is not killing (that is, staying alive) either. In brief, the actual way of being of all seeming phenomena (such as the triad of agent, object, and action, or cause and result) is that they are not established as such phenomena right from the very moment of their appearing. Thus, it is just in terms of how these phenomena appear that the production of entities that are the means to end a life (the opposite of being alive) is presented as "the karma of killing." So, in general, actions with improper mental engagement are presented as unvirtuous actions, while those with proper mental engagement are virtuous. Thus, all such presentations are made in accordance with those who mistake and cling to seeming dreamlike phenomena as being really existent. Moreover, in itself, the dream example is not suitable here because the mind in the dream state is impaired by sleep. Thus, since the power to accumulate karma differs in strength during the waking state and in dreams, also the results of having accumulated such karma are more or less powerful. Nevertheless, according to *Viṃśatikākārikā* 4ab (referring to ejaculating during a sexual dream), there is the accumulation of actions in dreams, so the example of actions not being accumulated in dreams is mistaken. Likewise, the prajñāpāramitā sūtras say here that if one rejoices in whatever virtue or nonvirtue one has committed in one's dreams, the mind of the waking state engages in these actions through clinging to them and reviving them mentally, which leads to a result. JNS concludes with a verse:

> Seeming saṃsāra and nirvāṇa being equal in their being empty
> And ultimate existence and peace being equal in their being permanent bliss—
> These two and their difference being clear in the mind
> Is through the power of being familiar with it from former lives.

133 JNS (vol. 2, pp. 221–23) says that, merely through the training in equality, one is able to manifest the dharmakāya of the relinquishment of the two obscurations. However, without the training in pure realms, one is not able to promote the welfare of others through producing the appearances of the rūpakāyas. Through gradually having purified the worlds of impure mistaken sentient beings, ultimate sentient beings are accomplished in a clearly manifest way. Likewise, the impure environmental world that appears from the perspective of mistakenness is purified. Through the training in accomplishing the pure remainder of this—the previously existent pure realm—in a clearly manifest way, this genuine buddha realm is completely pure of mistaken appearances. This complete purity is illustrated by examples of very marvelous things from the perspective of mistakenness (such as the ground of this realm being of blue beryl), but otherwise the arrays of such pure realms are not suitable to appear in the minds of impure beings. Some say, "During the path of learning, impure environments are worked on to become pure and eventually will become pure on the buddhabhūmi." This is not tenable because it is impossible for something impure to become pure. Also, in the absence of a worldly realm

that is a specifically characterized outer object, there is nothing to be transformed into anything else. Others say, "In fact, there is no such impure worldly realm as an outer object that could be transformed into something pure, but the actual pure realm is being brought forth on the path of learning and then becomes manifest on the buddhabhūmi." This is not tenable either because such a special buddha realm has the nature of being permanent and something permanent cannot be produced through causes and conditions. However, the same flaw does not apply to what was explained above. For though there is no permanent realm to be reestablished, it is made suitable to appear through eliminating the stains that obscure it. "But if it is explained before that it is tenable for something permanent to entail the triad of agent, object, and action, what is wrong with something permanent having been made existent through being accomplished by causes and conditions?" This is not the same because the reasonings in the systems of Madhyamaka and valid cognition say the following. In terms of training on the level of the seeming (such as in pure realms), it is in relation to what is permanent that impermanent is presented. Based on the latter, as mere appearances, it is suitable to function in terms of the triad of agent, object, and action. Karmapa Rangjung Dorje says that line IV.61c primarily identifies sambhogakāya realms and not nirmāṇakāya realms for the following reason. The two trainings here in the equality of saṃsāra and nirvāṇa and in pure realms, respectively, are the means to eliminate the stains that obscure the traces of having meditated—the two ultimate kāyas (dharmakāya and sambhogakāya), which are support and supported, respectively. However, when a nirmāṇakāya like Buddha Śākyamuni teaches on the mother, he does not need to cultivate this training in pure realms. For at that point, based on the totalities and so on, he is able to mature his retinue of disciples whom he had attracted before through blessing it as being a pure environment through his miraculous powers. Commenting on the *Vivṛti*, JNS (vol. 2, pp. 223–24) says that the retinues in pure buddha realms do not suffer from hunger, thirst, and so on, and that the ground is free from stones, thorns, and so on. Thus, the environment is similar to the god realms, but since even that is difficult to exemplify, these buddha realms are merely illustrated by saying that the ground is made of gold and so on. As for the boundary lines of the training in pure realms, according to JNS it exists from the level of heat of the path of preparation up through the end of the tenth bhūmi. For the *Vivṛti* on the culminating training of heat below says that, by virtue of previously having seen beings in the hells and so on, bodhisattvas are mindful of eliminating the unpleasant realms in their own buddha realms. NSML (p. 512) agrees in saying that the purification of realms is taught to exist below the seventh bhūmi, but the actual training discussed here is a special feature of the three pure bhūmis. YT (p. 519) limits it to the eighth bhūmi.

134 CZ, pp. 417–21.

135 The Tibetan of I.62a is *yul dang sbyor ba can 'di ni* (Skt. *viśayo 'sya prayogasya*) which CE takes to mean "entail joining" instead of "training" (as other commentaries do).

136 JNS (vol. 2, p. 224) glosses line IV.62a as "the profound object that is the dharmadhātu (the three knowledges) and the special training in skill in means to manifest it." As for what the nature of "training" and so on in this line is, JNS (p. 225) just says that there are many different positions among the great Indian and Tibetan masters (for the *Vivṛti*, see below). PSD (pp. 339–40) says the following on the object of this training. According to the sūtra in twenty-five thousand lines (see below) and the *Vṛtti* (D3787, fol. 161b.2–3), it is tenfold—the three doors to liberation and the seven sets of the dharmas concordant with enlightenment. According to the large sūtra, the object consists of the nine absorptions of progressive abiding, the ten powers, the eighteen unique buddha qualities, and so on. The subject (the nature of the training) is as follows. Though prajñā familiarizes with all phenomena, out of compassion the fruition of this (one's own welfare) is not manifested and thus bodhisattvas do not dwell in either of the two extremes of saṃsāra and nirvāṇa. The training in skill in means is the one that has the practice of equality, which was explained above, as its object. PBG (p. 580) refers to the ten above objects

as "the objects or trainings of bodhisattvas" and says that the single nature of the training in skill in means is explained as tenfold by way of differing manners of accomplishing these ten.

137 CZ, p. 424.

138 IX.32. The Second Pawo Rinpoche's commentary on the *Bodhicaryāvatāra* (Dpa' bo gtsug lag phreng ba n.d., pp. 675–76) explains this and the following verse (Once this "utter nonexistence"—the entity to be determined—cannot be observed, how should a nonentity without a basis remain before the mind?) as follows. One should familiarize with the discriminating notion that all phenomena are illusionlike. Once one is familiar with this [notion], [phenomena] will not even be observed as mere illusions [but] will be seen as empty aspects. **Through familiarity with the latent tendencies of emptiness, the latent tendencies of entities**—which apprehend all such varieties as the same and different—**will be relinquished.** All phenomena will be seen as nothing at all. You might wonder, "Is this very 'utter nonexistence' the ultimate?" Also this ["utter nonexistence"] is just some kind of discriminating notion, [a step in] a remedial sequence. However, it is not the perfect nature [itself] because it does not even abide as this very "utter nonexistence." Venerable Nāgārjuna [said] in [verse 23 of his] *Lokātītastava*:

> In order to relinquish all imagination,
> You taught the nectar of emptiness.
> However, those who cling to it
> Are blamed by you as well.

Nevertheless, this laxative of seeing nothing at all is applied as the remedy for the disease of apprehending reference points, [which exists] in sentient beings who are in trouble merely because of these reference points. **Utter nonexistence**, such as attaining something or not attaining it, being bound or being released, seeing or not seeing, means seeing [emptiness] as the aspect that is the extinction of all reference points. **Through** becoming increasingly accustomed to and **familiar with** exactly this [notion of utter nonexistence], **this** cognition that apprehends utter nonexistence **will be relinquished later on too.** Through one's seeing all phenomena as illusionlike, the reification that is entailed in the conception of reality is reversed. Then, even **this "utter** and complete **nonexistence"**—the very nonexistence that is **the entity to be determined** [here]—**cannot be observed. Once** [such is the case,] all phenomena do not exist as any entities or nonentities whatsoever, and there is freedom from all flux of discriminating notions, such as [notions] about a basis and something based on it. However, **how should** even this firewoodlike entity—**a** mere **nonentity without a basis—remain before the** immaculate prajñā of true reality that is a **mind** similar to the conflagration at the end of time? Once the firewood is consumed, the fire also subsides on its own. Likewise, also this very mind of immaculate prajñā subsides in this way within the expanse of true reality, which is always at peace in that it is the very nature of primordial nonarising and nonceasing.

139 The Tibetan omits "hordes of."

140 See also Appendix I4H.

141 The Tibetan of line IV.62c has "force" (*shugs*) instead of "hitting" (Skt. *vedham*), so a more literal translation of CE here would be "the force of dedicating virtues to perfect enlightenment . . ."

142 In Tibetan, "aspiration prayer" (Skt. *praṇidhi*) is rendered as "aspiration path" (*smon lam*), and CE splits up this term here.

143 JNS (vol. 2, pp. 224–25) comments by largely following the sūtra in twenty-five thousand lines (CZ, pp. 424–30). (1) The example of a hero who defeats his enemies and then is freed together with his friends and relatives from some wilderness shows that bodhisattvas are skilled in the means to overcome the enemies of existence and peace through prajñā and compassion,

respectively. (2) The example of a bird moving through the sky shows that they are skilled in the means of not abiding and settling in emptiness, though they engage in emptiness. (3) The example of an expert archer shows their skill in the following way. As long as their virtues have not matured into perfect enlightenment, they do not manifest the true end, and once these have matured, they manifest it. Through the force of their being familiar with this skill in means, just as it is, they are skilled in the means to manifest the true end without any difficulties. (4) They train in the true end through prajñā, but the cause for not falling into the extreme of peace at some point on the way is to not forsake sentient beings out of compassion. Furthermore, bodhisattvas are skilled in the means of (5) not being attached to personal identity and the four mistakennesses (regarding what is unclean as clean, what is suffering as happiness, what is impermanent as permanent, and what is without identity as an identity); (6) the two identities not being observed (or, these identities being empty); (7) having terminated characteristics and reference points; (8) having terminated prayers of aspiring for the three realms; (9) demonstrating their acquaintance with emptiness—the sign of the Buddha's prophecy about the unsurpassable enlightenment of these bodhisattvas who are endowed with skill in means; and (10) knowing unlimited knowable objects, such as attainment or nonattainment of signs. As for the boundary lines of this training, mere skill in means exists from the level of heat of the mahāyāna path of preparation onward, but the special training referred to here exists only on the three pure bhūmis. Commenting on the *Vivṛti*, JNS (vol. 2, pp. 230–31) says that (1) through having attained great enlightenment, one has gone beyond any phenomena that are obstacles and cannot be obstructed by the four māras. (2) Through having familiarized with all phenomena being equality in that they are empty, emptiness—the nonabiding of anything—abides because the true mode of being does not abide as anything else. (3) By way of profound means, the vast aspiration prayers to liberate sentient beings are accomplished. Through this, the fruitional welfare of others comes about through having been propelled by the force of the preceding cause of having generated bodhicitta. (4) Through having become greatly familiar, for the sake of others, with all the genuine kinds of conduct that are hard to grasp, bodhisattvas are skilled in the means of infinite ways of conduct that are not in common with śrāvakas and pratyekabuddhas. (5) Though they engage in pure phenomena, they do not cling to any phenomena in terms of the three spheres. (6) Through the door to liberation that is emptiness, nothing whatsoever is observed. (7) Through the door to liberation that is signlessness, there is no seeing of characteristics. (8) Through the door to liberation that is wishlessness, there is nothing to be accomplished, that is, nothing to be aspired for. (9) These bodhisattvas possess the signs of irreversibility since they describe the distinctive features of irreversibility to those who ask them about irreversibility. (10) They are skilled in unlimited knowledge by virtue of knowing all objects of the two realities. Thus, this training in the skill in means is the training in knowing whether the time in terms of the vast welfare of oneself and others arising or not arising is right or not for manifesting these ten kinds of objects of prajñāpāramitā (the subject) as fruitions for the sake of others.

144 *Prajñāpāramitāsaṃcayagāthā* XX.4. The two levels refer to those of śrāvakas and pratyekabuddhas.

145 JNS (vol. 2, p. 233) says that, in order to attain the complete training in all aspects, the progression of determining the three knowledges through study and reflection is taught as what makes one eventually gain mastery over these three knowledges oneself, but this is not a teaching that the culminating training must necessarily be preceded by the entire range of the complete training in all aspects. Thus, the culminating training represents the respective supreme realizations on the respective levels of the paths of preparation, seeing, and familiarization that are the consummations of having familiarized with the aspects of the three knowledges in a combined manner on the corresponding steps of the progression of the complete training in all aspects. Once the complete training in all aspects, through being endowed with profound skill

in means, has reached its respective culminations, it becomes irreversible. In order to facilitate the understanding that such culminating realizations are irreversible, they are explained here by first presenting their signs that occur in dreams and so on, which show that the respective culminating realizations have arisen in those who are endowed with such signs. However, these signs are not repetitions of the signs of irreversibility in the fourth chapter. YT (p. 526) says that the culminating training is explained after the complete training in all aspects because the latter is the cause and the former is its result. BT (p. 582) elaborates that the culminating training of the path of preparation arises from the training in all aspects on the path of accumulation and so on. NSML (p. 516) agrees and explains that, through bodhisattvas on the path of accumulation having familiarized with the 173 aspects of the three knowledges in a combined manner, experiences of the actuality that they familiarize with dawn, which arise primarily from meditation (and not from study and reflection). This is presented as the culminating training of the path of preparation and so on. Thus, it is explained following the complete training in all aspects. The signs of irreversibility taught in the fourth chapter refer to the signs of irreversible learners and nonlearners, while the signs taught in the fifth chapter specifically indicate the signs of the attainments of the respective levels of the culminating training through having cultivated the corresponding preceding levels of the complete training in all aspects. As for matching the culminating training with the prajñāpāramitā sūtras, according to CZ (pp. 431–546), it covers The Exposition of the Forsaking of Discrimination (Chapter Fifty-five) up through The Exposition of the Path-Development (Chapter Sixty-nine).

146 JNS (vol. 2, p. 234) says that (1) those who attain the culminating training of heat in meditative equipoise do not only see phenomena as dreamlike and so on during the waking state of subsequent attainment, but do so even in their dreams. Commenting on the *Vivṛti*, JNS (vol. 2, pp. 235–36) notes on (3) and the following points that, according to the sūtra in eight thousand lines, one dreams of oneself being a tathāgata teaching the four kinds of retinues, while the sūtras in one hundred thousand and twenty-five thousand lines speak of dreaming of other tathāgatas. (7) Through their blessed words, bodhisattvas accomplish the pacification of conflagrations of towns and so on, but are not proud of it. (8) They say, "If I am prophesied to become enlightened, may harm through nonhumans (such as yakṣas), be eliminated." (9) Bodhisattvas rely on spiritual friends by warding off all obstructing conditions through their supernatural knowledge as to whether these conditions obstruct their own liberation or not. (10) They train in eliminating the stains that obscure prajñāpāramitā—the permanent moment of Mahāmudrā, the supreme awareness that is other. Though a moment being permanent is untenable among the Niḥsvabhāvavādin-Mādhyamikas, among the Yogācāra-Mādhyamikas such being tenable is a philosophical system without any flaw. (11) Bodhisattvas do not cling to any phenomena as they appear and are labeled. (12) They are close to buddha enlightenment by virtue of practicing prajñāpāramitā. As for the boundary lines of these twelve signs in terms of whether they refer to the waking state or dreams, there are many differing assertions among Āryavimuktisena, Ratnākaraśānti, Ratnakīrti, the two Buddhaśrījñānas, Dharmakīrtiśrī, and so on.

147 CZ, p. 431 (as mentioned above, from here on CZ follows the sūtra in eighteen thousand lines).

148 CZ, pp. 442ff. JNS (vol. 2, pp. 236–37) adds that the last fourteen examples include their respective virtues being dedicated to buddhahood. These sixteen examples illustrate the increase in merit in those who have already cultivated the wisdom of heat (as illustrated through the twelve signs above) and thus have reached the culminating training of peak. The many examples here show that bodhisattvas who abide in this culminating training, through not being separated from the mental engagement of all phenomena being dreamlike, engage in prajñāpāramitā and teach it to others. This is far more meritorious than the merits in any of the sixteen examples. Commenting on the *Vivṛti*, JNS (vol. 2, pp. 237–39) says that this great increase in merit refers to eight primarily external and eight primarily internal forms of such increase. The first eight

are (1) being superior to the merit of worshipping as many buddhas as there are sentient beings in Jambudvīpa up through a trichiliocosm; in particular, (2) the one-pointed mental engagement of the culminating training of peak in the words and the meaning of prajñāpāramitā throughout day and night; (3) the attainment of the poised readiness of having gained certainty about the dharma of nonarising (and thus being free from doubts about it); (4) the nonobservation of the nature to be realized (Mahāmudrā) and what causes its realization (the dharmas that eliminate the seeming adventitious stains) because enlightenment has the nature of not being suitable to be observed as an object of (ordinary) mental states and because it is only from the perspective of being under the sway of ignorance that the seeming dharmas that cause enlightenment appear as if there are factors to be relinquished and remedies (or factors that cause enlightenment), but they are not focal objects that are real referents; (5) being superior to having attained the ten virtues, the dhyānas, and the formless absorptions; (6) all kinds of gods approaching those who have attained the culminating training and thus being taught the dharma by the latter; (7) all māras who obstruct becoming a buddha being outshone and thus not finding a chance for harm; (8) just like the Buddha, having a mind full of respect for all who have entered the mahāyāna. For these signs teach the results that arise from the causes that are the mahāyāna motivation and application of this motivation—if one has confidence in the results, it is reasonable to have confidence in their causes too. The eight kinds of the primarily internal increase in merit are (9) the training of those who attained this culminating training being pure of obstacles by virtue of being skilled in the means to promote the welfare of oneself and others in all respects; (10) their joy of knowing that they will soon become someone who has the nature of a buddha; (11) the virtues that are the complete accumulation of the causes for attaining the fruition of buddhahood; (12) due to the bodhisattva vows, the virtues of not giving rise to any states of mind (such as miserliness) that are antagonistic to the pāramitās; (13) the virtues of the accumulation of wisdom—not giving rise to any thoughts that mere appearances have characteristics (such as form); (14) knowing the prajñā of peak to be the yoga in which all pāramitās are combined; (15) attaining all the excellent types of realization of the three yānas; and (16) this culminating training of peak soon being close to completely perfect enlightenment free from all stains. As for the manner in which merit increases within these sixteen, it is said that, compared with the former, each of the latter are more distinguished roots of virtue. Some say that all sixteen are equal in being increases of the roots of virtue but that there is a difference in the degrees of such increase. However, this is a self-styled explanation. The first eight and the latter eight are called "external" and "internal," respectively, because the manner of accumulating roots of virtue in dependence on the mind streams of others is predominant in the first, while the latter refer to accumulating virtue in dependence on one's own mind stream.

149 JNS (vol. 2, p. 240) explains that the characteristics of the culminating training of poised readiness are, during subsequent attainment, to make dedications and not abandon the welfare of sentient beings. Through the dharmas of the three omnisciences (the qualities of the generation of bodhicitta and so on), the unsurpassable perfect realization on the bhūmi of a perfect buddha is taught. The abiding in nothing but the welfare of others means to never abandon the welfare of sentient beings—the means to eliminate the adventitious stains. These two are described as stability. What is explicitly stated here is the mere virtue that is defined by the three knowledges, but the meaning to be understood by this is that the virtues of the perfection of all eight clear realizations are dedicated to enlightenment. Commenting on the *Vivṛti*, JNS (vol. 2, p. 241) says that, through the power of being endowed with the skill in the perfect means to accomplish the welfare of others, even during the phase of nonconceptual realization in meditative equipoise and without needing to rise into subsequent attainment in order to dispel the suffering of others, the welfare of others is accomplished through the force of this culminating training that has the characteristic of not abandoning the welfare of others by virtue of its nature of manifesting great compassion. To dedicate all the individual dharmas of the three knowledges to unsurpassable enlightenment is definite stability in terms of enlightenment. For

through dedicating any roots of virtue to enlightenment by focusing on the welfare of others, there is no doubt about these virtues possibly being unstable with regard to eventually turning into enlightenment.

150 CZ, p. 458.

151 JNS (vol. 2, pp. 241–43) says that the culminating training of the supreme dharma is referred to as "complete settling of the mind" because it represents the samādhi of the mind completely settling in the threefold lack of arising (of the three knowledges) and the vast virtues of rejoicing that are induced through that samādhi. Due to not being able to measure the abundance of merit (such as rejoicing in roots of virtue) during this culminating training, its samādhi is said to have increased in merit to an extent that is beyond measure. The statement in the sūtras that rejoicing in roots of virtue is immeasurable virtue and the statement in the AA that cultivating samādhi is immeasurable merit are not contradictory. Through the attainment of the culminating training that consists of the samādhi of the supreme dharma, merit increases by way of the mind completely settling by virtue of the immeasurable accumulation of wisdom. This is the meaning of the mind completely settling in the perfection of the immeasurable accumulation of merit, such as rejoicing. Moreover, the following about the four levels of the culminating training of the path of preparation is to be understood. The sūtras and the AA do not say that "signs," "increase," "stability," and "mind completely settling" are the fully perfect nature of the factors conducive to penetration. Also, in the sūtras, it looks as if this culminating training of the path of preparation is presented from the perspective of subsequent attainment. However, the actual meaning of this needs to be explained as referring to the culminating training that is attained by way of the special powers right within the meditative equipoises with regard to each individual aspect of certainty. The function of the culminating training of the path of preparation is to suppress any of the four sets of conceptions that are the factors to be relinquished through seeing and familiarization. Commenting on the *Vivṛti*, JNS (vol. 2, pp. 243–44) says that measurable things (such as a four-continent world) can be measured. However, the extent of the two accumulations of merit and wisdom that characterize the samādhi of the supreme dharma, in which the nature of everything (such as the six pāramitās) is made a living experience, cannot be measured.

152 CZ, p. 459.

153 The Sanskrit of V.5–7 always has the dual case for "conceptions." This is absent in the Tibetan of V.5, but CE on this verse adds "two."

154 JNS (vol. 2, p. 245) says that the two sets of conceptions about the apprehended refer to engaging in certain objects by way of seeing them as something to be accomplished or to be affirmed and withdrawing from certain objects by way of the notion that they are something to be stopped or to be negated. The character of these conceptions is that their objects are not as they seem to be, that is, existing as having a nature of their own. In this context, the sūtras explicitly teach the remedies of these conceptions and thus implicitly indicate the factors to be relinquished, while the AA explains them in the opposite manner (JNS's comments on the *Vivṛti* on both the conceptions about the apprehended and the apprehender are found at the beginning of Appendix I5A).

155 CZ, p. 460 (against the sūtras, JNS, and so on, CE has "form" instead of "space").

156 Both CE and JNS comment on lines V.7ab in a somewhat different way (due to shifting the referent of "like that" in V.7a and reading *gang gis* instead of *gang gi* in V.7c) than most other commentaries, which all say that there is no apprehender without something apprehended. Both the *Ālokā* (D3791, fols. 289b.7–290a.2) and the *Vivṛti* (D3793, fol. 122a.5–6) say that when the entities that are the objects (or apprehended referents) of these two conceptions about the apprehender do not exist like that—that is, as actually having the nature of something

apprehended—these two conceptions cannot be said to be the apprehenders of anything whatsoever either. Thus, their nature is to be devoid of being apprehenders, which means that only mistaken appearances appear to them, but not the actual true object as it is (JNS's comments on the *Vivṛti* basically follow this; see Appendix I5A). BT (p. 593) says that since it is not tenable to assert these two conceptions about the apprehender to be apprehenders that engage the actual nature of any objects, they are conceptions of apprehending in a wrong way because they are mistaken consciousnesses whose apprehended referents do not exist in suchness.

157 JNS (vol. 2, p. 247) explains that, divided by the psychophysical supports of ordinary beings and noble ones, the conceptions that sentient beings exist substantially are asserted as the conceptions of ordinary beings about the apprehender and the conceptions that persons exist merely imputedly are asserted as the conceptions of noble ones about the apprehender. However, if apprehended referents—entities that are (outer) referents and entities that are objects of conceptions—do not exist, any substantial or imputed nature of them likewise does not exist. Therefore, can these two—substantial and imputed entities—be asserted as being apprehenders through anything? To assert such is not reasonable. Just as apprehended referents do not exist, these two are devoid of any nature of an apprehender. Therefore, they are nothing other than having the characteristic of emptiness (for more details on the four conceptions, see Appendices I1D in Volume One and I5A).

158 CZ, p. 463.

159 JNS (vol. 2, p. 256) comments that these nine conceptions are based on the purified phenomena of bodhisattvas, that is, the factors of engaging in (1) the basic nature, whose nature is devoid of any imputations; (3) perfect accomplishment of the path through purifying the basic element—the disposition of uncontaminated wisdom; (6) the bodhisattva's own realization of the three knowledges; (7) having realized these, bodhisattvas are the agents of distancing any mental engagement in their own welfare; (8) the function of the knowledge of the path—the welfare of sentient beings. Commenting on the *Vivṛti*, JNS (vol. 2, pp. 256–57) identifies the nine objects of clinging here as (1) the nature of not realizing what is void (enlightenment or the reality of cessation as the fruition) through what is void (the reality of the path as the cause). Here, the *Vṛtti* speaks of "not realizing" because, through not observing which results are to be attained by which causes and so on, bodhisattvas are free from anything to be realized and anything that realizes. (2) Through those with supreme fortune entering the three pure bhūmis, their disposition for buddhahood is certain. (3) Through realizing that all seeming phenomena are illusionlike (not existing through a nature of their own), the aims of the paths of seeing and familiarization, which accord with true reality, are accomplished. (4) Unmistakenness is the certainty that the appearing objects of consciousness are delusive appearances because the focal objects of the seeming are nothing but reflections, that is, nonexistents that appear. (5) Preceded by seeing the qualities and flaws in relation to true reality, bodhisattvas reject the antagonistic factors and adopt the remedies. (6) By virtue of being free from all stains that obscure the nature of phenomena, they realize this nature by themselves. (7) They are the agents of keeping away and going far beyond the two levels of śrāvakas and pratyekabuddhas since these are inferior yānas and deficient states. (8) They perform the activity of promoting the welfare of sentient beings through accomplishing the wishes of those to be guided accordingly. (9) Through the power of being skilled in the correct means that lead to liberation, they connect all beings with the fruition of establishing them in the nonabiding nirvāṇa. The nature of these nine conceptions about the apprehended is the clinging mind of thinking that flawless bodhisattvas should engage in these objects by conceiving them as what is to be adopted. These conceptions are held to be relinquished through training in the remedial path of seeing. In accordance with the sūtras, PSD (pp. 353ff.) lists a specific remedy for each one among the four sets of nine conceptions about apprehender and apprehended in the context of the path of seeing.

160 CZ, p. 467.

161 Both the Sanskrit *pṛṣṭhato gamana* and the Tibetan *rjes 'gro* can mean "(actively) pursuing" or "following after."

162 According to JNS (vol. 2, pp. 258–59), the nine inferior objects from which bodhisattvas withdraw are (1) the inferior realization of the path of the śrāvakas since this path lacks skill in means and falls into the extremes of either existence or peace; (2) the inferior mentoring of not being led to the bhūmis of the mahāyāna; (3) inferior paths since the aspects that are the constituents of the path to accomplish buddhahood are incomplete; (4) beings with inferior faculties since those who have attained the fruition of the śrāvakas, when progressing to the knowledge of all aspects, have to progress by virtue of the condition of another yāna—the one of prajñāpāramitā; (5) inferiority of the means for omniscience since śrāvakas turn away from the aim that is the knowledge of all aspects; (6) limited inferior relinquishment since śrāvakas relinquish only personal identity; (7) inferior wisdom by virtue of focusing on a variety of apprehending characteristics; (8) inferior welfare of others since śrāvakas are ignorant about abiding in the knowledge of all aspects and about introducing others to abide in it; and (9) despite having attained the fruition of śrāvakas, they progress to the buddhabhūmi by again subsequently following prajñāpāramitā and the five other pāramitās. Through these nine conceptions, bodhisattvas withdraw from the purified phenomena of the hīnayāna, thus giving rise to weariness of the levels of śrāvakas and pratyekabuddhas (here, JNS plays on the Tibetan *yid las 'byung ba*—"arising from mind"—rendering it as *las yid 'byung ba*—"weariness of"). Commenting on the *Vivṛti*, JNS (vol. 2, pp. 259–60) says that these nine conceptions are about (2) lacking a mahāyāna spiritual friend who is skilled in means; (3) the remedies for all cognitive obscurations being incomplete on the śrāvaka path and it thus not being the path to accomplish perfect buddhahood; (4) proceeding to the enlightenments of the inferior paths by virtue of the conditions that are other masters (buddhas and spiritual friends); (6) the śrāvaka path being a limited remedy for only the afflictive obscurations; (7) by virtue of the śrāvakas focusing merely on the sixteen aspects of the four realities, the realization in terms of their first fruition (stream-enterer) differing from mahāyāna stream-enterers; (8) by virtue of not having relinquished all latencies of ignorance, śrāvakas do not know how to abide in the dharmatākāya and then to display the rūpakāyas as appearing within the sphere of those to be guided; and (9) when śrāvaka arhats, subsequent to having manifested their specific nirvāṇa, engage in the knowledge of all aspects through the entire mahāyāna path that incorporates the realizations of the śrāvakas in the knowledge of all aspects, they all must practice the means to newly pursue the buddhabhūmi. The nature of these nine conceptions about the apprehended is to think that bodhisattvas should withdraw from these objects (which are based on the mind streams of śrāvakas) by conceiving them as what is to be discarded. These conceptions, which arise in the mind streams of śrāvakas and pratyekabuddhas as their factors to be adopted, are held to be relinquished through the primary minds and mental factors that serve as the remedial wisdom of the path of seeing of bodhisattvas.

163 CZ, p. 470.

164 JNS (vol. 2, p. 261) explains that these nine conceptions of apprehending the minds and mental factors of persons by clinging to them as substantially existent consist of clinging to (1) seizing phenomena as qualities and discarding them by conceiving of them as flaws; (2) mental engagement—the cause for adopting and rejecting; (3) adhering to the phenomena in which one mentally engages and the three realms of sentient beings; (4) abiding in real substances; (5) clinging to these as substantial entities; (9) clinging to one's proceeding to the buddhabhūmi, just as one wishes, being impaired through the power of apprehending substantial existence in these ways. Commenting on the *Vivṛti*, JNS (vol. 2, pp. 261–62) says that (1) bodhisattvas here seize seeming illusionlike phenomena through taking them to be real substances. (2) All phenomena, which do not exist as real substances, cannot actually be mentally engaged, but they mentally engage in them as such real substances. (3) Through the nature of there being mental

engagement in characteristics, they are attached by adhering to the three realms. (4) Through not abiding in emptiness, they abide in clinging to characteristics. (5) By virtue of not clinging to entities, they cling to all phenomena as real [NSML (p. 538) has "as lacking reality"]. (6) Since all phenomena do not exist substantially, they are mere imputations, but here, bodhisattvas conceive of the opposite. (7) Through knowing true reality, they are not attached to any phenomena and thus do not cling, but that is subsequently followed by developing the opposite—conceptions of attachment. (8) Through the very remedy of familiarizing with all antagonistic factors of the path as being emptiness and equality, bodhisattvas cling to the remedy as being a substantially existent entity. (9) Through not correctly understanding the actuality of prajñāpāramitā, bodhisattvas are separated from it and thus think that they are prevented from proceeding to buddhahood as they wish. By virtue of clinging to appearances that are empty of a nature of their own (or naturally empty) as ultimate entities, the nine conceptions about the apprehender are held to be factors to be relinquished through seeing.

165 CZ, p. 474.

166 JNS (vol. 2, p. 263) speaks about (1) śrāvakas not being finally delivered in accordance with proceeding to the aim that is the perfect buddhabhūmi and therefore focusing on the enlightenment of the hīnayāna; (2) identifying the mahāyāna path as not being the supreme path; (3) focusing on causes ceasing and results arising; (5) abiding in form and so on as imputed appearances; the absence of (7) striving to accomplish the path and (8) the cause that is the knowledge of the path; and (9) observing opposing forces, such as māras, as entities. Commenting on the *Vivṛti*, JNS (vol. 2, pp. 263–64) says that these nine are conceptions about the following. (1) Śrāvakas and pratyekabuddhas, through being delivered all by themselves, are not finally delivered according to the aim of the mahāyāna. (2) Since the śrāvakas' being content with just the path that they themselves desire is not explained as the mother, other paths are not the path of the mahāyāna. (3) Causes and results, respectively, are what arise and cease as the nature of the seeming. (4) By virtue of the appearance of being uninterrupted and interrupted, respectively, all entities are conceived as being joined, at their own time, with a continuum or not being joined with a continuum. (5) Just as a bird staying in the sky does not rely on any obstructive support, but stays there based on its own prowess, form and so on do not abide as real substances, but only as mere imputations. (6) Through generating bodhicitta and so on and thus progressing to great enlightenment, the dispositions of śrāvakas and pratyekabuddhas are destroyed, it thus being certain that their states are not manifested. (7) Since there is no dharma that is more distinguished than the suchness to be realized by oneself, there is no wish for great enlightenment. (8) In terms of ultimate reality, there are no causes—minute particles and states of consciousness. (9) By virtue of one's nature of being very much familiar with the antagonistic factors of the six pāramitās (such as avarice), opposing entities (such as māras) are observed. The nature of these nine conceptions about the apprehender is to cling to imputed entities and they are also factors to be relinquished through the remedial minds and mental factors of the path of seeing. As for the remedies for these four sets of conceptions, see the end of Appendix I5A. STT (pp. 136–37) explains the four conceptions about apprehender and apprehended to be relinquished through seeing as (a) clinging to the real existence of what appear as various kinds of apprehender and apprehended (such as saṃsāra and nirvāṇa, or what is to be adopted and to be rejected); (b) clinging to the absolutely real existence of the consciousness that clings to saṃsāra and nirvāṇa as being different and appears as various kinds of appearances; (c) clinging to the absolutely real existence of a personal self as being permanent, single, independent, clean, and so on; and (d) clinging to the absolutely real existence of phenomenal identities—mere imputed individuals being impermanent and such.

167 CZ, p. 477.

168 JNS (vol. 2, pp. 266–67) says that (1) it is certain that bodhisattvas who immerse themselves in prajñāpāramitā will attain unsurpassable enlightenment. Therefore, as exemplified in

the life stories of teachers from the past, other beings to be guided who are to be established in genuine enlightenment are prophesied to become buddhas, such as the present Buddha prophesying that certain six thousand monks who had immersed themselves in prajñāpāramitā will awaken to unsurpassable enlightenment and appear in the world as the tathāgatas who are all called Avakīrṇakusuma in the starlike eon. [This prophecy is related in the sūtras in eighteen thousand and eight thousand lines (CZ, p. 482; Conze 1973, p. 265).] (2) Therefore, those who wish for enlightenment must train in prajñāpāramitā. Since such training in turn depends on the unmistaken study of the words and the meaning of prajñāpāramitā, which are the causes that make one attain this enlightenment, they were entrusted to Ānanda by the Buddha, saying, "Take care of them without letting them get lost and assimilate them fully. Then teach them to others and spread them far and wide." (3) The familiarization with prajñāpāramitā by bodhisattvas who dwell on the level of the supreme dharma and make the words and the meaning that were entrusted in the above manner a living experience is the concordant causal condition for attaining enlightenment in an uninterrupted way and therefore induces the clear realization of the path of seeing. Thus, it has the characteristic of an abundance of immeasurable merit that arises in the mind streams of such bodhisattvas. In brief, as exemplified in life stories from the past, if the followers in the retinue of a teacher are immersed in prajñāpāramitā, they receive the prophecy of definitely becoming enlightened. The cause for this enlightenment (the words and meaning of prajñāpāramitā) is entrusted by the teacher to the mind streams of their followers. Through familiarizing with what has been entrusted to them in this way, they train in manifesting a part of enlightenment—the path of seeing that is taught in this context here. Therefore, the result of this has the nature of greatly increasing merit. Commenting on the *Vivṛti*, JNS (vol. 2, pp. 267–68) says that the first cooperative cause for manifesting enlightenment consists of buddhas and bodhisattvas teaching the cooperative conditions—the paths of seeing and familiarization (the wheel of dharma)—that are the aids for others to manifest this enlightenment, thus establishing them in the enlightenment that has the nature of the path of seeing. In order to implant the second cooperative cause for enlightenment in the mind streams of those to be guided, the words and meaning of prajñāpāramitā are entrusted to them through many means of pointing them out. The third cooperative cause is to be without any battles with antagonistic factors to be relinquished that interrupt the attainment of great enlightenment, which means to familiarize with prajñāpāramitā during meditative equipoise and engage in generosity and such during subsequent attainment. Therefore, this is a practice that has the characteristic of attaining the great abundance of the merit of fruitional enlightenment. Here, some assert that there is an appropriating or substantial cause of great enlightenment and present it as the mental continuum of becoming familiar with the appropriating mind being empty of real existence. This does not accord with the intention of any among all buddhas and bodhisattvas because the mental continuum of becoming familiar with mind being empty of real existence is an adventitious stain. Therefore, it is impossible for it to function as the appropriating or substantial cause of great enlightenment. In general, appropriating or substantial causes are presented as impermanent conditioned phenomena, while permanent and unconditioned great enlightenment does not have any appropriating or substantial cause. For it is free from any reference points, such as what is appropriated, what appropriates it, and how it is appropriated. However, in the manner of pointing out that the delusive stains that obscure great enlightenment are delusive, cooperative conditions function as the conditions for enlightenment becoming clearly manifest.

169 CZ, p. 480.

170 JNS (vol. 2, p. 271) explains that the wisdom of Mahāmudrā, in which the stains are terminated primordially and which does not arise as anything conditioned from the very start, is called and taught as "the nature of enlightenment." For there is no sudden termination of previously existing stains, nor is it the case that a previously existing arising, through suddenly being obstructed, has become the lack of arising. In due order, these two should be understood

as the wisdom of the termination of stains and the wisdom of nonarising. Commenting on the *Vivṛti*, JNS (vol. 2, pp. 271 and 278–79) says that realists think, "The stains of afflictive and cognitive obscurations, which have really arisen before, are rendered nonarisen later through the remedies." This is not justified because the Bhagavān Maitreya says in *Madhyāntavibhāga* V.19ab:

> Except for the dharmadhātu,
> There are thus no phenomena. [This quote appears in the *Vivṛti* (D3793, fol. 124a.6).]

Thus, the unfathomable nature of the dharmadhātu, which is unarisen and unceasing by virtue of being unconditioned like space, exists. Therefore, except for it, there is no phenomenon in any respect. Since there are no phenomena, any phenomena such as stains are established to be primordially nonexistent. Here, Haribhadra gives a trustworthy scripture as his reason to refute the above position of realists. Next, he teaches that there are also reasonings for this that operate through the power of entities. These consist of the reasoning of being free from a nature of unity and multiplicity (the negation through analyzing the nature of what is at hand); the vajra sliver reasoning (the negation through analyzing causes); the reasoning that negates an arising of existents and nonexistents (the negation through analyzing results); the reasoning that negates arising from the four possibilities (the negation through analyzing both causes and results); and the reasoning of dependent origination (analyzing mere appearances; for more details on these five reasonings, see Appendix I5C and Brunnhölzl 2004, pp. 231–62). If it is eliminated through the valid cognitions induced through these reasonings that the stains exist as entities which are justified as being established through a nature of their own, one realizes that they are nonexistent. Thus, just like a sky lotus, enlightenment is without any cessation of something previously existent and without any later arising. Consequently, according to such examples, the knowledge of termination means that the termination of stains is known as termination because they never existed in the first place. The knowledge of nonarising means that the unarisen buddha heart—Mahāmudrā—is known as unarisen. Hence, it is stated that great enlightenment has the character of the actual nature of the ultimate three kāyas, such as the dharmakāya, whose characteristic is the personally experienced wisdom of realizing the basic nature of all phenomena in an unmistaken way. See also Appendix I5B.

171 CZ, p. 488.

172 Commenting on the *Vivṛti*, JNS (p. 279) explains that Buddhist tīrthikas—realists—think, "Enlightenment refers to the knowledge that previously existing stains have been terminated and do not arise later. Therefore, the knowledge of termination means that the entities of adventitious stains are terminated through the mental states of destroying them through their remedies, and the knowledge of nonarising means that the entities that are these stains do not arise again by virtue of the mental states that discontinue their arising."

173 The Tibetan of the last two lines reads, "What type of conceptions could be terminated and what kind of nonarising could be attained?" (*rnam par rtog rigs ci zhig zad/ skye med rnam pa ci zhig 'thob*).

174 A more literal rendering of CE up to here (in accord with the Tibetan of V.19cd), which is not formulated as a question, would be " . . . any type of conceptions—the factors to be relinquished—has not been terminated and any kind of nonarising has not been caused to be attained newly because . . ."

175 I.51cd. Here, JNS (p. 281) also quotes *Uttaratantra* I.15cd: ". . . Is due to the natural complete purity [of the mind] and due to the primordial termination of the afflictions."

176 XV.8cd. Note that verses V.19–21 are without direct correspondences in the sūtras, but are supplementary topics introduced by the AA and elaborated in its commentaries. JNS (vol. 2, pp. 280 and 282) explains on V.19–20 that there is no need to again cease any adventitious stains

in great unconditioned enlightenment, in which these adventitious stains have never existed in the first place. Therefore, through the capacity of this pure nature nature without cessation (the path called "seeing"), what type of previously existing conceptions could have been terminated and which previously nonexisting kinds of wisdom realizing nonarising could be attained? No such conceptions have been terminated and there is no such wisdom to be attained. The gist of this is as follows. Some opponents may say, "In this case, it follows that enlightenment—purification and realization—is not justified because there is no termination of what is to be purified (previously existing real stains) and no new arising of what is to be realized (the knowledge of nonarising)." It is sufficient to answer this by saying either that the entailment is not certain or that the entailment is contradictory. As for the first option, great enlightenment does not have to be an enlightenment by way of previously existent stains having been terminated and the wisdom of nonarising arising later because it is primordial changelessness—the wisdom free from the extremes of the reference points of arising and ceasing—which is just like emptiness. As for the second answer, since it is impossible for really existing stains to become terminated, they are not suitable to be purified anyway. Since it is impossible for what is nonarising and unconditioned to arise newly, it is not suitable as being a newly arisen enlightenment. Therefore, the enlightenment as asserted by realists above is not tenable. In brief, the result of freedom of the path of seeing, which has the nature of enlightenment, neither terminates previously existent stains nor produces a later arising of the wisdom of nonarising because its nature is emptiness free from arising and ceasing. For śrāvakas, this reason is a reason that proves a fact, but in the mahāyāna, it is just a correct reason that proves a convention. Thus, its subject property is established through valid cognition and its entailment is too because something unconditioned free from arising and ceasing does not perform the activities of producing any results in terms of termination and attainment. Whoever accepts this has the good fortune of siding with the Madhyamaka that is my position. As for what Maitreya considers amazing, it is the following statement that contradicts reasoning. The phenomena that are other—adventitious stains—are said to exist primordially as something unsuitable to be relinquished, just as the nature of enlightenment. At the same time, this Bhagavān, who teaches what is to be adopted and to be rejected with respect to knowable objects, is supposed to have, through the path, suddenly terminated these primordially existent obscurations. The reason for this being amazing is that a postulated existent nature of entities cannot be transformed into something nonexistent, nor can the nonexistence of a nature of entities be transformed through anything whatsoever into existing. Commenting on the *Vivṛti*, JNS (vol. 2, pp. 281–82 and 302–3) says that the ultimate nature of suchness is free from any termination of what has arisen (the stains) and any recessation of these stains that obstruct the arising of what is unarisen (the nature of phenomena). Therefore, according to the realists who mistakenly cling to entities that are mere appearances as being real, through the power of the arising of the path of seeing what stains that have arisen and exist as the nature of conceptions and so on could be terminated? It follows that none of them can be terminated because they exist by a nature of their own. And what unarisen nonarising could possibly arise? Since it does not arise in the first place, such claims by realists just invalidate their own position. Since there are no such inconsistencies in our Madhyamaka scriptural tradition, it just seems reasonable that these realists accept it too. As for the explicit teaching of AA V.20, realists cling to the stains as being real permanent entities, which are as unchanging as space. This means that any arising of remedies and any relinquishment of factors to be relinquished are impossible. If they assert that the remedy here on the path of seeing has the nature of being just its momentary dharma cognition, while the factors to be relinquished (cognitive obscurations) exist ultimately, then, even through cultivating this remedy, the factors to be relinquished cannot be ceased. Just as when one meditates on space being nonexistent, said remedy cannot invalidate such supposedly ultimately existent factors to be relinquished even in the slightest. Thus, in the systems of realists, it is simply not tenable for the stains to ever be relinquished because they have not put an end to mistakenly clinging to real entities, which is the opposite of how things actually are. Consequently, Maitreya considers it amazing to hold the mutually exclusive positions that buddhas relinquish all cognitive obscurations, while the stains to be relinquished really exist. In this context, the *Vivṛti*'s above example of space as a permanent substance refers to the position of the śrāvakas, but not to what the mahāyāna understands as space. In brief, the Mādhyamikas assert that, let alone speaking about any real and permanent kind of factors to be relinquished, these factors have never existed in the first place. In order to prove that, first they prove that consciousness (which has the nature of adventitious stains) is impermanent, and that what is impermanent is established as empty. As verses 53–54 of Nāgārjuna's *Bodhicittavivaraṇa* say:

> For whom consciousness is momentary
> It is not permanent.
> If mind is impermanent,
> How could that be contradictory to emptiness?
>
> In brief, if the buddhas
> Hold mind to be impermanent,
> Why should they not hold
> Mind to be empty?

Accordingly, the manner of being impermanent here is not to be impermanent after having arisen, but to be impermanent by virtue of this very arising because arising per se is not established if it is not impermanent. You may think, "But if the stains to be relinquished were impermanent and empty in the sense of not existing at their own time, they would not be overcome through any remedy that is other than them either, and even if they were overcome, it would be unnecessary." When analyzed, momentary factors to be relinquished are not overcome through remedies because they have already ceased, once they come into existence. Nevertheless, the stains to be relinquished consist of the continuum of stains that arose by virtue of the condition of mistakenness, and it is this continuum that needs to be overcome through the remedies preventing the arising of this condition of mistakenness. If this continuum of mistakenness is not overcome, suffering is experienced by taking what is identityless to be an identity. For details on what is implicitly taught by AA V.20—the four stages of yoga—see Appendix I5D.

177 For the various sources of this verse, see Appendix I5D2d.

178 I.13a.

179 XXVIII.7 (D13, fol. 16b.2–3; Conze 1973, p. 67); CE quotes only lines b and half of c.

180 X.256–257 (D107; ACIP MDO SDE CA@270a.2–3). The translation corresponds to the Sanskrit and the Tibetan in the *Kangyur*, while CE only quotes X.256–257ab with some corruptions (the actual line 256c appears as 257a, while 256c in CE reads *snang ba med pa la brten nas*). For JNS's rather uncommon explanation of X.257 and general remarks on that verse's last line, see Appendix I5D2db. As for JNS own commentary on AA V.21 (vol. 2, pp. 304–10), which centers on nondual wisdom, it is found in Appendix I1G6 in Volume One. Commenting on the *Vivṛti*, JNS (pp. 304 and 310–11) starts by saying that V.21 ascertains the position of the "lack of nature," which is the system of Madhyamaka. Only this is what is to be accepted by those who wish for liberation. Next, referring back to its comments on the *Vivṛti* on the fourth stage of yoga (see Appendix I5D), JNS first has someone ask why it is not tenable for the nondual wisdom whose nature is dependent origination to exist. If it existed in the manner of being established as an entity through a nature of its own, it is not tenable to become liberated from clinging to it as being such an entity. Therefore, without removing anything from phenomena (mere appearances) by denying that they exist in accordance with dependent origination, or adding anything to them by superimposing that they exist as being established through a nature of their own, all these merely appearing phenomena have the conventional

nature of existing on the level of seeming reality as correct common worldly consensus that only satisfies as long it is unexamined. This is to be examined as having the actual nature of being without any nature, nonarising, primordial voidness, and so on. "But when examined in this way, if all phenomena had the illusionlike nature of mere dependent origination empty of any nature, the presentations of factors to be relinquished and their remedies would be untenable." They are not untenable—just as an illusory elephant may defeat another illusory elephant, through producing dependently originating remedies that are empty of a nature of their own, dependently originating factors to be relinquished that are empty of a nature of their own are put to an end. Once true reality is seen by virtue of that, one will be liberated from bondage. Ratnākaraśānti's *Sārottamā* (D3803, fols. 183b.7–184a.1) comments that there is nothing to be removed because neither persons nor phenomena exist. Nor is there anything to be added because personal and phenomenal identitylessness are without beginning and end. However, these two kinds of identitylessness are to be seen as actual reality as it really is because if the actual reality of personal identitylessness is seen, one is liberated from the afflictive obscurations, and, if the actual reality of phenomenal identitylessness is seen, one is liberated from the cognitive obscurations. LN (vol. 2, pp. 280ff.), YT (pp. 570ff.), PSD (p. 368), and NSML (pp. 551–52) all agree on this verse presenting the Madhyamaka view and closely follow the *Vivṛti*'s above explanation of all phenomena being free from complete nonexistence (by virtue of dependent origination) and real existence (by virtue of lacking any nature). As noted in the Introduction, AA V.21 is identical to one of the most essential verses of the *Uttaratantra* (I.154) and, in general, ranks among the most famous and often-cited verses in the literature of the mahāyāna. According to Gampopa's *Ornament of Precious Liberation* (Sgam po pa 1990, p. 289), it originally stems from the *Gaganagañjaparipṛcchāsūtra* (P815). Except for the third line, it is also found in the *Śrīmahābalatantra* (P36, fol. 34a.6–7). To my knowledge, there are at least ten more works in which it appears: Buddhaghoṣa's *Sumaṅgalavisāraṇī* I.12 (in Pāli, attributes the contents to the Buddha); Nāgārjuna's *Pratītyasamutpādahṛdayakārikā* (verse 7) and *Kāyatrayastotranāmasyavivaraṇa* (P2016, fol. 83a.7); Aśvaghoṣa's *Saundarananda* (paraphrase XIII.44) and *Śuklavidarśana* (a summary of the *Śālistambasūtra* that begins with this verse); Sthiramati's *Madhyāntavibhāgaṭīkā* (Pandeya ed., p. 23; P5534, fol. 36a.5); the *Nāmasaṃgītiṭīkā* ad VI.5 (which attributes it to Nāgārjuna); Nāgamitra's *Kāyatrayāvatāramukha* (paraphrase verse 106); the *Bodhisattvabhūmi* (Wogihara ed., p. 48; prose); and the *Mahāyānaśraddhotpāda* (Suzuki's translation, p. 57; prose).

181 As indicated in CE's outline, the path of seeing is presented here in terms of the four remedies (see below and Chart 20 in Volume One), with the supreme dharma of the path of preparation being the first one of these four (the invalidating remedy) and the path of seeing being the second one (the relinquishing remedy).

182 This means that there are specific applications of ethics, patience, vigor, dhyāna, and prajñā with regard to generosity, and the same principle applying to generosity, patience, and so on with regard to ethics and so forth (thus arriving at six sets of five). In this, CE agrees with JNS (see below).

183 Against CE, all other commentaries agree that the culminating training of the path of seeing consists of merely its very first moment—the uninterrupted path that is the poised readiness for the dharma cognition of suffering. JNS (vol. 2, pp. 311–12) adds that Haribhadra lists six sets of six pāramitās here, just as in the context of armorlike practice in AA I.43 (which is followed by most other commentators). However, some Tibetan scholars reject the *Vivṛti*'s explanation here, saying that to explain the same manner of combining the pāramitās in both contexts contradicts the sūtras (in the latter context, the sūtras indeed only speak of the ethics and so on of generosity etc., but not of the generosity of generosity etc.; see CZ, pp. 492ff.). In general, the culminating trainings of the path of seeing, the path of familiarization, and the uninterrupted path must be explained as consisting of four paths each, which are called the

four remedies. In dependence on the phases of (a) still being in the process of eradicating the respective factors to be relinquished on a given path or (b) having already eradicated them, these four are as follows. (1) The invalidating remedy is the path of preparation (focusing on the four realities of the noble ones and invalidating the obscurations in terms of their sixteen aspects). (2) The relinquishing remedy refers to the uninterrupted paths (the actual process of eradicating even the seeds of the respective factors to be relinquished). (3) The sustaining remedy refers to the paths of liberation (experiencing and sustaining the attained freedom from the factors that have been relinquished through the preceding uninterrupted paths). (4) The distancing remedy refers to the special paths (enhancing the realizations that were attained through the preceding paths of liberation). In this way, the first two remedies belong to phase (a) and the last two to phase (b). According to the Seventh Karmapa (Chos grags rgya mtsho 1985, vol. 1, p. 257), the first remedy weakens the factors to be relinquished; the second one eradicates them; the third one manifests liberation; and the fourth one distances the factors to be relinquished. JNS says that, according to the intentions of Āryavimuktisena and Haribhadra, the four remedies in the context of the culminating training of the path of seeing are as follows. (1) arises starting with the supreme dharma of the path of preparation. (2) is explained to be simultaneous with the moment of the readiness for the dharma cognition of suffering (which is the actual culmination of the path of seeing). (3) does not appear clearly in V.22, but the *Vivṛti* explains it as the realization of the sixteenth moment of the path of seeing, which is attained simultaneously with the relinquishment of both the 108 cognitive obscurations and the 108 latencies of the afflictions (which, as explained before, are a part of the factors to be relinquished through seeing). (4) is presented as the meditative equipoise of the lion's sport and its subsequent attainment. Commenting on the *Vivṛti*, JNS (vol. 2, pp. 312–13) says that the nature of the uninterrupted path of the path of seeing here (the dharma readiness of suffering) arises as being characterized by being pure of the three spheres (agent, object, and action) and entailing thirty-six uncontaminated aspects (the six times six pāramitās). This clear realization—the culmination of having familiarized with the aspects of the three knowledges in a combined way (during the training in all aspects)—is the culminating training of the path of seeing in this chapter here. As for its divisions, the 108 cognitive obscurations that are the factors to be relinquished through seeing (the four sets of nine conceptions about apprehender and apprehended multiplied by the three realms) are relinquished through the 108 aspects of the culminating training of the path of seeing (the six sets of six pāramitās times the three realms). Through the force of this, the relinquishment of the 108 afflictive latencies that give rise to afflictive conceptions is included, being attained by virtue of the nature of dependent origination. In this context, Āryavimuktisena and Haribhadra have the intention of not presenting the latencies of the afflictions as afflictive obscurations, though afflictive obscurations are relinquished here. Though the latencies of the afflictions are relinquished, it is not explicitly clear in either of their commentaries that the seeds of the afflictions have been relinquished. Still, some say that the assertion of the seeds having been relinquished here is the intention of Āryavimuktisena and Haribhadra. In brief, the two obscurations here consist of the two sets of 108 afflictive and cognitive conceptions (that is, two times thirty-six in terms of each one of the three realms). The culminating training of the path of seeing that focuses on these two different sets consists of two sets of 108 pāramitās (that is, two times six sets of six in terms of each one of the three realms). Therefore, the numbers of both the factors to be relinquished and their remedies here are certain to be 432.

184 CZ, p. 492.

185 CZ, p. 501. The latter phrase is missing in CZ, which follows the sūtra in eighteen thousand lines. BT (pp. 621–22) says that the examination of dependent origination during the subsequent attainment of the lion's sport is only mentioned in the sūtra in twenty-five thousand lines and its revised edition. For details on the lion's sport, see the general explanation of this samādhi within the context of the culminating training of the path of familiarization (see

Appendix I5F). Commenting on the *Vivṛti*, JNS (vol. 2, pp. 338–39) says that, in order to gain mastery over the wisdom of the path of seeing, one familiarizes with the realization of the path of seeing again and again. There is some slight qualm here in that some commentators include verse V.23 in the set of verses that belong to the culminating training of the path of familiarization, while Haribhadra includes it in the set of verses on the culminating training of the path of seeing. In fact, since both the lion's sport (as the meditative equipoise) and the manner of examining dependent origination (as its subsequent attainment) are not suitable as the path of seeing, they are not included in the culminating training of the path of seeing. However, Haribhadra includes them in the section on the path of seeing because they represent the special path of the path of seeing. You may wonder why this meditative equipoise of the lion's sport is not suitable as the culminating training of the path of seeing. The reason is that all sixteen moments of the path of seeing rely solely on their specific substantial cause, which is the wisdom of the supreme dharma of the path of preparation that in turn relies on any one among the six grounds of dhyāna. However since there is no time during these sixteen moments to shift one's faculties to other levels of samādhi (as is the case with the lion's sport), the lion's sport does not arise from the specific cause that is the wisdom of the supreme dharma. As for the *Vivṛti*'s actual comments, since yogins who have attained the path of seeing are without any fear of afflictive or cognitive obscurations, they absorb themselves in the samādhi with the name "the lion's sport" or "frolic." By virtue of having accomplished the mental support of this supreme samādhi of calm abiding, right upon that, the prajñā of superior insight examines dependent origination in its progressive and reverse orders. The purpose of realizing this lies in the explanation in the great collection of tantras about the accomplishment of the permanent kāya of having reached the state of the twelve bhūmis, which has the nature of the twelvefold actual reality free from obscurations, such as the twelve houses, the twelve links, and the twelve āyatanas.

186 VI.4cd.

187 The above is the first line of a verse that is quoted in Asaṅga's *Ratnagotravibhāgavyākhyā* (J 37.6) and at the beginning of the Third Karmapa's *Pointing Out the Tathāgata Heart*. Jamgön Kongtrul's commentary on the latter (Kong sprul blo 'gros mtha' yas 1990b, p. 133) identifies it as coming from the *Abhidharmasūtra* (I am not aware of any other source that confirms this; the *Abhidharmasūtra* is frequently quoted in Indian and Tibetan texts, but is not preserved in any language). As above, most Tibetan commentators on the verse in question gloss its first line as pertaining to saṃsāra, which makes sense. Note however that the first line in the Sanskrit (*anādibhūto 'pi hi cāvasānikaḥ*) clearly pertains to what is said in the second one (*svabhāvaśuddho dhruvadharmasaṃhitaḥ*). Thus, it indicates that what is beginningless and yet entails an end is that which is naturally pure and consists of permanent dharmas (the dharmadhātu). In terms of the meaning, however, there is no difference since "end" can only mean the end of the adventitious obscurations in relation to the naturally pure and unchanging dharmadhātu.

188 CE says "the latter one," which is emended in accordance with JNS (vol. 2, p. 321), which explicitly identifies the ignorance about the realities as the first link of dependent origination (see Appendix I5E).

189 Skt. *bhava*, Tib. *srid pa*. Both the Sanskrit and the Tibetan can also mean "existence," "being," "state," and so on. Depending on the context, both here and in the discussion of this link in Appendix I5E, any one of these meanings may apply.

190 Lines 2ac. For more details on dependent origination, see Appendix I5E.

191 JNS (vol. 2, pp. 358–60) starts here by remarking that the AA, in the context of the culminating training of the path of seeing, teaches the conceptions to be relinquished first and then their remedies. Here, in the culminating training of the path of familiarization, this order is reversed. Next, JNS criticizes the presentations of a number of other commentators. According to Ratnākaraśānti's *Śuddhamatī*, the preparatory lion's sport here is included in the above lion's

sport in the context of the path of seeing, while the phrase in V.24, "After the twofold progressing through the nine absorptions, including cessation" teaches the lesser and medium crossing in one leap; "returning" indicates the slight exiting of the Peak of Existence; and the remaining lines teach great crossing in one leap. The same author's *Sārottamā* explains that V.24a refers to the great crossing in one leap. Some say, "Haribhadra explains lines V.24ab as the preparatory lion's sport, but that is wrong because he already treated this preparatory lion's sport under the lion's sport (in the context of the path of seeing) above. As for the basis of error here, the *Vṛtti* creates some ground for being mistaken through citing the sūtra passages that pertain to the preparation and the actual crossing in one leap together." Others say, "Verse V.25 teaches the three stages of the actual crossing in one leap, with its lines ab referring to the lesser one; line d, to the medium one; and lines bc, to the great one. Lines V.24cd teach the phenomenon to be alternated with the other meditative absorptions in the great crossing in one leap." JNS's own interpretation is that lines V.24ab represent the preparatory lion's sport in this context of the path of familiarization. As for lesser crossing in one leap, by virtue of Maitreya having in mind that its mode of meditative absorption accords with that of the lion's sport, he did not teach lesser crossing in one leap in the AA, but intended it to be understood implicitly. Medium crossing in one leap is not contained in the AA either, but is explained in the *Vivṛti* in a supplementary way. The mode of great crossing in one leap is that bodhisattvas first assume the intermittent consciousness that belongs to the desire realm and then progressively enter the first, the second, the third, and the fourth dhyānas; then the first, second, third, and fourth formless absorptions; and finally the meditative absorption of cessation. Each one of these nine is alternated in disparate ways with this mind of the desire realm. Here, "disparate ways" means that one skips gradually increasing numbers of these meditative absorptions when entering the respective next one from said mind of the desire realm (according to JNS's general comments, this process of great crossing in one leap is performed in both its progressive and reverse orders.) For more details on the lion's sport and the crossing in one leap in general and JNS's comments on the *Vivṛti* on V.24–25 in particular, see Appendix I5E and Chart 23.

192 CZ, p. 502.

193 The Tibetan has "being abandoned."

194 Note that, in this and the following verses on the four sets of nine conceptions about apprehender and apprehended, there are recurring Sanskrit *bahuvrīhi* compounds ending in *-gocaraḥ* or *-viṣaya*, which are connected to *vikalpaḥ* (conception) or the like, meaning that these conceptions have the respective nine items in the verses as their spheres/objects. However, like CE and JNS, some Tibetan commentators take the typical Tibetan versions of these compounds—*spyod yul can/yul can*—simply to mean "subject" instead of "having as object." As in the above and following passages in CE and JNS, this usually results in differences in meaning.

195 In JNS (vol. 2, pp. 365–66), the Eighth Karmapa says that his own comments on these verses are based on his own analysis, while his comments on the *Vivṛti* directly reflect the intention of Haribhadra. The nine conceptions about the apprehended that are based on mere entities are with regard to (1) the concise explanation of the basic nature—the mother of the victors, the nature of nondual wisdom—as merely that; and (2) the detailed teachings on the general and specific characteristics of all phenomena, whether they operate as this basic nature or not. (3) That the buddhas are acting as protectors is stated here in an ancient terminology—"Those sentient beings who do not train in the mother are not adopted through being abandoned." Since those who do not adopt the buddhas as protectors do not seek refuge in the ultimate refuge, the buddhas are not able to adopt them because these beings do not properly engage, out of confidence in the three jewels, in adopting and rejecting as taught by the three jewels. Without doing so, even if they presume to be adopted by the three jewels, the latter cannot adopt them. Implicitly, if one thinks about the three jewels with confidence, one knows how to correctly adopt them as protectors. These conceptions (1)–(3) are in terms of the path to

be known; (4)–(6), in terms of the qualities of this path; and (7)–(9), in terms of the nature of this path [the last six are as above in CE]. These nine conceptions about the apprehended are the subjects that take the aspects of the training as their spheres or objects. Commenting on the *Vivṛti*, JNS (vol. 2, pp. 366–67) says that (1) and (2) refer to the concise and detailed teachings of the dharma for those who like it concise and detailed, respectively. As for (4)–(6), the wisdoms of the uninterrupted paths of the respective bhūmis lack the qualities of the path of preparation since these have ceased in the past; they lack the qualities of the path of seeing as reference points since—in actual fact—the latter are not endowed with the causes and conditions for the arising of entities; and, at their preceding times, they lack the qualities of the path of familiarization since the latter lie in the future. Here, some say that "lacking qualities" is intended to mean lacking qualities in terms of the seeming, while others say that it is intended to mean lacking qualities ultimately. Some also say that this is an explanation on the opposite of lacking qualities, that is, being endowed with these three qualities. In due order, (7)–(9) refer to the excellent path of preparation, which joins one with the nirvāṇa of the mahāyāna through pacifiying manifest mistakenness; the path of seeing, which makes one a noble bodhisattva through accomplishing emptiness; and the path of familiarization, on which one familiarizes with the lack of nature that has been seen already. The nature of these conceptions is to be the subjective cognitions that, first, take these nine objects as their apprehended objects and then are associated with them as conceptual referent objects. LN (vol. 2, p. 300) explains that these conceptions refer to (1)–(2) the two kinds of dharma that teach general and specific characteristics, respectively; (3) the persons who train or do not not train in the mother; (4)–(6) the qualities of the path of preparation (freedom from afflictions existing on the level of the seeming, but not ultimately), the common qualities of practicing the mother, and the qualities of the path of familiarization; and (7)–(9) the three paths of preparation for, seeing, and familiarizing with emptiness. YT (pp. 585–86) explains that these nine conceptions, in due order, are in terms of three kinds of persons (the first two liking concise or detailed explanations); the qualities of the paths of preparation, seeing, and familiarization existing on the level of the seeming, but not ultimately; and these three paths themselves. Both BT (pp. 625–26) and PBG (p. 595) identify these nine as being the innate conceptions that cling to the actual factors under (1)–(2) and (7)–(9), while clinging to (3)–(6) by way of isolates. As in most commentaries, BT identifies these nine as the aspects or subjects of the preparatory stage of the culminating training of the path of familiarization. PBG adds that they cling to the reality of various factors to be engaged in in terms of the mahāyāna path.

196 CZ, pp. 505–9.

197 CE interprets "the second ones" in V.27c as "dualistic" (*gnyis su*) and—as mentioned above—"have . . . as their objects" as "subject."

198 Skt. *bodhimaṇḍa*, Tib. *byang chub snying po*. This is usually the term for the place under the bodhi tree in Bodhgayā, where all buddhas on this earth are said to attain enlightenment.

199 According to JNS (vol. 2, p. 367), these nine conceptions about the apprehended are based on mere purified phenomena. Commenting on the *Vivṛti*, JNS (vol. 2, pp. 368–69) says that (1) bodhicitta does not arise by virtue of lacking spiritual friends of the mahāyāna and skill in means. (2) One does not not mentally engage in the nature of enlightenment—the sugata heart—because one lacks the distinguished accomplishment of merit that is the path of focusing on the state of perfect buddhahood. (3) By virtue of having the dispositions of śrāvakas and pratyekabuddhas, respectively, one mentally engages in the śrāvakayāna and manifests the pratyekabuddhayāna. (4) By virtue of lacking the practice of prajñāpāramitā (that which produces the knowledge of all aspects), one does not mentally engage in perfect enlightenment (that which is produced by such practice). (5)–(8) Neither familiarizing with the sixteen aspects (such as impermanence) through focusing on the four realities; nor not familiarizing with the aspect of the freedom from reference points through not focusing on suchness on the path of śrāvakas; nor focusing on prajñāpāramitā; nor not focusing on inferior objects to be realized—in

this manner, in due order, there is neither any familiarization with the wisdom free from reference points that is empty of the two identities, nor is it that there is no familiarization with mere personal identitylessness. In brief, (9) through mistakenly clinging to the basic nature, nirvāṇa, and ultimate reality as being established as such, one conceives of what is not in accord with true reality. In brief, this second set of nine conceptions about the apprehended conceives of the principles of the mahāyāna dharma in a manner that is the opposite of the first set of nine. BT (p. 628) takes Āryavimuktisena's comments (D3787, fol. 177a.2–177b.4) to mean that these nine conceptions represent mental factors of śrāvakas and pratyekabuddhas, which are to be engaged by them in a progressive fashion. Therefore, in terms of their objects, he asserts them as the conceptions about the apprehended in terms of engagement. In due order, they refer to (1)–(2) the paths of accumulation of śrāvakas and pratyekabuddhas; (3)–(4) their paths of preparation; (5)–(7) their paths of seeing, familiarization, and nonlearning, respectively; and (8)–(9) the focal objects and aspects of the mere way of thinking of śrāvakas and pratyekabuddhas. However, Haribhadra does not refer to the paths of śrāvakas and pratyekabuddhas, but comments on these nine objects as factors from which bodhisattvas must withdraw as above. Therefore, he says that these conceptions are the conceptions about the apprehended in terms of withdrawal. YT (pp. 589–90) and NSML (pp. 568–70) also say that these nine conceptions refer to the above paths of śrāvakas and pratyekabuddhas, and then say that it is these paths that bodhisattvas consider as the factors from which they must withdraw. PBG (p. 595) agrees with the above matching of the paths of śrāvakas and pratyekabuddhas. It adds that these nine conceptions are the factors to be relinquished that have as their objects the phases of the minds and mental factors of the uncontaminated path of familiarization engaging in the end of its uninterrupted path. LN (pp. 303–4) and YT add that these nine are held to be the subjects of said phase of the path of familiarization because they are the conceptions to be relinquished during this phase (LN glosses the primary mind of the path of familiarization as uncontaminated wisdom and its mental factors as prajñā and so on). LN further comments that the mistakenness in these conceptions lies in focusing on the dharmas of śrāvakas and pratyekabuddhas and seeing them as something to be rejected. However, differing from the above, in due order, the nine pertain to (3)–(6) the paths of preparation, seeing, familiarization, and nonlearning of śrāvakas and pratyekabuddhas; (7)–(8) the opposites of meditating and not meditating; and (9) what is to be eliminated.

200 CZ, p. 510. I could not locate this passage in the sūtras. JNS (vol. 2, p. 368) and other commentaries have what corresponds to CZ, pp. 509–10.

201 JNS (vol. 2, p. 370) says that these nine conceptions about the apprehender refer to mere persons. The first three among them are in terms of knowable objects—(1) reifying through imputing "sentient being" onto what is endowed with discrimination; (2) clinging to all phenomena as entities actually existing in just the way they are imputed; and (3) clinging to their not being emptiness ultimately. The next two conceptions are in terms of the ways in which śrāvakas and bodhisattvas, respectively, engage objects—(4) attachment to focal objects; and (5) the state of mind that has the character of completely discriminating the characteristics of phenomena. The following two conceptions are in terms of deliberate mental convictions—(6) clinging to all phenomena as entities that arise from the mental formation of entities; and (7) clinging to each one of the three yānas as being real. The two conceptions of regressing from the view and conduct, respectively, are (8) clinging to certain beings as being impure objects for offering by virtue of their not having merged with prajñāpāramitā; and (9) disordered conduct of the aspect of means, such as generosity. Commenting on the *Vivṛti*, JNS (vol. 2, p. 371) says that (1) since substantially existent referents that are entities do not arise, also sentient beings are merely imputed in this way. (2) Phenomena do not exist because they are nothing but mere mistaken appearances. Therefore, they are mere imputations. (3) By virtue of proceeding to the level of perfect buddhahood in all respects through the causes for buddhahood (phenomena such as the knowledge of all aspects, the knowledge of the path, and the knowledge of entities),

these causes are conventionally not empty. (4) By virtue of not having relinquished clinging to objects in all respects, there is attachment to all phenomena in the manner of clinging to them as being such phenomena. (5) Through realizing the lack of nature, the basic nature of phenomena is completely discriminated as to whether it exists or not. (6) One deliberately forms the entities of śrāvakas and pratyekabuddhas by virtue of not forming the aim of the three greatnesses. (7) Because of not focusing on form and so on, those of dull faculties gain final deliverance by virtue of the paths of the three yānas. (8) Because of incorrect engagement due to not having seen reality, or not engaging in the mahāyāna, one clings to objects for generosity as being impure objects for offerings. (9) Due to lacking the kind of focusing that is pure of the three spheres, one practices by focusing on the giver, the recipient, and generosity. Through this, one's conduct—the nature of phenomena—becomes disordered, and one wrongly aspires for stages of conduct other than the nature of phenomena. Differing from CE and in accord with almost all other Tibetan commentaries, JNS concludes by saying that, just like the first nine conceptions about the apprehender to be relinquished on the path of seeing, these nine here also cling to *substantially* existent persons. YT (pp. 591–92) explains this as follows. Some bodhisattvas cling to the focal object that consists of the clinging of those ordinary beings who cling to substantially existent persons (as in the first set of nine conceptions about the apprehender that are factors to be relinquished through seeing). Though, ultimately, sentient beings do not arise as something substantially existent, on the level of the seeming they arise as something that is endowed with a mental continuum. It is by virtue of this that they are imputed as sentient beings, to which some ordinary beings then cling as being substantially existent. The states of mind of bodhisattvas that focus on and cling to this kind of clinging of ordinary beings are the factors to be relinquished through familiarization here. These states of mind are said to be conceptions of clinging to substantial existence because they cling to the clinging of those ordinary beings who cling to substantially existent persons. LN (vol. 2, pp. 305–6), however, explains that these nine conceptions are the clinging to the substantial existence of persons who are ordinary beings, that is, to a substantially existent self (just like the first nine conceptions about the apprehender that are to be relinquished through seeing). In due order, (1)–(2) refer to objects and the remaining to subjects. Among the latter, (3)–(5) refer to the prajñā and (6)–(7) to the means of the paths of noble ones, while (8)–(9) refer to the paths of ordinary beings. BT (pp. 630–31) agrees that these nine conceptions cling to a substantially existent self by focusing on their nine objects. In due order, they are in terms of (1)–(3) knowable objects; (4)–(5) the prajñās of śrāvakas and bodhisattvas, respectively; (6)–(7) aim-oriented means and the means for final deliverance, respectively; and (8)–(9) the view and conduct of ordinary sentient beings. PBG (p. 596) agrees with this, saying that (4)–(5) and (6)–(7) are in terms of the prajñā and means of the mahāyāna and the hīnayāna, respectively. In general, it is not clear to me how the various explanations on substantially existent persons here match the statements and comments in the AA, the *Ālokā* (D3901, fol. 308b.3ff.), the *Vivṛti* (D3793, fol. 127b.1), JNS, and CE about beings, phenomena, and so on being merely imputed. NSML (p. 571) says that mental states of clinging to substantial existence do not arise in noble ones and comments on (1)–(2) as JNS does on the *Vivṛti* above.

202 CZ, p. 511.

203 This is the literal meaning of *bdag nyid ji bzhin*, which the Tibetan of line V.33b has for Skt. *yathāsvaṃ* ("each one," "respectively").

204 JNS (vol. 2, pp. 372–74) says that the imputations as sentient beings and the conceptions about the apprehender that are the subjects which function as the causes for imputing such sentient beings are overcome by the path of familiarization. Therefore, these conceptions and the path of familiarization (the factors to be relinquished and their remedy, respectively) are mutually exclusive phenomena that do not coexist. The nine conceptions are about (1)–(3) the three obscurations that obscure the pure nature of the three omnisciences of knowing the essential character of the basic nature, just as it is; (6) not being equal because there is nothing

other than the existence of true reality; (8) the nature of the afflictions—emptiness; and (9) the nature of nonduality. This last set of conceptions about the apprehender means to be ignorant about these nine objects in terms of apprehending all of them as being real such and such phenomena. Commenting on the *Vivṛti*, when read in accordance with the Sanskrit, JNS (vol. 2, pp. 373–75) identifies the factors to be relinquished here as the conceptions that have imputed sentient beings and the causes for their being imputed (mere other-dependent appearances) as their objects (when understood as above ["subject" versus "having as object"], this passage would read, "the factors to be relinquished here are imputed sentient beings and the causes for their being imputed—the conceptions about the apprehender that are their subjects and mere other-dependent appearances"). These nine conceptions have the nature of being ignorant about the obscurations of (1)–(3) the natures of the knowledge of all aspects, the knowledge of the path, and the knowledge of entities, respectively, which is by virtue of not knowing all aspects of causes and results, all paths of the three yānas, and all entities (such as the skandhas); (4) the path that pacifies all factors to be relinquished, which is due to not knowing the remedy—prajñāpāramitā; (5) the modes of knowable objects, such as form (the bearers of the nature of phenomena), and the basic nature of suchness (the nature of phenomena), which is due to not knowing that these two modes are not the same and thus not knowing whether suchness and knowable objects are conjoined or disjoined in nature; (6) the unequaled actuality that is difficult to realize, which is due to not knowing the nature of māras—desire and so on (the ordinary states of existence and peace); (7) the four realities, which is due to taking literally statements about the "existence" of referents that are able to perform functions on the level of the correct seeming; (8) the nature of the afflictions as the factors that obscure, which is due to not knowing that their nature is primordially empty; and (9) the actuality that cannot be made dual, which is due to not knowing the characteristic of apprehender and apprehended to be emptiness. Here, "ignorance" means to not know that the obscurations of (1)–(9) actually are obscurations. YT (pp. 593–94) explains these conceptions as follows. Bodhisattvas on the path of seeing conventionally impute noble beings onto the continuum of the five wisdom skandhas of having realized identitylessness and impute ordinary beings onto the continuum of the five skandhas that consist of afflictive ignorance. The factors to be relinquished through familiarization here are the states of mind of bodhisattvas that focus on and cling to said kind of clinging to imputations that exists in bodhisattvas on the path of seeing. PBG (pp. 597–98) phrases the general characterization of these nine conceptions about the apprehender as the subjects that take conventionally imputed sentient beings and the causes for their being imputed as their objects (most Tibetan commentaries gloss this as the skandhas being imputed as sentient beings and the causes for this being the mere appearances of the continuum of these skandhas). PBG adds that these nine conceptions are in terms of (1)–(3) the obscurations of the bodhisattva path; (4) its nature; (5) and (7) its focal objects; (6) its distinct feature; (8) its factors to be relinquished; and (9) its aspect. BT (p. 633) agrees with this except for saying that (5)–(7) are in terms of knowable objects. In sum, JNS concludes, it should be understood that, corresponding to the general fourfold division of these sets of conceptions about the apprehender and the apprehended as the factors to be relinquished, the division of training in the wisdom of the path of familiarization that represents the remedies for these four sets is also fourfold. As mentioned before, in the sūtras the remedies are taught explicitly, and the conceptions implicitly, whereas the AA teaches the conceptions explicitly and the remedies implicitly. NSML (pp. 576–77) adds that the remedies for these four sets of conceptions are not explicitly taught here in the fifth chapter because their nature was already taught in AA II.30. Also, these remedies being either divided into nine or four is not contradictory. For the ninefold division is in terms of the boundary lines of the nine degrees of the cognitive obscurations with regard to the nine levels of the three realms. The fourfold division is in terms of isolates in that each uninterrupted path on the nine levels of the path of familiarization functions as the remedy to relinquish the corresponding seeds among the four sets of conceptions to be relinquished through familiarization. PSD (p. 390) concludes by saying that the modes of apprehension of the four kinds of conceptions to be relinquished through familiarization and the manner in which they are relinquished through their remedies are similar to the conceptions to be relinquished through seeing. In general, most commentaries agree that the first set of the conceptions about the apprehended and the first set of the conceptions about the apprehender here are the subjects of the preparatory stages of the culminating training of the path of familiarization, while the second sets of the conceptions about apprehender and apprehended are the subjects of the uninterrupted paths of this culminating training. This means that they are respectively relinquished during these phases. See also the beginning of CE on the culminating training of the path of familiarization above; Appendices I1D (Volume One), I4B, and I5A; and Charts 17–18 in Volume One.

205 CZ, p. 518.

206 The Tibetan has "supreme" (*mchog*) instead of "desired" (Skt. *nikāma*). JNS (vol. 2, p. 377) points out that some Tibetans say that the former does not correspond to the Sanskrit text.

207 CZ, p. 524. JNS (vol. 2, p. 377) says that the pestilences here are the apprehended and the apprehender that arise in all sentient beings and are extinguished through the medicine-like knowledge of the path. The disease from which the bodhisattvas here are cured is the suffering of being worn out through one's imaginations since beginningless time. JNS relates the example of all rivers feeding into the ocean to the *Buddhāvataṃsakasūtra* (see *The Flower Ornament Scripture*, trans. T. Cleary, Shambhala, 1984–1987, vol. 2, p. 106). Commenting on the *Vivṛti*, JNS (vol. 2, pp. 375 and 377–78) says that, just as certain afflictive obscurations are relinquished as a matter of course during the relinquishment of the cognitive obscurations on the path of seeing, simultaneously with the relinquishment of the 108 cognitions that are the cognitive obscurations to be relinquished through familiarization the 108 latencies of the afflictions that are included in the factors to be relinquished through familiarization are relinquished. Therefore, all excellent qualities of realization sustain those bodhisattvas who dwell on the path of familiarization. The four kinds of conceptions about apprehender and apprehended are like harmful pestilences since they prevent one from attaining great enlightenment for all sentient beings equally. Once they are extinguished, there are no more obstacles to attaining enlightenment. Thus, just as when being joyfully relieved from suffering, by virtue of the three kinds of compassion bodhisattvas cannot help but eliminate the suffering of other beings. With their excellent qualities of being skilled in producing the happiness of beings, which consist of the entirety of the three yānas, bodhisattvas effortlessly dwell on the path of familiarization, just like the ocean collects the water of all rivers. They are beautified by their qualities of having almost attained the ultimate fruition of having practiced this path, which in turn support their mind streams.

208 The Tibetan has "śrāvakas."

209 The Tibetan of this line says, "With nothing between it and buddhahood" (*sangs rgyas nyid kyi bar med de*).

210 JNS (vol. 2, pp. 378–82) says that, after the culminating training of the path of familiarization, the culminating training of the uninterrupted path is taught because it accomplishes the immediately following attainment of the wisdom that is the knowledge of all aspects and relinquishes the stains that are the impregnations of negative tendencies. The following is to be understood here. The statement that the factors to be relinquished through this culminating training of the uninterrupted path are the impregnations of negative tendencies that were input by the two obscurations is not correct. They are not presented for the reason that they constitute some obscurations of a different substantial type that is other than the two obscurations themselves. Even if they were presented like that, they would then not be obscurations because such putative entities are of a different type than the obscurations and because whatever is concordant in type with the two obscurations has already been relinquished on the ten bhūmis of

the paths of seeing and familiarization, on which the two obscurations plus their seeds are relinquished. In brief, this culminating training of the uninterrupted path is an obstacle to entering the imminent cessation of the mind stream of a bodhisattva on the tenth bhūmi—in the second smallest moment in time right after it, the wisdom of the knowledge of all aspects is clearly manifest. If I thoroughly reflect on this since the factors to be relinquished and their remedies do not coexist, there is no earlier and later time within the triad of this obstacle arising, what is to be put to an end having ceased, and the result of this cessation. Therefore, even the clear manifesting of the knowledge of all aspects in the second moment is difficult. Consequently, I assert the mind stream of the tenth bhūmi here as the ālaya-consciousness, or the basic element of formations, or false imagination. This is called "the impregnations of negative tendencies" because it impregnates and takes in all the negative tendencies of saṃsāra. Some may say, "But since this is a knowable object, it is of a substantial type that concords with the cognitive obscurations." This statement only reflects the flawed understanding that arises from thinking, "Whatever is a knowable object must necessarily be a cognitive obscuration." In our opinion, by taking knowable objects as the bases of analysis, the factors that obscure the realization of their actual way of being and their way of appearing are presented as cognitive obscurations. Therefore, even when the obscurations that constitute the portion of ignorance about knowable objects have been relinquished, there still remains a mere knowable object that functions as the support for knowable objects. This entity is burned by the culminating training of the uninterrupted path because *Madhyamakāvatāra* XI.17ab says:

> With the dry firewood of knowable objects being incinerated without remainder,
> This peace is the dharmakāya of the victors.

Furthermore, whatever is a knowable object is not suitable to be a cognitive obscuration. For example, in terms of buddhas seeing the knowable objects of the seeming and these appearing to them, if knowable objects and cognitive obscurations were one, it would follow that buddhas see cognitive obscurations when they see knowable objects. If this is accepted, that is, if obscurations still appear to the wisdom of buddhas though they have exhaustively relinquished the obscurations, one must accept the existence of the triad of objects, sense faculties, and mind—the causes and conditions that cast these appearances—as being contained in the knowledge of these buddhas' own mind streams. However, if the above is not accepted, this contradicts the power of entities since appearances would not need any causes and conditions. But if such causes and conditions are necessary, it follows that buddhas have obscurations. A cottonclad guru who lived in Tibet said, "Since all logicians are familiar with the obscurations that are the impregnations of negative tendencies, they are not identified, but all venerable logicians just say that they are like smelling the scent of musk on the skin of a musk deer. Some say that these obscurations are not the seeds of the two obscurations, but some sort of general obscurations. This is wrong. So what are they? They are the remaining blank five sense consciousnesses without thoughts." His famous student claimed, "The blank five sense consciousnesses without thoughts that remain outside are what overflow from the ālaya to the outside. Not recognizing this blank remainder is saṃsāra. Recognizing it or it being aware of itself is called dharmakāya, nirvāṇa, and buddhahood. Thus, what recognizes this is called the vajralike samādhi. Therefore, after it has been relinquished through this samādhi, it is withdrawn into the thoughtfree ālaya." However since the five sense consciousnesses are relinquished or have changed state from the first bhūmi onward, how could they still be around on the tenth bhūmi? It may be asked, "What is the reason for their being relinquished on the first bhūmi?" The five sense consciousnesses of those who just see this life must arise from the coming together of the triad of object, sense faculty, and mental engagement. But on the first bhūmi, apprehender and apprehended are realized to be nondual, and the immediate condition (mental engagement) and so on have ceased. Therefore, their result—the consciousness that has the nature of the triad of apprehender, apprehended, and awareness—has ceased too. You may wonder, "But how do bodhisattvas on the bhūmis produce consciousnesses that engage objects?" They have consciousnesses that are based on samādhi and uncontaminated sense faculties [it may be added here that the eye sense faculties of bodhisattvas on the bhūmis are not only able to see, but also hear, smell, taste, and experience tangible objects, with the same applying to the other sense faculties]. The outcome of this explanation is the certainty that the obscurations that are the impregnations of negative tendencies are neither the latencies of the factors to be relinquished through seeing nor the seeds of the conceptions that are the factors to be relinquished through familiarization. The explanation of Āryavimuktisena on these impregnations of negative tendencies appears below under the sixteen mistaken notions that are to be relinquished (see the endnotes on AA V.40–42). However, certain Tibetan masters say, "This explanation is not good for the following reasons. Since these obscurations mostly appear as imaginary conceptions, they consist of either portions of the factors to be relinquished through seeing or portions of the factors to be relinquished through familiarization. Also, as long as these factors to be relinquished have not been eliminated, not even the preparatory stage of this culminating training here can arise. As for the intention of Maitreya here, he says that, without having eliminated this qualm, the culminating training of the uninterrupted path does not arise." From among the two parts of the uninterrupted samādhi here (preparation and main part), the preparation is to engage in the wisdom before the end of the continuum, while the main part is explained as the vajralike samādhi at the very end of the continuum. Therefore, they must be distinguished in terms of being nominal and actual, respectively. For more details on the vajralike samādhi and the impregnations of negative tendencies, see AA's Chapter Seven and Appendix I4B.

211 CZ, p. 526.

212 The definitions of the six causes and four conditions here agree with the respective lines in the second chapter of the *Abhidharmakośa* as referred to in Appendix I5G (for more details, see there).

213 JNS (vol. 2, p. 389) says that the focal object of this culminating training of the uninterrupted path is dependent origination—the lack of entity. Its dominant factor, which is directed toward manifesting the knowledge of all aspects, is the mindfulness that gives rise to samādhi. The cognitive aspect of this culmination is the peacefulness of being free from reference points. Commenting on the *Vivṛti*, JNS (vol. 2, pp. 389–91) says that the object condition of this uninterrupted samādhi is the correct focal object that is the opposite of all phenomena being established as entities—the nature of the lack of entity. Its dominant condition is mindfulness, and its aspect is the natural peacefulness of being primordially free from stains. As for the assertions of certain Tibetans about this, some say, "According to Vasubandhu, the passage in the sūtras about 'the lack of entity' does not refer to the object condition and the phrase 'its dominating factor is mindfulness' is stated in terms of the previous cause, but does not refer to the time of this culminating training here." With this in mind, they explain that this culminating training of the uninterrupted path is the cooperative cause in the production of the knowledge of all aspects. However, since this culminating training has the character of being very close to the knowledge of all aspects, it is free from causes and conditions (such as focal object, dominant condition, and cognition's own aspect). Others say, "The focal objects of this culminating training are the bases that are taken for cutting through superimpositions by discriminating prajñā focusing on them during the preparatory stage. Their characteristic is to be the mere appearing aspects of the dependent origination of the seeming, which are empty of a nature of their own. This is expressed in the sūtra passage, 'The focal object of the knowledge of all aspects is the lack of entity.' The aspect of this culminating training is to be without clinging to any extreme of reference points whatsoever ('its aspect is peacefulness'). Its dominant condition is the mindfulness of not forgetting the continuum of the progressive stages of how to mentally engage during meditative equipoise as these were determined through study and reflection since the sūtras say, 'Mindfulness is its dominant condition.'" Furthermore, the following is to be analyzed. One may

wonder, "With the object condition and the dominant condition being taught explicitly here, through what is the immediate condition taught?" Some say that is is taught implicitly. Others say, "The immediate condition is presented from the perspective of the previous moment of this continuum of the culminating training of the uninterrupted path having ceased and the following one not having arisen yet. Supplementing the object condition and the dominant condition, cognition is produced in the form of possessing an aspect." The omniscient Chötra Gyatso says that the expression "aspect" teaches nothing but cognition because without the experience of an aspect, it is hard to even speak of an aspect. But if this aspect is experienced, nothing but cognition is suitable to do so. Consequently, it is understood by implication that the three conditions (object, dominant, and immediate) for the arising of a cognition must be complete.

214 CZ, p. 527.

215 CZ, pp. 527–46. JNS (vol. 2, p. 401) says that those with little insight who are greatly affected by the latent tendencies of entities dispute these principles of focal object and aspect by saying, "If all phenomena do not exist as entities, the sixteen phenomena (such as the focal object) in dependence on the knowledge of all aspects are not tenable." Commenting on the *Vivṛti*, JNS (vol. 2, p. 401) says that since this point about the focal object and the aspect here is very profound and thus difficult to realize, the disputes of talkative dialecticians, who have not realized the skill in means with regard to the two realities, continually proliferate, starting from their first qualm (discussed below). Thus, these disputes should be quelled by those who are skilled in said means. Others identify the phrases "in this regard" in line V.39c and "this point" in the *Vivṛti* as referring to the culminating training of the uninterrupted path proper. But I think that they refer to the disputes that develop out of the explanation of the focal object and the aspect of this culminating training, with the meaning of such disputes amounting to a dispute on the culminating training of the uninterrupted path.

216 XXIV.10ab.

217 In debate style, JNS (vol. 2, pp. 402–3) lists the sixteen disputes that are eliminated by CE's presentation above and gives two general answers for all of them. (1) "It follows that a focal object of the culmination of the uninterrupted path is not justified because the nature of phenomena does not exist as an entity." If this consequence is put forth in terms of the ultimate, I accept. But if it is in terms of the conventional that this conseqeunce is put forth with said reason, the entailment is not established. In other words, there is no entailment if the above consequence is put forth in terms of the conventional because, utimately, the nature of phenomena does not exist as an entity. The same answers also apply to all the remaining fifteen consequences. (2) "It follows that the identification of the realization of the nature of this focal object is not justified because there is no focal object." (3) "It follows that there is no wisdom of the knowledge of all aspects because objects (both entities and nonentities) do not exist." (4) "It follows that ultimate reality and seeming reality are not justified because such a presentational division is not established." (5) "It follows that the training of bodhisattvas does not exist because the six pāramitās do not exist." (6)–(8) "It follows that the three jewels do not exist because there is nothing to be realized; the nature of dharmas (like all other dharmas) is a mere name; and the six pāramitās (the conduct of the saṃgha) do not exist." (9) "It follows that bodhisattvas are not endowed with perfect means because the six pāramitās do not exist." (10) "It follows that the realization of the sage does not exist because there is no realization of entities, nonentities, or both." (11) "It follows that the existence of the fourfold mistakenness of apprehending permanence, happiness, a self, and purity is not justified because it is impermanence and so on that pertain to the actual way of being." In this context, some also say, "It follows that the view and conduct of bodhisattvas are mistaken because they entertain reference points of permanence and impermanence." (12) "It follows that the path of the mahāyāna (the cause) and its fruition do not exist because the fruition (enlightenment) is not manifested." If this consequence is put forth because enlightenment is absolutely not manifested at all, the

reason does not apply. If it is put forth because enlightenment is not manifested until the triad of perfection, maturation, and purification has been completed, there is no entailment. (13)–(14) "It follows that remedies and antagonistic factors do not exist because there is nothing to be adopted and nothing to be rejected." (15) "It follows that the defining characteristics of all phenomena do not exist because there are no instances of them." (16) "It follows that familiarization does not exist because something to familiarize with (specifically characterized and generally characterized phenomena) does not exist." Some analytical Tibetans say that these sixteen are not the qualms of dialecticians, but must be understood as the Buddha's answers to these qualms, which are indicated in V.39d. Otherwise, it would mean that the Buddha did not give any answers to these qualms because Maitreya does not include any such answers in the AA. This is highly unreasonable because it would result in the defeat of the defender (in this case the Buddha) if they do not give an answer to the challenger. The Seventh Karmapa says that this is not reasonable because lines V.42bd explicitly count these sixteen only as wrong views and not as answers. JNS (vol. 2, p. 400) adds that Dölpopa also considers these sixteen as the answers to qualms. Commenting on the *Vivṛti*, JNS (vol. 2, pp. 404–6) identifies the sixteen wrong ideas as follows. (1) "It follows that a focal object of the knowledge of all aspects is not justified because conditioned and unconditioned phenomena do not exist as entities." If this consequence is put forth in terms of the ultimate, one can either accept it or say that there is no entailment. If it is put forth in terms of the seeming, the reason does not apply. The same also applies to all the following qualms. (2) "It follows that the nature of the focal object—appearance and emptiness inseparable—cannot be identified because the first two characteristics (the imaginary and the other-dependent) are without any nature in all respects." (3) "It follows that the wisdom of the knowledge of all aspects does not exist because entities and nonentities are not observed through any nature of their own and thus do not exist." (4) "It follows that the two realities—ultimate and seeming—are not justified because the nature of phenomena does not exist as anything other than the nature of suchness." (8) "It follows that the jewel of the saṃgha is not justified because focal objects, such as imaginary form, have been refuted." (9) "It follows that the skill in the means to promote the welfare of others does not exist because generosity, giver, and recipient are actually not observable." (10) "It follows that the sage's clear realization of the dharma does not exist because conceptions about any nature of entities, nonentities, or both have been put to an end." (11) "It follows that views about permanence and so on are not mistaken because the understanding of impermanence, suffering, and so on—which is set up through the nature of reference points—is mistaken when compared to true reality." (12) "It follows that the paths of śrāvakas and pratyekabuddhas are not justified because cultivating these paths does not manifest the fruition of great nirvāṇa." (15) "It follows that the defining characteristics of phenomena (the supported) do not exist because the supports that bear these characteristics do not exist." These qualms are raised by dialecticians (both childish beings and noble ones) who do not understand the bodhisattva's skill in means with regard to the distinction of the two realities and thus take them to be mutually exclusive with regard to a single subject in question. As for the skill in the means to eliminate such qualms that mistakenly attempt to confute the ultimate through the seeming, or the seeming through the ultimate, they must be countered by answers that pertain to ultimate reality in the first case and to seeming reality in the second. For example, the qualm, "The ultimate is not emptiness because sprouts and such exist" is answered by saying, "Just because they exist on the level of the seeming does not mean that they have to exist ultimately." Or the qualm, "Seeming sprouts and such do not arise because they are emptiness" is countered by saying, "Just because they are not established ultimately does not mean that they have to not be established on the level of the seeming" (for more details on this, see Appendix I1C2–6 in Volume One). Dharmakīrtiśrī from Suvarṇadvīpa asserts that qualm (10) is answered in terms of both realities; (12), in terms of both the false and the correct seeming; (1) and (3)–(6), in terms of the seeming; and the remaining ones, in terms of the ultimate. As for the manner in which the samādhi of the culminating training of the uninterrupted path is generated through eliminating these qualms, the bodhisattvas who wish for the virtue of this culminating training are skilled in the means of relying on both realities. Therefore, they correctly give rise to unmistaken certainty in all respects by way of this certainty being preceded by the elimination of the adverse conditions of innumerable wrong ideas to be eliminated. In this way, the samādhi of the uninterrupted path is to be generated.

218 Verse 75. CE only quotes the first three lines, with the second line saying, "Will increase step-by-step" (thus being almost literally the same as the fourth one).

219 CZ, pp. 548–49. JNS (vol. 2, pp. 407–8) says that, once mastery over the three knowledges has been attained through the culminating training, the serial training is the yoga that brings about the irreversible stability of this mastery. It has two parts—the part of relinquishing the factors to be relinquished and the part of liberation after they have been relinquished. The meaning of gaining stability is explained as being free from obstructions of the mastery of infinite qualities, which refers to the ability to manifest these infinite qualities in the next moment. To meditate in order to gain such stability in the yoga that manifests these qualities is the meaning of "cause" here (with the instantaneous training being its result). According to YT (p. 613), the serial training refers to bodhisattvas below the end of the continuum who have attained the culminating training and then sequentially familiarize with (a) the three knowledges individually, (b) all the points that were realized during the complete training in all aspects as their combined familiarization, and (c) all the points that were realized during the culminating training. They do so through mentally reviewing all of these points and realizations in order to gain stability in them. LN (vol. 2, p. 326) says that such a sequential familiarization applies to mentally reviewing, during three incalculable eons, everything that is realized during both meditative equipoise and subsequent attainment from the path of accumulation onward, which consists of all the individual natures taught through the respective paths and their being condensed in the wisdom of not conceptualizing the nature of phenomena. "In order to gain stability" is glossed as "in order to make them effortless and spontaneously present." NSML (pp. 590–91) explains that the wisdom of the subsequent attainment of bodhisattvas who have attained the culminating clear realizations mentally reviews the individual dharmas contained in the three knowledges, while the wisdom of their meditative equipoise reviews the points that were realized during the complete training in all aspects. This reviewing takes place in just the order in which these points and realizations have arisen in the mind streams of these bodhisattvas. The reason for explaining the serial training after the culminating training is as follows. Through the culminating training, all antagonistic factors of the bodhisattva path have been relinquished without exception. However, without the qualities that are accomplished through the serial training, the buddhabhūmi would just be a one-sided relinquishment without consummate realization being accomplished. Therefore, bodhisattvas need to cultivate the serial training for this purpose. As for matching the serial training with the prajñāpāramitā sūtras, according to CZ (pp. 547–54), it consists of The Exposition of the Consummation of the Training in Serial Activity (Chapter Seventy).

220 The sūtras speak of gods being reborn in the various god realms, which is followed by Āryavimuktisena, Haribhadra, BT (p. 647). LN (vol. 2, p. 328) and PSD (p. 406) say that, according to Dharmamitra's *Prasphuṭapadā*, this refers to recollecting (a) that ordinary saṃsāric gods attained their pleasant states through special virtuous karmas, thus making efforts in doing the same, and (b) the qualities of deities such as Tārā and Avalokiteśvara. In this vein, YT (p. 616) also speaks of mundane and supramundane deities. NSML (p. 593) adds the recollection of the qualities of buddhas and bodhisattvas as one's own supreme meditation deities as explained in the sūtras. According to LN, Tibetans speak of connate, spatial, pure, and ultimate deities. JNS (see Appendix I6) relates the recollection of deities to meditation deities. STT (p. 141) says that this refers to recollecting the deities, bodhisattvas, and buddhas in the desire and form realms, thinking, "Ultimately, any entities such as someone to be worried about (a self or me), someone who worries (the bodhisattvas), and their worrying are not established as any nature whatsoever.

Through knowing that, on the level of the seeming, if I do not relinquish in an attachment-free manner all the nonvirtues to be relinquished by bodhisattvas, the deities, bodhisattvas, and buddhas in the desire and form realms will be worried and I will be ashamed. Since they see me directly and are present as witnesses at all times, I shall absolutely not commit any nonvirtues."

221 According to JNS (vol. 2, pp. 409–10), it is neither the case that the fourth and fifth recollections are repetitions of the first two pāramitās, nor that the recollection of deities is a repetition of the three jewels since the *Prajñāpāramitāpiṇḍārthapradīpa* (D3804, fol. 239a.5–6) says:

> The two of generosity and ethics
> And the recollections of giving and ethics
> Are taught from the perspectives of actual [training]
> And fruition, respectively—so there is no flaw of repetition.
> The deities and the jewels represent the principles
> Of witnesses and supports, respectively, so there is no repetition.

Commenting on the *Vivṛti*, JNS (vol. 2, pp. 412–14) says that the thirteen recollections are divided into three groups—(a) excellent application; (b) excellent motivation; and (c) the dharma that purifies. (a) The excellent training or application of the motivation represented by the six recollections consists of (1)–(6) the six pāramitās. As for the four pāramitās of means, aspiration prayers, power, and wisdom among the ten pāramitās, they are not taught separately here since they are included in the pāramitā of prājñā. In due order (according to *Madhyāntavibhāga* V.6cd), skill in means is to render virtue inexhaustible through prajñāpāramitā. Through engaging in generosity and so on, the fruitions are accomplished as aspired. Power refers to vanquishing antagonistic factors. Through the wisdoms of knowing suchness and variety, sentient beings are matured. Therefore, through being embraced by prajñā, the other five pāramitās (such as generosity) are characterized by being pure of clinging to the three spheres. Through fully completing all these six pāramitās, the ten bhūmis are accomplished. (b) The six recollections as the excellent motivation have three subsets in terms of recollecting the supports of the path (the three jewels); the bases of the path (giving and ethics); and the witnesses of the path (the deities). As for (7)–(9) the three jewels, the thirty-seven dharmas concordant with enlightenment have the characteristic of ultimately lacking the recollection of their being free from reference points. During their subsequent attainments, the manner of recollecting the Buddha as being free from reference points takes place in three degrees (lowest, medium, and highest) during the phases of the factors conducive to penetration, the path of seeing, and the path of familiarization, respectively. The same applies to recollecting the dharma and the saṃgha—recollecting that all dharmas (virtuous, nonvirtuous, and neutral) and irreversible bodhisattvas, respectively, are free from reference points. Likewise, (10)–(12) giving, ethics, and the supreme deities are recollected as being unobservable. (c) The dharma that purifies is (13) the serial training that is the yoga of bodhisattvas realizing all phenomena as having the nature of the lack of entity. For more details on the serial training, see Appendix I6.

222 CZ, p. 549.

223 JNS (vol. 2, p. 415) says that the reason for becoming a buddha in an instant is as follows. The serial training consists of familiarizing with the 173 aspects of the three knowledges in order to attain mastery over them. Having familiarized with this for a very long time as the means to attain the dharmakāya, the instantaneous training means to familiarize with this very serial training in its entirety in a single moment. LN (vol. 2, p. 330) says that the instantaneous training is the end of the continuum of having cultivated the serial training and is cultivated in order to gain stability in the latter's spontaneously present great familiarity. It means to familiarize with the three knowledges in a combined manner, which happens in a single moment in the sense of the time it takes to complete this activity. According to NSML (p. 594), the need for having familiarized with the clear realization of the serial training before the instantaneous

training is to familiarize with all aspects of the three knowledges (the objects of familiarization) becoming manifest once a single aspect of them has become manifest. Once one has attained stability through familiarizing with this, one is finally able to manifest, through familiarization in a single instant, all uncontaminated phenomena once one has manifested a single one of them. As for matching the culminating training with the prajñāpāramitā sūtras, according to CZ (pp. 555–72), it covers The Dharma Is Signless and Cannot Be Apprehended (Chapter Seventy-one) and Exposition of Marklessness (Chapter Seventy-two).

224 CZ, p. 556.

225 As mentioned above, CE (fol. 13b) says that the "single instant" here refers to the time that it takes to complete a given action, while JG (p. 247) argues for it being the smallest moment in time. JNS (vol. 2, pp. 420 and 422) says that each one of the moments of uncontaminated wisdom (such as generosity and ethics) includes all uncontaminated phenomena. In order to manifest them, one should understand the sage's realization—the wisdom in a single instant at the end of the continuum of the tenth bhūmi that knows all aspects (JNS adds that, unlike Haribhadra, some Tibetan masters refer to "the sage" here as a buddha). This wisdom that knows all uncontaminated phenomena in a single instant resembles the example of a water-wheel, which is not found in the sūtras. Commenting on the *Vivṛti*, JNS (vol. 2, pp. 421–22) says the following. In the system of the great chariot, when one engages in the dharmadhātu's own nature through giving rise to serial clear realization and through fully complete knowledge, Āryadeva says the following (*Catuḥśataka* VIII.16). Emptiness—the single entity of ultimate reality—is the nature of all dependently originating entities in their entire variety, and all these dependently originating entities do not exist as anything other than the nature of the single entity of profound emptiness. Therefore, those who see a single dependently originating entity as suchness (emptiness) see all these entities as suchness (emptiness). Therefore, it is not only that many phenomena include a single phenomenon, but a single phenomenon can include many phenomena as well. Thus, the instantaneous training, which has the nature of nonobservation, is free from any seeds of mistakenness and ascertains each one of the entities to be observed in a single instant of observation through the wisdom at the end of the continuum. In this way, it familiarizes with many phenomena (from generosity up through the eighty minor marks) through including them in suchness. This realization of the sage—the bodhisattva—is to be understood as the training in becoming completely enlightened in a single instant. Through this explicit teaching of the manner in which one includes many, the manner of single emptiness including many—all nonempty phenomena—is taught. Through the training in this single instant at the end of the continuum (which resembles the single pivotal step on a waterwheel that enables one to move it), the entirety of the mind stream that has become familiar with the threefold lack of arising of the three knowledges throughout the path of learning operates simultaneously (just as said waterwheel moves smoothly in its entirety by virtue of having been well-crafted before by a skillful carpenter). In other words, through the power of bodhisattvas at the end of their continuum being propelled by their previous aspiration prayers and the power of the dharmadhātu, when they focus on the single uncontaminated wisdom in a single instant, they manifest all instances of uncontaminated wisdom that accord with this wisdom in type.

226 The Tibetan of this verse varies somewhat:

> When the nature of all spotless phenomena—
> Prajñāpāramitā, the state
> Of the true nature of maturation—is born,
> Then [it is] the wisdom in one single instant.

227 Verse 76 (CE only quotes the last two lines). JNS (vol. 2, p. 423) comments as follows. When the uninterrupted samādhi at the end of the continuum is attained, it seems as if the nature of all purified spotless phenomena—the mother of the victors, prajñāpāramitā,

Mahāmudrā, the fully complete nature of phenomena, which is matured right from the beginning, spontaneously present, and free from stains—arises since this is the state of its having become free from stains. At that point, this is the instantaneous training—the wisdom of simultaneous realization in one single instant, which realizes true reality in a fully complete manner. Therefore, *Dharmadhātustava* lines 76cd (see above) and verse 7 say:

> Once the vajra of samādhi
> Has completely smashed this vase,
> To the very limits of all space
> It will shine just everywhere.

Commenting on the *Vivṛti*, JNS (vol. 2, pp. 423–24) says that, at the end of the bhūmis, bodhisattvas have cultivated both contaminated and uncontaminated remedies and thus are free from all antagonistic factors to be relinquished through familiarization. Through that, they attain the state of the true nature of matured phenomena (the class of purified phenomena) and are free from all stains that obstruct becoming a completely perfect buddha. Therefore, when the nature of what is spotless arises just as the light of the autumn moon, the wisdom that realizes the uncontaminated dharmas and represents the effortless and spontaneously present state of maturation in one single instant is the training in perfectly realizing prajñāpāramitā through the single instant of maturation.

228 CZ, p. 564.

229 The Tibetan of line VII.4a has "all phenomena."

230 JNS (vol. 2, p. 424) says that bodhisattvas, through not rejecting the engagement in generosity and so on at this time, abide in the realization of all phenomena being dreamlike. In this way, through this single instantaneous training, they discover that the entirety of the fundamental being of phenomena and their nature is the lack of characteristics and thus manifest the knowledge of all aspects. Commenting on the *Vivṛti*, JNS (vol. 2, pp. 424–25) says that, through having become familiar with all phenomena being dreamlike on the paths of learning before, bodhisattvas have experienced the two accumulations. Then, at the point of realizing true reality, they are certain that the appropriating skandhas and so on, by virtue of their dreamlike nature, are emptiness. Therefore, they abide in all phenomena through regarding them in this way and thus practicing the six pāramitās. Just this single moment of the wisdom at the end of the trainings, which entails the aspect of realizing the nature of generosity and so on, discovers that all imaginary and conceived phenomena lack their own specific characteristics and instances. Thus, since it realizes that all afflicted and purified phenomena lack characteristics, it is the training in becoming perfectly enlightened in a single instant (as mentioned before, "imaginary phenomena" and conceived phenomena" in the prajñāpāramitā sūtras correspond to the imaginary and other-dependent natures among the three natures).

231 CZ, p. 565.

232 The Tibetan of line VII.5b adds "likewise" at the end.

233 JNS (vol. 2, pp. 425–26) says that both a dream and the seeing of it are not perceived in a dualistic fashion—they have the nature of a single imagination. Likewise, the instant of the wisdom of nonduality, which is free from superimposition and denial, clearly sees the dharmas of the svābhāvikakāya—luminosity—in a nondual manner in one single instant of true reality. Immediately upon that, one is fully and perfectly enlightened. Commenting on the *Vivṛti*, JNS (vol. 2, p. 426) says that, at this point, bodhisattvas have eradicated the latent tendencies of dualistic appearances through abiding in the one-pointed consummate familiarity with the yoga of relinquishing the dualistic appearances of apprehender and apprehended in an uninterrupted manner for incalculable eons. Such bodhisattvas view the principle of apprehender and apprehended as follows. Just as a dream and the seeing of that dream are not perceived as

apprehended and apprehender, respectively, at the end of the continuum, all phenomena have the nature of being nothing but entities of such dream imaginations. By virtue of realizing all buddha qualities through just this single instant of the true reality of phenomena (the nonduality of apprehender and apprehended), this is the training that makes one fully and perfectly enlightened in a single instant.

234 CZ, p. 571.

235 JNS (vol. 2, p. 429) says that the points of the three knowledges, which are ascertained through study and reflection, are made a living experience through the four trainings, through which the fruition of the dharmakāya arises. Therefore, being free from all obscuring stains in the very next moment right after having cultivated the instantaneous training that makes one enlightened, this enlightenment has the nature of the dharmakāya endowed with twofold purity. As for matching the dharmakāya with the prajñāpāramitā sūtras, according to CZ (pp. 573–652), it consists of The Perfection of the Imperishable Consummation of the Marks and Minor Characteristics (Chapter Seventy-three) up through The Manifestation of a Bodhisattva's Training (Chapter Eighty-three) in the sūtra in twenty-five thousand lines as well as certain passages in this sūtra's revised edition and the sūtra in eighteen thousand lines (CZ, Appendices I–II, pp. 653–65).

236 As mentioned before, the dharmakāya is often referred to as "dharmatākāya" or "svābhāvikadharmatākāya," with dharmakāya being explained as an abbreviation of these two terms.

237 Basically following JNS, CE's matching of the three kāyas with the four (five) buddha wisdoms differs from classical Yogācāra and the Third Karmapa's presentation, mainly through matching mirrorlike wisdom with the sāmbhogikakāya (instead of the dharmakāya) and not matching the wisdom of equality and discriminating wisdom with a particular kāya (JNS says that mirrorlike wisdom and the wisdom of equality are primarily the knowledges that perform activities from a buddha's own perspective, while the latter two are primarily the knowledges that perform activities from the perspective of others). The Yogācāra system matches the dharmakāya with mirrorlike wisdom; the sāmbhogikakāya with the wisdom of equality and discriminating wisdom; and the nairmāṇikakāya with all-accomplishing wisdom. The dharmadhātu is usually not counted as a fifth wisdom (which originally comes from the vajrayāna tradition), but represents the underlying matrix or space within which the four wisdoms display. When counted as a fifth wisdom, dharmadhātu wisdom is associated with the svābhāvikakāya. As mentioned before, the common Sanskrit grammatical forms svābhāvikakāya, sāmbhogikakāya, and nairmāṇikakāya indicate that these kāyas are related to the dharmakāya as its features or functions and not as three separate entities on their own. Thus, in terms of its nature, the dharmakāya is referred to as svābhāvikakāya (this is also the reason for these two usually being presented as equivalent); in terms of its bringing the enjoyment of the mahāyāna dharma to bodhisattvas, it is the sāmbhogikakāya; and in terms of its manifesting in all kinds of forms for all kinds of beings, it is the nairmāṇikakāya. For more details, see Appendix I8A and Chart 25.

238 As mentioned above and as CE makes very clear here again, the whole point in terms of mind's luminous nature (be it called dharmadhātu, natural purity, disposition, or buddha nature) is that there is absolutely no transformation of anything into anything at any point. The revelation of mind's primordially pure nature that appears as fruitional enlightenment represents a change of its state only from the perspective of deluded mind—it seems to be obscured before and then unobscured later. Obviously, as in the above example, this does not refer to any change in nature. Thus, when the process of uncovering mind's fundamental nature is sometimes described in Buddhist texts as if there were a transformation of something impure (such as mental afflictions) into something pure (such as wisdoms), this is just a conventional or expedient way of speaking.

239 As it stands, I could not locate this verse in Nāgārjuna's works, but it resembles verse 17 of his *Mahāyānaviṃśikā*.

240 For more details, see Appendix I8A and Makransky 1990 and 1997 (esp. Chapter 10).

241 This can also be translated as "The dharmakāya—the nature of the sage—. . ."

242 JNS (vol. 2, p. 446) says that the svābhāvikakāya of a bhagavān refers to the nature of someone having attained as many of the uncontaminated dharmas (the distinctive features of a tathāgata alone) as there are. This nature is pure because the factors to be relinquished, including their latent tendencies, have been relinquished in every respect. Since this represents being endowed with twofold purity, it means bearing the characteristic that defines the nature and the essence of a tathāgata. Commenting on the *Vivṛti*, JNS (vol. 2, pp. 446–50) first speaks about the nature of the svābhāvikakāya, which means being endowed in an inseparable manner with the nature of the dharmas of realization—the twenty-one sets of uncontaminated wisdom (such as the four foundations of mindfulness). This fundamental nature (the uncontaminated reality of cessation whose nature is the supramundane dharmadhātu), no matter whether it just looks as if obscured by adventitious stains to be relinquished (since these stains are not really existing entities in the first place) or is not obscured by them, always consists of the characteristics of being pure and naturally free of the hosts of such adventitious stains in every respect. These characteristics' own nature being of the nature of nonarising is the svābhāvikakāya of perfect buddhahood here. Through Haribhadra explaining the svābhāvikakāya to be established through or as the nature of nonarising, he does not teach it as an emptiness in the sense of extinction. Referring to the svābhāvikakāya with a plural ("these characteristics") is an explanation of the infinite natures that do not deviate from its own nature of nonarising. However, if one follows the explanation by others here that "being of the nature of nonarising" refers to nonarising's own nature since the nature of nonarising does not occur as a cause, the second word "nature" (in Haribhadra's above phrase, "These characteristics' own nature being of the nature of nonarising") would be meaningless. Secondly, as for the manner of attaining the svābhāvikakāya, in the sense of not being contrived through any formations, the svābhāvikakāya of the supramundane uncontaminated path is attained through the nature of phenomena, but it is not something that is produced through the natural dharmadhātu. Rather, this luminosity (of the svābhāvikakāya) exists within the ālaya-consciousness (that which obscures this luminosity) as having the remedial nature of the seeds for listening that are the natural outflow of the dharmadhātu (see also Appendix I1E1 in Volume One). Through their power increasing, the factors to be relinquished within the ālaya-consciousness are progressively relinquished. As for the manner in which this happens, illusionlike consciousnesses (which have the nature of listening and so on) realize all mistaken seeming phenomena to be free from any nature of their own. By virtue of the familiarity with this realization reaching its consummation, the two obscurations (the factors to be relinquished) cease through the gathering of the two accumulations (the remedies). Finally, when the power of the knowledge of all aspects of the buddhabhūmi (the indivisible vajralike samādhi, which is endowed with the unimpeded power of the enlightened activity of the dharmakāya) operates in a bodhisattva at the end of the continuum, the ālaya-consciousness ceases through not being able to withstand the power of this samādhi. Once it has ceased, the illusionlike consciousnesses that are based on it and represent the dispositions or causes for attaining the knowledge of all aspects—the virtues at the time of the path that bear the nature of the latent tendencies for listening—cease too. Therefore, this is the meaning of the roots of virtue being extinguished on the level of complete buddhahood. However, unlike that, to say that the uncontaminated virtues that make up the buddhabhūmi and exist as the nature of the knowledge of all aspects do not exist is not suitable. Since I explain the correct definitive meaning of Yogācāra-Madhyamaka here, there is no need for doubt. Thirdly, as for the purpose of presenting the remaining three kāyas as different, all three are ultimate and operate on the level of the fundamental nature, that is, they are not other than the nature of the dharmadhātu.

However, on the level of the correct seeming, they are distinguished through the manners in which the svābhāvikakāya is perceptually approached in terms of the buddhas' own appearances and the appearances of others (sentient beings). This means that the dharmakāya is presented as the sphere of buddhas; the sāmbhogikakāya, as the sphere of bodhisattvas; and the nairmāṇikakāya, as the sphere of śrāvakas, pratyekabuddhas, and ordinary beings. Here, the following concern by some people is to be analyzed. "This passage in the *Vivṛti* says that, ultimately, the nature of the three remaining kāyas is the nature of phenomena. Therefore, it explains that whatever is a buddhakāya is necessarily the svābhāvikakāya (the object) alone. In terms of the subject, two different appearances occur from the two perspectives of the self-awareness of buddhas seeing each other versus the referential awareness of pure and impure sentient beings. However, the svābhāvikakāya cannot be divided into the remaining three kāyas in terms of the substance of its actual way of being. Consequently, this contradicts the assertion in JNS's general presentation of the kāyas (see Appendix I8A) that the three remaining kāyas are divisions of the svābhāvikakāya in terms of the substance of its actual way of being." This is indeed true—what I say in this vein in my general presentation is in terms of the definitive meaning in the context of slight analysis, but this passage in the *Vivṛti* here is in terms of the context of thorough analysis. Therefore, the concern raised here is in fact the only reasonable thing to say in the latter context. Also, some may say, "The general presentation of JNS explains that the correct seeming does not appear to buddhas, which contradicts the *Vivṛti*'s statement here ("On the level of the seeming, they are distinguished through the manners of perceptual approaches . . .") explaining that the seeming does appear to buddhas." In the Sanskrit text of the above passage in the *Vivṛti*, "On the level of the seeming . . ." must be connected with "bodhisattvas." However, for prosodic reasons, this was not rendered in that way when the text was translated into Tibetan. Moreover, Karmapa Chötra Gyatso says the following. In actual fact, the unity or the dependent origination of the two realities not being mutually exclusive is never separate from buddhas and sentient beings throughout all three phases of the knowledges of entities, the path, and all aspects. Therefore, for buddhas, there is a correct seeming that consists of the buddhabhūmi, and the manner in which it exists is as follows. The ultimate of all buddhas exists as the svābhāvikakāya, from which the twenty-one sets of uncontaminated wisdom unfold. When buddhas see each other through this wisdom, they see their respective svābhāvikakāyas together with their wisdom kāyas as constituting their correct seeming. However, this is not actually true—for these respective wisdom dharmakāyas there is nothing that is produced through mistakenness. On the other hand, through applying the conventions of the seeming, the manner in which the aspects of the dharmakāyas of other buddhas appear in certain ways to certain facets of buddha wisdom is to appear as if they pertained to an awareness of something other. However, in terms of the actual way of being, since it is not reasonable for these aspects to be anything other than a buddha's own wisdom, they are established as self-awareness. Thus, this kind of correct seeming of buddhas is unlike the conditioned other-dependent appearances that arise from the latent tendencies of the mistaken appearances of ignorance and are suitable to appear for sentient beings. "So why not call them 'ultimately existent' then instead of speaking of a 'correct seeming?'" This is fine indeed, but the buddha heart being self-aware of its own nature is explained as the ultimate, while the buddha heart being self-aware of the nature of other buddha hearts is explained as correct seeming. You may think, "All dharmakāyas are of the single taste of equality, so for them there are no appearances of mutually being self and other. Therefore, such a presentation of the correct seeming on the buddhabhūmi is not explained in the *Vivṛti*." All dharmakāyas are indeed equal in being buddhahood, without any being better or worse. As the great emptiness free from reference points, they are free from being one or different and thus are of equal taste in that they cannot be differentiated. Nevertheless, it is not contradictory for them to appear to each other as profound dependent origination. It is clear in the sūtras and tantras that buddhas perceive each other directly without any obscurations—by way of the distinctive features of the pure realms of the five buddha families and so on appearing differently there are differences in the sāmbhogikakāyas, which in turn have different dharmakāyas as their respective supports. If such a presentation of the correct seeming were not explained here, the question arises whether, in terms of the buddhas' own appearances, the geese and so on that they see in the pure realms of other buddhas are the correct seeming or the ultimate. If they were the ultimate, it would follow that the ultimate is not free from coming and going. For the geese in this situation are the ultimate and they engage in coming and going since they beautify this pure buddha realm. But if these geese are the correct seeming of said buddhas here, our assertion is established because the two categories here (the ultimate and the correct seeming) are mutually exclusive and there is no third possibility either. Some also say that Haribhadra uses the term "correct seeming" here by him bearing in mind that he is a Sautrāntika-Mādhyamika. In conclusion, the tradition of the earlier learned ones says that any primordially void phenomenon is asserted as being void in a way that is not different from being void by nature (or of a nature of its own). [Note that that this last sentence in JNS comments on an (unidentified) two-line quote in the *Vivṛti* (D3793, fol. 131b.5) that says, "For it is asserted that what is discerned is not separate from the discernment" (*viviktāvyatirekitvaṃ vivekasya yato matam*). The full four-line quote is found in Triratnadāsa's commentary on Dignāga's *Prajñāpāramitārthasaṃgraha* (P5208, fols. 4b.8–5a.4), which says (abbreviated) that prajñāpāramitā is not other than suchness, but similar to a lamp and its light. "'Emptiness' does not exist as anything other than cognition. For it is asserted that what is discerned is not separate from the discernment." Otherwise, cognition would not be empty of duality, which would imply the existence of the two kinds of identity. Thus, the nature of suchness is the very Bhagavān. For both cognizer and what is cognized are based on cognition itself. Obviously, this is a typical explanation found in many Yogācāra texts. However, the *Vivṛti* uses the above two lines of this quote to support its own description of the svābhāvikakāya and the other three kāyas being ultimately not distinct in that they are the nature of phenomena (*dharmatā*) and the bearers of this nature (*dharmī*), respectively. Interestingly, Abhayākaragupta turns Haribhadra's quote against him, saying that it rather supports the very inseparability of emptiness (dharmatā) and wisdom (the uncontaminated dharmas) and not Haribhadra's distinction between them. JNS's entirely different interpretation of these two lines is based on their highly ambiguous Tibetan version (*gang phyir dben pa dben gyur las/ tha mi dad pa nyid du 'dod*) takes *dben pa* (which renders *viveka/vivikta*) to mean "void."] Since this is what pertains to the actual way of being, the remaining three kāyas are not different from the svābhāvikakāya. However, their ways of appearing are presented as different, just as different desirable and undesirable features may appear in the physical form of a single person. BT (pp. 657–58) explicitly follows Haribhadra in saying that there are four kāyas and phrases the above commentary in CE as follows. The svābhāvikakāya is endowed with three features. For it represents (a) the attainment of the uncontaminated dharmas (the twenty-one sets of wisdom) through the power of the supramundane path and (b) the ultimate reality of cessation of being pure of the adventitious stains in every respect. In addition, these two qualities of realization and relinquishment have (c) the characteristic of being devoid of a nature of their own. In other words, the suchness that is the ultimate realization and relinquishment is the svābhāvikakāya because it is the dharmadhātu of being free from all adventitious stains to be relinquished within the naturally pure dhātu. Summarizing the *Vivṛti*, BT says that the svābhāvikakāya is endowed with twofold purity because it has the characteristic of being naturally and primordially devoid of stains and also is pure of adventitious stains in every respect. That these stains have become pure through their remedies is by virtue of the very fact that they are adventitious. As for the remaining three kāyas, ultimately they are not different from the svābhāvikakāya because their ultimate nature is the nature of phenomena. Referring to all four lines of the above quotation in the *Vivṛti* on discernment, BT says that it implies the kāyas that are the nature of phenomena not being different from the kāyas that bear this nature. Nevertheless, on the level of the seeming, the remaining three kāyas are presented as different since they respectively appear in different ways to buddhas; bodhisattvas; and śrāvakas, pratyekabuddhas, and ordinary beings.

243 CZ, p. 653.

244 In Appendix I8A, JNS (vol. 2, p. 435) attributes this expression to Dölpopa, while Dpa' bo gtsug lag phreng ba n.d. (p. 692) gives the *Bodhisattvabhūmi* as the source of this number. As can be seen below, the sum total of all the qualities listed in AA VIII.2–6 is 144. Thus, without thoroughly investigating the actual sources of the number of 140 (which is beyond the scope of this volume), one can only speculate how it is arrived at. Usually verses VIII.2–6 are explained as describing the twenty-one sets of uncontaminated dharmas or wisdoms as numbered below.

245 The Tibetan has "lack of afflictions" (*nyon mongs med*).

246 The Tibetan has "nothing to guard" (*bsrung ba med pa*).

247 Commenting on the *Vivṛti*, JNS (vol. 2, p. 452) says that the first kāya is the dharmatākāya, while the second one is the dharmakāya, which has the character of wisdom free from reference points, whose nature consists of the uncontaminated foundations of mindfulness and so on.

248 CE reads *zla ba* ("moon"), but the *Vṛtti* (D3787, fol. 195a.1) and other commentaries have *lva ba*.

249 JNS (vol. 2, pp. 453–55) explains the following on the ten totalities. The first eight are based on the actual fourth dhyāna, their nature is the virtuous mental factor of detachment, and their focal objects consist of the āyatana of visible forms of the desire realm. The last two totalities are simply the pure actual meditative absorptions of Infinite Space and Infinite Consciousness, and their focal objects are one's own four mental skandhas (*Abhidharmakośa* VIII.36). In terms of the path of learning, the totalities can also be contaminated, but the ten totalities on the buddhabhūmi are uncontaminated in nature. As for the manner of meditating as illustrated by focusing on earth, during the preparatory stage one meditates that all elements are earth. During the main stage one meditates by focusing on the name "earth" (the same applies to the remaining nine as explained in CE). In addition to the signs of accomplishment described in CE, JNS speaks of the entire surface of the earth being as even as the palm of one's hand; water being still and without bubbles; fire being unmoving and of lucid colors; wind blowing gently from one direction and not ruffling the earth; the four colors (such as blue) appearing clearly without being mixed with any other colors; mountains and so forth appearing completely unobstructive and transparent; and there being no characteristics of appearances when there are absolutely no appearances of any referents other than consciousness. The formless meditative absorptions of Nothing Whatsoever and Peak of Existence are not presented as totalities because the mind is withdrawn and unclear in them. The six sense faculties are not presented as totalities because they cannot be externalized. The sound āyatana is not so presented because it has no continuum, while the totalities must expand in an uninterrupted and all-pervading manner. The āyatanas of smell and taste are not so presented because they cannot pervade the form realm. Thus, the samādhis of the appearance of earth and so forth expanding so that they pervade all apprehended aspects that appear to one are called "totalities." Most commentaries on the AA do not mention any specifics about the totality of earth, but traditional abhidharma sources speak of using a disc made of clay as one's focal object. In general, one takes the respective physical focal object as one's model, looking at it for a while. Then, one visualizes it internally, gradually imagining that the entire world appears like that. As an aid to focus on the physical and the mental image, one also repeats the name (or one of the epithets) of the respective object. Some sources also include the step of closing one's eyes and focusing on the retinal image that occurs after having looked at the outer object for an extended period.

250 This presentation is based on the *Abhidharmakośabhāṣya* on VIII.35. It is said that the eight liberations are the gateways for the eight kinds of overpowering, which in turn serve as

the gateways for the ten totalities. According to *Abhidharmakośa* VIII.35bd, the first liberation is identical to the first two kinds of overpowering; the second liberation, to the third and fourth kinds of overpowering; and the third liberation, to the remaining four. Also, these latter four are very similar to the above four totalities in terms of colors. However, according to the *Abhidharmakośabhāṣya* and JNS (vol. 2, p. 456), the specific differences between the liberations, overpowerings, and totalities are as follows. The liberations refer to the factor of turning one's back to formational mundane phenomena or the factor of being liberated from all obscurations with regard to them. The āyatanas of overpowering refer to gaining complete mastery over these phenomena and therefore being able to see and influence them as one pleases (thus overpowering other mundane focal objects—even those of others in the same environment). The totalities culminate in wisdom pervading all knowable objects, which is a buddha's mind of totality. As *Mahāyānasūtrālaṃkāra* XXI.44 says, a buddha's mind is liberated from all obscurations, overpowers the entire world, and pervades all knowable objects. In general, except for the meditative absorption of cessation, all the samādhis among the liberations, the āyatanas of overpowering, and the totalities can occur in both ordinary beings and noble ones. For more details, see *Abhidharmakośa* VIII.32–37 and its *Bhāṣya*.

251 JNS (vol. 2, p. 457) comments that (7) refers to a buddha's samādhi that severs the continuum of the afflictions of others. (8) means that the wisdom of buddhas knows all knowable objects by virtue of their previous aspiration prayers to be able to do so. Commenting on the *Vivṛti*, JNS (vol. 2, pp. 459–60) says that (8) refers to this wisdom engaging in the welfare of all sentient beings for as long as saṃsāra lasts and these beings are not liberated, which is by virtue of the buddhas' previous aspiration prayers to eliminate attachment, doubt, and so forth of those who entertain reference points and characteristics despite all phenomena being free from reference points and characteristics. For more details, see AA VIII.7–8.

252 The description of these four is literally taken from *Mahāyānasūtrālaṃkāra* XXI.50.

253 Commenting on the *Vivṛti*, JNS (vol. 2, p. 460) adds that the mastery over karma (d) can also be presented from the perspective of sentient beings having no control over their actions, while buddhas have complete control over theirs. Masteries (a)–(c) are the fruitions of generosity; (d)–(e), of ethics; (f), of patience; (g), of vigor; (h), of dhyāna; and (i)–(k), of prajñā.

254 As mentioned in the Introduction, most Indian AA commentaries other than Haribhadra's and many Yogācāra commentaries give one or more of three basic etymologies for "dharmakāya"—(a) the collection of the consummate uncontaminated qualities of a buddha (in certain pre-mahāyāna explanations, "dharma" is taken to refer to the Buddha's teachings); (b) the basis or substratum of uncontaminated qualities, or the basis of mastery over all phenomena; and (c) the embodiment of the nature of phenomena, or the embodiment of the nature of phenomena as perceived by wisdom. Though the prajñāpāramitā sūtras never speak about the dharmakāya in the sense of (a) (they discuss the above uncontaminated qualities, but not in relation to the dharmakāya) and almost always as (c), AA VIII.2–6 clearly presents the dharmakāya as a collection of uncontaminated qualities. However, most AA commentators explain this as applying only conventionally. For example, the *Vṛtti* (D3787, fols. 191b.7–192a.7) is very explicit on the unity of the svābhāvikakāya and the dharmakāya, with both referring to the unconditioned dharmatā. Yogācāra texts typically agree that buddhahood (the svābhāvikakāya/dharmakāya) cannot be defined through its qualities, which are merely associated with it from a phenomenological perspective, but do not represent its nature. Rather, the defining essence of buddhahood is the nondual wisdom of realizing the emptiness of all phenomena, including these very buddha qualities. For the above twenty-one sets of qualities, see also Charts 11, 12, and 14 in Volume One and "The explanation of the uncommon thirty-nine aspects of the knowledge of all aspects" under AA IV.4ac. As mentioned in the Introduction, these qualities are also found in *Mahāyānasūtrālaṃkāra* XXI.43–58 and its commentaries (most of them are also in the seventh chapter of the *Abhidharmakośabhāṣya*) and described in great detail in the

tenth chapter of the *Mahāyānasaṃgraha*. Commenting on the *Vivṛti*, JNS (vol. 2, pp. 458 and 462) says that certain portions of all these qualities may occur to certain degrees even in ordinary beings, but the ones of a perfectly enlightened buddha, which are described here, refer to the fully complete and clearly manifest qualities of uncontaminated wisdom free from all stains, which consist of the dharmadhātu. These qualities have the nature of wisdom—the perfect nature without any reference points of the other-dependent nature—which is the element of the change of all states to be relinquished in the sense of being liberated from them. Thus, all these dharmas of the perfect nature are described as the dharmakāya. To separate the dharmakāya from the svābhāvikakāya is the assertion of some masters, such as Vairocanabhadra. For the discussion of whether the AA teaches three or four kāyas in general and the *Vivṛti's* stance in particular, see Appendix I8A.

255 CZ, p. 653 (see also pp. 580–83 and 654–56).

256 The Tibetan of VIII.7ab (*nyan thos nyon mongs med pa'i lta/ mi yi nyon mongs yongs spong nyid*) says:

> The view of the dispassion of śrāvakas
> Means relinquishing the afflictions of people.

257 This Tibetan rendering (*yongs spong nyid*) in VIII.7b seems to be the reason why CE includes this line—against all other commentaries—under the Buddha's dispassion.

258 JNS (vol. 2, pp. 464–66) says that the dispassion of śrāvakas is regarded as the distinctive feature of the mere absence of any conditions for the arising of afflictions in their own mind streams. By virtue of that, they merely avoid the afflictions of other people. As for the samādhi of dispassion of the buddhas, when they enter into cities and so on, there is no need to examine whether there are any afflictions in their own mind streams or not, or whether they function as focal supports for the arising of the afflictions of others or not. Rather, since the samādhi of dispassion of the victors serves as the dominat condition for extinguishing the stream of all afflictions of those to be guided without exception, it overcomes the afflictions in both their own mind streams and those of others (as stated in *Mahāyānasūtrālaṃkāra* XXI.45). As for the samādhi of a buddha's knowledge through aspiration, JNS points to it being described in exactly the same way in *Mahāyānasūtrālaṃkāra* XXI.46. Commenting on the *Vivṛti*, JNS (vol. 2, pp. 465–66) says that the samādhi of dispassion of śrāvakas and pratyekabuddhas consists of avoiding serving as focal objects for the afflictions of others arising upon being seen by these others, but they are not able to extinguish the seeds of the afflictions of others.Therefore, the samādhi of dispassion of buddhas is far more distinguished because śrāvakas and pratyekabuddhas are not able to eradicate the afflictions of others merely through being seen by these others, whereas buddhas are able to do so. As for the knowledge through aspiration of buddhas, (a) it operates automatically for the welfare of others without any signs of effort; (b) is free from attachment to form and so on by virtue of not clinging to any inner or outer entities; (c) is unobstructed with regard to all knowable objects by virtue of having relinquished all afflictive and cognitive obscurations, including their latent tendencies; (d) remains forever because it remains for the welfare of sentient beings as long as saṃsāra lasts; and (e) solves all questions in the ten directions by virtue of having attained the fourfold discriminating awareness. Thus, in terms of these five features, it is the exact opposite of said knowledge of the śrāvakas.

259 The Tibetan has "appear" (*snang ba*).

260 The Tibetan says, "the king of the gods" (*lha'i rgyal po*).

261 I.5a.

262 JNS (vol. 2, pp. 467–70) says that, once the causes for seeing the buddhas, such as confidence, have matured, the forms of certain buddhas appear to whomever among those to be

guided in whichever forms of guiding them whenever the enlightened activities of their enlightened bodies and so on benefit these beings through their guiding activities. Just as in the example of rainfall, though buddhas have come forth in the world and showered down rains of nectar, those who are unsuitable for the dharma will not enjoy the good taste of the nectar of the teachings. *Mahāyānasūtrālaṃkāra* IX.16 says:

> Just as a water container, when broken,
> Does not show the reflection of the moon,
> The image of the Buddha does not show
> In bad sentient beings.

Therefore, the buddhas are not observed by such beings by virtue of not appearing to them. However, it is never the case that buddhas are not observed while all circumstances for them to appear are suitable. As for the meaning of sending down rainfall, the *Buddhāvataṃsakasūtra* explains that only the nāgas send down rainfall, while the vinaya texts explain that the gods belonging to the four classes of great kings (see Chart 1 in Volume One) stir the ocean by dipping their clothes into it and thus shower down rain. Dharmakīrtiśrī from Suvarṇadvīpa explains that it is Indra who sends down rain, which is in accord with the AA (the *Vivṛti* [D3793, fol. 134a.4] also explicitly says Surendra, which is an epithet of Indra). It is explained that the dharmakāya is permanent at all times and places, even if it does not appear to the unsuitable. Thus, by virtue of the vastness of the activities of enlightened body, speech, and mind, it is described as all-pervading since there is no one who is not a buddha and no one who is not pervaded by buddhahood (or by the buddhas). Since the dharmakāya is not conditioned and impermanent, it is also declared to be "permanent." Therefore, though the verses VIII.9–11 cannot be directly connected with the sūtras, verse VIII.11 is formulated as the basic probative argument that the wisdom dharmakāya is all-pervading and permanent. Verse VIII.9 teaches that, though it is all-pervading and permanent, there are the two possibilities of it appearing or not appearing as all-pervading and permanent to others. By way of a concordant example, verse VIII.10 teaches that it does not have to be not all-pervading and permanent, even when it does not appear to others in this way. As for the statement that the dharmakāya is contained within individual mind streams, it is made with a certain intention because *Uttaratantra* I.129 says that the stainless nature of the mind is primordially unconnected with the cocoon of the afflictions of sentient beings. Also, the statement that the dharmakāya has distinct moments is of expedient meaning because *Uttaratantra* I.5a says that it is unconditioned and effortless. Commenting on the *Vivṛti*, JNS (vol. 2, pp. 467–70) says that seeds of virtue were produced in former lifetimes through having met the external conditions of mahāyāna spiritual friends and so on. By virtue of these seeds, the causal conditions of focusing on the three jewels have unfolded. Then, through the activities of buddhas teaching the dharma and so on at the time of their having become enlightened and their doing so in ways that accord with sentient beings, the basic element of those to be guided and the enlightened activity of these buddhas meet for a while. During this time, as a result of their former aspiration prayers for the sake of accomplishing the welfare of those to be guided, the buddhas appear to certain ones among those beings and promote their welfare accordingly. However, though buddhas are engaged in accomplishing happiness and benefit at all times, just as a wish-fulfilling jewel, by virtue of the causes for the appearance of buddhakāyas being incomplete due to certain beings' self-produced karmic flaws, it may not appear to these beings that the buddhas are engaged in maturing the fruitions of promoting the welfare of beings. "Since the dharmakāya, which has the character of wisdom, exists in the supports that are the individually distinct mind streams of yogins and arises in each moment, how can the dharmakāya wisdom and its enlightened activity be described as all-pervading and permanent?" The dharmakāya is all-pervading because its activity for the welfare of others is vast by way of its appearing as potentially everything due its not being adventitious. Though it continually remains in each moment without any gap as long as saṃsāra lasts, the enlightened body, speech, and mind of the Bhagavān are without any change, transition, arising, ceasing, or exhaustion.

263 JNS (vol. 2, pp. 471–72) says that the sāmbhogikakāya of the sage is held by the Bhagavān to be the great sāmbhogikakāya that resides in Akaniṣṭha because it is the kāya with these major and minor marks that enjoys solely the dharma of the mahāyāna. The conventional expression of the sāmbhogikakāya being endowed with "the five certainties" was coined by way of inferring this from the meaning of *Madhyamakāvatāra* XI.18ff. Atiśa's *Prajñāpāramitāpiṇḍārthapradīpa* (D3804, fol. 239b.5–7) speaks of four, saying that, according to Haribhadra, (1) the retinue consists only of bodhisattvas on the tenth bhūmi, while Ratnākaraśānti speaks of bodhisattvas from the path of seeing onward; (2) the place is Akaniṣṭha; (3) the dharma is only the mahāyāna; and (4) the teacher is solely appearing in the form of being adorned with the major and minor marks (the fifth certainty refers to the time of this appearance lasting for as long as saṃsāra does). Dharmamitra explains that the kāya which passes into nirvāṇa is the nairmāṇikakāya, whereas this does not happen for the sāmbhogikakāya. Therefore, though the latter is momentary, it is permanent in terms of its continuum. Some scholars hold that the sāmbhogikakāya is permanent because, just as the birth and transition of Indra, its arising and ceasing are not perceived by others who are not buddhas. To say that the svābhāvikakāya does not have the major and minor marks is wrong—among buddhas, this fact that the svābhāvikakāya possesses the major and minor marks of the dharmakāya appears to each other. For bodhisattvas who are only a single birth away from buddhahood, this fact of the svābhāvikakāya possessing the major and minor marks of the dharmakāya appears as the major and minor marks of the sāmbhogikakāya.

264 CZ, p. 653.

265 In this regard, both CE and JNS (vol. 2, pp. 474–76) basically reproduce what the *Vivṛti* (D3793, fols. 134b.7–135b.3) says.

266 This is what the sūtras say and most commentaries agree with this, but PBG (p. 612), NSML (p. 636), and Samtani 2002 (p. 212) say that the first four protuberances refer to the backs of the hands and prominent insteps.

267 Ordinary humans are said to be three-and-a-half cubits tall (one cubit being the span between one's own elbow and fingertips).

268 The all-knowing horse is an Indian mythical figure, being one of the seven precious items of a cakravartin. Obviously, in the case of a buddha, "having many sons" is generally not to be taken literally, but refers to spiritual heirs. In particular, in the case of Buddha Śākyamuni, his physical son was Rāhula; the sons of his speech were the śrāvakas and pratyekabuddhas; and the sons of his mind were the bodhisattvas.

269 Other sources say that this is a single coil of hair between the eyebrows, which extends for many miles when uncoiled.

270 Usually the expression used here refers to the flesh between the shoulder blades and at the back of the neck.

271 This is the Indian fig tree, also called banyan tree.

272 There are sixty aspects to Brahmā's melodious voice, which include being gentle, pleasant, clear, worthy to listen to, understandable by all, pervasive, making everything known, having the force of a lion's roar, and resounding within any kind of retinue. For details, see the *Mahāvyutpatti* (section 20, nos. 445–504, which are explained in detail in Abhayākaragupta's *Munimatālaṃkāra*).

273 CZ, pp. 583–85 and 657–61. Note that this is just one from among a considerable number of more or less differing lists of these thirty-two marks that are found in various sūtras and treatises (for a rather comprehensive list, see Xing 2002, p. 27). Also, the comments on

them and their causes vary in different texts. Except for a few minor changes in the order and some additional features, Nāgārjuna's *Ratnāvalī* (II.77–96) gives basically the same list as above. The *Uttaratantra* (III.17–25) has another (slightly varying) list, which—except for minor differences in counting—corresponds to the one in TOK (vol. 3, pp. 619–22). Differing from the prajñāpāramitā sūtras as the source of the AA, this latter list (which includes also some of the minor marks explained below) is based on the *Ratnādārikāparipṛcchāsūtra*. For a detailed comparison of these sources, including Nāgārjuna's **Prajñāpāramitāśāstra*, see the footnotes in Takasaki 1966a on the translation of the *Uttaratantra*'s above-mentioned verses. For the most detailed presentation of the major marks apart from the prajñāpāramitā sūtras, see the *Lakkhaṇasutta* (*Dīgha Nikāya* III.142ff.; translated in Walshe 1995, pp. 441–60) and the *Arthaviniścayasūtra* (Samtani 2002, pp. 205–16), which however lists thirty-three marks. See also the *Lalitavistarasūtra* (Dharma Publishing 1983, vol. 1, pp. 155–56), the *Mahāvyutpatti* (section 17, nos. 236–67; translated in Thurman 1976, p. 156), and Pawo Tsugla Trengwa's commentary on the *Bodhicaryāvatāra* (Dpa' bo gtsug lag phreng ba n.d., pp. 720–23). YT (p. 656) refers to a **Dharmadānasaṃgrahasūtra* (Tib. chos kyi sbyin pa bsdu ba'i mdo) as the source for the causes that accomplish the thirty-two major marks, but the *Kangyur* does not contain a sūtra by that name (the *Tengyur* contains two short texts with similar names—D4398 and D4399—but they do not treat this subject).

274 The Tibetan is very clear on this line, while the Sanskrit *dhvāntapradhvastālokaśuddhatā* is very ambiguous and can also mean what Conze has ("his pure light dispels the darkness"). However, both the Sanskrit and the Tibetan of this minor mark in the *Mahāvyutpatti* (section 18, no. 300) confirm the above translation.

275 In the Tibetan, the order of "smooth" and "slender" is reversed.

276 The Tibetan has *bkra shis* ("auspicious") for *svastika*. In another Tibetan version of this verse, there is an additional line after the third one, which explicitly adds, "and are ornamented with swastikas" (*g.yung drung 'khyil bas brgyan pa ste*).

277 The Sanskrit and Tibetan words (*vyañjana* and *mtshan*) here can mean both "mark" and "genitals," but all other commentaries agree that this minor mark refers to all parts of the genitals being complete and fully developed.

278 The Sanskrit *bimba* can refer to both the plant *Momordica monadelpha* and its red berries. It can also mean "image" or "reflection."

279 Given the explanations in the *Vivṛti* and other commentaries (see below), "motivation" may (also) pertain to those to be guided.

280 These are a mirror, yogurt, *Panicum dactylon* grass, wood-apple fruits, a right-coiling conch shell, elephant bile, vermilion powder, and white mustard.

281 This probably refers to the *nandyāvarta* diagram (see Samtani 2002, p. 218, which also adds wheels, vajras, lotuses, and fish).

282 CZ, pp. 586–87 and 661–65. In the above, I did not follow CE's splitting up of verses VIII.21–32 according to the eight sets of ten marks. Differing from CE, the *Vivṛti* (JNS, vol. 2, pp. 481–85) gives the following reasons for these marks—(1) being free from desire for all formations; (6) having properly and progressively engaged in each virtue; (7) having guarded well his actions of body, speech, and mind as well as his livelihood; (9) being endowed with insight into very hidden phenomena; (10) liberating beings from all places difficult to access; (11)–(12) being skilled in outshining humans and nāgas, respectively; (16) being skilled in elegance; (18) perfectly proclaiming the qualities of others; (22) the mind being endowed with compassion; (27) teaching the pure dharma; (28) teaching the dharma in a way that is easy to understand [obviously due to a spelling variation in the Tibetan of the *Vivṛti* (*gos* versus *go*), JNS comments,

"teaching how to easily find dharma robes"]; (30) the roots of virtue being greatly distinguished; (33) teaching the utterly pure meaning of words; (40) his retinue being beautiful from all sides; (41) having a clean mind; (42) being free from dharmas that guide beings untimely; (43) teaching the dharmas of attaining a sound body, speech, and mind; (46) teaching the utterly pure dharma for as long as saṃsāra lasts; (48) having realized that the entire world is like a reflection; (60) being a person of excellent cleanliness; (61) the dharma being extremely vast; (65) being skilled in the gentle dharma of the vinaya; (66) the mind stream being moistened by virtue; (70) not letting the virtuous mind streams of all sentient beings deteriorate; (71) buddhas not changing into anything else through any actions by others due to their wrong views; (79) having spread the fragrance of the flowers of the branches of enlightenment; (80) being beautiful in all respects. For the minor marks, see also the *Lalitavistarasūtra* (Dharma Publishing 1983, vol. 1, pp. 156–57), Samtani 2002 (pp. 217–18), the *Mahāvyutpatti* (section 18, nos. 269–349; translated in Thurman 1976, pp. 156–57), Dpa' bo gtsug lag phreng ba n.d. (pp. 723–26), and TOK (vol. 3, pp. 622–25). As for the amounts of merit it takes to accomplish the minor and major marks, *Ratnāvalī* III.2–8 explains that the merits of all pratyekabuddhas, learners, nonlearners, and ordinary beings in all worlds in the universe are as infinite as these worlds. Through ten times these merits, just a single pore of a buddha is accomplished, and the same goes for all his pores. One hundred times the merit that produces all these pores together accomplishes one single minor mark. One hundred times the merit that it takes to accomplish all eighty minor marks produces a single major mark. One thousand times the merit that is necessary for accomplishing thirty of these major marks produces the ūrṇā hair. Finally, one hundred thousand times the merit of the ūrṇā hair brings forth the uṣṇīṣa.

283 JNS (vol. 2, pp. 486–87) says that, as Atiśa's *Prajñāpāramitāpiṇḍārthapradīpa* (D3804, fol. 240a.2–3) explains, the nairmāṇikakāya lacks the four (or five) certainties of the sāmbhogikakāya and thus can appear as anybody or anything in any way. Commenting on the *Vivṛti*, JNS (vol. 2, p. 487) says that the three kinds of nairmāṇikakāyas accomplish what sentient beings wish for in a manner that accords with these wishes and is equal for all. A buddha's nairmāṇikakāya is perpetual by virtue of its appearing continuously (though in different forms) from the perspective of countless beings. TOK (vol. 3, p. 599) explains the meaning of nairmāṇikakāya as its "definitely changing into something else [at some point] because it is a kāya that has the nature of being emanated [or created]."

284 CZ, p. 653.

285 JNS (vol. 2, p. 489) says that, just like the perpetual dharmatākāya, its enlightened activity is also perpetual as long as saṃsāra lasts [LN (vol. 2, p. 372) and BT (p. 688): According to Haribhadra (see below), the perpetual dominant condition for perpetual enlightened activity is the dharmakāya, whereas Āryavimuktisena speaks of the nairmāṇikakāya instead]. The reason for this is that the stream of sentient beings is perpetual and that thus the actions accumulated by them are also perpetual. Therefore, the enlightened activity of the dharmakāya operates as long as there are sentient beings. Commenting on the *Vivṛti*, JNS (vol. 2, pp. 488–89) says that the stains which obscure the essential character of the svābhāvikakāya (the feature of the nature) are eliminated through the remedies that arise through the power of cultivating the four trainings (the feature of the cause). By virtue of that, this nature is certain to appear as different objects (wisdom dharmakāya, sāmbhogikakāya, and nairmāṇikakāya, respectively) for the distinct modes of perception of buddhas, bodhisattvas, and śrāvakas as well as ordinary beings (the feature of the perceiving subject). Thus, it is based on these distinct appearances of the single nature of the svābhāvikakāya that it is labeled as one of the other three kāyas, respectively, by individual noble and ordinary beings [LN (vol. 2, p. 371) interestingly says that the nature of the three kāyas—the svābhāvikakāya—is labeled as dharmakāya in dependence on mirrorlike wisdom; as sāmbhogikakāya in dependence on the wisdom of equality and discriminating wisdom; and as nairmāṇikakāya in dependence on all-accomplishing wisdom]. How is

the welfare of others accomplished through these three kāyas? On the level of the seeming, it is the wisdom dharmakāya alone that promotes the welfare of sentient beings through giving rise to what appear as sāmbhogikakāyas and nairmāṇikakāyas to others (those to be guided) by virtue of their different inclinations. Thus, the activities of the dharmakāya arise in dependence on this wisdom kāya being the dominant condition for the perfect activities that are based on the appearances of the beings to be guided. Through these activities, the obscurations of the mind streams of sentient beings as its recipients are relinquished and their remedies are produced, so the question is what the agent of these activities is. Buddhas arrive in the world and teach the points to be adopted and to be rejected. Through training in these points, sentient beings as the recipients of such activity cease and primordial buddhahood—natural luminosity—is the actual recipient (see also Appendix I8B).

286 Commenting on the *Vivṛti*, JNS (vol. 2, pp. 491–95) says that enlightened activity is threefold—establishing beings in (a) the support of the path, (b) the path itself, and (c) the fruition of this path. (a) The beginning of a buddha's enlightened activity to lead sentient beings to nirvāṇa is (1) the activity of appeasing them—the characteristic of lacking any clinging to both higher and unpleasant realms. (b) Establishing humans on the path of accumulation is twofold. The techniques of gradually maturing the mind streams of others consist of (2) establishing them in the four means of attraction. Establishing them in the view of realizing the four realities refers to (3) making them realize the actual way of being through the prājñās that arise from study and reflection rejecting the antagonistic factors and adopting their remedies. Establishing humans on the path of preparation is threefold. The welfare of others means to (4) establish those on the path of accumulation in the true nature of the four immeasurables as the welfare of other beings through being free from attachment, anger, and the other bondages, just as illusionists do not have any of these bondages with regard to the illusory things they created. One's own welfare means to (5) establish them in cultivating the six pāramitās that are characterized by being pure of the three spheres. The welfare of both is twofold—establishing them in causal maturation and the pure view. The first means to (6) make them establish themselves and others in the buddha path (the ten virtuous actions) and the second refers to (7) them becoming familiar with all phenomena being natural emptiness. Establishing them on the path of seeing means to, (8) primarily based on the perfection of the pāramitā of generosity on the first bhūmi, establish them in the nondual nature of phenomena, which has the characteristic of realizing that the nature of the pure dharmadhātu is omnipresent. Establishing them on the path of familiarization is twofold in terms of the impure and pure bhūmis. The first one is threefold—through further completing the accumulations, (9) establishing them, on the second and third bhūmis, in the knowledge that all dharmas of the pāramitās of ethics and patience are mere imputed symbols; (10) establishing them, on the fourth, fifth, and sixth bhūmis, based on the pāramitās of vigor, dhyāna, and prajñā, respectively, in the nonobservation of all phenomena by virtue of the characteristic of not clinging to any entities that are knowledge and knowable objects; and (11) establishing them, on the seventh bhūmi, in maturing beings through the power of the pāramitā of means. Establishing them on the pure bhūmis is also threefold. On the eighth bhūmi, through the pāramitā of power, they are first established (12) on the path of bodhisattvas that is not in common with śrāvakas and so on and then (13) in relinquishing any clinging to any phenomena within the true reality of the actual way of being. (14) On the ninth bhūmi, they are established in swiftly attaining enlightenment through the power of the pāramitā of aspiration prayers. Being established on the tenth bhūmi is threefold. First, being established in the immediate attainment of this bhūmi means that (15) they purify various buddha realms through the power of the pāramitā of wisdom and thus are granted the empowerment of great light rays by all buddhas. Second, being established in the state of a tenth-bhūmi bodhisattva who is only obstructed by one single rebirth from buddhahood is threefold—(16) being established in such a bodhisattva's own nature being definite as being someone who is about to become a complelety perfect buddha; (17) being established in maturing means being established in promoting the

welfare of sentient beings of all worldly realms in the ten directions; and (18) being established in attending to the spiritual friend means being established in approaching the buddhas in all pure and impure worldly realms and in the qualities of studying the dharma with them and so on. Third, being established on the special path of the tenth bhūmi is eightfold. These bodhisattvas are established in (19) the special path's own nature—the branches of enlightenment, which have the characteristic to be the dharmas that swiftly induce all kinds of enlightenment in their own mind streams; (20) the certainty that nothing becomes lost within the actuality of karmic actions and their results being connected; (21) realizing the actual way of being of all entities, just as they truly are; (22) having relinquished all mistakenness; (23) the wisdom of having relinquished mistakenness in that it is nonsubstantial; (24) considering the attainment of the purification of bodhisattvas by virtue of the characteristic of natural complete purity; (25) the completion of the two accumulations—the collections of the causes for attaining the state of purification free from all stains; and (26) understanding conditioned and unconditioned phenomena as nondifferent by virtue of the nature of emptiness. (c) Being established in the fruition of the path means (27) being established in nirvāṇa on the bhūmi of a tathāgata. In this way, just like the dharmakāya, also its twenty-sevenfold enlightened activity is held to last as long as saṃsāra.

287 CZ, p. 576.

288 JNS (vol. 2, p. 497) says that the summary of all the points of prajñāpāramitā in six is as follows. (1) The characteristics in terms of defining the meaning of the mother of the victors consist of the three knowledges. The four trainings consist of (2) the complete training in all the aspects to manifest these three knowledges, which, (3) when being joined with one's mind stream through skillful means, is the culminating training. (4) In terms of the order of all these trainings, they are the serial training; and (5) in terms of their last moment, they are the instantaneous training. (6) The maturation of these trainings is the dharmakāya.

289 In linking "cause" in line IX.2a with the four trainings, CE (like PK, fol. 169.3–4) follows the *Vṛtti* (D3787, fol. 210a.4), the *Vārttika* (D3788, fol. 179b.2), and the *Ālokā* (D3791, fol. 339b.1–2), which agree on the four trainings being the cause of the dharmakāya. However, most Tibetan commentaries follow Haribhadra's *Vivṛti* (D3793, fol. 140a.1) in linking "cause" with "object" (see below). Though the Sanskrit and the Tibetan of this verse are not unambiguous on this point, the metrical structure of both rather suggests the latter reading.

290 JNS (vol. 2, p. 499) says that (1) the objects of engagement are the three knowledges, which are the cause. (2) The means to make this cause a living experience consists of the fourfold training. (3) What is attained through having made this cause a living experience is its result—the dharmakāya and enlightened activity. Commenting on the concluding remarks of the *Vivṛti*, JNS (vol. 2, pp. 500–501) says that, in the brief summary of the contents of the mother, only the meanings of the clear realizations are complete. In the other one (the medium version), not only the meaning but also the words are complete, and in yet another one (the detailed version), each meaning is extensively discussed through dividing it in terms of many different specifications of names and words. Thus, one should know that the manner of summarizing the meanings of the entire mother consists of just the eight clear realizations as explained by scholars like Maitreya and so on. Nevertheless, there is no flaw of redundancy through the contents of the mother being divided in different ways (such as brief, medium, and detailed) because these are nothing but distinct ways of turning the wheel of dharma in accordance with the individual dispositions of those to be guided. In the concluding verses of his *Vivṛti* (D3793, fol. 140a.3–6), Haribhadra says that he saw the meaning of the mother through Āryavimuktisena's power. Thus, in order to make this meaning understood easily, (unlike Vimuktisena) he avoided matching each passage of the sūtras with the verses of the AA. In this way, after having having paid homage to the excellent paṇḍita and guru Vairocana, he composed this commentary. Haribhadra dedicates the merit of this composition so that all beings may attain the prajñā of a sugata. He concludes that,

for beings with dull prajñā like him, the entire meaning of a treatise like the AA, which is the sphere of noble ones like Maitreya, lies beyond his mind. Nevertheless, in order to plant some good tendencies from the perspective of the welfare of both himself and others, he made some efforts here—may the learned be patient with his mistakes. Finally, he says:

> Through all kinds of scriptural traditions,
> I was tired out, but at long last,
> I saw my place of resting at ease—
> The approach of prajñāpāramitā.

291 CE has Vidyākāraprajñā, while JNS has the correct form as above.

292 Obviously, the author here refers to JNS (written by his guru, Mikyö Dorje) being as vast as an ocean and too difficult to understand for certain people. In comparison, he considers his own CE as being just a droplet from that ocean.

293 "Lightning" refers to the element of fire.

294 Vol. 2, pp. 3–11.

295 This section omits the parts of the descriptions of the four realities that correspond to CE 2.3.1.2.1.1.2.1.1.2.1.2.

296 Statements to that effect are found in Dharmakīrti's *Pramāṇavārttika* (III.338 and especially III.368-484) and *Pramāṇaviniścaya* (D4211, fols. 165a.4–5 and 167a.3).

297 See CE on AA IV.39ff. and Appendix I4d.

298 Vol. 2, pp. 14–25.

299 Examples of what is neutral yet obscuring are the afflictions of the two higher realms, their views about a real personality and extremes, and the ignorance that is congruently associated with these two views. An example of what is neutral and unobscuring is the reality of suffering.

300 Lines 5b–6ab.

301 According to JG (p. 191), some say, "Realization is completed on the first bhūmi and relinquishment is completed on the eighth bhūmi. For by virtue of the afflicted mind having changed state, all afflictive obscurations are relinquished without exception." It is not justified that all afflictive obscurations have been relinquished on the eighth bhūmi because the *Ālokā* explains that afflictive obscurations exist on all ten bhūmis; the *Abhidharmasamuccaya* (D4049, fol.73b.1–2) says, "During the path of familiarization on the ten bhūmis, [bodhisattvas] cultivate the path that is the remedy for the cognitive obscurations, but this is not a [direct] remedy for the afflictive obscurations. However, upon attaining enlightenment, afflictive obscurations and cognitive obscurations are [finally] relinquished simutaneously"; and also the *Madhyamakāvatārabhāṣya* (D3862, fols. 342b.7–343a.1) states, "The latent tendencies of ignorance, desire, and so on are only put to an end in the state of omniscience and buddhahood, but not anywhere else." Thus, it is explained that said latent tendencies exist until buddhahood.

302 Both the Sanskrit *jñeyāvaraṇa* and the Tibetan *shes bya'i sgrib pa* for "cognitive obscurations" can be understood in two ways. The more common explanation is found in the *Bodhisattvabhūmi* (Dutt ed., p. 26.8), which says, "The obscurations are what prevent cognizing the objects to be cognized" (*jñeyejñānasya pratighāta āvaraṇam*). Prajñākaramati's *Bodhicaryāvatārapañjikā* on IX.55 (Vaidya ed., p. 201) presents the alternative understanding that, "by virtue of their having the nature of being [merely] superimposed, the obscurations consist of the very objects to be cognized" (*jñeyam eva samāropita rūpatvād āvṛtiḥ*). Alternative descriptions of afflictive and cognitive obscurations are found in Mi bskyod rdo rje 2004, p. 514: "Through taking the five skandhas as a personal identity and, based on the views about a self,

discriminating between self and others, the triad of attachment, hatred, and ignorance exists in one's mind stream. Through this, one commits virtuous, nonvirtuous, or unmoving actions and thus circles in the three realms. This is the effect of being obscured by the afflictive obscurations. Through taking the five skandhas as a phenomenal identity and, based on that, discriminating between characteristics of reference points (such as existence, nonexistence, arising, and ceasing), false imagination exists in one's mind stream. Through the power of that, one commits actions of clinging to real existence and clinging to the lack of real existence, and thus does not transcend [saṃsāric] existence and peace. This is the effect of being obscured by the cognitive obscurations."

303 See Appendix I5d.

304 Skt. *dṛśyānupalabdhihetu*, Tib. *snang rung ma dmigs pa'i gtan tshigs*. This kind of argument is defined as "a reason with the three modes that proves both the fact and the conventional expression of 'nonexistence' by negating the cognizing subject of something suitable to appear." For example, "In this room, there is no elephant because none is observable in it through any kind of valid cognition." Usually, if there is an elephant somewhere, given sufficient light and nothing obscuring it, it is clearly observable to the people present whose sense faculties are intact. Thus, the inverse of this—that is, if an elephant is not observable in this place—means that it does not exist there. Likewise, if what seems to appear as an outer object cannot be verified as an actual outer object through either direct perception or valid inference, one has to conclude that it does not exist as such an object, and that what appears as it is merely a mental appearance (for more details, see Brunnhölzl 2004, pp. 179–81).

305 After "no reference points," JNS has *rtogs pa med pa dang/ rlom pa med pa*. However, these are not two distinct points in Vimuktisena's and Haribhadra's commentaries, but they speak about it as rendered above.

306 Section 2ca below also includes the factors to be relinquished through familiarization in this category.

307 On the impregnations of negative tendencies, the ālaya-consciousness, and the vajralike samādhi, see also JNS's remarks in the endnote on AA V.37–38 and Chapter Seven. According to the *Saṃdhinirmocanasūtra* (D106; ACIP MDO SDE CA@63b.3–5 and 64b.5–6) on the eleventh bhūmi (the buddhabhūmi), what is removed are (1) the ignorance that consists of a very subtle clinging to all knowable objects (the most subtle afflictive obscurations); (2) the ignorance that consists of the very subtle obstructions to knowable objects (the most subtle cognitive obscurations); and (3) all the remaining impregnations of the negative tendencies of (1) and (2).

308 JNS only has *gzung rtog*, but the conceptions about the apprehender are not treated separately below and—as is the case below and elsewhere—should obviously be included here too.

309 Though JNS does not indicate to what the above point 3) "boundary lines" refers, this paragraph seems to correspond to it. Mi bskyod rdo rje 2004 (pp. 520–22) says that, through the wisdom of realizing personal and phenomenal identitylessness, the true nature of the four realities with regard to the three realms is perceived in the sixteen moments of the path of seeing (during the dharma readinesses and dharma cognitions, the sixteen aspects of the four realities with regard to the desire realm; during the subsequent readinesses and subsequent cognitions, the sixteen aspects of the four realities with regard to the two higher realms). In this way, the afflictive and cognitive obscurations that are the factors to be relinquished through seeing are relinquished. Then, on the nine levels of the path of familiarization, the dualistic appearances of nonafflicted ignorance—false imaginations—are relinquished. Finally, through the vajralike samādhi, the most subtle impregnations of negative tendencies are eradicted. The reason for the remedies being able to eliminate these obscurations is as follows. It is nothing but this dependently originating self-aware and self-lucid cognition that is imagined as a self and what is mine.

Through the habituations of the imaginary cognitions of karma and afflictions, lucid appearances with regard to what is false are set up. This is the other-dependent nature appearing as saṃsāra with its three realms. However since none of this engages in the true nature of the mind, it is suitable to be relinquished. On the other hand, when this self-aware and self-lucid cognition sets up correct lucid appearances with regard to the two kinds of identitylessness and the creation and completion stages, this very self-aware cognition represents the wisdom of realizing emptiness and the wisdom of realizing identitylessness. This very cognition of realizing emptiness and identitylessness, through the power of being bound through the pure nāḍīs, vāyus, and tilakas in the body of the creation stage that lucidly appears as the supreme deity, is liberated as the completion stage—the nature of mahāmudrā, which consists of infinite kāyas and wisdoms. For as long as the mind stream is not liberated from the karma and the afflictions that are factors to be relinquished through seeing, the ten virtuous actions (the causes for divine and human rebirths) and all immovable virtues (the dhyānas and formless absorptions) that cause rebirth in certain realms and are contaminated propel one into saṃsāric suffering. Therefore, they have the nature of the origin of suffering. Once the karma and afflictions that are factors to be relinquished through seeing have been relinquished, the ten virtues and the immovable virtues are embraced by the prajñā of realizing identitylessness and therefore turn into the nature of the uncontaminated six pāramitās. Through these uncontaminated virtues becoming the causes of the pure realms, kāyas, and enjoyments of the buddhabhūmi, they represent the reality of the path that relinquishes the cognitive obscurations too and they also establish pure worldly realms.

310 JNS has *yod med* (in the blockprint, *med* appears to be inserted by hand), which is emended to *yod mod.*

311 JNS has *gral* (also being handwritten), which can only be *bral.*

312 On the afflictive and cognitive obscurations, see also Appendix I1H3 in Volume One.

313 Vol. 2, pp. 38–72.

314 The Tibetan word *dran pa* has a wide range of meanings, such as "mindfulness," "recollection," "memory," "thinking," and "something coming to mind." The distinction here is between the first one and the last two among these meanings.

315 For a detailed discussion of the four foundations of mindfulness from a mahāyāna point of view, see Pawo Rinpoche Tsugla Trengwa's commentary on *Bodhicaryāvatāra* IX.78–110 (translated in Brunnhölzl 2004, pp. 713–42).

316 The Sanskrit *prahāṇa* can not only mean "relinquishment," but also "effort" (as a corrupt form of *pradhāna*). In Tibetan, it is always rendered as the former (*spong ba*), with JNS's explanation of the term thus being based on that. As can be seen here, the term clearly refers to four activities in which one makes effort, only the first one among which is an actual relinquishment (the second one is to prevent future nonvirtue; the third one, to increase already existing virtue; and the fourth one, to newly produce virtue).

317 See Chart 12 in Volume One and the comments on AA VIII.4b.

318 Though JNS does not continue here, the same obviously applies for the remaining four faculties.

319 D4082. This is Śāntarakṣita's commentary on Candragomī's *Bodhisattvasaṃvaravimśaka* (D4081).

320 D4027, fol. 18.a1–2.

321 These "five" are (1) agitation and regret; (2) malice; (3) drowsiness and torpor; (4) sense pleasures; and (5) doubt.

322 Note that the thirty-seven dharmas concordant with enlightenment consist only of fourteen distinct factors, with twenty-eight among the thirty-seven being the same five factors of confidence, samādhi, prajñā, mindfulness, and vigor. Confidence appears twice—as a faculty and a power. Samādhi is listed four times—as a faculty, a power, a branch of enlightenment, and a branch of the eightfold path (in addition, it participates in all four limbs of miraculous powers). Prajñā features five times—as a limb of miraculous powers, a faculty, a power, a branch of enlightenment, and a branch of the eightfold path (in the form of right view). Mindfulness appears eight times—as the four foundations of mindfulness, a faculty, a power, a branch of enlightenment, and a branch of the eightfold path. Vigor shows nine times—as the four correct efforts, a limb of miraculous powers, a faculty, a power, a branch of enlightenment, and a branch of the eightfold path. Thus, the contents of the seven sets among the thirty-seven dharmas overlap greatly and are inextricably interwoven. When the same factors are named differently in different sets, this just serves to highlight their different functions, while their (often repetitive) arrangement in different sets indicates their progressive perfection and also shows how these factors cooperate in various patterns of mutual support. Also, as the boundary lines of these seven sets show, though they represent the main practices on their respective sections of the path, they remain to be practiced until the final fruition (arhathood or buddhahood). For an overview of the seven sets of the thirty-seven dharmas in relation to the paths of accumulation, preparation, seeing, and familiarization, see Chart 14 in Volume One.

323 Beyond the brief explanations on the paths of relinquishment and buddhahood in CE, JNS provides no further details.

324 *Mahāyānasūtrālaṃkāra* XVIII.77–79 and its *Bhāṣya* speak about the three doors to liberation as three samādhis, with the samādhis being the apprehenders and the three doors being their apprehended spheres. The sphere of the samādhi of emptiness consists of personal and phenomenal identitylessness; the sphere of the samādhi of wishlessness is the basis for clinging to these two kinds of identity, that is, the five appropriating skandhas; and the sphere of the samādhi of signlessness is the subsiding of this basis. In due order, the respective natures of these samādhis are nonconceptual since there are no conceptions about the two kinds of identity; turning away from the basis for clinging to them; and always being endowed with the pleasure in this basis subsiding.

325 *Mahāyānasūtrālaṃkāra* XVIII.80–81 treat the four epitomes of the Buddha's teaching—everything conditioned is impermanent; everything contaminated is suffering; all phenomena are empty and identityless; and nirvāṇa alone is peace. The *Bhāṣya* and Sthiramati's *Sūtrālaṃkāravṛttibhāṣya* (D4034, fols. 131b.1ff.) explain that they are the contents of the three doors to liberation.

326 There is no such text by Dignāga in the *Tengyur*, but the following stanza greatly resembles verse 5 of Nāgārjuna's *Cittavajrastava*.

327 The *Bhāṣya* on *Mahāyānasūtrālaṃkāra* XVIII.80–81 matches the three doors to liberation and the four epitomes as above and continues that, for bodhisattvas, the meaning of "impermanence" is "nonexistence." What does not exist as permanent is impermanent, which, for bodhisattvas, is the imaginary characteristic. The meaning of "suffering" is false imagination, which is the other-dependent characteristic. The meaning of "identityless" is mere "imagination." The imaginary does not exist as an identity, but as mere imagination. Thus, the meaning of "identityless" is the meaning of the nonexistence of the imaginary characteristic. The meaning of "peace" is the meaning of conceptions being at peace, which is the characteristic of the perfect nature—nirvāṇa. Following this explanation, *Mahāyānasūtrālaṃkāra* XVIII.82–104 and the *Bhāṣya* enter into a detailed discussion of the two aspects of "impermanence" and "identitylessness."

328 This refers to the three notions of forms being mutually dependent, mutually connected, and mutually of one taste (see below), which are illustrated in CE through the example of looking at three different vases.

329 As mentioned before, the *Bahubhūmivastu* is the largest one among the five major portions of the *Yogācārabhūmi*, with the *Śrāvakabhūmi* being a part of it.

330 Tib. 'phags pa chos kun tu 'gro ba'i mdo (I could not find such a sūtra in the *Kangyur*).

331 D4049, fol. 95a.6.

332 See CE's general topic on AA I.44a as supplemented by JNS (pp. 278–304).

333 JNS has "right after" (*rjes thogs*), but this should be read as above (*rjes thob*)—as it appears in CE.

334 JNS has "from the sixth bhūmi onward" (*phyin chad*), but given the explanations here and in CE, this must mean "up through the sixth bhūmi" (the same applies for the fifth bhūmi below).

335 The point here is that, as explained above, exactly these seven consciousnesses that could be the only dominant conditions of the mental consciousness have by definition ceased in the meditative absorption of cessation. Thus, a mental consciousness cannot arise either.

336 As for the thirty-nine aspects of the knowledge of all aspects, JNS offers no separate general explanation apart from its comments on the *Vivṛti* (vol. 2, pp. 73–79), which are found at the end of CE on AA IV.4–5.

337 Vol. 2, pp. 140–44.

338 CZ, p. 388.

339 In general, the Sanskrit *liṅgam* and the Tibetan *rtags* are used for both "sign" and "reason."

340 CZ, p. 388.

341 D3804, fol. 237b.2–3.

342 Vol. 2, pp. 156–67.

343 Throughout the twenty-two faculties, "pleasure" and "suffering" refer only to physical sensations based on the sense consciousnesses. The only exception is on the third dhyāna level (see below).

344 D4036, fol. 108b.3.

345 D4038, fol. 91a.2–3.

346 Ibid., fol. 178b.3.

347 JNS and the abhidharma texts distinguish here between "mental ease" (Skt. *sukhacitta*, Tib. *sems bde*) and "mental pleasure" (Skt. *saumanasyam/sumanaska*, Tib. *yid bde*).

348 As in this case, these two mental factors are not necessarily or exclusively understood in a conceptual sense, but as coarse and fine discriminations, respectively, which also apply in the context of sense perception.

349 For details on these questions and the faculties in general, see the first, second, and eighth chapters of the *Abhidharmakośa* and its *Bhāṣya* as referenced above.

350 Based on *Abhidharmakośa* II.22, JNS elaborates that, according to the Vaibhāṣikas, in the desire realm all eight atomic substances are complete in all those minute particles that do not make up the five sense faculties and are free from the āyatana of sound. According to the

Sautrāntikas, all eight atomic substances are not necessarily complete in minute particles. For the *Abhidharmasamuccaya* (D4049, fol. 77a.7) says that there are minute particles that consist of just one, two, three or all among the four elements. Also, the *Vyākhyāyukti* says that moon rays, sun rays, mountains, and the five sense faculties consist of only wind, fire and wind, the first three elements, and all four, respectively. The body sense faculty as asserted by the Vaibhāṣikas consists of nine atomic substances—the above eight plus its own one. Each of the other four sense faculties consists of ten atomic substances—the just-mentioned nine plus their respective own ones.

351 Pp. 184–87. This is an elaboration on the *Vivṛti* on I.31b.

352 The only prajñāpāramitā sūtra that contains such a threefold classification of all phenomena is the one in five hundred lines (D15; ACIP SHES PHYIN SNA TSOGS KA@163a.3–164b.5). This sūtra says that ordinary beings, due to not understanding the threefold classification of phenomena in terms of "nonexistent entity," "bad entity," and "existent entity," cling to phenomena, accomplish them, and are obscured, which means having to experience the six realms of saṃsāra for a long time. Thus, they cannot even be liberated through the śrāvakayāna or pratyekabuddhayāna, let alone through the mahāyāna. On the other hand, the learned, due to properly understanding this threefold classification of phenomena in accordance with true reality, neither cling to phenomena nor accomplish them, but clarify them, which means not having to experience the six realms of saṃsāra. Thus, they can be liberated even through the mahāyāna, let alone through the śrāvakayāna and pratyekabuddhayāna.

353 Skt. *param*, Tib. *dam pa*. This refers to *Uttaratantra* I.37, which says:

> Because the [dharmakāya] is naturally pure
> And free from latent tendencies, it is pure.
> It is the supreme self because the reference points
> Of self and no-self are at peace.

354 Vol. 2, pp. 188–197. This is an elaboration on the meaning of buddhahood as an example for the path of familiarization having the nature of unchanging suchness while still performing activity (*Vivṛti* on IV.57). On wisdom or buddha nature being a permanent entity, see also Appendix I1G6 in Volume One.

355 The first verse appears in the *Ratnagotravibhāgavyākhyā* (J57; P5526, fol. 108b.4–5), but is not considered as a part of the *Uttaratantra*. However, it is included in the Tibetan versions of the *Uttaratantra*. The following five verses are I.88–92 in the Sanskrit version.

356 The contemporary Jonang scholar Ngawang Yönden Sangbo (Ngag dbang yon tan bzang po 2000, pp. 272–76) says that the process of finally revealing the dharmakāya as it is described in the *Uttaratantra* is not taught in a hidden way as in the prajñāpāramitā sūtras, but very clearly and explicitly. Apart from that, the final intention of the eight clear realizations of the AA and the seven vajra points of the *Uttaratantra* is the same. The hidden meaning of the prajñāpāramitā sūtras is nothing but buddha nature, whose essence is undifferentiable from the three knowledges. This view is also clearly reflected in his definitions of the eight topics of the AA.

357 As for "instance-isolate" and "meaning-isolate" (technical terms mainly used by Gelugpas), as mentioned above, the first one refers to the instances that exemplify a definition and its definiendum (such as a camp fire being an instance of what defines fire). The second one is another term for the definition of something (such as fire being what is hot and burning). As for the above objection, it is correct for all the instances of what is usually considered as permanent and unconditioned, but not necessarily in terms of the defining characteristics "permanent and unconditioned" as they apply to the nature of phenomena.

358 The Seventh Karamapa's commentary on these lines (Chos grags rgya mtsho 1985, vol. 1, p. 18) says that the Buddha **embodies** ultimate **valid cognition** by virtue of the consummate cause and result. Said cause consists of the consummate motivation (the great compassion of **wishing to benefit beings**) and its consummate application (**teaching** the path to others). The consummate result consists of being a **sugata** (one's own welfare of consummate relinquishment and realization) and being a **protector** (proclaiming the four realities as the welfare of others). Thus, Dignāga **pays homage** to the Buddha who is endowed with the two consummate welfares.

359 The Seventh Karmapa (ibid., vol. 1, pp. 9–13) explains this verse through matching it with (1) the four kāyas according to Śākyabuddhi's commentary, (2) the three kāyas, and the two opening lines of the *Pramāṇasamuccaya*. (1) The hosts of **conceptions**, which consist of the minds and mental factors in any of the three realms and appear as the duality of apprehender and apprehended, constitute **the web** that fetters the beings who possess these conceptions in saṃsāra. The svābhāvikakāya is the nature of phenomena in which the adventitious stains that consist of said conceptions and their latent tendencies **are eliminated** by way of having made them into something that never arises again. The buddha wisdom that is not different from the nature of phenomena free from adventitious stains is **profound** because it is not the sphere of others. This is the dharmakāya. For noble bodhisattvas and various pure and impure beings to be guided, respectively, this very wisdom arises as the appearances of **vast** kāyas (the sāmbhogikakāya) and vast activity (the nairmāṇikakāya). This is **the ever-excellent one endowed with the** four **kāyas**. Their activity consists of establishing beings in the support of the path, the nature of the path, and the fruition of the path (see CE and JNS on AA VIII.34cd–40). The **light** of this enlightened activity **radiates everywhere** in accordance with the karmic dispositions of those to be guided. (2) As for matching this with the three kāyas, the svābhāvikakāya is the inseparable union of dhātu and awareness in which **the web of conceptions** as described above **is eliminated** for good through the remedies. Since this very kāya appears to the bodhisattvas who dwell on the bhūmis, which is not something in common with śrāvakas and pratyekabuddhas, it is **the profound** sāmbhogikakāya. Its teaching various pure and impure beings to be guided in a **vast** manner represents the nairmāṇikakāya. This is **the ever-excellent one endowed with the** three **kāyas** and the **light** of his activity **radiates everywhere**. (3) As explained above, the state of a buddha arises from the consummate motivation and its application. The former refers to being motivated by the great compassion of wishing to protect beings from suffering (the result). Its application is to eliminate the shackles of the beings who are fettered in saṃsāra by the web of the conceptions of clinging to the two kinds of identity, which consists of the origin of suffering—karma and afflictions (the cause). This web is eliminated through teaching them the remedy—the path of identitylessness—in exactly the same way as oneself has directly realized it. Respectively, this motivation and its application are the causes of being a "protector" (the welfare of others) and being a "sugata" (one's own welfare), with the word "eliminate" explicitly indicating said application, while implying its motivation. The result of one's own consummate welfare consists of consummate relinquishment and realization. The former refers to the nature of phenomena that is endowed with twofold purity. Since this is an object of buddha wisdom alone, it is profound and has the meaning of "excellent" or "bliss" (*su* in *sugata*; *bde ba* in *bde bar gshegs pa*)—the consummate relinquishment that is the svābhāvikakāya. Since the vast object (all knowable objects—the nature of phenomena and its bearers) is directly realized through the vast subject (the two wisdoms of knowing suchness and variety), it has the meaning of "gone" or "realized" (*gata* in *sugata*; *gshegs pa* in *bde bar gshegs pa*)—the consummate realization that is the dharmakāya. Thus, one's own consummate welfare in the first two lines of this verse in the *Pramāṇavārttika* that speak about profound relinquishment and vast realization is taught by "sugata" in the above two lines in the *Pramāṇasamuccaya*. By virtue of being endowed with said kāyas of one's own welfare, a buddha is "ever-excellent" due to always benefiting all sentient beings, not being mixed with what is not excellent, and all kinds of excellence being complete in an interrupted manner. The sāmbhogikakāya and nairmāṇikakāya of

someone who is designated as "ever-excellent" radiate the light of overcoming the darkness of the two obscurations through turning the wheel of dharma of proclaiming the path seen by oneself in accordance with the karmic dispositions of those to be guided. Thus, the last two lines of said verse in the *Pramāṇavārttika* teach the consummate welfare of others, which corresponds to "protector" in the *Pramāṇasamuccaya*. This sugata and protector embody valid cognition because he makes those to be guided newly understand the referents such as the four realities that they did not understand before and accomplishes all temporary and ultimate purposes (or aims) in an undeceiving manner (according to *Pramāṇavārttika* II.1a and II.5c: "valid cognition is an undeceiving cognition" and "illuminates unknown referents"). His being "the protector" who promotes the welfare of those to be guided is caused by his consummate motivation, while his being a "sugata" who is able to accomplish all purposes (or aims) is caused by his consummate application.

360 Here, JNS starts to play with the Tibetan word *zhi ba*, which refers to both "peace" and the Indian god Śiva (the latter literally means "auspicious," "gracious," "benevolent," "happy," and "liberation"). Thus, in the following, the word may well be understood in both ways.

361 These five are listed, for example in *Madhyamakāvatāra* VI.121ab: the ātman is eternal, the experiencer, not an agent, without qualities, and inactive.

362 This term usually refers to the supreme godhead in Hinduism since the time of the Vedas, who is mostly identified as the personal god who creates the universe. Later, this supreme godhead often became synonymous with the god Śiva. Several Indian non-Buddhist philosophical systems claim the existence of Īśvara, such as the Vaiśeṣikas and some subschools of the Sāṃkhyas. In Śaṅkara's Advaitavedānta, Īśvara is understood as the impersonal primordial nature of the universe, thus being identical with the brahman.

363 Note that the *Ratnagotravibhāgavyākhyā* (J 8.11–12) explicitly affirms activity arising from unconditioned buddhahood: "From tathāgatahood, even though it is unconditioned and has the characteristic of being inactive, all activities of a perfect buddha unfold without effort in an unimpeded and uninterrupted manner until the end of saṃsāra." The same text also equates the uncontaminated dhātu with *tathāgatagarbha* and the natural disposition (for example, J 55.10). Yamabe 1997 (endnote 32) also mentions "the *Hsien-yang sheng-chiao lun* (Taishō 31.581c5–8), which states that all the actions of the buddhas arise on the basis of the **asaṃskṛta-dharmakāya*."

364 More modern examples include inventing some medicine (such as antibiotics) which keeps performing its functions even after its inventor has died or a spaceship that keeps moving forever without any fuel, engines, or personnel once it has taken off the ground and reached the vacuum of outer space (just as the impetus of former aspiration prayers and compassion keeps enlightened activity occurring in a nonconceptual, nondual, and nonpersonal manner). The Second Pawo Rinpoche's (Dpa' bo gtsug lag phreng ba n.d., pp. 794–96) commentary on *Bodhicaryāvatāra* IX.35–37 says, "There is no question that at that point [of utter mental peace] all observed objects (such as oneself and others) completely vanish and that the motions of discrimination entirely discontinue. This [mental peace] is not something without discrimination, nor does it possess any motivational aspects at all. Still . . . since beginningless [time] before this [state], [bodhisattvas] had not even an atom of considering their own welfare. Rather, the benefit of others was simply all they had in mind. [At last,] supreme familiarity with this has reached its final culmination and inconceivable aspiration prayers are accomplished. Therefore, when discursiveness is at peace like space, the welfare of all sentient beings will be simultaneously and uninterruptedly accomplished without any effort through the impetus of aspiration prayers and enlightened compassion. Just as a wish-fulfilling jewel . . . and . . . a wish-fulfilling tree . . . , the enlightened activity [of buddhas] will interact with the assembly of those to be trained. For the pure ones to be trained, it appears as the sambhogakāya that is like a wish-fulfilling jewel

... For those who are [only] slightly pure, it appears as a supreme nirmāṇakāya that is like a wish-granting tree ... It promotes great welfare through appearing in all possible and impossible forms for those who are not yet ripened, starting with [appearances] such as bodhisattvas, hearers, solitary realizers, and Brahmā up to [appearances] such as ships and bridges. Thus, for those to be trained, the very dharmakāya that does not abide anywhere happens to be seen as the appearances of the rūpakāyas of the victors ... For example, an individual who has practiced the awareness-mantra of Garuḍa may have built a pillar out of jewels on the shore of the ocean and formed an effigy of Garuḍa on its top ... Likewise, through following enlightening conduct, the pillar of the victor is built too by the bodhisattva. The continuum of mind and mental factors that served as the basis to ascribe the name 'bodhisattva' terminates completely upon the realization of true reality through the vajralike samādhi. Thus, [the bodhisattva] has passed beyond the locations of saṃsāra and nirvāṇa. Through such enlightenment in dharmadhātu, there is no observation of oneself and others. However, even after [enlightenment], enlightened activity takes place and continues to promote the welfare of all sentient beings without exception in a nonconceptual way." For the full translation, see Brunnhölzl 2004, pp. 655–56.

365 Note that the Eighth Karmapa is not the only one who speaks about buddha nature and so on as a permanent entity. For example, a commentary on the *Uttaratantra* by a close disciple of Dölpopa, Sabsang Mati Paṇchen (Sa bzang ma ti paṇ chen blo gros rgyal mtshan 1999, pp. 122.6–123.5), says, "As for relinquishing the [unwanted] consequence that [the tathāgata heart] is a permanent entity, it may be said, 'The dhātu would be a permanent entity because it is without difference before and after and yet also is a result accomplished in dependence on causes and conditions.' It is surely permanent because it is unconditioned. So since it is free from the three characteristics of arising, abiding, and ceasing, how could it possibly be a conditioned entity? ... 'Though that is the case, since it is able to perform a function, it would [still] be an entity.' It certainly is endowed with the ability to bring the two welfares to completion in every respect. Therefore, it is not a limited conditioned entity because everything conditioned is delusive, deceiving, and without essence. However, there is no contradiction in saying that [the tathāgata heart] is both permanent and an unconditioned entity." Mati Paṇchen also says (ibid., pp. 16.1–17.2) that if it is claimed that the notion of mind's natural luminosity does not withstand Madhyamaka reasoning, the tantras should be subjected to the very same critique too (which all schools of the Tibetan tradition carefully avoid) since they also greatly discuss this natural luminosity. A commentary on the same text by the Sakya scholar Lodrö Tsungmé (thirteenth/fourteenth century; Blo gros mtshungs med 1999, p. 319.6) first says that "mind's natural luminosity is naturally abiding wisdom" and then (p. 336.1) defines the naturally abiding disposition as "primordially established dhātu and wisdom." The aspects of dhātu and wisdom are further qualified as follows: "The [tathāgata] heart, if identified under the aspect of dhātu, is the true nature (*chos nyid*) of the mind associated with stains and inseparable from the inconceivable buddha qualities. It is the primordially established dharmakāya (pp. 334.6–335.1) ... It may be said, 'If the naturally abiding disposition were a fully qualified cause, it would be an entity.' The beginningless naturally abiding disposition abides as the true nature (emptiness) that is associated with stains and inseparable from immeasurable qualities. Here, though the aspect that is the true nature (emptiness) is the cause for the change of state as the stainless dharmakāya, it is not a producing cause (*bskyed byed kyi rgyu*). Therefore, it is not an entity. As for the aspect of wisdom, since it is the cause that produces later [instances] of similar type, such as the [ten] powers of a buddha, there is no invalidation of its being an entity (p. 343.4–6)." As for the objection that the result would already abide in the cause (as in the Sāṃkhya system), Lodrö Tsungmé (p. 337.3) says, "The wisdom that is completely pure of all stains is the result, but it does not exist in sentient beings. Likewise, though the wisdom that is associated with stains exists in the mind streams of sentient beings, it is not the result."

366 Vol. 2, pp. 211–17.

367 CZ, p. 415.

368 Ratnakīrti's *Kīrtikala* (D3799, fol. 238a.4–5) says, "'Craving' appears as the minds that bear the aspects of the three realms together with their afflictions. 'Peace' appears as the minds without afflictions, which bear the aspects of the dharma[kāya], the sambhoga[kāya], and the nirmāṇakāya. In particular, it is expressed as 'completely perfect buddhahood.'"

369 XXV.20.

370 Part 2, III.31cd–32.

371 These and the following passages are found on pp. 415–16 in CZ. However, under (a), CZ includes in Śāriputra's question what is presented as its answer here. Also, large parts of (b) and (c) are not found in CZ.

372 See JNS's comments on the *Vivṛti* on IV.60cd.

373 Vol. 2, pp. 225–30.

374 In general, māra can mean "killing," "destroying," "death," "pestilence," "obstacle," "hindrance," "the passion of love," and "the god of love." Specifically, in Buddhism, māra as a single "individual" is the personified evil that tempts beings (especially spiritual practitioners) to indulge in their passions in order to prevent detachment and spiritual progress. As indicated above, the teachings also speak of "the four māras" as well as the millions of māras ruled over by the chief māra.

375 JNS only gives *bsdu ba* as the title of text in question. The only passage in the four *Saṃgrahaṇīs* in the *Yogācārabhūmi* that says anything about this is the *Vastusaṃgrahaṇī* (D4039, fol. 190b.5–6) in the context of describing three types of not being forgetful: "The hindrances of forgetfulness are the four māras. For the skandhamāra is connected with everything. The devaputramāra creates hindrances from time to time. The two māras of death and the afflictions are the bases of the sufferings that arise from dying, transiting, and being born."

376 D3793, fol. 120a.5–6 (see JNS on the *Vivṛti* on AA IV.62b).

377 Vol. 2, pp. 245–55 and 264–65; the first two paragraphs are JNS's comments on the *Vivṛti* on V.5–7.

378 D3787 (fol. 168a.6–7 and 168b.2–4) and D3791 (fol. 289b.1–2 and 289b.5–6).

379 D3804, fol. 238b.5.

380 Tib. stag bde ba seng ge rgyal mtshan (1212–1294), a master in the lineage of Ngog Lotsāwa's transmission of the prajñāpāramitā teachings.

381 See also Appendix I5F7: "As for the manner in which the conceptions that are factors to be relinquished through familiarization are relinquished, the conceptions taught here are in terms of imputation alone. For in those whose minds are not altered by Buddhist philosophical systems, the mental clinging to the characteristics of the objects of the conceptions explained here does not arise. An example for such conceptions is the clinging mind of thinking, 'For those to be guided who like the dharma in a brief form, the dharma was taught in a summarized manner.' The reason that the seeds of such conceptions cannot be eliminated merely through directly seeing the nature of phenomena lies not in their being unable to obstruct the direct realization of the nature of phenomena, but rather in the fact that imputational conceptions are not definite as factors to be relinquished through seeing. Examples for not all imputational conceptions being definite as factors to be relinquished through seeing are the conceptions of clinging to the lack of real existence that arise during the subsequent attainment of the impure bhūmis. Also, it is not by virtue of dividing the conceptions of clinging to imputations into imputational and innate ones that they are presented as two factors to be relinquished, but they are so

presented by virtue of dividing them into manifest ones and those that retain a certain potency. Among these, the manifest conceptions of clinging to imputations obstruct the direct seeing of the nature of phenomena, while those that retain a certain potency do not obstruct this seeing. The manifest conceptions of clinging to imputations obstruct the direct seeing of the nature of phenomena because if the nature of phenomena is seen directly, it must be seen by way of having put an end to the manifest entertaining of the reference points of the clinging to the lack of real existence. As for those conceptions that retain a certain potency not obstructing the direct seeing of the reality of the nature of phenomena, their case is similar to the latencies of the innate clinging to real existence not obstructing the direct seeing of the lack of real existence. Therefore, the conceptions to be relinquished through familiarization that are explained here do not refer to the innate clinging to real existence, but are explained as the manifest conceptions of clinging to characteristics during the subsequent attainments of the impure bhūmis."

382 D3801, fol. 175b.5–6.

383 The way the Tibetan is phrased here, it could also mean ". . . and two authors of the *Abhidharmakośaṭīkās*." The *Tengyur* in fact contains three texts with this name by three different authors, but probably JNS refers to the most well-known and widely used one by Yaśomitra (D4092).

384 Vol. 2, pp. 268–70.

385 The classic sources of this statement are *Madhyāntavibhāga* V.19ab and *Mahāyānasūtrālaṃkāra* XIII.11ab and XIII.12ab. For the *Vivṛti* on AA V.18 quoting these two lines, see CE.

386 Vol. 2, pp. 271–78. Although these reasonings are usually called "the five great Madhyamaka reasonings" in the Tibetan tradition, JNS does not refer to them in this way, but speaks of "the reasonings with regard to termination and nonarising." Also, JNS provides several scriptural sources (primarily by Dharmakīrti) for these reasonings outside of Madhyamaka texts, while (except for a single line) quotations from Candrakīrti's texts—the Tibetan tradition's all-time Madhyamaka champion—are conspicuously absent here. JNS obviously prioritizes the first two reasonings ("freedom from unity and multiplicity" and "negating arising from the four extremes"), also listing them by name in the outline, but treats the other three only briefly and refers to them summarily as "the remaining reasonings." On the primacy of said first two reasonings in Madhyamaka, TOK (vol. 3, pp. 79–80) says, "The essential point of all reasonings that analyze the ultimate is to first take some [phenomenon that serves as the] basis of certain properties. Then, one searches for an [internally] noncontradictory nature of this [phenomenon] and for something that is contradictory [to this nature], such as its properties. For example, the definition or nature of a vase may be explained as 'that which possesses a bulbous belly and a flat bottom and can perform the function of holding water.' Then, one analyzes [this definition with absurd consequences], such as, 'It follows that also the opening of the vase is the bulbous belly because [the opening too] is the vase.' Therefore, from among [all Madhyamaka] arguments, the two main reasonings through which one is able to determine that both outer referents and inner consciousnesses lack real [existence] are the freedom from unity and multiplicity (the negation of a nature) and the negation of arising from the four extremes (the negation of properties). The many other enumerations of arguments that are explained in Madhyamaka texts are merely their branches."

387 The Sanskrit has "if reddened" (*rakte*), while the Tibetan literally says "changed through color" (*tshon gyis bsgyur na*).

388 This is another name of the vajra sliver reasoning and thus not to be confused with (4) "the reasoning that negates arising from the four possibilities" below.

389 JNS only quotes line VI.36c.

390 In the context of these five reasonings, JG (pp. 164–65) distinguishes between what is to be negated (or ceased) in one's mind through the path and what is to be negated through reasoning. The first one consists of one's own longtime mistaken states of mind and the mistaken appearances that are their objects, which together make up the two obscurations that are to be relinquished directly and indirectly through the five paths. The second one is twofold—what is to be negated through the reasonings that analyze conventions (such as the notion of permanent sound) and what is to be negated through the reasonings that analyze the ultimate (the extremes of wrongly superimposing existence onto what does not exist and denying existence to what does exist). Thus, the object of such reasonings consists not merely of mental imputations onto phenomena, but of objects being apprehended as being established from their own side. The common cause for this is innate ignorance and the specific causes are the various forms of imputational ignorance of those who engage in philosophical systems. In other words, the object of these reasonings is what is apprehended through the particular mode of grasping that clings to mere imputations as being really established. Some people say, "First one negates any real existence in appearances and later one also negates appearances. For if one did not negate them, the characteristics of appearances would not be overcome." However, not a single text of *Prāsaṅgika and *Svātantrika Mādhyamikas explains any reasonings to negate appearances. Therefore, appearances are not what is to be negated through reasoning. These people may say, "Appearances are what is to be negated through reasoning because there are no appearances in the meditative equipoise of the noble ones." This reason does not apply because, in the meditative equipoise of the noble ones, it is possible for there being both phases in which there are appearances and phases in which there are no appearances. Though there are certain stages on the path when appearances of objects are ceased, appearances are never what is to be negated through reasoning.

391 Vol. 2, pp. 282–302. JNS presents this as the implicit teaching of AA V.20.

392 These three are usually presented as the criteria of a truly existing personal self.

393 Note that there is a shift in the third stage of yoga when compared to how it was explained above. Both times, this stage is said to refer to what the False Aspectarians say, but here it is said that the *apprehended* aspect is not real as consciousness, while above the *apprehending* aspect of consciousness is said to be equally unreal (due to there being no corresponding real apprehended aspect). In a way, these two explanations represent simply the subjective and objective sides of arriving at "self-aware self-luminous consciousness without the duality of apprehender and apprehended," which is implied as the position of the False Aspectarians in what JNS says right below about the fourth stage of yoga. Thus, as per JNS's above brief description of the third stage of yoga and the slightly more elaborate one below (2c), the False Aspectarians assert not only the aspect of the apprehended as being unreal, but also the aspect of the apprehender. These two assertions correspond exactly to the difference that JNS makes below (2d) between the wrong and the correct understanding, respectively, of the position of the False Aspectarian Mere Mentalists (many Tibetan doxographies present the former, while Yogācāras such as Asaṅga and Vasubandhu—no matter how they may have come to be classified later—state the latter). Note though that, under (2b) and (2c) below, JNS presents the second yoga as the stage of the pratyekabuddhas alone and the third one (in the manner of both apprehended and apprehender being unreal) as the one of the Mere Mentalists in general, without differentiating them into Real and False Aspectarians (for more details on these two categories, see below).

394 With occasional slight variations, the four stages of yoga as briefly described here and in more detail below are found in many mahāyāna texts in general. In particular, they are included in basically every Indian Madhyamaka work on meditation, such as Nāgārjuna's *Bodhicittavivaraṇa* and *Bhāvanākrama*; Bhāvaviveka's *Madhyamakaratnapradīpa*; Jñānagarbha's *Yogabhāvanāmārga*; Kamalaśīla's *Bhāvanākrama* and *Bhāvanāyogāvatāra*; Atiśa's two *Madhyamakopadeśa*s; Jñānakīrti's *Tattvāvatāra* and *Pāramitāyānabhāvanākramanirdeśa*;

and Vimalamitra's **Kramaprāveśikabhāvanāpada* (for more details, see Brunnhölzl 2004, pp. 295ff.). In addition, the second through fourth of these stages of yoga correspond in principle to the second through fourth among the classical "four yogic practices" (*prayoga*) as explained in Appendix I1D in Volume One. BT (pp. 612–13) explicitly combines the first two *prayogas* as the second stage of yoga.

395 As mentioned before, the followers of Vatsīputra (a disciple of Śāriputra) asserted an ultimately real person that is inexpressible as being either the same as or different from the five skandhas.

396 D4211, fol. 166a.4.

397 Ibid., fol. 166a.6.

398 Ibid., fol. 166a.3–4.

399 Ibid., fol. 166a.4.

400 Ibid., fol. 166a.2–3.

401 For details on reasons of nonobservation and this particular type, see Brunnhölzl 2004, pp. 179–81.

402 D4211, fol. 167a.3.

403 D4038, fol. 77b.7.

404 See also Appendix I3a1bb.

405 D4211, fol. 166a.4–5.

406 JNS gives *bden gnyis* as the source of these two lines, but they are not found in either Jñānagarbha's *Satyadvayavibhāga* or Atiśa's *Satyadvayāvatāra*.

407 With minor variations, this appears as verse 28 of the *Jñānasārasamuccaya* (ascribed to Āryadeva), as the first verse of Jetāri's *Sugatamatavibhāgakārikā* (D3899, fol. 7b.5), and in the *Vimalaprabhā* commentary on the *Kālacakratantra* (D1347, fol. 196b.3). The above translation follows the *Jñānasārasamuccaya*, while the last two lines in JNS read *mtha' bzhi las ni rnam grol ba/ de nyid dbu ma pa yis rig*. The first two lines are also found in the *Śālistambasūtra* (see *Mahāyānasūtrasaṃgraha*, Vaidya ed., pt. 1, p. 115).

408 *Hevajratantra*, part 2, III.36. JNS quotes only the last three lines and has line b as "the entire seeming as it appears" (*kun rdzob 'di ltar snang ba kun*). Note that this verse is very similar to verse 45 of the *Yuktiṣaṣṭikā*:

> Whoever holds that dependent things
> Are like [the reflection of] the moon in water,
> Neither real nor delusive,
> Is not carried away by views.

409 Compare Śākya mchog ldan 1975 (pp. 213–14): "As for the second [system (Niḥsvabhāvavāda)] since all knowable objects in terms of suchness and variety never existed from the beginning, the extreme of existence is eliminated. Because it is not the case that what previously existed is made nonexistent either through reasoning or the cognitive seeing of noble ones, the extreme of nonexistence is eliminated. Because nobody [and nothing] has ever existed, the extreme of being both [existent and nonexistent] is eliminated. If being both [existent and nonexistent]—the basis on which to depend—is impossible, not being either [existent or nonexistent]—the phenomenon that depends [on this basis] cannot be accepted either. For if one accepts phenomena that are not dependently established, they do not go beyond being really established."

410 On this section 2da, see also Appendix I1H2bb in Volume One.

411 I.13a.

412 I.15.

413 X.257 (D107; ACIP MDO SDE CA@270a). The translation corresponds to the Sanskrit and the Tibetan in the *Kangyur*, while JNS has line b as "One should rest in nonappearance" (*snang ba med la gnas par bya*). RT (fol. 128b.1–2) has the same, glossing "nonappearance" as referring to "no mistaken appearances." RT also says that the line "one must even go beyond nonappearance" is corrupt because it and the next line, "rests in nonappearance," are contradictory (however, see Kamalaśīla's commentary on these two lines as indicated below). Differing from JNS—which takes the whole verse to teach the third stage of yoga—LN, RT, and PK take it to be the fourth stage. As for line 257d, the Tibetan versions of the *Laṅkāvatārasūtra* say, "does not see the mahāyāna" (*de yis theg chen mi mthong ngo*), while the otherwise identical verse 55 of Nāgārjuna's *Bhāvanākrama* does not have this negative. In his translation of the sūtra, Suzuki (1979, p. 247) says that most Sanskrit manuscripts have *na* ("not"), but that one has *sa* ("he"). B. Nanjio's edition (Bibliotheca Otaniensis 1. Kyoto: Otani University Press, 1923) also has *sa*. The above two verses are also quoted in Śāntarakṣita's own *Madhyamakālaṃkāravṛtti* (D3885, fol. 79b) as well as in Kamalaśīla's *Madhyamakālaṃkārapañjikā* (P5286, fols. 137a–138a) and his first *Bhāvanākrama* (D3915, fol. 33a). The latter two texts explain these verses in detail, commenting on X.257 from a Madhyamaka perspective (see Brunnhölzl 2004, pp. 300–302). In said three texts, line X.257d also appears and is commented on without the negative.

414 This is verse 27 of Āryadeva's *Jñānasārasamuccaya*, which is also found in Jetāri's *Sugatamatavibhāgakārikā* (D3899, fol. 8a) and Kalkin Puṇḍārika's commentary on the *Kālacakratantra*, called *Vimalaprabhā* (D1347, fol. 26a). JNS differs in the last two lines—"This is what those who have gone to the other shore of the ocean of Yogācāra texts proclaim" (rnal 'byor spyod gzhung rgya mtsho yi/ pha rol phyin rnams de skad sgrog). Bodhibhadra's *Jñānasārasamuccayanibandhana* (D3852, fol. 43a.6ff.) confirms the above version and gives a number of explanations on "mind's ocean," but relates the verse to both Real and False Aspectarians (identifying the former as represented by masters such as Dignāga and the latter by such as Asaṅga).

415 Rendawa (1348–1412) was one of the most famous Sakya masters and also the early Madhyamaka teacher of Tsongkhapa before the latter developed his own differing approach. In his *Grub mtha' kun shes* (Beijing: Mi rigs dpe skrun khang, 1999, p. 170), the Sakya master Dagtsang Lotsāwa (Tib. stag tshang lo tsā ba shes rab rin chen, 1405–?) says that, starting with the four sons of Patsab Lotsāwa (Tib. pa tshab lo tsā ba, born 1055), the transmission of *Prāsaṅgika Madhyamaka reached Rendawa via the early Sakya masters Bang Lotsāwa Lodrö Denba (Tib. dpang lo tsā ba blo gros brtan pa, 1276–1342), Shongtön Dorje Gyaltsen (Tib. shong ston rdo rje rgyal mtshan), Jamsar Sherab Öser (Tib. 'jam gsar shes rab 'od zer, both thirteenth—fourteenth centuries), Butön (1290–1364), and Lochen Kyabchog Balsangbo (Tib. lo chen skyabs mchog dpal bzang po, 1257–1310). For another, more detailed, lineage of *Prāsaṅgika from Patsab Lotsāwa to Rendawa, see D. Jackson 1985, p. 31. The Eighth Karmapa's introduction to his commentary on the *Madhyamakāvatāra* identifies the two Madhyamaka lineages from Patsab Lotsāwa and Atiśa as "the early tradition of *Prāsaṅgikas" in Tibet (for details on these, see Brunnhölzl 2004, pp. 58–61). He says that even before, but especially after, the beginning of "the new tradition of Prāsaṅgikas" (Tsongkhapa's novel interpretation of Madhyamaka), the proponents of the earlier tradition had become as rare as stars in daylight—specifically mentioning Rendawa, Kyabcho Balsangbo, Dagtsang Lotsāwa, and the great tulkus of the Tagpo Kagyü together with some of their realized yogic disciples.

416 Note that this is precisely what is asserted in most Tibetan doxographies, also within the Kagyü School. See, for example, TOK (vol. 2, pp. 504–6, which, however, adds to this position

that the False Aspectarians assert solely self-aware self-lucid cognition empty of apprehender and apprehended as real; see also below).

417 In Indian philosophy in general, the distinction between "Aspectarians" (*sākāravādin*) and "Non-Aspectarians" (*nirākāravādin*) is very common. Somewhat simplified, the former assert that mind apprehends an object via or as a mental "aspect" or image that appears to consciousness, thus being mind's actual cognitive content. Non-Aspectarians deny such an aspect (or at least its real existence). The Tibetan tradition often refers to the former as "Real Aspectarians" (*rnam bden pa*) and the latter as "False Aspectarians" (*rnam brdzun pa*). Among Buddhist schools, the Sautrāntikas and certain Yogācāras are usually said to be Aspectarians, while the Vaibhāṣikas and certain other Yogācāras are held to be Non-Aspectarians (or False Aspectarians). With regard to the Yogācāras, however, the situation is rather complex and there are various (later) interpretations as to what exactly the terms Aspectarian and Non-Aspectarian refer. Often, Yogācāras such as Dignāga and Dharmapāla are classified as the former and Asaṅga, Vasubandhu, Sthiramati, Kambala, and so on as the latter (for further details on the distinction, see Lindtner 1997, pp. 175–82, 198–99). However, there is no mention of either such names or the corresponding positions in their own writings, and it is highly questionable whether the much later standard doxographic descriptions of these terms adequately represent their view (for example, Asaṅga, Vasubandhu, and others say that, in being the imaginary nature, *both* the apprehended and apprehending aspects are equally unreal, while not asserting any ultimately real or independent kind of consciousness). Also, it seems that, in their treatment of all beings except buddhas, all Yogācāras must be considered Aspectarians, just differing as to whether they take these aspects to be conventionally real as a part of consciousness (that is, as part of the other-dependent nature) or not even conventionally real (in being just the imaginary nature). Later Indian Mādhyamikas, such as Jñānagarbha, Śāntarakṣita, Kamalaśīla, and Haribhadra, refer to the notion of a really existent consciousness or self-awareness in both the Aspectarian and Non-Aspectarian versions and unanimously refute them (without, however, mentioning specific persons). It is mainly in a number of late Indian works dating from the eleventh and twelfth centuries—usually written as or containing doxographies from a Mādhyamika point of view—that the explicit distinction between Aspectarians and Non-Aspectarians with regard to the Yogācāras is found (though by no means always described in the same way). However, when looking at the ways in which the distinction between Aspectarians and Non-Aspectarians is described in some of these texts, one wonders what fundamental difference is at stake here since they rather seem to represent just two slightly different ways of describing the same fact—pure self-aware consciousness being ultimately free from all stains of the imaginary aspects of *both* apprehender and apprehended. For example, a passage in both Jetāri's *Sugatamatavibhāgabhāṣya* (D3900, fols. 46a.8ff.) and Mokṣākaragupta's *Tarkabhāṣā* (P5762; ed. R. Iyengar, 1952, p. 69.11–19) says, "Here, some say that everything that is commonly known as the natures of the body and objects is this very consciousness. Since this [consciousness] is self-awareness, it is in no way apprehender and apprehended. Rather, the natures of apprehender and apprehended are superimposed through imagination. Therefore, the consciousness free from the natures of imaginary apprehender and apprehended is real. Others say that, ultimately, consciousness is unaffected by all the stains of imagination, resembling a pure crystal. These [imaginary] aspects are nothing but mistaken, appearing [only] due to being displayed through ignorance. Thus, a so-called 'apprehended' is entirely nonexistent. Since this does not exist, an apprehender does not exist either." In any case, apart from all such doxographical references in mainly Madhyamaka texts, there is only one explicit and rather late (eleventh century) Indian dispute about various issues *within* the distinction between Aspectarians and Non-Aspectarians that is actually recorded. Here, the Non-Aspectarian stance is advocated by Ratnākaraśānti in his *Madhyamakālaṃkāropadeśa* (P5586), *Triyānavyavasthāna* (P4535), and *Prajñāpāramitopadeśa* (to wit, just as Asaṅga and others, he considers both the aspects of apprehended and apprehender as false, while saying that it is solely mind's underlying sheer lucidity—*prakāśamātra*—free from these two that is real;

P5579, fol. 161a.5–161b.4). The Aspectarian position is mainly represented by Jñānaśrīmitra's *Sākarasiddhi* and *Sākarasaṃgraha* (ed. A. Thakur, mainly pp. 368.6–10 and 387.8–23) and also by Ratnakīrti's *Ratnakīrtinibandhāvalī* (ed. A. Thakur, 1976, esp. p. 129.1–12; none of the texts in these two editions are contained in the *Tengyur*), both quoting and rejecting Ratnākaraśānti's Non-Aspectarian approach in the *Prajñāpāramitopadeśa*. However, it is still hard to regard this as a dispute purely within the Yogācāra School itself since at least Ratnākaraśānti consistently exhibits a clear synthesis of Yogācāra and Madhyamaka, thus being more often than not considered as a Mādhyamika. Also, it should be noted that the issues at stake in all these texts are rather complex and not just a matter of whether consciousness has aspects or not (which might be real or illusory). Thus, much more research needs to be done to correctly understand such debates within their respective contexts and perspectives. In any case, the much later Tibetan labels "Real/False Aspectarian Mere Mentalists" (with all their respective subclassifications) usually—and JNS's above presentation is definitely an exception here—refer to the objective aspect that appears to consciousness as being really existent as mind or just being an illusory and mistaken appearance, respectively. However, there are numerous discrepancies in various Tibetan doxographies as to which Indian masters belong to these categories and their supposed subschools (moreover, the adduced scriptural sources—especially for the latter—are usually everything but obvious). According to TOK (vol. 2, p. 545; obviously relying on Śākya Chogden's *Nges don gcig tu grub pa*, p. 538.2–4), the conventional terms "real aspect" and "false aspect," which are based on the system of the Mere Mentalists, are just applied by Tibetans as they please. All that is found in the original texts are the two types of passages that establish the consciousness that appears as an outer referent as being a real or a false aspect of consciousness. For more details, see Brunnhölzl 2007b (pp. 380–82 and endnote 542) and the translation of Sahajavajra's *Tattvadaśakaṭīkā* on stanza 2 in Brunnhölzl 2007a (pp. 150–59 and esp. endnotes 492 and 533).

418 Interestingly, in the introduction to his commentary on the *Madhyamakāvatāra* (Mi bskyod rdo rje 1996, pp. 16 and 20ff.), the Eighth Karmapa presents exactly this as the position of Śākya Chogden and then refutes it at length. In particular, he refers to the position of "those who propound the real existence of nondual wisdom being Mādhyamikas" as completely pointless. No matter which labels the False Aspectarians give to mind—be it wisdom, dharmadhātu, signlessness, or emptiness—the view of its being really existent is nothing but Mere Mentalism, but not Madhyamaka because the Mere Mentalists are distinguished by saying that mind exists ultimately as the perfect nature. Some texts of the Mere Mentalists speak of "nondual wisdom" and others of "nondual consciousness," "nondual mind," and so on. In general, terms such as *jñāna*, *vijñāna*, and their cognates are often used as equivalents as well as applied in different ways in various texts and contexts, but there is no evidence in the Buddha's teachings or the works on linguistics and such that the mind as asserted by the Mere Mentalists must be called "consciousness" and the mind as asserted by the Mādhyamikas should be called "wisdom." However, the Karmapa says, I certainly do not state that there is no difference between wisdom and consciousness in terms of cognizance having or not having undergone a change of state, respectively. In addition, in the vajrayāna, a wisdom without any aspects is not reasonable as the definitive meaning. For the wisdom that is endowed with the supreme of all aspects is presented as the definitive meaning through greatly praising it (while the cause of this wisdom is great prajñāpāramitā—the emptiness that is endowed with the supreme of all aspects). Also, it is refuted in the vajrayāna that wisdom's unique own object is without aspect, while it is taught that the fruition of omniscience is attained by virtue of familiarizing with the wisdom of realizing the emptiness that is endowed with all aspects. If no aspects appeared for nondual wisdom, the explanations of it as being omniscience or "all-knowing" would not be feasible because it is not suitable to apply a plural if wisdom is presented as having nothing but itself as its object. Thus, it is through the power of the cognitive obscurations of nondual wisdom having been relinquished that it is the knowledge of all the aspects that can be known. Unmistaken nondual

wisdom (as well as its samādhi) is self-awareness and not some blank inanimate emptiness or state without any mental activity at all.

419 Since this section of the *Vivṛti* on V.20 (D3793, fols. 124b.7–125a.4; virtually identical in the *Ālokā*, D3791, fols. 302b.7–303a.4) does not explicitly state JNS's names of the four stages of yoga, and in order to give a clearer picture of JNS's following comments on this section, it is translated here as it stands: "Here, the clinging to a self is given up through meditating by thinking, 'There is no self because of being empty by virtue of arising and ceasing.' Then, through focusing on the phenomena that bear the features of arising and ceasing, such as the skandhas devoid of such a [self], one mentally engages in the fact that since [something like] blue and the mental state that [perceives] this [blue] are invariably observed together, they are nothing but mere mind, while outer referents do not exist. Without giving up the clinging to the mind that has the aspect of the apprehender, the clinging to outer referents is relinquished. Then, through having gained certainty that if there is nothing apprehended, there is no apprehender, also the mere cognizance that has the characteristic of being the aspect of the apprehender is eliminated. Having gained certainty in the sense of thinking that this sheer nondual wisdom has the nature of existing truly, one meditates by thinking, 'It is without nature, like an illusion because it is dependently originating—truly, it is free from any conceptualized nature, such as definitely being an entity or a nonentity.' When the power of meditation is accomplished through that, just like the knowledge about gems, silver, and so on in some [persons], once the nonconceptual mental state of all characteristics of mistakenness having been relinquished (which appears with an illusionlike character and is to be experienced personally) arises truly, just as it is, the yogin perfectly relinquishes the cognitive obscurations."

420 D3793, fol. 125a.2.

421 Compare Śākya Chogden's *Nges don rgya mtsho sprin gyi 'brug sgra zab mo'i rgyas 'grel bdud rtsi'i char 'bebs* (Śākya mchog ldan 1988a, vol. kha, p. 364): "'Isn't it that this master [Haribhadra's *Vivṛti* (D3794, fol. 125a.2–3)] established nondual wisdom as self-empty [by saying], "because it is dependently originating?' He indeed explained it in this way in the context of cutting through superimpositions through reasoning that arises from reflection. Nevertheless, in the context of making it a living experience through [the prajñā] that arises from meditation, he explained this very wisdom as what is to be experienced. For [the *Vivṛti* (ibid., fol. 125a.4) continues], '. . . once the nonconceptual mental state of all characteristics of mistakenness having been relinquished (which appears with an illusionlike character and is to be experienced personally) arises truly . . .' Thus, if this very wisdom is not experienced, there will be no ground for the arising of said [personally experienced] self-awareness in this context."

422 JNS literally says, "The Seventh Avalokiteśvara."

423 D3793, fol. 125a.2.

424 On nondual wisdom, see also Appendix I1G6 in Volume One. According to LN (vol. 2, pp. 276–80), the four stages of yoga are to focus on (1) the lack of a self; (2) mere mind; (3) suchness; and (4) nonappearance. (1) and (2) basically correspond to what JNS above and PSD below say. As for (3), by virtue of meditating by thinking that the wisdom without the duality of apprehender and apprehended is the actually existing nature, without even abiding in mere mind, what happens is that it is not observed as anything whatsoever. (4) refers to the freedom from all extremes. Just as knowing a reflection to be empty of real existence yet clearly appearing, through having relinquished all mistaken characteristics of superimposition and denial as well as the clinging to real existence (their cause), the mind in which all entities appear with an illusionlike nature (appearing yet not really existing) and which does not conceive of existence or nonexistence at all is experienced by any given person by themselves alone. But it cannot be directly shown to others, nor are others able to rely on or apprehend it. Though it exists and arises at that point, it is difficult to label with conventional terms. Since Haribhadra asserts the

Yogācāra-Madhyamaka philosophical system, he holds that this mind appears during meditative equipoise like an illusion, while the *Prāsaṅgika-Mādhyamikas say that meditative equipoise refers to the mind not conceiving of the nature of phenomena free from reference points as anything whatsoever—by virtue of there not being anything to be seen, true reality is seen. On this, LN quotes *Laṅkāvatārasūtra* X.256cd–257 as a conclusion. PK (fols. 148a.6–149b.5) titles the four stages of yoga in the same way as LN. (1) As for the yoga of focusing on the lack of a self, after having accomplished calm abiding, one mentally engages in the aspect of emptiness by thinking that the skandhas and so on lack something that is a self because the latter is empty of arising and ceasing (whereas the former are not). Through becoming familiar with this, suppleness arises and, through the power of that, one engages in the meditative equipoise with regard to said focal objects. This represents the yoga of the lack of a self, which has the nature of superior insight. Through it, śrāvakas and pratyekabuddhas cast off the clinging to a personal self, gradually relinquish the afflictions, and thus become arhats. Hence, those who cultivate this yoga are mainly śrāvakas and pratyekabuddhas. Beginner bodhisattvas, through using this yoga to cast off the coarse clinging to identity, connect with the subsequent stages of yoga and find the focal objects of these yogas. (2) In the yoga of focusing on mere mind, through focusing on the skandhas and so on, which are devoid of a personal self and are dependently arising and ceasing, one mentally engages by thinking that blue and the cognition that appears as blue (which appear to be different in substance) are invariably observed together and therefore are nothing but mere mind, but not established as outer referents. Thus, the clinging to outer referents being established as such is relinquished, while the clinging to the aspect of the apprehender being established as such is not yet relinquished. Through seeing this, bodhisattvas connect with the subsequent stages of yoga and find the focal objects of these yogas. (3) During the yoga of focusing on suchness, one one-pointedly contemplates that the apprehender is not really existent either because the apprehended does not really exist. Through thus eliminating the clinging to what has the characteristic of being the apprehender and bears the name "mere cognizance," one thinks that solely nondual wisdom has the nature of actually existing. Through this, bodhisattvas connect with the subsequent stage of yoga and find its focal object. (4) In the yoga of focusing on nonappearance, through focusing on the true reality of being without, or empty of, the duality of apprehender and apprehended, one familiarizes with it by thinking that it too is dependent origination and therefore without nature, just as an illusion—in actual fact it is free from any nature that could be labeled as absolutely being an entity, a nonentity, and so on. Once the power of such familiarization is accomplished, just as when some people recognize reflections that appear on gems and silver, the nonconceptual mind in which all characteristics of mistakenness are relinquished, which appears as having an illusionlike nature, and which is to be personally experienced arises perfectly, just as it is. Through this, yogins perfectly relinquish the cognitive obscurations. In *Laṅkāvatārasūtra* X.256cd–257, lines X.257cd refer to the level of the supreme dharma and lines X.256cd–257ab, to the preceding levels of the path of preparation. In our own system, PK says, through wishing to solidify said nonconceptual mind, it is not tenable to become liberated from the clinging to entities. Therefore, in all phenomena there are no causes for denial to be removed and no causes for superimposition to be added. For on the level of the seeming, they are free from being delusive and, ultimately, they are free from being real. Having explaining the view like that since actual reality without dividing it into the two realities is called "the mode of actual reality," one familiarizes through this actuality that is to be viewed or examined. Once one completes such familiarization, just like an illusory elephant defeating another illusory elephant, when actual true reality is seen unmistakenly, one will be liberated, which indicates the fruition. PSD (pp. 366–68) explains that Mādhyamikas, based on the four stages of yoga, realize all phenomena as the nature of suchness free from reference points and thus are able to relinquish all cognitive obscurations of clinging to real existence without exception. These four stages of yoga are as follows. (1) Non-Buddhist and Buddhist tīrthikas assert a permanent self that is empty of arising and ceasing. Within seeming phenomena, there is nothing that is empty of arising and ceasing (any hypothetical entity that is permanent and a self), that is, there is no personal self, which is like the horns of a rabbit. Having determined that, by focusing on the focal object of the innate views about such a self one meditates by thinking, "In terms of negative determination, there is no self, and, in terms of positive determination, phenomena are just mere phenomena." Through this, the clinging to a self is put to an end, which is the yoga of focusing on the lack of a self. (2) Whatever is invariably observed together is necessarily not different in substance, such as happiness and the awareness that experiences that happiness. As for the appearance of blue and the mind that perceives this blue, by virtue of the reason of invariable co-observation, it is determined that what appears as a referent does not exist outside of the mind in which it appears. One familiarizes with the fact that what appears as an object, in terms of positive determination, is mere inner mind, and, in terms of negative determination, does not exist as an outer referent. Through this, the clinging to outer referents is relinquished. (3) Having determined that, without anything to be apprehended, there is also no apprehender because these two are mutually dependent, one familiarizes with this by thinking, "The two of apprehender and apprehended do not exist." Through this, the clinging to a mere apprehender is also eliminated, but what is not relinquished here is the clinging to mere nondual wisdom. (4) What originates dependently necessarily lacks a real nature (just as the appearances of illusory horses and elephants) and nondual self-awareness is also dependently originating. Having determined that, through familiarizing with all phenomena being free from reference points all cognitive obscurations of clinging to apprehended, apprehender, and self-awareness are relinquished without exception. Therefore, the Madhyamaka path relinquishes the two obscurations completely.

425 Vol. 2, pp. 314–37.

426 Dependent origination is usually classified as twofold—being established in dependence refers to being short in dependence on being long and so forth, while arising in dependence refers to what is known as causality, such as the arising of smoke due to the arising of fire.

427 The Sanskrit *saṃvara* (Tib. *sdom pa*) can mean "stopping," "controlling," "containing," "refraining," "keeping back," "shutting," or "closing." Obviously, the idea here is again that saṃsāra is naturally contained or under control in the sense of it never having arisen in the first place.

428 JNS says that this line is from the *Mahāyānasaṃgraha*, but it is not found or quoted there. As mentioned before, it is, for example, anonymously quoted in Asaṅga's *Ratnagotravibhāgavyākhyā* (J 37.6) and at the beginning of the Third Karmapa's *Pointing Out the Tathāgata Heart*.

429 D4035, fol. 117b.6.

430 Skt. *cetanā*, Tib. *sems pa*. This is the most fundamental mental factor from which all others derive and is defined as "the expression of mentation in the phase when mind moves toward an object." It belongs to the group of the five omnipresent mental factors that accompany each moment and type of consciousness.

431 As explained before, "immovable karma" consists of the karmic causes that consist of the dhyānas and formless absorptions, which are cultivated in order to be reborn on the corresponding levels of the form and formless realms. They result only in rebirth within their specific corresponding god realms and cannot be changed by anything into resulting in any other levels of rebirth. Another reason for these samādhis and their rebirths being called "immovable" is that they are not moved or stirred by the flaws of any levels below them.

432 JNS literally says "born," but—as in the explanation of the "becoming of birth" here—the intermediate state ends once one's consciousness enters the womb.

433 In the *Abhidharmakośabhāṣya* on III.14, Vasubandhu mentions four opinions (also found in the *Mahāvibhāṣā*), with the first one above ascribed to Vasumitra. The other two not

listed above say that the intermediate state lasts seven weeks or that it is very short since the beings in it greatly desire rebirth (the latter being the position of the Vaibhāṣikas).

434 The *Abhidharmakośabhāṣya* on the above verse provides a number of examples for each one of these cases, such as humans being born from eggs.

435 Ed. La Vallée Poussin, p. 5.1–4: "*Prati* means 'meeting' (*prāpti*). [The verbal root] *i* means 'going.' Here, the term *pratītya* (a continuative) refers to 'meeting' or 'relying' because the meaning of the verbal root is modified by the modifying [prefix] . . . [The verbal root] *pad* [('going')] prefixed by *samut* means 'manifesting,' 'appearing,' or 'arising' (*prādurbhāva*). Thus, the term *samutpāda* refers to 'manifesting,' 'appearing,' or 'arising.' Hence, the meaning of *pratītyasamutpāda* is 'the appearing of entities in reliance [or in dependence] upon causes and conditions.'" For an even more elaborate Sanskrit etymology, based on Candragomī's grammar, see Hopkins 1996, pp. 662–64.

436 The *Abhidharmakośabhāṣya* (D4090, fol. 125a.5–125b.1) says, "The confusion of killing under the sway of attachment constitutes ignorance. The intentions [or impulses during this killing] are the formations. To distinctly cognize entities represents consciousness. The four skandhas that arise together with consciousness are name and form. The sense faculties that abide in name and form are the six āyatanas. The coming together with the six āyatanas is contact. The experience of contact is feeling. The attachment [in this case] is craving. The [afflictive mental] fetters that are congruently associated with this [craving] represent grasping. The physical and verbal actions motivated by this constitute becoming. The arising of the actions [involved in killing] is birth. Their maturing is aging and their ceasing is death." The explanation in TOK (vol. 2, pp. 432–33) differs as follows. "A single moment" is said to refer to the time it takes to complete a certain action, such as killing. In detail, (1) the link of ignorance refers to the afflictions at the time of killing, that is, the hatred motivated by ignorance. (2) Karmic formations constitute the act of killing itself. (3) The link of consciousness refers to having affected one's mind in a negative way through this act of killing, with the result that one's consciousness is impregnated with the latent tendencies of being reborn in the hells or the like. (4)–(5) The links of name and form and the six āyatanas, respectively, refer to the aspects of one's own five skandhas and six āyatanas at that time being impregnated with this negativity. (6) Contact means the triad of object, sense faculty, and consciousness meeting and thus delimiting the object at that time. (7) Feelings refer to experiencing the killing of the being in question. (8) Craving means to crave for this act of killing. (9) Grasping is the desire to accomplish this act one craves for. (10) Becoming refers to planting the latent tendencies for one's next rebirth through said grasping. (11)–(12) Birth, aging, and death refer to the aspects of the changes of one's skandhas during that time.

437 As an example for this, TOK (vol. 2, p. 432) speaks of falling into the hell realms in this very lifetime by virtue of having committed any of the five actions without interval (such as killing an arhat).

438 Except for shifting the link of becoming from the category of completing factors into the category of completed results in the next life, TOK (vol. 2, pp. 431–32) presents the same. In addition, a single cycle of completing all twelve links over two lifetimes is explained, in which the same links as in TOK's presentation of completion over three lifetimes are identified as propelling, propelled, completing, and completed, respectively. However, in the completion over two lifetimes, both the propelling and completing links are included in this lifetime, while the propelled and completed links belong to the next life (the former are compared to planting seeds, while the latter are like these seeds being revived).

439 Obviously, this is the Sanskrit of the Seventh Karmapa's name.

440 The Sanskrit is a (somewhat abbreviated) form of "Lord Rangjung Dorje" (the Third Karmapa). His treatise on dependent origination is not preserved at present.

441 Vol. 2, pp. 339–57 and 360–64.

442 D3787, fol. 174b.4–5.

443 Note that the same is said in this context of the lion's sport (see CZ, p. 501).

444 JNS has "path of seeing." However, given the main point at stake here (denying that the lion's sport belongs to the path of seeing, while asserting it to belong to the path of familiarization alone), I can only make sense of this phrase if it reads "path of familiarization."

445 JNS has "from the first to the tenth bhūmi," but says "second" several times below, outlining that each one of these nine bhūmis has its own set of nine meditative absorptions of progressive abiding.

446 Note that neither the sūtras (CZ, pp. 501–2), nor the *Vṛtti*, the *Ālokā*, or the *Vivṛti* say that the lion's sport is the prepatory stage of the culminating training of the path of familiarization. In the *Vṛtti* (D3787, fol. 174b.2–4), the lion's sport is explicitly related only to the culminating training of the path of seeing. Though the text also mentions the lion's sport in two passages from the above-mentioned sūtra section under the heading of the path of familiarization's crossing in one leap (ibid., fols. 174b.7 and 175a.5), both passages only say that the crossing in one leap is entered subsequent to the lion's sport, but not that the latter belongs to the path of familiarization. Both the *Ālokā* (D3791, fol. 305a.2–3) and the *Vivṛti* (D3794, fol. 126a.1) explicitly relate AA V.23 on the lion's sport to the path of seeing, but do not mention this samādhi when very briefly treating V.24–25 on the crossing in one leap. Being a commentary on the sūtra in eight thousand lines (which does not discuss this topic in the first place), the *Ālokā* does not comment on V.24–25 at all, but explicitly refers to the sūtra in twenty-five thousand lines and just quotes the beginning of the relevant passage (CZ, p. 501, last paragraph). For the *Vivṛti's* comments, see below. Ratnākaraśānti's *Śuddhamatī* (D3801, fols. 181b.3–182b.5) comments on AA V.23 by suggesting that the lion's sport still belongs to the path of seeing. On V.24–25, the text explicitly states that it is the crossing in one leap (which follows the lion's sport) that represents the path of familiarization, without mentioning the lion's sport as being a part of the path of familiarization (RT [fol. 134a.4] praises "Ratnākaraśānti's excellent explanation of the lion's sport being only treated by V.23 and not being included at all in V.24–25"). By contrast, the same author's *Sārottamā* (D3803, fols. 184b.1–186b.1) does not mention the lion's sport in the context of the path of seeing, but explicitly comments on AA V.23–25 as relating to the path of familiarization, saying that, according to the sūtras, both the lion's sport and the crossing in one leap constitute "the entirety of the means in which bodhisattvas are skillful" (on this phrase, the *Ālokā* [D3791, fol. 305a.4] says that it here means the path of familiarization). In Abhayākaragupta's *Marmakaumudī*, the situation is not very clear. Though the text has a single commentarial section on AA V.23–25 (D3805, fols. 180b.5–181b.7) that discusses the lion's sport and the crossing in one leap together, the text first explicitly relates the lion's sport to the path of seeing and the crossing in one leap to the path of familiarization. Then, just as in the *Sārottamā*, these two samādhis together are referred to as "the entirety of means" and are again repeated with their outlines identical to those in the *Sārottamā*. This may suggest that the lion's sport *also* belongs to the path of familiarization, but there is no explicit statement to that effect or that the lion's sport represents the preparatory stage of crossing in one leap.

447 See "Specific explanation of what is difficult to understand" in CE on AA I.44a, supplemented by JNS (pp. 276–98).

448 As mentioned before, the *Bhāṣya* on VI.63 says that, among the two types of arhats who are liberated through prajñā alone and through both prajñā and samādhi, respectively, the former are not able to enter the meditative absorption of cessation, but are liberated from all

afflictive obscurations through the prajñā of realizing identitylessness. The latter are, in addition, able to enter said meditative absorption since they are liberated from the obscurations of meditative equipoise too.

449 See also Appendix I4c2bc (lower abhidharma).

450 D4038, fol. 9a.2–3.

451 D3854, fol. 288a.2–3.

452 The only approximate reference to this in said text is D4037, fol. 91a.7–91b.1.

453 D45.31, vol. ga, fol. 164b.5–7.

454 CZ, p. 397.

455 D4049, fol. 95a.5–6.

456 D4038, fol. 73a.4.

457 D4090, fol. 68b.2.

458 D4049, fol. 54a.6–7.

459 D3862, fol. 325b.1–2.

460 I could not locate this passage in said sūtra.

461 This and the following three quotes are found in CZ, pp. 501–3.

462 The Sanskrit terms *avaskandha, viṣkandha, vyutkrānta* for this literally mean "leaping," "skipping," "jumping over," or "striding over."

463 To reiterate, the first sixteen steps of the medium crossing in one leap consist of leaping from the first dhyāna to the meditative absorption of cessation, from which one leaps back to the second dhyāna and then again up to the meditative absorption of cessation and so on. From the last meditative absorption of cessation, one enters another Peak of Existence (a.k.a. Neither Discrimination Nor Nondiscrimination), and rises from it into the state of mind of the desire realm of not being in meditative equipoise (as explained below, the latter is considered as the pure subsequent attainment of bodhisattvas during this process of crossing in one leap). This is step seventeen. Unlike any other commentaries, JNS also describes a descent in the reverse order for the medium crossing in one leap. Though the literal description of the eighteenth step in this process is somewhat cryptic in JNS's above presentation, to make sense both logically and in terms of the numbers described it should be the exact reverse of the seventeenth step. That is, step eighteen means that one, from the state of mind of the desire realm enters a state of mind of the Peak of Existence, the latter then resting in the meditative absorption of this very level. Next—and this starts the actual descent in reverse order—from this meditative absorption of the Peak of Existence one enters the meditative absorption of cessation. Likewise, one descends through the remaining seven absorptions and dhyānas by alternating each one of them with the absorption of cessation, which covers steps nineteen through thirty-four. Finally, one emerges again in a state of mind of the desire realm—step thirty-five.

464 According to PK (fol. 154.a 5–154b.2), what is explained in the sūtra in eighteen thousand lines as "slight exiting" is the process of rising from the meditative absorption of cessation into the Peak of Existence and then into the mind of not being in meditative equipoise, again entering the meditative absorption of cessation, and again rising into the mind of not being in meditative equipoise.

465 D3793, fol. 126a.7–126b.1.

466 Nothing like that is mentioned in the corresponding very brief passage in Ngog Lotsāwa's brief commentary on the AA (Rngog lo tsā ba blo ldan shes rab 1993a, fols. 86b.6–87a.1). Thus, it may have been put forward in his—now lost—larger commentary on the AA.

467 This is yet another Sanskritized variation of "Karmapa Chötra Gyatso."

468 This is the Sanskrit for "Karmapa Teshin Shegba" (Tib. de bzhin gshegs pa; the Fifth Karmapa).

469 PSD (p. 384) says that alternating between the meditative absorption of cessation and the state of mind of the desire realm that is not in meditative equipoise represents alternating between the two extreme poles of an utterly peaceful and a nonpeaceful mind. Therefore, if one is able to do this, alternating between any one of the other eight absorptions and the state of mind of not being in meditative equipoise is easy. In general, it is said that the purpose of the samādhis of the lion's sport and the crossing in one leap is that bodhisattvas gain complete mastery over instantly entering into and rising from all kinds of meditative equipoises, even from the most unstable state of mind (the consciousness of the desire realm) directly into the most stable mental state (the absorption of cessation) and back. This dexterity in calm abiding serves then as the basis for the wisdom of familiarizing with the emptiness of all remaining obscurations in terms of the dualistic appearances of apprehender and apprehended plus the imputations that are based on such appearances. As the above presentation indicates, the details of the stages of crossing in one leap are explained in different ways in the prajñāpāramitā sūtras in one hundred thousand, twenty-five thousand, and eighteen thousand lines (see Chart 23 and also Ruegg 1989, pp. 165–67, who slightly differs). For Conze's schematic overview of the entire crossing in one leap as found in the sūtra in eighteen thousand lines, see CZ, p. 504 (however, he doubles the step of moving from the mind of the desire realm into cessation and back). In addition, these stages are presented in various ways in different commentaries—even JNS's own comments on the *Vivṛti* differ somewhat from JNS's above explanation of this topic. The Indian commentaries do not divide the crossing in one leap into lesser, medium, and great, nor do they comment much in addition to the plain overall progression as outlined in the sūtras. The clearest and most straightforward presentations of this entire progression are found in Ratnākaraśānti's *Sārottamā* (D3803, fols. 184b.5–185b.1) and Abhayākaragupta's *Marmakaumudī* (D3805, fol. 181a.2–181b.3). Both these commentaries also explicitly describe the lion's sport in this context and say that it precedes the crossing in one leap. As for the Tibetan commentaries at my disposal, most of them seem to—more or less—agree on the following model. The preparatory lion's sport consists of the seventeen or eighteen steps (depending on whether the culminating meditative absorption of cessation is counted as one or two) of traveling through the nine meditative absorptions of progressive abiding in both their progressive and reverse orders, without any skipping or alternating. The lesser crossing in one leap consists of the nine steps of traveling through these nine meditative absorptions in only their progressive order, again without any skipping or alternating (some commentaries say that this is the same as the lion's sport). The medium crossing in one leap has seventeen or eighteen steps (depending on whether the final Peak of Existence and the mind of the desire realm are counted as one or two). These consist of alternating each one of the four dhyānas and four formless absorptions with the meditative absorption of cessation (in only an upward progressing manner), which ends in rising from the last meditative absorption of cessation into the state of mind of the Peak of Existence, and from there into a state of mind of the desire realm (that is, not being in any meditative equipoise). The great crossing in one leap consists of the eighteen steps of alternating each one of the nine meditative absorptions of progressive abiding with said mind of the desire realm (in only a downward progressing manner), thus ending in the latter state of mind. For friends of simplified digital displays, the various models for the entire progression from the lion's sport up through the crossing in one leap are presented in Chart 23 (now, if all of this doesn't sound like the twentieth level of the notorious computer game . . .). On a more serene note, Haribhadra's

Subodhinī (his commentary on the *Prajñāpāramitāsaṃcayagāthā*; D3792, fols. 66b.7–67a.1) says in this context: "The path of familiarization, which has the defining characteristic of the meditative absorption of crossing in one leap, realizes prajñāpāramitā as being uncontaminated. Through this, just as the sun unobscured by clouds, on its own, has the power to dispel darkness through radiating its light rays, the self-arisen state of a bhagavān will be attained through overcoming dark ignorance, just as the tathāgatas [by name] Avakīrṇakusuma [do in Chapter Twenty-eight of the sūtra in eight thousand lines]."

470 Here and in some of the following instances, JNS just has "lesser and medium," but this seems to be a not uncommon shorthand for "lesser, medium, and great."

471 JNS has "ninefold," but says "threefold" throughout the following. Thus, this was emended accordingly.

472 The *Bhāṣya* on this explains that "the eight levels" are the four dhyānas and the four formless absorptions; "traveling back and forth" means going through these eight levels in their progressive and reverse orders; and "in two manners" refers to the contaminated and uncontaminated forms, respectively, of these eight levels. JNS's following explanations are partly based on these and the further comments in the *Abhidharmakośabhāṣya* on this verse.

473 The *Abhidharmakośabhāṣya* lists four preparatory stages. First, one sequentially travels through the eight contaminated meditative absorptions in their progressive and reverse orders. Second, one does the same for the uncontaminated forms of the first seven of them. The third and fourth preparations are as in the above "proximate preparation."

474 D4090, vol. khu, fol. 74b.3. Thus, two of the major differences between the crossing in one leap here and in the prajñāpāramitā sūtras are that the former is only able to skip one meditative absorption at a time and never reaches the meditative absorption of cessation, while the latter is able to skip up to eight meditative absorptions (this capacity is also mentioned in Jinaputra's *Abhidharmasamuccayavyākhyā*; see Ruegg 1989, p. 174) and includes the meditative absorption of cessation.

475 JNS repeats the example that both the *Vṛtti* (D3787, fol. 175b.5) and the *Ālokā* (D3791, fol. 305b.7) use to make their point here—the Sanskrit word *vāyasa* meaning both "crow" and "milk sweets/soup" (an English example would be "pen," signifying both a writing instrument and a corral).

476 To provide a clearer idea on how JNS comments on/breaks up this section of the *Vivṛti* ((D3794, fol. 126a.4–126b.3), a translation of the latter follows here (headings from JNS in [ ]). "[*Lion's sport*] Bodhisattvas progress from the first dhyāna up through cessation and then return from cessation down to the first dhyāna. Thus, through said two progresssive and reverse orders of ascending and descending, they progress and return through the nine meditative absorptions—the four dhyānas, the four formless [absorptions], and the one that has the characteristic of cessation. [*Medium crossing in one leap*] Again, they enter the meditative absorption of the first dhyāna and, after having risen from it, [they enter] cessation. Likewise, from [each absorption] up through Neither Discrimination Nor Nondiscrimination, they enter cessation. Having risen from that, they focus on the adjacent meditative absorption and then [*great crossing in one leap*] rest in a consciousness that engages in the desire realm, which has the nature of being a boundary line. Through the power of their skill in means, after having manifested such a consciousness that is not in meditative equipoise, they [again enter] cessation. From this, [they again enter the state of] not being in meditative equipoise. After that, they skip only cessation and [enter] the āyatana of Neither Discrimination Nor Nondiscrimination. From that, [they enter the state of] not being in meditative equipoise. Then, they skip two [meditative absorptions] and [enter] the āyatana of Nothing Whatsoever. From that, [they enter the state of] not being in meditative equipoise. Likewise, by skipping up to eight [meditative absorptions], [they

enter] the first dhyāna. From that, [they enter the state of] not being in meditative equipoise. [*Summary of the meaning of crossing in one leap*] According to this, through skipping one [meditative absorption] and so forth until they arrive at the meditative absorption of cessation, they progress by way of disparate [modes]. Therefore, this progression in disparate ways is the meditative absorption of crossing in one leap. [*The nature of the culminating training of the path of familiarization*] By virtue of manifesting the characteristic of mastering [this crossing in one leap], it is the path of familiarization."

477 As RT's (fols. 133b.8–134a.4) and CE's comments on AA V.24ab (the two lines at stake here) show, it seems at least not self-evident that these two lines must refer to the lion's sport rather than to the lesser crossing in one leap. However, most Tibetan commentaries interpret these lines similar to JNS here, saying that the lesser crossing in one leap is implied since it corresponds to (only) the ascending progression as in the lion's sport (note that, differing from here, JNS's above general presentation of the lesser crossing in one leap also says the latter).

478 Note that JNS's above general presentation of the medium crossing in one leap includes the step of going from the meditative absorption of the Peak of Existence into the state of mind of not being in meditative equipoise, while the latter is only mentioned here at the beginning of the next paragraph on the great crossing in one leap.

479 BT (p. 624) says that the wisdom of the second bhūmi is the culminating training of the path of familiarization since it is the clear realization subsequent to manifesting the crossing in one leap, which has the defining characteristic of mastering being absorbed in many different samādhis.

480 In Appendix I1D3 in Volume One, JNS gives another example in terms of noble ones having manifest conceptions that apprehend imputations and focus on persons—during the subsequent attainments of noble ones there is the apprehension that "all these persons are illusionlike, dreamlike, and mere designations."

481 What JNS says here is that the conceptions to be relinquished through seeing represent the imputational form of the clinging to real existence and also the manifest form of the clinging to the lack of real existence, while the conceptions to be relinquished through familiarization represent the manifest form of the clinging to characteristics on the first seven bhūmis (with all conceptions to be relinquished through familiarization being imputational). Following JNS's above distinction in terms of manifest factors to be relinquished and those that retain a certain potency, this seems to imply that the conceptions to be relinquished through familiarization on the last three bhūmis consist of the clinging to characteristics in the form of its retaining a certain potency (in Appendix I1D3 in Volume One, JNS says that, "on the pure bhūmis, there are no manifest conceptions at all because one has gained mastery over nonconceptual wisdom"). As for the above-mentioned innate clinging to real existence, JNS (Appendix I5A2) says, "The instances of the innate clinging to real existence are exclusively factors to be relinquished through familiarization and they do not occur in the mind streams of mahāyāna noble ones because these have directly realized that all phenomena lack real existence. 'But then it follows that the innate clinging to real existence represents a factor to be relinquished through seeing.' This does not follow because to render the innate clinging to real existence into something that does not arise anymore depends exclusively on the path of familiarization. Therefore, though said clinging has not been relinquished on the path of seeing, it does not become manifest on the path of familiarization." Thus, JNS subsumes both the innate clinging to real existence and the imputational manifest conceptions of clinging to characteristics under the factors to be relinquished through familiarization. However, their difference is that the former never becomes manifest in the minds of bodhisattvas on the bhūmis, while the latter manifests during the subsequent attainments of the seven impure bhūmis. Note in this context that, in general, a common threefold division of cognitive obscurations in the Tibetan tradition is into clinging to

(1) real existence, (2) characteristics, and (3) duality, which are—in certain explanations—relinquished on bhūmis 1, 2–7, and 8–10, respectively (see also Charts 17–18 in Volume One).

482 For the Second Pawo Rinpoche's commentary on this and the next verse of the *Bodhicaryāvatāra*, see CE on AA IV.62a.

483 Vol. 2, pp. 382–88.

484 This is an example for the counterparts of substantial causes—cooperative causes—which are defined as "that which primarily produces something that is not the continuum of its own substance as its specific result."

485 D3859, fol. 158a.6.

486 D4090, fol. 91b.3.

487 D4038, fol. 111a.6.

488 D4211, fol. 157a.4.

489 This is exactly what *Abhidharmakośa* II.62ab and the *Bhāṣya* say.

490 Tib. zhang tshe spong ba chos kyi bla ma (born eleventh century). Being the third abbot of the Kadampa seat of Sangpu, he was a student of Ngog Lotsāwa and a teacher of Chaba Chökyi Sengé.

491 Vol. 2, pp. 410–12.

492 JNS (p. 411) has "the lack of recollection of the deity is the supreme lack of recollection of the deity." Given the context and the following explanation, this is hard to make sense of, so I omitted the second occurrence of "lack of."

493 Obviously, JNS alludes here to the Tibetan stereotype of the Ch'an master Hvashang Mahāyāna from Tun-huang, who is said to have advocated an exclusive cultivation of a thought-free mental state—as representing the realization of the ultimate—along with a complete rejection of the aspect of means, such as the accumulation of merit and proper ethical conduct. However, there are at least two indigenous Tibetan versions of the "debate at Samyé," with the more verifiable one presenting a different account of Hvashang's position. Also, Tibetan and Chinese documents on this debate found at Tun-huang differ greatly from the "official" Tibetan story, eventually presenting Hvashang as the winner and not Kamalaśīla. In any case, in Tibet, Hvashang's name and purported view became the favorite polemical stereotype that continues to be freely applied—justified or not—by proponents of Tibetan Buddhist schools to the views and meditation instructions of other Tibetan schools. In particular, Mahāmudrā meditation as presented in the Kagyü School was often and wrongly accused of being nothing but this mistaken approach.

494 This obviously refers to the Eighth Karmapa's writings on Mahāmudrā, such as his *Pointing Out the Three Kāyas* (Tib. sku gsum ngo sprod). For details on mental nonengagement and its relation to Mahāmudrā (partially based on Mikyö Dorje's commentary on the *Madhyamakāvatāra*), see Brunnhölzl 2004 (pp. 52–57 and 310–20) and 2007a (pp. 133–34).

495 In the last three sentences, JNS has "former" and "latter" in the reverse order, but given its above statement about "the last serial training (realizing the nature of the lack of entity) during meditative equipoise . . ." and the sentence that follows said three sentences, I cannot help but take "former" and "latter" in the order they are presented here.

496 D3791, fol. 314a.2.

497 CZ, p. 549.

498 D3787, fol. 187b.6–7.

499 Vol. 2, pp. 415–20.

500 CZ, p. 165.

501 This is a rearranged and abridged paraphrase of the following passage in D3796 (fols. 90b.4–91a.1): "As for 'what is nonmatured being uncontaminated,' what is matured is threefold—the supramundane matured [phenomena] on the first bhūmi, the maturated [phenomena] of being without characteristics on the eighth bhūmi, and the inconceivable and spontaneously present matured [phenomena] on the buddhabhūmi. All the phenomena on these [bhūmis] are called 'matured' because they are matured in that they differ from the phases before them. As for 'what is not matured' in these ways, all the appearances of all the many phenomena that consist of apprehender and apprehended in those in whose mind streams the path of seeing has not arisen are called 'nonmatured. As for their 'being uncontaminated,' this is [said] in terms of their [fundamental] operation. Though they are nonmatured, the nature of these phenomena is uncontaminated, which is [to be understood] in the manner of it being said that, 'though childish beings do not know enlightenment, they abide in it.' Here, what is contaminated refers to both conceptions and afflictions. Second, as for 'the state of the matured nature of phenomena being uncontaminated,' this consists of the three maturations as explained before." Then the *Prasphuṭapadā* (ibid., fol. 91a.1–4) continues: "It is because all the many phenomena that exist in the mind streams of the noble ones have changed state that they are expressed as 'matured.' Their nature abides as nothing but the uncontaminated state of the nature of phenomena. You may wonder, 'If matured is expressed as "the fundamental change of state," what is this change of state?' It is that the appearances of the dharmadhātu have seemingly become pure, but . . . it is not reasonable to assert the existence of a so-called 'ālaya-consciousness' and to speak of being matured and nonmatured by virtue of this [ālaya-consciousness] having or not having fundamentally changed state."

502 Rngog lo tsā ba blo ldan shes rab 1993a, fol. 96a.6 (note that the following explanation seems to be JNS's own interpretation of what Ngog Lotsāwa says before this quote).

503 Vol. 2, pp. 429–45, 450–51, and 462–64. To be able to better follow some of the following discussions, it is helpful to consult Makransky 1990 and 1997 (esp. Chapter 10) for detailed accounts of the long-standing Indo-Tibetan debates about whether there are three or four kāyas and how many the AA teaches.

504 D3793, fol. 138a.4 (on VIII.33).

505 In brief, Haribhadra speaks about four kāyas by distinguishing the svābhāvikakāya as the nature of phenomena (*dharmatā*) and the other three kāyas as the bearers of this nature (*dharmī*). Thus, buddhahood is divided into the aspect of its unconditioned ultimate nature and its conditioned aspect of appearing and functioning on the level of correct seeming reality. Within the latter framework, the dharmakāya is presented as a conditioned collection of twenty-one sets of qualities of uncontaminated wisdom, which represents the way in which the nature of buddhahood (the svābhāvikakāya) conventionally appears to buddhas themselves as their correct seeming reality. For other beings (bodhisattvas, śrāvakas, pratyekabuddhas, and ordinary sentient beings), this nature appears in the forms of the correct seeming reality that consist of the sāmbhogikakāya and the nairmāṇikakāya, respectively. In this way, Haribhadra clearly replaces the traditional notion of the inseparable and ultimate unity (both epistemologically and "ontologically") of nondual wisdom and dharmadhātu/emptiness (which is not only standard in Yogācāra texts, but also in almost all sūtras) by separating the aspect of wisdom or realization from the aspect of dharmatā/dharmadhātu/emptiness and placing it on the level of seeming conventional reality. This is one of the main reasons for his being fiercely criticized by later commentators such as Ratnākaraśānti, Abhayākaragupta, and Dölpopa. In addition, the presentation of the dharmakāya as a collection of qualities (though only on the level of seeming reality) corresponds not only to its presentation in the abhidharma, but also differs from the prajñāpāramitā sūtras (and the Yogācāra tradition) never identifying the dharmakāya—the

ultimate realization of a buddha—as just a collection of conventional phenomena, no matter how uncontaminated these may be. Interestingly, similar to Haribhadra's description, Hsüan-tsang's *Vijñaptimātratāsiddhi* (La Vallée Poussin 1928–48, 703–16) reports Dharmapāla as explaining that the svābhāvikakāya is one of the three aspects of the dharmakāya and represents the foundation of the other two kāyas. In other words, the dharmakāya is the consummate makeup of buddhahood, the svābhāvikakāya represents its essence, and the sambhogakāya and nirmāṇakāya are its manifestations.

506 D3793, fol. 133a.4 (see also below under 2d). TOK (vol. 3, p. 596) lists the following eight characteristics of the dharmakāya: "(1) It is *equal* because there is no difference between the dharmakāyas of all buddhas. (2) It is *profound* because it is free from all reference points and therefore difficult to realize. (3) It is *permanent* because it is unconditioned and therefore lacks the three times, arising, and ceasing. (4) It is *single* because dhātu and wisdom are not different and therefore inseparable. (5) It is *truly real* because it is beyond the extremes of superimposition and denial and therefore is unmistaken. (6) It is *pure* because it is free from the stains of the three obscurations. (7) It is *luminous* because it is through nonconceptuality that it is observed as this very nonconceptuality. (8) It is *connected to perfect enjoyment* (*sambhoga*) because it serves as the support for the perfect enjoyment that has the character of vast qualities."

507 The following paragraph is inserted here from vol. 2, pp. 450–51 (JNS's separate explanation of the dharmakāya) due to belonging to the same topic.

508 In this and the next sentence, JNS obviously plays on the crucial and controversial expression "change of state."

509 For more details, see the beginning of Appendix I1E in Volume One.

510 Note that this corresponds to Sthiramati's commentary on *Mahāyānasūtrālaṃkāra* IX.12–17 (D4034, fol. 113b.1–5)—the classical Yogācāra source for the change of state of the eight consciousnesses into the four wisdoms: "Here, 'state' refers to the five skandhas from the skandha of form up through the skandha of consciousness. After the afflictive and cognitive obscurations that exist in these skandhas have been relinquished, the dharmadhātu has become pure and has become nonconceptual wisdom. This is called 'change of state into something else.' In this regard, when the four skandhas of form, feeling, discrimination, and formation as well as [everything] in the skandha of consciousness from the eye consciousness up through the afflicted mind have become pure, the dharmadhātu becomes pure. When the ālaya-consciousness has become pure, it becomes nonconceptual wisdom. Or when the emptiness that exists in form, feeling, discrimination, formation, and the eight consciousnesses has become pure, the dharmadhātu becomes pure. From among the eight consciousnesses, when the ālaya-consciousness has become pure, it becomes mirrorlike wisdom. When the afflicted mind has become pure, it becomes the wisdom of equality. When the mental consciousness has become pure, it becomes discriminating wisdom. When the five [sense] consciousnesses, from the eye [consciousness] up through the body [consciousness] have become pure, they become all-accomplishing wisdom. The attainment of these five—the four wisdoms and the pure dharmadhātu—are called 'the five changes of state into something else.'"

511 Note that the above passage is one of the few examples that explicitly state the crucial point of the division into the four or five wisdoms not being a static one, but one in terms of the operational dynamics of the single fundamental wisdom of buddhahood or the dharmadhātu. The same is expressed in the Third Karmapa's autocommentary on his *Profound Inner Reality* (Rang byung rdo rje n.d., fol. 163b). *Mahāyānasūtrālaṃkāra* IX.59–60 (these two verses are also found literally in the *Buddhabhūmisūtra*) says:

> The purity of the dharmadhātu
> Of the buddhas is explained

As its function varying in terms of
Nature, enjoying the dharma, and emanating.

The svābhāvika[kāya], the sāmbhogikakāya,
And the other one, the nairmāṇika[kāya],
Are the divisions of the kāyas of the buddhas.
The first one is the foundation of the [other] two.

512 For more details on the four (five) wisdoms, see Makransky 1997 (pp. 100–104). For more details on the change of state of the eight consciousnesses into the above wisdoms and kāyas as explained in Yogācāra and by the Third Karmapa, see Brunnhölzl 2009. In this context, it shall be mentioned again that Buddhaśrījñāna's *Saṃcayagāthāpañjikā* (D3798) interestingly discusses the last chapter of the *Abhisamayālaṃkāra* in terms of the change of state of the eight consciousnesses into the five wisdoms (adding dharmadhātu wisdom) and the four kāyas.

513 Topic d) consists of JNS's comments on the *Vivṛti* (vol. 2, pp. 462–64).

514 As described in *Uttaratantra* II.51, the five distinctive features of the sāmbhogikakāya (not to be confused with its five certainties) are (1) the uninterrupted display of a body, (2) the uninterrupted stream of speech, (3) the uninterrupted activities of mind, (4) being without any formations, and (5) appearing in great variety while not being really established. It is not clear to what the four distinctive features of the nairmāṇikakāya refer. *Uttaratantra* II.53–56 speaks of its displaying the twelve deeds out of great compassion, while not moving away from the dharmakāya, in all impure realms, and for as long as saṃsāra lasts. Based on *Uttaratantra* II.57–60, PSD (p. 414) says that it causes sentient beings to become weary of saṃsāra and thus strive for nirvāṇa, turns those who have entered the hīnayāna away from it and matures them through the mahāyāna, and causes beings to attain liberation through prophesying their supreme enlightenment. Thus, it functions as the cause for these three results and it arises under the influence of the sāmbhogikakāya. MPZL (p. 197) takes AA VIII.33 as teaching the nairmāṇikakāya's five distinctive features of (1) the rūpakāya (emanations such as the nairmāṇikakāya of a supreme buddha), (2) time (appearing until saṃsāra is emptied), (3) object (all kinds of beings in the ten directions), (4) fruition (all kinds of benefits in terms of higher realms and liberation), and (5) activity (guiding beings equally through effortless, spontaneously present, and unbiased enlightened activity). TOK (vol. 3, p. 601) gives five characteristics of each one of the three kāyas according to the *Uttaratantra*, with the five of the nairmāṇikakāya being that it (1) demonstrates the path of peace, (2) matures those to be guided, (3) gives the prophecies, (4) displays the stream of various enlightened activities (that is, it assumes various forms that guide beings), and (5) appears for the cognizance of others. TOK (ibid., pp. 597–98) also lists the following eight characteristics of the sāmbhogikakāya: "(1) Its *retinue* together with which it enjoys [the dharma] consists exclusively of bodhisattvas who dwell on the ten bhūmis. (2) The *[pure] realm* in which it enjoys [the dharma] is Richly Adorned Akaniṣṭha. (3) The *bodies* that enjoy are those of Vairocana and so on. (4) The *characteristics* that it possesses are the thirty-two major and the eighty minor marks. (5) The *dharma* that it fully enjoys is solely the mahāyāna. (6) The *enlightened activity* that it performs consists of the prophecies for the children of the victors and so on. (7) *Spontaneous presence* means that its performance [of enlightened activity] and so on happen effortlessly and spontaneously, just as in the case of a wish-fulfilling jewel. (8) Its *lack of nature* means that it appears as various [phenomena] (such as said kāyas), but cannot be identified [as said phenomena], just like a rainbow." On the eight characteristics of the nairmāṇikakāya, TOK (ibid., pp. 599–600) says, "(1) Its *support* is the dharmakāya—[it appears] while [the latter] is unmoving. (2) Its *cause* refers to its arising from great compassion, that is, the wish to benefit all beings. (3) The *realms* [in which it appears] are all kinds of pure and impure [realms]. (4) The *time* [of its activity] lasts for as long as saṃsāra [exists]. (5) Its *nature* consists of the forms of the three emanations of artistry, incarnation, and enlightenment. (6) *To cause engagement* means that it causes ordinary worldly people to strive for, and engage in, [one of] the three types

of nirvāṇa, as is individually appropriate. (7) *To cause maturation* means that it causes the maturation of the accumulations of those who have entered the path. (8) *To cause liberation* means that it, for those who are matured through what is virtuous, causes liberation from the bondage of [saṃsāric] existence."

515 TOK (vol. 3, p. 598) explains that the great sāmbhogikakāya is the one that appears in the Richly Adorned Akaniṣṭha, while the lesser one is the one that resides in the Akaniṣṭha that is one of the five pure abodes within the realm of form.

516 The latter is literally found as the heading that pertains to these five verses in CE.

517 The dharmakāya is also mentioned in VIII.6d, referring to the twenty-one sets of wisdom qualities.

518 PK (fols. 160b.1ff.) defines the svābhāvikakāya as "the fundamental character of being endowed with dharmadhātu wisdom and representing the complete purity of the final uncontaminated dharmas, which have been attained through the supramundane path; or abiding in the natural state, with its nature being unborn" and "the fruition that is attained through the final cultivation of the four trainings." The dharmakāya is said to be equivalent to the svābhāvikakāya, but is presented in the AA through the twenty-one sets of uncontaminated dharmas. Also, the svābhāvikakāya is the fundamental character of the buddhabhūmi (its true nature), while the dharmakāya is its radiance or creative display (the features of its true nature). The sāmbhogikakāya is explained as "that in which the thirty-two major and eighty minor marks are complete in number, lucid, and perfect and which has the character of the wisdom of equality and discriminating wisdom." The nairmāṇikakāya is explained as "the kāya that has the nature of all-accomplishing wisdom, which in any kinds of forms (such as Buddha Śākayamuni) equally performs various benefits for the beings in all worldly realms as long as saṃsāra exists." It is an "emanation body" because, on the level of the seeming, the capacity of this single wisdom appears as all the forms of enlightened activity.

519 D3791, fols. 317b.5–318a.6 and D3793, fols. 132b.7–133a.7. Except for the two answers by those who assert three kāyas and their refutation given below, the *Vivṛti* here is largely identical to the *Ālokā* and says, "Others accept [AA VIII.1] . . . literally [in the sense of the svābhāvikakāya being] precisely these uncontaminated supramundane dharmas and explain that the svābhāvikakāya has the defining characteristic of being the nature of these [dharmas]—the fact of nonarising. This [kāya] is the dharmatākāya, but it is taught [here] as 'dharmakāya' through the elision of the particle [-*tā* that indicates a] nature. Then, [they raise the rhetorical] question, 'What are these uncontaminated dharmas that have the characteristic of being of the nature of the dharma[tā]kāya?' [They take the answer as] referring to verses [VIII.2–6] . . . Others reply, 'In that case, as for the undoubtedly accepted nondual minds and mental factors, which are the change by virtue of the fundamental change of state and perform functions such as teaching the dharma by way of giving rise to appearances with specific purposes for the seeming [reality] of yogins, how are they included [in the three kāyas]?' Some say, 'In [AA I.17] . . . , the word "dharmakāya" does not appear immediately after the word "svābhāvikakāya." Therefore, there are only three kāyas.' Others reply, '[This verse] is phrased in this way due to the force of demonstrating the [above] purpose, from the perspective of prosody, and because of matching activity with wisdom alone. Therefore, this is not contradictory to all the statements about the four kāyas in other quarters.'"

520 Somewhat differing from what Haribhadra's texts report on it, the *Vṛtti* (D3787, fols. 191b.7–192a.7) says, "Now, the dharmakāya is to be discussed. This is to be known as threefold—svābhāvikakāya, sāmbhogikakāya, and nairmāṇikakāya. In terms of the svābhāvikakāya, [AA VIII.1] reads, . . . The svābhāvikakāya of the Bhagavān should be known as the nature of being pure as the uncontaminated dharmas, which is endowed with the dharmadhātu, with 'nature' having the sense of being unfabricated. It is common worldly consensus that what is

called 'nature' refers to 'being unfabricated.' The supramundane path is what makes one attain that [nature], but it is not its creator. Some may wonder, 'So what are these uncontaminated dharmas—this nature of being utterly pure in all respects that represents the dharmakāya?' They are stated in [AA VIII.2–6] . . . [The term 'dharmakāya' in VIII.6d is arrived at] through the elision of the particle [-*tā*, but actually] means 'dharmatākāya.' Otherwise, there are the following two flaws—by virtue of 'dharmakāyā' referring to a 'kāya of dharmas,' said nature would be negated, and since this has the meaning of engagement, [this kāya] would be conditioned. To call this a 'kāya' must be [taken as] metaphorical by following what preceded it." Note that, at least in part, the Indo-Tibetan discussions about three or four kāyas hinge on the multifaceted meaning of the term "dharmakāya" (see the endnotes on AA VIII.2–6). All Indian AA commentators before Haribhadra and most after him (the most prominent ones being the early Buddhaśrījñāna, Dharmamitra, Ratnākaraśānti, and Abhayākaragupta) speak of three kāyas instead of four, with many of the latter explicitly rejecting four kāyas. Apart from Haribhadra, the commentators who accept four kāyas are Prajñākaramati, the later Buddhaśrījñāna, and Kumāraśrībhadra. Among Tibetan commentators, those who rely on the *Vivṛti* here follow Haribhadra, while others (such as CE, STT, and Gorampa) explain only three kāyas. STT (p. 144) equates the svābhāvikakāya with the dharmakāya and defines them as "the nature of phenomena (nonarising) that has the nature of the wisdom and the relinquishment of a buddha." This, STT says, refers to the buddha wisdom that knows suchness and variety, which is actually without nature and free from reference points. This is what the *Prāsaṅgika Mādhyamikas call "dharmakāya."

521 Pawo Rinpoche's commentary on the *Bodhicaryāvatāra* (Dpa' bo gtsug lag phreng ba n.d., p. 701) explains the same and adds that, just as calling the complete collection of all body parts a "body," the dharmakāya refers to the manifestation of the nature of all phenomena, just as it is, in a complete, indivisible, and fully perfect manner.

522 As mentioned above, JNS on AA I.17 also says that the svābhāvikakāya and the dharmakāya are not different in both being the dharmatākāya.

523 This means that neither the svābhāvikakāya (when, as Haribhadra does above when reporting on Āryavimuktisena's position, interpreted as the nature of mere emptiness or nonarising and not as the union of wisdom and emptiness), nor the sāmbhogikakāya, nor the nairmāṇikakāya qualify as said uncontaminated wisdom minds and mental factors and their activities. Thus, Haribhadra obviously has in mind that these can only refer to the dharmakāya, which must consequently be presented as a separate fourth kāya. Note though, that, differing from the *Vivṛti*, the *Ālokā* (D3791, fol. 318a.1–3) does present—hypothetical or actual—replies by those who assert three kāyas and refutes them, saying, "It may be replied, 'The very teaching on the kāya that has the character of the nature of phenomena is a teaching on the dharmakāya that has the nature of nondual wisdom, which is by virtue of the principle [that is expressed in *Lokātītastava* 22ab]:

> That which is dependent origination
> Is precisely what you assert as emptiness.'

In that case, by the very same reasoning, [the teaching on the svābhāvikakāya] would also be a teaching on the sāmbhogikakāya and the nairmāṇikakāya, and therefore these would not have to be taught separately either. It may be held, 'But these two are taught as the seeming of yogins since such is stated in the Buddha's words.' It is by virtue of the very same reasoning that the dharmakāya, which has the character of nonduality, would then be taught separately too."

524 For more details on both Āryavimuktisena's comments and Haribhadra's *Vivṛti*, and how the latter (seemingly misrepresenting the former here) advances his own specific approach of combining Madhyamaka with the logico-epistemological and abhidharma traditions, see Makransky 1997, pp. 216–18 and 225–48. Just as an aside, Nāropa's *Sekoddeśaṭīkā*

(D1351, fol. 277a.7) says that the AA and so on teach the dharmakāya as being distinct from the svābhāvikakāya and the sambhogakāya.

525 Compare the Third Karmapa's autocommentary on *The Profound Inner Reality* (Rang byung rdo rje n.d., p. 203), which presents the more common position on this: "There is the assertion by some that this *is* sambhoga-buddhahood, but they just did not grasp the intention of master Vasubandhu's commentary [on line IX.69c], which says, 'It is *also* sambhoga-buddhahood.' Adding the term 'also' [serves as] a word that links dharmakāya and mirrorlike wisdom to sambhoga-buddhahood as the latter's causal condition, just as linking the ālaya to the seven collections of consciousness as their causal condition. If it were not like this, [that is, if mirrorlike wisdom were the sambhogakāya,] there would indeed be numerous flaws in terms of scriptures [(such as contradicting the above and other sources)] and reasoning [(such as messing up the basis of purification and the means of purification)], but that much elaboration shall suffice." Karma Trinlépa's commentary on this passage (Ka rma phrin las pa phyogs las rnam rgyal 2006b, p. 353) elaborates the intention behind all this by saying that, ultimately, all five wisdoms have the same nature, but are merely divided in terms of conceptual isolates. As for how the nature of buddhahood appears for buddhas themselves, it appears as the five wisdoms and the five buddha families not being different. As an appearance for others, buddhahood displays as the rūpakāyas. Therefore, though mirrorlike wisdom is not contradictory to the sambhogakāya, when making the conventional classification of three kāyas it is explained as the dharmakāya and not the sambhogakāya.

526 Sections 26a–b. The translation follows the Sanskrit as quoted in Makransky 1997 (p. 375). The last two lines in JNS vary somewhat: "The buddhas are dharmakāya—Regard the guides as the nature of phenomena."

527 Here, JNS has *nang* instead of *dang* (literally, "the merits of those to be guided, inner aspiration prayers"). It seems that, here, these aspiration prayers are meant to be those of the disciples (and not the former ones by the buddhas). Usually it is said that enlightened activity occurs by virtue of three conditions coming together—the blessings or the powerful capacity of the dharmakāya of a buddha, the ongoing impetus of their previous aspiration prayers as bodhisattvas, and the pure karma of those to be guided.

528 The same point is made in the *Dharmadharmatāvibhāga* (lines 213–216). TOK (vol. 3, pp. 601–2) comments, "[The *Uttaratantra*] explains that the two rūpakāyas represent buddhahood, while the *Suvarṇaprabhāsasūtra* explains that they do not. Some [other sources] say that buddhahood does not exist. The scholars who know the essential point [here] assert that these [explanations] represent the expedient meaning, the definitive meaning, and the final definitive meaning, respectively."

529 To note, technically speaking, this would put Dignāga into the Tibetan doxographical category of "False Aspectarians Without Stains," whereas he is usually classified as a "Real Aspectarian."

530 Tib. rgya chen rnal 'byor spyod pa'i dbu ma pa dang zab mo 'jigs med smra ba grags sde spyod pa'i dbu ma pa. This obviously refers to one of the standard Tibetan subdivisions of the sūtra teachings of the mahāyāna—the lineages of vast activity and the profound view, respectively.

531 The translation represents verse 17 as found in D3833. JNS replaces the above second line by the first one, while its first line says, "These are mistaken appearances" (*'di dag 'khrul pa'i snang ba ste*). In the third line, JNS has "mistakenness" instead of "darkness."

532 I could not locate these verses in Nāgārjuna's works.

533 As mentioned above, statements to that effect are found in Dharmakīrti's *Pramāṇaviniścaya* (D4211, fols. 165a.4–5 and 167a.3) and *Pramāṇavārttika* (III.371 and III.426).

534 The reformulation of the above probative argument as a three-part reasoning is: "All the various appearances of seeming reality do not appear to buddha wisdom because they are observed as knowable objects that appear under the sway of ignorance." Here, the reason ("what is observed as a knowable object that appears under the sway of ignorance") is a general category that is contradictory to the predicate to be negated ("what appears to buddha wisdom").

535 Vol. 2, p. 488.

536 For an explanation of this, see JNS on the *Vivṛti* on VIII.34–40.

537 For more details on enlightened activity, see Appendix I4f2.

538 These are identical with the thirty-seven dharmas concordant with enlightenment in the mahāyāna (see Chart 13 in Volume One).

539 See Chart 11 in Volume One.

540 See Chart 10 in Volume One.

541 For details on (a)–(d), see Chart 11 in Volume One.

542 Here, the nine meditative absorptions of progressive abiding are numbered as 1 – 9, while the state of mind of the desire realm of not being in meditative equipoise is indicated by 0. In this context of the culminating training of the path of familiarization as presented by the sūtra in twenty-five thousand lines, all the steps within the lion's sport and the crossing in one leap represent a single continuous sequence of different meditative equipoises (only alternated with phases of nonequipoise during the last part). Later commentators broke down this single sequence in different ways into different phases. Note that the explicit division of crossing in one leap into lesser, medium, and great is not mentioned in either the sūtras or any Indian commentaries, but only in certain Tibetan commentaries (LSSP, PSD, and PK do not mention this division either). In addition, some models do not count the state of mind of not being in meditative equipoise as an actual step, while others do. For the sake of conveniently comparing these various models, their respectively corresponding phases are presented here in separate lines. Clearly, the existence of all these (and more) models on this topic suggests that it is far from self-explanatory. Sources: CZ (pp. 501–4); *Vṛtti* (D3787, fols. 174b.4–175b.7); *Ālokā* (D3793, fols. 305a.3–306.a.1); *Vivṛti* (D3793, fol. 126a.4–126b.3); *Śuddhamatī* (D3801, fols. 181b.3–182b.5); *Sārottama* (D3803, fols. 184b.5–185b.1); *Marmakaumudi* (D3805, fol. 181a.2–181b.3); JNS (vol. 2, pp. 347–53); LN (vol. 2, pp. 296–300); YT (pp. 578–83); RT (fols. 131a.3–135a.2); PSD (pp. 383–84); LSSP (fols. 188b.6–189b.3); BT (pp. 622–24); and PK (fols. 154a.2–155a.5).

543 According to JNS's description in Appendix I5F, in terms of separately counted steps, the sequence 8 – 0 – 8 – 9 in the middle between the upward and downward progressions in the medium crossing in one leap represents three steps—8 – 0 is step seventeen, 0 – 8 is step eighteen, and 8 – 9 is the first step of the seventeen steps of descending in reverse order. The last 0 at the end of the descent is the final step thirty-five in the medium crossing in one leap.

544 Note that, according to LN (vol. 2, pp. 285–86), the lion's sport on the path of seeing and the above lion's sport on the path of familiarization differ. LN identifies the same passage as RT (see below) in the sūtra in eighteen thousand lines (CZ, p. 501, second paragr.) as pertaining to the lion's sport on the path of seeing, it thus consisting of the eight liberations and the nine meditative absorptions in their progressive and reverse orders.

545 Though the two models for the medium crossing in one leap here are slightly different, according to Yagtön both accord with the sūtra in eighteen thousand lines.

546 The basis for this is RT's (fol. 131a.4) identification of the same passage as LN as pertaining to the lion's sport, but taking it to apply to this samādhi on both the path of seeing and the path of familiarization. Other commentaries take the immediately following passage (ibid., last paragr.) as pertaining to the preparatory lion's sport of the path of familiarization.

547 BT (pp. 622–24) has the same presentation as this one in terms of the *Vivṛti*.

548 The above definitions of causes, conditions, and results are based on the *Abhidharmakośa* (II.49–54; 61–62; and 56–58). Those of causes and conditions are found in JNS (Appendix I5G), while those of the results are based on TOK (vol. 1, pp. 242–43).

549 Vol. II, p. 504 and vol. III, pp. 604–8.

550 Rang byung rdo rje 2004b. In parts, the following is a slightly abbreviated and paraphrased translation (mainly omitting repetitious outlines and enumerations), with some elements of the outline being supplemented.

551 Tib. *phyva* (sometimes translated as "fortune"). This refers to the creator principle in the Tibetan Bön tradition.

552 These are the *prakṛti* and the *puruṣa* of the Sāṃkhya system.

553 The text has no description of the dharma cognition of the reality of the path, so this sentence is tentatively added in accordance with the second one of the four aspects of the reality of the path.

554 This refers to the presentation of the sixteen moments of wisdom on the path of seeing as found in Asaṅga's *Abhidharmasamuccaya* (D4049, fol. 93a–b), which is adopted by Haribhadra. See CE's general topic on "The manner of the knowledge of the path of bodhisattvas" (fols. 65b–66a) as well as Appendices I1H (esp. section 3ad) and I2D2b in Volume One.

555 The Tibetan has "the definition of the three knowledges as such."

556 Obviously, "aspects" and "appearances" are taken to be equivalent.

557 The Tibetan first gives the three definienda of the above definitions, but then spells out only two definitions, saying, "The second one is the realization that all entities are without a self, clinging to characteristics, including the remedy" (*gnyis pa ni gzhi thams cad bdag med par rtogs pa mtshan mar 'dzin pa gnyen po dang bcas pa yin no/*). It seems that something is missing here in the Tibetan, but in any case, as explained below, "clinging to characteristics" belongs to the second definition, while "the remedy" pertains to the third one. Thus, I supplemented the third definition as above.

558 The Tibetan in Rangjung Dorje's *Collected Works* (p. 445.2) has "the first one," but as explained below, this must refer to the second one that is an antagonistic factor for bodhisattvas.

559 The Tibetan has "two."

560 Other commentaries, following Haribhadra, speak of fifteen situational trainings (see CE on IV.9bd–11).

561 CZ, p. 320.

562 Ibid., p. 549.

563 D3787, fols. 187b.6ff.

564 D3791, fol. 314a.2.

565 Note that, in the following, despite frequent divisions of the eight topics into (a), (b), and so on, the numeration of their individual points is continuous.

566 Usually the above point (1) is divided into two, which are considered the first two points of the knowledge of entities—the knowledge of entities of not abiding in saṃsāra through prajñā and the knowledge of entities of not abiding in peace through compassion. The above point (2) is usually not mentioned as one of the nine points of the knowledge of entities.

567 The Tibetan omits entry (8), but lists it below, so it is supplemented here too. Usually points (7) and (8) of the knowledge of entities are called "training" and "its equality," respectively.

568 Usually (3) and (4) are named as above—being distant from the mother due to lacking the means and not being distant due to possessing the means, respectively.

569 This may refer either to skandhas, āyatanas, and dhātus, or to what is otherwise known as the three spheres (agent, recipient, and action).

570 Again, usually the definienda of (5) and (6) are as above, that is, being an antagonistic factor of the mahāyāna knowledge of entities and its remedy, respectively.

571 Usually the complete training in all aspects is only characterized by eleven points, with the second one below not being included.

572 The Tibetan is somewhat peculiar here (*'khor 'das kyi chos nyid dam so so rang gi rgyu ma grub*) and may be corrupt. In any case, it seems that *chos nyid* is not to be taken here as "nature of phenomena" since the second door to liberation is related here to their "nature" (*ngo bo*). Usually the three doors to liberation are put as follows. The nature of phenomena is emptiness; causes lack any signs or defining characteristics; and the appearance of results is not bound to expectations or wishes.

573 Usually the culminating training has eight points, the last one being the erroneous notions of taking the two realities to be contradictory.

574 The Tibetan has the reverse (*rten* and *brten pa*), while the version in the *Collected Works* has *brtan* and *rten pa*. Usually the dharmakāya is described as the support for the rūpakāyas, functioning—as explained below—as their dominant condition.

575 This is the divine creative artist described in the Vedas, said to be a son of Brahmā.

576 IX.64.

577 This is a translation of Rang byung rdo rje 2006c.

578 This echoes the two opening verses of Nāgārjuna's *Mūlamadhyamakakārikā*.

579 The text has *ming yang gzugs* (emend to *ming dang gzugs*).

580 The text has "impure" (*dag ma yin*), which seems not to make any sense, especially when considering what follows.

581 The last two lines almost literally correspond to *Madhyāntavibhāga* I.16cd.

582 The text has *'di 'ong*; one would rather expect *'gro 'ong*.

583 These five examples for the skandhas are found in *Saṃyutta Nikāya* III.141–42.

584 The last two verses describe the fourfold application of mindfulness of body, feelings, mind, and phenomena (the first set of four among the thirty-seven dharmas concordant with enlightenment).

585 This verse speaks about the second and third set of four among the thirty-seven dharmas. These first three sets correspond to the lesser, medium, and greater path of accumulation, respectively.

586 As mentioned above, the five faculties correspond to the first two phases of the path of preparation (heat and peak), and the five powers to the latter two (poised readiness and supreme

mundane dharma). In due order, coarse conceptions about the apprehended and the apprehender are relinquished.

587 Tib. ka rma lha steng. This is a monastery in eastern Tibet founded by the First Karmapa in 1185.

588 Pp. 239–48.

589 Pp. 64–65.

590 Besides their definitions of the eight topics, JNS and CE provide only definitions for two among the seventy points (among the knowledge of all aspects, the generation of bodhicitta, and the factors conducive to penetration).

591 Fols. 12a–13b.

592 Pp. 103, 104, 106, 107, 109, 112, 114, and 115.

593 For the more usual enumeration and names of the first eight points of the knowledge of entities, see PSD below ("the hīnayāna knowledge of entities" is usually not mentioned as one of them).

594 Usually, as in PSD below, the complete training in all aspects is only characterized by eleven points, with the second one below not being included.

595 Usually the culminating training has eight points, the last one being erroneous notions (see PSD below). However, Atiśa's *Prajñāpāramitāpiṇḍārthapradīpa* also lists only seven points.

596 SLG (fols. 7a.6–38b.2). Except for a few among the eight topics and the seventy points (such as the dharmakāya, the generation of bodhicitta, the instructions, and the disposition, which accord with SLG), PK does not give definitions. For PK's distinct definitions/explanations on the four kāyas, see Appendix I8A.

597 SLG does not give actual definitions for points (2)–(5) and (8), so I summarized the respective explanations.

598 SLG does not present actual definitions, but rather explanations or divisions, for the respective points of the knowledge of entities and the four trainings.

599 SLG's heading says, "The eight points of the culminating training," but only lists the seven presented here.

600 LSSP, fols. 68b.4–69a.5, 77b.6–86b.6, and 94b.6–95a.1; PSD, pp. 31–32, 34, 37–43, and 46. Unless noted otherwise, the definitions and boundary lines in PSD and LNG are identical.

601 LNG adds that the boundary lines are also stated as ranging from the mahāyāna path of seeing up through the buddhabhūmi.

602 LNG: the actual knowledge one, on all five paths of the hīnayāna; the nominal one, in all mahāyāna noble ones. It is also said to exist in all noble ones.

603 LNG: the one mainly arisen from study and reflection, from the path of accumulation onward; the one arisen from meditation, from heat up through the end of the continuum.

604 LNG: the special mental consciousness that is endowed with the two welfares, induced by its cause (the resolve to strive for the welfare of others as its aim) and congruently associated with its aid (the desire for fully perfect enlightenment as what is to be attained).

605 LNG further glosses this as "great compassion."

606 LNG: the fully qualified ones, from the great path of accumulation of the mahāyāna onward; the approximately concordant ones, from not having entered the path up through the buddhabhūmi.

607 LNG: the basic state of the mind—the nature of the dharmadhātu that serves as the foundation for the thirteen [types of] practice discussed here and, in its emptiness aspect, functions as the cause of freedom for the svābhāvikakāya and, in its appearance aspect, as the cause of freedom for the genuine rūpakāyas.

608 LNG: the knowable objects that are the basis for cutting through the superimpositions of the practitioners of the mahāyāna.

609 This definition is to be supplemented at the beginning of each one of the following four definitions.

610 LNG adds that also the following is said: the mere practice of engagement, from the path of accumulation onward; the special one, from the medium level of the supreme dharma of the path of preparation onward.

611 LNG: from the great level of the supreme dharma up through the end of the continuum. In general, the mere equipments (or accumulations) exist from the path of accumulation onward, but since "equipment" here refers primarily to the realization of emptiness and the direct cause of enlightenment as its result, the first fifteen exist on the great level of the supreme dharma, while the two equipments of the bhūmis and the remedies exist on the ten bhūmis, which consist of the paths of seeing and familiarization.

612 Almost all other commentaries speak of five branches, the third one being the pervasiveness of the disposition as the foundation for all beings to potentially give rise to the knowledge of the path.

613 LNG: the limited knowledge that, by way of being embraced by threefold genuineness and for the sake of fully completing the relinquishments and realizations of the three yānas in a bodhisattva's own mind stream and taking care of those to be guided who possess the śrāvaka disposition, realizes merely that [all] knowable objects lack a personal self.

614 LNG: the limited knowledge that, by way of being embraced by threefold genuineness and for the sake of fully completing the relinquishments and realizations of the three yānas in a bodhisattva's own mind stream and taking care of those to be guided who possess the pratyekabuddha disposition, realizes that [all] knowable objects lack one-and-a-half [of the two types of] identitylessness.

615 LNG: the realization of the two [types of] identitylessness that newly sees supramundane reality.

616 LNG: both the eighth and the ninth bhūmis.

617 LNG: the uninterrupted path of the uncontaminated path . . .

618 LNG : the path of liberation of the uncontaminated path . . .

619 PSD does not provide boundary lines for (10) and (11), but LNG has "from the second up through the tenth bhūmis" for both.

620 LNG: from the mahāyāna path of accumulation up through the buddhabhūmi.

621 According to LNG, the boundary lines are up through the seventh bhūmi.

622 LNG: the approximately concordant one, from the mahāyāna path of accumulation onward; the manifest one, from the eighth bhūmi onward.

623 LNG: the approximately concordant one, from the path of accumulation onward; the special one, from the eighth bhūmi onward.

624 LNG: the approximately concordant one, from the path of accumulation onward; the primary one, from the eighth bhūmi onward.

625 According to LNG, the boundary lines of these thirteen correspond to the above-mentioned boundary lines of the serial training in general.

626 According to LNG, the boundary lines of these four correspond to the above-mentioned boundary lines of the culminating training in general.

627 LNG adds in the beginning, "The ultimate reality of cessation that is . . ."

628 According to LNG, the boundary lines are as follows. The factor of enlightened activity that exists in its agent exists only in buddhas, while the one that exists in terms of its recipients or objects exists for these recipients even before they enter the path. It is remarkable that there are only very few similarities between the respective definitions (and sometimes even the names) of the eight topics and the seventy points as listed above in JG, JNS, CE, STT, SLG/PK, and LSSP/PSD. For an overview of the eight topics and the seventy points, see also Chart 26.

629 Vol. 2, pp. 464–508.

630 The other three here are the uninterrupted path, the path of liberation, and the special path.

631 *Panthā* is an old form of *pathin* and also related to the more common *patha.*

632 Here, TOK has *pathi* ("traveler").

633 I.21b.

634 There are two commentaries on the prājñāpāramitā sūtras by a master of this name in the *Tengyur* (D2647 and D3819), but the quote is not found in them.

635 TOK mistakenly says "instance" (*mtshan gzhi*).

636 XV.3.

637 This refers to those roots of virtue that can still be shaken by adverse conditions.

638 TOK mistakenly has *mūrti* ("form" or "body").

639 TOK has *'phags pa'i lam gyis 'dren nus pa.*

640 I.26cd (TOK only quotes the first line).

641 TOK has "two."

642 VI.24ab.

643 I.34–35.

644 Conze 1973, p. 84.

645 II.4ac.

646 This quote is actually *Abhidharmakośa* VI.23ab.

647 Here, this term does not refer to the usual fourfold mistakenness of clinging to purity, happiness, permanence, and a self, but to the mistakenness of the conceptions about the apprehender and the apprehended with respect to each one of the two identitylessnesses.

648 TOK has "108," but below (as in the *Abhisamayālaṃkāra*) 112 afflicted factors to be relinquished through seeing are listed and the other number is refuted.

649 V.4.

650 D4038, fol. 114b.6–7.

651 D4049, fol. 84b.3–6.

652 As outlined above, the view of holding ethics and spiritual discipline as paramount engages in all four realities.

653 TOK omits the negation particle *mi.*

654 This means that relinquishment takes place in a way that the ceasing of the remedy and the ceasing of its factor to be relinquished are simultaneous. If relinquishment occurs due to a "path concurrent with arising," the process of the arising of a particular remedy and the process of the ceasing of its factor to be relinquished are simultaneous.

655 VI.77cd.

656 V.21ab.

657 IX.151ab.

658 Conze 1973, p. 84.

659 VI.25cd–26.

660 VI.28 and 31b.

661 Sparham 2006, p. 171.

662 Lines 11cd–12.

663 I.1.

664 XXI.11. TOK has "impaired" (*bslad pa*) instead of "seeing."

665 Verse 71.

666 XXIV.19

667 VI.7cd.

668 These are the five fears that are still present in bodhisattvas on the paths of accumulation and preparation—the fear of lack of livelihood, the fear of not being praised, the fear related to a retinue, the fear of dying, and the fear of the lower realms.

669 In addition to the three supramundane yānas of śrāvakas, pratyekabuddhas, and bodhisattvas, the Buddha also taught two mundane yānas—the yāna of gods and humans and the brahmayāna. The first one refers to all the mundane paths that lead to favorable rebirths as human beings or as gods in the desire realm. The second one is the general name for all the various cultivations of the dhyānas and formless absorptions that lead to rebirth on the different levels of the form realm and the formless realm. These two realms are called "pure" (*brahma*) since they are free from the afflictions of the desire realm. TOK explains these yānas in Chapter 6.1 (the presentation of the common sciences and the mundane paths; vol. 2, pp. 348–61).

670 XIII.5.

671 D3791, fols. 25b.7–26a.1.

672 The last two levels refer to śrāvaka arhathood and buddhahood, respectively. For the dharmas of nonlearning, see below.

673 VIII.55ab.

674 II.4.

675 V.40.

676 This refers to one of the chapters of the *Kālacakratantra.*

677 XX.39.

678 XX.40.

679 XXI.41.

680 XX.24.

681 XI.75cd.

682 I.48–70.

683 P. 99.

684 V.5 and V.30ab.

685 D45.31, vol. ga, fol. 96a.1–3.

686 I.67.

687 I.68.

688 II.7.

689 Here, this refers to both the paths of accumulation and preparation.

690 According to the *Bod rgya tshig mdzod chen mo* (pp. 903–4), this refers to a special meditation of signless yoga in the kriyātantras—"entering" is the realization that, upon thorough analysis, all phenomena (such as the skandhas) are without arising. "Abiding" is the perception of the nature of nonconceptuality. "Rising" means that one, from within this state, engages in great compassion for those beings who do not realize this.

691 Vol. 3, pp. 591–629.

692 XVIII.7.

693 D4049, fol. 91a.3.

694 Ibid., fol. 91a.3–4.

695 Ibid., fol. 91a.4–5 (the quote in TOK omits the result of a once-returner).

696 Ibid., fol. 91.5.

697 I.42.

698 These are suchness and the variety of all phenomena.

699 I could not locate the exact quote, but it is very similar to verse 2 of Candrakīrti's *Triśaraṇasaptatika*:

> Because of being liberated from the paths of the three times,
> Mind having unfolded toward knowable objects,
> And the closed state of ignorance having been overcome,
> Buddhahood unfolds like a lotus.

700 III.12.

701 There are three kinds of Akaniṣṭha—(1) the ultimate Akaniṣṭha (the formless state of the dharmakāya), (2) the Richly Adorned Akaniṣṭha (the sphere in which the sāmbhogikakāyas manifest), and (3) the highest pure level of the form realm, which is a natural sphere of nairmāṇikakāyas. The one referred to here is (2).

702 IX.65cd.

703 XIX.54. According to Vasubandhu's *Bhāṣya*, "what does not exist" refers to characteristics and "what exists" refers to suchness. This is "the change of state" because, through it, said such-

ness (which did not appear) appears. It "is liberation" since one became independent and gained mastery over one's own mind.

704 D3897, fol. 290a.4–5. The *Tengyur* contains only a single commentary on Nāgārjuna's *Ratnāvalī* (which is also called *Instructions for the King*), by Ajitamitra (D4159), and the *Saṃskṛtāsaṃskṛtaviniścaya* explicitly refers to a commentary on the *Rājaparikathāratnāvalī*, but this quote is not found in said commentary.

705 The same is explained in Āryavimuktisena's *Vṛtti* (D3787, fol. 192a.6) and Haribhadra's *Ālokā* (D3791, fol. 317b.6) and *Vivṛti* (D3793, fol. 133a.3).

706 VIII.1.

707 X.1 (D4048, fol. 37a.4).

708 These are afflictive obscurations, cognitive obscurations, and the obscurations to meditative absorption (agitation and dullness).

709 VIII.12cd.

710 VIII.12.

711 X.26.

712 D2219, fol. 41b.4–5.

713 D3897, fol. 290b.3.

714 In all versions of TOK, the passage that comments on the above section of the root text is missing.

715 This could also be read as "while not moving."

716 IX.64.

717 In *Uttaratantra* II.44–46, these five characteristics are said to be those of the svābhāvikakāya and the order of (3) and (4) is reversed. According to Jamgön Kongtrul's commentary on this text (Kong sprul blo gros mtha' yas 2005b, p. 150), in due order, (2)–(4) refer to having relinquished the two extremes of superimposing what does not exist and denying what exists; lacking the stains of the afflictions, not being the sphere of conceptions, and being the sphere of the personally experienced wisdom of the ultimate yogins who always rest in the meditative equipoise of the unity of means and prajñā; and being free from afflictive, cognitive, and meditative obscurations.

718 These five characteristics correspond to *Uttaratantra* II.51.

719 Characteristics (1)–(3) are found in *Uttaratantra* II.57–58, while (4) appears in several lines (such as I.145d and II.53d–56) and (5), in IV.71b.

720 IX.66ab.

721 IX.66cd.

722 This and the following quotes from the *Nighaṇṭa* are found on fol. 6a–b in P5833. It is a small Sanskrit-Tibetan etymological dictionary for some important key terms. It was compiled by various Indian paṇḍitas and Tibetan translators during the ninth century C.E.

723 II.38.

724 IX.68.

725 IX.70.

726 IX.72.

727 IX.74.

728 I.48 (P5549, fol. 11b.6–7).

729 IX.12.

730 X.76.

731 I was not able to locate this line and the quote by Candragomī.

732 I.28cd.

733 Verse 37.

734 D107 does not contain this passage in verse, but it is found in prose (ACIP MDO SDE CA@88b.1–2).

735 III.532.

736 III.1.

737 III.13a.

738 VII.28ab.

739 See the sixteenth of the twenty-one uncontaminated sets of qualities in the following section.

740 In other words, buddha wisdom deals not only with ordinary sentient beings in saṃsāra, but also with arhats and bodhisattvas on the bhūmis who are already liberated from saṃsāra, but have not yet attained buddhahood.

741 The term *śarabha* originally referred to a kind of deer and, later, to a fabulous animal with eight legs that inhabits the snowy mountains and is stronger than a lion and an elephant. Often, it is said to be an eight-legged lion.

742 In Hindu cosmology, this is the son of Mahāpuruṣa, the latter being the primeval man as the soul and original source of the universe. Also, Nārāyaṇa is variously identified as Brahmā, Viṣṇu, or Kṛṣṇa.

743 TOK has "nails" instead of "fingers and toes."

744 VIII.21–32. The numbers are as found in TOK and the last verse is as in the *Tengyur*, but the Sanskrit and several other Tibetan versions replace the third and fourth lines by the single line "[His hands and feet show] endless knots and swastikas." Usually the three aspects of ornamentation (80)–(82) are counted as a single minor mark, thus arriving at exactly eighty.

745 IV.25.

746 See its quote in the *Mahāyānasūtrālaṃkārabhāṣya* (D4026, fols.182b.2–183b.5; translated in Jamspal et al. 2004, pp. 156–58).

747 A mythical being whose lower body is eaglelike, while its upper body is human and has wings. It plays cymbals as it flies.

748 This refers to the god Indra.

749 These are also known as "the four seals"—everything conditioned is impermanent, everything contaminated is suffering, all phenomena are empty and identityless, and nirvāṇa alone is peace. It is said that the big drum of the gods, which is floating in the heavens, spontaneously utters these four defining characteristics of a buddha's speech.

750 IV.3.

751 IV.12.

752 Tib. mang yul ding ri glang 'khor.

753 Tib. ston pa chos dpal.

754 Tib. jo mo g.yang 'dren.

755 Tib. u rgyan pa rin chen dpal.

756 Tib. khro phu ba kun ldan shes rab.

757 Tib.tshur phu.

758 Tib. gnyan ras dge' 'dun 'bum.

759 Tib. slob dpon shes rab dpal.

760 Tib. rgya sgom ye shes 'od.

761 Tib. gnam mtsho ba mi bskyod rdo rje. In particular, the Karmapa received the transmission of Cutting Through (Tib. gcod) from him.

762 Tib. gzhon nu byang chub.

763 Tib. dge 'dun rin chen.

764 Tib. gsang phu.

765 Tib. shākya gzhon nu.

766 Tib. snye mdo ba kun dga' don grub.

767 Tib. tshul khrims rin chen.

768 Tib. sba ras.

769 Tib. bi ma snying thig. These are the main Dzogchen teachings by Vimalamitra.

770 Tib. ka rma yang dgon.

771 Tib. ka rma snying thig.

772 Tib. g.yag ston sangs rgyas dpal.

773 Tib. sgam po zang lung.

774 Tib. dvags po.

775 Tib. kong po.

776 Tib. rkungs (Chos kyi 'byungs gnas 1972 has *spungs*).

777 Tib. bde chen steng.

778 The only source that reports a meeting between the Karmapa and Dölpopa at all is Chos kyi 'byung gnas and 'Be lo Tshe dbang kun khyab 1972 (p. 208.1–2), but there is no mention of the latter being a disciple of Rangjung Dorje.

779 Tib. lkog phreng.

780 Tib. ka rma dgon. The main Karma Kagyü seat in Kham, established in 1173 by the First Karmapa.

781 Tib. sog chu.

782 Tib. ri bo rtse lnga.

783 Tib. phyag rgya chen po'i smon lam.

784 Tib. phyag rgya chen po lhan cig skyes sbyor khrid yig.

785 Tib. sku gsum ngo sprod.

786 Tib. rlung sems gnyis med.

787 Tib. rgyal ba g.yung ston pa.

788 Tib. grags pa seng ge.

789 Tib. spyi lha.

790 Tib. dpal 'byor don grub.

791 Tib. ban sgar 'jam dpal bzang po.

792 Tib. bkra shis rnam rgyal.

793 Tib. chos 'khor lhun po.

794 Tib. bkra shis dpal 'byor.

795 Tib. rin spungs.

796 Tib. bkra shis rnam rgyal.

797 Tib. chos kyi grags pa ye shes dpal bzang po.

798 Tib. dvags po rab 'byams pa chos rgyal bstan pa.

799 Tib. sa tam.

800 Tib. ngom chu.

801 Tib. dul mo bkra shis 'od zer.

802 Tib. dvags po bkra shis rnam rgyal.

803 Tib. mkhan chen chos grub seng ge.

804 Dpa' bo gtsug lag phreng ba 2003, p. 1240.

805 Tib. dvags po legs bshad gling.

806 Tib. sku gsum ngo sprod.

807 Tib. 'bri gung pa 'jig rten gsum mgon.

808 Tib. dam chos dgongs pa gcig pa.

809 Tib. thun bzhi la ma'i rnal 'byor.

810 Tib. bka' brgyud mgur mtsho (translated as *The Rain of Wisdom*).

811 The founder of this style, Tulku Namka Dashi (Tib. sprul sku nam mkha' bkra shis), was a student of the Eighth Karmapa and identified by the latter as one of his own emanations.

812 Both the statue and the impressed marble can still be seen at Rumtek (Tib. rum btegs), the Karmapa's present main seat in Sikkim, India.

813 Tib. grags pa dpal 'byor.

814 Tib. chos kyi go cha.

815 Tib. dga' ldan khang gsar.

816 Tib. kong po.

817 Tib. zab mo nang don.

818 Tib. dge bsnyen. These are the five Buddhist lay vows of refraining from killing, stealing, lying, and drinking alcohol, and maintaining celibacy (or at least monogamy).

819 Tib. dkon mchog 'bangs.

820 Tib. yangs pa can.

821 Tib. śā kya rgya mtsho.

822 Tib. zhig po gling pa gar gyi dbang phyug rtsal.

823 Tib. kun dga' chos bzang.

824 Tib. 'dzam thang rgyal ba seng ge. He was the second incarnation of the abbot of Dzamtang Monastery in far eastern Tibet, the only place in Tibet where the Jonang tradition survived after the sixteenth century to the present day.

825 Tib. stag lung rnam rgyal grags pa. Obviously, there is a problem with the dates of this master having been a teacher of the Shamarpa, but the biographies (which do not give these dates) agree that he was.

826 Tib. dbang phyug rdo rje.

827 English translation in Brunnhölzl 2007a.

828 Tib. grags pa don grub.

829 Tib. chos kyi rgyal mtshan.

830 Tib. gtsug lag rgya mtsho.

831 Tib. khyab bdag grub mchog dbang po.

832 Tib. rgyal ba rgod tshang ba (1189–1258).

833 Tib. bsod nams rgya mtsho.

834 Tib. gsung rab gling.

835 Tib. chos rgyal phun tshogs.

836 Tib. stag lung kun dga' bkra shis.

837 Tib. nam mkha' bkra shis.

838 Tib. yan pa blo dbe.

839 Tib pad ma gling pa (1450–1521).

840 Tib. rtse gdong bdag chen kun dga' legs pa'i byung gnas.

Index

The Nitartha Institute Series
published by Snow Lion Publications

Nitartha Institute was founded in 1996 by The Dzogchen Ponlop Rinpoche, under the guidance of Khenchen Thrangu Rinpoche and Khenpo Tsültrim Gyamtso Rinpoche, the leading contemporary teachers of the Karma Kagyü tradition of Tibetan Buddhism. The Institute, under the aegis of Nitartha *international*, aims to fully transmit the Buddhist tradition of contemplative inquiry and learning; it offers Western students training in advanced Buddhist view and practice, as taught by the Karma Kagyü and Nyingma lineages of Tibet.

The Institute is pleased to ally with the Tsadra Foundation and Snow Lion Publications in presenting this series of important works offering a wide range of graded educational materials that include authoritative translations of key texts from the Buddhist tradition, both those unique to the Kagyü and Nyingma lineages and those common to the wider scope of Indo-Tibetan Buddhism; modern commentaries by notable lineage scholar-practitioners; manuals for contemplative practice; and broader studies that deepen understanding of particular aspects of the Buddhist view. The initial releases are from the Kagyü tradition and will be followed by publications from the Nyingma tradition.

This publication is an Advanced Level Nitartha book.

Six-armed Mahākāla